D0622539

FOOD PRODUCTS FORMULARY

VOLUME 3

FRUIT, VEGETABLE AND NUT PRODUCTS

other AVI books with additional information on food processing

Agriculture Science

BASIC ENGINEERING PRINCIPLES in soft and hard cover Editions *Merkel*
COCONUTS: PRODUCTION, PROCESSING, PRODUCTS *Woodroof*
HANDLING, TRANSPORTATION AND STORAGE OF FRUITS AND VEGETABLES, VOL. 1 and 2 *Ryall and Lipton*
PEANUTS: PRODUCTION, PROCESSING, PRODUCTS, 2ND EDITION *Woodroof*
POSTHARVEST BIOLOGY AND HANDLING OF FRUITS AND VEGETABLES *Haard and Salunke*
POTATOES: PRODUCTION, STORING, PROCESSING *Smith*
POULTRY PROCESSING TECHNOLOGY, 2ND EDITION *Mountney*
PROCESSING AGRICULTURAL AND MUNICIPAL WASTES *Inglett*
PROCESSING EQUIPMENT FOR AGRICULTURAL PRODUCTS *Hall*
SMALL FRUIT CULTURE, 4TH EDITION *Shoemaker*
SWEET POTATOES: PRODUCTION, PROCESSING, MARKETING *Edmond and Ammerman*
TREE FRUIT PRODUCTION, 2ND EDITION *Teskey and Shoemaker*
TREE NUTS: PRODUCTION, PROCESSING, PRODUCTS, VOL. 1 and 2 *Woodroof*
WHEAT: PRODUCTION AND UTILIZATION *Inglett*

Food Science and Technology

COMMERCIAL FRUIT PROCESSING *Woodroof and Luh*
COMMERCIAL VEGETABLE PROCESSING *Luh and Woodroof*
ECONOMICS OF FOOD PROCESSING *Greig*
ENCYCLOPEDIA OF FOOD ENGINEERING *Hall, Farrall and Rippen*
ENCYCLOPEDIA OF FOOD TECHNOLOGY *Johnson and Peterson*
FABRICATED FOODS *Inglett*
FOOD DEHYDRATION, 2ND EDITION, VOL. 1 and 2 *Van Arsdel, Copley and Morgan*
FOOD FLAVORINGS: COMPOSITION, MANUFACTURE AND USE, 2ND EDITION *Merory*
FOOD PACKAGING *Sacharow and Griffin*
FOOD PROCESS ENGINEERING in soft and hard cover Editions *Heldman*
FOOD PRODUCTS FORMULARY, VOL. 1—MEATS, POULTRY, FISH AND SHELLFISH *Komarik, Tressler and Long*
FOOD PRODUCTS FORMULARY, VOL. 2—CEREALS, BAKED GOODS, DAIRY AND EGG PRODUCTS *Tressler and Sultan*
FOOD SCIENCE, 2ND EDITION *Potter*
FREEZING PRESERVATION OF FOODS, 4TH EDITION, VOLS. 1, 2, 3, and 4 *Tressler, Van Arsdel and Copley*
FRUIT AND VEGETABLE JUICE PROCESSING TECHNOLOGY, 2ND EDITION *Tressler and Joslyn*
HANDBOOK OF SUGARS *Junk and Pancoast*
LABORATORY MANUAL FOR FOOD CANNERS AND PROCESSORS, 3RD EDITION, VOL. 1 and 2 *National Canners Association*
PACKAGE PRODUCTION MANAGEMENT, 2ND EDITION *Raphael and Olsson*
POTATO PROCESSING, 3RD EDITION *Talburt and Smith*
PRINCIPLES OF PACKAGE DEVELOPMENT *Griffin and Sacharow*
QUALITY CONTROL FOR THE FOOD INDUSTRY, 3RD EDITION, VOL. 1 and 2 *Kramer and Twigg*
SEED PROTEINS SYMPOSIUM *Inglett*
SNACK FOOD TECHNOLOGY *Matz*
SOYBEANS: CHEMISTRY AND TECHNOLOGY, VOL. 1—PROTEINS *Smith and Circle*
SUGAR CHEMISTRY *Shallenberger and Birch*
SWEETENERS SYMPOSIUM *Inglett*
TECHNOLOGY OF FOOD PRESERVATION, 3RD EDITION *Desrosier*
TEXTURE AND RHEOLOGY IN FOOD QUALITY *DeMan*
TOMATO PRODUCTION, PROCESSING AND QUALITY EVALUATION *Gould*

FOOD PRODUCTS FORMULARY

VOLUME 3

FRUIT, VEGETABLE AND NUT PRODUCTS

by **DONALD K. TRESSLER, Ph.D.,**
President and General Manager,
The Avi Publishing Company,
Westport, Connecticut

and **JASPER GUY WOODROOF, Ph.D.,**
Alumni Distinguished Professor
Emeritus of Food Science,
University of Georgia,
Experiment, Georgia

THE AVI PUBLISHING COMPANY, INC.
WESTPORT, CONNECTICUT

THE AVI PUBLISHING COMPANY, INC.,

Westport, Connecticut

Library of Congress Catalog Card Number: 73-94091

ISBN-0-87055-202-3

Printed in the United States of America

Preface

This is the third volume of a series of books presenting formulas and procedures for the making and preservation of a large number of commercial and institutional food products. This volume presents formulas and methods of making and preserving many different fruit, vegetable, and nut products and sauces.

The fruit products described include, among others, frozen, canned, and dehydrated fruits of all kinds: jams, jellies, preserves, and fruit butters; fruit syrups, sauces, and purées, including those for variegated ice creams, and sundaes; many fruit confections (candied orange and grapefruit peel, syllabub, and velva fruit); fruit fillings for pies, puddings, desserts and baked goods; pickled peaches, and pears; fruit juices: both still and carbonated; fruit juice concentrates; fruit flavors and flavorings, and natural and imitation colors.

The vegetable products described include, among others, the following: frozen, canned, and dehydrated vegetables of all kinds, both straight and mixed (e.g., chop suey, hopping John, tamales, vichyssoise, succotash, and peas and snapbeans). The frozen vegetables include both blanched and cooked vegetables (e.g., frozen French-fried potatoes, onion rings) and many other convenience and fast food products. Formulas and procedures for making and preserving a large variety of pickled vegetables (e.g., beets, peppers, and cucumbers) are also presented. Methods of preparing and preserving a number of fermented vegetables (e.g., sauerkraut and dill pickles) are given. The making and preserving of tomato products are presented. Formulas for making catsup, chili sauce, and many other sauces are also included.

In most instances, the procedures that should be followed in making the products are not given in great detail, but anyone accustomed to handling and preserving fruits and vegetables can understand and follow the directions.

Many of the formulas and procedures were contributed by important companies producing fruit and vegetable products and those manufacturing ingredients used in making these products. Some of the formulas were developed in the authors' laboratories. A considerable number of the formulas and procedures have been published in Avi Publishing Company books. The authors of this volume are grateful to other Avi authors for the authorization to use these formulas.

Although care has been taken to check the accuracy of the formulas and procedures, the detailed methods should be checked further on a small scale before being adopted commercially. Also, the suggested processing times and temperatures for sterilization in containers should be approved by a can manufacturer or National Canners Association.

The formulas included in this book have three characteristics, as contrasted to kitchen recipes. They (a) are or have possible commercial applications; (b) are in relatively large quantities; and (c) utilize mechanical equipment insofar as possible.

About 500 of the formulas used are from companies, corporations, institutes, exchanges or cooperatives that manufacture or produce special ingredients for fruit, vegetable, nut, and sauce formulations; about 200 more are from State or Federal government institutions or agencies; about 100 are from private laboratories, and some are from anonymous sources. More specific information is found under "Sources" at the end of each formula.

DONALD K. TRESSLER
J. GUY WOODROOF

December, 1975

Grateful Thanks to Numerous Contributors

It would not have been possible to publish the wide range of formulas contained in this book without the generous cooperation of manufacturers, industry associations, government agencies, publishers, and individuals. Even though acknowledgement of contributions is given along with the formula which was contributed, we hereby gratefully extend thanks to the following:

Allied Chemical Company, New York, N.Y.
American Dry Milk Institute, Chicago, Illinois
American Maize-Products Company, New York, N.Y.
American Molasses Company Division, SuCrest Corporation, New York, N.Y.
American Mushroom Institute, Kennett Square, Pennsylvania
American Spice Trade Association, New York, N.Y.
American Viscose Company, FMC Corporation, Avicel Division, Marcus Hook, Pennsylvania
Archibald and Kendall, Inc., New York, N.Y.
Atkinson, F. E., and Strachan, C. C., Dominion of Canada, Department of Agriculture, Ottawa, Canada
Atlanta Journal, Atlanta, Georgia
Atlas Chemical Division, ICI America, Inc., Wilmington, Delaware
California Almond Growers Exchange, Sacramento, California
California Avocado Advisory Board, Newport Beach, California
California Bush Fruit Advisory Board, Fresno, California
California Dried Fig Advisory Board, Fresno, California
California Prune Advisory Board, World Trade Center, San Francisco, California
California Strawberry Advisory Board, Watsonville, California
Canadian Department of Agriculture, Ottawa, Ontario, Canada
Cargill Texturized Vegetable Protein, Minneapolis, Minnesota
Cling Peach Advisory Board, New York, N.Y.
Commercial Fruit Processing by Woodroof and Luh and published by Avi Publishing Company, Westport, Connecticut
Complete Course in Canning by Lopez and published by Canning Trade, Baltimore, Maryland
Corn: Culture, Processing, Products by Inglett and published by Avi Publishing Company, Westport, Connecticut
Cornell Hotel and Restaurant Administration, Ithaca, N.Y.
CPC International, Inc., Industrial Division, Englewood Cliffs, New Jersey
Davis Flavor Corporation, Clifton, New Jersey
Diamond Walnut Growers, Inc., Stockton, California
Dried Fig Advisory Board, Fresno, California
Durkee Industrial Food Service Group, Cleveland, Ohio
Eastman Chemical Products, Inc., D.P.I. Division, Kingsport, Tennessee
Far-Mar Company, Inc., Research Division, Hutchinson, Kansas
Florasynth Company, New York, N.Y.
Florida Agricultural Experiment Station, Gainesville, Florida

Foamat Foods Corporation, Corvallis, Oregon

Food Dehydration, Volume 2, Products and Technology by Van Arsdel, Copley, and Morgan and published by Avi Publishing Company, Westport, Connecticut

Food Engineering, Philadelphia, Pennsylvania

Food Flavorings, Composition, Manufacture and Use, 2nd Edition by Merory and published by Avi Publishing Company, Westport, Connecticut

Food Products Formulary, Volume 1, Beef, Poultry, Fish and Shellfish, by Komarik, Tressler and Long and published by Avi Publishing Company, Westport, Connecticut

Freezing Preservation of Foods, 3rd Edition by Tressler and Evers and published by Avi Publishing Company, Westport, Connecticut

Freezing Preservation of Foods, 4th Edition, Vol. 1 by Tressler, Van Arsdel and Copley and published by Avi Publishing Company, Westport, Connecticut

Freezing Preservation of Foods, 4th Edition, Vol. 2 by Tressler, Copley and Van Arsdel and published by Avi Publishing Company, Westport, Connecticut

Freezing Preservation of Foods, 4th Edition, Vol. 3 by Tressler, Van Arsdel and Copley and published by Avi Publishing Company, Westport, Connecticut

Freezing Preservation of Foods, 4th Edition, Vol. 4 by Tressler, Van Arsdel and Copley and published by Avi Publishing Company, Westport, Connecticut

Fruit and Vegetable Juice Processing Technology, 2nd Edition by Tressler and Joslyn and published by Avi Publishing Company, Westport, Connecticut

Gentry International, Inc., Gilroy, California

Georgia Agricultural Commodity Commission for Peanuts, Tifton, Georgia

Georgia Experiment Station, Department of Food Science, Experiment, Georgia

Georgia Pecan Growers Association, Albany, Georgia

Germantown Manufacturing Company, Broomall, Pennsylvania

Givaudan Corporation, New York, N.Y.

Gold Kist, Inc., Atlanta, Georgia

Griffith Laboratories, Chicago, Illinois

Hathaway Allied Products, Harbor City, California

Hawaii Agricultural Experiment Station, Honolulu, Hawaii

Heggblade-Marguleas-Tenneco, Bakersfield, California

Henningsen Foods, Inc., New York, N.Y.

Hoffmann-LaRoche, Inc., Nutley, New Jersey

Horticultural Experiment Station, Vineland, Ontario, Canada

Institutions Magazine, Chicago, Illinois

Kelco Company, Chicago, Illinois

Komarik, Stephan, Coral Gables, Florida

Land O'Lakes Creameries, Inc., Minneapolis, Minnesota

McCormick and Company, Hunt Valley, Maryland

Mallinckrodt Chemical Works, St. Louis, Missouri

Marine Colloids, Inc., Springfield, New Jersey

Massachusetts Agricultural Experiment Station, Amherst, Massachusetts

Meyer-Blanke Corporation, St. Louis, Missouri

Microbiology of Food Fermentations by Pederson and published by Avi Publishing Company, Westport, Connecticut

Military Specification 35051, 21 November 1960

Military Specification, U. S. Quartermaster Corps, Arlington, Virginia

Naarden, Inc., Owings Mills, Maryland

National Peach Council, Baldwin, Missouri
National Red Cherry Institute, East Lansing, Michigan
National Restaurant Association, Chicago, Illinois
National Starch & Chemical Company, New York, N.Y.; Plainfield, New Jersey
Nestlé Company, Food Ingredients Division, White Plains, N.Y.
New Mexico Agricultural Experiment Station, State College, New Mexico
North American Blueberry Council, Marmora, New Jersey
Oklahoma Peanut Commission, Madill, Oklahoma
Pacific Coast Canner Pear Service, Seattle, Washington
Peanut Growers of Alabama and Georgia, New York, N.Y.
Pineapple Growers Association of Hawaii, Honolulu, Hawaii
Potatoes: Production, Storing, Processing by Smith and Published by Avi Publishing Company, Westport, Connecticut
Processed Apple Institute, New York, N.Y.
Progressive Farmer, Memphis, Tennessee
Quick Frozen Foods, New York, N.Y.
Theodore R. Sills, Inc., Chicago, Illinois
SMC Durkee Industrial Foods Group, Cleveland, Ohio
Staley, A. E., Manufacturing Co., Decatur, Illinois
Stange Company, Paterson, New Jersey
Stauffer Chemical Company, Westport, Connecticut
Sunkist Growers, Inc., Ontario, California
Sweet Potatoes: Production, Processing, Marketing by Edmond and Ammerman and published by Avi Publishing Company, Westport, Connecticut
Swift Chemical Company, Winchester, Massachusetts
Technology of Food Preservation, 3rd Edition by Desrosier and published by Avi Publishing Company, Westport, Connecticut
Tragacanth Importing Corporation, New York, N.Y.
Tressler, D. K., and Associates, Westport, Connecticut
United Fruit Sales Corporation, Boston, Massachusetts
United States Department of Agriculture, Agricultural Research Service, Washington, D.C.
United States Department of Agriculture, Eastern Utilization Research and Development Division, Philadelphia, Pennsylvania
United States Department of Agriculture, Southern Utilization Research Division, New Orleans, Louisiana
United States Department of Agriculture, Western Utilization Research and Development Division, Albany, California
University of Georgia, College of Agriculture, Experiment Station, Experiment, Georgia
University of Massachusetts, Agricultural Experiment Station, Amherst, Massachusetts
Vacu-Dry Company, Emoryville, California
Waycross Womens Club, Waycross, Georgia

Contents

FRUIT BEVERAGES AND PURÉES

APPLE JUICE BLENDS

RECOMMENDED PERCENTAGES OF BLENDS

Fruit Blend	Other Fruit %	Baldwin Apple Juice %	Added Sugar, % of Blend	*pH*	Acidity (Malic Acid) (gm/100 ml)	Brix at 17.50
Plum[1]-apple	63 Plum	37	1.5	3.40	0.98	18.50
Cherry[2]-apple	55 Cherry	45	3.0	3.22	1.14	17.75
Apple-raspberry	25 Raspberry	75	2.0	3.32	0.72	16.50
Apple-strawberry[3]	40 Strawberry	60	5.0	—	0.70	17.00
Apple-strawberry[4]	53 Strawberry	47	5.0	—	—	—
Apple-grape[5]	50 Grape	50	None	—	—	—
Apple-elderberry	20.3 Elderberry	79.7	3.3	—	—	—
Apple-cranberry	22.6 Cranberry	77.4	2.5	3.10	—	13.0

[1] Italian prune variety.
[2] Blend of Montmorency and English Morello varieties.
[3] Dresden variety.
[4] Premier variety.
[5] Concord variety.

Each of these juice blends may be flash pasteurized at 180°-190°F, filled hot into fruit-enamel-lined cans or bottles which are immediately closed, and cooled.

SOURCE: *Fruit and Vegetable Juice Processing Technology, 2nd Edition* by Tressler and Joslyn published by Avi Publishing Co., Westport, Conn.

CHERRY-APPLE JUICE

The use of apple juice instead of sugar syrup for the dilution of strong-flavored cherry and other fruit juices has the advantage of maintaining the body of the juice. Further, the product may be called juice since it is not diluted with water. Hot-pressed cherry juice has a deep red color and has a much stronger flavor than cold-pressed juice and consequently is preferred for making an apple-cherry juice blend.

Plum-Apple Juice

The Italian prunes (plums) should be washed, then split and heated to 150°F in a steam-jacketed kettle with freshly pressed apple juice, using two gallons of apple juice for each bushel of fruit. The prunes are pressed hot in an hydraulic press; double muslin cloths should be used inside the regular press cloths to prevent the flesh of the fruit from coming through. The blend should be clarified, filtered, deaerated, flash pasteurized at 180°F and packaged according to the procedure described above for cherry-apple juice.

SOURCE: *Fruit and Vegetable Juice Processing Technology, 2nd Edition* by Tressler and Joslyn published by Avi Publishing Co., Westport, Conn.

APPLE JUICE, CIDER

All varieties of apples do not make apple juice of the same quality. The character of the juice made from the varieties of apples commonly grown in Ohio are:

Sweet subacid: Baldwin, Hubbardson, McIntosh, Northwestern Greening, Rome Beauty, Stark, Grimes Golden.

Tart: Jonathan, Stayman Winesap, Northern Spy, York Imperial, Rhode Island Greening, Wealthy.

Aromatic: Delicious, Golden Delicious, Winter Banana, McIntosh.

Astringent: Crab apple.

Neutral: Ben Davis, Black Ben, Gano.

In many cases, blends of the tart and aromatic varieties will give more flavorful juice than a single variety.

Washing

Before apples are used for juice they should be thoroughly washed to remove all adhering dirt. This washing may be done by dumping the apples into troughs of moving water in which they are conveyed into the plant after which they are separated from the water and given a final spray-wash on a roller type conveyor.

Sorting

The washed apples should then be passed over a moving inspection belt from which men or women pick out and eliminate rotten and partly rotten apples.

Grinding

The washed and sorted apples are elevated to the equipment that reduces them to a pulp suitable for juice extraction. Two types of equipment are most commonly used for this process, one type grates the apples to a pulp, the other type is a hammer mill. The former type of equipment is most common in Europe but is not being introduced into North America. The hammer mill or similar equipment has been most common in North America. Regardless of the type of equipment used, care must be taken to see that the apples are reduced to the proper consistency for economical juice extraction.

Juice Extraction

The smaller "cider mills," almost invariably use hydraulic presses to press out the juice from the apple pulp.

Press racks are square lattices of wooden slats varying in total dimensions according to the press for which they are required. The wooden slats are approximately ¾-in. wide by ¼-in. thick and are spaced about ¼-in. apart. The outer slat on each side is usually about 3 in. wide for added strength. The top surface of each slat should be rounded for easy cleaning and rapid draining. The usual wood used for racks is either elm or poplar although oak has proved very strong and durable. In all cases a coat of chemical resistant varnish on the racks will make them nonabsorbent and more easily cleaned. Nails used for the racks should be brass or preferably stainless steel.

In loading a press, a rack is placed in the press truck; a form or bottomless box (slightly smaller than the rack) is placed on the rack; a press cloth is placed on the rack so that the corners hang over the sides of the form and then sufficient apple pulp is allowed to run on to the cloth so that the evenly spread depth of apple pulp fills the volume of the form. The apple pulp is then wrapped up in the cloth by folding the corners across the top. Another rack is then placed on the filled cloth and the whole process repeated until a sufficient number of "cheeses" have been made for the capacity of the press. The truckload of "cheeses" is then pushed under the press and pressure is applied.

A continuous screw-type press followed by a continuous belt-type filter are used in some apple juice plants.

The yield of apple juice to be expected is from 7.0 to 8.5 U.S. gal. or 6.0 to 7.0 Imperial gal. per 100 lb of apples. The yield will vary with such factors as variety, season, location, condition of the fruit, type of grinder, and method of extraction or pressing. Freshly picked fruit will yield more juice than similar apples that have been stored. A general observation is that after a dry season the juice will be higher in soluble solids but less in quantity than after a wet season.

Screening

Apple juice, as it comes from the press, contains more or less finely divided pomace and if the cloths are precoated, some rice hulls. To remove these particles the juice is usually screened. This is most commonly done by means of a "cider" screen. This screen is a cylinder of monel or stainless steel screen of approximately 100–150 mesh which revolves on a system of rollers.

Juice Processing

Before apple juice is placed in containers for distribution it is treated or processed in various ways depending on the type of final product desired. These treatments are given prior to pasteurization or other preservation.

Unclarified Juice

Apple juice in the unclarified state is generally sold in the fresh state or preserved by 0.1% sodium benzoate for prompt consumption. Juice of this type has the coarse particles removed by screening or settling but is not otherwise treated.

Centrifuged Apple Juice

A type of apple juice that is slightly clearer than the unclarified juice, but is considerably more opaque than the filtered juice can be made by passing the pressed, screened juice through a centrifuge. The use of a centrifuge to clarify the juice makes it possible to process juice by an almost continuous method and plants of this type were designed with this in mind. No large storage or holding tanks are required so the juice can usually be turned out in its final container within 30 min of being pressed from the apples.

Filtered Apple Juice

A large proportion of processed apple juice is sold in the filtered or brilliantly clear condition. This product is produced by passing the juice through some type of filter that removes all particles, giving a final product that is brilliantly clear.

Filtering freshly pressed apple juice is very difficult unless the juice is treated to reduce the pectinaceous nature of the product. Much of the suspended solid material is colloidal and can only be retained on a very retentive filter. Such filters are easily clogged and therefore have a low production rate. Various treatments have been developed to overcome this difficulty by making the juice more easily filtered.

Filtered juice is produced in the following general types: untreated, tannin and gelatin treated, enzyme treated, heat treated, and bentonite treated. Treated filtered juices should be brilliantly clear and are demanded in certain markets.

Untreated Juice.—A filtered juice that will have a superior flavor with excellent body can be produced without any pretreatment if the freshly pressed and screened juice is filtered and processed rapidly. Modern filters with large filter areas and resultant large capacity which are easily and quickly cleaned have been used successfully for this method. The juice has 0.5–2.0% of filter aid added and then filtered. The juice carries a slight haze but has the full flavor of the original fruit. The finished product develops no objectionable sediment during storage although a slight increase in cloudiness may occur.

Pasteurization

Flash pasteurization or HTST pasteurization means rapidly heating the juice to temperatures just below the boiling point. The usual temperatures are between 180° and 190°F with times of between 25 and 30 sec. Under usual operating conditions the juice is exposed to high temperatures for not over 3 min including heating, holding, and filling. Numerous types of HTST heat exchangers are available. The basic procedure in all of them is to heat the juice very rapidly by passing it in a thin film between plates or through small diameter tubes that are heated by steam or hot water. The high speed flow causes turbulence in the juice which prevents scorching the product. The hot juice is filled into containers which are immediately sealed and cooled. The HTST method causes little reduction in the flavor of apple juice because the short exposure of heat causes no scorched flavor. This method is the one most commonly used because of its adaptability to continuous operations.

Fruit-enamel-lined cans or glass bottles are the best containers for apple juice.

SOURCE: *Fruit and Vegetable Juice Processing Technology, 2nd Edition* by Tressler and Joslyn published by Avi Publishing Co., Westport, Conn.

"CRUSHED" APPLE JUICE

"Crushed" apple juice is an extreme type of unclarified apple juice containing a large quantity of fine cellular material. In this process no cider press is used; instead the sorted and washed apples are passed through a rough slicer and then into a Schwartz comminutor extractor. This is a vertical mill which grinds the fruit and forces the juice and fine particles through a special rubber screen. The perforations in the screen vary from 1600 to 3600 per sq in. The Schwartz machine may be varied to give any desired amount of pulp in the extracted juice. The amount of solids is usually between 3 and 10%. The pulpy juice is drawn by vacuum into a deaerator and then through a homogenizer to the pasteurizer. The juice is pasteurized at 190°F and filled into the containers, then cooled and cased. As this type of juice should be very light or pale in color, it is essential that every precaution be taken to prevent oxidation. The process is, therefore, continuous with the juice never being exposed to the air.

SOURCE: *Fruit and Vegetable Juice Processing Technology, 2nd Edition* by Tressler and Joslyn published by Avi Publishing Co., Westport, Conn.

FROZEN APPLE JUICE

All kinds of apple juice can be frozen without notable change, except for browning because of enzyme action. This can be prevented either by flash heating the juice to 170°F and promptly cooling and freezing, or by the addition of a small amount (e.g., 0.1%) of ascorbic acid prior to freezing. The frozen juice keeps best in airtight containers.

SOURCE: *Fruit and Vegetable Juice Processing Technology, 2nd Edition* by Tressler and Joslyn published by Avi Publishing Co., Westport, Conn.

STRAINED APPLES AND APRICOTS

Dried apricots are washed, and then soaked overnight in about three times their weight of water. The next day the fruit is cooked in the soaking water for about 15 min. A quantity of applesauce, either frozen or freshly prepared, twice the weight of the dried apricots used, is added to the cooked apricots and mixed thoroughly. The mixture is then converted into a purée by running it through a rotary finisher fitted with a screen with 0.027-in. openings. The resulting purée is homogenized, pumped through a flash sterilizer (tubular heat exchanger), cooled to the proper filling temperature by passage through another heat exchanger, and then packaged and quick frozen.

SOURCE: *Freezing Preservation of Foods, 4th Edition, Vol. 4* by Tressler, Van Arsdel and Copley published by Avi Publishing Co., Westport, Conn.

CRANBERRY CIDER

Ingredients	Qt	Lb
Cranberry juice	10	
Apple juice, fresh, flash pasteurized	1½	
Sugar		3

Procedure

Mix ingredients, use immediately, or freeze or flash pasteurize and pack in cans.

SOURCE: *Cranberry Products*, University of Massachusetts Agricultural Experiment Station Bull. *481*.

VITAMIN C-ENRICHED CANNED OPALESCENT APPLE JUICE

1. Thoroughly wash the apples to remove dirt and spray residue. It is advantageous to chill the the washed fruit to about 34°-40°F before grinding.

2. Rapidly grind the apples in a hammer mill or disintegrator. A stainless steel mill is preferred. Under no circumstances should a mill having exposed copper surfaces be used.

3. Press the pomace in the usual manner. Nylon press cloths and clean hardwood press racks coated with glyptol are preferred. Bulky press cloths introduce excessive air into the juice. All metal parts of the press which are exposed to the juice should be stainless steel or lined with stainless steel. The juice should be collected in a stainless steel trough and any large particles which may have been squeezed out in processing should be removed by passing the juice through a 100-mesh stainless steel sieve. Pipe lines, pumps, and other equipment should be of stainless steel.

A proportioning pump is used to introduce the L-ascorbic acid solution (10% L-ascorbic acid in apple juice) into a metered flow of juice from the press. If holding tanks are at times necessary, then L-ascorbic acid may be introduced at that point. In either case, it is important to add the L-ascorbic acid to the pressed juice as soon as possible. Usually 1000 mg pure ascorbic acid is added per gallon of juice.

4. After screening, the juice is immediately deaerated, flash pasteurized at 180°F, and canned. Headspace in the container should be kept at the lowest practical minimum.

5. Rapidly cool the cans in cold water; then air cool to as low as 34°F before casing. *Insufficient cooling greatly reduces storage life.* Store the juice below 70°F if possible.

SOURCE: Hoffmann LaRoche, Inc., Nutley, N.J.

APRICOT FRUIT PUNCH

Ingredients	Amount
Canned apricot nectar	2 46-oz cans
Canned pineapple juice	2 46-oz cans
Frozen orange juice	2 12-oz containers
Frozen lemonade	2 12-oz containers
Sugar	¾ cup
Cold water	1 gal.
Ginger ale	2 qt
Lemon sherbet (optional)	2 qt

Yield: About 3½ gal.

Procedure

Combine apricot nectar, pineapple juice, orange juice, lemonade, sugar, and cold water. Stir to mix well and refrigerate until the punch is to be served. Add ginger ale and sherbet to punch just before it is to be served. If the punch is to be served over a period of time, it is best to omit the lemon sherbet and serve the punch with a block of ice in the bowl.

SOURCE: D. K. Tressler and Associates, Westport, Conn.

CANNED APRICOT NECTAR

The process now used for making and preserving apricot nectar may be briefly described as follows: Soft ripe apricots are thoroughly washed, then passed over an inspection belt to eliminate damaged fruit and foreign matter. The fruit is steamed in a continuous steam cooker for approximately 5 min. The hot fruit is then run through a brush finisher equipped with a fine screen, having holes approximately 0.025 in. in diameter. The resulting purée is then passed through a steam heated tubular heat exchanger where it is brought to a temperature of 190°-200°F.

The purée is then sweetened with approximately an equal quantity of 15°-16° Brix sugar syrup acidified with citric acid. The amount and concentration of sugar syrup and citric acid is adjusted so as to maintain a constant total solids-acid ratio throughout the season. The resulting nectar is filled into plain tin cans, exhausted for approximately 6 min and sealed. No. 1 tall cans are cooked for 15 min at 212°F; larger cans are given a longer process.

In some canneries the purée is mixed with the acidified sugar syrup, flash heated to 205°F in a steam heated tubular heat exchanger and filled immediately; the cans are sealed then cooled with sprays of water.

SOURCE: *Fruit and Vegetable Juice Processing Technology, 2nd Edition* by Tressler and Joslyn published by Avi Publishing Co., Westport, Conn.

CANNED APRICOT PURÉE

Apricot purée can be prepared by steaming washed, pitted apricots until soft; passing through an expeller screw extractor of the type commonly used for making tomato juice; adding 1 part of sugar to 3 of pulp; canning in plain tin cans; exhausting 8-10 min (No. 1 tall cans); processing 20-25 min at 212°F; and cooling immediately. The undiluted product prepared in this way is of purée consistency, and requires dilution with water before use as a beverage.

Apricot purée diluted with sugar syrup prior to canning gives an especially attractive ready-to-drink beverage which is very popular.

SOURCE: *Fruit and Vegetable Juice Processing Technology, 2nd Edition* by Tressler and Joslyn published by Avi Publishing Co., Westport, Conn.

BANANA PURÉE

The delicate flavor of properly ripened bananas is successfully maintained when L-ascorbic acid is used.

Procedure

1. Ripen bananas properly. Green bananas have an astringent taste; over-ripe bananas lack flavor.
2. Wash and peel the fruit.
3. Pack bananas tightly into containers. Several variations of packing may be used. The whole bananas may be mashed into the can or the fruit may be puréed or ground prior to packing. In either case, the finished pack must not contain any air pockets. The grinding used should not incorporate air into the purée.
4. After the containers are full of purée, a dry paper (not waterproof) disc is firmly placed on the surface and up the sides of the container for at least ½ in.
5. Pour over the disc, a water solution of L-ascorbic acid as indicated below.

Addition of L-Ascorbic Acid Solution to Banana Pulp

No. of Cans	Wt of Pulp or Pulp and Sugar in Can (Lb)	Volume of Solution Added on Disc of Each Can (Fl Oz)
1000	6[1]	1
1000	15	3
1000	30	5-6

Total Solution Required per 1000 Cans (Gal.)	Ounces of Dry L-Ascorbic Acid to Add per 1000 Cans to Obtain Per Pound of Finished Pack		
	Mg	Mg	Mg
	75	100	150
8	16	21	32
23	40	53	80
39-46	80	106	159

[1] Packed in No. 10 cans.

6. Put container, still in upright position, into -20°F freezer. For packs of banana purées which will be held a month or so, sugar addition is not necessary. For better flavor retention during long storage, the addition of about 1 part (by weight) of sugar to 10 parts of purée is suggested. The sugar is thoroughly mixed with the purée and the L-ascorbic acid added as indicated above.

Sliced Bananas

Sliced or broken banana pieces may be processed by spraying with L-ascorbic acid solution just prior to, or after, packaging. A spray of 200 mg of L-ascorbic acid in ½ oz of water per pound of fruit is used. The tightest possible packing should be used and the fruit should be immediately frozen.

SOURCE: Hoffmann-LaRoche, Inc., Nutley, N.J.

CANNED ACIDIFIED BANANA PURÉE

Good mature raw bananas at color index No. 6 and 7 are selected and peeled carefully with attention to removal of peel, rag, and rot. The bananas should be blanched whole in steam or boiling water (or a combination or both) until a center temperature of 190°F is reached. A medium size, peeled banana requires about 6-8 min to attain this center temperature. The blanched bananas are checked for sugar content and pH value. They are puréed or macerated to the desired viscosity in a comminution machine. Either during the comminuting process, or after it, sugar and citric acid are metered and blended into the banana purée to obtain the desired sugar level and the necessary pH of 4.1-4.3. The purée is heated to approximately 200°F and filled into enameled No. 1 cans. The cans are closed immediately, inverted, and held for 5 min followed by water cooling to 100°F. The entire operation from peeling to filling into cans should be carried out as rapidly as possible to ensure a high quality product.

SOURCE: *Fruit and Vegetable Juice Processing Technology, 2nd Edition* by Tressler and Joslyn published by Avi Publishing Company, Westport, Conn.

BERRY JUICES

Sort and wash fully ripe blackberries, boysenberries, gooseberries, loganberries, raspberries, strawberries, or youngberries; put through a hammer mill fitted with ¼-in. screen, and press as indicated below.

Cold Pressing Fresh Berries

To the crushed fresh berries add 3-10% filter aid (see cherry juice), and press immediately in a bag-type press. The amount of filter aid used depends on the firmness of the berries, and should be enough to produce a firm, dry press cake. The yield of juice depends on the kind, variety, and maturity of berries.

Treat the cloudy juice from the press immediately with a pectic enzyme preparation to remove pectin. Treat with 0.5% Pectinol M at 75°F, for 3 hr, then filter under pressure using filter aid-precoated plates in addition to 0.25% filter aid in the juice. Flash pasteurize the juice at about 207°F for 15 sec, fill completely at 180°F or higher.

Hot Pressing Fresh Berries

Heat the sorted, fully ripe, washed berries in a steam-jacketed kettle to 140°-180°F, with continuous agitation. Press immediately in an hydraulic rack-and-cloth press (using a muslin liner on the cloths), with a yield of 68-70% juice. The use of a continuous screw expeller will give about 2% higher yield of juice, but with less clarity and more astringency. Pasteurize as with cold pressed juice.

Cold Pressing Thawed Berries

Freezing and thawing berries before pressing has the following advantages: (a) coagulates mucilaginous compounds to facilitate pressing and rendering heating unnecessary; (b) increases yield of juice up to 10%; (c) operates juice plant throughout the year; (d) obtains juice with deeper color; and (d) with more fresh fruit flavor.

SOURCE: *Fruit and Vegetable Juice Processing Technology, 2nd Edition* by Tressler and Joslyn published by Avi Publishing Co., Westport, Conn.

CANNED AND BOTTLED BERRY JUICES

(Blackberry, Boysenberry, Loganberry, Raspberry, and Youngberry)

Methods of Preparation

Berry juices may be prepared from either fresh or frozen fruit. When fresh fruit is used, the process generally employed for blackberries, boysenberries, loganberries, raspberries, and youngberries is the following: Fully ripe, washed, and sorted berries are placed in a steam-jacketed kettle where they are heated to 140°-175°F. During heating the fruit is agitated continuously either by mechanical means or by paddles. This agitation and heating partially crushes the berries, thus aiding in the extraction and fixation of the color. The heating also reduces the mucilaginous character of the partially crushed berries and so facilitates the pressing. As soon as the berries reach the desired temperature, they are pressed preferably in an hydraulic rack-and-cloth press. Long continued heating should be avoided as otherwise tannin and other disagreeably flavored substances may be extracted from the seeds.

Continuous screw expeller presses are sometimes used, but because of the excessive maceration of the pulp the resulting juice is very pulpy and is usually difficult to clarify.

Frozen berries, usually those prepared without sugar, are sometimes used for juice. Their use has three definite advantages. Freezing effects a coagulation of the mucilaginous components which otherwise make pressing difficult, thus making heating of the berries unnecessary. A higher yield of juice is obtained from frozen berries than is the case when heated fresh berries are used. A third advantage is that when frozen berries are used as raw material, the juice plant may be operated throughout the year instead of only during the season when fresh berries are available.

Clarification

Since most berry juices are ordinarily marketed as clear juices, filtration is necessary. During the heating required to effect pasteurization, clouding and possibly coagulation and deposition of colloidal matter may occur if the juice has not been preheated at a temperature slightly above that used in pasteurization. For this reason, berry juices should be heated to a temperature of approximately 190°F and then cooled, and filtered through an aluminum or wooden filter press using Hyflo Super-Cel[1], Dicalite[2], or some similar substance as a filter aid.

Treatment of berry juices with a pectic enzyme preparation aids materially in effecting clarification. According to this clarification procedure, the juice is centrifuged for 5 min at 3500 rpm, then decanted and prepared for filtration by digestion at 113°F with a strong enzymatic extract of *Aspergillus oryzae*. After the suspended matter has been thrown down, the juice can easily be filtered. The commercial pectic enzyme preparation, Pectinol, may be used for loganberry, strawberry, and other fruit juices.

Loganberry juice is usually not filtered prior to canning but is merely carefully strained.

Deaeration of berry juices prior to pasteurization is recommended in order to prevent undesirable changes caused by oxidation during storage of the pasteurized juice. These changes include loss of color and flavor, and the clouding of the clear juice. Deaeration may be effected either by the batch process in which the juice is run into a tank and then subjected to a high vacuum (28 in. or higher) for 30 min, or by a continuous process. By the latter process, the juice is sprayed into an evacuated chamber, thus deaerating the juice almost instantaneously.

Pasteurization

Berry juices are best preserved by flash pasteurization. The juice should be heated to 190°F for about 1 min as it passes through a flash pasteurizer; filled at this temperature into the warm bottles or the proper type (enamel-lined) can; the can sealed, then turned on its side and cooled immediately by passage through a trough of water. The so-called berry enameled charcoal Type L tinplate can is recommended for berry juices, with the exception of strawberry juice.

[1] Hyflo Super-Cel is made by Johns-Manville, New York.
[2] Dicalite is made by the Dicalite Co., New York.

SOURCE: *Fruit and Vegetable Juice Processing Technology, 2nd Edition* by Tressler and Joslyn published by Avi Publishing Co., Westport, Conn.

BLUEBERRY JUICE

Hot Pressing

According to the process worked out at the New York State Agricultural Experiment Station, the washed blueberries should be heated in a steam-jacketed aluminum or stainless steel kettle, agitating the berries slowly during the heating process. When the berries reach 180°F, they should be put through a screw impeller type of tomato juice extractor. The temperature of the extracted juice should be raised to 180°F by passage through a heat interchanger. The hot juice should be run into carboys which are completely filled and then closed with a paraffined cork according to the process used for grape juice (p. 13). After standing in a cool cellar for at least two months, the juice is siphoned from the heavy sludge on the bottom of the carboys. It is then flash pasteurized at 180°F, according to the usual procedure, filled into bottles or cans (fill each container completely) which are promptly cooled.

Cold Pressing

Instead of heating the berries to release the juice, sort, wash, and macerate the fresh blueberries; crush; and then mix with 0.1% Pectinol M. After standing for 2 hr at 65°-70°F the product is pressed in an hydraulic press, using a pressure approximately 6000 lb per sq in. A yield of nearly 88% of juice is obtained, which is slightly more than when the berries are heated prior to pressing. Thus, 1 bushel of blueberries yields approximately 4 gal. of juice. Juice prepared by this method is red in color and translucent in layers approximately 2 in. in thickness. By contrast, the juice from cooked blueberries is almost opaque in layers of this thickness. The cold pressed juice is flash heated and filled into containers at a temperature of at least 180°F; fill each container completely.

SOURCE: *Fruit and Vegetable Juice Processing Technology, 2nd Edition* by Tressler and Joslyn published by Avi Publishing Co., Westport, Conn.

CHERRY JUICE

Make juice from fully ripe, washed, sour cherries (Montmorency or Early Richmond for brilliant juice, or English Morello for dark red juice), and sweet cherries (Bing) separately, and blend and sweeten to taste.

Hot Pressing

Heat washed cherries to 150°F, and press while hot, using medium press cloth and corrosion-resistant metal containers. Chill juice to 50°F and let settle over night. Siphon off clear juice; add small amount of filter aid (e.g., Hyflo Super-Cel[1] or Dicalite[2]) and filter through canvas in a plate and frame filter press.

Cold Pressing

Soak washed fruit in chilled water over night; drain, comminute into coarse pulp, and press in a rack-and-cloth hydraulic press. Heat freshly pressed juice quickly to 190°-200°F; cool to 120°F; add 0.1% by weight of pectic enzyme (Pectinol M) and hold for 3 hr. Heat to 170°-180°F, then cool and filter through plate and frame filter press.

Mix cold pressed (light colored) and hot pressed (dark colored) juice in ratio of 2:1, or otherwise, to produce a more desirable color. Add sugar to bring density to about 17° Balling, and if juice is too "heavy" add up to 50% 17° Balling syrup.

Pack in bottles or cans, using type L charcoal plate lined with sanitary or berry (Improved R) enamel, and pasteurize at 140°-145°F for 30 min, or flash pasteurize at 207°F for 15 sec.

Carbonated cherry juice may be prepared by adding three volumes of carbon dioxide.

Make cherry syrup by concentrating the juice to one-half volume either by low temperature vacuum evaporation or freezing concentration.

---

[1] Hyflo Super-Cel is made by Johns-Mansville, New York.

[2] Dicalite is made by The Dicalite Co., New York.

SOURCE: *Fruit and Vegetable Juice Processing Technology, 2nd Edition* by Tressler and Joslyn published by Avi Publishing Co., Westport, Conn.

CANNED CHERRY "COCKTAIL"

Blends of hot-pressed and cold-pressed cherry juice are somewhat superior to either alone. Four lots of cherry juice are prepared: (1) hot-pressed Montmorency juice, (2) cold-pressed, pectinol-clarified Montmorency juice, (3) hot-pressed English Morello juice, and (4) cold-pressed Pectinol-clarified English Morello juice. Each lot of juice is filtered, and then all are blended together. The mixture is diluted with an equal volume of 15% sugar syrup. The composition of the final blend, which contains approximately 15% total solids, is as follows:

	%
Cold-pressed Montmorency juice	28.1
Hot-pressed Montmorency juice	9.4
Cold-pressed English Morello juice	9.4
Hot-pressed English Morello juice	3.1
15% sugar syrup	50.0
	100.0

The blend is strained, deaerated, flash pasteurized at 180°F and packed in cans lined with "berry enamel."

Care should be taken to fill each can completely with hot (180°F) juice and close immediately; invert and cool the cans before labeling.

SOURCE: *Fruit and Vegetable Juice Processing Technology, 2nd Edition* by Tressler and Joslyn published by Avi Publishing Co., Westport, Conn.

FROZEN CHERRY JUICE

Fully ripe, red, sour (tart) cherries of either the Montmorency or English Morello variety should be used. The English Morello variety yields a juice of much darker color and richer flavor than the Montmorency, but it is so strong that it is best when diluted or blended with apple juice.

The first step in the preparation of cold-pressed cherry juice is the crushing of carefully washed Montmorency or English Morello cherries. The crushing can be effected either between rolls spaced so that the seeds are not broken, or in an apple grater adjusted for coarse grating. The crushed cherries are pressed in an hydraulic press using either fine press cloths, or coarse cloths lined with muslin or some similar material. If a clear juice is desired, it should be treated with the pectin enzyme preparation, Pectinol, prior to filtration. Details concerning the preparation of both cold-pressed and hot-pressed juice are given above for Cherry Juice.

When Montmorency or English Morello cherries are pitted, much juice leaks from the fruit. This juice is usually saved, and some of it is preserved by freezing. Although this juice is a fine flavor, it is very pale in color and so it is not considered to be of high quality.

Hot-pressed cherry juice is prepared by first heating in steam kettles either whole or crushed cherries to 150°-180°F. The hot cherries are pressed in hydraulic presses using the same kind of press cloths that are used in cold-pressing. Hot-pressed juice may be clarified by filtration without treatment with Pectinol.

A juice of superior quality can be made by blending juice from Montmorency cherries with that from English Morellos. Further, it has been found that the blending of hot-pressed with cold-pressed juice is desirable.

The juice may be packed in either large or small containers taking care to allow about 10% head-space and then freezing in an air blast freezer.

SOURCE: *The Freezing Preservation of Foods, 2nd Edition* by Tressler and Evers published by Avi Publishing Co., Westport, Conn.

FLAVOR BASE FOR A SINGLE-STRENGTH CHERRY POWDER BEVERAGE MIX

A cherry flavor base powder, to make a single-strength cherry beverage mix for reconstitution with water.

Ingredients	%	For a 32-Oz Serving Gm
Cherry flavor base powder	3.56	4.1296
Sugar	91.30	105.9121
Citric acid, anhydrous	5.00	5.8000
Ascorbic acid	0.10	0.1195
FD&C Red No. 2*	0.04	0.0387
FD&C Yellow No. 6	0.00	0.0001
Total	100.00	116.0000

Procedure

Blend all ingredients thoroughly with rapid agitation until a homogeneous suspension is obtained.

---

*This coloring has been de-listed. It is no longer on the FDA-approved list of food colors and cannot be used. Consult your food color supplier for recommended color substitution.

SOURCE: Foamat Foods Corp., Corvallis, Oregon.

FROZEN CITRUS PURÉES

Sound, fully mature fruit is first thoroughly washed, preferably with a good detergent, and rinsed well with clean cold water to reduce microbial contamination to a minimum. If made from immature fruit certain citrus varieties yield purées that have a tendency to be bitter. Medium to small fruit is preferred because of the better yield and quality of the juice. After the fruit is washed, the stem end may be cut off and discolored spots removed so that no dark specks will be mixed in with the bright-colored purée. If Washington Navel oranges are used, the navel end should first be removed.

After the whole fruit has been trimmed, it is either crushed in a machine, such as an apricot pitter, or sliced by means of circular saws. The crushed or sliced fruit is then put through a rotary or tapered screw press fitted with stainless-steel screens of appropriate mesh, so that most of the fruit is reduced to the form of a purée. Screen openings of 0.027-0.044 in. in diameter are usually employed, depending on the end use of the purée. Screen sizes of 0.027 and 0.033 in. are preferable when purées are intended for sherbets, ices, pies, and beverages, but larger sizes are better for purées intended for marmalades, jams, cake, and sundae toppings.

Yield of purée from the whole fruit is approximately 50-60%, and should contain 0.40-0.75% peel oil depending on the variety of fruit. With some lots of fruit the peel-oil content of the purée may be considerably higher and too strong for most uses. Then the oil content of the purée can be controlled if various proportions of the fresh fruit are passed through an abrasive machine prior to crushing to remove most of the oil sacs or flavedo. Another method of standardizing the oil content of purées is by adding different proportions of single-strength juice.

After a purée of the required oil content is obtained, it is run into a stainless-steel tank, and dry sugar gradually added with thorough mixing in the proportion of 1 part of sugar to 5 parts of purée. Purées may be packed without the addition of sugar. The sweetened or unsweetened purée is filled into enameled tin containers of 1 to 2½ gal. capacity, the cans are hermetically sealed or closed with slip tops, and the contents are frozen at subzero temperatures. The product is stored at 0° to -10°F. The time of freezing can be reduced if the purée is first frozen to a slush in a mechanically agitated heat exchanger before filling into cans.

Frozen citrus purées are used in the commercial preparation of milk sherbets and water ices. According to the USDA Agricultural Marketing Service, milk sherbets having approximately 2.5% butterfat have a more pleasing flavor than water ices. Lemon and lime purées find use in the making of ades and other fruit drinks. Other uses for frozen citrus purées are in puddings, cakes, pies, marmalades, and jams and in making ice cream toppings.

SOURCE: *Fruit and Vegetable Juice Processing Technology, 2nd Edition* by Tressler and Joslyn published by Avi Publishing Co., Westport, Conn.

CRANBERRY JUICE

Cranberry juice may be obtained by either cold or hot extraction methods. Heat-extracted juice is bright red, syrupy, and high in pectin content. To make a palatable beverage or "cranberry cocktail," the pure juice is diluted with 1½-2 parts of water and sufficient sugar added to raise the total sugar content to 15-20%.

Cold-extracted juice is obtained by grinding the cranberries and allowing them to set for several hours before pressing. The yield from a barrel (100 lb) of cranberries is approximately 7 gal. The juice has the consistency of syrup and contains some sediment, which is removed by adding a commercial pectolytic enzyme preparation such as Pectinol and then by filtering with a filter aid.

Juice may also be extracted by running raw frozen and thawed cranberries through a screw extractor. This method gives a yield of 8-8½ gal. of juice to a barrel of cranberries.

Frozen cranberries are more suitable than fresh fruit for juice manufacture. They have a deeper color and require less cooking to make heat-extracted juice. Moreover, after grinding, frozen cranberries do not need to set before pressing. Juice from frozen fruit contains considerably more pectin and is more viscous than juice from fresh fruit. Because of its greater viscosity, it has to be treated with Pectinol before it can be filtered.

Sweetened cranberry syrup (65% solids) can be prepared only after destroying the natural pectin content of the juice by Pectinol. The clear syrup is very attractive and useful as a fountain syrup or for preparing beverages.

Unless highly colored fruit is used, the color of the final product, because of dilution with water, is light and unsatisfactory rather than an attractive, rich red. Early Black is one of the best juice varieties.

This frozen sweetened juice is diluted with two parts of water to make a ready-to-drink cranberry cocktail.

One of the major problems in the commercial manufacture of cranberry juice and cocktail is obtaining sufficient quantity of dark, richly colored cranberries.

Both straight cranberry juice and cranberry juice cocktail are preserved by flash pasteurizing at 180°F and filling hot into bottles or fruit enamel-lined cans, taking care to fill the containers with the hot juice within ¼ in. of the top and inverting them before cooling.

SOURCE: *Cranberries*, Bull. 481, Massachusetts Agriculture Experiment Station, Amherst, Mass.

CRANBERRY JUICE COCKTAIL

The most common commercial procedure followed in making cranberry juice cocktail is to put thawed cranberries through a tapered screw extractor. A yield of 8-8½ gal. of juice is obtained from each 100 lb of fruit. For cocktail, this product is diluted with twice its volume of water and sufficient sugar is added to bring the specific gravity up to 15° Brix. The pomace may be used for making strained cranberry sauce.

SOURCE: *Fruit and Vegetable Juice Processing Technology, 2nd Edition* by Tressler and Joslyn published by Avi Publishing Co., Westport, Conn.

BOTTLED BLACK CURRANT JUICE

Black currants are steamed at about 176°F in a continuous steamer which simultaneously comminutes the fruit. The pulp is mixed with about 3% of a filter aid (filter cel) and then pressed in an hydraulic press. Usually the pomace from the press cloths is disintegrated and repressed. The juice is sufficiently acid (low pH) so that it can be preserved by flash pasteurization. The product can be diluted with 3 volumes of water, filtered, and heated to 170°F; then it is filled into clean hot bottles to produce a popular British beverage.

SOURCE: D. K. Tressler, and Associates, Westport, Conn.

BOTTLED RED CURRANT JUICE

Although currant juice is extensively used for making jelly and is used in a limited way for punches and other mixed fruit beverages, its use for beverage purposes is not of great importance in this country.

The methods used for making Concord grape juice may be employed in making currant juice. However, since the juice does not contain potassium bitartrate, it is not necessary to hold currant juice to eliminate argols. The hot-pressed juice may be flash pasteurized and bottled immediately after filtration.

SOURCE: *Fruit and Vegetable Juice Processing Technology, 2nd Edition* by Tressler and Joslyn published by Avi Publishing Co., Westport, Conn.

FREEZING FRUIT JUICES AND FRUIT JUICE CONCENTRATES

Quick freezing methods may be subdivided into (1) those in which the juice is slush-frozen before being packaged, (2) those in which the containers are rotated while immersed in a refrigerated liquid, (3) those in which the juice is frozen in small containers in contact with refrigerated metallic surfaces, and (4) those in which the juice is frozen in small containers in an air blast tunnel at a low temperature. Method No. 1 effects very rapid freezing, but in the case of orange and other easily oxidizable juices, care must be taken to prevent exposure to air during freezing and also the inclusion of air in the container during packaging of the slush.

SOURCE: *Fruit and Vegetable Juice Processing Technology, 2nd Edition* by Tressler and Joslyn published by Avi Publishing Co., Westport, Conn.

FRUIT JUICE DRINK FORMULATIONS

Drink	Formula	Soluble Solids (%)	Acidity as Tartaric Acid (%)	Brix/Acid Ratio
Apple	Apple concentrate—36.4 lb (70% soluble solids) Sugar—91.0 lb Citric acid—2.7 lb Sodium citrate—7.2 oz Water to make—100 gal.	11.5-12.0	0.41-0.44	28
Apricot-grapefruit	Apricot concentrate—8.32 gal. (24% soluble solids) Grapefruit concentrate—3.25 gal. (39% soluble solids) Sugar—131 lb Citric acid—1.8 lb Rapid-set pectin 150 grade—1.8 lb Water to make—100 gal.	14.5-15.0	0.47	31
Cherry (sweet)	Sweet cherry juice—50 gal. Water—50 gal. Sugar to give 14% soluble solids Citric acid to give 0.43% total acid Fruit punch flavor—5 fl oz	14.0	0.43	33
Grape	Grape concentrate—5.5 gal. (50% soluble solids) Sugar Citric acid Concord grape flavoring Concord coloring Water to make—100 gal.	12.0-12.5	0.45	28
Orange-apricot	Orange concentrate—1.80 gal. (63% soluble solids) Apricot concentrate—5.25 gal. (22% soluble solids) Sugar—90 lb Rapid-set pectin 100 grade—2.75 lb Water to make—100 gal.	12.5	0.65	19.3
Raspberry	Raspberry juice—33.3 gal. (7.7% soluble solids) Water—66.6 gal. Sugar—102 lb	16.0	0.68	23

SOURCE: Canadian Department of Agriculture, Ottawa, Ontario, Canada.

FRUIT JUICE NECTAR FORMULATIONS

Fruit Juice Blends	Formula	Soluble Solids (%)	Acidity as Hydrous Citric Acid (%)	Brix/Acid Ratio
Apple-apricot	Opalescent apple juice—47.50 gal. (11.9% soluble solids) Apricot purée—26.25 gal. (12% soluble solids) Sugar syrup—26.25 gal. (22% soluble solids)	14.5	0.51	29

Fruit Juice Blends	Formula	Soluble Solids (%)	Acidity as Hydrous Citric Acid (%)	Brix/Acid Ratio
Apple-black currant	Opalescent apple juice—74 gal. (14.3% soluble solids) Black currant juice—22 gal. (9.6% soluble solids) Sugar—43 lb	16-17	0.68	24
Apple-cranberry	Clarified Delicious apple juice—86 gal. (12% soluble solids) Depectinized cranberry juice—14 gal. (12% soluble solids) Sugar—35 lb	15	0.68	22
Apple-grape	Clarified apple juice—50 gal. (12.6% soluble solids) Red or purple grape juice conc—10 gal. (50% soluble solids) Sugar—25 lb Concord grape essence—0.5 gal. Water to make—100 gal.	15	0.64	25
Apple-orange	Single-strength orange juice—20 gal. (12% soluble solids) Opalescent apple juice—45 gal. (11.9% soluble solids) Sugar syrup—35 gal. (22% soluble solids) Orange oil (cold press)—4 fl oz	16.2	0.72	23
Apple-raspberry	Delicious apple juice (clarified)—75 gal. (12.5% soluble solids) Raspberry juice—25 gal. (7.7% soluble solids) Sugar—52 lb	16.5	0.80	20
Orange	Brazilian type orange concentrate—84.2 lb (63% soluble solids) Valencia type concentrate—45.3 lb (59% soluble solids) Sugar—57.8 lb Orange oil (cold press)—1.6 fl oz Water to make—100 gal.	12.0-12.5	0.68	18
Opalescent apple-lime	Opalescent Delicious apple juice—97 gal. (14% soluble solids) Top pulp lime juice—3 gal. (8% soluble solids) Citric acid to give 0.7% total acid Sugar—14 lb	15	0.70	21.5
Pineapple-grapefruit	Pineapple concentrate—102 lb (61% soluble solids) Grapefruit concentrate—113 lb (39% soluble solids) Sugar—56.5 lb Citric acid—90 oz Sodium citrate—36 oz Water to make—100 gal.	15.0	1.24	12

SOURCE: Canadian Department of Agriculture, Ottawa, Ontario, Canada.

PECTINIZED FRUIT PURÉE

Ingredients	Berry Lb	Berry Oz	Peach Lb	Peach Oz
Fruit	100		100	
Sugar	80		76	
Slow-set citrus pectin 150 grade		17.3		17
Monocalcium phosphate		1.7		1.7
Citric acid		0		4

Procedure

The amount of sugar used is such that the final soluble solids content is about 50%.

(1) The purée is divided into two portions in the ratio of 60 to 40.

(2) Slow-set citrus pectin, approximately 0.6% of the weight of final product (purée plus sugar) for 150 grade, is dispersed and dissolved as follows: The pectin is mixed with about ten times its weight of sugar. An amount of purée equal in weight to this sugar is taken from the 60% portion and added to the pectin-sugar mixture. The mixture is stirred until all of the sugar is dissolved. This step helps dispersion by allowing the particles to become wetted without much swelling. The concentrated pectin mixture is then added to the remainder of the 60% portion of purée to form mixture A, and is mixed for about 20 min with a mechanical mixer of a type that does not beat air into the product. The soluble solids content at this stage should not exceed 25%. A higher sugar concentration will interfere with proper dissolving of the pectin. As an alternative and somewhat simpler procedure, the dry pectin can be mixed with approximately 2.5 times its weight of glycerin or 10 times its weight of invert sugar, and then added slowly to the 60% portion with constant stirring for about 20 min.

(3) The calculated amount of sugar, required to increase the soluble solids of the purée to 50% is mixed into the 40% portion. This will be referred to as mixture B. The greater part of the sugar will dissolve. Amount of sugar required to increase soluble solids to 50% can be calculated from the following equation:

$$x = \{0.50y - [(s.s/100)(y)]\}/0.50$$

where x = weight of total amount of added sugar, y = weight of fruit purée, and $s.s$ = percent soluble solids determined by refractometer using the sucrose scale.

The amount of sugar to be added to the 40% portion then becomes x, less the amount of sugar, glycerin, or invert sugar added to the pectin.

(4) The mixture B is added to the 60% pectinized portions, (mixture A) and stirring is continued until all of the sugar is dissolved and a uniform mixture is obtained (approximately 5 min).

(5) Monocalcium phosphate is made into a slurry by the addition of small amount of water. This slurry is then mixed into pectinized purée. When desired, citric acid (50% solution) is also added at this stage.

(6) Two parts of the pectinized purée are then packed with 1 to 1.5 parts of sliced fruit (peaches or strawberries) or whole berries (raspberries and other similar berries).

(7) After packaging, the product is frozen in an airblast at −20°F or lower, and stored at 0°F, and then placed into freezing storage.

SOURCE: *The Freezing Preservation of Foods, 4th Edition, Vol. 2* by Tressler, Van Arsdel and Copley published by Avi Publishing Co., Westport, Conn.

PASTEURIZED GRAPE JUICE

The most popular grape juice is that of the Concord variety which is the first variety preserved for year round use.

Juice is expressed from grapes by hot-pressing, i.e., heating and then pressing. Concord grapes are almost always heated to extract color from the skin.

The fully ripened grapes are washed and crushed and the grape mass is heated in a heat exchanger to 140°F. Grapes may be heated to higher temperatures for longer times if additional color extraction is desired. After crushing, the grapes may be treated with enzymes to break down the pectin. The juice may be pressed either in a hydraulic rack-and-frame press similar to those described for apple juice (p. 2) or by more modern equipment using a Garolla, Zenith, Willmes, Vincent, or other type of press. Practically all of the latter pressing techniques require the addition of a filter aid. Stainless steel screw-presses have been successfully used commercially and are more sanitary and require less labor than the hydraulic rack and frame press. The juice yield per ton of grapes is 175-185 gal.

The extracted juice is flash-heated in a plate-type or tubular heat exchanger to 175°-185°F for pasteurization. It is then cooled to 32°F and pumped into storage tanks, glass carboys, or wood barrels, where it is held at cool temperatures for 1 to 6 months to allow the mixture of potassium bitartrate, tannins, and other substances commonly known as argols to settle.

Pasteurization and Bottling

After settling for 3-6 months, the grape juice is siphoned off the argols, filtered and then flash pasteurized in a heat exchanger, either tubular or plate, filled hot into bottles or cans (taking care to fill completely) which are immediately closed. Grape juice is very corrosive of tinplate; therefore fruit enamel-lined cans must be used.

Frozen Concentrated Grape Juice

Detartrated grape juice is concentrated under vacuum by equipment very similar to that used for concentrating apple juice. For the 6-oz, 4-fold retail size, juice is concentrated and sweetened to 48° Brix, and grape essence is added before packing and freezing.

SOURCE: *The Freezing Preservation of Foods, 4th Edition, Vol. 4* by Tressler, Van Arsdel and Copley published by Avi Publishing Co., Westport, Conn.

FLAVOR BASE FOR A SINGLE-STRENGTH GRAPE POWDER BEVERAGE MIX

A grape flavor base powder to make a single-strength grape beverage mix reconstituted with water.

Ingredients	%	For a 32-Oz Serving Gm
Grape flavor base powder	2.13	2.470
Sugar, baker's special	93.72	108.714
Citric acid, anhydrous	4.00	4.640
Ascorbic acid	0.10	0.119
FD&C Red No. 2*	0.02	0.029
FD&C Yellow No. 6	0.01	0.015
Tricalcium phosphate	0.01	0.007
FD&C Blue No. 1	0.01	0.006
Total	100.00	116.000

Procedure

Blend all ingredients thoroughly with rapid agitation until a homogeneous suspension is obtained.

---

*This coloring has been de-listed. It is no longer on the FDA-approved list of food colors and cannot be used. Consult your food color supplier for recommended color substitution.

SOURCE: Foamat Foods Corp., Corvallis, Oregon.

CANNED GRAPEFRUIT JUICE

Fruit is generally brought to the canning plant in bulk form by truck, weighed in, dumped from the trucks, given a primary grading, sampled for analysis, and lifted by elevators to the storage bins. It is necessary to remove all split and decayed fruit before storage to eliminate possible contamination of sound fruit. The fruit is given another grading inspection before washing where additional inferior fruit is removed by hand; then it is treated in a soaking tank or "hot pit," which has the multiple purpose of soaking, washing, and oil control. These tanks are fitted with steam spargers and the temperature maintained is determined by the degree of oil control required. Synthetic detergents are generally used to assist in the washing as are the polyphosphates in particular. The fruit is finally washed by means of revolving brushes and high pressure sprays.

Extraction of Juice

Modern extractors (Bireley, Brown, FMC) mechanically extract substantially all of the juice at a very rapid rate obtaining a yield of about 80 gal. per ton of fruit at the beginning of the season to a high of about 130 gal. at midseason; yield then drops considerably toward the end of the season. Average yield is about 115 gal. or 36 cases (basis No. 2's) per ton in Texas and some 3-4 gal. more in Florida. Once the juice is extracted it must be handled in stainless steel or aluminum, since ascorbic acid (vitamin C) is catalytically oxidized by the presence of iron and copper.

SOURCE: *Fruit and Vegetable Juice Processing Technology, 2nd Edition* by Tressler and Joslyn published by Avi Publishing Co., Westport, Conn.

CANNED GUAVA NECTAR

The following formula, having 20% purée by weight, is calculated so that the soluble solids of the finished product will be approximately 11%, and the pH (depending on that of the original fruit pulp) will be between 3.3 and 3.5.

Ingredients	Lb
Guava purée (average soluble solids 7%)	100
Cane sugar	48
Water	352
Yield of guava nectar	500

Procedure

In a stainless steel mixing kettle or tank the water and sugar are mixed. The purée is added at a steady rate while mixing thoroughly again. The mixture is pumped through a heat exchanger at 180°-190°F and held there for 60 sec. The product is filled into enameled cans. The cans are sealed, inverted, held for 3 min, and cooled with water to 100°F. After labeling and casing, the cans are ready for shipping or warehousing.

Some processors believe that the addition of a

small amount of acid, such as citric acid, enhances the natural flavor of guava.

Sodium benzoate may be added as a preservative up to the limit prescribed by law, provided that such an addition is stated on the label. The use of this or any other preservative, however, does not assure the processor that his product will not spoil.

SOURCE: *Fruit and Vegetable Juice Processing Technology, 2nd Edition* by Tressler and Joslyn published by Avi Publishing Co., Westport, Conn.

CLARIFIED GUAVA JUICE

Two methods for making clarified guava juice have been developed. In the first method, whole guavas are frozen to help break down their internal structure and are kept in frozen storage until needed. In the second method, the starting material is frozen guava purée. From here on both processes are essentially the same, except that when whole guavas are used, the yield of juice is less due to interference of the seeds in pressing out the juice. After thawing, the fruits or purée are placed in a press cloth and the clear juice squeezed out by applying mechanical pressure. When purée is used, it is advisable to warm it to about 100°F, and to add a filtering aid before pressing. Celite, a diatomaceous earth, at the rate of 1% by weight, thoroughly mixed with the purée, is a good filtering aid.

The clarified juice may be blended with other juices, made into jelly or clarified nectar, or heated and canned using process specified for guava nectar then stored for future use. Since the flavor and odor of this juice are weaker than that of the guava purée, more of it must be used in juice products.

SOURCE: *Fruit and Vegetable Juice Processing Technology, 2nd Edition* by Tressler and Joslyn, published by Avi Publishing Co., Westport, Conn.

GUAVA PURÉE

Guava is one of the easiest fruits to process. The whole fruit can be fed into a paddle pulper for maceration into a purée. If the fruits are rather firm, it may be necessary to attach a chopper or slicer to the hopper which feeds into the machine. Several food machinery companies manufacture pulpers and chopping attachments in enough sizes to fit the needs of different-sized plant operations. To remove seeds and fibrous pieces of skin tissue, the pulper should be fitted with 0.003- or 0.045-in. perforated screens. Chopping of all fruit before feeding into the pulper may be desirable since it allows for a more uniform rate of feed. This is important because the rate of feed, as well as the speed and adjustment of the paddles, controls the amount of waste being discharged from the machine. Nonuniform movement of the material through the pulper may cause discoloration of the purée.

Removal of Stone Cells

The outer flesh of nearly all guava types found in Hawaii has a considerable number of hard stone or grit cells. Removing the majority of the stone cells not only improves the texture of the final product but also enhances the color. Being yellowish or tan in color, the stone cells "dilute" the bright pink that is sought for finished guava purée. The flesh of guavas grown in Taiwan does not have a bright pinkish color. The nectar made from such fruit resembles milk in appearance, although it is slightly more translucent.

One good method for getting rid of these unwanted cells is to pass the purée through a paddle finisher equipped with 0.020-in. screens. This machine is exactly like the pulper except that the steel paddles are replaced by neoprene rubber strips held in place by stainless steel or hardwood cleats. The rubber paddles can be adjusted so that they almost touch the screen and the angle should be decreased from that at which the paddles are set for the pulping operation. For this operation, the speed of the machine is reduced to 600–800 rpm and the purée is fed into the hopper at a uniform rate.

Another method of finishing is to run the purée through a mustard mill so that the stone cells are pulverized. This does reduce the grittiness but does not improve the color. Both methods are used by guava processors.

Deaeration

After pulping and finishing to remove the seeds and stone cells, it would be advisable to pump the purée through a deaerator to remove entrapped air. The advantages of deaerating are apparent. First, the removal of oxygen lessens the deterioration caused by this gas during prolonged storage. Oxidation is one of the chief causes for loss in color, breakdown of vitamins, loss of flavor, and production of off-flavors. Second, the removal of air makes for a more uniform and smoother-looking product with improved color. Third, the prevention of foaming, as caused by mixture with air, allows correct and uniform fill of containers. This last advantage of deaeration is important, especially if a mechanical filler is used in the processing line.

Flash Pasteurization

There are two methods adaptable for heat preservation of canned guava purée. One, the so-called batch process, involves heating the purée in a steam-jacket kettle until it reaches 185°F. The second method uses a flash pasteurizer or heat exchanger to heat the product to a high temperature for a much shorter period of time. For guava purée the recommended time-temperature relationship would be 60 sec at 195°F. Other time-temperatures can be used. The flash pasteurization does less damage to the flavor of guava purée than the low temperature pasteurization method.

After heating, the purée should be filled immediately into enameled cans, type "N" enameled container with 2 coats of enamel (citrus enamel and vinyl), or type "H" with 2 coats of enamel (fruit enamel and vinyl). The cans are sealed, inverted, held for 3 min and then cooled by water sprays or some other method to lower the temperature of the cans rapidly to 100°-120°F. The cans are then air-cooled until they reach room temperature.

SOURCE: *Fruit and Vegetable Juice Processing Technology*, *2nd Edition* by Tressler and Joslyn published by Avi Publishing Co., Westport, Conn.

FROZEN CONCENTRATED LEMONADE

Frozen concentrate for lemonade is second only to orange juice concentrate in production. This product is primarily single-strength lemon juice with sugar added. A small amount (approximately 10%) of concentrated lemon juice is added to give the proper balance of sugar and citric acid. A typical frozen concentrate for lemonade would be prepared as follows: Add sufficient concentrated lemon juice to a mixture of 280 gal. of single-strength lemon juice plus 2800 lb sucrose so that the citric acid level of the final product will be from 3 to 3.5%. This will make approximately 500 gal. of 55° Brix concentrate. To give the characteristic appearance of fresh lemonade, some of the juice cells which are screened from the lemon juice after extraction are returned to the concentrate. Unlike most other juice concentrates, which are 4-fold (3 parts water to 1 part concentrate), lemonade concentrate is reconstituted to lemonade by adding 4 to 4½ vol of water to each volume of concentrate.

The product is slush frozen and then filled into small retail-size containers.

SOURCE: *The Freezing Preservation of Foods*, *4th Edition*, *Vol. 4* by Tressler, Van Arsdel and Copley published by Avi Publishing Co., Westport, Conn.

FROZEN LEMON JUICE

Lemons from storage bins are conveyed along an inspection or sorting table, where defective fruit is eliminated. The lemons pass to a washer, then to a scrubber, and on to size graders. Next the fruit goes to reamers. The juice passes through a finisher which removes seeds and coarse particles. It is then pumped to a special centrifuge called a deoleomizer, in which the excess oil is removed. Then it passes through an homogenizer and on through a deaerator to eliminate dissolved oxygen. Next it is cooled in a precooler (heat exchanger). The juice is slush-frozen in a Girdler Votator. The slush is automatically filled into cans which are checked for proper weight. The cans are closed by double reamers, then passed through a freezing tunnel (at -40°F), after which they are put into cases and stored at 0°F or lower.

Canned Lemon Juice

Lemon juice for canning is prepared by the same procedure as lemon juice which is to be frozen. However, after the juice has been deaerated, it is flash pasteurized at 170°F in a stainless steel heat exchanger and filled into fruit enamel-lined cans or into bottles immediately, taking care to fill each container completely. The containers are closed, inverted, and then cooled. The pH of the juice is so low that no other treatment is required.

SOURCE: *Fruit and Vegetable Juice Processing Technology*, *2nd Edition* by Tressler and Joslyn published by Avi Publishing Co., Westport, Conn.

FLAVOR BASE FOR A SINGLE-STRENGTH LEMON POWDER BEVERAGE MIX

A lemon flavor base powder, to make a single-strength lemonade beverage mix for reconstitution with water.

Ingredients	%	For a 32-Oz Serving
Lemon flavor base powder	11.45	13.05
Sugar, baker's special	88.45	100.83
Ascorbic acid	0.10	0.12
Total	100.00	114.00

Procedure

Blend all ingredients thoroughly with rapid agitation until a homogeneous suspension is obtained.

SOURCE: Foamat Foods Corp., Corvallis, Oregon.

FROZEN LIME JUICE

The methods used in Florida for lime processing have been largely those developed for handling citrus in general. In one processing plant of California, lime juice is handled and pasteurized in the same way as lemon juice as described above.

With the Persian variety, the juice is passed through a finisher, after extraction with standard (orange) juicing equipment. In these steps it is important to keep the pressure comparatively light to avoid extraction of bitter constituents from the peel. Deaeration combined with flash pasteurization of 195°-205°F gives the best retention of vitamin C and overall juice quality.

In the case of lime juice obtained by crushing the whole fruit in a screw press, it may be desirable to reduce the peel oil content by vacuum deoiling. The lime juice also may be clarified by mixing with a filter aid and passing through a plate-and-frame press. Clarified juice is useful in compounding formulas for bottled drinks and fountain use.

As compared to other citrus juices, the marketing of canned lime juice has been limited, mainly because the products deteriorate rapidly at room temperature.

Single-strength, pasteurized, canned limeade was known to develop off-flavors which were described, in part at least, as "terpeney," a difficulty believed to be caused by the peel oil present in the juice. For these reasons most lime juice is frozen after cooling and filling into citrus enamel-lined cans. Some is sweetened with sugar so that when diluted with water limeade is obtained.

SOURCE: *Fruit and Vegetable Juice Processing Technology, 2nd Edition* by Tressler and Joslyn published by Avi Publishing Co., Westport, Conn.

CANNED MANGO NECTARS

Mango nectars can be made either from fresh mangoes or frozen purée. A procedure for canning mango purée follows:

Procedure

Frozen purée is thawed overnight at room temperature and transferred to a large stainless steel container in which the ingredients are mixed with a power stirrer. The basic formula for the nectar is as follows:

	Lb
Mango purée	100
Sugar	30
Water	170
Citric acid	10

After thorough mixing, the nectar is filled into No. 2 cans and vacuum sealed. The cans are processed 3 min at 212°F in a spin cooker in which the cans are rotated at 125 rpm on their long axis. The product should be spin-cooled with water at 72°F, which is sufficient to reduce the temperature to about 100°F in 4 min.

Processing time should be checked with can supplier or the National Canners Association.

SOURCE: Hawaii Agricultural Experiment Station, University of Hawaii, Honolulu.

FROZEN MANGO PURÉE

Haden mangoes are sorted, washed in a rotary spray washer, and the seeds removed with knives by hand. (A mechanical scraping device was used to remove the peel for some of the experimental lots.) The fruit is put through a cutting mill and a paddle pulper fitted with a screen with 0.033-in. perforations to remove coarse fibers and particles. The purée is then pumped through a plate heat exchanger for rapid heating and cooling to inactivate the enzyme catalase. In the heat exchanger the purée is heated to 195°-200°F, held at that temperature for 1 min, and then cooled to 90°-100°F. It is then filled into 30-lb tins with polyethylene liners and frozen at -10°F.

SOURCE: Hawaii Agricultural Experiment Station, University of Hawaii, Honolulu.

CANNED ORANGE JUICE

In Florida, the principal varieties of oranges used for processing are Pineapple (mid season) and Valencia (late season). Relatively little juice is processed in California where the principal variety used is the Valencia.

Upon reaching the processing plant the fruit goes through inspection lines, where bruised or broken fruit are removed, and then is conveyed to storage bins which permit an accumulation of fruit sufficient for continuous operation of the cannery over a reasonable length of time. These bins are constructed so that the fruit is never piled to a depth of more than 3-4 feet. Fruit should not be kept in bins longer than required to permit orderly plant operation.

After inspection, the oranges are washed. The fruit is soaked briefly in water containing a detergent then scrubbed with revolving brushes. The oranges are halved and the juice extracted, usually by reaming with revolving rubber or plastic burrs.

Finishing.—The juice from the extractor passes through a finisher where seeds, pieces of peel, and excess pulp are removed. These finishers usually consist of cylindrical screens through which the juice is forced by means of a screw. The pulp and peel escape through an adjustable annular orifice at the end of the screen.

Blending and Sweetening.—After finishing, the juice flows to large stainless steel tanks where it is checked for acidity and soluble solids. Sugar is added, if needed.

Deoiling.—Deoilers are essentially small vacuum evaporators in which the juice is heated to about 125°F and from 3 to 6% of the juice evaporates. The vapors are condensed, the oil separated by centrifuging or by decantation, and the water layer returned to the juice. This treatment is sufficient to remove about ¾ of the volatile peel oil present. Government standards for U.S. Grade A orange juice permit not more than 0.03% recoverable oil by volume and the level should be kept well below this figure. Peel oil is essential to flavor and the juice should contain from 0.01 to 0.02% by volume.

Deaeration.—Deoilers simultaneously deaerate juice though deaerators are seldom seen in juice canneries. Oxidation has long been considered as a mechanism of flavor deterioration in citrus juices and the oxygen level should be kept low. Dissolved oxygen disappears rapidly in canned juice, especially at high temperature. This reaction has been associated with loss in vitamin C. A decided benefit is a decrease in frothing in the filler bowl if deaeration is used.

Pasteurization.—Pasteurization of citrus juices accomplishes two things. First, it destroys microorganisms which would otherwise cause fermentation in the can and, second, it inactivates enzymes which would otherwise cause cloud loss and other changes in the juice. Generally, higher temperatures are needed for enzyme inactivation than for destruction of microorganisms. Heating to about 160°F is sufficient to prevent fermentation in experimental packs but from 185° to 210°F is required to achieve cloud stability. This is accomplished by heating in tubular or plate type heat exchangers in which the heating medium is either steam or hot water. Pasteurization is accomplished in 30-60 sec and the juice is then piped to the filling machine. The juice is maintained at about 185°F in the filler bowl and filled directly into either plain or fruit enamel-lined cans. The juice should not be kept longer than 2 min at this temperature.

Cans are closed in automatic machines, inverted for about 20 sec, and rapidly cooled by spraying with cold water while spinning in a conveyor. Live steam may be injected into the headspace as the can is closed so as to replace the air with steam. High speed filling and closing machines have been developed and some will handle up to 500 cans a minute.

It is considered desirable to minimize the amount of oxygen in the final container.

Frozen Orange Juice

Finished, deoiled orange juice may be chilled, then frozen. Frozen single-strength orange juice is of high quality but little is frozen without concentration.

SOURCE: *Fruit and Vegetable Juice Processing Technology, 2nd Edition* by Tressler and Joslyn published by Avi Publishing Co., Westport, Conn.

CANNED ORANGE-GRAPEFRUIT JUICE

Orange-grapefruit juice is a popular blend of fruit juices. This blend was first packed commercially in 1935, and has been an important product since about 1940. Considerable quantities of orange-grapefruit, tangerine-grapefruit, and other citrus juice blends are also packed commercially. The great bulk of the citrus juice blends are packed in Florida although small quantities are canned in Texas and California.

The methods employed in the production of citrus juices to be blended are the same as those used in preparing these same juices for canning.

The proportion of orange to grapefruit juice used in preparing an orange-grapefruit blend will depend upon the color desired, the acidity and Brix of the juices to be blended, on the relative price of the fruit, and other factors. As a rule, not less than 50% orange juice is used, and if the orange juice is light in color, as much as 75% may be used.

In order to be graded U.S. Grade A or Fancy, the blend must contain not more than 0.2% free and suspended pulp and not more than 0.030% by volume of recoverable oil; it must not contain seeds or seed particles or other defects that more than slightly affect the appearance of the product.

After blending, the blend should be deaerated. It is then flash pasteurized at 190°-200°F, filled immediately into cans, and cooled.

SOURCE: *Fruit and Vegetable Juice Processing Technology, 2nd Edition* by Tressler and Joslyn published by Avi Publishing Co., Westport, Conn.

CHILLED ORANGE JUICE

Chilled juice is extracted and prepared by the same process as canned orange juice as described above. The fresh juice is heated to 180°F or above to inactivate pectinesterase (to stabilize cloud) and reduce microorganisms; then it is chilled rapidly to 30°F, deaerated, and filled into stainless steel tanks in which it is shipped to market.

The juice should be kept as near 30°F as possible during distribution. Shelf-life is estimated at about two weeks. One Florida company ships juice in bulk in refrigerated tanks by ship and packages the product in the New York area.

SOURCE: *Fruit and Vegetable Juice Processing Technology, 2nd Edition* by Tressler and Joslyn published by Avi Publishing Co., Westport, Conn.

FROZEN ORANGE CONCENTRATE

Juice Extraction and Finishing

Juice extraction and finishing is done in essentially the same manner as for canned juice (see Canned Orange Juice) with some variations. For the preparation of fresh "cutback" juice, to be added to restore fresh flavor after the bulk of the juice has been overconcentrated, the strainer tube in the FMC extractor or the screen in the finisher used after the Brown extractor may have larger holes to permit larger pulp pieces to give the appearance of juice freshly extracted in the home. In Florida, State regulations prohibit the addition of sugar to frozen concentrated orange juice, the idea being to delay harvesting until the juice is naturally sweet and to permit marketing a product which is 100% orange juice.

Large automatic "desludging" centrifuges are used at times to reduce the amount of finely divided pulp, if an adequate job is not done at the finisher. These are disc-type units with nozzles at the periphery of the bowl which open periodically to discharge a thick slurry. These centrifuges are helpful in reducing viscosity in juice passing through an evaporator and are used particularly after a freeze when the fruit tissue tends to disintegrate more readily.

Pasteurization

Most juice which is to be concentrated either by freezing or vacuum evaporation and that which is added to the concentrated juice to improve its fresh flavor is flash pasteurized in order to reduce the pectin esterase (enzyme) activity and at the same time reduce the microbial activity. A temperature of approximately 180°F for 30 sec to 1 min is used. Some pasteurizers are tubular and some are of the plate type. In most cases the juice is pasteurized before being fed to the evaporator and this has the advantage of decreasing bacterial count in the entire evaporator as well as inactivating enzymes. In a few plants, pasteurization is after partial concentration. This decreases the energy needed as the weight of material to be heated is much less. In a few cases heating of the concentrate between stages is by direct steam injection, a method which involves very little equipment and permits very rapid heating.

Vacuum Concentration

Several types of vacuum concentrators are used, but the most common is known as the TASTE evaporator (Temperature Accelerated Short Time Evaporator). In a typical design, there are 7 stages and 4 effects plus a flash cooler. The juice passes through each stage only once so the time the juice is in the evaporator can be measured in minutes instead of an hour or two in the usual low-temperature unit. One or more stages operate at 200°-212°F and one result is the pasteurization of the product. Other stages and effects range down to about 105°F. Approximate operating conditions in an evaporator of 65,000 lb/hr water evaporating capacity are:

Stage	Product Lb	Temp °F	Conc °Brix
Feed	80,000	70	12
First	75,000	105	13
Second	60,000	205	16
Third	40,000	190	33
Fourth	25,000	170	40
Fifth	20,000	145	48
Sixth	18,000	115	56
Seventh	15,200	105	63
Flash	15,000	60	65

These evaporators are of the falling-film type using fairly small tubes in bundles.

TASTE evaporators have advantages in a minimum of product residence time, comparatively low initial cost, high efficiency, and relative ease for "in place" cleaning. They also have some disadvantages. They are relatively inflexible because the product goes through each stage only once and changes in concentration of feed are soon reflected in a change in pump-out concentration. It is not convenient to blend "add-back" concentrate with the feed juice and send it through the evaporator as this would increase the concentration of the pump-out. Also, the higher temperatures cause more rapid fouling of heat exchanger tubes and necessitate more frequent cleaning. Fortunately, cleaning takes only a few minutes and can be done without disassembly. Intervals between cleaning may be as short as 6 hr.

Addition of Fresh Cutback Juice

Concentrate from the evaporators is collected in cold-wall tanks. Cutback is added at this point and the concentrate adjusted to 45° Brix. In order to assure optimum flavor, cold-pressed peel oil may be added to bring the recoverable oil value to about 0.025% v/v on a reconstituted basis.

While in the mixing tank, the temperature of the

concentrate is reduced to 30°-40°F. Further cooling may be achieved by pumping through Votators before filling into the final containers. In some plants automatic blending units replace the blending tanks.

Containers

The familiar 6-oz can which reconstitutes to 24 oz when 3 volumes of water are added is still the most popular size. Some 12-oz cans are also marketed and offer savings in container cost per unit of product.

Enamel-lined tin cans were the regular container for many years. Then a series of changes began to occur, including the replacement of the soldered side seam with a heat sealed side seam, aluminum bodies, aluminum ends, and finally composition bodies. Zip tops were introduced then modified so that concentrate is not flipped about on opening. Composition bodies are in general use and a favorite combination is a fiberboard body with polyethylene liner, aluminum ends and a zip-strip in the body where it joins an end. Rectangular cardboard boxes with plastic liners are being made and they offer advantages in a savings in space.

Because of the relatively high freezing point of the concentrate, temperatures of -10°F or lower should be used in freezing the packaged product. Storage should never be higher than 0°F.

SOURCE: *Fruit and Vegetable Juice Processing Technology, 2nd Edition* by Tressler and Joslyn published by Avi Publishing Co., Westport, Conn.

FLAVOR BASE FOR A SINGLE-STRENGTH ORANGE JUICE POWDER BEVERAGE MIX

An orange juice drink base powder to make single-strength orange juice drink beverage mix for reconstitution with water.

Ingredients	%	For a 32-oz Serving Gm
Orange juice flavor base powder	37.25	43.214
Sugar, baker's special	54.23	62.893
Citric acid, granular	4.08	4.729
Beatreme No. 3442 (Beatrice Foods)	2.55	2.955
Tricalcium phosphate	1.32	1.535
Syloil 244 (free-flow agent)	0.45	0.527
Ascorbic acid	0.10	0.119
FD&C Yellow No. 5	0.02	0.023
FD&C Yellow No. 6	0.00	0.001
Total	100.00	116.000

Procedure

Blend all ingredients thoroughly with rapid agitation until a homogeneous suspension is obtained.

SOURCE: Foamat Foods Corp., Corvallis, Oregon.

FLAVOR BASE FOR A SINGLE-STRENGTH ORANGE POWDER BEVERAGE MIX

An orange flavored base powder to make single-strength orange-flavored beverage mix for reconstitution with water.

Ingredients	%	For a 32-oz Serving Gm
Orange flavored drink base powder,	5.78	6.702
Sugar, baker's special	84.28	97.761
Citric acid, anhydrous	6.00	6.960
Beatreme No. 3442 (Beatrice Foods)	2.50	2.900
Tricalcium phosphate	1.30	1.508
Ascorbic acid	0.10	0.119
FD&C Yellow No. 5	0.04	0.046
FD&C Yellow No. 6	0.00	0.002
Total	100.00	116.000

Procedure

Blend all ingredients thoroughly with rapid agitation until a homogeneous suspension is obtained.

SOURCE: Foamat Foods Corp., Corvallis, Oregon.

FROZEN PAPAYA PURÉE

The fresh papayas are inspected and sorted to remove damaged and undesirable ones. The fruits are immersed in water at 120°F for 20 min. The warm water treatment is used to prevent undue spoilage losses during ripening. The fruits are ripened at room temperature for 5-6 days. It is advisable to cool the product to 35°F prior to processing to lessen the possibility of gel formation. The chilled fruits are washed, trimmed with a stainless steel knife or an hydraulic cutter to remove the ends, and then cut into four pieces in a slicer. The skins are separated in a skin separator. The mixture containing the seeds is passed through a paddle pulper over a 0.033-in screen. In this operation the seeds are removed. The purée is pumped through a scraped-surface heat exchanger at 210°F or higher, and held there for 1 min. It is necessary to heat inactivate the pectin esterase enzyme in the purée immediately after seed removal. The product is cooled to 85°F in a second scraped-surface heat exchanger, and then passed through a paddle finisher with a 0.020-in. screen to remove specks and fibers. The purée is then filled into polyethylene-lined 30-lb cans, sealed, and deep frozen to -10°F or below.

SOURCE: Hawaii Agricultural Experiment Station, University of Hawaii, Honolulu.

PASSION FRUIT NECTAR AND NECTAR BLENDS

Passion fruit nectar base is a combination of passion fruit juice and sugar in suitable proportions for dilution with water to produce a palatable drink. The recommended ratio of ingredients is as follows:

	Parts
Passion fruit juice	100
Sugar	55-65

One part of this mixture is diluted with 4 to 4½ parts of water to give a pleasant and refreshing beverage.

These find ready acceptance as canned products and for distribution through dairy outlets as pasteurized chilled products packed in waxed cartons. To achieve attractive flavor combinations, passion fruit is frequently blended with orange and pineapple juices. A suitable balance of flavor is achieved by the addition of citric acid, sodium citrate, and essential oils with algin derivatives added to control viscosity and appearance. These blends are frequently fortified with vitamin C.

The canned products should be mixed in blending tanks and normally pasteurized at 190°F; fill hot into enameled cans, seal, and then cool in rotary coolers. A better flavored product can be prepared using the spin cooker process.. The juice is filled into enameled cans at room temperature, sealed in a vacuum closer, and then spin processed to a can center temperature of 190°F. The cans are then rapidly cooled before storage.

Nectar intended for packing in waxed-paper cartons is normally processed in a tubular or plate type pasteurizer and then run through a refrigerated milk cooler to drop the temperature below the melting point of the wax coating used in the carton manufacture.

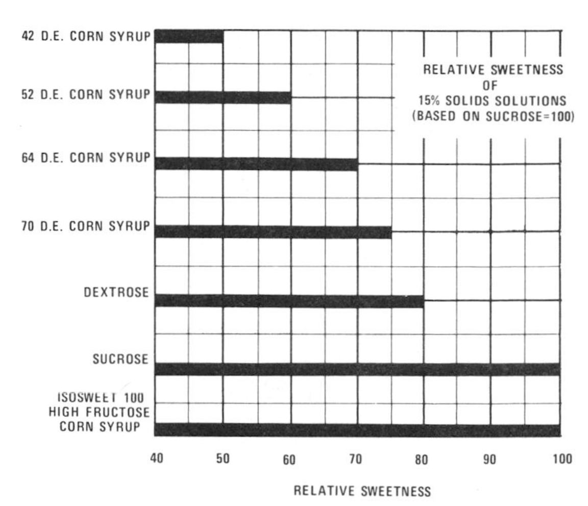

Courtesy of A. E. Staley Manufacturing Co.

FIG. 1.1. RELATIVE SWEETNESS OF SIX SUGARS

SOURCE: Hawaii Agricultural Experiment Station, University of Hawaii, Honolulu.

CLEAR PEACH JUICE CONCENTRATE

This product is suitable for jelly, syrup, wine, ice cream, punch, and flavoring.

Pass peach pulp through a 0.060-in screen; add a pectinase enzyme (K-200 Kleerzyme) at the rate of 1 gm per lb of pulp; add rice hulls at the rate of 1 lb per 30 lb of pulp (cellulose acetate fiber may be used at the rate of 1 lb per 100 lb of pulp as an alternate filter aid to rice hulls).

Hold treated pulp for 1 hr at 80°F, preheat to 160°F, and filter with a pneumatic filter press. Spray juice under reduced pressure into a vacuum evaporator and concentrate at 130°-140°F, to 20°-70° Brix.

Flash pasteurize at 195°-200°, and flash cool to 35° in 30 sec. Pack aseptically in sterile tin, glass, or plastic containers; or hold in freezing storage.

SOURCE: *Production and Utilization of Peach Pulp, Juice Drink and Concentrates*, University of Georgia College of Agriculture Experiment Station Research Bull. 136.

PEACH NECTAR

Peach concentrate may be used to prepare beverage "peach nectar" by altering the Brix-acid ratio by addition of sucrose, equal to 93% of the soluble solids in the juice, prior to flavor recovery. Increasing the Brix also results in reduced vaporization required to achieve desired concentration in a single pass. In determining the amount of pomace add-back, effect of seasonal variation of insoluble solids content of the fruit must be taken into account.

Desired consistency is obtained by adding 100% of recovered pomace.

Sweetened concentrate, pomace, and recovered aromas are blended, then the mixture is homogenized for smoothness. Soluble solids content of the nectar is established at 51.4° Brix, so that dilution with 3 volumes of water results in a 15° Brix beverage. This is a very palatable drink having a fresh flavor and natural color.

SOURCE: USDA Eastern Regional Research Laboratory, Philadelphia, PA.

PEACH PURÉE BEVERAGE BASE

The steps in the preparation of the peach purée base are as follows:

(1) Receive 100 lb of fruit within 12 hr after picking.

(2) Cool fruit to be held overnight, and ripen that which is not yet soft.

(3) Grade for ripeness and freedom from defects. Select worm-free, rot-free, soft fruit of any variety.

(4) Peel by immersing in, or spraying with, 5% lye at 210°F for 30 sec; then expose to air for 1-2 min.

(5) Wash with rotary or spray washer.

(6) Wash lightly in soft brush washer, remove rotten spots by trimming, and rewash.

(7) Heat whole fruit in a continuous thermoscrew for 2 min at 200°F to aid in pulping, prevent oxidation, and stabilize cloud in purée. A jacket around the screw should maintain 20 lb steam pressure.

(8) Pulp by passing through a continuous rotary unit with ¼-in. perforated screens to remove soft flesh from seed and unripe portions.

(9) Finish the pulp by passing through rotary unit with 0.033-in. or 0.024-in perforated, stainless steel screen. This reduces pulp to liquid and removes fiber.

(10) Accumulate in tank, add 0.14% ascorbic acid and mix, then feed uniformly to pasteurizer.

(11) Pasteurize at 190°-200°F and cool quickly to 35°F.

(12) Fill aseptically into sterile 55-gal. drums or large cans for refrigerated storage. Filling hot in No. 10 or smaller size cans also may be used; fill hot in No. 10 cans or smaller sizes.

(13) Close cans using vacuum and nitrogen, or vacuumize with steam jet.

(14) Cool cans (which were not already cool) in canal or water spray.

(15) Dry cans with warm air to remove water drops and avoid rusting or staining of labels.

(16) Label containers, use code identification.

(17) Store in cool dry place.

SOURCE: *Fruit and Vegetable Juice Processing Technology, 2nd Edition* by Tressler and Joslyn, published by Avi Publishing Co., Westport, Conn.

PEACH JUICE DRINK

For a peach juice drink, peach purée base should be modified by (a) adjustment of the sugar-acid ratio, (b) the color so as not to confuse it with orange juice, and (c) an increase in the consistency to resist settling.

Ingredients	Lb	Oz
Peach purée base (1 drum) (see Peach Purée Beverage Base given above)	430	
Water (43.5 gal.)	444	
Invert syrup 50% (76.5° Brix)	143	
Vegetable gum (Kelcoloid S)	2	
Color (yellow No. 6)		0.4

Procedure

Flash pasteurize at 195°-200°F and flash cool to 35°F in 30 sec. Pack aseptically in consumer-size sterile cans or bottles.

SOURCE: *Production and Utilization of Peach Pulp, Juice Drink and Concentrates*, University of Georgia College of Agriculture Experiment Station Research Bull. 136.

PEACH-ORANGE DRINK

Peach purée base may be blended with orange juice to make a household beverage.

Ingredients	Lb
Peach purée base (1 drum)	430
Orange juice concentrate, 42° Brix (4.25 gal.)	48
Water (94 gal.)	760
Invert syrup 50% (76.5° Brix)	167
Malic acid crystals	1½
Orange oil, for flavor	trace

Procedure

When mixed, the beverage is ready to serve with 40% fruit juice solids of a 3 : 1 peach-orange ratio.

Flash pasteurize at 195°-200°F, and flash cool to 35°F in 30 sec. Pack aseptically in consumer-size sterile cans or bottles.

SOURCE: *Production and Utilization of Peach Pulp, Juice Drink and Concentrates*, University of Georgia College of Agriculture Experiment Station Research Bull. 136.

PEACH PURÉE BASE

Most varieties of peaches are suitable for purée when soft ripe. These include orchard run fruits or overripe pickouts from packing sheds and canning and freezing operations. Fruit should be carefully inspected for defects and inedible portions.

Peel the whole peaches with steam, or 2% lye followed by thorough rinsing; then preheat to 140°-150°F in a thermoscrew; and immediately pulp using a 0.25-in. screen, with finishing using a screen having 0.024-0.033 in. perforations operated at 1000-1200 rpm.

Flash pasteurize the purée at 195°-200°F and flash cool to 35°F in a total time of about 24 sec. The sterile product may be sealed aseptically in tin, glass, or plastic containers; and stored under refrigeration, or preferably frozen. The soluble solids should be 13.0-13.5%, pH 3.75-3.78, total acidity 0.41-0.42%, and viscosity 96.2-104.0 cps.

SOURCE: *Production and Utilization of Peach Pulp, Juice Drink and Concentrates*, University of Georgia College of Agriculture Experiment Station Research Bull. 136.

BIRTHDAY PARTY PUNCH

Ingredients	Qt
Tropical punch	1
Orange drink	½
Grape drink	½
Lemonade concentrate	¼
Ginger ale	2
Rum	¼

Procedure

This is a very simple punch formula. Chill all ingredients and mix together adding ginger ale last, and serve over ice.

Yield: 40 servings.

SOURCE: A. E. Staley Mfg. Co., Oak Brook, Illinois.

CHRISTMAS PUNCH

Ingredients	Qt	Pt
Grapefruit drink	1	
Orange drink		1
Apricot nectar	2	
Club soda	1	
Rum, vodka, or wine	1	

Procedure

Chill, blend together all ingredients and serve over ice. Garnish with orange slices and mint leaves.

Yield: 54 servings.

SOURCE: A. E. Staley Mfg. Co., Oak Brook, Illinois.

GRADUATION PUNCH

Ingredients	Qt	Pt
Grape drink	1	
Cranberry juice		3
Lemon juice		¼
Ginger ale	4	
Sliced lemon		

Procedure

Chill all ingredients well, blend in large punch bowl, adding ginger ale last.

Yield: 42 3-oz servings.

SOURCE: A. E. Staley Mfg. Co., Oak Brook Illinois.

NEW YEAR'S EVE PUNCH

Ingredients	
Water	1 qt
Brown sugar	½ lb
Cinnamon	2 tsp
Cloves, ground	½ tsp
Orange drink	1¼ qt
Lemon juice	3 tsp
Apple cider	1¼ qt
Light rum	1 qt

Procedure

Heat water, brown sugar, cinnamon and cloves; strain and add other ingredients. Mix and heat again. Ladle into heated mugs and serve warm.

Yield: 40 servings.

SOURCE: A. E. Staley Mfg. Co., Oak Brook, Illinois.

PICNIC PUNCH
(In Watermelon punch bowl)

Ingredients	Qt	Pt
Orange drink	2	
Orange-pineapple drink	1	
Cranberry juice	1	
Lemon juice		½
Strawberries, unsweetened		1
Sugar		1

Procedure

Chill all ingredients thoroughly; in a large punch bowl, blend together all ingredients except strawberries. Float strawberries and ice on top.

Slice top off watermelon horizontally. Scoop out melon in chunks and use for dessert. Remove seeds from bottom and scrape smooth with spoon. Scallop edges of "punch bowl" and chill thoroughly. Fill with punch and surround base with lemon slices.

Yield: 42 3-oz servings.

SOURCE: A. E. Staley Mfg. Co., Oak Brook, Illinois.

APRIL FOOL'S DAY PUNCH

Ingredients	Qt	Pt
Orange drink	1	
Orange-flavored gelatin 6-oz packet		
Orange-pineapple drink	1	
Lime juice		¼
Ginger ale	1	
Peppermint sticks		24

Procedure

Dissolve gelatin in hot orange drink; add orange-pineapple drink and lime juice, mix and chill. Before serving, add chilled ginger ale, mix, serve, and sip punch through peppermint sticks as you would a straw.

Yield: 32 3-oz servings.

SOURCE: A. E. Staley Mfg. Co., Oak Brook, Illinois.

POLYNESIAN PUNCH

Ingredients	Parts
Passion fruit juice	18
Pineapple concentrate	5
Acerola purée	4
Pineapple juice	3
Lemon juice	2
Water	8
Citric acid to give 1.7% acid	

Procedure

Mix; put into enamel-lined cans and use, can, or freeze. Dilute each can with 4½ cans of water.

SOURCE: *Commercial Fruit Processing* by Woodroof and Luh published by Avi Publishing Co., Westport, Conn.

SPRINGTIME PUNCH

Ingredients	
Orange drink	1 qt
Milk	½ pt
Strawberries, frozen, whole	1 pt
Sugar	3 tbsp
Ice cubes—containing strawberries	1 qt

Procedure

Chill orange drink and milk. Put strawberries, sugar, orange drink, and milk into blender, and blend. Pour blended mixture into punch bowl with ice cubes and mix well. Garnish with strawberries.

Yield: 21 3-oz servings.

SOURCE: A. E. Staley Mfg. Co., Oak Brook, Illinois.

SWEETHEART PUNCH

Ingredients	Qt	Pt
Orange drink		3
Lemonade concentrate, frozen		1½
Water		1½
Cranberry juice		1½
Ginger ale	2	

Procedure

Chill all ingredients, mix well and pour over ice in chilled punch bowl. To add pink color to punch, use heart-shaped salad mold, fill with water tinted pink with cranberry juice and freeze.

Yield: 42 3-oz servings.

SOURCE: A. E. Staley Mfg. Co., Oak Brook, Ill.

WEDDING PUNCH

Ingredients	Qt	Pt
Orange drink	1	
Grapefruit drink		1
Apple juice	1	
Cranberry juice		1
Light rum		½
Pineapple chunks in own juice	1	1

Procedure

Chill all ingredients well; blend in punch bowl and garnish with mint leaves and pineapple.

Fill two small ring molds with water. Freeze solid, and interlock by melting small section of one and refreeze together to form a double ring, then float in punch.

Yield: 32 3-oz servings.

SOURCE: A. E. Staley Mfg. Co., Oak Brook, Ill.

CANNED PEAR JUICE

Pears should be ripened to a pressure test of 3 to 5 before processing, as is customary prior to canning. Slicing is suggested to shorten time required in the blancher. The residence time in the screw-type blancher will depend upon the particular unit used, but should lie between 2 and 4 min. The time is determined by testing purée from the finisher with catechol solution and setting the time in the blancher at a figure slightly (about 25%) longer than that needed for a negative test. The screen size in the finisher may range from 0.03 to 0.05 in. The purpose is to remove seeds and fiber and to convert the pears to a pulp or purée. Treatment with a pectic enzyme serves three purposes: treated purée is easier to press, juice yields are appreciably higher, and the juice can be filtered to a sparklingly clear product.

Enzymatic degradation of pectins requires a certain length of time and may vary to some extent with the characteristics of various lots of fruit. The measure for completion of treatment is whether a sparkling juice can be obtained from the purée. Two simple tests can be used. (1) A sample of purée can be filtered through filter paper, the first few drops of filtrate discarded, and the remainder examined for clarity. (2) If a small centrifuge is available, a sample can be centrifuged and the upper layer in the tube examined for clarity.

The amount of filter aid needed will vary with type of press, desired thickness of press cake, and variety of fruit used. Experience under conditions in a particular plant will enable the operator to arrive at a figure representing the minimum quantity that will produce a firm, dry press cake. Filter aid used here and in clarification should be both tasteless and odorless, because the juice will readily absorb odors or flavors. The presence of flavor or odor in the filter aid can be determined by smelling and tasting a water suspension of the particular type and shipment under consideration.

The pear juice which has a pH of 3.6-3.8 may be flash pasteurized at 190°F filled hot into fruit enamel-lined cans which are immediately closed and inverted and then cooled or the juice may be perfectly preserved by freezing.

SOURCE: *Fruit and Vegetable Juice Processing Technology, 2nd Edition* by Tressler and Joslyn published by Avi Publishing Co., Westport, Conn.

CANNED PINEAPPLE JUICE

Sources of Beverage Juice

In general, there are seven types of fruit, portions, or derivatives used in the preparation of commercial pineapple beverage juice. These constituents are derived from various stages in the processing of the solid packs of pineapple. Four of the sources are solid matter, i.e., fruity tissues. Three of the sources are liquids. The seven common constituents are: (1) cores, (2) juice trimmings, (3) eradicator meat, (4) small fruit, (5) juice drained from crushed pineapple (kettle-drained), (6) juice drained from eradicator meat, and (7) juice drained from the cylinders and slices during processing.

Cores.—The cores are removed from the central axis of the individual fruits by the Ginaca machine.

Juice Trimmings.—The cylinders of fruit prepared by the Ginaca machine for subsequent trimming and slicing yield portions suitable for juice which are prepared as described below.

Eradicator Meat.—The eradicator meat (flesh adhering to the shells) produced if the Ginaca machine is employed either totally or in part as a primary source of beverage juice.

Small Fruit.—Fruit primarily from older ratoons which, owing to their small size, is unsuited to the production of slices is generally used as a juice constituent in its entirety after peeling and trimming.

Juice Drained from Crushed Pineapple (Kettle-drained).—During the cutting or crushing of pineapple tissues in the preparation of crushed pineapple, a surplus of liquids is frequently developed. This excess, if left in the crushed product, would dilute the solids disproportionately. Accordingly, a part of this juice is drained to become a constituent of the beverage juice.

Juice Drained from Eradicator Meat.—In the removal of the flesh adhering to the shells, a surplus of juice is developed which, if removed at the Ginaca machine, can be pumped to the Juice Department to become a constituent of the beverage juice product. This separation of the juice at the eradicator improves the ease of conveying the eradicator solids to the juice plant.

Juice Draining from Cylinders and Slices During Processing.—In the handling of the fruit cylinders and the slices derived therefrom, free-flowing juice is produced. This becomes a minor constituent in potable juice production.

Extraction

Extraction of the potable juices from the combined comminuted solids is accomplished by different means in the several canneries. At least three types of equipment are employed: (a) pressure-screw extractors, (b) Hoyt-Botley extractors, and (c) Schwarz extractors.

Specially designed pressure screw extractors of the general type frequently used in tomato juice production are employed in many canneries to separate the liquids from the comminuted solids of pineapple. These extractors generally are operated in at least two stages; the first, often having a drum-type rotor, provides a light pressing and the second, having a screw-type of rotor, provides a firmer pressing of the cake from the first-stage extractors. Preheating of the in-going solids may be practiced by some canners, but is not universally used.

In the Hoyt-Botley process inert coarse, sharp filter aid is mixed with the comminuted fruit solids prior to its extraction by pneumatic pressure in a special filtering system.

The juice extracted in the Hoyt-Botley extractor is conveyed for ultimate blending with the free-flowing juices from the crushed product as well as from the eradicator meat and slices. A part of the Hoyt-Botley system also separates the spent pulp from the filter aid. The spent pulp is conveyed to the by-products plant and the filter aid is washed and reprocessed for return to succeeding batches of disintegrated pulp.

The Schwartz extractor is employed in some canneries either for the processing of cores primarily to which a bit of eradicator meat or trimmings has been added, or may be used for the final comminution and the extraction of all of the solid portions of fruit employed in beverage juice production.

Inasmuch as the characteristic pineapple flavor is volatile, the steps of comminution and extraction are carried out at room temperature in a number of canneries. This practice is not universally followed, however, since in some of the canneries it is felt that improved extractions from the fruit pulp are realized through heating the pulp prior to pressing it.

Blending

The juices derived from the several liquid sources and those expressed from the solid portions of the fruit may be blended either prior to passing through heaters, in the heater, or following heating. In any event, the juices are thoroughly mixed, not only from the different fruit portions but from succeeding batches of fruit as well.

Heating

The juices derived from whatever source are heated to approximately 140°–145°F in suitable heat exchangers. The juices then may be passed through revolving screens or other types of finishers or strainers to separate out large fragments of solids which may be passed through the extractors. In the case of the juices extracted by the Schwarz or by the Hoyt-Botley processes, it is not necessary to use the revolving screen since other provision is made in these systems for an appropriate sizing of the suspended solids.

Finishing

The hot juices are passed into centrifuges to remove the excess of suspended solids and other suspended material which may have been carried through prior processing steps. Control of the quantity and character of the suspended solids is one of the important operations affecting quality. It is possible by controlling the centrifuge cycle to control both the amount and size distribution of cellular fragments remaining in the beverage juice.

Pasteurizing

From the blending tank into which the centrifuges discharge, the juice may be handled according to either of two alternative processes. In the first alternative, the juice passes directly into the filling machines and thus is filled at a temperature of approximately 140°F. The filling machine commonly employed is manufactured by the Food Machinery and Chemical Corporation of San Jose, Calif. In a number of the larger canneries, the 24-valve juice filler is used. In smaller installations, the 18- or 12-valve filler is employed. It is believed, however, that fillers of a number of other manufacturers might be used successfully.

Following the filling of the juice at a temperature approximating 140°F, the filled cans pass through the usual double seamers and then the juice receives its final pasteurizing in the can. This is generally accomplished by passing the cans through a standard reel and spiral cooker and cooler combination. The processing time of the several can sizes is regulated to bring the temperature of the contents to no less than 190°F. Many canneries prefer to heat to 195°F and then to cool. Many types of rapid coolers are employed in the several canneries.

The second alternative procedure for handling the juice during its final pasteurizing is to pump it directly from the centrifuge discharge tank into a flash pasteurizer which heats the product to approximately 195°F. The cans are filled with the juice at this temperature, and the filled cans are conveyed to allow a brief lag of 1–3 min prior to cooling them in various types of high-speed coolers.

SOURCE: *Fruit and Vegetable Juice Processing Technology, 2nd Edition* by Tressler and Joslyn published by Avi Publishing Co., Westport, Conn.

FROZEN CONCENTRATED PINEAPPLE JUICE

Frozen pineapple concentrate is used both as a beverage base in 6-oz cans or as an ingredient in the manufacture of blended, canned fruit drinks, such as pineapple-grape, pineapple-grapefruit, and other fruit drinks. Pineapple juice comes from several sources. These include the juice obtained by pressing the shell scrapings from the Ginaca machine which both peels the pineapple and forms the cylinder from which the slices are made; cores; trimmings; broken pieces from the canning lines; fruit too small for canning; and the juice drained from crushed pineapple preparation, the peeled cylinders, trimming tables, and the slicing operation. The solid material is shredded by various machines and filter aid such as infusorial earth is mixed with the finely ground material before it is fed to an hydraulic press. The liquid material is heated to coagulate some of the solids and the resulting thin slurry is passed through a continuous centrifuge which removes most of the suspended solids, including the fibers and other small pieces. Pineapples too small for canning may be peeled and pressed for juice by machines similar to those used for oranges, or they may simply be crushed, heated, and pressed. Pineapple juice is sometimes homogenized to stabilize the slightly cloudy appearance, since it is believed that the finely divided solids give the juice a better flavor.

For pineapple juice concentrate the juice is concentrated in multiple-effect vacuum pans. Where the method of evaporation is such that the juice must be heated for a long period—say an hour—it is necessary to use pans which operate at temperatures below 140°F. Where short-time evaporators are used, temperatures as high as 180°F have been successfully used. The fresh pineapple juice at about 12° Brix is concentrated to 60°-65° Brix for remanufacturing purposes, or to 45° Brix for packing in retail size 6-oz cans.

Essence is added and mixed with the pineapple concentrate, which is then slush-frozen and packed either into 6-oz metal containers at 45° Brix or in 75-lb, 3-mil polyethylene-lined fiberboard containers at 65° Brix. Freezing is completed by holding at -10°F.

SOURCE: *The Freezing Preservation of Foods, 4th Edition, Vol. 2* by Tressler, Van Arsdel and Copley published by Avi Publishing Co., Westport, Conn.

FLAVOR BASE FOR A SINGLE-STRENGTH PINEAPPLE POWDER BEVERAGE MIX

For pineapple flavor base powder to make a single-strength pineapple beverage mix for reconstitution with water.

Ingredients	%	For a 32-Oz Serving Gm
Pineapple flavor base powder	8.14	9.44
Sugar, baker's special	66.35	76.97
Dextrose, anhydrous	15.00	17.40
Citric acid, anhydrous	5.20	6.03
Maltrin 15, (malto-dextrin, Grain Processing Corp.)	5.00	5.80
Beatreme No. 3442 (Beatrice Foods)	0.20	0.23
Ascorbic acid	0.10	0.12
FD & C Yellow No. 5	0.01	0.01
Total	100.00	116.00

Procedure

Blend all ingredients thoroughly with rapid agitation until a homogeneous suspension is obtained.

SOURCE: Format Foods Corp., Corvallis, Oregon.

PLUM (PRUNE) JUICE

1. Wash and drain fresh prune plums.
2. Steam 8-10 min to soften the prunes and prevent browning by the fruit's enzymes.
3. Pass the heated fruit through a tomato pulper equipped with very coarse screen to remove pits and obtain a coarse purée containing the skins. Discard the pits.
4. Cool the purée to below 120°F in a heat interchanger such as used for tomato juice, fruit nectars, etc.
5. To the purée add about 0.2% (2 gm per 100 gm, or 2 lb per 1000 lb) of Pectinol 0 or other pectic enzyme preparation of similar activity. Mix thoroughly to dissolve and distribute the enzyme.
6. Let stand until juice can be obtained readily when tested by draining a sample on cheese cloth; normally about 6-12 hr.
7. Add 2% of infusorial earth such as Hyflo Super-Cel or other filter aid. Mix well. It greatly aids in pressing.
8. Place the purée on light canvas, or heavy white muslin, which in turn lies on heavy apple press cloth. This gives double press cloths, which prevent bursting of the cloths and give a clearer juice. Build up a "cheese" of press cloths of the purée and racks. Press as for crushed apples, using an hydraulic press.
9. Filter the juice. Take its Brix degree. If above 25° Brix dilute to about 22.5°-23° Brix. Or blend with other juice to obtain the desired Brix degree.
10. Flash pasteurize the juice in a continuous heat interchanger type pasteurizer to about 190°F. Fill into steamed bottles or into reenameled (double enameled) Type-L berry cans at 180°-185°F. Seal at once. Place on sides 4-5 min to sterilize tops. Cool cans in cold water and bottles in warm water.

Or fill bottles with cold juice. Crown cap the bottles. Pasteurize by placing the bottles in cold water, bottles lying on sides, and heating the water to 180°F for 30 min for quart and smaller bottles. Cool slowly with tempered water.

SOURCE: *Fruit and Vegetable Juice Processing Technology, 2nd Edition* by Tressler and Joslyn published by Avi Publishing Co., Westport, Conn.

CANNED STRAINED PRUNES (INFANT)

Dried prunes are washed, then soaked overnight in water, using about twice as much warm water by weight as prunes. The drained fruit is placed in a steam-jacketed kettle and covered with the soaking water, cooked for 10-15 min, then converted into a purée and pitted in a paddle-type finisher fitted with a screen with 0.027-in. openings. The finisher should have steam inlets at both ends so that there will be a steam atmosphere at all times inside. The resulting purée is homogenized at about 2000 lb psi pressure, pumped through a tubular sterilizer (of the small-tube, high-velocity type) in which the temperature is quickly raised to about 270°F and then immediately cooled to the desired filling temperature in a tubular heat exchanger.

The product may be either packed into small cans or glass jars and sterilized; or the product may be put into cartons and frozen at -20°F or below and stored at 0°F.

SOURCE: *The Freezing Preservation of Foods, 4th Edition, Vol. 4* by Tressler, Van Arsdel and Copley published by Avi Publishing Co., Westport, Conn.

CHOPPED PRUNES FOR INFANT FOOD

Dried prunes are washed, then placed in twice their weight of warm water, and soaked overnight. The next day after they are pitted, the prunes are chopped in a chopper which will produce an average particle size of 1/16 in. in diameter or less. The chopped prunes are cooked in the soaking water for about 25 min. Additional water is added, if necessary, to produce the desired consistency. If packed in cans, the chopped prunes can be filled without cooling. If the product is to be put into cartons or composite cartons with metal ends, it should be cooled. This may be done by pumping it through a heat exchanger, provided the pump used will handle a product containing the small pieces of prunes. The product is then quick frozen.

SOURCE: *The Freezing Preservation of Foods, 4th Edition, Vol. 4* by Tressler, Van Arsdel and Copley published by Avi Publishing Co., Westport, Conn.

PRUNE (DRIED) JUICE

Two different methods are used commercially for making prune juice from dried prunes. One of these, the diffusion method, involves extracting the soluble components from the dried fruit by means of successive leachings with hot water. The other, sometimes called the disintegration method, consists of breaking up the dried fruit by vigorous cooking in water, followed by separation of the juice by pressing the disintegrated fruit in an hydraulic press.

Diffusion Method

Dried prunes are thoroughly washed to free them from adhering dust and lint. The washed fruit is placed in large wood tanks, usually about 5 ft in diameter and 7 ft deep, each fitted with a perforated steam cross or a closed coil in order to keep the extracting water at 185°F or slightly higher. Tanks of this size hold 350-400 lb of prunes and 25 gal. hot water per each 100 lb fruit. Steam is employed to maintain the water at 185°F or slightly higher. Higher temperatures may result in loss of prune aroma and cause a "burned taste" in the product. After 2-4 hr extraction, the liquor is drained and stored. Fresh hot water is placed upon the fruit in the proportion of 15 gal. for each 100 lb fruit in the extractor and maintained at the extraction temperature (185°F) for the second extraction which again requires 2-4 hr. At the end of this period the liquor is drawn off and combined with that from the first extraction. Hot water is again added to the prunes, this time in the proportion of 10 gal. of water for each 100 lb of prunes used in the batch. At the end of the third extraction, the three extracts are combined, and the exhausted fruit, which is practically free of soluble matter, discarded. The extracts can either be used to extract a fresh batch of prunes and thus build up the desired concentration of soluble solids, or the liquor can be evaporated until the concentration reaches 19°-21° Brix, the strength ordinarily desired.

If the combined extracts are used to treat a fresh lot of prunes, the resultant juice usually attains a concentration of 22°-24° Brix and, consequently, must be diluted.

A modification of the process is to pulp the fruit prior to the third extraction, then add a quantity of water and filter the product through coarse bag filters. Infusorial earth may be used as a filter aid. This adds considerable body to the juice because of the pectin from the pulp.

Disintegration Process

The disintegration process involves thoroughly cooking the washed prunes in a wood or stainless steel tank equipped with an agitator and a heating unit of sufficient size to obtain vigorous boiling. In some instances an apple butter cooker, which can be sealed and operated under a few pounds pressure, is used. This shortens the time required for cooking.

To 122 lb of washed prunes in a cooker (approx 6 ft in diameter and 5 ft in depth) 700 gal. of hot water are added. The water is brought to a boil and the fruit digested for 60-80 min, or until it is well disintegrated. The resulting prune mush is dropped from the cooker onto a cloth on an hydraulic press of the type commonly used in converting apples into juice. When a "cheese" has been built up, it is subjected to hydraulic pressure which ordinarily does not exceed 1000 lb. The juice or liquor obtained in this way is about 10° Brix. It is allowed to settle, then the clear juice is siphoned off, concentrated to about 20° Brix, and bottled. Or, it may be clarified by filtering through a filter press using about 1.0% infusorial earth (Hyflo Super-Cel or Dicalite) as a filter aid.

When the extract has attained the desired concentration (19°-21° Brix), it is heated to 180°F prior to filling into bottles. At this point citric acid may be added to make the juice more tart; 2 lb of citric acid per 100 gal. improves the flavor noticeably. If used, the presence and amount of citric acid added must be declared on the label. Quart bottles of prune juice are usually pasteurized in a water bath at 190°F for 35 min. Cans and smaller bottles require less sterilization.

Processing time and temperature should be checked with container supplier or with the National Canners Association.

SOURCE: *Fruit and Vegetable Juice Processing Technology, 2nd Edition* by Tressler and Joslyn published by Avi Publishing Co., Westport, Conn.

FLAVOR BASE FOR A SINGLE-STRENGTH RASPBERRY POWDER BEVERAGE MIX

A red raspberry flavor base powder to make a single-strength red raspberry beverage mix for reconstitution with water.

Ingredients	%	For a 32-Oz Serving Gm
Red raspberry flavor base powder	5.10	5.9160
Sugar, baker's special	92.27	107.0292
Citric acid, anhydrous	2.50	2.9000
Ascorbic acid	0.10	0.1195
FD & C Red No. 2*	0.03	0.0348
FD & C Blue No. 1	0.00	0.0005
Total	100.00	116.0000

Procedure

Blend all ingredients thoroughly with rapid agitation until a homogeneous suspension is obtained.

---

*This coloring has been de-listed. It is no longer on the FDA-approved list of food colors and cannot be used. Consult your food color supplier for recommended color substitution.

SOURCE: Foamat Foods Corp., Corvallis, Oregon.

STRAWBERRY MILK SHAKE

Ingredients	
Frozen strawberries, sliced	5 lb
Instant vanilla pudding and pie filling mix	30 oz
Nonfat dry milk crystals, liquid as directed	40 cups
Red food coloring	as desired

Procedure

Force strawberries through sieve or food mill. Combine pudding mix and milk; beat until smooth. Add strawberries and few drops of food coloring.

Yield: 3 gal.

SOURCE: California Strawberry Advisory Board, Watsonville, Calif.

PEAR SHAKE

Ingredients	
Pears, canned halves	2½ lb
Pear syrup	1 lb
Cold milk	1¼ qt
Vanilla Ice cream	2 qt
Nutmeg	2 tbsp

Procedure

Combine pear halves and syrup, milk, and ice cream in blender and mix until smooth and thick. Pour into tall glasses and sprinkle with nutmeg. Serve with straws.

Yield: 20 servings.

SOURCE: Pacific Coast Canned Pear Service, Sixth Ave. North, Seattle, Washington.

BOTTLED STRAWBERRY JUICE

Cold Pressing Fresh Strawberries

Cold fresh strawberries are put through a hammer mill fitted with a ¼-in. screen. Then filter aid is added to the crushed berries in amounts varying from 3 to 10%, after which the slurry is immediately pressed in a bag-type press. The amount of filter aid used depends on the firmness of the berries, and this is added in sufficient quantity to produce a firm, dry cake in the press. The yield of juice varies from 70 to 80% depending upon the variety, maturity, etc., of the berries. The cloudy juice from the press is treated immediately with a pectic enzyme preparation (Pectinol), in order to remove the pectin component. Treatment for 3 hr at 75°F with 0.5% Pectinol degrades the pectic substances sufficiently to produce a clear stable juice. After this treatment it is filtered under pressure using filter-aid precoated plates and an addition of 0.25% of filter aid to the juice. The juice is flash pasteurized at 180°F and bottled at this temperature.

Cold Pressing Thawed Berries

Frozen berries, usually those prepared without sugar, are sometimes used for juice. Their use has five definite advantages. Freezing effects a coagulation of the mucilaginous components which otherwise make pressing difficult, thus making heating of the berries unnecessary. On the average a higher yield of juice (65-79% of the weight of the fruit) is obtained from frozen berries than is the case when heated fresh berries are pressed in an hydraulic press. A third advantage is that when frozen berries are used as raw material, the juice plant may be operated throughout the year instead of only during the season when fresh berries are available. Juice obtained by cold pressing thawed berries has a much deeper color than that produced by cold pressing fruit that has not been frozen, and is nearly equivalent in this regard to hot-pressed juice. Further, it has a fresh fruit flavor and lacks the astringency often characteristic of hot-pressed juice.

The juice from thawed fruit is preserved by flash pasteurization at 180°F, followed by bottling at this temperature, in the same way as the juice made from fresh berries.

SOURCE: *Fruit and Vegetable Juice Processing Technology, 2nd Edition* by Tressler and Joslyn published by Avi Publishing Co., Westport, Conn.

FLAVOR BASE FOR A SINGLE-STRENGTH STRAWBERRY POWDER BEVERAGE MIX

A strawberry flavor base powder to make a single-strength strawberry beverage mix for reconstitution with water.

Ingredients	%	For a 32-Oz Serving Gm
Strawberry flavor base powder	4.00	4.640
Sugar, baker's special	93.89	108.912
Citric acid, anhydrous	2.00	2.320
Ascorbic acid	0.10	0.119
FD & C Red No. 2*	0.0	0.009
Total	100.00	116.000

Procedure

Blend all ingredients thoroughly with rapid agitation until a homogeneous suspension is obtained.

---

*This coloring has been de-listed. It is no longer on the FDA-approved list of food colors and cannot be used. Consult your food color supplier for recommended color substitution.

SOURCE: Foamat Foods Corp., Corvallis, Oregon.

FRESH TANGERINE JUICE

The methods used in extracting, preparing, and canning orange juice (pp. 17-20) are also used for tangerine juice. The procedures followed in concentrating orange juice and freezing the concentrate (p. 18) are also those used in preparing frozen tangerine concentrate. However, there are certain precautions that should be observed.

Tangerines are quite fragile and must be handled with care. They cannot be hauled at the usual depth in citrus trucks or placed in bins. They are handled in boxes or in shallow layers in trucks. Some orange conveyers and washers would crush tangerines and would need remodeling or replacing in order to efficiently handle the latter fruit. Regular citrus juice extractors can be used, especially those fitted to handle small fruit which would otherwise contribute to off-flavor development in storage. The capacity of a given plant handling tangerines is about half that when handling oranges. Canned tangerine juice has a very limited shelf-life; the frozen concentrate is quite stable. Many of the volatiles of unusual flavor are removed during vacuum concentration and the product is not as harsh in flavor as is the canned juice.

SOURCE: *Fruit and Vegetable Juice Processing Technology, 2nd Edition* by Tressler and Joslyn published by Avi Publishing Co., Westport, Conn.

CANNED FRUITS

CANNED APPLES

Firm apples, having white flesh and pronounced apple flavor, should be used. The apples are first washed and then sorted to eliminate bruised, rotten, and misshapen fruit. Then they are placed by hand on mechanical peeling and coring machines. The peeled and cored fruit pass onto a long belt before women who trim the apples free from skin, eliminate defective fruit, and cut them into quarters or slices.

Blanching

The next step is to pass the quartered or sectioned apples through a steam box to soften them, to expel the air from the fruit, and to destroy the oxidase enzyme.

Canning

After blanching, the hot apples are immediately solidly packed into cans having type-L or other corrosion-resistant tinplate. To eliminate any air pockets in the cans a small amount of boiling water is added. The cans are then passed through an exhaust box in which live steam replaces the air in the headspace above the apples. The cans are immediately closed and processed in an agitating sterilizer. A processing time of 10 min at 212°F is considered adequate, if the cans have been filled and sealed at 160°F or higher.

Processing time and temperatures should be checked with can supplier or with the National Canners Association.

SOURCE: D. K. Tressler and Associates, Westport, Conn.

CANNED APPLE HALVES

Winter apples, (e.g., Cortland, McIntosh, and Red Delicious) that retain their good color and flavor are canned using ascorbic acid to prevent browning. Peel and core firm ripe apples. Cut in halves, and immerse in 1% salt brine for 5 min. Then fill cans with the halves, add ascorbic acid at the rate of 300 mg per lb of apples. Cover with hot (200°F or hotter) 25% sugar syrup. Seal cans immediately, then process in boiling water (212°F) for 10 min. Cool with sprays of water.

Check processing time with can supplier or the National Canners Association.

SOURCE: D. K. Tressler and Associates, Westport, Conn.

CANNED APPLESAUCE

Varieties that are rather tart and give a sauce of light color, pleasing texture, and have a pronounced apple flavor are preferred.

First, the apples are washed, then sorted to remove badly bruised, partly rotten, and wormy apples. The apples are then placed by hand on a peeling and coring machine. The peeled and cored fruit is then wet with dilute brine to prevent browning. Next the apples are run over a slowly moving belt along which women trim off peel left by the machines and pick out defective fruit. The apples are rinsed with water to wash off the salt brine, after which they are sliced or chopped by machine. Then heavy syrup (e.g., 67° Brix) is slowly added as the apples are cooked in a continuous steam cooker. The cooked apples are pulped by a machine, similar to a tomato pulper, which removes any remaining seed cells and fiber. The sauce is then inspected as it flows over a brightly illuminated transparent plate where any "specks" are removed. It is then heated to 192°-195°F and filled into cans at this temperature. After "double seaming" the cans, they are cooled with water to 100°F, allowed to dry on a conveyor, and are either labeled and cased, or cased and labeled later.

SOURCE: D. K. Tressler and Associates, Westport, Conn.

CANNED BAKED APPLES

Select choice, firm winter apples (Baldwin, R. I. Greening, Gravenstein, Northern Spy, or Rome Beauty varieties) about 3 in. in diameter. Wash thoroughly, remove core by making a small cut and removing the core without cutting through the stem end, then put apples in a 3% salt brine until needed for baking. After rinsing in fresh water, bake at 350°F for 45 min. Put 2 or 3 hot baked apples in a can of suitable size and fill the can with 40° Brix syrup. To prevent apples from floating in the syrup, exhaust air from the head space of the cans in a steam box; then close cans and process for 20-30 min (depending on the size of the cans) in boiling water. Cool the cans with a spray of cold water and stack.

Check processing time with can supplier or the National Canners Association.

SOURCE: D. K. Tressler and Associates, Westport, Conn.

CANNED WHOLE GLAZED APPLES

Choice winter apples should be washed and cored from the blossom end without cutting through the stem end.

Core apples and cook in a 50° Brix sugar syrup for about 14 min. Depending upon the size of the can, 2 or 3 apples are then placed in each can while apples are hot and covered with the hot syrup in which they were cooked; cans should be filled with the hot syrup. Cans are closed and processed in boiling water for 20-30 min depending upon size of the can. Cans are then cooled in running cold water.

Check processing time with can supplier or the National Canners Association.

SOURCE: D. K. Tressler and Associates, Westport, Conn.

CANNED APRICOTS

Select firm-ripe, well-colored apricots; run them through a size grader. The usual sizes are those "counting" 12 or less and those running 14 to the pound.

After thorough washing, the apricots should be split along the natural dividing line to obtain symmetrical halves. This is done in a hand-operated splitter which also removes the seeds.

Apricots may be lye-peeled by the process described for **Canned Peaches** but the demand for peeled apricots is not great.

Fill the apricots into cans by the "hand-pack" method. Cans with plain tin bodies and enameled ends should be used. An automatic syruper is used to "syrup" the apricots, or "cots" as they are commonly called. Use the following concentrations: 55° Brix for the fancy grade; 40° for choice; 25° for standard; 10° Brix for seconds or "Pie." Plain water may also be used for pie cots.

The cans of apricots are exhausted in the manner described for canned peaches. After exhausting and sealing, the cans are immediately sterilized at 212°F. No. 2½ cans should be processed 17 min and No. 10 cans 20-30 min depending on the texture of the fruit. Check processing time with the can supplier or the National Canners Association.

SOURCE: D. K. Tressler and Associates, Westport, Conn.

CANNED BLACKBERRIES

Sort freshly picked blackberries carefully, eliminating mouldy and overripe fruit. Then wash the berries in gentle sprays of cold water. Fill the berries into fruit-enamel lined tin cans. If the berries are to be sold at retail, pack them in No. 303 or No. 2 cans. Fill the cans with boiling 20° Brix syrup (208 lb sugar to 100 gal. water). Pack berries for the wholesale market in No. 10 cans and cover them with boiling water.

Give the cans a short exhaust (4-5 min for No. 2, and 6-10 min for No. 10). Then seal and process in boiling water. The usual process is 15 min for No. 2 or No. 303 cans and 25 min for No. 10 cans. Check processing time with can supplier or the National Canners Association.

SOURCE: D. K. Tressler and Associates, Westport, Conn.

CANNED BLACKBERRIES, BOYSENBERRIES, DEWBERRIES, LOGANBERRIES, AND YOUNGBERRIES

The berries are carefully sorted, thoroughly washed and size graded. Berries to be used in pie making are packed in water or light syrup. Berries packed for "dessert purposes" are placed in heavy syrup 40°-55° Brix.

The smaller berries are usually packed in No. 10 cans (type L plate, coated inside with "berry" enamel) for use by bakers. The larger berries are packed in No. 303 cans for use as dessert in the home. The small cans are thoroughly exhausted, then closed and processed at 212°F for 11-14 min. The No. 10 cans should be processed at 212°F for 25 min or longer. Check processing time with can supplier or the National Canners Association.

SOURCE: D. K. Tressler and Associates, Westport, Conn.

CANNED BLUEBERRIES

First clean the blueberries in a fanning mill which removes the greater proportion of the leaves, sticks, and stems. Then run the berries over a white sorting belt where workers should eliminate most of the remaining foreign material. Next, wash the berries in a shaker washer to remove insecticides and any remaining dirt. Drain the water from the berries and fill them into fruit-enamel-lined, hot dipped tin cans. Shake the berries down in cans with vibrator. Cover berries in retail size cans with boiling 40° Brix syrup. The institutional pack in No. 10 cans should be covered with boiling water. After exhausting small cans for 4-6 min and No. 10 cans for 8-12 min, close the cans preferably with a steam flow closer.

Process the smaller retail size cans for 10 min in boiling water; larger cans (e.g., No. 10) require about 25 min processing. Check kind of can used and processing time with can supplier or with the National Canners Association.

SOURCE: D. K. Tressler and Associates, Westport, Conn.

CANNED RED SOUR PITTED CHERRIES

The Montmorency is the standard variety used for canning. The cherries should not be picked until they are fully ripe and should be picked without stems and then transported to the cannery in shallow lug boxes. After inspection the cherries should be dumped into a tank of cold water (the colder the better), where they are held at least 3 hr and often overnight. This soaking plumps and washes the cherries. Wormy cherries are lighter than sound fruit and usually float; they should be skimmed off. The soaked cherries are passed over a sorting belt where defective cherries are picked out and discarded; then the cherries go to a mechanical pitter. The pitted cherries are mechanically filled into enamel-lined heavily plated (usually Charcoal 2-A plate) cans. Then hot water or syrup at, or near, the boiling point is added. Water is usually used in No. 10 cans; fancy cherries in No. 2 cans receive 70° Brix syrup; 50° Brix syrup is commonly used on choice and extra standard grades. The cans should then be given an exhaust sufficiently long to raise the temperature of the center of the can to 170°F for the No. 2 size and 160°F for No. 10's.

After closing, the cans are processed in boiling water. The No. 2 cans for 12-15 min, the No. 10 cans for 25-30 min. The cans should be cooled to about 90°F before casing.

Processing times should be checked with the can supplier or the National Canners Association.

SOURCE: D. K. Tressler and Associates, Westport, Conn.

CANNED SWEET CHERRIES

Sweet cherries are mechanically stemmed, and then inspected to eliminate imperfect fruit. The cherries should then be washed and size graded into 22/32, 24/32, 26/32, 28/32, and 32/32 in. sizes. The larger the size of the fruit the heavier the syrup used. The syrups used on black and white cherries should be the following: 40° Brix on 32/32 in.; 30° Brix on 28/32 in.; 20° Brix on 26/32 in.; 10° Brix on 24/32 in.; and water on the 22/32 in. size. In the case of Royal Anne cherries, the syrup concentrations used should be the following: 55° Brix on 32/32 in.; 40° Brix on 28/32 in.; 25° Brix on 26/32; 10° Brix on 24/32 in.; and water on the 22/32 in. size. The syrup or water used should be at about 120°F. The cans of cherries should be slowly but well exhausted requiring about 15 min at 190°-200°F. Hot dipped tinplate enamel-lined cans are best.

The exhausted cans should be immediately closed and then processed in boiling water for the same periods as recommended above for **Canned Red Sour Pitted Cherries.**

SOURCE: D. K. Tressler and Associates, Westport, Conn.

CANNED KADOTA FIGS

Figs are first placed on a slowly moving belt and sorted to remove overripe and split figs, which are diverted to the "dry yard." The nearly perfect figs are washed in a long spray washer, and then again sorted. The riper figs are put in No. 10 cans, and the firmer fruit in smaller cans. The filled cans are conveyed through a long steam chamber for 18 min to bring the fruit to about 200°F. Then a 48° Brix syrup acidified with lemon juice to a pH of 3.8 is added. The cans are exhausted in a steam box for about 9 min and processed in a continuous agitating cooker at about 212°F for No. 2½ and smaller cans and 60 min for No. 10 cans. Then the cans are cooled in sprays of cold water. Some plants process the canned figs at 220°F for 30 min in a continuous agitating pressure cooker.

Check processing time with can supplier or the National Canners Association.

SOURCE: D. K. Tressler and Associates, Westport, Conn.

CANNED GOOSEBERRIES

Gooseberries are picked when they have attained full size but before they have begun to soften. The stem and blossom ends should be snipped by an Urschel snipper. After snipping, the gooseberries should be put over a sorting belt where all defective berries and foreign material are removed. Then the berries should be washed, drained, and filled into plain tin cans. Most gooseberries are sold to bakeries. These are packed in No. 10 cans and should be covered with boiling hot water. If the gooseberries are for table use, they are packed in No. 2 cans and should be covered with boiling hot heavy syrup. The cans should then be passed through an exhaust box in order to bring the center of the can up to a temperature of 140°F.

Berries in heavy syrup in No. 2 cans should be processed for 15-20 min at 212°F. Berries in water in No. 10 cans may require only processing for 15 min at 212°F.

Processing times and temperatures should be checked with can supplier or the National Canners Association.

SOURCE: D. K. Tressler and Associates, Westport, Conn.

CANNED GRAPEFRUIT SECTIONS

Tree-ripened fruit should be used in order to obtain a product of maximum flavor. The grapefruit should first be placed in boiling water from 3 to 7 min, the length of time depending on the size, variety, and maturity of the fruit. Then the grapefruit should be "quarter-scored" with a knife and the rind peeled off. The peeled fruit should then be passed under sprays of a boiling caustic soda solution (1-3% sodium hydroxide or lye). This treatment causes the disintegration of the membranes covering the segments. The grapefruit should then be passed under cold water sprays, sufficiently strong to wash off the particles of membrane as well as all traces of caustic soda. After the fruit has been thoroughly washed, it should be conveyed on a belt in front of workers who separate sections and remove broken and defective pieces.

The use of Type L tinplate cans is desirable. The proper amount of 40° Brix syrup is first placed in each can, then the can is filled by hand with segments (17 oz in a No. 2 can). Sufficient headspace (5/16 in.) should be left to permit thorough exhaustion. The lids should be given the first crimping before the cans are passed through the exhaust (steam) chamber. The cans are then closed and moved through a processing bath of water at a temperature of 180°F or higher until the center of each can reaches 170°F which takes 25-50 min depending on the size of the can. Check time and temperature of processing with can supplier or the National Canners Association.

SOURCE: D. K. Tressler and Associates, Westport, Conn.

CANNED PEACHES

The first step in preparing peaches for canning is grading for size and maturity. The fully mature fruit is promptly prepared for canning. Immature fruit is held until it softens.

Clingstone peaches are halved and lye-peeled. The halving is carried out mechanically. The halves are placed on a conveyor belt, cup side down, and put through a 5-11% lye solution maintained at 215°F or slightly hotter. This treatment loosens the skins in 45-60 sec. The immersion time, temperature, and concentration of the lye used are dependent on the maturity of the fruit. The peaches are then conveyed under strong sprays of cold water to wash off the skins and all traces of lye.

Freestone peaches should be peeled by steaming. This is effected by conveying the halved peaches, cup side down through a steam scalder for ½-2 min after which the peaches pass under sprays of cold water. This loosens the skins so that they can be picked off without lifting the peaches. The peeled peaches then pass before inspectors who remove off-color, partially peeled, and otherwise imperfect fruit. These imperfect halves are canned as pie stock.

Peaches are canned both sliced and as halves. Machines are available for slicing halves. Cans with electrotin plate bodies and electrotin enameled ends should be used.

Peach halves are filled into cans by in-line and rotary type fillers. Slices should be passed over an inspection belt for the removal of imperfect pieces before passing on to hand-pack fillers.

Syruping.—With the top grade of peaches 55° Brix is used; with lower grades 40°, 25° or 10° Brix syrup is used. Syruping is accomplished by rotary and straight line syrupers or by prevacuumizing syrupers. The syrup should be very hot (190°F). When sufficiently hot syrup is used, the exhaust step may be omitted. However, exhausting for 6 min at 190°F will ensure obtaining a product that will retain its quality (color and flavor) during storage.

The peaches should be 160°F or hotter when the cans are closed. If the temperature of the peaches is below 160°F, "Steam-Vac" closing should be employed; the headspace should be 5/16 in. or slightly greater. The peaches should be processed immediately after closure assuming that the temperature of the peaches is 160° or higher at the beginning of processing. The following processing times in boiling water are recommended:

Can Size	Water Pack Min	Syrup Pack Min
307 × 409 and smaller	10-15	12-17
401 × 411	15-20	20-25
603 × 700	25-30	30-35

Process times should be checked either with can supplier or the National Canners Association.

After processing, the cans should be water cooled to about 95°F.

SOURCE: D. K. Tressler and Associates, Westport, Conn.

CANNED PEARS

The two principal varieties of pears canned are the Bartlett and the Kieffer. The Bartlett is the best variety because of its large regular size and thin skin, which makes it easy to peel. The Kieffer is largely grown in the East. It is rather irregular in size and has a thick skin and rather grainy flesh.

The Bartlett can be machine peeled and cored but the Kieffer must be peeled and cored by hand. Kieffer pears are easier to peel if they are given a 20-30 sec blanch in steam or boiling water. Pears begin to turn brown as soon as they are peeled; therefore, unless they can be canned immediately, they must be held under water.

The pear halves must be carefully graded by workers who fill the cans. The halves must be placed in layers in order to fill the space and get the proper weight in each can. Cans with hot dipped or electrolytic bodies and enameled ends should be used.

Pears are not tart; for this reason, they are not covered with heavy syrup. The heaviest syrup used is 40° Brix; 30°, 20°, 10° Brix, and water are also used. If hot (190°F) syrup is added with a prevacuumizing syruper, there is no need to exhaust the cans. If a steam-flow closer is not available, the cans should be exhausted in steam until the center of the can reaches about 160°F; about 10 min is required.

The pears should be processed in boiling water. The No. 303 and the No. 2½ cans will require from 15 to 25 min, the time required depending on the closing temperature and the syrup used. Pears in heavy syrup will require a longer time than those in light syrup. The process time should be checked with can supplier or the National Canners Association.

SOURCE: D. K. Tressler and Associates, Westport, Conn.

CANNED SLICED PINEAPPLE

Pineapples are not harvested until they are fully ripe and then are canned the same day. When the pineapples arrive at the cannery they are graded mechanically for size and each size goes to a different Ginaca machine. This machine is entirely automatic in operation. It cuts a cylinder from the center portion of the fruit, removes the shell, cuts off the shell portion at each end of the cylinder, and removes the core. The flesh on the inside of the shell is scraped out for use either as crushed pineapple or for juice. The cylinders of pineapple are conveyed to trimmers who inspect the cylinders and trim away any bits of shell still adhering.

The trimmed cylinders are conveyed through a spray washer to a slicing machine which slices them transversely into rings ½-in. thick for the No. 2½ cans, and 25/64-in. thick for the No. 2 tall cans. The slices are conveyed by belt to women who inspect the slices and put them in cans. The slices are graded into three grades: Fancy, Choice, and Standard. The grade depends on color, texture, and appearance. Broken and other defective slices are conveyed to a shredder which prepares them for the crushed pineapple pack. The filled cans are passed on to a vacuumizing chamber in which they are subjected to a 25 in. vacuum for a few seconds. The vacuum removes air from the tissues and improves the uniformity of color of the fruit. Syrup is then added. The syrup is made in part from juice expressed from the shells and other by-products. This juice has been neutralized with lime heated to precipitate calcium and slightly concentrated before it is mixed with cane sugar syrup. The Fancy or No. 1 Grade receives 40° Brix which produces a 24° Brix "cut-out" syrup in the finished product. The No. 2 and No. 3 grades receive 20° Brix syrup.

If a prevacuumizing syruper is employed either mechanical vacuum or a steam-flow closer is satisfactory when hot (190°F) syrup is used. The cans should be processed in continuous pressure cookers until the center of the can reaches 195°F. This requires from 7 to 10 min, the time depending upon the initial temperature of the pineapple, the size of the can, and the temperature of the steam in the cooker. Check process time and temperature with can supplier or the National Canners Association. After processing, the cans should be cooled to 100°F in water.

SOURCE: D. K. Tressler and Associates, Westport, Conn.

CANNED CRUSHED PINEAPPLE

The shredded pineapple obtained from the scraping of the interior shell by the "eradicator" of the Ginaca machine and the shredding of defective slices, is pumped into a steam-jacketed kettle and heated to 195°F. Some of the juice is drained off and packed as pineapple juice. If the remainder is not sufficiently sweet, heavy sugar syrup is added. The hot crushed pineapple is then automatically filled into cans, which are sealed and given a short process. The time and temperature of processing should be checked with the can supplier or the National Canners Association.

After processing, the cans should be cooled in water to 100°F.

SOURCE: D. K. Tressler and Associates, Westport, Conn.

CANNED PLUMS

The Green Gage and the Yellow Egg give the best canned product. The plums are washed and then run over an inspection belt where defective plums and foreign matter (stems and leaves) are eliminated. Then they are size-graded on vibrating screens. The fancy grade measures 56/32 in.; the choice, 50/32 in.; and the standard, 42/32 in. in diameter. The plums are then packed directly into cans. Type L tinplate is recommended for plums. The cans are then filled with boiling hot syrup: 55° Brix is used on the Fancy Grade; 40° Brix on Choice; and 25° Brix on Standard Grade No. 2 cans should be given a 6–8 min exhaust; and No. 10 cans, 10–12 min. The cans of plums are processed in boiling water usually 12–15 min for No. 2 and 28–35 min for No. 10 cans. Check process time with can supplier or the National Canners Association.

The cans should be cooled to 100°F or lower in cold water immediately after processing.

SOURCE: D. K. Tressler and Associates, Westport, Conn.

CANNED DRIED PRUNES

First the prunes are sorted to eliminate broken and defective fruit. Next, they are washed, then blanched in water near the boiling point, after which they are filled into cans. Since the prunes will absorb part of the hot syrup added, allowance must be made so that after canning the "cut-out" will be 22 oz for a No. 2½ can. This must be determined by preliminary trials. The cans should be exhausted for 15 min and closed with steam flow. The usual process time for No. 2½ cans is 20 min in boiling water. After processing, the cans must be cooled to below 100°F in running cold water.

Processing time should be checked with can supplier or the National Canners Association.

SOURCE: D. K. Tressler and Associates, Westport, Conn.

CANNED FRESH PRUNES

The Italian variety of prune plum should be used, as the "French prune" has such a tough skin that they must be peeled. The procedure followed in canning the fresh Italian prunes is the same as that described previously for plums. The prune plums are rather tart so a 40° Brix syrup should be used.

SOURCE: D. K. Tressler and Associates, Westport, Conn.

CANNED RED RASPBERRIES

Both red and black raspberries are canned. The procedure used is the same for both. Raspberries are easily bruised and mold quickly if held for more than a few hours. Because of their fragility, they cannot be passed over an inspection belt. The berries in each small box should be inspected as they are washed over a small sink. Mouldy berries and foreign matter are eliminated and the good berries filled directly into the hot-dipped tin can in which they are processed. The filled cans are inverted in order to drain off any free water. The filled cans (usually No. 2's) then should be passed on to the syruper where hot 50° Brix syrup, preferably at 200°F is added leaving only ⅝-in. headspace. The cans should then be passed through a steam exhaust box and should be given a sufficiently long exhaust to bring the temperature in the center of the cans to 165°–170°F. The exhausted cans should be closed on seamers equipped with steam-flow. No. 2 cans filled with light syrup should be processed for 10 min at 212°F; those with heavy syrup require 15 min processing. Check exact processing time with can supplier or the National Canners Association. The processed cans should be cooled to 100°F in water before casing.

Black raspberries should be packed in No. 10 cans following the handling, sorting, and washing procedure outlined above. When the No. 10 cans are filled with berries, hot water (instead of syrup) is added and the cans are put through an exhaust box long enough to raise the temperature in the center of the can to 160°F. The cans should be closed with steam-flow seamers and then processed for 25 min at 212°F. No. 10 cans will require much longer cooling in running water than No. 2 cans.

SOURCE: D. K. Tressler and Associates, Westport, Conn.

CANNED STRAWBERRIES

In small canneries, the berries are capped by hand, larger operations use mechanical cappers. Following capping the berries should be sorted and washed.

If the washed berries are placed in cans, then covered with hot syrup, the cans exhausted, closed and processed, according to the procedure followed in canning other fruit, the berries collapse so much that the cans will only be about ½ full of fruit. To obtain a satisfactory product, other procedures must be used.

The best procedure is that which the housewife uses: The berries and sugar and a very little water should be placed in a steam-jacketed preserve kettle and boiled very rapidly. The partially collapsed berries should then be filled into cans, the syrup partially evaporated, then added to the cans. The cans are closed and processed.

Another method which gives a satisfactory product is to put into the cans ⅓ of the berries which it is intended to hold, add ⅓ of the sugar, then add another ⅓ of the berries and sugar, and finally place a wide-mouthed funnel on the top of the can with the last ⅓ of berries and sugar. Then the cans should be run through a slow steam exhaust which cooks the berries and causes those in the funnel to sink into the can, simultaneously forming hot juice which dissolves the sugar and forms a syrup, thus giving a satisfactory fill.

The cans should be of the best tinplate and lined with a fruit enamel. The cans should be closed with a steam-flow seamer. The usual process for No. 2 and 2½ cans is 10 min in boiling water. Process time should be checked with can supplier or the National Canners Association. Cooling must be promptly carried out in order to reduce the effect of the cooking on the tissues of the berries.

SOURCE: D. K. Tressler and Associates, Westport, Conn.

FRUIT FLAVORS, CONCENTRATES, AND ESSENCES

FROZEN APPLE CONCENTRATE

The process may be divided into the following major operations: pressing, essence stripping, clarification, concentration, blending, freezing, and packaging.

Pressing is accomplished in the customary manner, with standard equipment readily available for this purpose. No changes from operations as performed for single-strength juice are required. Strict sanitary practices are recommended.

After removal of essence, the residual or stripped juice is clarified by treatment with a pectic enzyme and filtration. Methods of clarifying fresh apple juice are described in Section 1 under **Apple Juice, Ciders.**

After clarification, the stripped juice is concentrated. A low temperature, as used for citrus concentrates, is not required to prevent changes in flavor. In view of the smaller dangers of localized overheating, with production of off-flavors, a forced-circulation evaporator unit is recommended in preference to a pan or calandria type of evaporator.

The concentrated stripped juices are blended in agitator-equipped, cold-wall tanks. This operation is regulated on a volumetric basis. The solids content of the final product can also be adjusted in the same blending tanks. If the juice has been concentrated to a slightly higher degree than is required, the solids content in the final product can then be controlled accurately by dilution with a small amount of juice from the clarification operation.

The concentrate is then slush frozen and packed into cans in which freezing is completed at 0°F or lower.

SOURCE: *The Freezing Preservation of Foods, 2nd Edition* by Tressler and Evers published by Avi Publishing Co., Westport, Conn.

APPLE ESSENCE

The most efficient process for recovering the volatile flavor constituents from apple juice is the process of stripping these substances from juice by heating in a rapid evaporator to obtain a 10% flash vaporization which removes all of the volatile substances. The condensate is then treated in a fractionating column where the volatile flavoring constituents can be concentrated up to 150 times that of the original juice at atmospheric pressures.

The more complete removal of volatile constituents, which is obtained by the rapid evaporation, and their subsequent enrichment through fractional distillation make it possible to prepare full-flavored apple juice concentrates which, when reconstituted with water, are indistinguishable in taste and aroma from fresh apple juice. This process for recovering and concentrating the volatile, aromatic components of apples also proved to be a practical method for the commercial preparation of volatile fruit concentrates from a variety of fruits.

This process of producing a true fruit essence may be used to obtain essences from other fruit juices, e.g., apricot, blackberry, blueberry, cherry, grape, loganberry, black raspberry, red raspberry, pear, peach, plum, strawberry and others. The essences obtained have the characteristic aroma and flavor of the kind and variety of fruit used in making the juice.

SOURCE: *Food Flavorings, Composition, Manufacture, and Use, 2nd Edition* by Merory published by Avi Publishing Co., Westport, Conn.

APPLE FLAVORS

Apple Fruit Flavor Essence

Mixture of:

	Gm
Freshly recovered apple essence 100-fold	850
Ethyl alcohol 95%	150
	1000

Apple Syrup Flavor

Mixture of:

	Gm
Full-flavored concentrated juice 68° Brix	500
Recovered volatile apple essence	350
Ethyl alcohol 95%	150
	1000

Liquid Apple Flavor

Mixture of:

	Gm
Full-flavored apple concentrated juice 70° to 72° Brix	150

	Gm
Recovered volatile apple essence	20
Citric acid 50% (aqueous solution)	30
Sugar syrup 73.9° Brix	800
	1000

Procedure

All of the ingredients of these three formulas are liquid and merely require thorough mixing until an homogeneous solution is obtained.

SOURCE: *Food Flavorings, Composition, Manufacture, and Use, 2nd Edition* by Merory published by Avi Publishing Co., Westport, Conn.

APRICOT FLAVOR

Ingredients

2500 lb	frozen apricots (preferably Blenheim variety)
510 lb	or 75 gal. alcohol, 95%
415 lb	or 50 gal. water
125 gal.	menstruum of about 25% alcohol content
10 lb	Pectinol (a commercial enzyme preparation)

Procedure

(a) 2500 lb frozen apricots are partly defrosted at room temperature and mixed with:
925 lb or 125 gal. menstruum of 25% alcohol content. The mixture is run through a comminuting machine and then pressed. The expressed juice and flavoring extract is mixed with:
10 lb enzyme Pectinol and left to clear.

Yield
300 gal. expressed juice and flavoring extract of about 15% alcohol content. The expressed portion of about 878 lb is processed in **(g)**.

(b) 50 gal. of the clear juice and flavoring extract of **(a)** is put aside for use in **(h)**.

(c) 150 gal. of the clear juice and flavoring extract of **(a)** is distilled, slowly at atmospheric pressure to yield:
First fraction: 5 gal. flavor distillate of about 66.5% alcohol content, which is used in **(h)**.

(d) The distillation is immediately interrupted and the remaining juice and flavoring extract in the still is cooled to about 77°F; to it is added approximately:
90 gal. remaining clear juice and flavoring extract of **(a)** for concentration. The rest of **(a)**, about 10 gal., is used in the distillation of the pressed remains of **(a)**, which is processed in **(g)**.

(e) The concentration of **(d)** continues under vacuum distillation and yields:
Second fraction: 10 gal. flavor distillate, of about 62% alcohol content, which is used in **(h)**.

(f) The vacuum distillation continues to recover all the alcohol and yields:
Third fraction: 70 gal. distillate of about 30% alcohol content, which is used in **(g)**;
Fourth fraction: About 120 gal. of distillate, nonalcoholic, and is used in **(g)**; the concentrate in the still is 31.25 gal. soluble solids which are used in **(h)**.

(g) Distillation at atmospheric pressure of:
878 lb remains of **(a)**, which are mixed with:
70 gal. distillate of 30% alcohol content, of **(f)**
10 gal. juice and flavoring extract remaining after sedimentation of the juice of **(a)** and
120 gal. distillate, nonalcoholic, of **(f)** to yield:
Fifth fraction: 3.75 gal. flavor distillate of 60% alcohol content; it is used in **(h)**.
Sixth fraction: 120 gal. distillate of about 40% alcohol content; it is redistilled if necessary and then used in the next production batch.

(h) Mixture of:

Gal.	
31.25	concentrated soluble solids of **(f)**
50.00	juice and flavoring extract of **(b)**
5.00	first fraction—flavor distillate of **(c)** of 66.5% alcohol content
10.00	second fraction—flavor distillate of **(e)** of 62% alcohol content
3.75	sixth fraction—flavor distillate of **(g)** of 60% alcohol content
100.00	apricot fruit flavor of about 19% alcohol content

Flavor Property

One gallon of apricot fruit flavor is derived from 25 lb of fruit.

SOURCE: *Food Flavorings, Composition, Manufacture, and Use, 2nd Edition* by Merory published by Avi Publishing Co., Westport, Conn.

ASPIC EXTRACT

Extraction of comminuted botanical ingredients:

Ingredients	Gm
Laurel	1.65
Clove	6.65
Pepper	33.35
Leek	41.65
Parsley	41.65
Celery	41.65
Total	166.60

and menstruum consisting of:

Alcohol, 95%	842.00
Water	158.00

Recommended use

Use 1 oz av for 1 gal. jelly or tomato juice.

SOURCE: *Food Flavorings, Composition, Manufacture, and Use. 2nd Edition* by Merory, published by Avi Publishing Company, Westport, Conn.

BANANA FRUIT FLAVOR

Ingredients

Lb	
2500.0	bananas
166.0	(or 20 gal.) water
190.4	(or 28 gal.) alcohol, 95%
3.0	enzyme Pectinol
50.0	filter aid

Procedure

(a) Spread out 2500 lb bananas and allow them to become overripe, but not too soft, in order to permit easy peeling.
1500.0 lb peeled fruit (60% yield of 2500 lb bananas) is run through the comminuting machine and mixed with:
20.0 gal. water and
3.0 lb Pectinol
The mixture is to be well agitated to form a uniform mash which is then allowed to stand for one day in order to thin its consistency and to dissolve the pectins.
28.0 gal. alcohol, 95%, is then added and thoroughly mixed with the banana mash.

(b) 50.0 lb filter aid is added to the mixture of **(a)** and the juice separated by draining and then by pressing; the yield is about:
95.0 gal. banana juice and flavoring extract; it is used in **(d)**.

(c) The remaining mash is mixed with:
30.0 gal. water and distilled at atmospheric pressure to yield:
First fraction:
5.0 gal. flavor distillate of about 60% alcohol content; it is used in **(d)**.
Second fraction:
5.0 gal. distillate of about 40% alcohol content; it is used in the next production batch.

(d) Mixture of

Gal.	
95.0	extract of **(b)**
5.0	first fraction—flavor distillate of **(c)**
100.0	banana fruit flavor of about 15% alcohol content

Flavor Property

One gallon of banana fruit flavor is derived from 25 lb of fruit.

SOURCE: *Food Flavorings, Composition, Manufacture, and Use, 2nd Edition* by Merory published by Avi Publishing Co., Westport, Conn.

BLACKBERRY JUICE AND FLAVORING EXTRACT

Ingredients

1000.0 lb	frozen blackberries
115.6 lb	(or 17.0 gal.) alcohol 95%
2.0 lb	enzyme Pectinol
Yield:	
100.0 gal.	juice and flavoring extract

Procedure

(a) 1000.0 lb partly defrosted blackberries are mixed with:
115.6 lb (or 17.0 gal.) alcohol 95% and left to thaw entirely; the fruit is pressed and yields:
98.0 gal. juice and flavoring extract; it is used in **(c)**.

(b) The pressed remains are mixed with:
100.0 lb water and distilled at atmospheric pressure to obtain:
2.0 gal. flavor distillate of about 50% alcohol content; it is used in **(c)**.

(c) Mixture of:
98.0 gal. juice and flavoring extract of (a)
2.0 gal. flavor distillate of (b)
Yield:
100.0 gal. juice and flavoring extract of about 15% alcohol content.

Flavor Property

One gallon of juice and flavoring extract is derived from 10 lb of fruit.

SOURCE: *Food Flavorings, Composition, Manufacture, and Use, 2nd Edition* by Merory published by Avi Publishing Co., Westport, Conn.

BLACKBERRY FRUIT FLAVOR

(a) Vacuum distillation of:
300 gal. blackberry juice and flavoring extract manufactured according to formula above for **Blackberry Juice and Flavoring Extract.**
First fraction:
25 gal. flavor distillate of about 62% alcohol content; it is used in (b);
Second fraction:
90 gal. distillate of about 30% alcohol content; it is used in redistilling to higher proof alcohol and used in the next production batch;
Concentrate: 75 gal. soluble solids; they are used in (b).
(b) Mixture of:
75 gal. concentrated soluble solids of (a)
25 gal. first fraction—flavor distillate of (a)
100 gal. blackberry fruit flavor of about 15.5% alcohol content

Flavor Property

One gallon of blackberry fruit flavor is derived from 30 lb of fruit.

SOURCE: *Food Flavorings, Composition, Manufacture, and Use, 2nd Edition* by Merory published by Avi Publishing Co., Westport, Conn.

BLACK CURRANT FRUIT FLAVOR

Ingredients

3000.0 lb	black currants
122.4 lb	(or 18.0 gal.) alcohol, 95%
4.0 lb	enzyme Pectinol

Procedure

(a) 3000.0 lb frozen black currants are allowed to thaw entirely, then are pressed. The espressed juice is mixed with enzyme Pectinol and allowed to stand for 24 hr to separate pectins. The clear juice is then concentrated by vacuum distillation to yield the concentrate:
80.0 gal. soluble solids; it is used in (c).
(b) The pressed remains are mixed with:
8.0 gal. alcohol, 95% and
20.0 gal. water.
The mixture is then distilled at atmospheric pressure to yield:
10.0 gal. flavor distillate of about 65% alcohol content; it is used in (c).
(c) Mixture of:

Gal.	
80.0	concentrate of (a)
10.0	flavor distillate of (b)
10.0	alcohol, 95%

Yield:
100.0 gal. black currant fruit flavor of about 16% alcohol content.

Flavor Property

One gallon black currant fruit flavor is derived from 30 lb fruit.

SOURCE: *Food Flavorings, Composition, Manufacture, and Use, 2nd Edition* by Merory published by Avi Publishing Co., Westport, Conn.

CUSTARD FLAVOR (WITH RUM FLAVOR)

Ingredients	Gm
Oil of nutmeg	1.0
Oil of orange, cold pressed	2.0
Ethyl vanillin	23.0
Vanillin	192.2
Rum or rum ether	60.0
Diacetyl	0.3
Oil of lemon, cold pressed	0.3
Ethyl butyrate	0.2
Alcohol, 95%	721.0
Total	1000.0

Procedure

Mix together all ingredients.

SOURCE: *Food Flavorings, Composition, Manufacture, and Use, 2nd Edition* by Merory published by Avi Publishing Company, Westport, Conn.

EXPRESSED JUICE OF PITTED MORELLO CHERRIES

Procedure

(a) 3000.00 lb frozen pitted Morello cherries (to which no sugar was added) are to be partly defrosted and mixed with:

170.00 lb (or 25 gal.) alcohol, 95%, and then coarsely ground. The mixture is to be pressed and the expressed juice is to be mixed with:

170.00 lb (or 25 gal.) alcohol, 95%. The yield should be about:

3036.25 lb (or 347 gal.) of about 15% alcohol content.

(b) The pressed remains or pomace are to be mixed with an equal quantity of water and then distilled at atmospheric pressure to obtain a yield of:

22.50 lb (or 3 gal.) flavor distillate of about 55% alcohol content. The distillation is to be stopped and the remains of the still discarded.

(c) The finished product is made by mixing:

3036.25 lb (or 347 gal.) of expressed juice of **(a)** with:

22.50 lb (or 3 gal.) flavor distillate of **(b)**. The yield will be:

3058.75 lb (or 350 gal.) cherry juice and flavoring extract with an alcohol content of 15%. Its weight per gallon is about 8.75 lb.

Flavor Property

One gallon of the finished cherry juice and flavoring extract of **(a)** is derived from 8.57 lb. of pitted Morello cherries. If no alcohol were added to the fruit, about 9 lb of pitted cherries would yield 1 gal. of expressed juice.

SOURCE: *Food Flavorings, Composition, Manufacture, and Use, 2nd Edition* by Merory published by Avi Publishing Co., Westport, Conn.

CONCENTRATED FULL FLAVOR MORELLO CHERRY JUICE

Partly defrosted Morello cherries (5,100 lb. straight pack and 22,440 lb. 5 + 1) are expressed with the use of large presses. The juice of both cherries, with and without sugar, is mixed together and to it added enough Pectinol to eliminate the pectins. The total of the expressed juice is about 2754 gal. Thus, 1 gal. of juice is obtained from 10 lb of Morello cherries and pits. The addition of sugar to fruit increases the yield of juice and lowers the quantity of fruit needed per gallon expressed juice. Normally, 12 lb of cherries with pits yield 1 gal. of juice.

After 6 hr the juice is channeled into a still to strip the volatile aroma. The distillation is performed at atmospheric pressure at a temperature of 214°F. About 15 sec are required to strip 1 gal. of volatile aroma and to concentrate it 100-fold. The juice is then immediately cooled down to about 100°F. The yield is 27 gal. of 100-fold essence, each gallon stripped from 100 gal. of expressed juice. The distillate is filled in 1-gal. glass containers and stored at room temperature.

The juice is then piped directly to filter presses. From there it is channeled, without interruption, into the vacuum still. Concentration of the juice is carried out by distillation at a vacuum of about 27.12 in. and a temperature of 110°F. The yield is about 758 gal. of concentrated Morello cherry juice of 68° Brix. Considering the presence of added sugar to the fruit, each gallon of the concentrated Morello cherry juice is derived from 36.33 lb of fruit. The concentrated juice should be stored without the addition of volatile essence in stainless steel drums in a cold warehouse at 35°F temperature.

Five years of tests and observation of the full flavor Morello cherry concentrated juice 68° Brix, indicate that it will remain stable indefinitely at 35°F.

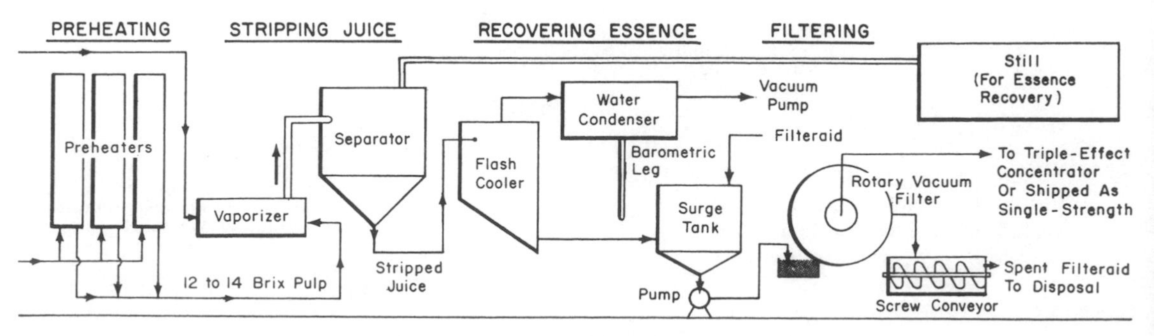

FIG. 3.1. STILL FOR ESSENCE RECOVERY

Flavor Property

One gallon of this full flavor concentrated Morello cherry juice is equal in flavor strength and natural fruit color to about 4 gal. of juice expressed from freshly picked fruit with pits. The characteristic cherry note is enhanced by the completely retained acids of the fruit and by the traces of benzaldehyde which are present in the juice.

Flavor Measurements

Threshold of perception: 1.50%; color: faint
Threshold of identification: 2.50%; color: distinct

SOURCE: *Food Flavorings, Composition, Manufacture, and Use, 2nd Edition* by Merory published by Avi Publishing Co., Westport, Conn.

CHERRY PIT FLAVOR

Procedure

200.00 lb of pits of cold pressed cherries and
1900.00 lb of pomace of hot pressed Morello cherries and pits are mixed with:
2100.00 lb (or 253 gal.) water to produce a uniform mixture. The pomace and pits then coarsely ground with the hammers of a comminuting machine. The mixture of the ground pomace and water is put into the still and heated to 131°F, with agitation, and kept at this temperature for 6 hr to hydrolyze the amygdalin of the cherry seeds to benzaldehyde. The hydrolysis is brought about by the emulsin enzyme which is present in the seeds. The mixture is then allowed to stand overnight. Then:
204.00 lb (or about 30 gal.) 95% alcohol is added and the mixture agitated. Distillation at atmospheric pressure is conducted slowly until all the alcohol is recovered. The still is emptied and the distillate returned to the cleaned still for fractional distillation. Hydrocyanic acid, which is formed during the hydrolysis, is lost during the distillation. The distillate is collected in 7 fractions, of 5 gal. each. The 1st fraction contains high aldehyde and very little flavor. The 2nd, 3rd, 4th, 5th, and 6th fractions have the clean aroma of cherry and benzaldehyde flavor. The 7th fraction has an alcohol content of 26%, with little flavor and the distinct odor of the tails. The first six fractions are combined to yield:
213.00 lb (or 30 gal.) with an alcohol content of 76%.

Flavor Property

The mixture of the first six fractions has the characteristic flavor of the cherry fruit enhanced by the presence of benzaldehyde.

One gallon of the cherry pit flavor distillate is derived from 70 lb of pomace or expressed remains of Morello cherries with pits.

Flavor Measurement

Threshold of perception: 0.05%
Threshold of identification: 0.08%

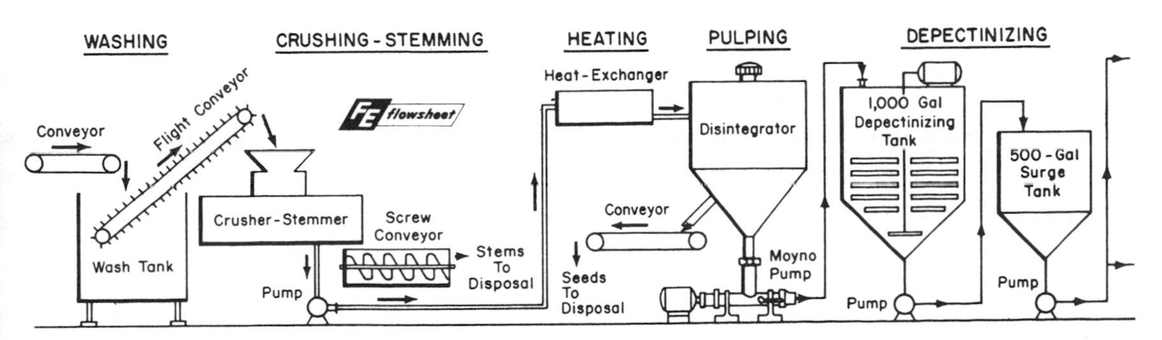

FIG. 3.2. JUICE-CONCENTRATE RECOVERY

SOURCE: *Food Flavorings, Composition, Manufacture, and Use, 2nd Edition* by Merory published by Avi Publishing Co., Westport, Conn.

FULL AROMATIC CHERRY FRUIT FLAVOR

Mixtures of full aromatic fruit flavors can be made in various strengths and adjusted to required needs. The compounding of full aromatic Morello cherry fruit flavors requires the use of full flavor concentrated juice and expressed cherry flavoring extract or fruit flavors. The following mixture is recommended for best flavor.

Ingredients

40 gal. **Concentrated Full Flavor Morello Cherry Juice** (formula given above) made from soluble solids of 68° Brix to which is added the proportionate quantity of recovered volatile aroma.

10 gal. genuine **Cherry Pit Flavor** (formula also given above) of 76% alcohol content

50 gal. **Expressed Juice of Pitted Morello Cherries** (see formula given above)

100 gal. finished full aromatic fruit flavor of 15% alcohol content.

SOURCE: *Food Flavorings, Composition, Manufacture, and Use, 2nd Edition* by Merory published by Avi Publishing Co., Westport, Conn.

DALMATIAN CHERRY EXTRACT

Procedure

(a) 110.00 lb of semi-dried Dalmatian cherries are to be coarsely ground and mixed with:

217.50 lb (or about 25 gal.) of expressed Morello cherry juice and flavoring extract as described above for **Expressed Juice of Pitted Morello Cherries.** To it are also added:

20.40 lb (or 3 gal.) of alcohol, 95%, which adds up to a menstruum of about 28 gal. of approximately 23.5% content. The menstruum is to be circulated twice daily through five days, to soak, soften, and extract the fruit. The extract is then taken off and expressed. The yield will be about:

216.00 lb (or 24 gal.) flavoring extract.

(b) The drained and pressed fruit remains are to transferred to the still and mixed with:

83.00 lb (or 10 gal.) of water. The mixture is to be heated to 131°F and left at this temperature for 6 hr to hydrolyze the seeds to benzaldehyde. The distillation is then performed at atmospheric pressure without fractionating; the heat is applied gradually to allow a slow rate of distillation. The yield will be:

31.70 lb (or 4 gal.) of distillate, of about 25% alcohol. The remains of the still are then discarded and the still cleaned. The distillate is then redistilled to yield a middle fraction of:

7.65 lb (or 1 gal.) flavor distillate of about 50% alcohol content. The tail fraction is to be used in the next production in place of alcohol.

(c) The finished product is made by mixing:

216.00 lb (or 24 gal.) flavoring extract of **(a)** with:

7.65 lb (or 1 gal.) flavor distillate of **(b).** The total yield will be:

223.65 lb (or 25 gal.) Dalmatian cherry flavoring extract with about 15% alcohol content. The weight of 1 gal. extract is about 9 lb.

Flavor Property

One pound of semi-dried Dalmatian cherries is equivalent to about 3.75 lb of freshly picked fruit without stems. Consequently, 1 gal. of finished Dalmatian cherry extract of **(c)** is derived from about 24 lb of cherries.

SOURCE: *Food Flavorings, Composition, Manufacture, and Use, 2nd Edition* by Merory published by Avi Publishing Co., Westport, Conn.

WILD CHERRY FRUIT FLAVORING EXTRACT

Procedure

(a) 600.00 lb of dried wild cherries are to be coarsely ground in a comminuting machine, then mixed with a menstruum of about 19% alcohol content consisting of:

867.00 lb (or 102 gal.) cherry juice and:

170.00 lb (or 25 gal.) alcohol, 95%. The total menstruum is:

1037.00 lb (or 127 gal.) which is to be circulated twice daily for 8 days in order to soak, soften, and extract the fruit. The extract is then drained off and the remaining fruit pressed to yield:

902.00 lb (or 97.50 gal.) of wild cherry extract.

The fruit remains are to be transferred into the still and mixed with:

(b) 332.00 lb (or 40 gal.) water and then heated to about 131°F, and kept at this temperature for about 6 hr to permit the seeds to hydrolyze to benzaldehyde. The distillation is performed at atmospheric pressure. The heat is applied gradually to allow a slow collection of the distillate. The yield is about:

18.70 lb (or 2.50 gal.) of distillate of about 65% alcohol content. Hydrocyanic acid evaporates during the distillation.

(c) The finished product is made by mixing:

902.00 lb (or 97.5 gal.) wild cherry extract of **(a)** with:

18.70 lb (2.50 gal.) distillate of **(b)**. The yield is:

920.70 lb (or 100 gal.) wild cherry fruit flavor of about 15% alcohol content.

Flavor Property

The analysis of the finished wild cherry flavoring extract shows a content of benzaldehyde.

SOURCE: *Food Flavorings, Composition, Manufacture, and Use, 2nd Edition* by Merory published by Avi Publishing Co., Westport, Conn.

WILD CHERRY BARK FLAVOR DISTILLATE

Procedure

825.00 lb of pulverized wild cherry bark is mixed with:

1801.00 lb (or about 217 gal.) water, advisably in the still, and heated to 131°F. The mixture is kept at this temperature for 6 hr to hydrolyze the prunasin of the bark, which is similar to the amygdalin of the almond seed. To the mixture is then added:

365.00 lb (or about 53.68 gal.) alcohol, 95%. The total of the menstruum will be:

2166.00 lb (or 270 gal.) of about 19.25% alcohol content; the weight of 1 gal. of this menstruum is about 8 lb. The distillation is carried out at atmospheric pressure with the collection of fractions of 5 gal. each. The temperature is increased gradually to facilitate a slow flow of the condensate with a high alcohol content.

The yield of distillate is as follows:

Middle Fraction	Quantity, (Gal.)	Alcohol Content, (%)	Absolute Alcohol, (Gal.)
(1)	5	85	4.25
(2)	5	72	3.60
(3)	5	69	3.45
(4)	5	68	3.40
(5)	5	64	3.20
(6)	5	64	3.20
(7)	5	63	3.15
(8)	5	60	3.00
(9)	5	58	2.90
(10)	5	56	2.80
(11)	5	56	2.80
Total	55		35.75

The total of the middle run fraction is 55 gal. distillate of 65% alcohol content.

SOURCE: *Food Flavorings, Composition, Manufacture, and Use, 2nd Edition* by Merory published by Avi Publishing Co., Westport, Conn.

CHERRY FRUIT FLAVOR (WITH OTHER NATURAL FLAVORINGS)

This compound is prepared by weight to secure uniformity of flavor.

Dissolve:

18.75 lb acid citric (may be omitted) in:

2.50 gal. water (weight: 8.3 lb = 1 gal.); then mix with:

25.00 gal. Enocianina—desugared grape extract, nonalcoholic, fruit color (weight: 9 lb = 1 gal.)

25.00 gal. **Wild Cherry Fruit Flavoring Extract** (formula given above), alcohol content (weight: 9.25 lb = 1 gal.)

18.75 gal. **Morello Cherry Full Aromatic Cherry Fruit Flavor** (formula above), 15% alcohol content (weight: 8.75 lb = 1 gal.)

12.50 gal. caramel, acid proof (weight: 11.375 lb = 1 gal.)

6.65 gal. **Wild Cherry Bark Flavor Distillate** (formula given above), 63.65% alcohol content (weight: 7.3 lb = 1 gal.)

6.25 gal. **Dalmatian Cherry Extract** (formula given above), 15% alcohol content (weight: 9.125 lb = 1 gal.)

4.00 gal.	alcohol 95% (weight: 6.8 lb = 1 gal.) add to the alcohol:
70.50 oz av	oil of bitter almond, free from prussic acid
100.75 gal.	finished flavor of 15% alcohol content, less:
0.75 gal.	allowed for sedimentation
100.00 gal.	total finished flavor

Recommended Use.—3-5 gal. flavor per 100 gal. syrup, to which are added 1-1.25 gal. citric acid 50% according to required taste.

SOURCE: *Food Flavorings, Manufacture, Composition, and Use 2nd Edition* by Merory published by Avi Publishing Co., Westport, Conn.

BLACK CHERRY CONCENTRATE

Formula per 100 gal:

47.92 gal.	Cherry Fruit Flavor (With Other Natural Flavorings—without acid citric (see formula given above)
22.14 gal.	citric acid solution (see below)
5.99 gal.	salt solution (see below)
4.17 lb	magnesium concentrate
2.08 gal.	caramel color, acid proof
0.70 lb	pectinase concentrate
0.26 gal.	sodium benzoate solution (see below)
qs	processed water
100.00 gal.	yield

Citric Acid Solution

Formula to make 1 gal. solution:

4.388 lb	acid citric, anhydrous
qs	processed water (heated to warm)

Salt Solution

Formula to make 1 gal. solution, which is to be filtered:

2 lb	sodium chloride
qs	processed water (heated to warm)

Benzoate Solution

Formula to make 1 gal. solution, which is to be filtered:

2 lb	sodium benzoate
qs	processed water (heated to warm)

SOURCE: *Food Flavorings, Composition, Manufacture, and Use, 2nd Edition* by Merory published by Avi Publishing Co., Westport, Conn.

SUGAR-FREE CHERRY FRUIT FLAVOR

200 lb	of comminuted cherries are mixed with:
4 gal.	95% alcohol or cherry brandy of equivalent alcohol content and pressed.
20-22 gal.	and 24 lb of press-cake are set aside for future use (**residue a**). The pressed juice is distilled at atmospheric pressure to remove ½ gal. of aromatic essence (**flavor distillate f**) containing volatile flavor. The remaining juice is vacuum distilled until a cherry concentrate of 36°-40° Baumé sugar content is obtained. The recovered alcohol of this fraction is put aside and called **distillate d**. The cherry concentrate is mixed with:
200 lb	cherries,
110 lb	imported Dalmatian cherries and a yeast culture. The mixture is placed in a fermentation tank and fermented. After a period of time, a sample is taken out and analyzed to determine the alcohol and sugar content. When no more sugar can be detected, the fermentation is terminated and the contents of the tank pressed to yield approximately
22 gal.	of concentrate (**concentrate b**). The press-cake is stored for future use (**residue c**). After comminution, **residue c**, which contains the cherry pits, is mixed with:
8 gal.	of water, warmed, and agitated, and then left at 131°F to stand for about 24 hr. The crushed pits of the residue develop an aromatic cherry essence (benzaldehyde) by enzymatic action. After a total of 24 hr have elapsed, the flavor **distillate d** and the
24 lb	**residue a** are added and the mixture distilled to yield:
2.5 gal.	of distillate (**flavor distillate e**).

A fully constituted authentic sugar-free cherry fruit flavor is obtained by compounding

22 gal.	of the **concentrate b** and
2.5 gal.	of **flavor distillate e** and
0.5 gal.	of **flavor distillate f** to yield:
25 gal.	of sugar-free fruit flavor with an alcohol content of approximately 20% and being equivalent to 31.4 lb of fresh cherries per gallon of fruit flavor. One pound of dried cherries is the equivalent of 2.75 lb fresh cherries. The quantity of 30 lb of fresh cherries per gallon of flavor concentrate is that concentration which can be considered the minimum of acceptable flavor strength for commercial use without the further

addition of so-called natural flavorings.

SOURCE: *Food Flavorings, Composition, Manufacture, and Use, 2nd Edition* by Merory published by Avi Publishing Co., Westport, Conn.

COLD-PRESSED CITRUS OILS (ORANGE, TANGERINE, GRAPEFRUIT, AND LEMON)

General Processing Procedure

To secure the oil from the peel of citrus fruits, oil sacs must be punctured by either pressure or rasping. Citrus peel oils are expressed in Florida by four different types of equipment: (1) Pipkin roll, (2) screw press, (3) Pipkin juice extractor, and (4) Fraser-Brace extractor. All of the above methods of extraction give an emulsion of oil and water. The oil is separated centrifugally from the aqueous phase by passing the emulsion through a sludger and then through a polisher. Following separation, the oil is stored for approximately 1 week at 32°-40°F and during this winterizing treatment undesirable waxy materials separate from the oil and are allowed to settle. The clear oil is decanted into stainless steel storage tanks or tin-dipped containers, which are then maintained at a storage temperature of about 40°F. Air usually is excluded from the container to prevent deterioration. This is accomplished either by filling the container full of oil or by displacing the air with carbon dioxide.

SOURCE: Citrus By-Products of Florida, Florida Agricultural Experiment Station, Gainesville, Florida

DISTILLED CITRUS OILS

Distilled oil of orange, grapefruit, or tangerine is secured by some processors as a by-product in the canning of citrus fruit juices. Some of the citrus peel oil becomes mixed with the juice as it is extracted by the various types of juice extractors used in the canneries. Excessive amounts of peel oil in the juice are harmful to the quality of canned juice; therefore, in most canning plants the oil content of the juice is reduced to a desirable level by passing the juice through a de-oiler. The juice is usually flashed in the de-oiler, which is operated under a vacuum of 11 in. (190°F) to 25.5 in. (130°F), and a vapor mixture of oil and water is removed. Then the mixture of oil and water vapors is condensed and the oil is separated from the condensate by decanting or centrifuging. Vacuum steam distilled oils manufactured in this manner will have properties slightly different from oils obtained by steam distillation at atmospheric pressure.

SOURCE: Citrus By-Products of Florida, Florida Agricultural Experiment Station, Gainesville, Florida

COFFEE CAKE FLAVOR

Ingredients	Gm
Vanillin	92
Alcohol, 95%	850
Oil of cinnamon bark,	20
Oil of bitter almond, free from prussic acid	8
Oil of lemon, cold pressed	10
Oil of coriander	8
Oil of nutmeg	10
Oil of cardamom	2
Total	1000

Procedure

Dissolve vanillin in alcohol; then mix with the oil flavorings.

SOURCE: *Food Flavorings, Composition, Manufacture, and Use, 2nd Edition* by Merory, published by Avi Publishing Co., Westport, Conn.

CONCENTRATED DATE FLAVORING EXTRACT

See *Concentrated Prune Flavoring Extract.*

FRUIT-FLAVORED GELATIN

Ingredients	350-Lb Batch (Lb)	3-oz av Package (Gm)
Sucrose (extra-fine granulated cane or beet)	300	72.8
Gelatin (pure food, 225 Bloom)	37	9.0
Citric acid, anhydrous	9.8	2.4
Buffer salt (sodium citrate or 1:1 mix of mono- and disodium phosphate)	1.6	0.4
Sodium chloride	1.6	0.4
Color and flavor	qs	

Yield: 1870 3-oz av packages

NOTE: A stronger or a weaker gelatin may be used but the sugar content per batch should be adjusted so that the combined sugar and gelatin ingredients would still add up to 337 lb.

Procedure

The general method in preparing gelatin desserts is to plate the sugar with flavoring and coloring; the gelatin and buffers are mixed separately and then slowly added to the flavored and colored sugar; mixing is continued until a uniform dry powder has been obtained.

Mixing of Colorings.—About 3 fl oz of water added to the sugar fraction (300 lb) of the 350-lb batch with 2 min agitation serves to moisten it sufficiently to cause the added powdered color to adhere to the sugar. This gives a fairly uniform color to the mass. In the case of the berry and cherry types, the true fruit extracts give enough moisture so that water need not be added.

To avoid a mottled appearance when FD&C Blue No. 1 is a component of the color, the color manufacturer will, upon request, prepare a special blend, dissolve it in water, dry, and grind it. Such a color powder will remedy the difficulty.

Use of Citrus Oils.—Citrus oils are dissolved in a volatile solvent: e.g., 95% alcohol. A DeVilbis-type sprayer is useful for plating the liquids on the sugar.

For a 3-oz av package of lemon gelatin, use 0.0044 gm of oil of lemon, 5-fold.

For a 3-oz av package of lime gelatin, use 0.0620 gm of oil of limes distilled, 5-fold.

For a 3-oz av package of orange gelatin, use 0.0440 gm of oil of orange, 5-fold.

Typical Color Formulas for 3-Oz Av Package

For Lemon.—FD&C Yellow No. 5, 0.00280 gm; and FD&C Yellow No. 6, 0.00011 gm; for a total of 0.00291 gm of coloring.

For Lime.—FD&C Blue No. 1, 0.0013 gm; and FD&C Yellow No. 5, 0.0183 gm; for a total of 0.0196 gm of coloring.

For Orange.—FD&C Red No 2,* 0.0074 gm; and FD&C Yellow No. 5, 0.0034 gm; for a total of 0.0108 gm of coloring.

For Cherry.—FD&C Red No. 1, 0.0120 gm; FD&C Red No. 2,* 0.0400 gm; and FD&C Blue No. 1, 0.0002 gm; for a total of 0.0522 gm of coloring.

For Raspberry.—FD&C Red No. 1, 0.0210 gm; FD&C Red No. 2,* 0.0100 gm; and FD&C Blue No. 1, 0.0001 gm; for a total of 0.0311 gm of coloring.

For Strawberry.—FD&C Red No. 2,* 0.004 gm; and FD&C Red No. 4, 0.004 gm; for a total of 0.008 gm of coloring.

---

*This coloring has been de-listed. It is no longer on the FDA-approved list of food colors and cannot be used. Consult your food color supplier for recommended color substitutions.

SOURCE: *Food Flavorings, Composition, Manufacture, and Use, 2nd Edition* by Merory published by Avi Publishing Co., Westport, Conn.

CONCENTRATED FIG FLAVORING EXTRACT

See *Concentrated Prune Flavoring Extract.*

GRAPE JUICE CONCENTRATE CONTINUOUS MANUFACTURE

Boxes of grapes are unloaded onto a variable-speed belt at rates from 10 to 20 tons per hour. Grapes are dumped into wash tank equipped with water sprays, and empty boxes are conveyed to outbound trucks. An inclined wire-mesh drains the washed grapes as they are transferred to a de-watering vibrator feeding a crusher-stemmer.

Crushed grapes are pumped through a tube-type heat-exchanger (Chisholm-Ryder) for a short 140° F preheat to extract color (as with Concords) and sugars from skins. Stems are conveyed to disposal. Fruit then continues through a vertical-type disintegrator that is operated by a 100-hp electric motor.

Pulp passes through 0.063-in. screens, as dry unbroken seeds are separately discharged for disposal. A variable-speed Moyno pump delivers pulp to 8 1000-gal. agitator-equipped, depectinizing tanks. Here, about 2 lb of pectinase is added per 1000 gal. of pulp. After about a 45 min reaction time and confirmation of a negative pectin test, the 140° F depectinized pulp is pumped into a 500-gal. surge tank.

Another Moyno pump pumps pulp through a preheating vaporizing section of an essence-recovery unit (Mojonnier). Juice is preheated to 220° F, and concentrated to 20°–25° Brix. Vapor proceeds to the unit's distillation column. Vapor-free stripped juice at the bottom of the cyclone separator continues to the vacuum flash-cooling tank that is equipped with condenser (with barometric leg) and vacuum pump.

Juice is flash-cooled from 220° to 120° F and run into surge tank, into which a filter aid is mechanically fed at a rate of about 2% (by weight). From the surge tank, 120° F juice is pumped to a continuous Eimco drum vacuum filter. Filtered juice is then bulk shipped or fed through a 2nd- and 3rd-effect evaporator (Monjonnier) for concentrating to 70° Brix. The concentrate's density is continuously measured and controlled by a radioisotope-gauging unit (Accuray). The concentrate then goes to cold-wall tanks (in a 38° F room), or into light 30,000-gal. vats for underground storage.

SOURCE: Food Engineering, J. A. Merch and N. F. Roger, 1964.

CONCORD GRAPE FLAVOR

Mix together the following ingredients:

	Fl Oz
Desugared grape extract, imported from Italy	32.0

	Fl Oz
Concord grape full flavor concentrated juice, 68° Brix	64.0
Concord grape recovered flavor essence 100-fold	2.0
Alcohol, 95%	20.0
Concord grape flavor	Total 118.0

Recommended use: 5 gal. flavor per 100 gal. syrup; a solution of citric and tartaric acid is added according to required taste.

SOURCE: *Food Flavorings, Composition, Manufacture, and Use, 2nd Edition* by Merory published by Avi Publishing Co., Westport, Conn.

FROZEN CONCENTRATED GRAPEFRUIT JUICE

Frozen concentrated grapefruit juice is processed essentially the same way as frozen orange concentrate. This juice has a tendency to gel because of enzyme activity, so it is heated to 150°–180°F for a few seconds before it goes to the evaporator.

Evaporation should be continued until the volume has been reduced to ¼ of the original. The concentrate is then slush frozen and filled into retail (usually 4 oz) size enamel or lined cans or cans with moisture proof cardboard bodies. Product should be stored at 0°F.

Seasonal Changes in Brix, Acid, and Ratio

	Acid %	Brix	Ratio
	Texas		
Nov.	1.35	10.80	8.00
Dec.	1.45	11.10	7.65
Jan.	1.41	11.35	8.05
Febr.	1.31	11.30	8.62
Mar.	1.18	11.20	9.48
Apr.	1.07	11.00	10.28
May	0.95	10.75	11.32
Avg	1.245	11.07	9.05
	Florida		
Nov.	1.47	10.05	6.84
Dec.	1.44	10.25	7.12
Jan.	1.38	10.25	7.43
Febr.	1.34	10.30	7.69
Mar.	1.29	10.30	7.95
Apr.	1.22	10.15	8.32
May	1.11	9.80	8.84
Avg	3.32	10.15	7.79

SOURCE: *The Freezing Preservation of Foods, 4th Edition, Vol. 4* by Tressler, Van Arsdel and Copley published by Avi Publishing Co., Westport, Conn.

GRENADINE (POMEGRANATE) FRUIT FLAVOR

Pomegranate fruit flavor is used in preparing grenadine syrup for cocktails and other mixed drinks.

The juice of the fruit is in the pulpy mass surrounding the seeds. The outer shell, or husk, contains tannin and the pulpy edible portion must therefore be removed without undue contact with the husk.

Fully ripe pomegranates yield a sweet deep-colored juice of rich flavor. The juice is expressed from halved or quartered fruit. It is high in sugar and in citric acid.

Procedure

(a) Comminute (using a No. 5 sieve) the fresh edible pulp of:

1600.0 lb	pomegranates, and mix with:
108.8 lb	(or 16.0 gal.) alcohol, 95%, then press. The yield is:
97.0 gal.	juice and flavoring extract.

(b) The pressed remains are mixed with water and distilled at atmospheric pressure to yield:

3.0 gal.	flavor distillate of 45% alcohol content.

(c) Mix

97.0 gal.	extract of (a)
3.0 gal.	flavor distillate of (b)
100.0 gal.	grenadine fruit flavor.

SOURCE: *Food Flavorings, Composition, Manufacture, and Use, 2nd Edition* by Merory published by Avi Publishing Co., Westport, Conn.

LEMON CUSTARD FLAVOR

Ingredients	Gm
Oil of cinnamon bark	4.25
Oil of nutmeg	9.50
Oil of Mandarin	19.25
Oil of lemon, cold pressed	277.00
Ethyl vanillin	7.75
Vanillin	160.25
Alcohol, 95%	522.00
Total	1000.00

Procedure

Dissolve all ingredients in the alcohol.

SOURCE: *Food Flavorings, Composition, Manufacture, and Use, 2nd Edition* by Merory published by Avi Publishing Co., Westport, Conn.

LEMON EMULSION

Ingredients

16.0 fl oz	oil of lemon, cold pressed
32.0 fl oz	propylene glycol
2.0 oz av	gum tragacanth
80.0 fl oz	water
0.18 oz av	(or 5.11 gm) acid citric
0.36 oz av	(or 10.22 gm) castor oil

Procedure

(a) 0.18 oz av (or 5.11 gm) acid citric are dissolved in:
2.00 fl oz water

(b) 2.0 oz av gum tragacanth are mixed with:
32.0 fl oz propylene glycol, and whipped until dissolved; to the mixture are added:
16.0 fl oz oil of lemon, cold pressed, and
0.36 oz av (or 10.22 gm) castor oil; the mixture is constantly kept agitated and to it are added:
80.0 fl oz water; agitated.

(c) The solution of (a) is added to the mixture of (b) and agitated until evenly dissolved; pass through sieve and run through emulsifier.

SOURCE: *Food Flavorings, Composition, Manufacture, and Use, 2nd Edition* by Merory published by Avi Publishing Co., Westport, Conn.

LEMON ESSENCE (TERPENELESS)

Procedure

(a) 20 lb Oil of lemon, cold pressed, are mixed with
58 lb alcohol 95%
The mixture is then diluted with:
32 lb water, to facilitate the separation of terpenes.
The composition is allowed to stand for 24 hr in a separator so that the separated terpenes can contract and reduce in volume.

(b) The terpene-free essence is then taken off and yields approximately:
92 lb flavor compound, which is mixed with
8 lb alcohol, 95% to clear it.

Yield:
100 lb lemon essence, terpeneless.

This flavor is most useful in pastry and cakes. Four fluid ounces of lemon essence, terpeneless, is sufficient to flavor 100 lb of bakery dough.

SOURCE: *Food Flavorings, Composition, Manufacture, and Use, 2nd Edition* by Merory published by Avi Publishing Co., Westport, Conn.

LEMON AND LIME ICE EMULSION

Disperse in

16.000 fl oz	propylene glycol
2.000 oz av	gum tragacanth, or (1.0 oz av gum tragacanth and 6.0 oz av gum acacia); then add:
0.750 fl oz	oil of lemon, cold pressed—10-fold—(terpenes have been removed by vacuum distillation)
2.000 fl oz	oil of limes, distilled
0.100 gm	antioxidant; then add:
80.000 fl oz	water; agitate rapidly and mix with prepared color solution consisting of:
32.000 fl oz	water
4.000 oz av	FD&C Yellow No. 5 (640 Tartrazine) certified color
2.000 oz av	FD&C Blue No. 1 (Brilliant blue FCF) certified color
0.125 oz av	benzoate of soda

Yield: 1 gal. lemon and lime emulsion.

Recommended Use

Use 1.0 fl oz flavor per 5 gal. ice pop mix or 6.25 fl oz per 32 gal.

SOURCE: *Food Flavorings, Composition, Manufacture, and Use, 2nd Edition* by Merory published by Avi Publishing Co., Westport, Conn.

FROZEN CONCENTRATE FOR LIMEADE

Frozen concentrate for limeade is prepared by adding enough sucrose to single-strength lime juice to raise the Brix to about 48°. Sufficient lime purée is added to give an oil content of 0.003% in the reconstituted limeade.

The product is slush-frozen, then filled into small cans for sale at retail. Product is stored at 0°F or below.

SOURCE: *The Freezing Preservation of Foods, 4th Edition, Vol. 4* by Tressler, Van Arsdel and Copley published by Avi Publishing Co., Westport, Conn.

ORANGE EMULSION

(a) Formula per 100 gal.

Lb	
100.000	cottonseed oil, brominated
51.870	gum arabic (acacia)
9.380	oil of orange (Valencia)
26.250	oil of orange, 5-fold
1.875	oil of orange, 15-fold (terpeneless)
65.000	oil of orange, cold pressed, California
9.375	oil of tangerine
qs	processed water

Procedure

(b) Combine all oils and mix well at high speed: Separately prepare gum and water emulsion by using approximately 3 lb warm water and add to it the gum, and agitating the mixture at high speed for 15 min; then cool mixture down to 70°-75°F (room temperature).

(c) Continue the rapid agitation and add to the mixture of **(b)** the oils, then pour additional cold water, to obtain:
100 gal. emulsion.

(d) Homgenize at 3000 lb per sq in.

SOURCE: *Food Flavorings, Composition, Manufacture, and Use, 2nd Edition* by Merory published by Avi Publishing Co., Westport, Conn.

CONCENTRATED ORANGE OIL EXTRACT
Free of Terpenes and Waxes

Lb

(a) 250.00 oil of orange, cold pressed, is concentrated 10-fold by vacuum distillation and the terpenes removed. The yield is:
25.00 oil of orange, cold pressed, 10-fold, which is used in **(b)**.

(b) Mixture of:

Lb

25.00 concentrated 10-fold oil of orange, cold pressed, of **(a)** and
68.00 alcohol, 95% and to it add:
31.25 water. The mixture has to be well agitated and is then allowed to stand in separator for 24 hr to effect separation of terpenes and waxes. It yields:
86.25 terpeneless orange essence which is to be mixed with:
13.75 alcohol, 95%
100.00 concentrated orange oil extract.

SOURCE: *Food Flavorings, Composition, Manufacture, and Use, 2nd Edition* by Merory published by Avi Publishing Co., Westport, Conn.

ORANGE FRUITY ICE POP FLAVOR
(TRUE FRUIT)

Ingredients	Gm
Alcohol, 95%	28.5
Oil of orange, cold pressed, California, 10-fold, terpenes removed by vacuum distillation,	2.5
Oil of orange, cold pressed, Florida, 10-fold, terpenes removed by vacuum distillation,	1.5
Oil of tangerine	2.0
Oil of lemon, cold pressed	1.0
FD&C Yellow No. 6 (Sunset yellow FCF)	3.5
Orange juice	50.0
Water	33.0
Acid citric, 50%	1.0
Benzoate of soda	1.0
Salt	4.0
Syrup—74.9° Brix (40° Bé)	870.0
Total	998.0

SOURCE: *Food Flavorings, Composition, Manufacture, and Use, 2nd Edition* by Merory published by Avi Publishing Co., Westport, Conn.

ORANGE OIL EMULSIONS

Keltrol ® stabilized bakery flavor emulsions have excellent stability and a smoothly-textured, pourable body. When compared to conventially stabilized bakery flavor emulsions, this formulation offers savings in preparation time and overall costs.

Ingredients	%
KELTROL*	0.70
Gum arabic, USP powdered	2.00
Orange oil, USP cold pressed	10.80
Sodium benzoate, USP	0.20
Citric acid anhydrous	0.39
Water	85.91
Total	100.00

Procedure

Add above ingredients in the order listed to water using a high rate of mix such as can be obtained with a "Lightning" mixer.

*Keltrol is Kelco's xanthan gum especially developed and authorized for use in foods as a stabilizing emulsifying, suspending, and bodying agent.

SOURCE: Kelco Company, 20 N. Wacker Drive, Chicago, Illinois.

TERPENE-FREE ORANGE OIL ESSENCE

Ingredients

Oil of orange, cold pressed	4.0 lb
Oil of orange, 10-fold, whose terpenes have been removed by vacuum distillation,	3.2 oz av
Citral	1.5 oz av
(or 6.25 gal.) Alcohol, 95%	42.5 lb
(or 4.0 gal.) Freshly expressed orange juice	39.2 lb

Procedure

(a) Dissolve 1 gm finely powdered magnesia oxide (MgO) with water.
(b) Add water and magnesia mixture to the oil and stir for 5 min.
(c) Let settle for separation of terpenes, and filter if necessary.

SOURCE: *Food Flavorings, Composition, Manufacture, and Use, 2nd Edition* by Merory published by Avi Publishing Co., Westport, Conn.

PASSION FRUIT JUICE EXTRACTION

This is an efficient method of volume production and high extraction yields. This method involves a centrifugal extraction, which necessitates a preliminary slicing of the fruit into ⅝-in.-thick slices. This operation is performed by a gang of serrated-edge blades, mounted on a common shaft with ⅝-in. spacers. The fruit is fed down a tubular inlet, and the serrated edges of the blades assist in pulling the fruit through the slicing operation. This innovation gives a considerable increase in cutting capacity, with no risk of fruit jamming between the blades.

The cut fruit then drops into a centrifugal extractor, which consists essentially of 19¾-in. holes at ⅝-in. spacings. Four ¾-in. high radial vanes are welded within the walls to form 4 compartments, to ensure that the sliced fruit rotates at the same speed as the basket (175 rpm). The basket is balanced on a slotted ball-and-socket joint, with a slender vertical drive shaft to permit considerable angular movement of the basket.

Under the influence of centrifugal force, the slices move up the inclined walls, and seeds, juice, and pulp are ejected radially through the perforations, while the rinds move upwards to leave the basket above the juice-retaining cover. This unit has a capacity of up to 3800 lb of fruit per hour and an extraction efficiency of 94%. Its main advantages are (1) that a number of seeds are cut in the slicing operation, which necessitates the use of a very fine screen in the final finishing operation, and (2) there is some extraction of skin juice and presumably enzymes under the influence of the gravity produced in the centrifuge.

Canning

The juice is filled into fruit enamel-lined cans, which are sealed in a vacuum closer. The heat sensitivity of passion fruit makes it difficult to heat process passion fruit juice without markedly changing the flavor of the juice. Many attempts have been made to process a satisfactory pasteurized product. The use of tubular and plate-type heat exchangers results in a darkened product with poor flavor. The most successful method has been the use of a spin cooker designed by L. J. Lynch of the Canning Section Division of Food Preservation, CSIRO, Australia. This is a cheap and easily-constructed unit that utilizes optimum can rotation speed to provide rapid heat transfer with mild effects on the product. The can is spun on an inclined belt at approximately 140 rpm in an enclosed chamber, with steam sprays impinging on the can surface. Pasteurization is achieved in about 1¾ min with a 190°F temperature in the center of the can, after which the can is immediately and rapidly cooled with a cold water spray in a similarly constructed water spray system.

SOURCE: Hawaii Agricultural Experiment Station, University of Hawaii, Honolulu.

PEACH CONCENTRATE

Briefly, the technique consists of pitting, peeling, purèeing, enzyme inactivation, depectinization, juice-fiber separation, aroma recovery, juice concentration, and restoration of aroma and fibers to concentrate.

Preparing the Product

In the processing steps, every effort is made to minimize exposure of fruit to flavor- and color-damaging conditions.

Preliminary Steps.—Pitted peach halves of mature fruit are purèed immediately following steam peeling, by means of a cylindrical juice extractor having an 0.033-in. screen. Discharge of the unit is modified to combine tailings with material passing through the screen.

Elimination of rapid enzymatic browning is accomplished by rapid heat treatment employing two heat exchangers with a holding coil between.

Purée is heated to 180°F, in first unit, held for 2 sec in the coil, then cooled to 100°F, in second unit. Residual activity of polyphenolase is 0.1% or less.

Purée leaving the second heat exchanger is treated with Pectinol 10M (Rohm & Haas) (8.6 oz/100 gal.) for ¾ hr to facilitate juice-fiber separation and permit high juice concentration without gel formation.

L-ascorbic acid is added (1.5 oz/100 lb of purée) during depectinization to prevent normal oxidative browning. In the nectar type concentrate, this has the additional advantage of placing it on a comparable level with other beverages that are rich in natural occurring vitamins.

Juice-Fiber Separation.—Removal of fibers from the juice is achieved with a Harris bag press. Fibrous material is held for blending with essence and concentrate.

Flavor Recovery and Juice Concentration.—This is done by stripping aroma from the juice and fractionating the vapors involved. The stripped juice is concentrated by a single-pass atmospheric technique.

The manufacture and sale of volatile fruit concentrates containing alcohol are subject to the regulations of the Alcohol, Tobacco and Firearms Division, U.S. Internal Revenue Service, Washington, D.C.

For the purée concentrate, the entire pomace from the juice extraction along with the recovered volatiles are blended with the concentrate, and the mixture homogenized to a smooth consistency. The product is made 7-fold with respect to the single-strength purée. Degree of concentration of the juice is dependent upon desired fold of finished product and moisture (juice) content of pomace.

NOTE: For application of the above process to grapes see "These Concentrating Advances Bring Superior Flavors" (*Food Engineering*, Dec. 1957, p. 90).

SOURCE: USDA Eastern Regional Research Laboratory, Philadelphia.

PEACH SYRUP (68° BRIX AND PEACH FRUIT COLOR)

Ingredients

350 lb dried peaches

Procedure

(a) 350 lb dried peaches are mixed with sufficient cold water to cover the fruit. The mixture is allowed to soak for 24 hr, is then comminuted and additional cold water is added to extract the fruit. The menstruum is circulated for about 1 hr and then drained off to yield:
600 lb extract; it is filtered and used in **(c)**;

(b) to the remaining mash is added sufficient water to extract the fruit without circulation of the menstruum and to yield:
400 lb extract; it is filtered and used in **(c)**; the extract remains are then discarded.

(c) Concentration by vacuum distillation of:
600 lb peach extract of **(a)**
400 lb peach extract of **(b)**
Yield: 110 lb peach syrup of 68°-70° Brix.

SOURCE: *Food Flavorings, Composition, Manufacture, and Use, 2nd Edition* by Merory published by Avi Publishing Co., Westport, Conn.

PEACH JUICE AND FLAVORING EXTRACT

Procedure

	Lb	
(a)	1000	of partially defrosted frozen freestone Elberta peaches (ascorbic acid is added before packing solely to retard discoloration) are mixed with:
	200	95% alcohol, and
	50	water, and
	2	enzyme Pectinol
		Agitate well and pass the mixture through the comminuting machine. Separate the juice from the fruit in the extractor by drainage after 24 hr extraction. Then press the remaining fruit. The yield is about:
	945	juice and extractive matter of about 15% alcohol content. It is used in **(c)**.

(b) The pomace or pressed remains are mixed with with 1.5 times its weight of water. The mixture is distilled at atmospheric pressure to obtain a yield of:
55 lb flavor distillate of about 15% alcohol content; it is used in **(c)**.

(c) Mixture of:
945 lb juice of **(a)**
55 lb flavor distillate of **(b)**
1000 lb peach juice and flavoring extract of about 15% alcohol content.

SOURCE: *Food Flavorings, Composition, Manufacture, and Use, 2nd Edition* by Merory published by Avi Publishing Co., Westport, Conn.

PEACH FRUIT FLAVORING EXTRACT

Ingredients

500.0 lb dried peaches
1050.0 lb **Peach Juice and Flavoring Extract** (formula given above) of 15% alcohol content
150.0 lb alcohol, 95%

Procedure

(a) 500.0 lb dried peaches are mixed with
1050.0 lb peach juice and flavoring extract and allowed to soak until they soften so that the fruit can be comminuted. The comminuted mixture is then extracted with:
150.0 lb alcohol, 95%, for 5 days; the menstruum is to be circulated twice daily over the fruit mash. The extracting menstruum is of about 30% alcohol content.

(b) On the sixth day the liquid is drained off to yield:
1070.0 lb peach extract
600.0 lb of the extract is put aside for use in **(f)**
470.0 lb of the extract is used in **(d)**

(c) To the remaining mash in the extractor is added sufficient water to cover the fruit; additional liquid is then drained off to yield:
150.0 lb extracted matter; which is used in **(d)**; the remaining mash is used in **(e)**.

(d) 470.0 lb extract of **(b)** is mixed with
150.0 lb extract of **(c)** and then distilled at atmospheric pressure to recover the alcohol and to yield:

First fraction:
40.0 lb flavor distillate of 60% alcohol content; which is used in **(f)**.

Second fraction:
200.0 lb distillate of 25% alcohol content is used in **(e)**.

Concentrate:
340.0 lb soluble solids, non-alcoholic, which are darkened in color by distillation at atmospheric pressure. This yield is used as color in **(f)**.

(e) The remaining mash of **(c)** is mixed with:
200.0 lb distillate—the second fraction of **(d)** and the distilled at atmospheric pressure to yield:

Third fraction:
20.0 lb flavor distillate of 60% alcohol content; which is used in **(f)**;

Fourth fraction: The rest of the alcohol is recovered and redistilled to higher proof for use in the next production batch.

(f) Mixture of:

Lb	
600.0	peach extract of **(b)**
340.0	concentrated soluble solids—peach color, non-alcoholic, of **(d)**
40.0	first fraction—flavor distillate of 60% alcohol content of **(d)**
20.0	third fraction—flavor distillate of of 60% alcohol content of **(e)**
1000.0	peach fruit flavoring extract of 15-18% alcohol content.

SOURCE: *Food Flavorings, Composition, Manufacture, and Use, 2nd Edition* by Merory published by Avi Publishing Co., Westport, Conn.

POUND CAKE FLAVOR OIL

Mix together the following ingredients:

Ingredients	Gm
Ethyl vanillin	27.5
Vanillin	126.0
Oil of bitter almond	66.0
Oil of cinnamon bark	420.0
Oil of cloves	66.0
Oil of cardamom	33.0
Oil of nutmeg	66.0
Oil of lemon, cold pressed	195.5
Total	1000.0

SOURCE: *Food Flavorings, Composition, Manufacture, and Use, 2nd Edition* by Merory published by Avi Publishing Co., Westport, Conn.

CONCENTRATED PRUNE FLAVORING EXTRACT

Extracts of dates and figs are made by this same procedure.

Procedure

(a) Extract
250.0 lb dried prunes and
370.0 lb cold water
Duration: 12 hr. The menstruum is then circulated until the extract runs sparkling clear. Yield of extraction:
187.5 lb prune juice.

(b) The remaining fruit is covered with:
187.5 lb cold water; however, the menstruum is not circulated over the fruit. After 2 hr the extracted juice is drained off.
Yield of extraction:
196.25 lb prune juice.

(c) Vacuum distillation of:
383.75 lb mixture of **(a)** and **(b)** extracted prune juices. Yields:

5.0 lb first fraction—flavor distillate, non-alcoholic; the other fractions are discarded.
95.0 lb soluble solids of 72° Brix remain in the still after the concentration by vacuum distillation.

(d) Both The 5 lb of flavor distillate and the 95 lb of concentrated soluble solids are mixed together and yield:
100.0 lb concentrated prune flavoring extract of approx 68.4° Brix; it is pasteurized at 158°F, then cooled to 140°F and bottled.

SOURCE: *Food Flavorings, Composition, Manufacture, and Use, 2nd Edition* by Merory published by Avi Publishing Co., Westport, Conn.

RAISIN TRUE FRUIT CONCENTRATED EXTRACT

Ingredients

1025 lb unbleached seedless raisins
1025 lb water

Procedure

(a) First extraction: the unbleached seedless raisins are soaked with:
1025.00 lb water, and then comminuted using No. 4 screen; the mash is put into an extractor or tank and mixed with:
10.00 lb Pectinol enzyme; after 6 hr
50.00 lb filter aid are added to the mixture.

(b) The soaked raisins and added ingredients of (a) are then mixed with:
3112.50 lb (or 375.00 gal.) hot water of 175°-180°F, agitated, and kept at that temperature for 1 hr. The mixture is allowed to cool and then pressed.

(c) Second extraction: The pressed remains of (b) are mixed with:
2490.00 lb (or 300 gal.) hot water of 140°-150°F, agitated, and kept at the same temperature for 2 hr; expressing follows without delay.

(d) Both extracts are then mixed, filtered, and concentrated under vacuum to approximately 68° Brix to yield the finished raisin true fruit concentrated extract, non-alcoholic.

SOURCE: *Food Flavorings, Composition, Manufacture, and Use, 2nd Edition* by Merory published by Avi Publishing Co., Westport, Conn.

GENUINE RASPBERRY (RED) FLAVOR DISTILLATE

(a) 150.0 lb frozen red raspberries. Allow to defrost at room temperature then comminute in a Fitzpatrick mill using No. 5 sieve. The ground mash is allowed to stand and ferment until its alcohol content is above 0.5% and below 1% strength.

It takes 6 days from the time of thawing up to the height of fermentation. The mash is to be agitated three times daily to avoid accumulation of fruit on the surface.

(b) At the height of fermentation add:
10.2 lb (or 1.5 gal.) alcohol 95% are mixed with the partly fermented mash. The mixture is allowed to stand for extraction until the following day.

(c) The partly fermented mash and flavoring extract is distilled at atmospheric pressure, very slowly, to yield:
20.0 lb raspberry flavor distillate of approximately 50% alcohol content.

SOURCE: *Food Flavorings, Composition, Manufacture, and Use, 2nd Edition* by Merory published by Avi Publishing Co., Westport, Conn.

RASPBERRY (RED) FRUIT FLAVOR

Properties and Treatment of Fruits

Red raspberries of the Cuthbert, Washington, and Newburgh varieties are of good use in flavors. Freshly picked full ripe raspberries are cold washed and rapidly processed within a few hours after picking to cut down the exposure to air and oxidation. The use of frozen fruit permits operation through the year. Thawing of frozen fruit and exposure to air inevitably deteriorates the flavoring and coloring substances. The addition of alcohol to partially defrosted fruit eliminates the deterioration of flavor and preserves the brilliancy of color. After the juice is expressed from the fruit it is advisable immediately to process the pomace, which contains a significantly large amount of flavor and is successfully utilized in the production of raspberry flavor. Frozen raspberries which are used in fruit flavors are packed in barrels. The following formula refers to a large-scale batch production.

Ingredients

4500 lb (12 bbl of 375 lb each) frozen red raspberries
72 gal. alcohol, 95%

Procedure

Consists of application of various manufacturing processes to obtain maximum recovery of aroma and taste from the fruit. The formula is divided into two batch procedures with the yield of each combined to make a finished fruit flavor.

Batch No. 1

(a) 4 bbl of 375 lb each, totaling 1500 lb of frozen red raspberries are allowed to defrost at room temperature for 2 days. To the partially defrosted fruit is added:

24 gal. alcohol, 95%.

The mixture is immediately charged into the comminuting machine with a ¼-in. sieve and comminuted, then pressed. The addition of alcohol to partially defrosted fruit prevents loss of the volatile aroma and change of color. It also separates pectins and other insoluble matter. Comminuting the fruit mixed with alcohol also facilitates the instantaneous extraction of flavor from all parts of the raspberries including the slightly crushed seed. It is important to know that a similar treatment cannot be applied to seeds of heated fruit for tannin and seedy flavor may be extracted. The expressed juice is stored in stainless steel containers at a room temperature of about 65°F and allowed to clear in order to separate impurities. The juice can then be filtered. However, it is rather advisable to omit filtration in order to cut down exposure of fruit juices to air. The yield of expressed juice and flavoring extract is about:

(b) 142 gal. The yield is then divided into two parts: 100 gal. of expressed juice and flavoring extract is put aside for use in the compound of the finished fruit flavor, while the remaining 42 gal. of the same yield is used in Batch No. 2 (g).

(c) The fruit cake, also called pomace, which is the pressed remains of extracted skin, fruit flesh, and seeds is mixed with the pomace of Batch No. 2(f), and to it added the second fraction.

Batch No. 2

(a) 8 bbl of 375 lb each totaling 3000 lb of frozen red raspberries are opened and the covers left on the barrels. The raspberries are stored at a room temperature of about 70°F and allowed to defrost partially so that the fruit can then be coarsely ground. The ground fruit is left at room temperature to defrost completely. After thawing, natural fermentation sets in, during which it is necessary to agitate the fruit frequently. The fermentation is interrupted when the alcohol content is above ½% but below 1%. The fermentation of red raspberries facilitates the change of acids to esters and thus increases the flavor strength of the fruit. The partly fermented fruit is then mixed with:

(b) 48 gal. alcohol, 95% and pressed.

Yield approximately 429 gal. expressed juice and flavoring extract.

(c) 42 gal. of expressed juice and flavoring extract which were put aside in Batch No. 1(b) are mixed with the

429 gal. of expressed juice of Batch No. 2(b) and left in stainless steel containers at room temperature for a few days during which time ester formation continues and sedimentation of pectins and other impurities takes place.

(d) The clear juice is taken off and transferred, for fractional distillation, into the still equipped with two receivers, a speedy agitator, a water jacket with built-in steam coil to facilitate both heating and cooling, and a reliable vacuum pump to assure uniform operation. The procedure begins with the removal of the flavor by a fractional distillation at atmospheric pressure. Heat is slowly applied to the water by means of a steam coil in the jacket of the still, and a slow flow of the first flavor fraction is collected which yields approximately 23 gal. of flavor distillate of about 50–55% alcohol content. The first fraction contains all the volatile flavor of extracted fruit and expressed juice. The temperature during the distillation at atmospheric pressure may go up to 190.4°F for a short period of time without impairing the juice and flavoring extract in the still. The first flavor fraction of the distillation at atmospheric pressure is set aside for use in the compound of the finished flavor in (g).

(e) After the first fraction is collected, the heat to the steam coil is cut off and the hot water rapidly removed by the influx of cold water into the jacket of the still. After the contents of the still have cooled to about 77°F, vacuum is applied gradually, until 28 in. of pressure is reached. Then the water in the jacket is again slowly heated to start the vacuum distillation to recover additional flavor and the remainder of the alcohol as well as to remove the water from the juice and flavoring extract. The vacuum distillation continues until the concentrate in the still is reduced to a quantity of 40 gal. of about 65°–70° Brix. The concentrate is then cooled and used in the compound mixture of the finished fruit flavor in (g). The yield will then be approximately 120 gal. distillate of about 26.5% alcohol and is used in the distillation of the pomace in (f).

(f) The pomace, consisting of the pressed remains of the first and second batch pressings, is mixed with the 120 gal. distillate of 26.5% alcohol content of Batch No. 2(e) and 80 gal. water. The mixture is slowly distilled at atmospheric pressure. The distillate is collected in two fractions, the first with a yield of approximately 17 gal. flavor distillate of about 56–70% alcohol content, containing all the flavor which was left in the pressed remains of the fruit. The second fraction with a yield of about 100 gal. distillate of about 29% alcohol content is redistilled to obtain a higher alcohol proof. The rectified yield is used in a next production batch.

(g) To make finished red raspberry fruit flavor, mix:

Gal.	
40	concentrate of Batch No. 2(e);
100	expressed flavoring extract juice of Batch No. 1(b);
23	flavor distillate of 54% alcohol content of Batch No. 2(d);
17	flavor distillate of 69% alcohol content of Batch No. 2(f); obtaining a yield of:
180	red raspberry fruit flavor of about 15% alcohol content.

Yield: 1 gal. concentrate from 25 lb frozen red raspberries

SOURCE: *Food Flavorings, Composition, Manufacture, and Use, 2nd Edition* by Merory published by Avi Publishing Co., Westport, Conn.

RASPBERRY (BLACK) FLAVOR CONCENTRATED JUICE

Procedure

(a) 28,284 lb frozen black raspberries are allowed to partially defrost at room temperature for 24 hr. The partially defrosted fruit is then heated rapidly to 180°F, and immediately pressed. The yield of 2357 gal. expressed juice should be concentrated without further delay.

(b) The 2357 gal. of black raspberry juice of 11.2° Brix should yield in one single procedural batch concentration 285 gal. full flavor concentrated black raspberry juice of 70.5° Brix. The concentrate should be filled into 5-gal. lacquered cans, vacuum sealed, and stored at room temperature. The 100-fold essence should be packed separately in glass containers.

The recovered volatile aroma of black raspberries does not have much flavor value. However, the soluble solids of the concentrated juice retains the full taste and color of the black raspberry fruit. The product should retain during at least 6 yr of storage at room temperature the aroma, taste, color, and consistency of full flavor black raspberry concentrated juice.

Flavor Measurements

A test made in 100 parts water should indicate:

Threshold of perception: 0.075% equivalent to 0.525 gal. concentrated juice mixed in 700 gal. water; color: faint.

Threshold of identification: 0.1% equivalent to 0.7 gal. concentrated juice mixed in 700 gal. water; color: distinct.

Threshold of consumers' acceptance: 0.15% equivalent to 1.05 gal. concentrated juice mixed in 700 gal. water; color: sufficient.

Threshold of full aromatic flavor: 0.5% equivalent to 1.40 gal. concentrated juice in 700 gal. water; color: brilliant.

Flavor Property

One gallon of full flavor black raspberry concentrated juice 8.15-fold of 70.5° Brix was obtained from 97 lb of fruit.

SOURCE: *Food Flavorings, Composition, Manufacture, and Use, 2nd Edition* by Merory published by Avi Publishing Co., Westport, Conn.

RASPBERRY (BLACK) FRUIT FLAVOR (For Use in Syrup and Carbonated Beverages)

Mix together

1.0 gal. Black Raspberry Flavor Concentrated Juice of 70.5° Brix, nonalcoholic

0.3 gal. Genuine Red Raspberry Flavor Distillate of 50% alcohol content (formula given above).

3.7 gal. Red Raspberry Fruit Flavor (formula also given above).

Total

5.0 gal. black raspberry fruit flavor of 15% alcoholic content.

Recommended Use.—From 3 to 5 gal. flavor in 100 gal. syrup to make 700 gal. carbonated black raspberry soda; acid citric solution is added according to required taste.

SOURCE: *Food Flavorings, Composition, Manufacture, and Use, 2nd Edition* by Merory published by Avi Publishing Co., Westport, Conn.

RASPBERRY (BLACK) FRUIT FLAVOR (With Other Natural Flavors and Certified Color)

(a) Formula for color mixture:

24 fl. oz.	boiling water mixed well with
16 gm.	amaranth FD&C Red No. 2*
16 gm.	umbria brown shade
16 gm.	concordine grape shade

(b) To the dissolved color mixture are then added, while agitating:

8 fl. oz.	caramel, acid proof, and left to cool.

(c) Mix together the following:

Fl Oz	
32	black raspberry juice, single-fold
32	Red Raspberry Fruit Flavor (formula given above)
20	Black Raspberry Flavor Concentrated Juice (formula also given above)
2	Raspberry With Other Natural Flavors (formula given below)
10	alcohol, 95%
32	color mixture of (b)
128	black raspberry fruit flavor with other natural flavors and certified color

(d) Use 4 fl oz in 1 gal. syrup including 1¼ fl oz citric acid solution.

(e) Formula for 1 gal. citric acid solution:

4.388 lb.	acid citric, anhydrous
qs	processed water (heated to warm)

---

*This coloring has been de-listed. It is no longer on the FDA-approved list of food colors and cannot be used. Consult your food color supplier for recommended color substitution.

SOURCE: *Food Flavorings, Composition, Manufacture, and Use, 2nd Edition* by Merory published by Avi Publishing Co., Westport, Conn.

RASPBERRY WITH OTHER NATURAL FLAVORS

Ingredients	Gm.
Alcohol	500.00
Oil of cassie	2.00
Oil of rose	2.00
Oil of lovage	0.50
Oil of jasmin	1.00
Oil of tangerine	3.50
Oil of carotte	1.00
Distilled water	520.00

Procedure

(a) Agitate mixture of alcohol and oils for 3 min, then add 520 gm distilled water and continue agitating for another 3 min. Transfer mixture into separator and leave it there covered overnight. The terpenes will separate to the surface, while the extract below will become clear.

(b) Take off the clear extract; discard terpenes.

(c) Approximate yield: 1000.00 gm.

Recommended Use

Use 10 gm of (b) and up per 1000 gm raspberry fruit flavor.

SOURCE: *Food Flavorings, Composition, Manufacture, and Use, 2nd Edition* by Merory published by Avi Publishing Co., Westport, Conn.

SLOE FLAVORING EXTRACT

Ingredients

Lb	
400.0	dried sloe berries
129.2	(or 19 gal.) alcohol 95%
437.5	(or 50 gal.) expressed Morello cherry juice, non-alcoholic
415.0	(or 50 gal.) water.

Procedure

(a) 400.0 lb. dried sloe berries are comminuted (using No. 4 sieve) and then mixed with:
50.0 gal. boiling water. After 24 hr a menstruum consisting of:
50.0 gal. Morello cherry juice and
19.0 gal. alcohol 95% is added. The menstruum is circulated over the berries twice daily for three days. The extract is separated to yield:
95.0 gal. sloe extract

(b) The remaining mash is distilled at atmospheric pressure to yield:
5.0 gal. flavor distillate of about 60% alcohol content.

(c) Mixture of:
95.0 gal. sloe extract
5.0 gal. flavor distillate
100.0 gal. sloe flavoring extract of about 15% alcohol content.

SOURCE: *Food Flavorings, Composition, Manufacture, and Use, 2nd Edition* by Merory published by Avi Publishing Co., Westport, Conn.

STRAWBERRY FRUIT JUICE AND FLAVORING EXTRACT

(a) 1000.0 lb frozen whole Marshall strawberries without, or with sugar (4 + 1), are defrosted; and to the partly defrosted fruit are added:
2.0 lb Pectinol and
163.2 lb (or 24 gal.) alcohol, 95%. The mixture is comminuted with the Fitzpatrick mill using a No. 4 sieve; after which the fruit is pressed as rapidly as possible.

(b) The pressed remains are mixed with:
199.2 lb (or 24 gal.) water and distilled at atmospheric pressure to obtain a distillate of about 3 gal. of flavor distillate of approximately 60% alcohol content. This flavor distillate is set aside for use in the finished mixture of **(c)**.

(c) The expressed juice of **(a)** is mixed with the 3 gal. of flavor distillate of **(b)** to yield about 100 gal. with approximately 19-20% alcohol content.

Strawberry juice and flavoring extract are usually prepared with an alcohol content of above 18%. Below this strength the juice ferments easily.

Flavor Property

One gallon of expressed juice is derived on an average from 10 lb strawberries without sugar or 8.5 lb strawberries with sugar.

SOURCE: *Food Flavorings, Composition, Manufacture, and Use, 2nd Edition* by Merory published by Avi Publishing Co., Westport, Conn.

STRAWBERRY TRUE FRUIT FLAVOR

The concentration of expressed strawberry juice by vacuum distillation yields an optimum flavor when derived from 20 lb of fruit per gallon of flavor. Strawberry true fruit flavor derived from more than 20 lb of fruit per gallon and concentrated by vacuum distillation yields an inferior product.

This formula is based on the strawberry juice being expressed from fruit without sugar according to the formula given above.

Procedure

(a) 200 gal. **Strawberry Fruit Juice and Flavoring Extract** (formula above) expressed from an average of 10 lb of fruit per gallon, with an alcohol content of 19%, is loaded into the still and concentrated by vacuum distillation to obtain the first fraction of:
28 gal. (or 210 lb) distillate of about 50% alcohol content to be used in **(b)**.

(b) The second fraction of the vacuum distillation yields:
72 gal. (or 568 lb) distillate of about 30% alcohol content which is redistilled to higher proof and is used in the next production of strawberry flavor.

(c) The third fraction is nonalcoholic and can be used in the next production batch in place of water, where it is mixed with the pressed remains and to distill the flavor. This third fraction yields about:
64 gal. (or 531 lb) distillate. The yield of the concentrate in the still is:
36 gal. strawberry concentrated soluble solids. It is used in **(d)**.

(d) The finished mixture consists of the cooled
36 gal. strawberry concentrated soluble solids of **(c)** to which is added in the still, to avoid loss of concentrated juice by the transfer into another container
36 gal. of expressed **Strawberry Fruit Juice and Flavoring Extract** of the above formula and

28 gal. of first fraction flavor distillate of (a). The total is:
100 gal. finished strawberry flavor true fruit concentrate of about 19% alcohol content.

Flavor Property

One gallon of this flavor concentrate is derived from 20 lb of strawberries without sugar.

SOURCE: *Food Flavorings, Composition, Manufacture, and Use, 2nd Edition* by Merory published by Avi Publishing Co., Westport, Conn.

TUTTI-FRUTTI FLAVOR

Ingredients	Gm
Allyl caproate	9.25
Citral	18.75
Vanillin	22.50
Amyl butyrate	37.00
Oil of orange, cold pressed	46.00
Ethyl butyrate	73.50
Ethyl acetate	185.00
Amyl acetate	185.00
Oil of lemon, cold pressed	423.00
Total	1000.00

Procedure

Mix thoroughly until all are in an homogeneous solution.

SOURCE: *Food Flavorings, Composition, Manufacture, and Use, 2nd Edition* by Merory published by Avi Publishing Co., Westport, Conn.

VANILLA EXTRACT

Vanilla flavor is extracted from cured vanilla beans with 95% alcohol. Distillation destroys the fragrance of the aromatic compounds. The color of vanilla extract is influenced by the quality of the beans, the strength of the alcoholic menstruum, the duration of the extraction, and the presence of glycerin, which is added to retard evaporation and to retain the flavor in the extract. Dry beans give a darker color than moist beans. Glycerin deepens the color of the extract. The amount of extracted color decreases as the strength of the alcohol is decreased.

Aging

The purpose of aging is to bring out improved aromas. Vanilla extract should not be stored in new wooden barrels. The vanilla absorbs from the wood tannin and other substances which have undesirable flavors. They should be removed by frequent washing. Vanilla extract should not be stored in containers made of aluminum, lead, nickel, zinc, or copper. Storage of vanilla in stainless steel or glass containers is commonly practiced.

An alcohol content of 42–45% accelerates the chemical changes and formation of esters from acids while aging. During this period, the total ester content of vanilla extract, as ethyl acetate, remains fairly constant. However, the nature of the esters changes considerably. The esters of higher alcohols liberate the higher alcohols upon hydrolysis, and the acids formed reunite with lower alcohols, forming volatile esters. The higher alcohols slowly oxidize to give aldehydes. This reaction takes place during storage and is often called "alcoholysis of the esters."

There is a direct dependency between the time of aging and the tempo of oxidation. The slower the oxidation the better are the forthcoming changes in the esters which produce the quality of aroma and taste in vanilla.

Yield

Approximately 180 lb of vanilla beans should produce 100 gal. of vanilla extract.

SOURCE: *Food Flavorings, Composition, Manufacture, and Use, 2nd Edition* by Merory published by Avi Publishing Co., Westport, Conn.

DRIED, DEHYDRATED, AND DIETETIC FRUIT PRODUCTS

DRIED OR EVAPORATED APPLES

When received at the drying plant the apples are dumped into a tank of running water. The washed apples are elevated by means of a bucket elevator or conveyor to an inspection belt. Here, rotten, wormy, bruised, and cut apples are eliminated. The good apples pass on to peelers, where workmen place each apple in a vertical position in the cup of the peeling machine. The cup is a revolving arm and delivers the apple to a vertical decending fork that impales the apple and spins it rapidly. A guarded peeling knife ascends vertically and removes the peel in ribbons. The coring knife ascends vertically and removes the core.

The peeled and cored apples are conveyed on a belt before women who trim off the remaining peel left by the peeling machine and any badly bruised portions. The peeled, trimmed, and cored apples are then cut by machine into rings about ¼ in. in thickness or into slices.

The apple rings or slices are dipped for about 30 min in a solution of sulfur dioxide or sodium bisulfite, which prevents browning. The sulfured apple slices are dried with hot air either in an air blast tunnel dehydrator or a "kiln" equipped with fans. The temperature of the air blast used should be in the range of 145° to 165°F. If the apples are dried in kilns, they must be frequently turned with aluminum or stainless steel shovels. About 7 tons of fresh apples yields 1 ton of dried fruit of about 24% moisture content. The dried apples are frequently moistened and given a second treatment with sulfur dioxide gas before packing for shipment.

SOURCE: D. K. Tressler and Associates, Westport, Conn.

SUN-DRIED APRICOTS

The Royal is the principal variety of apricots grown in California for drying, with the Tilton's coming second. The fruit should be ripe enough to be eaten from the hand before being picked for drying. The "Cots" are picked with as little bruising as possible, brought to the plant, dumped on slowly moving belts which convey the fruit past cutters who place the fruit in mechanical pitters. These cut each apricot in half around the suture and remove the pit. The halves with cups up are spread, one layer deep, on shallow trays for drying, while the pits are placed on other trays for drying for later use.

The trays, filled with apricot halves, should be stacked on "dry-yard" cars which are run into the "sulfur box," where the cots are exposed to sulfur dioxide fumes from burning sulfur for 3 hr or more, to give them a bright color and juicy appearance. Properly sulfured cots will not turn brown during or after drying. The trays of sulfured cots are spread on racks in the sun to dry. When the cots are about half dry the trays are stacked in such a way that the prevailing wind will pass freely between them. Properly dried cots should contain about 18% moisture and be soft and pliable, without being adhesive.

The trays of dried cots are emptied into boxes or bags which are delivered to the packing house. Here they are stored in bins to permit equalization of moisture. They are size-graded either before or after storage. The sizes are: Extra Fancy, over $^{48}/_{32}$ in. in diameter; Fancy, $^{48}/_{32}$ in. in diameter; Extra Choice, $^{40}/_{32}$ in. in diameter; Choice, $^{32}/_{32}$ in. in diameter; and Standard, below $^{32}/_{32}$ in. in diameter.

The graded cots pass first over a vibrating screen to remove leaves, stems, and other debris, and to break up lumps of matted fruit. Then they pass through a tank of cold water to remove dust, to make the cots more absorptive of sulfur dioxide, and to make them more pliable. The cots then pass under sprays of water on a vibrating screen, after which they are spread on large wooden trays. The trays are stacked on a car which is moved into the "sulfur house" and allowed to absorb sulfur dioxide for several hours. This treatment destroys insect eggs and prevents darkening of color, fermentation, and molding. The finished product usually has a sulfur dioxide content of 3000 ppm. The fruit is commonly packed in fiberboard boxes holding 25 or 50 lb. The filled boxes are weighed and the cots are pressed into the containers as they are closed.

SOURCE: D. K. Tressler and Associates, Westport, Conn.

DEHYDRATED BANANAS

Peels and "strings" are removed, and the fruit is passed through a disintegrator if it is to be drum dried or spray dried. Discoloration can be avoided by sulfuring lightly before cutting or grinding. The disintegrated pulp may be dried on an atmospheric double-drum drier, or it may first be finely ground in a homogenizer and then be spray dried, first being diluted somewhat with water if necessary to reduce its viscosity. The flakes produced by drum drying may be ground and bolted in order to produce a fine powder.

SOURCE: *Food Dehydration, 2nd Edition, Vol. 2* by Van Arsdel, Copley and Morgan published by Avi Publishing Co., Westport, Conn.

DRIED BANANAS

Fully ripe bananas should be peeled (usually by hand), mechanically sliced lengthwise, and placed one layer deep on perforated trays. The trays are placed on cars that are moved into sulfuring tunnels, for 20 min for treatment with sulfur dioxide to prevent browning. The cars then are moved directly into the dehydration tunnel until the slices are almost crisp. Dried bananas are hygroscopic and will pick up moisture on exposure to room humidity; therefore, they should be immediately packed in moisture-proof containers.

SOURCE: K. K. Tressler and Associates, Westport, Conn.

DEHYDRATED CHERRIES

Cherries should be dipped in lye solution (½% sodium hydroxide) to crack the skins. If cherries are pitted, they require no lye dipping. They are then rinsed with water and sulfured prior to dehydration. The fruit can be dried in about 8 to 12 hr in a countercurrent tunnel, with hot-end air temperature no higher than 170°F, wet-bulb temperature level 105°-115°F, and wet-bulb depression at least 15° at the cool end.

SOURCE: *Food Dehydration, 2nd Edition, Vol. 2* by Van Arsdel, Copley and Morgan published by Avi Publishing Co., Westport, Conn.

FOAMAT DRYING CITRUS JUICES

Citrus juice concentrates may be rapidly dried to a powder containing only about 1% moisture by the "foamat" process.

Orange Juice Procedure

Orange juice concentrate, 60° Brix or higher, should be foamed with 1.5% of a stabilizer consisting of 4 parts of enzymatically hydrolyzed soya protein and 1 part of 10 cps methyl cellulose (Methocel, Dow Chemical Co., Midland, Mich.). The actual foaming should be carried out in a Hobart mixer using a wire whip. The foam is spread in a thin (⅛-in.) layer on perforated sheet metal traps, then it is cratered by blowing thin jets of hot dry air through the tray perforations. The orange concentrate is dried in a stack of trays in a crater drier in 12-15 min to 2-2.5% moisture level. The dried product is cooled, detrayed, and packaged in a low humidity room maintained at 15% RH or less.

Lemon Juice Procedure

Lemon juice concentrate (e.g., 52° Brix and 29% citric acid) can be dried to a powder using similar techniques. About 1.4% glyceryl monostearate should be added in the form of a 10% water emulsion at 130°F. The foam obtained by whipping this emulsion should be spread on a perforated tray, cratered and dried using hot dry air according to the procedure used for drying orange concentrate.

SOURCE: USDA Western Regional Research Laboratory, Albany, Calif.

COCONUT (DESICCATED, SWEETENED, TOASTED)

The processing of desiccated coconut is accomplished in six main steps: shelling, paring, shredding, drying, sieving, and packing. The hard shell and tough brown skin of the nut are removed by hand. After shelling and paring, the broken nutmeats are passed through a water spray on their way to the shredding or dividing machines where they are reduced to the desired size in 2-3 sec. From the shredder, the coconut is taken to endless belt driers where the moisture content is reduced from 52 to 2.5%. After drying, the coconut is graded to size by a series of sieves. Finally the desiccated coconut is packed according to grade in 4-ply natural kraft bags, fitted with glassine or polyethylene liners. Each bag contains 100 lb of a specific grade.

Some desiccated coconut is reprocessed in tumbling mixers with powdered sugar, propylene glycol, salt, and added moisture to produce white, sweetened coconut products. To produce the toasted variety, desiccated coconut is treated with powdered sugar, dextrose, and salt and passed through an endless belt toasting oven.

White, sweetened coconut is packed in 50-lb, 25-lb and 10-lb corrugated cases which are fitted with polyethylene liners. (Toasted coconut flake is packed also in 10-lb corrugated cases fitted with polyethylene liners.)

SOURCE: J. G. Woodroof, Griffin, Georgia.

DRIED COCONUT (COPRA)

Copra is the trade name for the dried coconut meat or kernel. The first step in making copra is to remove the husk from the mature nuts. The second step consists of opening the husked nut by striking it at the "equator" with a heavy knife. This operation splits the nut in two and the milk spills out on the ground.

Sun Drying

The open halves are placed in trays and turned up to the sun. The trays can be stacked one upon another and quickly covered with a roof in the event of sudden rain. After 4-6 days of sunning, the partly dried meat is removed from the shell halves by prying with a sharp, curved steel spoon. The meat is further dried by sun or, if frequent rains prevent sun drying, it is cured by the use of one of several types of driers which pass heated air, or heat and smoke, through the trays of the meat placed under a shelter. The shells and husks of the nuts are frequently burned to provide the heat used in flue curing.

Tapahan Drying

The tapahan or artificial-drying method is faster than sun drying, but the copra is often discolored and of poorer quality. The husked coconuts are split into halves and arranged upside down on the tapahan, one over the other. After 4-6 hr of continuous heating the meat is removed, sliced into small pieces, and drying is resumed.

The drying time for coconut halves on platforms using artificial heat with rapidly circulating air may be as short as 40 hr. The coconut meat is reduced from 50 to 40% moisture in 1 hr, to 30% moisture in 3 hr, to 20% moisture in 5 hr, to 10% moisture in 10 hr, and to 5% moisture in 40 hr.

Kiln Drying

Kiln drying is supplementing and replacing sun drying in many cases and thereby affording better control of the operation. Optimum economic load for farm drying kilns is 200 coconuts, or 400 halves, arranged on 4 grills and heated to 122°-138°F. The quality is comparable with that of the best sun-dried product. Kilns are fired 4 months—from June to September—and have a life of 10 yr.

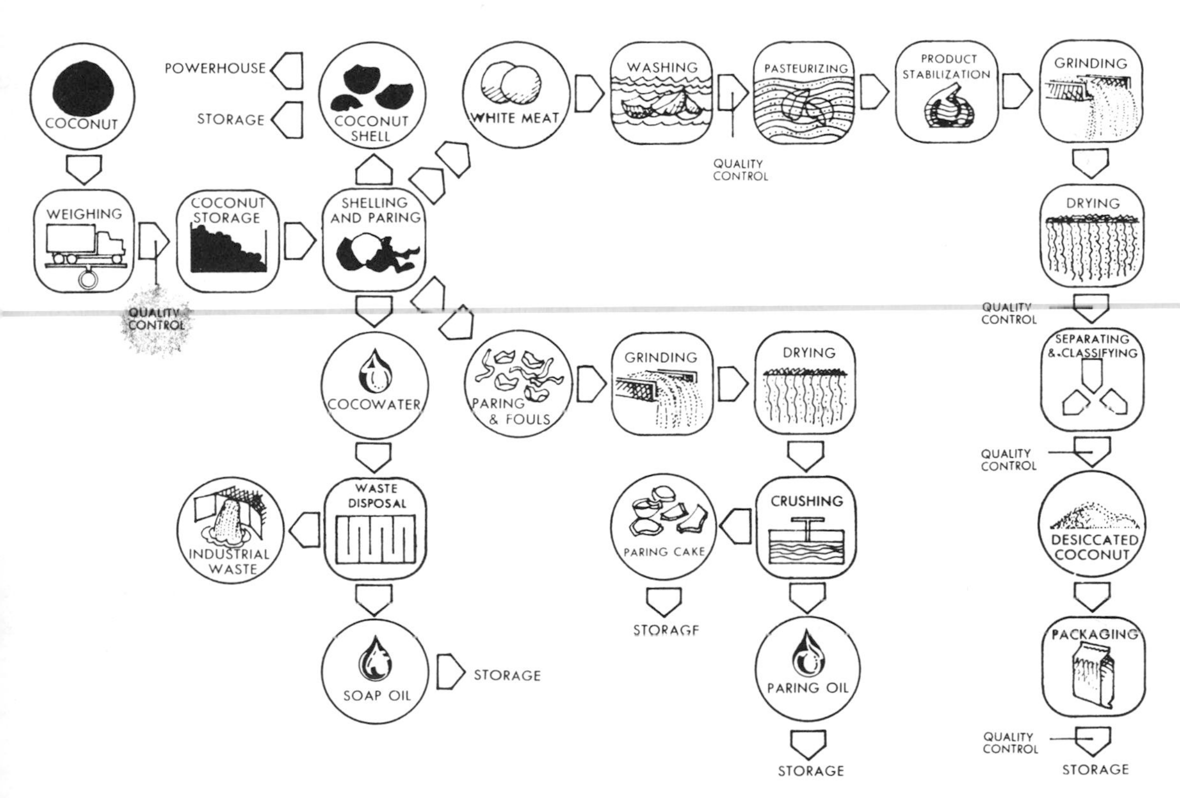

FIG. 4.1. PROCESS FLOW DIAGRAM OF A DESICCATED COCONUT PLANT

As with sun drying, kiln-dried coconut halves are dried until the meat loosens, then the shells are discarded and drying is continued to a moisture content of 5-7%.

Treating copra with sulfur fumes during drying prevents discoloration, wards off insects, and temporarily protects the product against mold and putrefaction. However, it should not be used as a means of attempting to restore brightness to already-discolored copra.

SOURCE: J. G. Woodroof, Griffin, Georgia.

DEHYDRATED CRANBERRIES

Cranberries are washed, inspected, and either sliced in a kraut cutter or similar type machine, or perforated, depending upon whether dehydrated flakes or whole berries are desired. The prepared berries are loaded on trays at about 1 lb per sq ft. The trays are loaded into trucks and wheeled into the dehydrator. Drying may be accomplished in either a countercurrent or cross-flow drier. With countercurrent flow of 500 ft per min air velocity and a hot-end temperature of 170°F, the material can be dried from 88% moisture content to about 10% moisture in 6-10 hr depending upon the method of preparation. The drying is then finished in bin driers in which the moisture content is lowered to about 5%. After inspection the dried product is pressed into bricks, and packaged into cartons or cans.

Cranberry Flakes

Cranberry flakes and cranberry powder are produced by drum drying. The berries are washed, and then cooked in a continuous steam-jacketed screw conveyor. The cooked berries are put through a pulper or finisher, and the resultant purée dried on stainless steel drum driers.

SOURCE: *Food Dehydration, 2nd Edition, Vol. 2* by Van Arsdel, Copley and Morgan published by Avi Publishing Co., Westport, Conn.

DEHYDRATED CRANBERRIES

Moisture is removed from cranberries by either of two ways.

(1) Pierce uniformly ripe, defect-free berries 20-30 times with needles, to allow escape of moisture. Dry 8-12 hr at 120°-150°F in forced air, with repeated turning, until moisture is reduced to 5%; 100 lb of cranberries yield about 10 lb of dehydrated product. The dried whole berries may be (a) compressed whole, (b) compressed sliced, or (c) powdered; then packed in hermetically sealed containers, for many months of storage.

(2) Boil cranberries in small amount of water for 2-3 min; reduce to a pulp, and dry immediately in rotating drum dryer to a crepe-paper-thin film; 100 lb of cranberries yield about 12 lb of film. Pulverize dried film is for use in sauce, jelly, beverage or other products.

SOURCE: *Cranberry Products*, University of Massachusetts Agricultural Experiment Station Bull. *481*, Amherst, Mass.

DRIED DATES

Fumigation is the first step in preparation of dates for drying. This is done by placing the trays of freshly picked dates in a gas-tight chamber where they are treated with methyl bromide. The dates are then cleaned either with toweling or with a brush under streams of water.

The cleaned dates are then put in shallow boxes in which they are held at 90°-95°F for a few days to ripen and dry. The dates soften and lose their astringency. The fully ripe dates are packed in cartons, a few drops of propylene oxide (a fumigant) are added before sealing the cartons.

Dried Pieces

Lower grade dates and culls of good quality are pitted mechanically and are dried "bone-dry," then broken into small pieces with rollers for use by bakers and confectioners.

SOURCE: D. K. Tressler and Associates, Westport, Conn.

DRIED FIGS

Figs to be dried should not be picked but should be allowed to partially dry on the tree and then fall to the ground. However, the figs should not be allowed to lie on the ground for more than three days. California and Adriatic figs should be dipped in a solution containing 10 lb of salt and 10 lb of hydrated lime for 100 gal. of water. This removes some of the hairs from the surface, improves the color, and softens the skins. Mission figs should not be dipped before drying; and Adriatic figs may be sulfured before drying.

All figs should be fumigated with methyl bromide before drying in order to kill the insects with which they are infested. This is done in small tight rooms. After fumigating the figs, the trays on which they are spread, are stacked and dried without exposure to the sun. Then the dry figs are placed on inspection belts and all green, bird-pecked, split, and otherwise cull fruit is eliminated. The sound figs are put in "sweet boxes" to obtain a product of uniform moisture content. At the packing plant the figs are graded for size, using equipment similar to that on which apricots are graded.

Before packing, the figs are immersed for 45-90 sec in boiling water or dilute corn syrup. They are carried through the hot solution in perforated sheet metal buckets. This softens the skins, makes the fruit pliable, and destroys insects. After the heat treatment, the figs are allowed to stand over night, then they are passed before women inspectors, who slit one side of each fig from the stem to the "eye" with a sharp knife. The figs are then rolled in the hand in such a manner that the cheeks are spread wide apart and the stem is hidden. The fruit is then packed into hardwood forms. When filled, the figs are pressed into the forms. After standing overnight the bricks of figs are removed from the forms and wrapped in waxed paper or cellophane.

SOURCE: D. K. Tressler and Associates, Westport, Conn.

OSMOVAC DRIED FRUITS

The osmovac process consists of two steps: (1) partial dehydration of fruit pieces to approximately 50% weight reduction by osmosis in either dry sugar or a heavy syrup; (2) completion of dehydration in a vacuum drier, operated at 150°-200°F shelf temperature and a pressure below 5 mm of mercury, to a moisture content of 1-2%. Fruit dried by this process has the following characteristics: (1) The sugar/acid ratio is increased in the osmotic step by removal of some of the fruit acid and addition of some sugar. (2) The texture is crisp but very friable. (3) The natural volatile flavors are protected by the high sugar content from loss during vacuum drying. These characteristics result in a product that is very pleasant to eat out of hand as a snack food or in conjunction with dry or cooked cereals.

With Dry Sugar

Mix 100 parts by weight of peeled, sliced, or diced fruit, or whole berries, with 100 parts of dry sugar (sucrose or dextrose). Let stand 20-24 hr at about 70°F, or 3-5 hr at 120°F. Drain fruit and place on vacuum drier trays, which are preferably lined with Teflon or other nonstick material. Place trays in drier on shelves heated to 150°F or higher. Lower pressure in the drier to 5 mm mercury or less and dry 5 hr, or more if necessary, to reach a moisture content of 1-2%. Cool shelves to 75°-80°F before releasing vacuum. Package in a moisture vapor-proof container.

With Syrup

Mix 100 parts by weight of prepared fruit with 400 parts of 70% sugar syrup, made from sucrose, corn syrup, or invert syrup. Procedure thereafter is the same as when dry sugar is used. Syrup drained from fruit can be used on another batch after concentrating back to original sugar concentration.

SOURCE: D. K. Tressler and Associates, Westport, Conn.

DIETETIC GELATIN DESSERT
(Hydrolyzed Cereal Solids)

Ingredients	Parts by Weight (%)
10 DE hydrolyzed cereal solids and artificial sweetener	(approx) 75.0
Gelatin	20.0
Citric acid	2.0
Flavor	2.0
Color	(to suit)

Procedure

The above dry mix is a typical gelatin dessert made with hydrolyzed cereal solids and an artificial sweetener. To prepare the dessert, the above should be added to one pint of boiling water, stirred, and allowed to jell in the refrigerator.

Serves 4 at approximately 60 cal per serving compared to approximately 100 cal per serving for regular gelatin dessert.

SOURCE: CPC International Inc., Industrial Division, Englewood Cliffs, N.J.

DIETETIC (ARTIFICIAL) FRUIT JELLY THICKENED WITH TRAGACANTH

Ingredients	%
TIC gum tragacanth pretested 500 USP powder	0.15
TIC colloid 600	0.05
Low methoxy pectin	0.20
Sodium saccharin	0.35
Sorbitol	4.00
Sodium benzoate	0.10
Potassium sorbate	0.05
Dicalcium phosphate	0.15
Citric acid	0.30
Water	40.00
Fruit juice (14°-15° Brix)	54.65

Procedure

Mix all dry ingredients. Heat water and fruit juice to 180°-185°F. Add dry ingredients with agitation, and mix for 5 min. Fill at temperature of at least 175°F.

SOURCE: Tragacanth Importing Corp., 141 E. 44th St., New York, N.Y.

POWDERED ORANGE JUICE

Powdered orange juice may be prepared by "puff-drying." In this process concentrated orange juice is made to "puff" into a porous structure under high vacuum and the product dried in a vacuum shelf drier. The material from the drier contains about 3% moisture. The product is very hygroscopic. It is packaged with an "in-package" desiccant which further reduces the moisture content to below 1% in which condition it has excellent stability at room temperature. Most of the volatile flavors are lost during drying, but typical orange flavor may be restored by adding cold-pressed orange oil entrapped in sorbitol or "locked-in" orange oil in sugars may be added. The Chain-Belt vacuum drier has been adapted to the puff drying on a commercial scale.

The newer process that has been developed is called "Foam-mat" drying. Edible stabilizers such as fatty acid monoglycerides are added to aid in the formation of a stiff foam produced by a wire beater. The foam is spread on a perforated sheet and crater holes are opened by passing the sheet over an air blast (the "crater" technique). Drying is accomplished by passing air through a stack of loaded sheets.

SOURCE: *Fruit and Vegetable Juice Processing Technology, 2nd Edition* by Tressler and Joslyn published by Avi Publishing Co., Westport, Conn.

DEHYDRATED PEACHES

Clingstone peaches of canning varieties should be halved, pitted, and lye-peeled, as described for **Canned Peaches** in Section 2. The halves are thinly spread on slab trays, cups up. Then the trays are placed on racks on cars that are moved into the sulfuring tunnel where they are exposed to sulfur dioxide from burning sulfur for 4-6 hr. The peaches are then dried in dehydrating tunnels. The dehydrated peaches are graded for size on mechanical graders. The dried and graded peaches are moistened and packed as described for apricots.

SOURCE: D. K. Tressler and Associates, Westport, Conn.

DEHYDRATED PEARS

Pears are halved, peeled, and sliced, or peeled, halved, and cored before sulfuring and dehydration. The drying time varies from 6 to 48 hr, depending on piece sizes to be dehydrated and whether peeled or not. Trays may be loaded about 2½ lb per sq ft. Recommended drying conditions in a countercurrent tunnel are a maximum hot-end air temperature of 150°F, a wet-bulb temperature level of 100°-110°F, and at least a 15°F wet-bulb depression at the cool end.

SOURCE: *Food Dehydration, 2nd Edition, Vol. 2* by Van Arsdel, Copley and Morgan published by Avi Publishing Co., Westport, Conn.

DIETETIC PRESERVES AND JELLIES

These products are generally produced from fruit or fruit juices, artificial sweetening agents, low-methyl-ester pectinates, a phosphate, sodium citrate, sodium benzoate, and water. FDA standards also include the addition of an acidulant "in quantities to reasonably compensate for deficiency, if any, of the natural acidity of the fruit (or fruit juice) constituent."

Dietetic Jelly and Preserve Formulas

Dietetic Jelly

Juice of fruit	55 lbs
Low-calorie sugar substitute	to suit
"Exchange" pectin LM No. 3466	1 lb 6.5 oz
Sodim citrate	2 oz
Monocalcium phosphate	2.75 oz
Benzoic acid	1 oz (Na salt)
Water	5 gal. 1 pt
Acidulant	to give a pH of 3.5

Sodium-Free Jelly

Juice of fruit	55 lb
Low-calorie sugar substitute	to suit
"Exchange" pectin LM (No. 3466)	1 lb 6.5 oz
Benzoic acid	1 oz
Water	5 gal. 1 pt
Acidulant	to give a pH of 3.5

Dietetic Preserves

Fruit	55 lb
Low-calorie sugar substitute	to suit
"Exchange" pectin LM (No. 3466)	1 lb
Sodium hexametaphosphate	8 oz
Benzoic acid	1 oz
Water	5 gal. 1 pt
Acidulant	to give a pH of 3.5

SOURCE: D. K. Tressler and Associates, Westport, Conn.

DRIED PRUNES (PLUMS)

Prunes are prepared either by sun drying or dehydrating. Before drying, the fully ripe fruit is dipped in either dilute (1%) lye or in hot water in order to check the skins and permit rapid drying. Another method is to roll the plums over multiple needles to puncture the skins. They are then rinsed and spread thinly on trays, which are placed in carts for drying in the air or in hot air-blast dehydrating tunnels. In either case, they are finished in a drying tunnel with the air at the finishing end not to exceed 165°F for the French variety and 140°F for the Imperial variety. Drying the French variety takes about 24 hr; the Imperial variety requires much longer.

Dried prunes are specially processed before they are packed. First they are sorted to remove any foreign material, split fruit, and culls. Next they are washed and immersed in boiling water for 2-4 min. This treatment cleanses the product, destroys insects, renders it soft and pliable, and gives it a glossy appearance. The hot, practically sterile prunes, should be packed in fiberboard boxes, lined with waxed or parchment paper, holding 25 to 50 lb each, and closed under pressure. The boxes of prunes should then be stacked so that air circulating around them will cool the dried fruit as rapidly as practical.

SOURCE: D. K. Tressler and Associates, Westport, Conn.

RAISINS

Eight methods of drying grapes to produce raisins are used commercially. These are (1) California soda-oil dip with sun drying; (2) Australian mix dip with rack drying; (3) Australian cold dip with rack drying; (4) soda dip with dehydration; (5) soda dip with sun drying; (6) natural sun drying; (7) sulfur bleach; and (8) golden bleach.

The soda-dip process involves dipping fresh grapes in a solution of 0.2-0.3% sodium hydroxide (caustic soda) at a temperature of about 200°F for a few seconds. They are then rinsed with cold water before sun drying or dehydration. The dipping in the lye solution removes the waxy bloom and checks the skins to hasten drying.

In the Australian mix dip method, the grapes are dipped in a solution of 0.3% sodium hydroxide, 0.5% potassium carbonate, and 0.4% olive oil at a temperature of about 180°F for 2-3 sec. The solution is not rinsed off the grapes before drying. Commercial practice in Australia is to dry the grapes on specially-constructed racks in the shade, where the fruit receives a weekly spray of 5% solution of potassium carbonate in which has been emulsified 0.4% olive oil. For the last day or two of drying, the raisins are placed in direct sunlight to change the greenish color to yellow or light brown.

With the Australian cold dip method, the grapes are dipped in a solution containing 5% potassium carbonate, in which has been emulsified 0.4% olive oil, for 1 to 4 min at 95°-100°F. The commercial drying procedure is about the same as for the Australian mix dip. When practically dry, the raisins are washed in a 0.5% solution of potassium carbonate containing 0.4% olive oil to remove the heavy deposit of carbonate left by dipping and spraying. The washed raisins are exposed to direct sunlight for 1 or 2 days to allow the surface to dry and change color.

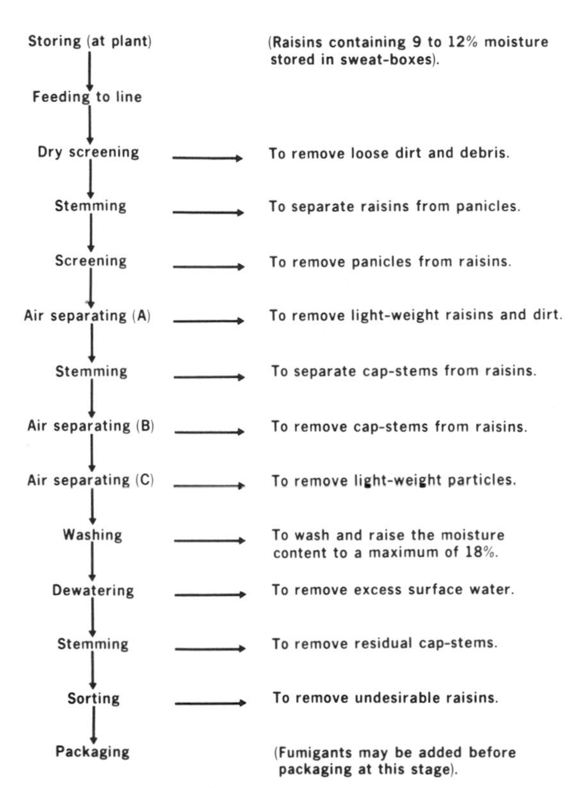

SOURCE: *Food Dehydration, 2nd Edition, Vol. 2, Avi Publishing Co., Westport, Conn.*

FIG. 4.2. FLOW SHEET FOR RAISIN PROCESSING

The California soda-oil dip, with sun drying, was once used extensively, but has now been largely abandoned. With this process, the grapes are dipped in a 4% solution of commercial anhydrous sodium carbonate on which is floated a thin film of olive oil. The dipping time is from 30 to 60 sec at a temperature of 95°-100°F.

Grapes that are to be dehydrated and processed to golden bleached raisins are dipped in a hot lye bath (0.25%). They are washed and spread on wooden trays and sulfured by allowing carloads of trays to remain in the sulfur house in fumes of burning sulfur for about 4 hr; 4-5 lb of sulfur is burned per ton of grapes. After sulfuring, the cars are transferred to tunnel dehydrators where they remain until dried to the desired moisture content (12%).

SOURCE: *Food Dehydration, 2nd Edition, Vol. 2* by Van Arsdel, Copley and Morgan published by Avi Publishing Co., Westport, Conn.

FROZEN FRUITS

FROZEN SLICED APPLES

Receive orchard-run fruit in boxes.

Remove rotten and under-sized fruit.

Wash fruit. (This step depends on the condition of the fruit as clean fruit may not require washing.)

Peel fruit by automatic peelers, corers, and seed cellers.

Seed celling of the apple improves the appearance and pie value of the thawed sliced fruit and helps to delay browning on the trimming tables during processing as the seed cell area in many apples browns more readily than the rest of the slice.

Trim peeled fruit immediately (otherwise, the fruit may be held in water or 1% salt solution to temporarily retard browning).

Slice fruit through cutters designed to yield either the ⅜-in. square slice or the ¼-in. flat slice. Knife heads (with a ½-in. stainless steel rod perpendicular to the cutting surface at its center to guide the apple) and a slicer foot (to force the peeled, cored, and seed-celled fruit through the cutter) are required. Most apple sectioning machines can be adapted to produce these types of slices.

Hold "square" sliced fruit in a 4% salt solution (1½ lb salt per 5 gal. of water) for 10-15 min. "Flat" slices are held for approximately 10 min.

All slices should be held below the liquid level. The salt solution should be replaced several times a day depending on the amount of use. The bath, like any dipping solution, collects finely divided fruit tissue and decreases in salt content with use. From a sanitary viewpoint occasional changes are also desirable. Directions for determining the salt content of brines are available.

If soft tissue apples are being processed, it is desirable to increase the firmness of the sliced fruit. This can be done by including some calcium salt in the dipping solution. Calcium chloride in amounts from 0.05 to 0.5% of the brine (½ to 6 oz of calcium chloride per 10 gal. of salt solution) are suggested concentrations. The processor should make several small scale tests when using this firming agent in order to check the texture of the finished apples of a specific variety and condition of storage before large trial runs are made. Overfirming produces a rubbery texture. Over-ripe apples or apples stored for very long periods of time do not respond as well to the calcium treatment as ripe apples or apples stored for a few months. The use of excessive amounts of calcium chloride should be avoided as it introduces a bitter flavor in the apples. The calcium salt (calcium chloride or other calcium salts) should be of a suitable degree of purity and the pack should be properly labeled.

Remove slices from the salt solution, drain but do not rinse. If fruit is to be packed with dry sugar, place the slices in a mixer, sprinkle dry sugar over the fruit, add a small volume of ascorbic acid solution and rotate slowly until uniformity is obtained. On the basis of a 30-lb pack, use 25 lb of sliced apples, 5 lb of sugar and 5 gm (1/16 oz) of ascorbic acid dissolved in 4-8 oz of water. Slow tumbling of fruit and sugar does not injure the fruit. The fruit-sugar-ascorbic acid mixture is then poured into lacquer-lined friction top cans holding 10 or 30 lb of product. When emptying the mixer, all liquid should be removed and evenly distributed to the containers.

Frozen sliced apples are usually packed in 30-lb slip cover, enamel-lined, tin cans and frozen in an air blast at -20°F or lower.

SOURCE: Hoffman La Roche, Inc., Nutley, N.J.

FROZEN APRICOTS

Upon arrival at the processing plant, the apricots are first inspected on a conveyor belt and then passed through a halving and pitting machine. After separation of the halved fruit from the pits, the halves are inspected again. Then they are washed and finally treated to prevent browning before they are syruped, packaged, and frozen.

Three methods have been successful for the prevention of browning: the fruit may be blanched in hot water or steam, dipped in a bisulfite solution, or treated with ascorbic acid. Blanching in a single layer on a mesh belt for 3-4 min in steam is satisfactory for firm fruit. It is probably best to treat softer fruit with SO_2 or ascorbic acid. The latter may be incorporated at a level of 0.05% or more into the syrup used for packing. The SO_2 treatments should be adjusted to leave a residue of 75-100 ppm in the frozen apricots.

For the baking, jam, or preserve trade, the SO_2 treatment is satisfactory and results in better color. The packing medium can vary from 15° Brix syrup, to dry sugar at 3 parts of apricots to 1 part of sugar or even a higher proportion of fruit, depending on the specifications of the buyer. When dry sugar is used, it may be sprinkled on the fruit as it is filled into the container or can be distributed evenly by light mixing. Apricots which are to be reprocessed and filled into cans should not be treated with SO_2 since the SO_2 will be reduced by tin to hydrogen sulfide.

Retail packages of apricot slices or halves have been marketed from time to time, but have never been produced in any great volume. Unless the fruit is peeled, the skins give a tough texture. Browning has been a serious problem, too, and can best be controlled by a combination of blanching and packing in heavy syrup containing 0.1% by weight of ascorbic acid.

SOURCE: *The Freezing Preservation of Foods, 4th Edition, Vol. 2* by Tressler, Van Arsdel and Copley published by Avi Publishing Co., Westport, Conn.

FROZEN BLACKBERRIES, BOYSENBERRIES, AND LOGANBERRIES

Since the methods used in preparing blackberries, Boysenberries and Loganberries are substantially identical, the procedure used for all three berries will be presented together.

The berries intended for manufacture into preserves, jam, and jelly, are washed with sprays of water in a conventional berry washer, then passed over an inspection belt where leaves and other extraneous materials are removed before the berries are put into 30-lb enamel-lined cans or barrels. Formerly, barrels were the principal containers used for this product, but more and more enamel-lined cans are used. Usually, sugar in the proportion of 5 lb of berries to 1 lb of sugar is added, unless the buyer specifically requests some other ratio.

Relatively small quantities of blackberries and Boysenberries are packed in small containers for sale through retail channels; however, Loganberries are not commonly packed in small containers. The retail demand for blackberries and Boysenberries has decreased in recent years.

Usually, the retail packs are made by filling the washed and cleaned berries into small cartons or enamel-lined tin cans, covering the fruit with a medium sugar syrup, closing the containers, and freezing the packaged product in either an airblast tunnel or plate freezer.

Some berries are individually quick frozen (IQF) by passing them on a wire mesh belt through a freezing tunnel, after which the frozen berries are packaged in flat rectangular fiberboard cases each holding 20 or 25 lb, or in the enamel-lined, slip-cover cans of the type commonly used for frozen fruit. No sugar is used in the IQF packs.

SOURCE: *The Freezing Preservation of Foods, 3rd Edition* by Tressler and Evers published by Avi Publishing Co., Westport, Conn.

FROZEN SWEET CHERRIES

Sweet cherries (Bing) are more meaty than sour cherries (e.g., Montmorency) and consequently do not collapse when frozen and thawed. However, they oxidize readily and brown, causing loss of both color and flavor. Therefore, they should be covered with a dilute (10%) sugar syrup containing ascorbic acid, and packed in air tight containers. Pitting causes loss of juices and texture, and for dessert purposes they may be frozen without pitting. Sweet cherries are one of the most desirable of all fruits for freezing.

SOURCE: D. K. Tressler and Associates, Westport, Conn.

FROZEN RED SOUR CHERRIES
Preferably the Montmorency Variety

Cherries are stripped from the tree and placed in boxes holding 40–50 lb. In many places the fruit is sorted in the orchard in order to eliminate foreign matter, defective cherries, etc. When received at the packing plant, the fruit is weighed and then immersed in ice water contained in large wooden tanks for a period varying from 4 to 18 hr. If the cherries are over-ripe, a small amount of calcium chloride is sometimes used in the ice water. The soaking and chilling cleans and also firms the cherries, so that much less juice is lost when the cherries are pitted. The cherries are drawn from the tanks as needed and conveyed to a grader which consists of accurately spaced belts which drop fruit under ⅝-in. in diameter. Those passed by the grader move on to rubber inspection belts where women eliminate all foreign matter and defective cherries which were overlooked in the inspection in the orchard and not separated in the chilling tanks. Those under ⅝-in. in diameter pass on to a second grading belt, where cherries under ½-in. in diameter are eliminated. In some plants the cherries between ½-in. and ⅝-in. in diameter are brined for later use in making maraschino cherries, and those under ½-in. are crushed for juice. The largest size graded fruit is then passed to the pitting machines where the pits are punched out.

One cherry drops into each hole in the pitters and the pits are punched out of three rows of cherries in a single operation of the continuously moving machine. Because the cherries are now firm, the pits are removed easily with a minimum of waste and without tearing the fruit. The bulk of the pitted cherries are packed with sugar in 30- or 50-lb enamel-lined slip-cover cans or in 50-gal. barrels. The latter were formerly almost exclusively used, but now almost all of the pack is put into cans. The 3 + 1 pack is most popular although a considerable quantity of cherries is packed 4 + 1, and smaller amounts are packed with other proportions of fruit to sugar. In the case of the 4 + 1 pack in 30-lb cans, 5½ lb of sugar is distributed through the pack as the cherries are poured in and the final ½ lb is placed on top before the lid is put on.

The cans or barrels of cherries are placed in a sharp freezer at 0°F or lower.

SOURCE: *The Freezing Preservation of Foods, 3rd Edition* by Tressler and Evers published by Avi Publishing Co., Westport, Conn.

FROZEN COCONUT

Coconut can be almost perfectly preserved by merely freezing the shredded flesh in its own milk plus the water taken from the center of the fruit. Enough coconut milk should be added to cover the shredded product and protect it from exposure to air. Airtight containers are preferable.

SOURCE: *The Freezing Preservation of Foods, 3rd Edition* by Tressler and Evers published by Avi Publishing Co., Westport, Conn.

FROZEN CRANBERRIES

Commercially, cranberries are harvested by raking in much the same way as low-bush blueberries. In preparing them for freezing they must be carefully cleaned. This is done in a type of fanning mill called a Hayden separator. This machine blows out leaves and chaff, eliminates most of the soft and partially rotten berries, and grades them according to size. From the separator the cranberries are emptied into a tank of cold water. The berries are then stemmed. In one plant this is accomplished by whirling and washing in a vegetable peeler, fitted with a relatively smooth rotor which is geared to operate at a low speed. The rolling and rubbing of the berries against each other breaks off the stems. After washing for a short time, the cranberries are allowed to drain in a small bin with a screen bottom. After draining, the berries are passed over an inspection belt where any trash which was not eliminated by the separator and any poor berries are picked out by hand.

The cranberries are placed in containers for freezing. A satisfactory temperature for freezing and storage is 0°F.

SOURCE: *The Freezing Preservation of Foods, 3rd Edition* by Tressler and Evers published by Avi Publishing Co., Westport, Conn.

FROZEN RED AND WHITE CURRANTS

Currants are frozen for use later in making jelly. After harvesting, the berries are cleaned, washed, sorted, and stemmed. They may be packed whole, without sugar or syrup, and frozen at 0°F. However, they retain flavor better if packed with sugar (e.g., 4 parts currants to 1 part sugar); and 30-lb enamel-lined tin cans are commonly used as containers.

SOURCE: *The Freezing Preservation of Foods, 4th Edition, Vol. 3* by Tressler, Van Arsdel and Copley, published by Avi Publishing Co., Westport, Conn.

FROZEN FIGS

Figs are one of the most perishable of fresh fruits. They are difficult to transport and cannot be stored long even under refrigeration. Since figs can be satisfactorily preserved by freezing, one might suppose that fig freezing would be of considerable commercial importance, but relatively small quantities are packed. The peeled fruit may be packed in 50% sugar syrup, preferably containing 0.05% of ascorbic acid or 0.05% ascorbic and 0.10% citric acid. The sliced or crushed fruit may be frozen with sugar in the proportion of 4 parts fruit to 1 part sugar. The addition of 0.05% ascorbic acid to the pack prevents discoloration during freezing and later thawing, in preparation for the table.

The packaged figs should be frozen either in an airblast or a plate freezer at 0°F or below.

SOURCE: *The Freezing Preservation of Foods, 3rd Edition* by Tressler and Evers published by Avi Publishing Co., Westport, Conn.

FROZEN GRAPEFRUIT SECTIONS

Plant operations begin with the arrival of the ripe fruit at the plant by truck. It is held in a receiving bin, with sloping bottom, that feeds down to an elevator of endless canvas belt type. The elevator has pick-up lugs of wood that move the fruit upward to a chute that supplies the processing line.

A thorough wash for the whole fruit is the first step in processing.

Next, operators remove the washed fruit from water-filled pans beside them and place it on a cutting block raised 2 in. above the work table. The top of the fruit now hangs over the edge of the cutting block and above a hole in the table through which the peel cuttings fall as they are removed.

Standard sectionizing knives are used, the wedge-shaped blunt-nosed type with two cutting edges. It is a 1-2-3 movement for the operator, entering the knife along a section wall of the grapefruit, turning in and then out against the next section wall of the fruit, to offer an all-fruit-cell segment of the ripened fruit.

The sweet, juicy segments of the grapefruit go on to white porcelain trays, about 12 × 16 in. in size, that are immediately in front of the workers. Filled trays are placed on the conveyor belt that rolls between two rows of operators, working on opposite sides of the work tables.

Seeds remaining in the grapefruit segments are removed when the sections are placed on the tray. As trays are filled, they are pushed onto the belt moving to the packing section.

Here is an inspection of the sections to eliminate from the select pack any that may be broken in the line processing, to see that no seeds get by, and that these segments meet requirements for the firm's unbroken sections pack. Any broken segments move aside here to enter a special pack for institutional trade that does not require the unbroken product.

Packaging is in three sizes, the 12-oz of select segments for domestic trade and a 4-lb package of the same for hotel and restaurant trade. The broken segments are in 5-lb packages for the institutional users.

Open spaces between the packed sections are filled by light sugar syrup. The syrup serves a triple purpose. By making contact with all fruit sections, it then presents a liquid front to speed freezing and provides a barrier against rupture of fruit cells in freezing; also color of the natural fruit is maintained through storage to table serving. Fresh fruit flavor is maintained by using a syrup only sweet enough to balance the sweetness of the fruit itself.

The filled cartons are check-weighed, closed, placed on trays on a wheeled truck, on which they are transported to an airblast freezing tunnel.

SOURCE: *The Freezing Preservation of Foods, 3rd Edition* by Tressler and Evers published by Avi Publishing Co., Westport, Conn.

FROZEN MELONS

Muskmelon and Honeydew melon flesh cut into 1⅛-in. balls and mixed in about 50:50 proportions makes a delicious frozen product; the mixture is now preferred to 100% Honeydews. After washing, the melons are cut into halves, deseeded, and cut into round balls with spoons. After inspection to remove imperfect pieces, the fruit is washed with water sprays and filled into either retail or institutional-sized containers, along with 28° Brix syrup. Racks of the packages are transported into an airblast tunnel for freezing.

SOURCE: *The Freezing Preservation of Foods, 4th Edition, Vol. 2* by Tressler, Van Arsdel and Copley published by Avi Publishing Co., Westport, Conn.

FROZEN RIPE OLIVES

The Mission variety is the only olive that produces a frozen product of desirable texture without heating prior to freezing.

Freshly pickled ripe olives should be packed in paraffined paper containers, covered with 12° Salometer brine and then frozen and stored in a room maintained at approximately 0°F.

Olives frozen without heating do not have the characteristic flavor of canned ripe olives, therefore it may be advisable to heat them in brine long enough to develop the flavor of canned olives before quick freezing them.

SOURCE: *The Freezing Preservation of Foods, 3rd Edition* by Tressler and Evers published by Avi Publishing Co., Westport, Conn.

FROZEN PEACHES

Only fully mature, table ripe peaches should be selected for freezing. In the case of some varieties, it is necessary to sort the fruit as it comes from the orchards. The peaches that are not fully ripe must be held until they soften, since immature fruit will be hard to peel and the frozen product may be bitter.

Procedure

Peaches are immersed in a lye bath at about 140°F. The usual concentration employed is 1 part of sodium hydroxide in 12 parts of water, although some packers use only 1 part of lye to 15 parts of water. After immersion for about 1 min, the peaches are usually discharged into a covered shaker-washer in which the lye-treated peaches are subjected to powerful sprays of water which remove the lye and the remnants of skins. In many plants, the peaches coming from the shaker-washer pass on a conveyor belt before women who place each peach on a hand-operated mechanical cutter which cuts each peach in half and loosens the pit. The women put the halves back on the conveyor belt. Other girls, at the lower end of the belt, pick out the pits and trim off any remaining skin, etc. Defective halves are also eliminated. The halves are then again washed with powerful sprays of water. The halves then pass over a shaker which turns most of them cut side down. They then pass through a slicer which cuts each into slices—usually tenths.

The peels of peaches can also be loosened satisfactorily by scalding in boiling water or steam. The length of time that peaches should be scalded varies with both the variety and maturity of the fruit. If the fruit is soft ripe, 1 min should be long enough. Firm peaches may require as long as 1½ min. After scalding, the fruit should be sprayed with or immersed in, cool water for a few moments so that they will not become hot throughout, as the heat softens the peaches unnecessarily. The cooling also helps to loosen the skins.

Another system sometimes employed for loosening the skins is to cut the peaches in half, remove the pits, either by hand or by the use of the hand-operated mechanical cutter described above, and place the halves, cut side down, on a tray which, when filled, is put on a moving belt which passes through a steam chamber in approximately 75 sec. After the peaches have passed through the steam, cold water is sprayed on them long enough to cool them. Then the trays are removed from the conveyor by women seated at either side of the belt who rub off the skins.

Peaches which are to be sold at retail are usually packed in paperboard cartons or paperboard cartons with metal ends. A few packers use enamel-lined tin cans. Formerly, 4 oz of 50° Brix syrup were metered into each container, then 12 oz of peaches were added by hand. Now, smaller cartons are ordinarily used. A common size holds 8 oz peaches and 2½ oz 50° Brix syrup. Another size contains 10 oz peaches and 2½ oz syrup.

If a 60% sugar syrup containing 0.2% L-ascorbic acid (crystalline vitamin C) is used on the sliced peaches in the proportion by weight of 1 part of syrup to 3 parts of sliced or halved peaches, a superior product is obtained. Peaches containing this amount of ascorbic acid, even when packed in paraffined paperboard cartons, will not darken during storage for 2 yr at 0°F. Further, they can be thawed and held at room temperature overnight without darkening, provided they are held under the syrup.

Considerable quantities of sliced peaches are packed in 10-lb and larger enamel-lined cans for use in baking and the making of ice cream. In filling 30-lb cans, 24 lb of sliced peaches are usually placed in a can, then 6 lb of 50° Brix syrup. Then they are quick frozen at -20°F or below.

SOURCE: *The Freezing Preservation of Foods, 3rd Edition* by Tressler and Evers published by Avi Publishing Co., Westport, Conn.

FROZEN PEARS

The process of preparing and freezing sliced apples should be followed in freezing pears, with a few exceptions. Of the important varieties, the Bartlett gives the best product. It is important to select soft ripe fruit for freezing, otherwise the texture of the thawed product will be poor. Heavy syrup containing ascorbic acid should be used on the sliced pears; and neither blanching nor sulfur dioxide treatment is satisfactory.

SOURCE: D. K. Tressler and Associates, Westport, Conn.

FROZEN PINEAPPLE

Considerable quantities of pineapple are frozen in Hawaii. This fruit is also frozen in Australia, Brazil, and South Africa.

Slices or chunks of this fruit need no pretreatment, and fully ripe fruit keeps satisfactorily at 0°F even without the addition of either sugar or syrup.

Sliced pineapple and pineapple chunks frozen with light sugar syrup are excellent products. Fully ripe pineapples should be carefully peeled, and the cores and other woody portions removed. The slices or chunks should be covered with a 20 or 30% syrup. During storage, off-flavors sometimes develop in frozen pineapple. This occurs more often in the Red Spanish than in other varieties. These undesirable flavors may be caused by the action of proteolytic enzymes. Under-ripe fruit are more subject to these off-flavors than uniformly well-ripened fruit.

The packaged fruit, preferably covered with a 30% sugar syrup should be frozen in an airblast or plate freezer at 0°F or below and stored at 0°F.

SOURCE: *The Freezing Preservation of Foods, 3rd Edition* by Tressler and Evers published by Avi Publishing Co., Westport, Conn.

FROZEN PLUMS AND PRUNES

Plums and prunes may be prepared for freezing and frozen in much the same way as peaches, except that they need not be peeled. Halved or quartered plums are superior to the sliced product.

Halved and sliced plums frozen with sugar or syrup yield an excellent product for use in pies. The product has a better flavor when sugar alone is used, but the skins are somewhat tougher. If syrup is employed it should contain at least 60% sugar. An amount just sufficient to cover the sliced or halved fruit should be used.

If dry sugar is used, about 1 part should be added for each 3 parts of fruit, and the mixture stirred until enough juice is drawn out of the fruit to cover the slices. Then the plums or prunes should be packed in containers of a size convenient for bakers, frozen quickly, and stored at 0°F or lower.

SOURCE: *The Freezing Preservation of Foods, 3rd Edition* by Tressler and Evers published by Avi Publishing Co., Westport, Conn.

FROZEN RASPBERRIES (BLACK)

Desirable varieties have minimum seediness, large, plump, juicy-fleshed berries, and deep dark color.

The Bristol is about the best blackcap for freezing under New York conditions, while in the Pacific Northwest, the Munger is the principal variety grown. Munger is superior to other varieties in yield, fruit quality, and plant characteristics.

Black raspberries are handled in the same manner as are red raspberries; see **Frozen Raspberries (Red)** given below. Blackcaps are packed in 30-lb cans or larger containers for the bakery, confectionery, preserve, and other remanufacture trade.

SOURCE: *The Freezing Preservation of Foods, 3rd Edition* by Tressler and Evers published by Avi Publishing Co., Westport, Conn.

FROZEN RASPBERRIES (RED)

Red raspberries are picked into hallocks measuring about 5 X 5 X 2 in. deep. They are delivered to the plant in flats of 12 hallocks each. In some areas in Oregon hallocks of 4 X 4 X 3 in. dimensions are used. The berries are delivered to the freezing plant as soon after picking as practical, usually as soon as a pickup load of flats has been filled.

In the plants the flats are emptied into an air cleaner (if used). From the air cleaner the berries go to the washer and then go over a dewatering shaker and onto an inspection belt. For the retail trade, 6 oz. of sound berries are weighed into a Sefton or another type of retail container; 4 oz of 60% sucrose syrup is added to the container and it is sealed. When larger containers are used, the amounts of berries and syrup in the 6:4 ratio are adjusted to make the declared weight. Freezing may be done by traying the sealed containers and placing the filled trays on buggies which are pushed into an airblast in the freezing tunnel maintained at -10°F or lower. As each cart is placed in the tunnel, the carts preceding it are moved along through the tunnel. In some plants, especially those plants not physically tied in with the freezing facilities, the berries may be cased, palleted, and frozen in a commercial warehouse by the pallet load.

Raspberries for ice cream, baking, and preserving trades are packed in 10- or 30-lb slip-covered cans or in plastic lined steel drums of 55-gal. capacity. Washed raspberries are filled into these larger containers without added sugar, unless the buyer specifies that sugar be added.

SOURCE: *The Freezing Preservation of Foods, 4th Edition, Vol. 3* by Tressler, Van Arsdel and Copley, published by Avi Publishing Company, Westport, Conn.

FRUIT SHERBET

	Ingredients	Weight
(A)	Canned apricots,* plums, or peaches	11¼ lb
(B)	Corn syrup (light)	2¼ lb
	Sugar	1 lb 14 oz
	Water	1 lb 8 oz
(C)	Egg whites	12 oz.
	Fruit juice (or water)	1 lb 8 oz
	Nonfat dry milk	8 oz
	Lemon juice	12 oz
	Sugar	1½ lb

Yield: 3 gal.
96 portions using No. 8 scoop

Procedure

(A) Drain fruit, press through strainer. Save juice for step C.

(B) Combine syrup, sugar and water. Bring to a boil over medium heat, stirring until sugar is dissolved. Boil 5 min. Cool. Add to above fruit pulp, mix well. Turn into flat pans and put in freezer until mixture is firm.

(C) When mixture in freezer is firm, combine fruit juice (or water) and egg whites; add nonfat dry milk; whip until soft peaks form. Add lemon juice and continue beating until stiff; add sugar slowly, whip until blended.

Place frozen fruit mixture in bowl, beat until light and fluffy. Fold in whipped egg whites-nonfat dry milk mixture. Return to freezer pans and freeze until firm. For best results do not make more than 3 gal. at a time. (Counter pans may be used.)

---

*Apricot Nectar may be substituted for apricot purée.

SOURCE: American Dry Milk Institute, 130 N. Franklin St., Chicago, Illinois.

COLD-PACKED WHOLE STRAWBERRIES

Berries are hauled to the freezing plant as soon as a truck load is ready. Berries are ordinarily frozen the same day they are picked. The freezing plants start up as early as sufficient berries are on hand to ensure continuous operation and continue throughout the afternoon and night until all berries received that day have been placed in the freezer.

The berries are picked without caps and are placed in 1-lb wood veneer hallocks (baskets) arranged 12 to the tray; 16 trays or hallocks are weighed at a time on a two-wheeled hand truck as the berries are unloaded on the receiving platform where they are stacked awaiting use. The stacks of trays are trucked 16 at a time to the washer where a wire grid is placed over each tray as it is inverted, thus emptying the berries but retaining the hallocks in the tray. When working at top speed, each worker empties about a truck load (16) of trays of hallocks per minute. Rapidly running water carries the berries to a bucket elevator which elevates them about 5 ft where they are emptied into a flume in which they pass to a shaker grader. The larger berries roll down over the slightly inclined slats, fall onto a belt moving at right angles to the grader and are conveyed in front of a line of women who eliminate any foreign matter, any berries from which hulls have not been removed, and pick out the over-ripe, damaged, and green berries. The good berries are allowed to remain on the belt and are conveyed into a barrel standing on a rocker. A man rocks the barrel about 100 times per minute as the berries fall in from the conveyor belt. He adjusts the flow of granulated sugar from a bin above by means of a stop in a chute so that a weighed amount of sugar in the proportion of 2 + 1 (i.e., 2 parts of berries to 1 part of sugar) or 3 + 1, or other desired proportion is uniformly mixed with the berries as they are run in from the belt.

The smaller berries are similarly sorted and then packed with sugar either in barrels or in 30-lb slip cover enamel-lined tin cans. In some plants all of the strawberries are packed with sugar in cans. Many plants use less sugar than 2 + 1. The strawberries should be frozen at -10°F or lower.

SOURCE: *The Freezing Preservation of Foods*, *4th Edition*, *Vol. 4* by Tressler, Van Arsdel and Copley published by Avi Publishing Co., Westport, Conn.

INDIVIDUALLY QUICK FROZEN STRAWBERRIES

A novel development in IQF strawberries is the cryogenic freezing of the fruit. When immersion freezing in liquid nitrogen (LN) is used, the berries are immersed long enough to freeze a shell equal in thickness to 0.5–0.6 of the radius of the cross section of the berry. The rest of the freezing is accomplished in the cold gas above the LN, or in conventional 0° to -10°F storage. Prolonged immersion in liquid nitrogen results in the freezing of a hard outer shell which becomes stronger at low temperatures. As freezing continues, internal pressures build up. The faster the freezing, the greater the pressure build-up. Relief of the pressure comes about by expansion of the frozen exterior layers, resulting in cracking or shattering. At any rate, prolonged immersion in liquid nitrogen results in shattered berries.

Liquid nitrogen-frozen strawberries do not leak as badly on defrosting as do conventionally IQF berries. In one experiment thawed IQF berries lost ⅓ of their weight in the first 1½ hr, while berries frozen in liquid nitrogen lost only 6–8% during the same time.

SOURCE: *The Freezing Preservation of Foods*, *4th Edition*, *Vol. 3* by Tressler, Van Arsdel and Copley published by Avi Publishing Co., Westport, Conn.

FROZEN HALF-SLICED STRAWBERRIES

Half-sliced strawberries are handled in much the same way as the regular sliced berries (see formula given below) except that the berries are cut in a half-berry slicer. This is a machine equipped with a series of parallel Vee-troughs which move back and forth with a reciprocating action. As the berries go down the troughs, they tend to line up with the tip down and are cut in half by rotating circular knives located at the discharge end of the Vee-shaped troughs. Mixing with sugar is carried out as in the regular sliced berries.

A very recent development is the packing of half-sliced berries with syrup or liquid sugar in pouches or in shallow plastic boxes which can be sealed shut. These berries, not having gone through the churning sugar mixing process, retain their slice character. By immersing the frozen pouches in cool running water, they can be thawed in a very short time and the resulting product is of excellent quality.

SOURCE: *The Freezing Preservation of Foods*, *4th Edition*, *Vol. 3* by Tressler, Van Arsdel and Copley published by Avi Publishing Co., Westport, Conn.

FROZEN SLICED STRAWBERRIES

On delivery to the plant, the berries are in flats and are dumped into a washer. The most commonly-used washer in the Pacific Northwest is the McLaughlan washer. The washer consists of a shallow pan with water running in it and sharp sprays playing onto the fruit from above. The pan is continuously in sharp reciprocal motion, thus moving the fruit through the washer. As the berries move forward in the pan they are subjected to sharp sprays from above which knock sand, dirt, leaves, and other foreign material from the berries. After washing, the berries pass over a dewatering shaker and onto inspection belts where women remove foreign material, rots, and defects from the berries. When sliced, sugared berries are being packed, the berries are cut into slices of ¼- to 7/16-in. thickness. The trend is toward thicker slices. Slicing is done mechanically in high-speed circular blade slicers separated by proper spaces to give the desired thickness of slice (McLaughlan slicer), or by slow-speed centrifugal slicer (Urschel).

The sliced berries then go into a mixer where 1 part sugar by weight is mixed with 4 parts of sliced berries. Mixing is by ribbon or screw type agitators. The length of time the berries are in the mixer varies a great deal from plant to plant. Sometimes, when tie-ups occur in other parts of the line, the berries may be mixed for prolonged periods. This should be avoided, because mixing longer than is necessary to thoroughly distribute the sugar with the berries tends to destroy the slices and results in a product which should more properly be labeled "crushed strawberries." In the ribbon-type mixer, sliced berries and sugar are weighed into one end of a stainless-steel, U-shaped tank from 3 to 5 ft long and 3 ft wide. The tank is equipped with slowly revolving stainless steel ribbon mixers, which, as they slowly revolve, mix the sugar with the berries, and move the berries and sugar to the discharge end of the tank. The sugar dissolves during the mixing and a slurry of slices, crushed berries, and syrup results.

The screw-type mixer consists of a hopper at the feed end into which the berries and sugar are metered continuously. From the hopper the berries and sugar pass into a cylindrical stainless steel tube or U-trough about 8 in. in diameter and several feet long. Inside the tube, or trough, a slowly turning screw, slightly smaller than the inner diameter of the tube, propels the berry-sugar mixture toward the discharge end. By the time the discharge is reached, the sugar is dissolved. Another way of sweetening berries is performed in two stages. The sliced berries are filled volumetrically into the packages and the partially filled containers then go to a syruper which adds the correct amount of high-density syrup. The packages are closed, placed on trucks, and frozen.

The sealed containers may be frozen singly on a belt moving through the freezing tunnel, tray-frozen on carts which are moved through the tunnel, or cased, palleted, and frozen in a sharp room or in a tunnel. Case freezing is all too common and is not the preferred method.

SOURCE: *The Freezing Preservation of Foods, 4th Edition, Vol. 3* by Tressler, Van Arsdel and Copley, published by Avi Publishing Co., Westport, Conn.

JAMS, JELLIES, MARMALADES, AND PRESERVES CANDIED AND GLACÉD FRUITS FRUIT SYRUPS AND SAUCES

JAMS, JELLIES, MARMALADES, PRESERVES

OPEN-KETTLE COOK FOR JELLIES USING DRY PECTIN

Measure or weigh fruit juice (or fruit juice and water) into the kettle and turn on the steam.

Thoroughly mix the proper amount of citrus pectin, slow set, with 5 to 8 times its weight of granulated sugar (taken from the total amount of sugar required for the batch) in a dry pan.

Stir the mixture of pectin and sugar into the hot juice (temperature 160°-180°F) in the kettle and allow the mixture to come to a brisk boil to completely dissolve the pectin. It is desirable to stir the batch occasionally during the time that it is coming to a boil. Then boil vigorously for about ½ min Note: Experience has shown that pectin dissolves best in solutions containing not more than 25% soluble solids (sugar).

Add the fruit juice, if it was not added in the beginning, and the remainder of the sugar. (When fruit juice taken from cold pack fruit is used, it is added at this point.*) Boil the batch as vigorously as possible until the desired temperature is reached, then turn off the steam.

Immediately add the specified amount of the acid solution and mix thoroughly. Draw off and fill into containers as quickly as possible. Cap the containers hot (above 190°F) and there will be no necessity to sterilize them. If the jelly is not filled hot, it will be necessary to sterilize the filled and capped containers.

*NOTE: If fruit juice obtained from 4+1 cold pack fruit is to be used for jellies, care must be taken not to add the juice to the kettle until the pectin is completely dissolved in the water.

SOURCE: Sunkist Growers, Inc., 720 E. Sunkist St., Ontario, Calif.

VACUUM COOKING OF PRESERVES AND JELLIES

In the modern production of high quality preserves and jellies vacuum cooking has become increasingly more important during the past few years. Cooking under vacuum has been found to be very beneficial in preserving the natural color, flavor, and appearance of the fruits used in these products. The rate of sugar penetration into the fruit also is greatly accelerated thus minimizing flotation problems.

Stainless steel is recommended and generally preferred for all equipment which will come in contact with the product in the preserving plant although Pyrex glass is sometimes used for connecting lines. Stainless steel has the advantage of durability but the cleaning of the glass line is more easily observed. All piping should be equipped with sanitary fittings to facilitate cleaning.

The transfer of product is best accomplished by gravity or air pressure and vacuum. When necessary, a slow speed, positive action pump may be used without causing too much maceration of the fruit.

Recommended vacuum pans normally have a finished batch size of about 200 gal. although some larger ones are in use. Many of the new pans have several separate steam jackets or a separate coil, part of which may be shut off for making smaller batches. Some of these pans are equipped with a water spray for washing down the pan after completion of the batch. A built-in refractometer is also a very useful addition to the modern vacuum pan.

A steam pressure of 25-30 lb is usually used with these pans which operate at a product temperature of 125°-140°F. Under special conditions a temperature as low as about 100°F may be used.

Vacuum pans may be obtained with either a wet or dry condenser. Where essence recovery is desired it is necessary to use the dry surface condenser.

All holding, mixing, pasteurizing tanks and filling bowls should be equipped with agitators. It is especially important that these agitators used on the finished product be of a slow type which will prevent fruit flotation but not cause disintegration of whole fruit (especially important with strawberries).

Some preservers use a small pilot vacuum cooker for pretesting new batches of fruit to determine pectin and acid requirements as well as other fruit characteristics.

To avoid preset in the vacuum cooking of jellies and preserves, it is important to have the pH of the fruit above the critical pH for gel formation. In the case of very acid fruit, the pH may be adjusted by the addition of sodium citrate. (Up to 3 oz of sodium citrate per 100 lb of sugar permitted.)

With an Exchange slow set pectin, added before the final heating of the product, the fruit pH should be 3.35 or higher. With an Exchange rapid set pectin, this pH should be 3.45 or higher. The final pH adjustment should be done with the product temperature at least 170°F using slow set pectin and at least 180°F using the rapid set product. This assumes a final pH of 3.2 and 3.3, respectively.

An alternative method is to add the pectin solution after the product has been heated to the filling temperature. As a general rule it is better to use a slow set pectin in vacuum pan work as there is less chance of preset with this pectin.

In certain preserves some producers prefer to have a slight amount of preset to give a viscous, flowing type of product. In such cases, the final acid addition may be made at a lower temperature and some setting allowed to occur before filling. A medium rapid set pectin may be used for such products.

A somewhat similar viscous product, without preset, may be obtained by using a mixture of Exchange Pectin L.M. (low methoxyl) and regular slow (or rapid, if desired) set pectin. The ratio of low methoxyl pectin and regular pectin may be in the order of 1 part L.M. to 3 parts regular up to equal parts of L.M. and regular depending on the exact character desired. About the same total amount of pectin should be used except in certain cases where considerable preset occurs. In these cases the total pectin requirement may be somewhat smaller.

Most preservers prefer to use a pectin solution in preparing their jellies and preserves. The formula recommended in the Exchange Preservers Handbook is easily prepared and used. This formula calls for 8⅓ lb of pectin, 24 lb of granulated sugar, and 22 gal. of water. The resulting solution contains ⅓ lb of 150 grade pectin and about 1 lb of sugar per gallon.

This solution may be conveniently prepared by dry blending the sugar with the pectin and dispersing this mixture in the water. A 50-gal. kettle equipped with a high speed agitator works very satisfactorily. If the kettle is steam jacketed the water may be warmed to 100°-130°F and the pectin-sugar mixture added quickly with good agitation. The batch should be heated simultaneously to about 180°F. This pectin solution may be strained through a coarse screen. However, this should not be necessary when the solution is prepared in the proper manner.

The pectin solution should be stored in a secondary tank, somewhat larger, from which it may flow by gravity to the desired place in the production line. It is best to use the pectin solution the same day it is prepared. However, small residual amounts may be held overnight in a cool, sanitary place for use the following day. Pectin solution containers and piping should be thoroughly cleaned and sanitized daily to prevent possible mold growth.

The pectin solution may be added before or after concentration of the batch as mentioned previously. Addition of the pectin after concentration results in a faster cooking rate due to the lower viscosity of the batch during concentration. However, in making jellies, it is best to add the pectin solution before cooking is completed as this helps remove any bubbles which may be added with the pectin solution.

In cooking strawberries, cherries, and other fruits where flotation may be a problem, it is customary to use the pectin solution as cutback to reduce the density of the juice syrup. The following procedure is typical for the vacuum cooking of strawberry preserves.

(1) Place 4+1 cold pack strawberries (which have been allowed to thaw for 2-3 days) in the mixing and preheating tank and separate the juice from the whole berries. Heat juice to 140°F.

(2) Add the sugar to the juice and dissolve by heating to 160°F.

(3) Draw into vacuum pan and cook to about 75-82% soluble solids (or as found correct for exact procedure being followed).

(4) Transfer syrup back to whole berries in mixing tank and return mixture to vacuum pan.

(5) Bring to boil and break vacuum to impregnate berries with sugar by cracking valve in bottom of pan. Repeat, if needed, to prevent floating of berries.

(6) Finish cooking batch to desired soluble solids (about 72°-73° Brix depending on pectin solution strength and amount being used).

(7) Draw batch off into pasteurizing and holding tank. Add pectin solution and heat to 170°-190°F.

(8) Add citric acid solution to adjust to proper pH.

(9) Fill immediately.

(10) Cap, cool, and case.

It is common practice to add 15-25% of the sugar as corn syrup solids. This eliminates any danger of crystallization resulting from the small amount of sugar inversion obtained during low temperature vacuum cooking. If this is not wanted, some of the acid may be added to low acid fruits to ensure adequate sugar inversion. Care must be taken when adding acid to not lower the pH beyond the critical gelling point for the pectin being used.

Theoretical yields of batches of strawberry preserves made from 1400 lb of 4+1 cold pack fruit at various percentages of soluble solids in the finished product:

Percent soluble solids in finished preserve from vacuum pan (%)	Theoretical yield of finished preserve in pounds (Lb)	Pounds of sterile water to be added or water to be cooked out of the batch to obtain normal yield at 68% soluble solids (Lb)
67	2243	cook out 34
68	2209	—
69	2178	add 31
70	2147	add 62
71	2116	add 93
72	2088	add 121
73	2080	add 149

SOURCE: Sunkist Growers, Inc., 720 E. Sunkist St., Ontario, Calif.

FRUIT JAM

Fruit jam or preserve is the product made by cooking to a suitable consistency properly prepared fresh fruit, cold-pack fruit, canned fruit, or a mixture of two or all of these with sugar, or sugar and dextrose with or without water. In its preparation not less than 41 lb of fruit are used with 55 lb of sugar or sugar and dextrose. A product in which the fruit is whole or in relatively larger pieces is customarily designated a preserve rather than a jam (U.S. Food and Drug Administration).

Some fruits, for example currants, Concord grapes, and sour blackberries, contain sufficient pectin and are sufficiently acid to produce jam of good consistency without the admixture of pectin, acid, or another fruit high in acid or pectin. Other fruits, e.g., strawberries, require the addition of pectin to obtain a jam. Still others have sufficient natural pectin but are not sufficiently acid to jell and require the addition of a fruit acid such as citric acid.

The first step in making jam or preserves is the preparation of the fruit. If frozen or canned fruit is used, much or all of the work of preparation has been done prior to freezing or canning. However, if seedless jam is to be made from fruits with small seeds, e.g., raspberries, the thawed fruit or the jam must be put through a finisher to remove the seeds.

If fresh fruit is used to make jam or preserves, it must be carefully sorted and any wormy or decaying fruit discarded, after which the sound fruit is washed. Large fruit such as peaches and some small fruits, e.g., cherries, must be cut and pitted. Other fruits, such as the pineapple, require special treatment.

PRESERVING FRUITS WITH SULFUR DIOXIDE

Prepare berries, cherries, citrus fruits, peaches, or other fruits as for freezing or use in fruit butter, jam, jelly, marmalade, sauce, vinegar, or wine. Cover with solution of 2000 ppm sulphur dioxide in wood or corrosive-resistant vessel with tight cover. Add 1 lb of calcium carbonate per 100 gal. Agitate or turn daily for 1 week, and weekly for 6 months or longer storage.

Freshen fruit by boiling in open steam-jacketed kettle for 45 min with frequent stirring. Proceed to process fruit as if it were freshly-cooked.

SOURCE: Dept. of Food Science, Georgia Experiment Station, Experiment, Georgia.

STANDARD 45-55 JAMS AND PRESERVES

The following six formulas may be labeled "PURE" on the basis of the Federal Standards.

Apricot-Pineapple

Using Straight Fruit

Ingredients		
Water	(approx 2½ gal.)	20 lb
Apricots		41 lb
Pineapple		41 lb
150 Grade rapid set citrus pectin		4¾-6 oz
Sugar		100 lb
Standard fruit acid solution		(adjust pH to 3.3)

Approx yield: 150 lb at 68% soluble solids

Procedure.—Cook to 223°F at or near sea level, or 11°F above the boiling point of water at higher altitudes.

SOURCE: Sunkist Growers, Inc., 720 E. Sunkist St., Ontario, Calif.

For Apricots, Nectarines,* Peaches, Pears*

Using Straight Fruit

Ingredients		
Water	(approx 2½ gal.)	20 lb
Fruit		82 lb
150 Grade rapid set citrus pectin		5½-6¾ oz
Sugar		100 lb
Standard fruit acid solution		(adjust pH to 3.3) (approx 14½ fl oz)

Approx yield: 157 lb at 65% soluble solids

Using 5+1 Cold Pack Fruit

Ingredients		
Water	(approx 2½ gal.)	20 lb
150 Grade rapid set citrus pectin**		5½-6¾ oz
Fruit		99 lb
Sugar		83 lb
Standard fruit acid solution		(adjust pH to 3.3) (approx 14½ fl oz)

Approx yield: 157 lb at 65% soluble solids

Procedure.—Cook to 221°F at or near sea level, or 9°F above the boiling point of water at higher altitudes.

---

*Nectarines and pears are not included in the Federal Standards. Consequently, ingredients should be listed on the label.

**Caution: Do not add the 5+1 cold pack fruit until the pectin is dissolved in the water.

SOURCE: Sunkist Growers, Inc., 720 E. Sunkist St., Ontario, Calif.

For Blackberries, Strawberries, Grapes, Pineapples, Raspberries

Using Straight Fruit

Ingredients		
Water	(approx 2½ gal.)	20 lb
Fruit		82 lb
150 Grade rapid set citrus pectin		4-5½ oz
Sugar		100 lb
Standard fruit acid solution		(adjust pH to 3.3) (approx 13 fl oz)

Approx yield: 150 lb at 68% soluble solids

Procedure.—Cook to 223°F at or near sea level, or 11°F above boiling point of water at higher altitudes.

SOURCE: Sunkist Growers, Inc., 720 E. Sunkist St., Ontario, Calif.

For Cherry Jam or Preserve

Using Straight Fruit

Ingredients		
Water	(approx 2½ gal.)	20 lb
Fruit		82
150 Grade rapid set citrus pectin		8-10 oz
Sugar		100 lb
Standard fruit acid solution		(adjust pH to 3.3) (approx 11 fl oz)

Approx yield: 150 lb at 68% soluble solids

Using 5+1 Cold Pack Fruit

Ingredients		
Water	(approx 2½ gal.)	20 lb
150 Grade rapid set citrus pectin*		8-10 oz
Fruit		99 lb
Sugar		83 lb
Standard fruit acid solution		(adjust pH to 3.3) (approx 11 fl oz)

Approx yield: 150 lb at 68% soluble solids

Procedure.—Cook to 224°F at or near sea level, or 12°F above the boiling point of water at higher altitudes.

---

*Caution: Do not add the 5+1 cold pack fruit until the pectin is dissolved in the water.

SOURCE: Sunkist Growers, Inc., 720 E. Sunkist St., Ontario, Calif.

For Loganberries

Using Straight Fruit

Ingredients		
Water	(approx 2½ gal.)	20 lb
Fruit		82
150 Grade rapid set citrus pectin		2¾-4 oz
Sugar		100 lb
Standard fruit acid solution		(adjust pH to 3.3) (approx 5½ fl oz)

Approx yield: 150 lb at 68% soluble solids

Procedure.—Cook to 223°F at or near sea level, or 11°F above the boiling point of water at higher altitudes.

SOURCE: Sunkist Growers, Inc., 720 E. Sunkist St., Ontario, Calif.

For Plums (Except Damsons)

Using Straight Fruit

Ingredients		
Water	(approx 2½ gal.)	20 lb
Fruit		82
150 Grade rapid set citrus pectin		4-5½ oz
Sugar		100 lb
Standard fruit acid solution		(adjust pH to 3.3) (approx 11 fl oz)

Approx yield: 157 lb at 65% soluble solids

Procedure.—Cook to 221°F at or near sea level, or 9°F above the boiling point of water at higher altitudes.

SOURCE: Sunkist Growers, Inc., 720 E. Sunkist St., Ontario, Calif.

PRESERVED CITRON

Ingredients	Lb
Water	1 cup
Citron	4 lb
Sugar	4 lb
Lemon, thinly sliced	1
Ginger root, broken	1 tsp

Procedure

Peel and cut citron into strips, the full length of the fruit. Combine sugar and water in pan, heat to boiling, and boil gently for 20 min. Add citron and continue to boil for 1 hr, or until the fruit is tender. Do not stir while boiling. Add lemon and ginger root and boil for only 1 min. Remove immediately from heat. Pour into sterilized containers and seal.

SOURCE: *The Atlanta Journal*, Atlanta, Georgia.

FIG JAMS OR PRESERVES

Fancy 50-50 Formula Using Straight Fruit

Ingredients		
Water	(about 2½ gal.)	20 lb
Fruit (see note below)		100 lb
Rapid set citrus pectin (150 grade)		6¾-8 oz
Sugar		100 lb
Standard fruit acid solution		19 fl oz

Approx yield: 154 lb at 68% soluble solids

Cooking Temperature.—Cook to 221°F at or near sea level, or 9°F above boiling point of water at higher altitudes.

NOTE.—If only dried figs are available, it will be necessary to cook the ground figs to thoroughly soften them (see footnote* below).

Standard 45-55 Formula Using Straight Fruit

Ingredients		
Water	(about 2½ gal.)	20 lb
Fruit (see note below)		82 lb
Rapid set citrus pectin (150 grade)		6¾-8 oz
Sugar		100 lb
Standard fruit acid solution		19 fl oz

Approx yield: 151 lb at 68% soluble solids

Cooking Temperature.—Cook to 221°F at or near sea level, or 9°F above boiling point of water at higher altitudes.

NOTE.—If only dried figs are available, it will be necessary to cook the ground figs to thoroughly soften them (see footnote* below).

35-65 Formula Using Straight Fruit

Ingredients		
Water	(about 3 gal.)	25 lb
Fruit (see note below)		54 lb
Rapid set citrus pectin (150 grade)		6¾-8 oz

Sugar	100 lb
Standard fruit acid solution	19 fl oz

Approx yield: 161 lb at 65% soluble solids

Cooking Temperature.—Cook to 221°F at or near sea level, or 9°F above boiling point of water at higher altitudes.

NOTE.—If only dried figs are available, it will be necessary to cook the ground figs to thoroughly soften them (see footnote** below).

Economical Formula Using Straight Fruit

Ingredients	
Water (about 3 gal.)	25 lb
Fruit (see note below)	45½ lb
Rapid set citrus pectin (150 grade)	9½-10¾ oz
Sugar	100 lb
Standard fruit acid solution	22 fl oz

Approx yield: 160 lb at 65% soluble solids

Cooking Temperature.—Cook to 220°F at or near sea level, or 8°F above the boiling point of water at higher altitudes.

NOTE.—If only dried figs are available, it will be necessary to cook the ground figs to thoroughly soften them (see footnote** below).

---

*If using dried figs in the standard 45-55 formula, for example, 20½ lb of dried figs should be ground and mixed with 61½ lb of water to take the place of the 82 lb of fruit. Cook to thoroughly soften. The addition of about 1 lb of ground lemons greatly improves the flavor of the standard 45-55 formula.

**If using dried figs in the economical formula, for example, 11½ lb of dried figs should be ground and mixed with 34 lb of water to take the place of the 45½ lb of fruit. Cook to thoroughly soften. The addition of about ¾ lb of ground lemons greatly improves the flavor of the economical formula.

SOURCE: Dried Fig Advisory Board, Fresno, Calif.

GLAZE, APRICOT

Ingredients	Lb	%
Apricot powder (Vacu-Dry)	1	6.67
Sugar (granulated)	8	53.33
Water	6	40.00
	15	100.00

Procedure

Blend dry ingredients. Combine dry ingredients with the water and bring to a boil. Simmer for 5 min.

To Use

Brush hot glaze on sweet goods while they are still warm after baking.

SOURCE: Vacu-Dry Company, 1311 63rd St., Emeryville, Calif.

BLUEBERRY CONSERVE

Ingredients	
Water	3 pt
Blueberries	3 qt
Sugar	2 lb
Lemon, thinly sliced	12
Raisins, yellow	6 cups
Walnuts, coarsely broken	6 cups
Cinnamon, ground	6 tsp

Yield: approx 2 gal.

Procedure

Combine water and blueberries. Cover and cook over low heat, crushing berries occasionally, until berries are tender. Measure berries, and for every cup add 1 cup of sugar. Add remaining ingredients. Cook while stirring until jam is thick and holds its shape. Pour into sterilized glasses, seal, and cool. Store in cool, dry place.

SOURCE: North American Blueberry Council, Marmora, New Jersey.

BLUEBERRY BUTTER

Ingredients	Lb	Gal.
Blueberries		2
Apples, green cooking, peeled, sliced		2
Sugar	8	
Allspice	1/16	
Mace	1/16	
Nutmeg	1/16	

Yield: approx 4 gal.

Procedure

Combine all ingredients in a large saucepan. Bring to a boil, lower heat and simmer for 1 hr, stirring occasionally. Cook until mixture is thick. Spoon hot mixture into sterilized glasses. Seal and cool. Store jars in a cool dry place.

SOURCE: North American Blueberry Council, Marmora, New Jersey.

CRANBERRY-ORANGE RELISH

Ingredients	Lb
Cranberries	4 (or 4 qt)
Sugar	2

Ingredients	Lb
Orange, chopped, without seed or membrane	2
Apple, peeled, cored, chopped	1

Procedure

Mix, chill, use immediately or pack into containers and freeze.

SOURCE: *Cranberry Products*, Bull. 481, University of Massachusetts Agricultural Experiment Station, Amherst, Mass.

GRAPE CONSERVE

These are similar to jams with chopped nuts (pecans, walnuts, or others) added for texture and flavor. Conserves are mixtures of two or more fruits with the chief ingredients in specific conserves being figs, peaches, pears, plums, oranges, and carrots. Conserves contain higher proportions of fruit than preserves or marmalades. While the formulas vary to suit individual tastes, the following formula for grape conserve is an example.

Ingredients	Lb
Grape pulp and hulls, ground	36
Sugar	12
Raisins, ground	6
Oranges, chopped	9
Pecan meats, chopped	3

Procedure

Boil the grape pulp and hulls about 15 min, or until tender. Add sugar, raisins, and finely chopped oranges. Cool slowly until moderately thick, add nuts, and boil for 5 min. Pack hot in sterile jars, seal, and cool quickly. Store in cool place.

SOURCE: *Commercial Fruit Processing* by Woodroof and Luh published by Avi Publishing Co., Westport, Conn.

HONEY JELLY CONTAINING 75% HONEY

Ingredients	Lb	Oz
Water (about 1 gal. or)	8	
150 Grade Exchange citrus pectin rapid set		2½
Honey (extracted or strained)	24	
Standard tartaric acid solution,* approx 1 fl oz or adjust pH to 3.3-3.6		

Procedure

Heat the honey slowly to 155°F in a jelly kettle or in a steam- or water-jacketed pan. In another kettle, heat the water to about 180°F (open-fire or steam-jacketed kettle may be used).

Remove a pint or so of the honey from the kettle into a sauce pan or small bucket and stir the dry pectin into it, making a smooth paste. When the pectin and honey have been well mixed, pour into the hot water and rinse the small pan or bucket with the pectin solution until all the honey-pectin mixture has been transferred to the water solution. Stir and heat until the pectin is completely dissolved and be sure there are no lumps remaining. (A baker's wire whip is recommended for stirring the batch.) Heat just to boiling.

Add the pectin solution at once to the honey, which should be at 155°F. The batch should then come to a temperature of 170°F or slightly above. Do not heat hotter, but be sure the temperature is at least 170°F.

After the containers are ready, stir the standard tartaric acid solution into the batch, avoiding the incorporation of an excessive amount of air. Keep the temperature of the batch at 170°F.

Immediately fill the batch into small containers of desired size. (Be sure the temperature of the batch is 170°F when poured into containers.) Cap at once while hot. Air cool promptly before labelling so honey jelly can set before being disturbed.

When the preserver wishes to package these jellies in large containers of 10 to 30 lb, it will be necessary to increase the amount of pectin by 20 to 30%. This is due to the fact that the jelly must be more rigid in the large containers in order to withstand commercial handling.

NOTE: It has been found that when honey or honey jellies are heated much above 170°F, as in the usual jelly-making procedure, the products develop a toughness, a darker color, and a rather strong flavor after a few weeks of storage. When 170°F is the maximum temperature attained, the materials are fluid enough for proper mixing to be accomplished with freedom from entrapped air bubbles, and at the same time proper sterilization may be effected.

From the standpoint of equipment, most anyone who is in a position to pack honey in glass would have the necessary equipment to produce honey jelly, and the process of producing honey jelly is quite simple. It is especially important, however, that the temperature suggested in the preceding directions and formula be observed closely to avoid adversely affecting the color and the flavor of the honey used. This is no place to use up buckwheat or other dark honeys for it takes good light-colored, mild-flavored honey to begin with to produce a mild-flavored attractive honey jelly for table use.

---

*Standard Tartaric Acid Solution: Dissolve ½ lb tartaric acid crystals or powder in 1 pt of hot water. One fluid ounce of this solution contains approximately 0.392 oz of tartaric acid.

SOURCE: Sunkist Growers, Inc., 720 E. Sunkist St., Ontario, Calif.

"INSTANT" JAM MIX FORMULAS

For Apricot "Instant" Jam

Ingredients	Gm per Package	(%)
Apricot powder	40	30.77
Apple pectin	2	1.54
Citric acid	3	2.31
Dextrose	85	65.38
	130	100.00

For Peach "Instant" Jam

Ingredients	Gm per Package	(%)
Peach powder	40	30.77
Apple pectin	2	1.54
Citric acid	3	2.31
Dextrose	85	65.38
	130	100.00

For Orange "Instant" Marmalade

Ingredients	Gm per Package	(%)
Whole orange granules	20.0	18.18
Apple pectin	2.6	2.36
Citric acid	3.0	2.73
Dextrose	84.4	76.73
	110.0	100.00

Procedure

Thoroughly mix together ingredients and package in moistureproof pouches or packages.

To Use

Mix contents of package with 1 cup (8 oz) of cold water in a saucepan. Heat slowly to a full rolling boil, stirring continuously. Slowly stir in 11½ oz (1½ cups) sugar and continue heating. Stir until completely dissolved. Reheat to a boil. Remove from heat and let stand 10 min or until slightly thickened. Stir the jam slightly and pour into glass jars.

SOURCE: J. G. Woodroof, Griffin, Georgia.

ORANGE MARMALADE

Ingredients	With Fresh Fruit	With Conc Juice
Water	25 lb (3 gal.)	30 lb (3½ gal.)
Oranges	50 lb	
Orange peel		21 lb
Concentrated orange juice		5.5 lb (½ gal.)
Cold-pressed orange oil		1 oz
150 Grade citrus pectin, rapid set	8 oz	8 oz
Sugar	100 lb	100 lb
Acidulant (50% solution of malic or citric acid)	14 fl oz	14 fl oz

Approx yield: 152 lb at 68% soluble solids

Procedure Using Fresh Fruit

Thoroughly wash the oranges and remove the stem "buttons." Fruits are then cut into halves and the juice removed by any available type of reamer. The juice is then strained through several thicknesses of cheese cloth or other suitable material to remove the pulp and is set aside until needed. If a brilliantly clear marmalade is desired, the orange juice should be filtered.

The orange peels are sliced into very thin, long pieces. These thin slices are placed in a kettle, covered with 3 gal. of water and heated to boiling. Cook the peel to soften it completely. The water which evaporates should be replaced several times during the cooking of the peel. After the peel has been softened, strain off and discard the water in which it was cooked. Add the same quantity of fresh water to the softened peel as was removed, also add the juices originally extracted from the fruit, place all in a kettle, and heat to 180°F.

Thoroughly mix the pectin with 8 lb of granulated sugar and add the pectin-sugar mixture to the cooked pulp and juice as they are being stirred. While the stirring is continued, the batch is raised to boiling and boiled vigorously for about 1 min. Then the remainder of the sugar (92 lb) is added and the batch cooked to 222°F at sea level or 10°F above the boiling point of water at your factory. The steam is then turned off and the batch is allowed to stand for a few minutes to permit the steam bubbles to come to the surface.

Just before placing into containers, add 14 fl oz standard citric acid solution to the marmalade, stirring well to obtain thorough mixing with the batch. The marmalade should then be packed into containers as quickly and as hot as possible, preferably above 190°F. If the marmalade is not packed hot, it will be necessary to sterilize the filled and capped containers.

SOURCE: Sunkist Growers, Inc., 720 E. Sunkist St., Ontario, Calif.

PASSION FRUIT JELLY

Because of the low pH of passion fruit juice, the use of the normal fruit to sugar ratio of 45 to 55 results in a product which is extremely prone to syneresis, resulting from the high inversion of sucrose during the boiling process. Most manufacturers, therefore, market their product under some alternative name, such as "Passion Fruit Supreme." A typical formula for this product is:

Passion fruit juice	40 lb
Sugar	60 lb
Pectin (150 grade, slow set)	6 oz

Procedure

The extracted juice is heated to boiling in a steam-jacketed kettle and the pectin, dispersed in 5 times its weight of sugar, is then added. After allowing 2 min for dispersion of the pectin, the balance of the sugar is added in 3 increments, allowing a short boil between each addition. Boil to 222°F and fill into containers. Cap, invert for 2 minutes to sterilize the closure, and then cool as rapidly as practicable. Due to the prolonged heating in the manufacture of jelly, some darkening and flavor loss are inevitable.

SOURCE: Hawaii Agricultural Experiment Station, University of Hawaii, Honolulu, Hawaii.

PINEAPPLE-PASSION FRUIT JELLY

The blending of passion fruit with other juices for jelly manufacture is a logical step to overcome the problems of high acidity and heat-sensitivity. The following process gives a significant improvement in flavor and color.

Ingredients	Gal.	Lb	Oz	Gm
Pineapple juice, or reconstituted concentrate		30		
Passion fruit juice		15		
Sugar		55		
Water	1			
Pectin (150 grade, slow set)			6	
Citric acid			1½	
Antifoam emulsion				4

Procedure

Bring the water to a boil and agitate vigorously with a mechanical stirrer. Add the pectin, dispersed in 5 times its weight of sugar. Allow to stand for air bubbles to clear. Add the pineapple juice, antifoam, and 15 lb of sugar to a steam-jacketed kettle and bring to a boil. Add the balance of the sugar and boil to about 224°F; add the pectin solution and boil to 226°F. Cool to 218°F, when trapped air bubbles will disappear. Then carefully add passion fruit juice and citric acid. The batch will be cooled by this juice addition to about 190°F, which results in minimum heat effect on the sensitive passion fruit ingredient. Care must be exercised to prevent incorporation of air bubbles. Fill into containers, seal, invert for 2 min, and then cool as rapidly as possible.

This basic method of processing can also be applied to passion fruit jelly, but shows its best results when used in blends where the passion fruit juice can be used as the final addition ingredient.

SOURCE: Hawaii Agricultural Experiment Station, University of Hawaii, Honolulu, Hawaii.

FRESH PEACH PRESERVES

Ingredients	
Peaches, sliced	9 lb
Sugar	11 lb
Pectin	0.85 oz
Citric acid	0.89 oz

Procedure

Mix the pectin with about ½ lb of dry sugar. Add the remainder of the sugar and 1 pt of water to the peaches in a steam-jacketed kettle; heat slowly until the sugar is dissolved, then cook rapidly to 220°F. Dip out enough syrup to dissolve the pectin-sugar mix, then remix; add the citric acid dissolved in about 1 cup of water. Continue boiling to 222°F (65% soluble solids).

SOURCE: Georgia Experiment Station, Dept. of Food Science, Experiment, Georgia.

CANNED PEACH PRESERVES

Ingredients	
Canned peaches, packed with sugar without water	11¼ lb
Sugar	8¾ lb
Pectin	23 gm
Citric acid	24 gm

Procedure

Mix the pectin with about ½ lb of dry sugar. Add the remainder of the sugar and 1 pt of water to the peaches in a steam-jacketed kettle; heat slowly until the sugar is dissolved, then cook rapidly to 220°F. Dip out enough syrup to dissolve the pectin-sugar mix, then remix; add the citric acid dissolved in about 1 cup of water. Continue boiling to 222°F (65% soluble solids).

SOURCE: Georgia Experiment Station, Dept. of Food Science, Experiment, Georgia.

FROZEN PEACH PRESERVES

Ingredients

Peaches, freshly thawed, packed with 20% sugar	11¼ lb
Sugar	8¾ lb
Pectin	23 gm
Citric acid	24 gm

Procedure

Mix the pectin with about ½ lb of dry sugar. Add the remainder of the sugar and 1 pt of water to the peaches in a steam-jacketed kettle; heat slowly until the sugar is dissolved, then cook rapidly to 220°F. Dip out enough syrup to dissolve the pectin-sugar mix, then remix; add the citric acid dissolved in about 1 cup of water. Continue boiling to 222°F (65% soluble solids).

SOURCE: Dept. of Food Science, Georgia Experiment Station, Experiment, Georgia.

SULFITED PEACH PRESERVES

Ingredients

Sulfited peaches, 10% water added	10 lb
Sugar	1 lb
Pectin	23 gm
Citric acid	24 gm

Procedure

Boil off sulfur dioxide from the peaches by adding two volumes of water and boiling for 30 min, making further additions of water as necessary to keep the volume from falling below that of the original.

Then mix the pectin with about ½ lb of dry sugar. Add the remainder of the sugar and 1 pt of water to the peaches in a steam-jacketed kettle; heat slowly until the sugar is dissolved, then cook rapidly to 220°F. Dip out enough syrup to dissolve the pectin-sugar mix; then remix; add the citric acid dissolved in about 1 cup of water. Continue boiling to 222°F (65% soluble solids).

SOURCE: Georgia Experiment Station, Dept. of Food Science, Experiment, Georgia.

ZESTY PEAR RELISH

Ingredients

Pear halves, canned	7¼ lb
Sugar	4 tbsp
Salt	4 tsp
Mustard, dry	4 tsp
Cayenne pepper	1 tsp
Vinegar	1 cup
Salad oil	3 cups
Celery, chopped	1⅓ cup
Pickle relish	1⅓ cup
Pimientos, canned, chopped	4 tbsp

Yield: 32 servings

Procedure

Drain pears. Combine sugar, salt, mustard, cayenne, vinegar, and oil in jar and shake until blended. Pour over pears and marinate several hours. To serve, drain pears. Combine chopped celery, pickle relish, and pimiento. Spoon into centers of pears.

NOTE: Reserve and use marinade drained from canned pears for summer salads; e.g., toss sliced canned pears with crisp greens or thinly-sliced new cabbage.

SOURCE: Pacific Coast Canned Pear Service, Sixth Ave., North, Seattle, Washington.

STRAWBERRY JAM
(50 Parts Fruit—50 Parts Sugar)

Using Fresh Fruit

Ingredients

Water	2.5–3 gal.
Strawberries, capped, washed, and crushed	100 lb
Sugar	100 lb
Citrus pectin	8 oz

Using Frozen Fruit

Strawberries are frozen with added sugar: 2+1 (2 lb of strawberries with 1 lb of sugar); 3+1; or 4+1. In calculating the components of a batch, allowance must be made for the added sugar in the frozen pack. Other components are the same.

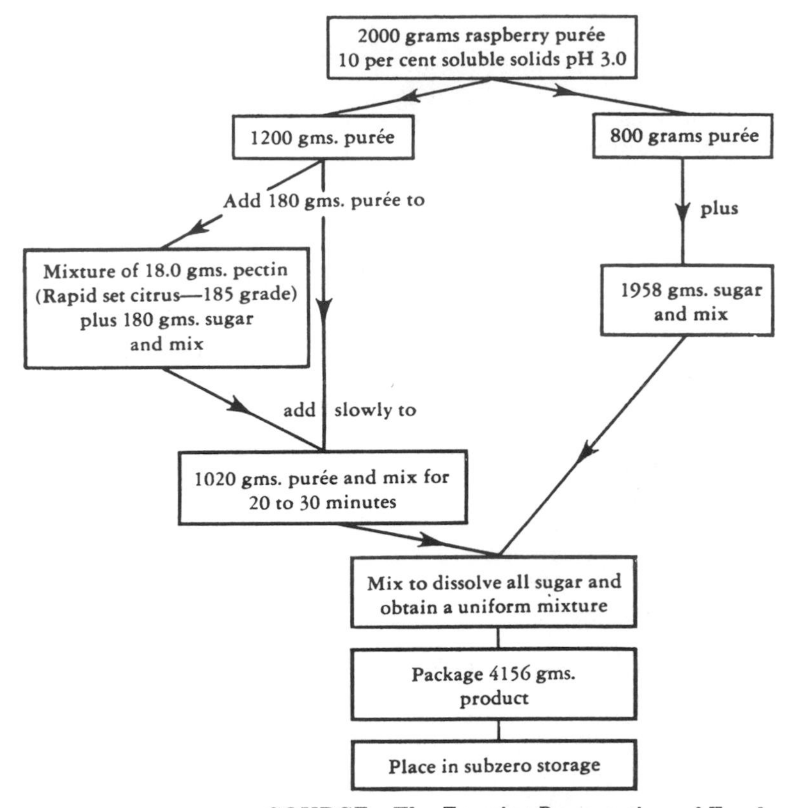

SOURCE: *The Freezing Preservation of Foods, 3rd Edition, Vol. 2, Avi Publishing Co., Westport, Conn.*

FIG. 6.1. PREPARATION OF RASPBERRY GELLED FRUIT

For the 2+1 Pack

Water	2.5–3 gal.
Frozen strawberries	150 lb
Sugar	50 lb
Citrus pectin	8 oz

For the 3+1 Pack

Water	2.5–3 gal.
Frozen strawberries	133.3 lb
Sugar	66.7 lb
Citrus pectin	8 oz

For the 4+1 Pack

Water	2.5–3 gal.
Frozen strawberries	125 lb
Sugar	75 lb
Citrus pectin	8 oz

Procedure

Heat the water to about 180°F in a steam-jacketed kettle. Mix a portion of the sugar with the pectin and add to the hot water; stir and continue heating until the pectin is dissolved. Add remaining sugar and fruit. Boil the batch until soluble solids content reaches 68%. At this point the boiling point will be about 221°F at sea level, or 9° above the boiling point of water at higher elevations. Pour the hot jam into clean hot glass jars and close immediately.

If the berries are not crushed, preserves are obtained. The same procedure is followed.

Fruits which are low in natural acid (e.g., sweet cherries and quinces) require citric or other fruit acid as otherwise the jam or preserve will not jell. A 50% solution of citric acid is usually added to low-acid fruits near the end of boiling.

SOURCE: Sunkist Growers, Inc., 720 E. Sunkist St., Ontario, Calif.

FIRMING WATERMELON RINDS FOR PICKLES OR PRESERVES

Rinds must be firmed after they are cut to the desired shape, in order to produce crispness in finished products. Otherwise, they become spongy and soggy, and sometimes leathery.

Firming is best accomplished by soaking rinds in a calcium salt solution. Most satisfactory results are obtained with solutions kept at 50°-70°F, especially for overnight firming.

Rinds treated 4 hr in a 0.4% calcium hydroxide solution (75°F) proved excellent and superior in texture to those treated for only 30 min; and they have better texture than those similarly treated at 110° and 145°F.

Covering rinds with firming solution and subjecting them to a 28-in. vacuum for 10 min proved unsatisfactory.

Satisfactory firming can be achieved by adding approximately 2 parts water and 1 part rinds (by weight) in a kettle, with either 0.1% calcium hydroxide solution for 15 hr, 0.2% calcium hydroxide for 4 hr, or 0.4% calcium hydroxide for 2 hr.

After firming, excess calcium hydroxide is removed from the rinds by washing and soaking. This can be accomplished by draining the calcium solution from the kettle and replacing it with fresh water 3 times at 15-min intervals. It is best to discard the calcium hydroxide solution each time.

If rinds are directly used, they must be parboiled immediately. If not, then a preservative can be added after freshening.

Parboiling is a continuation of the freshening process. It is necessary in order to produce the desired texture, color, and translucent appearance and to make the rinds "take the sugar" in the next operation. Parboiling can be carried out by boiling 3 successive changes of water at 15-min intervals. Rinds are now ready for processing into different products.

SOURCE: Dept. of Food Science, Georgia Experiment Station, Experiment, Georgia.

WATERMELON RIND PRESERVES

Prepare rinds by removing outside green peel and inside red portion, by hand or machine. Cut into cubes or domino-shaped pieces. Cover with solution of 0.2% calcium hydroxide for 4 hr, or 0.1% for overnight. Freshen in 3 changes of water for 45 min, and parboiling in 3 changes of water for 45 min. The prepared and firmed rinds may be held (a) under refrigeration for 1 week; (b) in 0.1% benzoate of soda at pH 2.5-3.9 for 24 months; or in 1500 ppm sulfur dioxide for 1 yr (see **Preserving Fruits with Sulfur Dioxide**).

Ingredients	
Prepared rinds	10 lb
Sugar	12 lb
Corn syrup	5 lb
Sliced lemons (or imitation lemon juice base 2 oz)	1 lb
Water	2 gal.

Procedure

Bring sugar and water to boil with stirring. Add watermelon rinds and lemons and boil until translucent and syrup reaches 222°F. Remove and pack immediately into sterile jars.

SOURCE: Dept. of Food Science, Georgia Experiment Station, Experiment, Georgia.

WATERMELON RIND CONSERVE

Prepare rinds as described above for Watermelon Rind Preserves.

Ingredients	
Prepared rinds, ground coarsely	10 lb
Whole oranges, ground coarsely	1 lb
Lemon juice	2 oz
Raisins, ground (white preferred)	1¼ lb
Pecan meats, finely chopped	1 lb
Sugar	10 lb
Water	2 qt

Approx yield: 26 10-oz jars

Procedure

Cook watermelon rinds, oranges, lemon juice and 1 qt of water in preserving kettle about 20 min, or until rinds are tender. Add sugar, raisins, and 1 qt of water; boil rapidly for an additional 30 min, or until mixture is thick and the temperature reaches 221°F with 65% soluble solids. Add nuts, mix well, and fill into hot jars; seal and cool rapidly.

SOURCE: Dept. of Food Science, Georgia Experiment Station, Experiment, Georgia.

IMITATION JAMS AND JELLIES

There are a large number of jams and jellies now produced that do not meet the FDA standards with respect to fruit (or juice)-sugar ratios or optional ingredients. These are sold as "imitation" jams or jellies. Many of them are now made with large amounts of corn syrup and imitation flavors. Since no standards have been set up for such products, any of the edible food acids may be used in their formulas provided it appears on the label under the title for an imitation product. Malic acid, fumaric acid, adipic acid, or succinic acid, when used in whole or part, offer some interesting flavor possibilities.

Formulations for some of the better-grade products based upon natural fruits and their juices, contributed by Sunkist Growers, Ontario, Calif., are given below.

All of the following four formulas must be labeled "IMITATION" on the label of the product and ingredients listed on the basis of the Federal Standards for fruit jams, jellies, and preserves since these products do not meet the FDA Standards with respect to fruit (or juice)-sugar ratio.

Apricot-Pineapple

Ingredients	
Water	25 lb (about 3 gal.)
Apricots	23 lb
Pineapple	23 lb
150 Grade Exchange citrus pectin, rapid set	9½-10¾ oz
Sugar	100 lb
Standard fruit acid solution	approx. 15 fl oz (adjust pH to 3.0-3.4)

Approx yield: 153 lb at 65% soluble solids

For Any of the Following Fruits

Apricots, nectarines, peaches, or pears:

Ingredients	
Water	25 lb (about 3 gal.)
Fruit	45 lb
150 Grade exchange citrus pectin, rapid set	9-11 oz
Sugar	100 lb
Standard fruit acid solution	approx 16½ fl oz (adjust pH to 3.0-3.4)

Approx yield: 153 lb at 65% soluble solids

For Any of the Following Using Straight Fruit

Blackberries, grapes, plums (except Damsons), pineapples, strawberries, raspberries:

Ingredients	
Water	25 lb (about 3 gal.)
Fruit	45 lb
150 Grade exchange citrus pectin, rapid set	9-11 oz
Sugar	100 lb
Standard fruit acid solution	approx 13 fl oz (adjust pH to 3.0-3.4)

Approx yield: 153 lb at 65% soluble solids

For Any of the Following Using Straight Fruit

Cranberries, currants, quinces, Damson plums, gooseberries, Loganberries, guavas:

Ingredients	
Water	25 lb (about 3 gal.)
Fruit	45 lb
150 Grade exchange citrus pectin, rapid set	8-9 oz
Sugar	100 lb
Standard fruit acid solution	approx 13 fl oz (adjust pH to 3.0-3.4)

Approx yield: 153 lb at 65% soluble solids

Procedure

Cook ingredients to 221°F at or near sea level, or 9°F above the boiling point of water at higher altitudes.

SOURCE: Sunkist Growers, Inc., 720 E. Sunkist St., Ontario, Calif.

REDUCED-SUGAR, IMITATION APRICOT PRESERVES USING HI-POLY CITRUS PECTIN

	500-Gm Batch	50-Lb Batch	100-Lb Batch
Apricots (frozen 5 + 1)	300	6.0 lb	60 lb
Hi-poly citrus pectin (No. 3475)	3.75	1.20 oz	12 oz
Sugar	83	1 lb 11 oz	16 lb 12 oz
Citric acid, anhydrous*	1.5	0.48 oz	4.8 oz
Sodium benzoate	0.35	0.10 oz	1.0 oz
Apricot flavor (WONF, #26887) (Fritzsche D & O)	2	0.55 fl oz	5.5 fl oz
FD&C Yellow No. 6	0.030	0.27 gm	2.7 gm
Calcium chloride, hydrate	0.034	0.31 gm	3.1 gm
Water (approx)	110	34 fl oz	2 gal 81 fl oz
Total	500 gm	50 lb	100 lb

Procedure

Dry mix the pectin with about five times its weight of sugar.

Add the pectin-sugar mixture, citric acid, and sodium benzoate to the water with good agitation and heat to boiling.

Add the remainder of the sugar and the food color and heat to boiling.

Add the apricots and heat to about 200°F for 3-4 min.

Prepare a calcium chloride solution by dissolving the calcium chloride into water at a rate of about ½ oz to 1 qt of water.

Heat the calcium chloride solution to boiling and add to the kettle with good agitation.

Add the flavor.

Fill product into containers at 170°F or higher and cool.

---

*This product is intended to have a pH of 3.4-3.5 and 32° Brix. The product will contain 50% fruit.

SOURCE: Sunkist Growers, Inc., 720 E. Sunkist St. Ontario, Calif.

REDUCED-SUGAR IMITATION GRAPE JELLY USING HI-POLY CITRUS PECTIN

Ingredients	500-Gm Batch Gm	10-Lb Batch	100-Lb Batch
Grape juice (16° Brix)	250	5.0 lb	50 lb
Citrus pectin, "Hi-Poly"	5.5	1.75 oz	1 lb 1.5 oz
Sugar	116	2 lb 5 oz	23 lb 6 oz
Citric acid, anhydrous*	1.2	0.38 oz	3.8 oz
Sodium benzoate	0.35	0.10 oz	1.0 oz
Grape flavor, Dosix WONF (Fritzsche D & O)	2.0	0.55 fl oz	5.5 fl oz
Calcium chloride, hydrate	0.15	1.3 gm	0.48 oz
Water (approx)	130	40 fl oz	3 gal. 16 fl oz

Procedure

Dry mix the pectin with about five times its weight of sugar.

Add the pectin-sugar mixture, citric acid, and sodium benzoate to the water with good agitation and heat to boiling.

Add the grape juice and the remainder of the sugar and heat to near boiling.

Prepare a calcium chloride solution by dissolving the calcium chloride into water at a rate of about ½ oz to 1 qt of water.

Heat the calcium chloride solution to boiling and add to the kettle with good agitation.

Add the flavor.

Fill product into containers at 170°F or higher and cool.

---

*This product is intended to have a pH of 3.4-3.5 and a °Brix of 32. The addition of citric acid may not be required depending on the pH of the grape juice. The product will contain 50% fruit.

SOURCE: Sunkist Growers, Inc., 720 E. Sunkist St., Ontario, Calif.

REDUCED-SUGAR IMITATION GRAPE JELLY USING HI-POLY CITRUS PECTIN AND SLOW-SET CITRUS PECTIN

Ingredients	500-Gm Batch Gm	10-Lb Batch	100-Lb Batch
Grape juice (16° Brix)	250	5.0 lb	50 lb
"Hi-Poly" citrus pectin	4.0	1.30 oz	13 oz
Slow-set citrus pectin	1.5	0.45 oz	4.5 oz
Sugar	116	2 lb 5 oz	23 lb 6 oz
Citric acid, anhydrous*	1.2	0.38 oz	3.8 oz
Sodium benzoate	0.35	0.10 oz	1.0 oz
Grape flavor, Dosix WONF (Fritzsche D & O)	2.0	0.55 fl oz	5.5 fl oz
Calcium chloride, hydrate	0.11	0.035 oz	0.35 oz
Water (approx)	130	40 fl oz	3 gal. 6 fl oz

Procedure

Dry mix the pectin with about five times its weight of sugar.

Add the pectin-sugar mixture, citric acid, and sodium benzoate to the water with good agitation and heat to boiling.

Add the grape juice and the remainder of the sugar and heat to near boiling.

Prepare a calcium chloride solution by dissolving the calcium chloride into water at a rate of about ½ oz to 1 qt of water.

Heat the calcium chloride solution to boiling and add to the kettle with good agitation.

Add the flavor.

Fill product into containers at 170°F or higher and cool.

---

*This product is intended to have a pH of 3.4-3.5 and a °Brix of 32. The addition of citric acid may not be required depending on the pH of the grape juice. The product will contain 50% fruit.

SOURCE: Sunkist Growers, Inc., 720 E. Sunkist St., Ontario, Calif.

IMITATION FLAVORED JELLY

Ingredients	Spray-Dried Lemon (%)	Durkee Synthesized Essential Lemon Oil (%)	Durkee Synthesized Essential Lime (%)	Durkee Synthesized Essential Peppermint (%)	Spray-Dried Peppermint (%)	Spray-Dried Lime (%)
Sugar	40.75	40.80	40.80	40.80	40.80	40.74
Water	40.66	40.81	40.81	40.86	40.76	40.66
Corn syrup	16.34	16.34	16.34	16.34	16.34	16.34
Citric acid	0.57	0.57	0.57	0.57	0.57	0.57
Sodium citrate	0.57	0.57	0.57	0.57	0.57	0.57
Agar-agar powder	0.81	0.81	0.81	0.81	0.81	0.81
Liquid flavors* (Durkee)	—	0.10	0.10	0.05	—	—
Spray-dried flavors* (Durkee)	0.30	—	—	—	0.15	0.31
Total	100.00	100.00	100.00	100.00	100.00	100.00

Add Durkee flavors after boiling the basic jelly mixture. Either liquid or spray dried flavor may be used at levels of 0.05–0.3%. Color should be added at 0.005–0.2%; consult your color supplier for details.

---

*Any of the Durkee Synthesized Citrus Oils may be used. Usage levels should be adjusted for each oil.

SOURCE: Durkee Industrial Food Service Group, 900 Union Commerce Bldg., Cleveland, Ohio.

REDUCED-SUGAR IMITATION ORANGE MARMALADE USING HI-POLY CITRUS PECTIN AND SLOW-SET CITRUS PECTIN

	500-Gm Batch (Gm)	10-Lb Batch	100-Lb Batch
Orange peel	76.0	1.0 lb 8.0 oz	15.0 lb
Concentrated orange juice, 65° Brix	20.0	6.5 oz	4.0 lb 1.0 oz
Hi-Poly citrus pectin	2.5	0.80 oz	8.0 oz
Slow-set citrus pectin	1.25	0.40 oz	4.0 oz
Sugar	140.0	2.0 lb 13.0 oz	28.0 lb
Citric acid, anhydrous*	1.63	0.50 oz	5.0 oz
Sodium benzoate	0.35	0.10 oz	1.0 oz
Cold-pressed orange oil	0.40	3.6 gm	1.3 oz
FD&C Yellow No. 6	0.011	0.10 gm	1.0 gm
Water (approx)	257.859	5.0 lb	48.0 lb 30.0 oz

NOTE: A calcium salt may or may not be required in this formula depending on available calcium provided by the orange peel.

Procedure

Dry mix the pectin with about five times its weight of sugar.

Add the pectin-sugar mixture, citric acid, and sodium benzoate to the water with good agitation and heat to boiling.

Add the remainder of the sugar, the orange peel, and the food color and heat to boiling and shut off steam.

Add the concentrated orange juice.

Add the orange oil.

Fill product into containers at 170°F or higher and cool.

*This product is intended to have a pH of 3.4–3.5 and a °Brix of 32. The product will contain 37% fruit.

SOURCE: Sunkist Growers, Inc., 720 E. Sunkist St., Ontario, Calif.

REDUCED-SUGAR IMITATION STRAWBERRY PRESERVES USING HI-POLY CITRUS PECTIN

	500-Gm Batch Gm	10-Lb Batch	100-Lb Batch
Strawberries (straight pack)	250.0	5.0 lb	50.0 lb
Citrus pectin, Hi-Poly	3.75	1.20 oz	12.0 oz
Sugar	135.0	2.0 lb 11.0 oz	27.0 lb
Citric acid, anhydrous*	1.63	0.5 oz	5.0 oz
Sodium benzoate	0.35	0.10 oz	1.0 oz
Strawberry flavor Dosix WONF, (Fritzsche D & O)	2.0	0.55 oz	5.5 oz
FD&C Red No. 2 (amaranth)**	0.023	0.20 gm	2.0 gm
FD&C Yellow No. 5 (tartrazine)	0.008	0.07 gm	0.7 gm
Calcium chloride, hydrate	0.07	0.63 gm	6.3 gm
Water (approx)	107.169	33.0 oz	20.5 lb

Procedure

Dry mix the pectin with about five times its weight of sugar.

Add the pectin-sugar mixture, citric acid, and sodium benzoate to the water with good agitation and heat to boiling.

Add the remainder of the sugar and the food color and heat to boiling.

Add the berries and heat to about 200°F for 3–4 min.

Prepare a calcium chloride solution by dissolving the calcium chloride into water at a rate of about ½ oz to 1 qt of water.

Heat the calcium chloride solution to boiling and add to the kettle with good agitation.

Add the flavor.

Fill product into containers at 170°F or higher and cool.

*This product is intended to have a pH of 3.4–3.5 and 32° Brix. The product will contain 50% fruit.

**This coloring has been de-listed. It is no longer on the FDA-approved list of food colors and cannot be used. Consult your food color supplier for recommended color substitutions.

SOURCE: Sunkist Growers, Inc., 720 E. Sunkist St., Ontario, Calif.

REDUCED SUGAR IMITATION STRAWBERRY PRESERVES USING HI-POLY CITRUS PECTIN AND SLOW-SET CITRUS PECTIN

	500-Gm Batch Gm	10-Lb Batch	100-Lb Batch
Strawberries (straight pack)	250.0	5.0 lb	50.0 lb
Citrus pectin, Hi-Poly	2.50	0.80 oz	8.0 oz
Citrus pectin, slow-set	1.25	0.40 oz	4.0 oz
Sugar	135.0	2.0 lb 11.0 oz	27.0 lb
Citric acid, anhydrous*	1.63	0.5 oz	5.0 oz
Sodium benzoate	0.35	0.10 oz	1.0 oz
Strawberry flavor Dosix WONF (Fritzsche D & O)	2.0	0.55 oz	5.5 oz
FD&C Red No. 2 (amaranth)**	0.023	0.20 gm	2.0 gm
FD&C Yellow No. 5 (tartrazine)	0.008	0.07 gm	0.7 gm
Calcium chloride, hydrate	0.046	0.41 oz	4.1 oz
Water (approx)	107.193	33.0 oz	20.5 lb

Procedure

Dry mix the pectin with about five times its weight of sugar.

Add the pectin-sugar mixture, citric acid, and sodium benzoate to the water with good agitation and heat to boiling.

Add the remainder of the sugar and the food color; heat to boiling.

Add the berries and heat to about 200°F for 3–4 min.

Prepare a calcium chloride solution by dissolving the calcium chloride into water at a rate of about ½ oz to 1 qt of water.

Heat the calcium chloride solution to boiling and add to the kettle with good agitation.

Add the flavor.

Fill product into containers at 170°F or higher and cool.

---

*This product is intended to have a pH of 3.4–3.5 and 32° Brix. The product will contain 50% fruit.

**This coloring has been de-listed. It is no longer on the FDA-approved list of food colors and cannot be used. Consult your food color supplier for recommended color substitutions.

SOURCE: Sunkist Growers, Inc., 720 E. Sunkist St., Ontario, Calif.

CANDIED AND GLACÉ FRUITS

CANDYING FRUITS

The initial steps in preparing candied fruit are the same as for canning the respective fruits. Variety and maturity are important, as well as freedom from defects and bruises. To avoid excessive softening and to preserve the fresh aroma and flavor, heating and freezing are avoided. Sulfur dioxide and other chemical preservatives are used instead. Cherries are pitted and brined. Brining with sulfur dioxide and firming with calcium are also followed with strawberries, raspberries, citron peel, and other berries. The same general procedure is followed with sliced apples, pears, pineapples, and other fruits to be held for more than a few days. Addition of calcium up to 0.04% of final product leads to 50% greater firmness.

While details for candying varies, the following procedure is followed with citrus peels. The fresh peels are thoroughly washed and checked for all defects. They are then diced and cured in polyethylene-lined barrels with sulfur dioxide. While this brining proceeds, the product is checked for constant temperature, even brine concentration, pH content, and cell structure.

Before use, the fruit is debrined by continuous washing until both sulfur dioxide and calcium are reduced to the desired level. It is then colored, the penetration of which depends upon the kind of fruit, acidity, and firmness. The fruit is then pumped into the glacéing vats for processing.

Sugar-Coated Candied Fruits

Ingredients	Lb
Fruit	20
Sugar	20
Water	10
Light corn syrup	2
Cinnamon, cloves, ginger, each	(trace)
Color	(as desired)

Boil all ingredients together except the fruit to 234°F or until syrup spins a thread when dropped from the paddle. Add fruit and simmer without crowding until transparent. Remove from syrup, drain, roll in granular sugar, allow to dry until pieces do not stick together, seal in moisture-proof containers, and store in cool place. It may be held for many months.

SOURCE: *Commercial Fruit Processing* by Woodroof and Luh published by Avi Publishing Co., Westport, Conn.

ALTERNATIVE METHODS FOR GLACÉING FRUITS

Slow Process

Glacé fruits may be prepared by equilibrating the fruit with syrups of concentrations ranging from 30° to 75° Brix. Usually, equal parts of sucrose and corn syrup are used. It is necessary to heat the fruit and syrup to 180°-190°F. After removing from the heat, the fruits are allowed to remain in the syrup bath for about 1½ to 2 days or longer. After removal from the syrup, they are again heated in a syrup of higher concentration, again allowed to stand for about 2 days. This heating, cooling, and standing is repeated until the sugar level of the fruit has been increased to 70° Brix or higher. Fruit is then removed and heated to drain excess syrup.

In preparation of whole fruit glacé specialities, preliminary boiling in water or a dipping in 2% sodium hydroxide may be carried out to hasten the subsequent syrup impregnation.

If straight sucrose is used with no invert sugar or glucose, the candied fruit will dry too much and be hard and granular. The glucose (preferably high-conversion—enzyme-converted—corn syrup) or invert sugar prevents over drying and improves the appearance of the finished product by making it more translucent.

Rapid Process

Impregnation of the fruit with the concentrated syrup can be greatly hastened by first cooking the fruit in 30° Brix syrup at 140°-150°F in stainless steel or glass-lined tanks. Then from time to time additional sucrose and corn syrup are added. When the syrup concentration reaches 68° Brix, the fruit is allowed to stand in the syrup for 24 hr. Then the syrup is drained, the fruit is rinsed with water, and dried before packaging.

SOURCE: D. K. Tressler and Associates, Westport, Conn.

METHODS FOR BRINING FRUITS

In the industry there are different methods of formulating calcium bisulfite brines as follows: (1) bubbling sulfur dioxide gas into a suspension of calcium hydroxide; (2) bubbling sulfur dioxide gas into a suspension of calcium carbonate; (3) dissolving calcium chloride and sodium bisulfite in water and adjusting pH with commercial hydrochloric acid. Listed below are formulations which have been widely used and can be expected to give satisfactory brined cherries and with fruit produced in the western States. Individual briners occasionally employ modifications of these formulations for certain lots of fruit. Commercial grades of the chemicals are not 100% pure; amounts used for making brine must be adjusted according to the composition given on the label.

Brine No. 1

Add commercial hydrated lime ($Ca(OH_2)$) to water at the rate of 6 lb per 100 gal. Stir well to form a suspension. Introduce sulfur dioxide gas into the lime slurry by means of a perforated tube or other submerged bubbling device. Dissolve 10.5 lb of sulfur dioxide. The brine will turn nearly clear when the proper amount of sulfur dioxide has been dissolved. The pH of this brine will be about 2.7 ± 0.2. Check the sulfur dioxide and calcium contents.

Brine No. 2

Add commercial whiting ($CaCO_3$) to water at the rate of 8 lb per 100 gal. Stir well to form a suspension. Introduce sulfur dioxide gas into the slurry of whiting by means of a perforated stainless-steel tube or other submerged bubbling device. Dissolve 10.5 lb sulfur dioxide per 100 gal. to give a solution containing about 1.25% of sulfur dioxide. During the addition of sulfur dioxide gas, considerable bubbling will usually take place due to the formation of carbonic acid and evolution of carbon dioxide. Loss of sulfur dioxide may be minimized by keeping a floating lid on the surface of the tank in which the brine is made. The brine will turn nearly clear when the proper amount of sulfur dioxide is dissolved. The pH of this brine will be 2.0 ± 0.2. Check the sulfur dioxide and calcium contents.

Brine No. 3

Add 14 lb of anhydrous sodium bisulfite ($NaHSO_3$) or 12.5 lb of anhydrous sodium metabisulfite ($Na_2S_2O_5$) to 100 gal. of water with stirring. Add 5 fl oz of commercial hydrochloric acid. Add 7 lb of commercial anhydrous calcium chloride and adjust the acidity to about pH 3.5 by adding more acid. This brine will contain about 1% sulfur dioxide and 0.85% calcium chloride (or 0.3% calcium ion). Check the sulfur dioxide and calcium levels. If the ingredients are mixed in a different order from that indicated here, the solution may become very cloudy and much insoluble material may be precipitated.

Sweet cherries become bleached and firm to the touch after several weeks in any one of the three bisulfite brines described above.

SOURCE: Western Utilization Research and Development Division, USDA, Albany, Calif.

CANDIED CITRON

Citron (a citrus tree fruit) are halved and placed in casks, which are filled with sea water. The casks are placed on their sides. The bung is removed and the citron allowed to ferment. After 10 days the casks are opened and the citron sorted, eliminating any spoiled fruit. With the addition of 15% salt brine containing 200 ppm sulfur dioxide, the citron is allowed to cure.

Candying is effected by removal of the central juice tissue and boiling the fruit in several changes of water to eliminate the salt and tenderize the citron. Candying is carried out by the "slow process" described above.

SOURCE: D. K. Tressler and Associates, Westport, Conn.

CANDIED CITRUS PEEL

The standard commercial procedure is to pack the orange or other citrus fruit peel in a 15% salt solution containing 2000 ppm sulfur dioxide. After a storage period, during which the peels become preserved by the salt, the peels are removed and boiled in several changes of water to remove salt and make the peel tender. The tender, refreshed peel is then candied by the slow process described above which involves cooking the peel in syrups of progressively increasing sugar content. Equal weight of invert syrup and cane sugar or of corn syrup and cane sugar are used in the proper amounts. The initial syrup is about 30° Brix, and the final is 75° Brix. The process requires about 10 days to get the peel to the desired 75° Brix sugar content. The fruit is stored in this final syrup for several weeks; then drained, wiped free of syrup with a wet cloth, and dipped in a saturated hot syrup. On drying, the fruit then requires a sugar coating.

SOURCE: D. K. Tressler and Associates, Westport, Conn.

CANDIED FRUIT

Ingredients	Lb
Fruit (apples, peaches, pears, cherries, berries, or plums) prepared (peeled, cored, graded, sliced)	10
Sugar	10
Light corn syrup, 42 DE	1
Flavor: ginger, clove, cinnamon (trace) (singly or in combination)	
Color: yellow, green, or red (as desired) (singly or in combination)	
Water	5

Procedure

Boil water, sugar, and corn syrup to 234°F or until the syrup spins a thread when dropped from the paddle. Add fruit and simmer with gentle stirring until transparent. Remove from syrup and drain. Roll in granular sugar and allow to dry until pieces no longer stick together. Seal in moisture-proof containers and store in cool place.

To prepare less tender fruit—cranberries, figs, pineapples, quinces—simmer first in clear water until tender, then transfer to boiling syrup and proceed as above.

A variation in flavor may be had by using honey instead of corn syrup.

Candied fruit is hand packed since there is no satisfactory automatic filling equipment.

SOURCE: J. G. Woodroof, Griffin, Georgia.

GLACÉ FRUIT

Candied fruit is usually coated with a thin transparent layer of heavy syrup that dries to a solid texture. Syrup for glacéing can be prepared by boiling 3 parts of sucrose, 1 of corn syrup and 2 of water to a boiling point of 236°-238°F. This is cooled to about 200°F; then the dried, candied fruit is dipped in this heavy syrup and dried a short time at 120°F; when cool glacé fruit thus coated should not be sticky.

SOURCE: D. K. Tressler and Associates, Westport, Conn.

FRUIT SYRUPS AND SAUCES

BOTTLED SYRUPS

Apple Syrup

Apples used for syrup must be sound, carefully sorted to eliminate rotten and wormy fruit, and then thoroughly washed to eliminate spray residues. Crushing and pressing are carried out as in the preparation of juice for bottling or canning (see Section 1). The juice should be treated with Pectinol to eliminate most of the pectin and then filtered. The juice should be concentrated in vacuo (28–29 in. vacuum) in a stainless steel vacuum to 60° Balling. This syrup should be bottled at 170°F.

Pear Syrup

Pear syrups can be prepared by the same method as described above for apple syrup. The flavor resembles that of baked pears.

Grape Syrup

Detartrated Concord grape juice may be similarly concentrated to 60°–65° Brix in vacuo. Grape essence should be added to the syrup if the syrup is used in making beverages.

Loganberry, Boysenberry, Currant, and Blackberry Syrups

Berry syrups may be prepared from berry juices (see Section 1) by treating the juices with a pectic enzyme (e.g., Pectinol) followed by filtration. Sufficient sugar should be added to give syrups 50° Brix. The syrups should be bottled at 170°F.

Sweet Potato Syrup

Oversized blemished, and mis-shaped sweet potatoes may be made into a palatable table syrup, as follows:

The sweet potatoes are carefully washed and trimmed; then boiled in three changes of water to eliminate soluble solids that otherwise would give the product off-color and undesirable flavor. The blanched sweet potatoes are steamed to gelatinize the starch and soften them for blanching. Water equivalent to twice the weight of the sweet potatoes is then added, and the potatoes are stirred, mashed, and mixed with the water. The mixture is then warmed to 140°F and about 1% of ground barley malt, free from sprouts, is added and mixed with the mashed sweet potatoes. The product is held at 140°F until all of the starch is hydrolyzed by the diastase of the malt. This takes 50–60 min. When the starch is all converted, a drop of the solution will not give a blue color with an iodine solution. The mash is then filtered in a hydraulic press (e.g., a cider press). The filtrate is boiled, then filtered. The filtrate is evaporated to obtain a syrup. It may be purified by a second filtration with charcoal which removes unwanted color and off-flavor. The yield of syrup is about ⅓ that of the sweet potatoes treated.

SOURCE: D. K. Tressler and Associates, Westport, Conn.

INVERT SYRUP

Invert syrup can be made from cane sugar by using 2 oz of citric or tartaric acid or ¼ oz of 36% hydrochloric acid per 100 lb of sugar. The sugar is made into a 70% syrup by adding 43 lb of water and is then maintained at 212°F for 30 to 60 min. The most feasible hydrogen ion concentration for maximum inversion and highest quality syrup is said to be in the neighborhood of 2.5.

SOURCE: F. E. Atkinson and C. C. Strachan, Dominion of Canada Agriculture Department, Ottawa, Canada.

BLUEBERRY SAUCE

Procedure

Simmer 4 qt of fresh or dry-pack frozen blueberries, 2 qt water, 6 cups corn syrup, and 1 cup lemon juice for 10–15 min. Remove from heat, add 1 cup butter, stir and let cool slightly. Stir in another 4 qt of blueberries and serve warm over French toast or hot cakes.

SOURCE: North American Blueberry Council, Marmora, New Jersey.

BLUEBERRY VELVET

Ingredients	
Blueberries	3 gal.
Water	1 qt
Sugar	4 lb
Lemon juice	½ cup
Salt	1 tsp
Gelatin, unflavored	½ cup
Water	2 cups

Yield: 4 gal.

Procedure

Combine blueberries and water. Cover and cook over low heat until berries are soft. Crush them as they are cooking. Press berries through a food sieve or mill. Add sugar, lemon juice, and salt. Soak gelatin in water 5 min. Add to hot purée. Cool. Pour into large container or bowl and freeze until half frozen. Remove from freezer and beat until fluffy. Fill small containers ¾th full with mixture. Cover tightly and freeze until firm. Store until needed.

SOURCE: North American Blueberry Council, Marmora, N.J.

CHERRY SYRUP

Cherry syrups of excellent color and good flavor may be prepared from hot-pressed Montmorency cherry juice. The method involves merely the sweetening of the juice, adding to each 100 lb of filtered juice 100 lb of 43° Baumé enzyme converted corn syrup (Sweetose) and 75 lb of granulated sugar. The product is approximately 63° Brix and is of a viscosity suitable for use on ice cream or in a soda. If a syrup of higher total solids content is desired, the proportion of sucrose should be increased. If the percentage of total solids in the syrup is under 67, a small amount of sodium benzoate should be added in order to avoid danger of spoilage.

SOURCE: *Fruit and Vegetable Juice Processing Technology, 2nd Edition* by Tressler and Joslyn published by Avi Publishing Co., Westport, Conn.

TEN-MINUTE CRANBERRY SAUCE

Ingredients	Lb
Sugar	4
Water	2
Cranberries	4 (4 qt)

Procedure

Add sugar to water and boil 5 min; add cranberries and boil an additional 5 min, without stirring. Pack hot into cans and allow to stand undisturbed.

SOURCE: *Cranberry Products*, Bull. *481*, University of Massachusetts Agricultural Experiment Station, Amherst, Mass.

CRANBERRY SYRUP

Cold-extracted cranberry juice is clarified with a pectolytic enzyme preparation and neutralized to pH 4.7 with potassium carbonate. Sugar is added, and the juice is concentrated in a vacuum pan to approximately 67% total solids content. The resulting syrup has a pleasing and characteristic color, flavor, and clarity.

SOURCE: *Cranberries*, Bull. *481*, Massachusetts Agriculture Experiment Station, Amherst, Mass.

MINT-FLAVORED FOUNTAIN SYRUP

Base syrup

Ingredients	%
Water	29.60
Corn syrup (Sweetose No. 4400)	19.00
High fructose corn syrup (Isosweet 100)	51.40
	100.00

Mint-Flavored Syrup

Ingredients	%
Base syrup	99.50
5% Green color solution	0.33
Mint flavor	0.17
	100.00

Procedure

Mix Sweetose and Isosweet in water to make base syrup. Add flavoring and color, to base syrup. Mix well.

SOURCE: A. E. Staley Mfg. Company, Decatur, Ill.

ORANGE ALMOND SAUCE

Ingredients	
Sugar	2 cups
Cornstarch	¼ cup
Orange juice (fresh or frozen)	1½ qt
Orange (halved and thinly sliced)	1
Angostura bitters	½ tsp
Roasted almonds, diced	3⅓ cups

Procedure

Combine sugar and cornstarch and add to orange juice in sauce pot. Bring to boil, stirring constantly and cook until thickened. Add sliced orange, bitters, and almonds. Simmer 10 min longer. Serve hot over meats such as ham steaks, etc.

SOURCE: California Almond Growers Exchange, Sacramento, Calif.

ORANGE-STRAWBERRY SAUCE

Ingredients	
Frozen strawberries, sliced	5 lb
Orange juice	3 lb
Cornstarch	12 tbls
Lemon extract	4 tsp
Salt	dash

Yield: 12 cups

Procedure

Drain strawberries; reserve syrup. Combine strawberry syrup, orange juice, salt, and cornstarch; blend. Cook over low heat, stirring constantly until thickened and clear. Add strawberries and lemon extract; mix well. Chill and serve as a sauce for cake or ice cream.

SOURCE: California Strawberry Advisory Board, Watsonville, Calif.

ORANGE SYRUP (BOTTLERS)

Ingredients

Sugar syrup. 65° Brix	105.47 fl oz
Processed water	16.19 fl oz
Benzoate solution (see below)	1.218 fl oz (36 ml)
FD&C Yellow No. 6	1.56 gm
Salt solution (see below)	0.1523 fl oz (4.5 ml)
Concentrated orange juice, 65° Brix	3.2 fl oz (90.2 ml)
Citric acid solution (see below)	1.46 fl oz (43.17 ml)
Orange emulsion (see Orange Emulsion formula in Section 3)	0.46 fl oz (13.6 ml)

Yield: 1 gal.

Procedure

Mix together all ingredients well.

To Use

Throw 5.35 fl oz of syrup per 29 oz.

Benzoate Solution

To make 1 gal. solution, which is to be filtered:

Sodium benzoate	2 lb
Processed water, heated to warm	qs

Salt Solution

To make 1 gal. solution, which is to be filtered:

Sodium chloride	2 lb
Processed water, heated to warm	qs

Citric Acid Solution

To make 1 gal. solution:

Acid citric, anhydrous	4.388 lb
Processed water, heated to warm	qs

SOURCE: *Food Flavorings, Composition, Manufacture, and Use, 2nd Edition* by Merory published by Avi Publishing Co., Westport, Conn.

PECTIN IN CRUSHED FRUITS OR FRUIT TOPPINGS FOR ICE CREAM SUNDAES

Ingredients

Fruit	40 lb
Sugar	34 lb
Corn syrup, 43° Baumé	20 lb
150 Grade No. 3430 Exchange citrus pectin	5 oz
Benzoate of soda, USP	1 oz
50% Citric acid solution	8 fl oz
Certified color (optional)	
Flavor (optional)	

Yield: 92 lb

Procedure

Place the fruit in a kettle and with constant stirring, heat until the fruit is warm (120°F). Thoroughly mix the pectin with 2 lb of granulated sugar. Add this pectin-sugar mixture to the warm fruit, stirring until it is all dissolved. Heat to

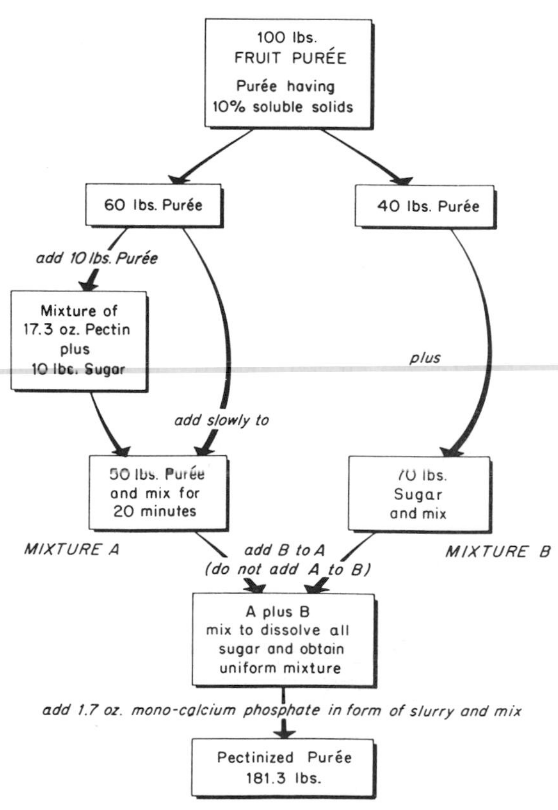

SOURCE: *The Freezing Preservation of Foods, 3rd Edition, Vol. 2, Avi Publishing Co., Westport, Conn.*

FIG. 6.2. PROCEDURE FOR PREPARING PECTINIZED PURÉE

200°F, then add the remaining sugar (32 lb) and stir gradually until completely dissolved; add corn syrup and the benzoate of soda which has been dissolved previously in a little water. Add certified color and flavor if used, then the acid solution. Fill hot (190°F) into jars, seal immediately, and store in a cool place.

Since this formula depends upon osmotic pressure to equalize the sugar solids within the fruit particles and in the syrup surrounding them, any separation may be eliminated after 24-48 hr by inverting or mildly shaking the jars to redistribute the fruit.

In some sections it is the practice to cook the batch in the above type formula sufficiently high to produce a distinct set, in which case the fountain operator cuts the jellied fruit with simple syrup to produce his fruit topping.

Fruits, especially strawberries, frequently are packed with sugar. 4 + 1 fruit means 4 parts fruit plus 1 part sugar; when used in the above formula, the total amount of 4 + 1 fruit would be 50 lb and the added sugar would only be 24 lb.

SOURCE: Sunkist Growers, Inc., 720 E. Sunkist St., Ontario, Calif.

STRAWBERRY FOUNTAIN SYRUP

Base Syrup

Ingredients	%
Water	29.60
Corn syrup (Sweetose No. 4400)	19.00
High fructose corn syrup (Isosweet 100)	51.40
	100.00

Strawberry-Flavored Syrup

Ingredients	%
Base syrup	99.28
Strawberry flavor	0.21
Certified color 5% FD&C No. 2*	0.16
Citric acid	0.35
	100.00

Procedure

Mix Sweetose and Isosweet in water to make base syrup. Add flavoring, color, and citric acid to base syrup. Mix well.

*This coloring has been de-listed. It is no longer on the FDA-approved list of food colors and cannot be used. Consult your food color supplier for recommended color substitution.

SOURCE: A. E. Staley Mfg. Company, Decatur, Illinois.

HOT STRAWBERRY SAUCE FOR ICE CREAM

Ingredients	
Fresh Strawberries	16 pt
Sugar	4 lb
Water	½ gal.
Cornstarch	16 tbls
Orange juice	1 cup

Yield: 3 qt

Procedure

Purée half of strawberries; cut remaining in halves. Combine sugar and 1 qt of water in saucepan and bring to boil; reduce heat and simmer 5 min. Stir in strawberries (halves and purée). In separate container, blend cornstarch and 1 qt of water. Stir into strawberry mixture in saucepan. Heat and stir until sauce boils ½ min. Cool slightly and stir in orange juice. Serve over ice cream.

SOURCE: California Strawberry Advisory Board, Watsonville, Calif.

VARIEGATED FRUIT SYRUPS

Ingredients	Weight Lb	%
Sherbelizer*	1.50	1.50
Sugar	35.00	35.00
Water	33.30	33.30
Fruit purée (4 purée : 1 sugar)	30.00	30.00
Citric acid, powdered	0.20	0.20
Color and flavor	as desired	
	100.00	100.00

Procedure

Dry mix Sherbelizer with three times its weight of sugar and add to water with good agitation. Continue agitation and heat to 190°F. Add and dissolve remaining sugar. Add purée and mix to uniform syrup. Add citric acid, and color and flavor (as desired). Mix 3-5 min and pack.

*Sherbelizer is an algin product for optimum body and smooth texture.

SOURCE: Kelso Company, Chicago, Illinois.

FRUIT BUTTERS
FRUIT SAUCES
SPICED AND PICKLED PRODUCTS

FRUIT BUTTERS

Fruit butters for which definitions and standards are prescribed by FDA cover apples, apricots, grapes, peaches, pears, plums, prunes, and quinces. Malic acid is one of the permitted acidulants and since it is a natural ingredient of all of these fruits, a smooth, fruity flavor is to be expected with its use.

Fruit butters are concentrated to 43% soluble solids.

For Apple, Apricot, Pear, Peach, Plum, and Prune Butters

First, the apples and pears are thoroughly washed to remove spray residue. The fruit is then passed over an inspection belt where any rotten, badly bruised, or wormy fruit is eliminated. The clean, sound fruit is put through a slicer or crusher; then it is cooked until soft in a steam-jacketed kettle with a small amount of water.

Peaches should be peeled and pitted before cooking. Apricots, prunes, and plums should be pitted before being thoroughly cooked.

The cooked fruit is pulped or puréed in a finisher of the type commonly used in making tomato catsup (with about ⅛-in openings).

Preparation Without Adding Sugar.—Apple juice (or apple syrup is often used instead of sugar; this produces a rather tart butter of high quality. One gallon of fresh juice is added per gallon of purée. The apple juice (cider) and purée are concentrated by rapid boiling to a thick consistency, then spices (cinnamon, cloves, and allspice) are added near the finishing point which is commonly determined by consistency. About 1½ oz of each of the 3 spices is commonly used per 100 lb of butter. Smaller amounts of ginger and nutmeg are also often used. The butter, when cold, should be thick enough to stand when a spoonful is placed on a plate. It should not flow; however, it should be thin enough to spread easily on bread.

Fruit Butters with Sugar.—Pear, peach, apricot, prune, and plum butters are usually made with sugar instead of juice. Brown sugar is often used instead of refined sugar because a finished product of dark color is desired.

As a rule, ½ lb of sugar is used per 1 lb of purée. The sweetened purée is concentrated and spiced as described above.

At the end of the concentration, lemon juice is often added to peach, apricot, and pear butters. Prune and plum butters are sufficiently tart without lemon juice.

Fruit butters require no sterilization if they are packed boiling hot (e.g., 221°F) and sealed at once.

SOURCE: D. K. Tressler and Associates, Westport, Conn.

APPLE BUTTER

Formulas for apple butter vary depending upon the ideas of the manufacturer, the variety of apples used, and the demand of the particular trade. Following is a basic formula which may be modified when made from fresh, frozen, or canned apples.

Ingredients	
Apple pulp	100 gal.
Cider, concentrated to ¼ volume	30 gal.
Ground cinnamon	8 oz
Ground cloves	4 oz
Ground allspice	4 oz
White or brown sugar	150 lb

Procedure

Add apple pulp, cider, and sugar and cook to about 45° Brix; run through a finisher to remove particles of peel, cores, or seed; add spices and mix thoroughly. Pack into cans at 190°F, with immediate sealing. No further heat treatment is necessary. If cans are filled at temperatures below

190°F, they should be heated in boiling water for 15 min.

SOURCE: J. G. Woodroof, Griffin, Georgia.

MUSCADINE GRAPE BUTTER

Muscadine grape butter is delicious with meats or with hot buttered rolls. It is similar to spiced grapes except it is less "chewy" and more lightly spiced.

Ingredients	
Grape pulp and ground hulls	5 lb
Sugar	2½ lb
Powdered cinnamon	2½ tsp
Powdered mace	2 tsp
Clove oil	2 drops

Yield: Approx 8 pt

Procedure

Wash and crush grapes. Separate hulls and pulp. Heat pulp with juice and put through a colander to remove seed, grind hulls in a food chopper using fine blade. Combine deseeded pulp, juice, and hull. Cook until hulls are tender. Add sugar and spices. Cook very slowly, stirring repeatedly until the mixture is very thick, with a jelly-like consistency. Pack in hot, sterile jars, and seal.

SOURCE: Dept. of Food Science, Georgia Experiment Station, Experiment, Georgia

APPLE BUTTERSCOTCH SAUCE

A rich and flavorful topping for rice pudding, cornstarch pudding, ice cream, cottage pudding, or cake a la mode.

Ingredients	Weight	Measure
Butter	1-½ lb	3 cups
Dark brown sugar, firmly packed	2 lb 10 oz	6 cups
Salt		1 tbsp
Canned apple slices	(1 No. 10 can)	3 qt
Cornstarch		4 tbsp
Cold water		1-½ cups

Yield: 50 (½-cup) portions; scant 4½ qt

Procedure

Combine butter, sugar, and salt in saucepan. Cook and stir over medium heat until sugar melts and sauce comes to a boil. Add apples and heat until sauce simmers. Combine cornstarch and water, blend well. Slowly add to hot sauce, stirring constantly. Simmer 1 min.

SOURCE: Processed Apple Institute, 666 Fifth Ave., New York, N.Y.

SPICY APPLE JUICE SAUCE

A tangy-sweet sauce to serve hot on apple pie, apple dumplings, bread pudding, rice pudding, cake a la mode, cottage pudding, or steamed pudding.

Ingredients	By Weight	By Measure
Sugar	12 oz	1½ cups
Cornstarch	4 oz	¾ cup
Nutmeg		1 tsp
Ground cinnamon		1 tsp
Ground cloves		½ tsp
Apple juice	6 lb	3 qt
Egg yolks		6

Yield: 48 (¼-cup) portions (3 qt)

Procedure

Combine sugar, cornstarch, nutmeg, cinnamon, and cloves. Add apple juice. Cook over medium heat, stirring constantly until sauce simmers for 1 min and thickens. Beat egg yolks; gradually add some of the hot sauce. Add egg mixture to remaining hot sauce. Cook, stirring constantly until slightly thickened, about 1 min. Chill and hold under refrigeration.

SOURCE: Processed Apples Institute, 666 Fifth Ave., New York, N.Y.

APPLESAUCE

Unsweetened

Ingredients	Lb	Oz	%
Apple powder (Vacu-dry)	1		16.67
Water	5		83.33
	6		100.00

Sweetened

Ingredients	Lb	Oz	%
Apple powder (Vacu-dry)	1		15.35
Granulated sugar		8	7.67
Salt		⅛	.12
Citric acid		⅛	.12
Water	5		76.74
	6	8¼	100.00

Procedure

Combine the dry ingredients. Gradually stir the dry ingredients into the water using a wire whip. Allow applesauce to rehydrate 5 min.

NOTE: For replacing canned applesauce with Vacu-dry apple powder in bakery formulas, just add the dry ingredients of either the unsweetened or sweetened applesauce formula to the bakery formula and use the water to complete the mix.

SOURCE: Vacu-Dry Company, 1311 63rd St., Emeryville, Calif.

APPLESAUCE BROWN BETTY

Ingredients	By Weight	By Measure
Soft bread cubes	4 lb	2 gal.
Butter or margarine, melted	4 lb	4 cups
Canned applesauce	(2 No. 10 cans)	6 qt
Dark brown sugar, firmly packed	1 lb 1 oz	3 cups
Lemons, grated rind and juice		4
Ground cinnamon		3 tbsp
Ground nutmeg		1 tbsp

Yield: 48 portions

Procedure

Mix bread cubes with butter in a skillet. Cook over low heat until crumbs are lightly browned, stirring constantly. Pour 2 qt of the cubes into each of two 20 × 12 × 2-in. baking pans. Spread evenly over bottom. Mix remaining ingredients; spoon 3½ qt of the apple mixture evenly over the cubes in each pan. Top each pan with 2 qt of the remaining cubes. Bake in a moderate 350°F oven 40 min or until top is deeply browned. Cool. To serve, spoon or scoop into dessert dishes. Or cut each pan into 24 squares. If desired, serve with cream, ice cream, lemon sauce, or hard sauce.

SOURCE: Processed Apples Institute, Inc., 666 Fifth Ave., New York, N.Y.

NOODLE AND APPLESAUCE BAKE

Ingredients	By Weight	By Measure
Broad noodles, cooked and drained	3 lb	12 cups
Butter or margarine, melted	¾ lb	1½ cups
Eggs, beaten		12
Canned applesauce	(1 No. 10 can)	3 qt
Salt		1 tbsp
Ground cloves		2 tsp
Light brown sugar, firmly packed		1½ cups
American cheese, grated	1-½ lb	6 cups
Bread crumbs		4 cups
Butter or margarine, melted	¼ lb	½ cup

Yield: 48 portions

Procedure

Combine hot noodles, 1½ cups melted butter and beaten eggs. Spread ½ of the noodle mixture into two greased 20 × 12 × 2-in. baking pans. Combine applesauce, salt, cloves, and brown sugar; blend well. Spread ½ of the applesauce mixture evenly over the noodles. Top with ½ of the grated cheese. Repeat layers, using remaining noodles and applesauce mixture. Combine remaining cheese with bread crumbs and ½ cup melted butter. Sprinkle over each pan. Bake in a moderate 350°F oven 45 min. To serve, cut into squares.

SOURCE: Processed Apples, Institute, Inc., 666 Fifth Ave., New York, N.Y.

FROZEN APPLESAUCE

The frozen product is superior in flavor to most of the canned applesauce on the market. If made from a given variety and maturity of apple, the canned sauce is somewhat lighter in color than the frozen product, owing to the bleaching of the sauce caused by the action of the malic acid of the apple on the tin of the can. This action also somewhat modifies the flavor of the canned product.

The process used by one important company in making and freezing applesauce is summarized as follows:

The apples are first cored by a battery of seedcellers. The cored apples are then elevated to a continuous steam peeler and then conveyed to a rotary spindle-type washer, where powerful jets of water knock off the loosened skins and force them through the bottom openings in the revolving cylinder to a waste conveyor below. The apples then pass over a long trimming and inspection table where adhering bits of skin, bruises, etc., are removed by women. The fruit is conveyed to a slicer, and then to a continuous cooker where the proper quantities of sugar and water are added. From the cooker the slices pass into a stainless steel pulper or puréer. The purée is pumped to a stainless steel tank, equipped with an agitator and heater. Then the purée is pumped through a Votator in which it is rapidly cooled. From the Votator the sauce passes to an automatic filler which fills measured amounts into cartons. The filled cartons are put in trays which, in turn, are placed on racks on pallets. The racks are moved into air-blast freezing tunnels. When frozen, the cartons are put into fiberboard shipping containers for storage or shipment.

SOURCE: *The Freezing Preservations of Foods, 4th Edition, Vol. 2* by Tressler, Van Arsdel, and Copley published by Avi Publishing Co., Westport, Conn.

FROZEN STRAINED APPLESAUCE

The procedures used in preparing applesauce for freezing have been described above. The same general methods are used in preparing strained applesauce for infant food, except for three additional steps: (1) Sugar equivalent to 10% of the total weight of apples and water is usually added to the cooked mixture just before the cooking is finished. (2) The sauce coming from the finisher is put through an homogenizer. (3) It is then pumped through a tubular sterilizer (small tube, high-velocity type) in which its temperature is raised to about 200°F and then through a tubular heat exchanger in which it is rapidly cooled to the filling temperature. If it is to be packed in tin cans, filling and closing temperatures preferably should be about 200°F, so that there will be a vacuum in the headspace when the sauce cools. If the product is put into cartons or composite cartons, the temperature should be much lower (e.g., 100°F); the exact temperature will depend upon the type of carton used and the methods used in cooling and freezing the product.

SOURCE: *The Freezing Preservation of Foods, 4th Edition, Vol. 2* by Tressler, Van Arsdel and Copley published by Avi publishing Co., Westport, Conn.

INSTANT APPLESAUCE FILLING

Ingredients	Lb	Oz	%
Apple powder (Regular Vacu-dry)	1		9.67
Sugar	4		38.67
Citric acid		½	0.30
Cinnamon		½	0.30
Instant starch		4½	2.72
Water (160°–180°F) for preparation	5		48.34
	10	5½	100.00

Procedure

Blend all dry ingredients thoroughly. Slowly pour blended ingredients into the hot water, stir continuously until the dry ingredients are well incorporated.

SOURCE: Vacu-Dry Company, 1311 63rd St., Emeryville, Calif.

INSTANT SPICY APPLE SPREAD

Ingredients	Lb	Oz	%
Apple nuggets or granules (Vacu-Dry)	1		9.68
Water (boiling)	5	8	53.24
Sugar	3	8	33.88
Salt		⅜	0.23
Cinnamon		¼	0.15
Cloves		⅛	0.08
Nutmeg		⅛	0.08
Mace		⅛	0.08
Citric acid		⅛	0.08
Malic acid		⅛	0.08
Instant starch		4	2.42
	10	5¼	100.00

Procedure

Combine apples with boiling* water and rehydrate for 5 min. Blend in combined sugar, starch, and spice mix. Mix thoroughly to disperse ingredients. Cool filling.

---

*NOTE: If boiling water is not available, increase the rehydration period by 5 min for each 10° below 212°F, but do not use water at less than 150°F for this formula.

SOURCE: Vacu-Dry Company, 1311 63rd St., Emeryville, Calif.

CANNED CRANBERRY SAUCE

Three kinds of sauce are packed: whole berries; chopped, sliced, or comminuted; and strained. A very large percentage of the total pack consists of the strained sauce.

Preparation

Cranberries are usually hauled from the fields to the packing houses or canneries in ½-barrel field boxes holding 50 lb. They are usually stored in these boxes before being cleaned. The berries are passed into the hopper of a separator where a blower removes chaff, leaves, and debris; they then fall on bounding boards to separate the good from the soft, decayed fruit. Good berries possess considerable resiliency and bound over the boards, while the soft, decayed berries remain to be discarded. A grading device grades the fruit for size.

Canning Strained Sauce

From the separator the cranberries are usually elevated to storage bins, and then flow by gravity into steam-jacketed cooking kettles. Hoppers just above the kettles are designed to hold a certain fixed weight of fruit; by releasing the door, the proper amount of fruit is delivered into each kettle.

The usual method of cooking is to boil approximately equal parts by weight of cranberries and water, until the skins are broken and the pulp thoroughly softened. The pulp is then passed through a cyclone-type pulper to remove the skins and seeds, and finally flows by gravity, or is pumped, into concentrating kettles where sugar is added in the proportion of 0.9-1.2 lb per pound of original fruit. More recently, because some packers have preferred liquid sugar to dry sugar, the liquid sugar is added to the pulp. An allowance for the water in the liquid sugar is made in the preparation of the pulp. Originally, the pulp and sugar were then boiled vigorously and concentrated to a finish point of 216°-218°F with a soluble solids content in the range of 39 to 41%. Now, however, the cranberry pulp (containing water) is mixed with the sugar in proper proportions so that the final sauce contains 38-40% soluble solids. The temperature in the steam-jacketed kettles is maintained below 200°F. Higher temperatures hydrolyze the pectin and decrease yields. After thorough heating and mixing, the sauce is dropped into the filler where it is filled hot into enamel-lined cans, sealed, and cooled. Cranberries require no additional heat-processing because the temperature for filling is sufficiently high. The high acidity (pH 2.5) and probably the content of benzoic and quinic acids prevent microbiological spoilage of cranberry sauce. The high vacuum in the canned sauce containers eliminates nearly all the oxygen of the headspace and thus aids further in preservation.

Cool storage temperatures are recommended because canned cranberry sauce deteriorates in storage, with a loss of its deep red color and fresh flavor.

SOURCE: *Cranberries*, Bull. *481*, Massachusetts Agricultural Experiment Station, Amherst, Mass.

FROZEN CRANBERRY SAUCE

Procedure

The first step in making the jellied cranberry sauce is to prepare a cranberry purée. This may be done either (1) by boiling cleaned and washed cranberries with an equal weight of water in a steam-jacketed kettle for 3 min, then partially cooling and puréeing in a tomato juice extractor or similar device; or (2) the berries may be steamed on stainless steel trays for 2 min, cooled to 125°F, puréed (waste about 15% of the weight of the fruit), and diluted with water in the proportion of 118 lb of water to 100 lb of purée. The second step is the addition of pectin. For each 100 lb of diluted purée, 0.42-0.58 lb of rapid-set 150 grade citrus pectin is mixed with 13 lb of granulated sugar. The sugar-pectin mixture is stirred into the purée; stirring is continued for 15 min in order to dissolve the pectin. Then 53.7 lb of sugar are added to the purée-pectin mixture, which is stirred until all of the sugar dissolves. After the sugar has dissolved, the liquid mix is packaged in liquid-tight, moisture-proof cartons, or fruit-enamel-lined cans which are closed and allowed to stand at 70°-80°F for approximately 24 hr. During this time, the gel structure forms and strengthens.

The product is then frozen and stored at 0°F or lower.

Yield from 100 lb of cranberries (85 lb purée), 100 lb water, 123.3 lb sugar, and 0.8 lb pectin is 309 lb of frozen jellied cranberry sauce. Jellied sauce prepared from the Howes, Early Black, and McFarlin berries do not differ significantly in gel strength or syneresis.

SOURCE: *The Freezing Preservation of Foods, 4th Edition, Vol. 4* by Tressler, Van Arsdel and Copley published by Avi Publishing Co., Westport, Conn.

FROZEN CRANBERRY-ORANGE RELISH

Frozen cranberry-orange relish freezes well, retaining its color, flavor, and texture almost perfectly.

The process of manufacture is relatively simple. Fresh washed cranberries are ground in a food chopper. The oranges are quartered, the seeds removed, and then the orange quarters (without peeling) are put through a food chopper. Then ground cranberries, ground oranges, and sugar are mixed together in equal proportions by weight. The product is packaged in liquid-tight, moisture-vapor-proof cartons or fruit-enamel-lined cans, and frozen at 0°F or lower.

SOURCE: *The Freezing Preservation of Foods, 4th Edition, Vol. 4* by Tressler, Van Arsdel and Copley published by Avi Publishing Co., Westport, Conn.

CALIFORNIA-VERMONT SAUCE

Ingredients	Lb	Oz
California dried figs (32 figs)		
Maple syrup	2	3
Water	2	

Yield: Serves 12 to 16

Procedure

With scissors, snip stems from figs. Cut figs into small bits and place in saucepan with syrup and water. Place over heat, bring to boil, lower to simmer and cook gently until figs are tender and sauce slightly thickened, about 15 min.

SOURCE: Fig Advisory Board, Fresno, Calif.

LEMON CUSTARD SAUCE

Ingredients	Lb	Oz
Egg yolks, 12		
Sugar		4
Salt		1/8
Scalded milk	2	
Lemon extract or flavoring		1/8

Yield: Serves 36

Procedure

Beat egg yolks slightly with fork; add sugar and salt. Add milk gradually, stirring constantly. Cook and stir in double boiler for 7 min over hot, but not boiling, water until mixture coats a spoon. Add flavoring and chill before using.

SOURCE: Dried Fig Advisory Board, Fresno, Calif.

ORANGE FIG SAUCE

Ingredients	Lb	Oz
California dried figs, coarsely chopped		8
Water		8
Orange marmalade	1	2
Chopped walnuts		6

Yield: 4 cups

Procedure

Rinse figs; cut up with scissors; add water, and simmer about 10 min, until figs are tender but not too soft. Add marmalade and heat just to boiling, stirring. Add nuts and serve.

SOURCE: Dried Fig Advisory Board, Fresno, Calif.

SPICED MUSCADINE GRAPES

The flavor of spiced grapes blends nicely with the flavor of white meat such as pork, turkey, and chicken, and this product is excellent when served in the same manner as cranberry sauce. For spiced grapes, rare-ripe or red fruit gives a more desirable product.

Ingredients	Lb	Oz
Deseeded grapes	5	
Sugar	4½	
Vinegar		8
Powdered cinnamon		1/12
Powdered mace		¼

Yield: 9-10 pt

Procedure

Boil deseeded grapes for 15 min or until hulls are tender. Add sugar and cook until thick. Add spices and vinegar and cook until the product gives a very light jell test (219°F). Pack hot in hot jars and seal. Yield nine to ten pints.

SOURCE: Dept. of Food Science, Georgia Experiment Station, Experiment, Georgia.

BRINED GREEN OLIVES

Green olives are harvested when fully sized, but before fully ripe. The fruit at this point contains a bitter alkaloid oleuropein, which must be controlled. The bitterness is removed by treating olives with a 2% sodium hydroxide solution at room temperature. The lye is permitted to penetrate nearly ⅔ through the fruit, but not completely to the pit. By stopping the alkaline penetration at this point, a small amount of bitterness remains in the flesh, and imparts a pleasing flavor. The lye-treated olives are then washed until lye-free. Care must be taken not to remove fermentable sugars. As grown in the United States, olives have a composition of about 70% moisture, 20% oil, 5% carbohydrates, 3% protein, and 2% ash.

After debittering, the fruits are packed into barrels and permitted to ferment slowly in a salt brine at 75°-80°F. The salt content is built to 25°-30° Salometer, as acid develops up to 1.5%. Fermentable sugar may be added. The pH of the treated olives should be 3.8 or less.

Olives may be pitted and stuffed with pimiento or other suitable material prior to being distributed. After stuffing, the olives may be given a further fermentation in a 30° brine prior to packaging.

The olives are packed in glass or in kegs and covered with fresh brine containing about 9% salt and about 1½% lactic acid. The brine should be about pH 3.8. They may be pasteurized at 140°F if they are to be stored long.

SOURCE: *The Technology of Food Preservation, 3rd Edition* by Desrosier published by Avi Publishing Co., Westport, Conn.

BOTTLED RIPE OLIVES

Ripe olive preservation includes a firming treatment in brine, treatment with lye, to promote oxidation of the color of ripe olives, a further lye treatment to debitter the fruit, washing to remove lye, curing in 8°-10° brine for upwards to a week, and preserving. The pH value of ripe olives is near 7.0 and requires heat sterilization in hermetically sealed containers for preservation.

SOURCE: *The Technology of Food Preservation, 3rd Edition* by Desrosier published by Avi Publishing Co., Westport, Conn.

PICKLED PEACHES

Procedure

Peaches are boiled in water until tender, then removed and the loose skins pulled off. The fruit is placed in a hot spiced syrup, having the following approximate composition: water 7 lb, sugar 14 lb, vinegar 3 lb, ginger root (broken) ½ oz, whole cloves ½ oz, stick cinnamon ½ oz. The peaches are heated to boiling in this syrup and allowed to stand overnight. Sufficient sugar is then added to bring the syrup to 60° Brix. The peaches are boiled in this syrup for 3-4 min, then are packed boiling hot into jars and covered with syrup. If the spices are tied in a bag they may be removed before the peaches are put into jars. If preferred, spice oils may be used instead of the spices.

SOURCE: D. K. Tressler and Associates, Westport, Conn.

SPICED PEARS

Spiced pears are a delicacy having characteristics of both preserved and pickled pears. They are popular for buffets, to be eaten with meats, vegetables, salads or alone.

Ingredients	Lb	Oz
Peeled whole or quartered pears	20	
Sugar	10	
Vinegar	4	
Stick cinnamon into broken 20 2-in. pieces		
Allspice, whole		¼
Ginger root	¼	
Lemons, sliced, 2		

Procedure

Peel pears in 2% boiling lye, rinse and dip in weak citric acid solution, trim and core. Mix together sugar, vinegar, lemon, and spices and bring to a simmer; add pears and bring to a boil. Boil slowly until fruit is tender and clear. Pack gently into sterile jars, cover with hot syrup that has been boiled down to half volume; seal and cool with water spray or water bath.

NOTE: A more crisp texture results if the cooked pears are allowed to cool overnight in the syrup, and reheated the following morning. The texture is further perfected if this procedure is repeated 2 or 3 times. The pears may also be colored red, green or yellow.

SOURCE: Georgia Cooperative Extension Service Bull. *602*.

PICKLE SPREAD OR BUTTER

This spread is an alternative to pickle relish and mustard. It is a smooth liquid-free product easily spread on bread or meats. It is adaptable to squeeze-type containers or aerosol containers. The process does not involve heating and so does not change the original flavor.

Procedure

For products involving free liquid, such as sweet mixed pickles, drain completely and chop to relish consistency. While grinding, slowly add the following: 1% by weight of rapid set cirtus pectin, ½ of 1% by weight of concentrated lemon juice.

Continue grinding to obtain desired consistency and to mix thoroughly the added ingredients. It may be necessary to add back a small amount of the previously drained juice in order to handle effectively. Additional mixing may be required following a Fitz Mill grinding to ensure good distribution of the pectin and lemon juice throughout the product. Fill into glass jars, or squeeze-type or aeorsol containers.

SOURCE: Sunkist Growers, Inc., Ontario, Calif.

PICKLES, SWEET FRUIT

Figs, grapes, peaches, pears, and watermelon rind make excellent sweet fruit pickles. Cook sliced or diced peaches, pears, figs, or watermelon rind in either water or dilute syrup until tender. Then boil fruit for about 10 min in a syrup containing 24 lb sugar, 2 gal. water, 1 gal. vinegar and 1½ oz each of whole cloves, stick cinnamon, and ginger. The syrup should then be drawn off and concentrated by boiling to a boiling point of 220°F. The syrup is returned to the fruit, heated to boiling and jars are filled while near the boiling point. No further processing is necessary.

SOURCE: D. K. Tressler and Associates, Westport, Conn.

SPECIALTY FRUIT ITEMS AND CONFECTIONS

ROLE OF GELATIN IN SPECIALTIES AND CONFECTIONS

The primary role of gelatin in the preparation is to form the gel. However, the pH of the preparation will determine how much gelatin has to be used to obtain the desired gel strength. Thus, the physical property of pH is also a primary factor of formulation. In turn, pH is a function of the amount and type of acid and buffering agent used and they also have to be considered.

Since the function of tartness is related to the amount of acid present, this value will be set by taste preference. Obviously in formulating a dessert or salad preparation for physical properties, these three primary variables of gel strength, pH, and acidity must first be selected. For this, the manufacturer should have a definite conception of consumers' desires and the effects of geographical location since these will govern what he can sell.

Amount of Gelatin

The amount of gelatin needed to produce a given gel strength varies with the type and quality of gelatin used. Nonetheless, the pH is the predominant factor governing the amount to be used. Certain anions, particularly those of the food acids that may be used in these preparations, also exert some influence on the gel strength; but this is relatively small. In fact, the amount of acid present usually is far in excess of the minimum necessary to obtain the maximum effect.

Tartness

Tartness is the property contributed by the type and amount of acid present. In gelled solutions, the amount of acid necessary to give an equivalent tartness is greater than that required in the liquid state. Laboratory analyses have indicated that the amount of acid (titratable acidity) is primarily indicative of tartness whereas the pH within fairly broad limits is relatively unimportant. The pH is read by means of a calomel-glass electrode potentiometer. The acidity is the amount of standard solution to reach neutrality as measured by a phenolphthalein end point (pH 7-9). Usually this is expressed as milliequivalents of acid per gram of powder.

pH Value

When sufficient acid is used to impart the proper tartness, the resulting pH is well below the optimum for gelatin usage. The pH can be raised by using a buffer which is the salt of a weak acid.

A pH of 3.5 is usually considered optimum in a gelatin dessert. This is obtained by the use of a buffer, either sodium citrate or disodium phosphate. In the formulas given below, sodium citrate is the buffer used with each of the acids commonly used in gelatin desserts.

Typical Gelatin Dessert Formulations

	I	II	III	IV	V	VI	VII	VIII	IX	X	XI	XII
Desired gel strength*	55	55	55	55	55	55	55	45	30	40	50	60
(Gm/100cc)	18	18	18	18	18	18	18	18	18	18	18	20
Titratable acidity (meq/100cc)	8.0	8.0	8.0	8.0	8.0	6.0	6.0	8.0	8.0	8.0	8.0	8.0
pH	3.0	3.5	3.5	3.5	4.0	3.5	4.0	3.5	3.5	3.5	3.5	3.5
Gelatin (Celero) (%)	10.5	9.7	9.7	9.7	9.3	9.7	9.3	8.7	7.2	8.3	9.3	9.1
Fumaric acid (%)	2.5	2.5	—	—	—	—	—	2.5	—	—	—	—
Citric acid (%) (anhydrous)	—	—	2.8	—	—	2.1	2.1	—	2.8	2.8	2.8	2.6
Malic acid (%)	—	—	—	2.9	—	—	—	—	—	—	—	—
Adipic acid (%)	—	—	—	—	3.2	—	—	—	—	—	—	—
Sodium citrate** (%) (buffer)	0.7	2.1	1.1	0.8	0.5	0.7	1.7	2.3	1.2	1.2	1.1	1.1

NOTE: Add color and flavor to suit. Add sugar to make 100%.

*The gel strength is obtained with 18 gm powder per 100 ml water except for the 60-gm test, which uses 20 gm.
**Disodium phosphate will require almost the same levels to maintain the pH, so it can be substituted for the sodium citrate pound for pound.

SOURCE: Swift Chemical Co., Winchester, Mass.

AMBROSIA FLUFF

Ingredients	By Weight Lb	Oz
Boiling water	1	8
Orange gelatin	1	2
Unsweetened frozen orange juice concentrate	1	8
Finely diced ripe bananas	4	5
Cold water	1	4
Nonfat dry milk	1	
Lemon juice		12
Sugar	1	8

Yield: 3 gal. (96 servings)

Procedure

Dissolve gelatin in boiling water. Combine orange juice and diced bananas and add to gelatin. Chill until slightly thickened. Whip until frothy. Sprinkle nonfat dry milk on water. Whip at high speed until soft peaks form. Add lemon juice and continue whipping until stiff. Add sugar slowly; whip until blended. Fold into whipped gelatin mixture. Chill. Full volume of yield depends on careful handling. For best results do not make over 3 gal. at a time.

SOURCE: American Dry Milk Institute, 130 N. Franklin St., Chicago, Illinois.

FROZEN SCALLOPED APPLES

Scalloped apples are prepared by covering the greased bottom of an aluminum foil container with bread crumbs to which melted butter has been added. Then the container is half filled with sliced apples which are sprinkled with sugar, nutmeg, lemon juice, and grated lemon rind. After this, the container is filled with sliced apples which are again sprinkled with sugar, nutmeg, lemon juice, and grated lemon peel. The sliced apples are covered with buttered bread crumbs. Bake for 40 min in a moderate oven. Cool before serving.

SOURCE: *The Freezing Preservation of Foods, 4th Edition, Vol. 2* by Tressler, Van Arsdel and Copley published by Avi Publishing Co., Westport, Conn.

FROZEN BAKED APPLES

Freezing preserves very well the flavor, color, and texture of baked apples.

Procedure

Apples are cored in the usual fashion, cutting out the core from the stem end, but leaving the blossom end undisturbed so as to prevent loss of syrup during the baking process. The skin is peeled off the top of the apple. To the core cavity of each apple is added approximately ½ oz of a granulated sugar-ground cinnamon mixture (approximately 99% sugar and 1% cinnamon).

The prepared apples are baked at 400°F until soft. After cooling, the apples are packed into quart-size plastic cups, three to a cup, placing two pieces of moisture-proof cellophane on top of each of the apples except the top one, which is covered with a single sheet of transparent film. The apples are frozen in an airblast at about −20°F and stored at 0°F.

SOURCE: *The Freezing Preservation of Foods, 4th Edition, Vol. 2* by Tressler, Van Arsdel and Copley published by Avi Publishing Co., Westport, Conn.

INSTANT APRICOT SPREAD

Ingredients	Lb	Oz	%
Apricot powder (Vacu-Dry)	1		9.50
Sugar (granulated)	4		38.01
Citric acid		¼	0.14
Instant starch		8	4.76
Salt		⅛	0.07
Water (160°-180°F)	5		47.52
	10	8⅜	100.00

Procedure

Blend all dry ingredients thoroughly. Slowly pour blended ingredients into the hot water, stir continuously until the dry ingredients are well incorporated.

SOURCE: Vacu-Dry Company, 1311 63rd St., Emeryville, Calif.

APRICOT NUGGET SPREAD
(For Sweetdough and Danish Pastries)

Ingredients	Lb	Oz	%
Apricot nuggets (Vacu-Dry)	1		11.41
Water	4		45.65
Sugar (granulated)	1		11.41
Glucose		8	5.70
Citric acid		¼	0.17
Modified starch (waxy maize)		4	2.85
Water		8	5.70
Sugar (granulated)	1	8	17.11
	8	12	100.00

Procedure

Combine apricot nuggets with water, granulated sugar (1 lb), glucose, and citric acid. Bring to a boil and simmer 5 min. Suspend the starch in 8 oz of water. Add to above and cook until the starch clears. Incorporate remaining sugar. Cool filling before using.

The above spread contains the equivalent of 68% fresh, pitted apricots.

SOURCE: Vacu-Dry Company, 1311 63rd St., Emeryville, Calif.

APRICOT BANANA FRUIT GELATIN

Ingredients	
Canned apricot halves	1 No. 2½ can
Fruit flavored gelatin	1-lb pkg
Boiling water	1 qt
Cold apricot juice and water	1¾ qt
Bananas	4 lb

Yield: 35 portions from a 12 × 20 in. steam table pan

Procedure

Drain apricots. Reserve juice for later use. Dissolve gelatin in boiling water. Add cold apricot juice. (Add water to apricot juice to total 1¾ qt.) Pour gelatin into steam table pan and chill until slightly thickened. Peel bananas and slice them into the slightly thickened gelatin; add apricots and stir to distribute fruit evenly. Chill until firm. Cut gelatin 5 × 7 to make 35 servings.

SOURCE: *Tested Recipes for Nursing Homes* published by Thedore R. Sills, Inc., 39 S. LaSalle St., Chicago, Illinois.

APRICOT WHIP

Ingredients	
Boiling water	2¼ cups
Orange gelatin	13½ oz
Apricot juice	3 cups
Almond flavoring	¼ tsp
Canned apricots, drained	4 lb 3 oz
Water	3 cups
Egg whites	1½ lb
Nonfat dry milk	15 oz
Lemon juice	½ cup
Sugar	1½ lb
Salt	1 tbsp

Yield: 3 gal. (96 No. 8 scoops)

Procedure

Mix gelatin with boiling water until it is completely dissolved. Add apricot juice to gelatin mixture; chill until slightly thickened. Chop fruit and nuts; add to thickened gelatin mixture and beat until frothy. Combine water and egg whites; sprinkle nonfat dry milk over surface and whip at high speed until soft peaks are formed; add lemon juice and continue beating until very stiff; then gradually add mixture of sugar and salt and continue beating until blended. Fold whipped nonfat dry milk mixture into apricot mixture, using French whip. Chill.

For best results do not make batches larger than 3 gal.

SOURCE: American Dry Milk Institute, 130 N. Franklin St., Chicago, Illinois.

FROZEN AVOCADO PASTE OR GUACAMOLE

Ingredients	Parts
Avocado purée	100
Lemon or lime juice	8-10*
Salt (sodium chloride)	1-2*
Dehydrated onion powder	0.3**

Procedure

Sound ripe fruit is thoroughly washed, preferably with a good detergent, and rinsed well with cold water so as to reduce microbial contamination to a minimum. The fruit is pared and all discolored spots, damaged portions, and the seed are removed. The fruit is then puréed by sieving or passing through a grinder. Sieving gives a product with a smoother texture, but many persons prefer the coarser texture produced from grinding. The avocado purée is then mixed with lemon or lime juice, salt, and onion powder.

After blending, the finished product is filled into a suitable container and frozen at 0° to −10°F.

When lime juice is employed instead of lemon juice, the amount added should be sufficient to bring the mixture to pH 4.5 for the preservation of green color.

---

*These values represent the permissible range for satisfactory retention of color for six months or more in the frozen state.

**Quantity may be varied according to taste, or the onion powder may be omitted if desired. Garlic powder may be used to vary the flavor of the product.

SOURCE: *The Freezing Preservation of Foods, 4th Edition, Vol. 4* by Tressler, Van Arsdel and Copley published by Avi Publishing Co., Westport, Conn.

BANANA PUDDING

Ingredients	Lb	Oz
Graham cracker crumbs	2	
Margarine or butter	2	
Sugar	2	
Whipped topping	4	
Bananas, mashed	10	
Lemon juice		4

Yield: 100 portions

Procedure

Blend graham cracker crumbs, melted butter, and sugar. Cover bottoms of baking pans with half of crumbs, press down and reserve other half to sprinkle over top.

Whip topping until stiff and add mashed bananas with lemon juice. Pour over crumbs in pans and cover with remaining graham cracker crumbs. Cut in squares and serve plain or with whipped topping rosette.

SOURCE: United Fruit Sales Corp., Prudential Center, Boston, Mass.

BANANA COTTAGE CHEESE SALAD

Ingredients	Lb	Oz
Cottage cheese	6	
Nonfat dry milk		4½
Lemon juice		8
Bananas, mashed	3	12
Plain gelatin		7
Sugar		10½
Boiling water	1	
Whipped topping		12

Yield: 100 portions

Procedure

Beat cottage cheese until curd is fine and smooth; then add dry milk powder, lemon juice, and mashed bananas. Combine gelatin and sugar, then add to boiling water and stir until dissolved. Pour slowly into cheese and banana mixture while beating. Pour into pans 2 in. deep. Chill.

To Serve

Serve in squares on lettuce, with orange section and cherry. For dessert, serve square in dessert dish with graham cracker crumbs over top. For pie, pour into graham cracker crusts.

SOURCE: United Fruit Sales Corp., Prudential Center, Boston, Mass.

BANANA LEMON PUDDING

Ingredients	Lb	Oz
Lemon gelatin	1	9
Boiling water	3	2
Cold water	3	2
Whipped topping	1	8
Sugar	1	
Nonfat dry milk		9⅓
Bananas, mashed	5	

Yield: 100 portions

Procedure

Add gelatin to boiling water and stir until dissolved, then add cold water. Chill until it is the consistency of unbeaten egg whites. Mix sugar and dry milk powder and add to whipped topping and then to mashed bananas. When gelatin mixture is set, whip until frothy, and add banana mixture toward end of beating.

Pour into pudding pans to set and keep refrigerated until time to serve. Put a spoonful of whipped topping on each portion and sprinkle with red sugar.

SOURCE: United Fruit Sales Corp., Prudential Center, Boston, Mass.

BANANA MARSHMALLOW RICE PUDDING

Ingredients	Lb	Oz
Rice, cooked, cold	3	2
Bananas, mashed	15	10
Sugar	1	
Lemon juice		6
Whipped topping	1	8
Vanilla		1
Miniature marshmallows	1	12
Maraschino cherries, chopped	1	

Yield: 100 portions

Procedure

Combine all ingredients and let stand in refrigerator 6 hr to blend flavors; then serve in dessert dishes garnished with half of maraschino cherry.

SOURCE: United Fruit Sales Corp., Prudential Center, Boston, Mass.

STRAWBERRY BANANA PARFAIT

Ingredients	Lb	Oz
Strawberry gelatin	1	9
Boiling water	5	
Sugar	1	5
Bananas, mashed	12	8
Whipped topping	2	8

Yield: 100 portions

Procedure

Add gelatin and sugar to water and dissolve. Cool until it is the consistency of unbeaten egg white, then add mashed bananas and whipped topping.

Serve in parfait glasses, leaving room at top for garnish of whipped topping and half of fresh strawberry. Alternate layers of strawberry-banana mixture and whipped topping make an attractive serving.

SOURCE: United Fruit Sales Corp., Prudential Center, Boston, Mass.

STRAWBERRY BANANA WHIP SALAD

Ingredients	Lbs	Oz
Strawberry gelatin	2	6½
Boiling water	6	
Whipped topping	3	4
Cottage cheese, large curd	6	
Bananas, mashed	15	10

Yield: 100 portions

Procedure

Add gelatin to water and stir until dissolved. Chill until it is the consistency of unbeaten egg whites then whip until frothy. Add whipped topping, cottage cheese, and mashed bananas.

Pour into pans so it will be 2 in. thick, chill and keep refrigerated until time to serve. Cut in squares and serve on lettuce leaves.

SOURCE: United Fruit Sales Corp., Prudential Center, Boston, Mass.

BANANA-RAISIN PUDDING

Ingredients	Lb	Oz
Bananas, mashed	3	12
Raisins	1	
Graham cracker crumbs	1	2
Sugar		12½
Nonfat dry milk		14
Water, cold	3	12
Salt		½
Vanilla		1
Whipped topping	1	6
Gelatin, plain		2

Yield: 100 portions

Procedure

Combine sugar, milk powder, 3 lb of the water, salt, vanilla, raisins, and half of the whipped topping. Add gelatin to 12 oz of water, place over hot water until dissolved, add slowly to mashed bananas while stirring. Combine all ingredients and fold in graham cracker crumbs. Serve in dessert dishes garnished with whipped topping and half of a maraschino cherry.

SOURCE: United Fruits Sales Corp., Prudential Center, Boston, Mass.

BANANA TOPPING

Ingredients	Lbs	Oz
Bananas, mashed	5	
Whipped topping	2	4
Vanilla		½

Yield: 100 portions

Procedure

Whip topping with wire whip on high speed until stiff as desired. Add mashed bananas and vanilla and beat to blend.

Refrigerate until ready to use. Spread on sheet cakes as topping or use on angel, sponge, or sunshine cakes.

SOURCE: United Fruit Sales Corp., Prudential Center, Boston, Mass.

BANANA WHIP

Ingredients	Lb	Oz
Gelatin, plain		2⅓
Sugar	1	5
Hot water	1	8
Orange juice		10
Bananas, mashed	1	14
Whipped topping	2	12
Maraschino cherries	1	

Yield: 100 portions

Procedure

Combine gelatin and sugar, and add to hot water; when dissolved add orange juice, mashed bananas, and whipped topping. Refrigerate until time to serve. Serve in ½-cup portions with maraschino cherry on top.

SOURCE: United Fruit Sales Corp., Prudential Center, Boston, Mass.

CHERRY CHIFFON

Ingredients	
Frozen red sour pitted cherries	1 lb 14 oz
Cherry juice and water	1½ qt
Cherry gelatin	¾ lb
Almond flavoring	1 tbsp
Water	3¾ cups
Nonfat dry milk	15 oz
Lemon juice	¾ cup
Cherry juice	¾ cup
Sugar	1 lb

Yield: 3 gal. (96 No. 8 scoops)

Procedure

Defrost cherries; drain and reserve juice. Chop cherries coarsely. Mix juice and water and bring to a boil; add gelatin; stir until dissolved; then add flavoring and chill until slightly thickened. Sprinkle nonfat dry milk on water; whip on high speed until soft peaks form; add lemon and cherry juice and continue beating until very stiff. Slowly add sugar, continuing to whip until well blended. Whip gelatin mixture until frothy; fold in drained cherries using French whip, then whipped nonfat dry milk mixture. Chill before serving. To obtain best results do not make more than 3 gal. at a time.

SOURCE: American Dry Milk Institute, 130 N. Franklin St., Chicago, Illinois.

MARASCHINO CHERRIES

Maraschino cherries are used in foods, chiefly for decorative purposes. They are prepared from sulfured cherries by leaching out the sulfur dioxide and then dyeing with a certified color.

Removal of Sulfur Dioxide

If the cherries are to be used in canned products, such as canned fruit salads, the sulfur dioxide must be reduced to below 20 ppm.

The stemmed and pitted cherries are soaked from 24 to 48 hr in running water to remove most of the sulfur dioxide. Fresh water is introduced at the bottom of the soaking tank, permitted to flow up through the cherries, and then discharged at the top of the tank. The fruit is then boiled in several changes of water until it is tender and the sulfur dioxide is below 20 ppm.

In preparing cherries for use in cocktails, they are drained from the bleach solution and then washed. They may or may not be stemmed and pitted, depending upon the type of pack desired. Remaining sulfur dioxide is removed by slowly boiling for 2 hr, or until tender. The water should be changed about 4 times during this boiling.

Dyeing and Syruping

Dissolve 5½ lb of sugar in 1 gal. of water. This will give about 1½ gal. of a 40° Brix syrup. To this syrup add 1.1 gm FD&C Red No. 2* and 0.3 gm FD&C Red No. 4, 14 gm of sodium benzoate, and 33.5 gm of citric acid.

If larger quantities are desired, add to every 100 gal. of 40° Brix syrup 2.55 av oz of FD&C Red No. 2 and 0.45 oz. of FD&C Red No. 4, 2 lb sodium benzoate, and 4¾ lb of citric acid.

Cover the fruit with this syrup mixture and bring to a boil. Set aside overnight. The next day add sufficient sugar to restore the Brix back to 40°. Bring to a boil and set aside for 24 hr.

Drain and replace with fresh 40° Brix syrup, to which has been added artificial maraschino flavor to suit.

Packing

Heat the cherries in the fresh syrup to 175°F and pack at this temperature into clean ½-pt jars. Seal and allow to cool in the air. The cherries in the jar should be completely covered with the hot syrup.

If sodium benzoate has been omitted, the sealed jars should be processed at 180°F for 30 min.

The presence of artificial flavor, artificial color, citric acid, and sodium benzoate (if present) must be declared on the label.

---

*This coloring has been de-listed. It is no longer on the FDA-approved list of food colors and cannot be used. Consult your food color supplier for recommended color substitution.

SOURCE: Bureau of Agricultural and Industrial Chemistry Publication *CA-14-12*.

COCONUT FIG CANDY

Ingredients	Lb	Oz
Corn syrup	12	
Cane or beet sugar	12	
Vegetable fat (confectioners)	2	11

	Lb	Oz
Coconut (for con-(fectioner's use)	10	8
Fig paste	17	7
Vanilla	to suit taste	
Water	12	12
Lecithin		½
Salt		2

Procedure

Cook corn syrup, water, sugar, vanilla, salt, and coconut slowly to a boiling point of 230°F (cook slowly so that the coconut will better absorb the sugar and flavoring).

Remove the mixture from the fire and add the fat and lecithin. Mix very thoroughly.

While the candy is still warm, mix in the fig paste. A considerable time may be required to mix in adequately. It should be broken up into small pieces before adding to the mix.

Spread on an oiled slab which has been sprinkled with corn starch, or rice powder. Form into bars by extrusion machine or spread on oiled slab to harden and then cut into bars, or pieces, of desired size. Coat with chocolate if to be sold as bars. The candy manufacturer can, of course, make modifications in this formula to better suit the conditions in his plant.

Chopped walnuts or almonds may be included, although the coconut takes the place of nuts to a considerable extent.

SOURCE: Dried Fig Advisory Board, Fresno, California.

SOFT COCONUT CANDY CENTERS

Ingredients	Lb	Oz
Sugar	8	
Water	3	
Corn syrup, 42 DE	24	
Invert syrup	16	
Coconut, unsweetened macaroon desiccated	28	
Salt		5
Flavors (optional): vanilla, orange, berry		

Yield: about 50 lb

Procedure

Heat sugar and water until dissolved; then add corn syrup, invert syrup, and salt; mix well and heat to 175°F. Cool in wax paper-lined trays, then place into rolled cream center machine to be formed into pieces of desired size and shape.

SOURCE: J. G. Woodroof, Griffin, Georgia.

CRANBERRY CRUNCH

Ingredients	
Rolled oats	1 lb
Flour	1 lb 8 oz
Nonfat dry milk	1 lb
Light brown sugar	4 lb 8 oz
Cinnamon	1 tbsp
Salt	2 tsp
Butter	2 lb
Cranberry sauce, jellied or whole	1⅓ No. 10 cans

Yield: 96 servings

Procedure

Use pastry blender attachment and mix all ingredients except cranberries at low speed until crumbly. Spread half of mixture in bottom of 4 buttered 12 × 20 × 2¼ in. pans. Spread 1 qt of the cranberries evenly in each crumb-lined pan and cover cranberries with remaining crumbs. Bake 45 min at 350°F. Cut in squares and serve warm with scoop of ice cream.

Variations

Apple Crisp.—Instead of cranberries, 15 lb of sliced, pared, tart apples may be used. Add ⅓ cup lemon juice and ½ tbsp nutmeg.

Apple Cheese Crisp.—To the Apple Crisp (above) add 3 lb of shredded cheese to crumb mixture and decrease butter to 1 lb 8 oz.

SOURCE: American Dry Milk Institute, 130 N. Franklin St., Chicago, Illinois.

DATE SLAB JELLIES

Ingredients	Lb	Oz
Water	58	
150 Grade rapid set citrus pectin	1½	
Dried pitted dates (ground)	30	
Glucose (43° Baumé)	30	
Granulated sugar	30	
Black walnut flavor		½
Tartaric acid (crystals or powdered)		5½
Caramel color	as desired	

Yield: about 107 lb

Procedure

Put water in the kettle and heat to 190°F. (Open fire or steam-jacketed kettle may be used.) Thoroughly mix pectin with about 12 lb of granulated sugar and add this pectin-sugar mixture to the hot water as it is being stirred vigorously with a paddle or baker's wire whip. Continue to stir and heat to boiling. Boil vigorously for a moment.

Add the pitted dates (ground), heat to boiling, then add the glucose. Heat to boiling again. Now add the remainder of the granulated sugar and cook as rapidly as possible to 222°F or 10°F above the boiling point of water at your factory. (This temperature corresponds to 75% soluble solids.)

Turn off the steam or remove from the fire, add the caramel color and black walnut flavor. Stir thoroughly. Finally add the tartaric acid dissolved in a small amount of hot water, stirring the batch thoroughly to obtain a uniform mixture. Pour on the slab as quickly as possible and allow to congeal. After the batch has "set," cut into desired shapes with a knife. The finished pieces may be sanded, crystallized, iced, or coated with chocolate.

SOURCE: Sunkist Growers, Inc., Products Sales Division, 720 E. Sunkist St., Ontario, Calif.

FIG AND GRAPEFRUIT CUP

Ingredients	25 Servings	50 Servings	100 Servings
California dried figs	1 lb	2 lb	4 lb
Orange juice	1 pt	1 qt	2 qt
Grapefruit sections	1 No. 2½ can	2 No. 2½ cans	1 No. 10 can
Mint leaves or maraschino cherries			

Procedure

Cover dried figs with hot water for 5 min. Drain and, with scissors, snip off the stems. Snip figs into thin slices and cover with sweetened orange juice.

Add an equal quantity of peeled grapefruit segments and chill mixture until almost frozen. Serve as a fruit cup for the first course of the dinner. Garnish with a sprig of mint dipped in powdered sugar or with a cherry.

SOURCE: Dried Fig Advisory Board, Fresno, Calif.

GLAZED FIGS, GOURMET

Ingredients	
California dried figs	48 figs (approx 2 lb)
Cold water	6 cups
Cider vinegar	½ cup
Whole cloves	2 tsp
California brandy (or water and brandy flavoring)	2 cups
White corn syrup	2 tbsp
Lightly browned almonds	48

Approx yield: 16 servings, 3 figs each

Procedure

Place figs and water in saucepan. Bring to hard boil, then lower heat to simmer. Cover and let cook 20 min. Add all ingredients except almonds. Stir gently in order not to break figs. Cover and simmer again for about 20 min or until figs are plump and transparent. Cool in syrup. Add a little water, if needed, but keep it rich. Just before serving, insert toasted almond in each fig. Delicious with roast turkey, baked chicken, beef, pork or ham.

SOURCE: Dried Fig Advisory Board, Fresno, Calif.

GINGERED FIGS

Ingredients	
California dried figs	45
Cold water	6 cups
Light molasses	2 tbsp
Powdered ginger	4 tsp
Sugar	1 cup

Yield: 15 servings of 3 figs each

Procedure

Place figs and water in saucepan. Bring to hard boil, then lower heat and simmer. Cover figs and cook for 20 min. Add molasses, ginger, and sugar. Stir gently in order to avoid breaking figs. Simmer for 15 min more or until figs are plumped and tender. Serve as an accompaniment with ham, pork, chicken, steak, or roast beef.

SOURCE: Dried Fig Advisory Board, Fresno, Calif.

FIG PUDDING

Ingredients	
Eggs, whole	12 oz (8 eggs)
Granulated sugar	1 lb 2 oz
Cake flour	1 lb 4 oz
Baking powder	2 tbsp
Salt	2 tsp
Powdered citric acid	½ tsp
Ginger	2 tsp
Mace	4 tsp
Cinnamon	2 tsp
Cardamom	2 tsp
Whole fresh milk	½ cup
Suet, finely chopped	1½ cups
Dried white figs, finely chopped	1¼ cups
Vanilla flavor	4 tsp

Yield: 4 14-oz puddings

Procedure

Beat eggs very lightly, add sugar and continue beating until thick and creamy. Sift flour, baking powder, salt, citric acid, and spices together 3 times, and fold ½ of mixture into egg-sugar mixture. Add milk and remainder of flour mixture and blend. Add suet, figs, and flavoring and beat. Pour into well-oiled molds, filling about ⅔ full; cover and steam over hot water. A 14-oz pudding will require about 2 hr steaming.

For a richer color, add ½ tsp caramel coloring (burnt sugar) to sugar and egg mixture in beater.

SOURCE: Dried Fig Advisory Board, Fresno, Calif.

BAKED BANANA FIG PUDDING

Ingredients	
Sugar	6⅔ cups
Flour	1¼ cup
Salt	⅝ tsp
Milk	7½ cups
Eggs, separated	15
Grated orange peel	1¼ tsp
Orange juice	⅔ cup
California dried figs, diced	3¾ cups
Oranges, pared and diced	5
Medium sized bananas, all yellow	15

Yield: 30 servings

Procedure

Mix 3⅓ cups sugar with flour and salt in saucepan; stir in milk. Cook over medium heat, stirring constantly until mixture boils 1 min. Beat some of hot mixture into yolks. Return to saucepan. Stir constantly and boil 1 min longer, or until thickened. Cool thoroughly. Stir in orange peel and juice, figs, and orange. Slice in bananas. Turn into quart baking dishes. Beat egg whites until soft peaks form; gradually add 3⅓ cups sugar, beating until stiff. Spread meringue over pudding to edges of dish. Bake at 400°F 4 min or until lightly brown. Serve warm or chilled.

SOURCE: Dried Fig Advisory Board, Fresno, Calif.

QUICK FIG WHIP

Ingredients	25 Servings	50 Servings	100 Servings
Gelatin, plain unflavored	2 tbsp	¼ cup	½ cup
Cold water	½ cup	1 cup	2 cups
Egg whites	12	24	48
Grated lemon rind	4 tsp	3 tbsp	⅓ cup
Lemon juice	½ cup	1 cup	2 cup
Salt	¼ tsp	½ tsp	1 tsp
Sugar	2 cups	1 qt	2 qt
California dried figs, cooked and chopped	2 cups	1 qt	2 qt

Procedure

Add gelatin to cold water and let stand to soften. Combine egg whites, lemon rind and juice, salt, and sugar in top of double boiler and beat with rotary beater until fluffy mixture will hold its shape when beater is lifted (about 5 min). Remove from heat.

Melt gelatin over hot water; fold into fluffy mixture and then fold in chopped figs. Heap in dessert glasses, garnish with figs and chill.

Serve with chilled custard sauce made of egg yolks, sugar, and scalded milk cooked in double boiler until custard coats metal spoon. Flavor with vanilla and serve cold.

SOURCE: Dried Fig Advisory Board, Fresno, Calif.

STEAMED WINE-FIG PUDDING

Ingredients	
Holland rusk or zweiback crumbs	6 cups
Baking soda	1 tbsp
Salt	1½ tsp
Cinnamon	1½ tsp
Nutmeg	1½ tsp
California dried figs	4½ cups
Mixed diced candied fruits (prepared glacé fruit mix is excellent)	3 cups

Butter or margarine	1½ cups
Sugar	3 cups
Eggs	6
California muscatel, white port or angelica wine	1½ cups
Milk	1½ cups

Yield: Approx 25 servings

Procedure

Cover figs with boiling water and let stand for 10 min. Drain. With scissors, snip off the stems and then snip the figs into small bits. Mix crumbs, soda, salt, and spices; stir in figs and candied fruits. Cream butter and sugar together until fluffy; add unbeaten eggs, one at a time; add dry ingredients alternately with wine and milk, heating well after each addition. Pour into 3 well-greased molds, filling not more than ⅔ full; cover tightly; steam 4 hr.

Serve with wine hard sauce.

SOURCE: Dried Fig Advisory Board, Fresno, Calif.

FIG TAPIOCA CREAM

Ingredients	25 Servings	50 Servings	100 Servings
Eggs, separated	6	12	24
Milk	3 qt	1½ gal.	3 gal.
Quick-cooking tapioca	1 cup	2 cups	1 qt
Salt	¾ tsp	1½ tsp	1 tbsp
Sugar	¾ cup	1½ cups	3 cups
Grated orange rind	3 tbsp	6 tbsp	¾ cup
Vanilla	1 tbsp	2 tbsp	¼ cup
Lemon extract	1½ tsp	1 tbsp	2 tbsp
California dried figs, chopped	2¼ cups	1 qt	2 qts

Procedure

Place egg yolks in saucepan and add enough milk to mix smooth. Mix tapioca with salt and half of the sugar and combine with milk and egg yolks in saucepan.

Stir in remaining milk, heat to boiling, stirring constantly. When it boils up well, remove from heat.

Add grated orange rind, vanilla, and lemon extract.

Beat egg whites stiff, then gradually beat in the remaining sugar. Stir hot tapioca gradually into the beaten whites. Fold in the chopped figs and chill.

SOURCE: Dried Fig Advisory Board, Fresno, Calif.

FIG DELIGHT

Ingredients	25 Servings	50 Servings	100 Servings
California dried figs	¾ lb	1½ lb	3 lb
Lemon-flavored gelatin	1½ cups (9 oz)	3 cups (18 oz)	6 cups (*or* 2 lb 4 oz)
Boiling water	3 cups	6 cups	3 qt
Evaporated milk	3 tall cans	6 tall cans	12 tall cans (*or* 1½ Inst. size)
Nuts, coarsely chopped	½ cup	1 cup	2 cups
Cookie crumbs (vanilla wafer, gingersnap, or graham cracker)	1 lb	2 lb	4 lb

Procedure

Cover figs with boiling water and simmer for 10–15 min, or until tender. Drain, clip off stems and cut in coarse pieces.

Dissolve gelatin in boiling water; allow to cool. Add evaporated milk and chill until beginning to thicken, then whip until very fluffy. Add figs and nuts.

Spread half the cookie crumbs in an oblong pan and pour gelatin mixture over them. Cover with remaining crumbs and chill until firm.

SOURCE: Dried Fig Advisory Board, Fresno, Calif.

FROZEN FRUIT COCKTAIL

Excellent frozen fruit cocktail can be prepared by the following procedure. Soft ripe peaches and pears are peeled, pitted and diced, and mixed with pineapple pieces, sliced maraschino cherries, and whole Thompson seedless grapes. The cocktail mix is covered with 40° Brix syrup then boiled for five min. After cooling the fruit mix is packaged in airtight packages and frozen in an airblast at −20°F and stored at 0°F.

SOURCE: *The Freezing Preservation of Foods*, *4th Edition*, *Vol. 2* by Tressler, Van Arsdel and Copley published by Avi Publishing Co., Westport, Conn.

FROZEN MOLDED FRUIT SALADS

Molded fruit salads can be prepared either from a mixture of frozen or fresh fruits. If frozen fruits are used, the fruits are thawed and drained. Gelatin, which has been dissolved in warm water, and a little ascorbic acid are added to the drained syrup. The drained fruits are mixed in the desired proportions. The fruit mixture is placed in cartons or other containers. The syrup containing the gelatin is allowed to cool until it forms a soft jelly, and is then poured over the fruit mixture in the cartons, which are then closed, overwrapped, and placed in a freezer.

The procedure is much the same if fresh fruit is used, except for the preliminary preparation of the fruit and the addition of corn or sugar syrup. Soft-ripe fruit is selected and washed. Pineapples are peeled, cored, sliced, and cut into pieces of the proper size. Peaches are peeled, pitted, and sliced. Sweet cherries are pitted. Seedless grapes are stemmed. Maraschino cherries are sliced. Pears are peeled, cored, and sliced. The fruits are mixed together. Gelatin and a small amount of ascorbic acid are dissolved in warm water. The solution of gelatin and ascorbic acid is mixed with corn or sugar syrup and the solution allowed to cool until it forms a soft jelly. The fruit mixture is placed in cartons or other containers and covered with the soft jelly. The containers are closed and placed in the freezer.

Fruit Salads in Defrost Pouches

A noteworthy method of packaging, freezing, and defrosting fruit salad and prepared fruits involves the packing of the fruit salad to which has been added a little sugar and ascorbic acid, or a small amount of a sugar syrup containing a little ascorbic acid, in a heat-sealable polyethylene pouch, pulling a high vacuum, then sealing the pouch, after which it is packaged in a rectangular carton and quick frozen. When desired for use, the pouch is immersed in a pan of running cold water, or lukewarm water, until the fruit is thawed but is still cold.

The packaging of the fruit under a vacuum maintains the color and flavor of the product almost perfectly. Rapid freezing and rapid thawing of the fruit aids materially in retaining both the color and flavor and also results in a product of better texture than that obtained if the fruit is thawed slowly while exposed to air.

SOURCE: *The Freezing Preservation of Foods, 4th Edition, Vol. 4* by Tressler, Van Arsdel and Copley published by Avi Publishing Co., Westport, Conn.

FRUITED SLAW

Ingredients

Canned apricot halves (No. 10 can)	3 qt
Cabbage, cleaned and quartered	6 lb
Chopped, red maraschino cherries	1 pt
Drained, crushed pineapple	1 pt
Sugar	½ pt
Salt	4 oz
Vinegar	½ pt
Salad dressing	1 qt
Light cream or evaporated milk	¼ pt
Celery seed	2 tbsp

Yield: 50 portions of approx ½ cup (1½ gal.)

Procedure

Drain apricots well; chop coarsely. Shred cabbage. Combine cabbage, apricots, cherries, and pineapple. Mix together remaining ingredients and pour over cabbage mixture. Toss lightly and refrigerate 2–3 hr before serving. Toss again lightly just before serving.

SOURCE: Theodore R. Sills, Inc., One E. Wacker Drive, Chicago, Illinois.

FRUIT SALAD DRESSING

Ingredients

Sugar	2 lb
Flour	8 oz
Pineapple juice	1¾ qt
Egg yolks	10 oz
Lemon juice	2 cups
Water	2 cups
Nonfat dry milk	8 oz

Yield: 1½ gal.

Procedure

Mix sugar and flour together in top of double boiler; blend in pineapple juice and cook over boiling water until mixture thickens. Beat egg yolks; add a small portion of cooked mixture to yolks then combine both mixtures and cook 3 min. Remove from heat and chill. Mix lemon juice and water; sprinkle nonfat dry milk over mixture and whip with wire whip attachment until mixture stands in stiff peaks. Fold into cooled pineapple cooked mixture.

Good dressing to use with all fruit mixtures, chicken and pineapple salad, or tossed vegetables.

SOURCE: American Dry Milk Institute, 130 N. Franklin St., Chicago, Illinois.

1000 ISLAND DRESSING

Ingredients

Finished salad dressing	100 gal.
B.D. complete 1000 Island seasoning	25 lb
Tomato paste (30–32% solids)	35 lb
Sweet pickle relish (drained)	70 lb
Water	3–5 gal.
	approx 118 gal.

Procedure

Since it is imperative that the particle size and mouth feel of the pickle relish and seasoning ingredients be maintained, it is necessary for the salad dressing base (30-35% vegetable oil content) to be completely milled and emulsified before the balance of ingredients are added and thoroughly mixed.

A particularly appealing modification of the above formula can be made by using liquid invert sugar or a high fructose corn syrup in place of the water.

SOURCE: Archibald and Kendall, Inc., 487 Washington St., New York, N.Y.

JELLIED FRUIT DESSERT USING LOW METHOZYL PECTIN

Ingredients	Lb	Oz	Gal.
Low methoxyl pectin	1.5		
Sugar	14		
Fruit, drained from canned fruit cocktail	23		
Calcium chloride, hydrate		¾	
Salt	1.5		
Sodium citrate		¾	
Citric acid, anhydrous	6		
Sodium benzoate	1		
Water			8
Color		(as desired)	

Yield: approx 100 lb

Procedure

Add the salt, sodium citrate, sodium benzoate and citric acid to 7½ gal. of water in the cooking kettle and begin to heat.

Mix the pectin and sugar thoroughly and add to the heating water in kettle using good agitation. Bring to a boil. Slowly add the hot calcium chloride solution (the ¾ oz of calcium chloride in the remaining ½ gal. of water) and mix well. Turn off heat and add the fruit. Cool the batch until the fruit no longer tends to float (approximately 120°-130°F) and fill into containers.

With a vegetable salad, the citric acid may be reduced to obtain the desired flavor. The sugar level may also be adjusted as desired.

The consistency of the gel may be adjusted as desired by the use of an ounce or so more or less of low methoxyl pectin. If desired, the juice from the canned fruit may be used instead of water. The sugar in this syrup would allow the use of somewhat less sugar than that called for in the formula; and the gel in this case would probably be slightly cloudy.

SOURCE: Sunkist Growers, Inc., 720 E. Sunkist St., Ontario, Calif.

JEWELED BEAUTY MOLD

Ingredients	Weight
Fruit-flavored gelatins: 1 each of lime, grape, cherry, orange	4 3-oz pkg
Boiling water	2 qt
Strawberry-flavored gelatin	12 oz
Sugar	8 oz
Pineapple juice	1 qt
Lemon juice	2 cups
Water	2 cups
Nonfat dry milk	8 oz

Yield: 2 gal. (96 servings)

Procedure

Dissolve each package of gelatin (except strawberry) separately in 1 pt of boiling water according to package directions. Pour in shallow pans. When congealed cut in ½-in. cubes, save for "jewels" in dessert. Place strawberry gelatin in bowl. Mix sugar with pineapple juice; heat to boiling, add to gelatin and stir until gelatin is dissolved. Add lemon juice, stir well and let set until slightly thickened. Using wire whip or electric beater, beat water and nonfat dry milk at high speed until very stiff. Add partially-congealed strawberry gelatin. Beat until well mixed. Remove beater and fold in jewels made in first step. Turn into pans* or molds. Refrigerate until firm. Cut in squares or unmold.

---

*For variety, pans may be lined with buttered grapham cracker crumbs.

SOURCE: American Dry Milk Institute, 130 N. Franklin St., Chicago, Illinois.

LEMON PUDDING

Ingredients	Lb	Oz
Nonfat dry milk		13
Pastry flour	1	4
Sugar	3	12
Salt		¼
Butter	1	4
Egg yolks, beaten	2	
Lemon juice	2	4
Grated lemon rind		5
Water	7	13
Egg whites	3	
Sugar	3	12

Yield: 2 counter pans (12 × 20 × 2¼)

Procedure

Mix dry ingredients with French whip. Cream butter until light and fluffy; add beaten egg yolks; blend in dry ingredients. Combine lemon juice, grated rind, and water and add to above mixture and blend. Beat egg whites until stiff but not dry; add sugar slowly, beating with each addition. Fold egg whites into above mixture. Pour into 2 greased counter pans and bake 50 min at 350°F.

Serve warm or chilled.

SOURCE: American Dry Milk Institute, 130 N. Franklin St., Chicago, Illinois.

LIME PUDDING

Ingredients	Lb	Oz	%
Water	664		61.85
Dextrose	35		3.26
Guar gum	1	8	0.14
Carrageenan		14	0.09
Sugar	180		16.76
Shortening	83		7.73
Modified tapioca starch*	4	2	0.39
Modified food starch**	34	7	3.21
Textured soy protein (SUPRO 350)	19		1.77
Corn syrup solids (24 DE)	47		4.37
Emplex	2	6	0.23
Salt	1	3	0.12
Citric acid (dry)		13	0.08
Color*** (to suit)			
Flavor**** (to suit)			100.00

Procedure

Preblend dextrose, guar gum, and carrageenan thoroughly. Make a slurry of about 100 lb of the cold water and the starch. Add balance of the water to a steam-jacketed kettle and heat to 160°F. Add gum mixture and agitate thoroughly. Add sugar and salt and dissolve. Add fat and Emplex and melt completely with agitation. Blend corn syrup solids and citric acid with SUPRO 350 and add to the batch with agitation. Add starch slurry at a temperature of 130°F or below and mix thoroughly. Mix in color and flavor. Process at 285°F for 17 sec for aseptic pack. Cool to 210°F, fill containers completely, close and seal aseptically immediately.

---

*Staley Fruitfil No. 4 Starch

**Staley Mira-Cleer 340 starch

***23 fl oz 5% solution lime green (Warner-Jenkinson 6508)

****19 fl oz Glidden synthesized lime oil

SOURCE: Ralston Purina Company, Checkerboard Square, St. Louis, Missouri.

ORANGE PUFF

Ingredients	Lb	Oz
Frozen orange concentrate	1	8
Water	4	
Orange gelatin	1	
Water	3	
Nonfat dry milk	1	8
Lemon juice		12
Sugar	2	4
Grated coconut	1	14

Yield: 3 gal. (96 No. 8 scoop servings)

Procedure

Mix concentrate and water. Bring to a boil. Add gelatin; stir until dissolved. Chill until slightly thickened. Sprinkle nonfat dry milk on water; whip at high speed until soft peaks form. Add lemon juice; continue whipping until stiff. Add sugar slowly continuing to whip until blended. Whip thicken gelatin until frothy. Fold in coconut, then whipped nonfat dry milk-water mixture, using French whip. For best results do not make over 3 gal. at a time. Chill.

Full volume of yield depends on careful handling.

SOURCE: American Dry Milk Institute, 130 N. Franklin St., Chicago, Illinois.

PANOCHE WITH FIGS AND NUTS

Panoche may be described as a fudge made with brown sugar and without chocolate. It is yellow-to-golden in color. The following formula makes a fig panoche:

Ingredients	Lb	Oz
Water		8
White sugar (cane or beet)	2	
Brown sugar	3	
Invert syrup or confectioner's corn syrup	1	
Unsweetened condensed (evaporated) milk		8
Chopped walnuts or almonds		8
Fig paste	3	
Butter or margarine		3

Procedure

Cook the water, condensed milk, brown sugar, and invert syrup or corn syrup to 240°F (241°F, soft ball). Remove from heat. Allow to cool about 5 min. Stir until creaming begins. Then add and mix in thoroughly the fig paste, nuts, and butter or margarine. Spread on oiled slab or pan, or on waxed paper to harden. Cut into pieces of desired size.

SOURCE: Dried Fig Advisory Board, Fresno, California.

PEACH FRITTERS

Ingredients	Lb	Oz
Flour, sifted	1	1
Sugar		7
Baking powder		7/8
Salt		3/8
Eggs, fresh or frozen, beaten		6
Milk		14
Shortening, melted		1 1/8
Peach halves	4	
Flour for coating peach halves		4

Procedure

Sift flour, sugar, baking powder, and salt. Combine eggs, shortening, and milk. Add to dry ingredients and mix until smooth. Roll peach halves in flour. Dip into batter, completely coating each peach with batter. Fry in deep fat at 375°F 4-6 min, turning frequently. Drain on a rack. Sprinkle with powdered sugar.

SOURCE: National Peach Council, Ballwin, Missouri.

HONEY-GLAZED PEARS AND SWEET POTATOES

Ingredients	
Pears, canned	4 lb
Sweet potatoes, peeled, cooked	4 lb
Butter or margarine	1/4 lb
Pear syrup	2 cups
Honey	2 cups
Salt	2 tsp
Cinnamon	4 tsp
Lemon juice	4 tbsp
Lemon peel, grated	4 tsp

Yield: 20 servings

Procedure

Drain pears, reserving 2 cups syrup. Place pear halves and sweet potatoes in buttered 1½ qt casseroles. Combine remaining ingredients in saucepan. Bring to a boil and cook 2-3 min. Pour over pears. Bake at 350°F 20-25 min, basting frequently.

SOURCE: Pacific Coast Canned Pear Service, Sixth Ave. North, Seattle, Washington.

LIQUID PECTIN FOR HOUSEHOLD USE

Manufacturing Directions

Ingredients	
150 Grade slow-set citrus pectin	3 lb 1 oz
USP citric acid	3 lb
Granulated sugar	10 lb 9 oz
Water	7 gal. 104 fl oz

Total: approx 1152 fl oz or 9 gal. which will make about 144 8-oz bottles of 6 cases of 24 bottles to the case.

Procedure

Put the water in a kettle and heat hot (about 180°F). Thoroughly mix the slow-set citrus pectin with the granulated sugar and add this mixture to the water as it is being vigorously stirred, preferably with a mechanical mixer. Continue to stir and heat to 180°F. When the pectin and sugar are completely dissolved (this will require less than 5 min), the citric acid is added. The batch is then stirred thoroughly until the citric acid is completely dissolved and thoroughly mixed. (To save time and to ensure complete solution of the citric acid at this stage of the process, it could have been previously dissolved in a little hot water taken from the kettle just before the pectin-sugar mixture was added).

With the temperature of the batch maintained at 180°F, the liquid pectin preparation is filled into bottles, the bottles capped, and inverted for not less than 1 min, and then the cooling process is started, first in water at 140°F, and finally in cold water. The bottles may then be labelled and packed into cases. *Bottles should be allowed to cool approximately to room temperature before packing into cases.* Caps should be spot crowns or should have enamelled or lacquered liners. Crowns must be clean from freshly opened containers or hot washed.

NOTE: All liquid pectin by its very nature is subject to loss in jellifying strength during storage, the amount of the loss, generally small, depending upon the length of time that the liquid pectin has been packed and the temperature to which it has been subjected. Manufacturers should always sell their oldest stock first, and should urge their brokers, jobbers, and retailers to do the same.

Directions for Household Use

For Jams

In this standard procedure, 4 cups of fruit, pulped or cooked, are required; the amount of the various fruits and water required to make about 4 cups after simmering are indicated below. Simmer the fruit until thoroughly softened. In measuring the cooked fruit or pulp when making the jam, add water if necessary to make exactly 4 cups. Never use more than 4 cups. Use the regular household measuring cup of 8 fl oz.

Apricots, canned: 1 lb 14 oz can + 1 cup water
fresh: 2 lb + 1 cup water
Blackberries: 2 lb + 1 cup water
Cherries: 2 lb + 1 cup water
Cranberries: 1½ lb + 1 cup water
Currants: 2 lb + 1 cup water
Figs: 2 lb + 1 cup water
Loganberries: 2 lb + 1 cup water
Mulberries: 2 lb + 1 cup water
Nectarines: 2 lb + 1 cup water
Peaches, canned: 1 lb 14 oz can + 1 cup water
fresh: 2 lb + 1 cup water
Pears: 2 lb + 1 cup water
Pineapple, canned: 1 lb 14 oz can + 1 cup water
fresh: 1 pineapple + 1 cup water
Plums, Santa Rosa: 2½ lb + 1 cup water
Satsuma: 2 lb + 1 cup water
Prunes, fresh: 2 lb + 1 cup water
Quinces, diced: 1 lb + 2 cups water
Raspberries: 2 lb + 1 cup water
Strawberries: 2 lb + 1 cup water
Youngberries: 2 lb + 1 cup water

To make the jam, the following procedure should be used.

Ingredients	
Cooked fruit or pulp (prepared as described above)	4 cups
Granulated cane or beet sugar	7 cups
Liquid pectin preparation	½ cup (4 fl oz)

Put cooked fruit or pulp in an 8-qt kettle and add sugar. Bring to a boil. Boil vigorously for 2 min and add liquid pectin preparation. Stir thoroughly, remove from fire, and skim. Pour at once into clean, dry glasses and cover with a thin layer of paraffin. (If the fruit has a tendency to float, cool the batch with stirring before pouring into containers).

This will make about 5¼ lb of jam or about 10½ 8-oz glasses.

For Jellies

This standard formula for jellies requires 4 cups of juice (or juice and water to make a total of 4 cups of liquid). The amounts of fruit and water to be simmered together to make about 4 cups are tabulated below. After the juice has been strained from the pulp, water should be added to make exactly 4 cups. Under no circumstances use more than 4 cups of liquid per batch. Always use a standard household measuring cup of 8 fl oz.

Apples: 3 lb + 3 cups water
Apple cider: 4 cups
Blackberries: 3 lb + 1 cup water
Cherries: 3 lb + 2 cups water
Crabapples: 3 lb + 3 cups water
Currants: 3 lb + 1 cup water
Figs: 3 lb + 1½ cups water
Grapes: 3 lb + 1½ cups water
Loganberries: 3 lb + 1 cup water
Oranges: Let grated orange peel from 2 oranges stand with the juice of 6 oranges and 3 lemons for 10 min, then strain juice through cloth
Peaches: 3 lb + 1½ cups water
Plums, Santa Rosa: 2½ lb + 1½ cups water
Satsuma: 4 lb + 1 cup water
Prunes, fresh: 2½ lb + 1½ cups water
Quinces: 3 lb + 4 cups water
Raspberries, fresh: 2 lb + 1½ cup water
canned: 1 lb 14 oz can + 1 cup water
Strawberries, fresh: 2 lb + 1½ cups water
canned: 1 lb 14 oz can + 1 cup water
Youngberries: 3 lb + 1 cup water

To make the jelly, the following procedure should be used.

Ingredients	
Fruit juice (prepared as described above)	4 cups
Granulated cane or beet sugar	7½ cups
Liquid pectin preparation	1 cup (8 fl oz)

Put juice in an 8-qt kettle and add sugar. Bring to a boil. Boil vigorously for 1 min and add 1 cup of liquid pectin preparation. Stir thoroughly and remove from fire, then skim. Pour at once into clean, dry glasses and cover with a thin layer of paraffin.

This will make about 5½ lb of jelly or about 11 8-oz glasses.

Home Use Suggestions

(1) Follow recipe exactly.

(2) Have all materials measured and at hand before starting the cooking process.

(3) Use standard 8 fl oz household measuring cup (½ pt size).

(4) A quick, hot fire and vigorous boiling give best results in the actual cooking of the jelly or jam. Precooking, when indicated, need be a simmer only.

(5) Use fully ripe fruit for which the recipes were designed. Immature fruits will generally require somewhat longer time of precooking.

(6) In measuring juice or fruit pulp, make up any slight shortage in the last cup by adding water

(7) A small piece of butter added to a batch will reduce foaming.

(8) Stirring jam for 5 min after removing from fire prevents fruit pieces from floating to top of jar.

(9) Give jellies and jams time to set; some fruits set more slowly than others. Usually the jam or jelly will be of the correct firmness in 24 hr but some kinds require 3-4 days.

(10) Store jellies and jams in a cool place. Inspect occasionally for breaks in the paraffin seal. Reseal with paraffin if necessary.

SOURCE: Sunkist Growers, 720 E. Sunkist St., Ontario, Calif.

PINEAPPLE-LIME PARFAIT

Ingredients	%
Gelatin, 225 Bloom	1.0
Sugar	8.0
Guar gum	0.08
Oil of lime	0.017
Water	26.80
Ice cream (10.5% butterfat)	26.84
Crushed pineapple	37.053
Green color (McCormicks)	0.01
Citric acid, 50% dilution	0.20
	100.000

Procedure

Mix sugar, gelatin, gum, and oil of lime. Dissolve in boiling water. Cool and add softened ice cream. Add pineapple. Spread in pan over crust. Cover and freeze. (500 gms filling used per sample).

SOURCE: D. K. Tressler and Associates, Westport, Conn.

INSTANT PRUNE SPREAD

Ingredients	Lb	Oz	%
Prune powder (Vacu-Dry)	1		15.02
Sugar (granulated)	2	4	33.80
Citric acid		¼	0.24
Cinnamon		¼	0.24
Instant starch		6	5.63
Water, hot	3		45.07
	6	10½	100.00

Procedure

Blend all dry ingredients thoroughly. Gradually pour blended ingredients into the hot water. Stir continuously until the dry ingredients are well incorporated. Cool filling.

This makes an ideal spread or filling for Danish or sweet dough items.

SOURCE: Vacu-Dry Company, 1311 63rd St., Emeryville, Calif.

PRUNE WHIP

Ingredients	
Dried prunes (dry weight)	6 lb 12 oz
Grated lemon rind	1 tbsp
Cold water	3 cups
Egg whites	1½ lb
Nonfat dry milk	15 oz
Lemon juice	½ cup
Sugar	3 lb
Cinnamon	1 tsp
Salt	1 tbsp

Yield: 3 gal. (96 servings)

Procedure

Cook prunes according to package directions; drain excess juice; pit and cut in small pieces or grind coarsely. Combine cold water and egg whites; sprinkle nonfat dry milk on mixture and whip on high speed until soft peaks are formed. Add lemon juice and continue whipping until very stiff. Combine dry ingredients; add gradually to whipped mixture. Continue whipping until blended. Fold whipped mixture into prunes, using French whip. Chill. For best results do not make over 3 gal. at a time.

SOURCE: American Dry Milk Institute, 130 N. Franklin St., Chicago, Illinois.

RASPBERRY FRUIT TOPPING

Ingredients	Lb	Fl Oz	%
Sherbelizer*	1.25		1.25
Sugar	47.00		47.00
Raspberry (4:1 Fruit:sugar)	30.00		30.00
Raspberry extract (approx)		5	0.10
Citric acid powdered	0.35		0.35
Water	21.40	(2½ gal.)	21.30
	100.00		100.00

Procedure

Dry mix Sherbelizer with three times its weight of sugar and dissolve in water with good agitation. Heat batch to 160°F. Add remaining sugar and citric acid. Add raspberries. Agitate constantly while heating. Hold at 160°F for 30 min and cool to 40°F.

*Sherbelizer is an algin product for optimum body and smooth texture.

SOURCE: Kelso Company, Chicago, Illinois.

SYLLABUB

Ingredients	
Light cream	2 qt
Juice and grated peel of oranges	4
Sugar	1 cup
Sherry, semidry	4 oz

Yield: 12 servings

Procedure

Put ingredients in deep bowl, blend at low speed of electric blender until very foamy. Remove froth with spoon and serve in tall glasses or goblets. Continue to blend skimming froth periodically until mix is used up.

SOURCE: D. K. Tressler and Associates, Westport, Conn.

VELVA FRUIT

Formula A for fruits with high acid and low pectin content

Ingredients	Lb	Oz
Fruit purée	640	
Sucrose	265	
Gelatin (275 Bloom)	5	13
Water	60	

Formula B

Ingredients	Lb	Oz
Fruit purée	610	
Sucrose	170	
Enzyme-converted corn syrup (43°Bé)	125	
Gelatin (275 Bloom)	5	13
Water	60	

Formula C for fruits with low acid and high pectin content

Ingredients	Lb	Oz
Purée	680	
Sucrose	225	
Gelatin (275 Bloom)	5	13
Water	60	
Citric acid	1	14

Procedure

For high acid and low pectin fruits, the soluble solids content, including the sugar of the fruit, should be about 37–38%.

A soluble solids content of 34–35%, including the natural sugar of the fruit is sufficient for the lower acid content of these fruits. A 3-to-1 ratio of fruit to sugar is usually satisfactory, though even less sugar can sometimes be used.

In the preparation of a mix, the purée, sugar, and citric acid (if used) are mixed until the sugar and acid are completely dissolved. The gelatin is mixed with 10 times its weight of water, and then heated to 180°F to dissolve and sterilize it. The mix itself is not pasteurized. During the addition of the gelatin solution, the mix should be stirred in order to prevent the formation of a stringy mass.

The Velva Fruit purée mix is frozen in an ice cream freezer with sufficient agitation to produce about 100% overrun.

The USDA Western Research and Development Laboratory especially recommends raspberries, strawberries, Loganberries, Boysenberries, and Youngberries for making Velva Fruit. Apricots, Santa Rosa plums, and prune plums also give smooth-textured products of excellent flavor. Cantaloupe purée is said to produce a remarkable fine dessert. Peaches and nectarines are also suitable for making Velva Fruit. The USDA Western Utilization Research and Development Division also recommends blends of berry with pear and apple purées.

SOURCE: *The Freezing Preservation of Foods, 4th Edition, Vol. 2* by Tressler, Van Arsdel and Copley published by Avi Publishing Co., Westport, Conn.

VEGETABLE BEVERAGES AND PURÉES

CANNED ASPARAGUS JUICE

Asparagus juice may be used as an ingredient of mixed vegetable juices or in soup blends. Although it has a pleasant flavor, it possesses the well-known odor of asparagus. The asparagus stalks should be washed, then steam blanched on a wire screen for 3-4 min and extracted twice in an American Utensil juicer. The canned juice, flavored with 0.75% salt, is processed at 240°F for 20 min in 8-oz cans. Juice acidified with citric acid may be processed at 212°F for 30 min in 8-oz cans, or flash pasteurized and filled into heated containers at 200°-212°F.

Processing time and temperature should be checked with the can supplier or with the National Canners Association.

SOURCE: *Fruit and Vegetable Juice Processing Technology, 2nd Edition* by Tressler and Joslyn published by Avi Publishing Co., Westport, Conn.

CANNED CARROT JUICE

Carrot juice may be made either as a clear juice or as a pulpy viscous juice with or without acidification. Nonacidified carrot juice processed at 250°F, when compared with acidified juice processed at 212°F, is inferior in flavor.

A pleasing blend is carrot juice adjusted to an acidity of pH 4.05 with orange juice. Acidification of the carrot juice with an equal quantity of high acid sauerkraut juice also produces a desirable product. The proportions are based upon relative amounts of the sauerkraut juice necessary to raise the acidity to pH 4.0-4.1. Blends of the various vegetable juices with sauerkraut juice are more palatable than similar blends acidified with pure acids or with rhubarb juice. In fact, the blends are considered superior to the pure juices before processing.

SOURCE: *Fruit and Vegetable Juice Processing Technology, 2nd Edition* by Tressler and Joslyn published by Avi Publishing Co., Westport, Conn.

CANNED CELERY JUICE

If fresh celery is ground and pressed, a fair yield of juice is obtained, but the juice soon darkens and changes in flavor. If, however, the celery is blanched in live steam for a few minutes, a light-colored juice is obtained which retains its flavor well. When 0.5% salt and 0.3% citric acid (or enough deterpinated lemon concentrate) are added to give 0.3% added citric acid to the celery juice it may be processed in small cans for 30 min at 212°F in a continuous agitating cooker. The product has a pH of 4.14 which is sufficiently acid to permit safe processing at 212°F and yet not sour enough to be displeasing. There is little doubt that flash pasteurization at 200°-212°F would be a better and a safer process.

Processing time and temperature should be checked with can supplier or with the National Canners Association.

SOURCE: *Fruit and Vegetable Juice Processing Technology, 2nd Edition* by Tressler and Joslyn published by Avi Publishing Co., Westport, Conn.

BOUILLON COCKTAIL MIX

Ingredients	Formula A %	Formula B %
Maggi HPP type super BE powder	58.80	
Maggi HPP type 4BE powder		29.40
Maggi HPP type 3H3 powder		29.40
Maggi autolyzed yeast extract (standard dark powder)	14.70	14.70
Sugar	8.25	8.25
Celery salt	0.57	0.57
Monosodium glutamate	12.75	12.75
Citric acid	4.93	4.93
	100.00	100.00

Procedure

Blend together well all ingredients.

To Use

Dissolve ½ oz (14.2 gm) of bouillon dehydrated mix in 8 oz of water and add 1 oz of V-8 tomato-vegetable juice. Serve over ice.

SOURCE: Food Ingredients Division, Nestlé Company, 100 Bloomingdale Road, White Plains, N.Y.

FROZEN RHUBARB JUICE

A thick juice resembling tomato juice in viscosity may be made from washed rhubarb stalks by blanching (scalding in steam for 1-2 min) and then extracting the juice in an hydraulic press using a fine press-cloth with a muslin lining. The viscous turbid juice is sweetened by the addition of sugar to 18° Brix, flash heated to 160°F and canned. It may also be preserved by freezing. The frozen juice retains its color and flavor better than the canned product.

SOURCE: *Fruit and Vegetable Juice Processing Technology, 2nd Edition* by Tressler and Joslyn published by Avi Publishing Co., Westport, Conn.

PREPARING AND PASTEURIZING RHUBARB JUICE

In harvesting rhubarb, the leaves should be cut off as they are high in oxalic acid. In preparing the stalks for pressing, they are very thoroughly washed in order to remove adhering earth, then they are shredded in an apple grinder made of acid-resistant metals. The shredded rhubarb is pressed in an ordinary rack and cloth hydraulic press such as is used for pressing apples. The yield should be about 170 gal. of juice per ton.

Regardless of whether or not the juice is to be clarified, oxalic acid may be removed. This is done by the addition of 0.32% of calcium carbonate (precipitated chalk) to juice heated to 180°F. The treated juice is allowed to remain at this temperature for about 30 min to facilitate the formation of large crystals and to prevent their settling. The juice is then chilled and allowed to stand overnight in a cool place; during this period the calcium oxalate and much of the cellular debris settle. The juice is then carefully racked off from the sediment and strained through a fine screen or cheesecloth. The screened juice is centrifuged, and then heated in a flash pasteurizer to 165°-170°F, canned while hot in tin cans or bottles which are inverted for 3 min, and then cooled.

Clarification

In order to get the juice in a filterable condition, it is heated immediately after pressing to 120°F. A commercial pectic enzyme preparation is added at the rate of about 20 oz to each 100 gal. of juice. The juice is held at 120°F for 3 hr in order to permit the enzyme to act on the pectin and thereby bring about flocculation of the suspended material. At the end of the holding period, the temperature of the juice is raised to 180°F and about 0.3% of precipitated chalk is added, with slow agitation to prevent loss by foaming. After 10 min standing at 180°F, to inactivate the enzyme, the juice is cooled and held in a refrigerator overnight, after which it is filtered through an ordinary plate and frame filter press using a small amount of a filter aid (Hyflo Super Cel or Dicalite). The filtrate should be brilliantly clear and remain so after pasteurization.

SOURCE: *Fruit and Vegetable Juice Processing Technology, 2nd Edition* by Tressler and Joslyn published by Avi Publishing Co., Westport, Conn.

CANNED SAUERKRAUT JUICE

Before sauerkraut is removed from the vat most of the juice is drained or pumped out. When kraut is repacked in small containers for sale as fresh kraut and also when the kraut is canned, a considerable proportion of the juice may be used. Even so, much is not utilized unless it is bottled or canned for sale as a beverage. The clear brine from the bottom of the vat will invariably be lower in acid and higher in salt than the brine that is in direct contact with the solid kraut. This clear brine is less satisfactory in flavor as well as in salt-acid balance than the cloudier juice. The difference is much more marked when juice is marketed as a bottled and refrigerated product rather than a processed juice.

The procedure usually followed in canning sauerkraut juice is very simple involving no processing other than exhausting and flash pasteurizing. Surplus juice from several vats is blended in a tank, ordinarily giving a blend containing from 1.5 to 1.6% lactic acid and less than 2.25% salt. The blended juice is strained through a fine screen and then run by gravity to a pasteurizer and a filler. The cans, filled to within ½ in. of the top, are slowly conveyed through a steam chamber. This exhaust heats juice packed in No. 2½ cans in 4½-min up to 165°-170°F. As the cans are conveyed to the closing machine, they pass under streams of hot water which fill the cans almost completely. The addition of hot water dilutes the juice and consequently reduces its salt content and acidity. By varying the proportion of hot water added it is a simple matter to produce a canned juice of uniform acidity. The closed cans are rolled in a continuous cooler, where they are cooled to 100°F with water. Sauerkraut juice is ordinarily packed in tin cans, although a small amount is packed in glass. The acid juice needs no further processing.

SOURCE: *Fruit and Vegetable Juice Processing Technology, 2nd Edition* by Tressler and Joslyn published by Avi Publishing Co., Westport, Conn.

BOTTLED SPINACH JUICE

Juice prepared from spinach is unattractive in appearance but possesses a fairly pleasing flavor. The spinach after trimming and washing is steam blanched for 3 min, then passed through an American Utensil tomato juicer to prepare a purée. Since the green color, chlorophyll, is not soluble in water or in the juice, one must grind the leaves to a fine purée. Since the purée is fairly thick, it should be diluted with more or less clear juice obtained by pressing the milled product in an hydraulic press. The purée and juice should be put through a tomato finisher. Salt 0.5-1.0 gm per 100 ml is desirable.

Similar to juices from many other vegetables, spinach juice coagulates quickly during processing at 252°F or at 212°F. The color turns the usual gray-green of retorted spinach, when processed at 250°F. Less change in character is obtained when the juices are acidified to pH 4.0-4.2 and then flash pasteurized and bottled at 200°-212°F.

Processing time and temperature should be checked with container supplier or with the National Canners Association.

SOURCE: *Fruit and Vegetable Juice Processing Technology, 2nd Edition* by Tressler and Joslyn published by Avi Publishing Co., Westport, Conn.

CANNED PURÉED SWEET POTATOES

The procedure followed in cleaning, washing, inspection, and trimming are the same for the preparation for canning of puréed potatoes. The trimmed roots should be sliced into ½ in. slices and then blanched for 30 min in atmospheric steam.

The hot blanched roots are puréed using a conventional pulper involving blades which force the purée through a screen with 0.055-in. holes and carry the fibrous material out through a waste port.

The hot sweet potato purée should be packed into cans, filling completely. The cans should be closed using a steam-flow closer and immediately processed. The National Canners Association or can supplier should be contacted in order to learn the proper process for the various size cans packed.

SOURCE: D. K. Tressler and Associates, Westport, Conn.

FROZEN MASHED OR PURÉED SWEET POTATOES

Fully cured sweet potatoes should be washed. If the operations are conducted on a large scale, the washed sweet potatoes should be graded according to size, then immersed in a boiling lye solution containing 7-10% of caustic soda for 5-6 min. The treated potatoes should be washed in a squirrel-cage washer equipped with powerful sprays of water to wash off the peels and cool them. The peeled potatoes should be trimmed to eliminate pieces of peel and dark spots and then cooked in a retort under 10 lb steam pressure long enough to bring the temperature in the center of the potatoes to 190°F. The time required for steaming under 10 lb pressure varies depending on the size of the potatoes:

Diameter of Potato (In.)	Steaming Time (Min)
4.5	30
4.0	25
3.5	23
3.0	20
2.5	15
2.0	7

Steam pressure higher than 10 lb is undesirable because the exterior of the potato will become too soft before the interior reaches 190°F.

The cooked, peeled sweet potatoes may be pulped in a ricer or in a rotary pulper. The riced or puréed potatoes are placed in the portable bowl of a large mixer. For each 100 lb of the riced or puréed sweet potatoes, 4-6 oz of citric acid, 1 lb of salt, and some sugar (if desired) are added and the mixer operated until a uniform mix has been obtained. Then the product is packaged and frozen.

If the operations are conducted on a relatively small scale, the washed sweet potatoes may be cooked and the skins loosened in the same operation by steaming under 10 lb pressure. After the potatoes have cooled, the skins are removed with a knife. After trimming the potatoes are puréed, and mixed with citric acid etc., as directed above.

SOURCE: *The Freezing Preservation of Foods, 4th Edition, Vol. 4* by Tressler, Van Arsdel and Copley published by Avi Publishing Co., Westport, Conn.

TOMATO JUICE

On arrival at the juice plant the fully ripe tomatoes are dumped into a small tank of water to avoid bruising. From this tank the tomatoes are conveyed by a roller belt through a washer where they are sprayed with a powerful spray of water. Then the washed tomatoes, on the roller belt, are passed before women who remove and trim off green portions of otherwise ripe fruit and eliminate rotten and partially decayed tomatoes.

The tomatoes are then chopped or crushed mechanically and immediately pumped through a heat exchanger in which the chopped or crushed product is heated to about 190°F, in order to inactivate enzymes which would otherwise break down the pectin and damage the body of the juice. The hot product is then put through a juice extractor, usually a tapered screw revolving type, within a perforated screen. Next the juice is put through a "finisher" which removes the seed and pieces of tomatoes.

The smooth juice is then pumped through a pasteurizer in which it is heated to 240°-250°F for about 60 sec. The juice is then cooled in a heat exchanger to a temperature of 200°-205°F before being filled into cans; 0.5%salt should be added by placing a salt tablet of the suitable size in each can before it is filled with juice.

After filling, the cans are immediately closed, allowed to stand for 5 min then cooled with sprays of cold water.

SOURCE: D. K. Tressler and Associates, Westport, Conn.

CANNED TOMATO JUICE

Under the Federal Food, Drug and Cosmetic Act enacted June 25, 1938, as corrected by amendments to May 15, 1969, tomato juice is defined in the Standard of Identity, promulgated July 27, 1939, effective January 1, 1940, as follows:

> "53.1 Tomato Juice: Identity.—Tomato juice is the unconcentrated liquid extracted from mature tomatoes of red or reddish varieties, with or without scalding followed by draining. In the extraction of such liquid, heat may be applied by any method which does not add water thereto. Such liquid is strained free from skins, seeds, and other coarse or hard substances, but carries finely divided insoluble solids from the flesh of the tomato. Such liquid may be homogenized, and may be seasoned with salt. When sealed in a container it is so processed by heat, before or after sealing, as to prevent spoilage."
>
> "53.5. Yellow Tomato Juice: Identity.—Yellow tomato juice is the unconcentrated liquid extracted from mature tomatoes of yellow varieties. It conforms, in all other respects, to the definition and standard of identity for tomato juice prescribed in 53.1."

Tomatoes selected for juice must be fully ripe, without green spots and stems. Partially rotten or decayed fruit cannot be used as it would impart an off-flavor and poor flavor to the juice.

Upon arrival at the cannery the tomatoes are first dumped into a soaking tank or sluiced to it by water in a flume. From the soaking tank, where they are washed in running water in a squirrel cage or on roller belts though high-pressure sprays of water the tomatoes are conveyed to the sorting and trimming belts.

Sorting and trimming are critical operations; the workers require training and the lighting, design, and operation of the belts must be such as to permit thorough inspection. The lighting should be such as to give bright illumination on the tomatoes without shining into the eyes of the operators. The width of the belt should be such that no operator has to reach more than 18-20 in., and the speed should not be more than 25 ft per min. Beyond this, the belts should not be loaded so heavily that all tomatoes cannot be turned and inspected on all sides.

Chopping and Preheating

Tomatoes may be preheated whole, and occasionally this is done when juice is produced simultaneously with the canning of whole tomatoes. In that case, all of the trimmed and sorted tomatoes are conveyed on a mesh belt through a steam box, after which part are selected for peeling and canning, the remainder going to the juice extractors. This is not a "hot-break" procedure, since, although the surface reaches a fairly high temperature, the interior of the tomatoes does not get above 100°-120°F.

More commonly the cold, clean tomatoes are delivered directly to a chopper and, usually but not always, are then pumped through a continuous preheater. Either before or after preheating, the chopped tomatoes are sometimes put through a vibrating screen. It is claimed for vibrating screens that they tend to remove black spots, green portions, hard cores, and yellow sunburn, thereby producing better color and flavor in the juice.

In the hot-break method, the temperature of preheat may range from 160°-210°F. Temperatures of 120°-140°F have been used, but this practice increases the hazard of spoilage by thermophilic bacteria. This temperature range would permit establishment of contamination foci in various parts of the equipment.

Extraction

Extractors of several types are available, but preference is given to the principle of pressing the juice from the pulp rather than using a churning or agitating action, which would incorporate air in the juice.

The typical extractor has a worm conveyor within a cylindrical or truncated conical screen. Extraction is frequently done in 2 stages; in the first the chopped tomatoes are pressed through a screen having 0.040-0.060-in. openings, this being followed by pressing or screening through a second "finisher" having 0.020-0.025-in. openings. The extractors can be adjusted to vary the yield of juice; usually this is about 70%.

The residue, especially with low yield extraction, is rather moist and is sometimes re-extracted for use in making other tomato products such as purée, sauce, or catsup. If this is done, however, the products must be labeled to show the use of such residual material from partial extraction of juice.

Deaeration

Since heating tomato juice containing dissolved or occluded air impairs the retention of vitamin C as well as, to some extent, that of color and flavor, some canners employ deaerators, in which the cold or slightly warm product is subjected to a vacuum of 25-26 in. Ideally, this should be done as soon as possible after the tomatoes are crushed and before they are heated at all, in order to remove the oxygen before it can do harm. For practical reasons, however, deaeration is usually applied immediately after extraction of the juice. If a hot-break is used, deaeration at this stage loses some of its advantage but is still capable of averting serious loss of vitamin C in subsequent sterilization of the juice.

Deaeration may also be applied after pasteurization or high temperature presterilization, to remove air incorporated by pumping, to prevent foaming in the filler bowl, and, in the case of presterilized juice, to cool the juice to filling temperature. At this stage, since the juice is hot, a vacuum of 10-15 in. is briefly applied to the juice before it goes to the fillers.

Salting and Filling

If the juice is accumulated in tanks prior to filling, it may be salted in batches at this stage. More commonly salt is added to the individual cans by means of dry salt or salt tablet dispensers, which make unnecessary the accumulation of batches. Usually from 4 to 6 lb of salt per 100 gal. (0.5-0.7%) is added or an equivalent amount per can.

Filling machines are adjusted to give a maximum fill, since this gives best retention of quality and of vitamin C, as well as best service value from metal containers. All these factors suffer when the headspace is excessive. In No. 10 (603 X 700) and No. 3 cylinder (404 X 700) cans the net headspace after cooling should not be over 7/16 in. (10/16 in. to the top of the double seam) and in shorter cans not over 3/16 in. below the cover 6/16 in. gross headspace), for best results.

Containers

Tomato juice is packed in plain or enameled tin cans, and, less frequently, in glass. The use of enameled as against plain cans is a moot point, with general agreement that a flavor difference exists but no unanimity as to which is preferable.

Some packers homogenize the juice before filling it into cans. This is done in an homogenizer in which the juice is forced under 1000 lb per sq in. pressure through narrow orifices. This increases the viscosity and prevents settling and separation of the solid particles.

Tomato juice may be processed by heat either before or after filling into the can and sealing. When processed before sealing, the juice is heated in continuous heat exchangers to temperatures of 240°-270°F, then cooled to a suitable filling temperature, usually 195°-205°F, depending on the size of container. Processing after sealing includes several variants in which the cans are sealted hot, after which they may be air cooled, held for a time before water cooling, or given a further process before water cooling. If the juice has been given no presterilization heat treatment and the cans are processing in boiling water, the following processes are usually given:

Can Size	Initial Temp[1] °F	Time (Min)
300 X 407	170	35
	180	30
	190	20
307 X 409	170	40
	180	35
	190	25
404 X 700	170	60
	180	45
	190	30
603 X 700	170	90
	180	70
	190	35
All sizes	195	15
	200	10

[1] The average temperature of the juice at the time the process is started.

If an agitating type of cooker or if the juice is given special treatment prior to filling, the packer should consult the can supplier or the National Canners Association for processing times and temperatures.

SOURCE: *Fruit and Vegetable Juice Processing Technology, 1st Edition* by Tressler and Joslyn published by Avi Publishing Co., Westport, Conn.

CANNING TOMATO PULP OR PURÉE

Whole tomatoes are washed, then passed over an inspection belt from which partially rotten and wormy tomatoes are picked out and eliminated, and green parts and other defects are trimmed by workers. The sound tomatoes are then heated with live steam until every part of the tomato is scalding hot. The hot tomatoes pass directly to a pulper or "cyclone" which converts the tomatoes to juice and eliminates seeds, skins, and fiber. The juice then goes to an evaporator which may be a tank with coils or a vacuum pan. The juice should be evaporated to the desired consistency in 30 min or less. Juice evaporated to ½ its volume yields purée or pulp of about 1.035 sp gr. By longer evaporation pulp of 1.040, 1.045 or even higher can be produced. The hot purée or pulp is put through a finisher to eliminate any rough particles or fiber. If the pulp is filled into No. 10 or 5 gal. cans at 190°F or higher then is no need for further processing. The cans should not be packed solidly but should be stacked not more than two deep for cooling.

SOURCE: D. K. Tressler and Associates, Westport, Conn.

CANNED STRAINED VEGETABLES

The procedure suggested for the manufacture of strained baby foods from vegetables may be summarized as follows.

Frozen vegetables, packed for remanufacture, or institutional-size packs, are allowed to thaw partially by standing overnight in a cool room. Circulating air may be provided by fans to hasten thawing. The partially or completely thawed product is placed in a steam kettle, covered with water, and cooked until tender; the amount of water used and the length of time required for cooking will depend, of course, on the kind, maturity, and size of pieces of the vegetable used. If the product is to be salted, salt (0.25%) and monosodium glutamate (0.15%) are added, then the cooked vegetable is converted while still hot into a purée by putting it through a paddle-type finisher with a screen having 0.027-in. holes. The purée is homogenized at 3,000–4,000 lb per sq in. pressure. It is then sterilized by pumping through a tubular heat exchanger of the small-tube, high-velocity type, in which it is heated to about 280°F. If tin cans are used as containers, the purée is filled, after cooling to 200°–210°F in a tubular heat exchanger. If it is packed into cartons, or composite cartons with metal ends, the purée should be continuously cooled without delay to 100°F or lower before filling. This cooling is best effected in another tubular heat exchanger.

SOURCE: *The Freezing Preservation of Foods, 4th Edition, Vol. 2* by Tressler, Van Arsdel and Copley published by Avi Publishing Co., Westport, Conn.

FROZEN STRAINED VEGETABLES
(From Fresh Vegetables)

Owing to the fact that fresh beets and carrots are generally available throughout much of the year, and further, since these fresh vegetables can be stored for several months, they are not commonly frozen for remanufacture, but the fresh vegetables are used for making infant foods. These vegetables are usually cleaned, trimmed, and thoroughly washed (first in a soaker, then in powerful sprays of water), and inspected, after which they are peeled, usually by first subjecting the vegetable to high-pressure steam, and then to high-pressure water sprays. The peeled vegetables are passed over an inspection belt where vegetables with crowns not completely removed, or discolored and improperly peeled portions, etc., are hand trimmed. The vegetables are then chopped in a stainless steel chopper or otherwise comminuted into small pieces. The chopped vegetables are cooked until tender in a steam-jacketed kettle with about 3 times their weight of water; 0.15% of monosodium glutamate and 0.25% of salt are usually added. After cooking, the mixture (vegetables plus cooking water) is passed through a stainless steel paddle type finisher equipped with a screen having 0.027-in. diameter perforations. This finisher should be equipped with steam inlets on either end so that there will be a steam atmosphere at all times during the straining operation. The chopped product is homogenized at 3,000–4,000 lb per sq in. pressure, after which it is sterilized at about 270°F by pumping it through a tubular heat exchanger of the small-tube, high-velocity type. This will effect almost complete sterilization of the product. The purée is then passed through another heat exchanger in which it is cooled to the desired filling temperature. If packed in tin cans, they should be filled at 200°–212°F, closed immediately, and promptly cooled by cold water sprays. If packed in composite or other moisture-vapor-proof cartons, the filling temperature should be 100°F or lower.

The product is then quick frozen and then stored at 0°F.

SOURCE: *The Freezing Preservation of Foods, 4th Edition, Vol. 2* by Tressler, Van Arsdel and Copley published by Avi Publishing Co., Westport, Conn.

CANNED VEGETABLES

CANNED ASPARAGUS

Both white and "all-green" asparagus are canned. The white is obtained by cutting the stalks at least six inches below the surface of the ground and before the stalks have turned green. The all-green stalks are allowed to grow 4–6 in. above the ground and then cut a little below the surface. The asparagus must be thoroughly washed promptly after cutting.

White asparagus is usually graded into three grades: No. 1, No. 2, and No. 3, the grade depending largely on the shape of the heads.

Green asparagus is usually graded into four grades, the grade depending largely on the size of the stalks.

After grading the butt ends are cut off and discarded. Then the "grass" is cut to the proper length to fit the cans in which it is to be packed. Stalks 4 in. in length are packed in the No. 2, the No. 300 and the tall No. 1 cans. The asparagus should be cut 5¾ to 7⅞ in. in length for the 304 × 604 cans.

The various grades of asparagus are blanched separately. Each lot is placed in a galvanized wire basket and lowered into water at 170°–200°F. The tender tips should not be immersed in the hot water until near the end of the blanching period of 1–3 min; the length of the blanch depends largely on the size of the stalks.

The blanched asparagus is filled into cans by hand. After the cans have been filled a 2% hot (200°F) salt brine is added, then the cans are exhausted for 3–5 min in water at 190°F. A steam-flow closure is best. Small cans of white asparagus (No. 2½ and smaller) should be processed for 23 min at 240°F or 14 min at 248°F. The "all-green" should be processed slightly longer. Process times and temperatures should be checked with can supplier or National Canners Association.

Immediately often processing the cans should be cooled to 100°F.

Since the yield of asparagus stalks of the proper size to fit the cans is low, it is important to use the remainder. Much of it can be canned as "cuts," the remainder used for making soup.

SOURCE: D. K. Tressler and Associates, Westport, Conn.

CANNED GREEN AND WAX BEANS

Pole beans (Kentucky Wonder and Blue Lake) have an excellent flavor but must be picked by hand. In most localities bush beans, both green and wax, are machine harvested. Upon receipt at the cannery, the mechanically harvested beans must be put through an air cleaner in order to eliminate dirt, leaves, and other foreign matter. The beans should then be washed. Next the beans are "pregraded" (separated into three sizes) and snipped. Then the beans are passed over an inspection belt where "rusty" and other defective beans are picked out and discarded. Next, the beans are graded into seven sizes. The three smallest sizes (Nos. 1, 2, and 3) are canned whole. The larger sizes $^{21}/_{64}$ in. in thickness and larger are either cut transversely into 1- to 1½-in. cuts or slit lengthwise into French-style or Julienne beans.

After grading the beans should be thoroughly washed in cold water and then blanched at 170°–180°F, the length of the blanching period depending upon the size and maturity of the beans. Smaller beans are blanched 2–3 min, larger ones 3–5 min. Following blanching, the beans are cooled by sprays of cold water.

Whole beans may be packed into cans "asparagus-style." In this pack the beans are cut to the length of the can, and arranged parallel for insertion into the can. Cut beans are filled mechanically. The cans of beans are filled with hot (200°F or hotter) brine containing 2–2½% salt. The small cans should be exhausted for 3–5 min, No. 10 cans should be given a much longer exhaust. No. 2 cans of cut beans filled with hot brine should be processed for 20 min at 240° or 11 min at 250°F; asparagus style beans in No. 2 cans should be given 25 min processing at 240°F. Process times and temperature should be checked with can supplier or with the National Canners Association.

SOURCE: D. K. Tressler and Associates, Westport, Conn.

CANNING LIMA BEANS

When a large proportion of the beans are of proper size but are still green and tender, the vines are hauled to viners where they are vined in equipment similar to that used in vining peas, except the holes in the screen are larger. The Henderson Bush Lima is the variety commonly grown for "baby limas." The vined beans are cleaned in clipper mills and then are thoroughly washed. They are graded for size by passing them over screens with holes $^{28}/_{64}$, $^{30}/_{64}$, and $^{34}/_{64}$ in. in diameter. The beans that pass through the $^{28}/_{64}$ and $^{30}/_{64}$ openings are mostly green and those which pass over are lighter in color.

The different sizes are blanched separately. The usual blanch is at 200°F but sometimes boiling water is used through a brine solution of a density that overmature beans sink and the tender green beans float. The tender beans are run over a picking belt where women pick out and discard defective beans and any foreign matter still remaining.

The beans are filled into cans, covered with boiling hot 2% salt solution; then the cans are closed and processed usually at 240°F. No. 2 cans require 35 min if the initial temperature is 140°F. Processing time should be checked with can supplier or the National Canners Association.

SOURCE: D. K. Tressler and Associates, Westport, Conn.

CANNING BEETS

Small beets are preferred for canning. The flesh of the beets must be of uniform color. They should be dug by special mechanical diggers which dig, top, and discharge the beets into a truck in which they are transported to the cannery. Washing is the first operation. If the beets are grown in clay soil, washing is difficult, and, therefore, they are soaked in tanks of water and sprayed with high pressure sprays of cold water.

The washed beets should be size-graded "tiny," small, and medium, so that they can be blanched uniformly. Water blanching causes loss of color; therefore, the beets should be steam blanched at 220°–240°F for 5 to 20 min. The length of the blanch depends upon the size and the length of time the beets have been out of the ground. The beets should be blanched long enough to loosen the skin and heat the beets to the center. Mechanical peelers should be used to peel the beets. The beets should be mechanically filled into enamel-lined cans. The cans are then completely filled with either boiling hot water or brine. If hot brine is used, it is made by dissolving 10 to 27 lb salt and the same quantity of sugar per 100 gal.

Usual Count of Whole Beets per Can

Size	No. 303 Can or Jar	No. 2½ Can or Jar	No. 10 Can
Tiny (size 1)	35 and over	70 and over	250 and over
Tiny (size 2)	25–34	50–69	175–249
Small (size 3)	18–24	35–49	125–174
Small (size 4)	10–17	20–34	75–124
Medium (size 5)	7–9	15–19	50–74
Medium (size 6)	less than 7	less than 15	less than 50

Sizes larger than 2 in. in diameter should be sliced, diced, or cut in narrow strips (to make shoestring beets).

The No. 303 cans need not be exhausted. The larger size cans should be steamed long enough to heat the center of the can to 150°F.

After closing, the canned beets should be processed at 250°F, the length of the process depends upon the temperature of the beets. Diced and sliced beets require about 5 min longer process than whole beets.

The processed beets should be promptly cooled to 100°F.

Processing time and temperature should be checked with can supplier or the National Canners Association.

SOURCE: D. K. Tressler and Associates, Westport, Conn.

CANNED BROCCOLI

Broccoli heads should be sorted and any heads which show yellow blossoms or are loose should be discarded. Heads with numerous aphids should not be used. All of the leaves should be trimmed off and the heads cut into pieces about ¾-in. across. The pieces of broccoli should be blanched for 3–4 min in boiling water containing about 1 oz of citric acid per gallon. The blanched broccoli should then be washed with water. It should then be drained and packed into cans (usually enameled-lined No. 2's) and covered with a boiling hot salt brine which contains about 2% of salt.

Next the cans should be thoroughly exhausted by holding them in the exhaust for 8 min. The cans should then be immediately closed and processed at 240°F for 30 min. The time and temperature of the process should be checked with can supplier or the National Canners Association.

The broccoli should be cooled to 100°F immediately after processing.

SOURCE: D. K. Tressler and Associates, Westport, Conn.

CANNED CABBAGE

Small, very solid heads of cabbage should be used. The outer leaves should be cut off and discarded. The core is cut out and also discarded. The heads are cut into sections. Small heads into 4 quarters; larger heads into 6 sections. The sections are blanched in boiling water or steam until soft. The hot cabbage is filled into cans and covered with a 1½% boiling hot brine.

No. 2½ cans should be processed for 40 min at 240°F or 25 min at 250°F.

Processing times and temperatures should be checked with can supplier, or the National Canners Association.

SOURCE: D. K. Tressler and Associates, Westport, Conn.

CANNED CARROTS

The red cored Chantenay and the Danvers Half Long are considered the best carrots for canning. The carrots are pulled while still young. The tops are removed in the field, and the carrots are delivered to the cannery in field boxes or burlap bags. The first step in processing is washing, which is carried out in a rotary drum with heavy sprays of water. They are then size-graded in order to separate the young smaller carrots from the larger sizes. The sizes usually are: 1 in. or less in diameter, 1–1¼ in., and those above 1¼ in.

The washed carrots may be peeled in any one of several ways: by abrasion, by hot lye, or by high temperature steam. For lye peeling a solution containing 3 to 10% lye (NaOH) is used in a spray-type peeler. Abrasion peeling is usually a combination of a short blanch at about 180°F to loosen the skin followed by abrasion.

The peeled carrots are trimmed by women working along a slow moving belt, and consists of removing roots and green portions.

The larger carrots are sliced, diced, or cut into shoestrings by Urschel or Food Machinery Company machines. Diced or julienne-cut carrots are washed or sprayed to remove small pieces before blanching. Diced carrots should be ¼–⅜ in. in diameter. The smaller carrots are usually canned whole after blanching in live steam or water at 190°F for 2–4 min. The whole carrots are carefully packed into cans by hand. Salt tablets are added by a dispenser, to each can as it filled with water, or the cans containing the carrots may be filled with hot dilute brine (6–8° salinometer). After passing through an exhaust box the cans are sealed and processed according to the following times and temperatures as recommended by the National Canners Association.

Can	Initial Temp (°F)	Process Time at 240°F (Min)	Process Time at 250°F (Min)
No. 2½ and smaller (401 X 411 and smaller)	70	35	23
	140	30	20
No. 10, not sliced (603 X 700)	70	45	30
	140	40	25
No. 10, sliced (603 X 700)	70	50	35
	140	45	30

If other packs are processed the processing times and temperatures should be checked either with the can supplier or the National Canners Association.

CANNED CARROTS AND PEAS

Prepare fresh carrots following procedure described above for **Canned Carrots**. Dice the carrots into ¼-in. cubes. Frozen peas prepared as described in Section 12 (**Freezing Green Peas**) should be mixed with the carrots either in a 50–50 proportion or 60% carrots and 40% peas. The carrots and peas should be carefully and slowly mixed so as not to crush the peas. The carrot-pea mixture should be filled into No. 2 cans or smaller for retail and into No. 10 for the institutional trade. Boiling hot 2% brine with or without 2% sugar should be added. If the brine addition is near boiling, no exhaust is necessary. Assuming boiling hot brine is added, the process for No. 2 and smaller cans should be 40 min at 240°F or 18 min at 250°F. No. 10 cans should be processed at 240°F for 55 min or for 25 min at 250°F.

The processing times and temperatures should be checked with can supplier or with the National Canners Association.

SOURCE: D. K. Tressler and Associates, Westport, Conn.

CANNED CAULIFLOWER

The procedure followed in canning cauliflower is much the same as that used in preparing and canning broccoli (as described above) but the canned product is better. The heads are broken apart and cut into pieces about ¾ in. across, and then thoroughly washed. The cauliflower pieces should be blanched 3–4 min in 0.75% citric acid solution. After blanching, the cauliflower pieces should be rinsed with water, filled into cans, and boiling hot 1½% salt brine added. Exhaust the cans long enough to bring the temperature in the center of the can to 140°F.

No. 2½ and smaller cans should be processed for 20 min at 240°F. Processing times and temperature should be checked with can supplier or the National Canners Association.

SOURCE: D. K. Tressler and Associates, Westport, Conn.

CANNED CELERY

Both celery hearts and pieces (or cuts) are canned. Upon receipt, the root is cut off and the stalks broken apart, thoroughly washed, and cut into pieces about 1 in. in length.

The solid heart is thoroughly washed, then cut into long pieces or sticks which are again washed. Then the pieces of celery hearts are blanched in 1-2% citric acid solution at about 190°F for 3-4 min. Following blanching, the sticks are packed in small cans "asparagus style" (like small whole beans). Hot 1½% brine is added and the cans exhausted for about 5 min.

The celery cuts (used principally in soup) are not blanched but are filled into either No. 2 or No. 10 cans, covered with hot 1% brine and exhausted for 8 min.

No. 2 and smaller cans of celery cuts should be processed for 25 min at 240°F; No. 10 cans require 40 min at 240°F.

No. 2 cans (and smaller) of celery hearts require 25 min at 240°F.

Time and temperature of processing should be checked with can supplier or the National Canners Association.

SOURCE: D. K. Tressler and Associates, Westport, Conn.

CANNED HOMINY

The first step in canning hominy is to treat the dried kernels of white field corn in boiling 2% lye solution with stirring until the skins will slip easily. This requires about 25 min or longer.

After the lye treatment, the corn kernels are washed with fresh water and then run through a hominy huller which resembles a truncated tomato pulper with a coarse wire screen. The hulled corn is transferred to a tank where it is washed and then boiled in several changes of water. The product is canned directly after cooking. If canned without additional soaking, less corn is filled into the cans in order to allow for increase in volume of the kernels during retorting.

The hominy may be bleached by boiling in water containing 1000 ppm sodium bisulfite for approximately 15 min. The bisulfite must be leached from the hominy thoroughly before canning. Proper lye peeling, washing, and precooking are usually sufficient to prevent discoloration without the sulfite bleaching process.

The hominy is canned in C-enamel cans with a brine containing 1.5% salt and 3% sucrose. The cans are exhausted, sealed, and retorted. The National Canners Association recommends the following processes (initial temperature 140°F or higher):

No. 2 cans	75 min at 240°F
No. 2½ cans	90 min at 240°F
No. 10 cans	100 min at 240°F

Stainless-steel tanks and equipment should be used to avoid contamination with iron. Overtreatment in lye solution or failure to thoroughly remove residual lye from the kernels by washing and cooking may cause dark spots or darkened kernels. The canned product is water cooled, dried and labelled.

SOURCE: *Commercial Vegetable Processing* by Luh and Woodroof published by Avi Publishing Co., Westport, Conn.

CANNED MUSHROOMS

Sorted, fresh mushrooms are steam blanched and filled into glass or tin containers in 4-oz lots and covered with hot water. Salt and citric acid tablets are added, the tablet consisting of 1.6 gm citric acid and 38.4 gm salt. A tablet containing 150 mg ascorbic acid is also added. Processing time is 20 min at 250°F for the tin-packed product, compared to 23 min at 240°F for the glass pack.

Time and temperature of processing should be checked with container supplier or the National Canners Association.

SOURCE: Hoffmann-LaRoche Inc., Nutley, N.J.

CANNED FRESH OKRA

Okra toughens quickly after picking, therefore it should be canned the same day it is harvested. The larger, tougher pods should be picked out and eliminated. The tender pods should be thoroughly washed and then blanched in boiling water for 2 min. Pods should then be cut crosswise in a string bean cutter. The cut okra should be filled into No. 2 or No. 2½ cans and covered with boiling hot brine. No. 2 cans should be processed at 240°F for 30 min and No. 2½ cans for 35 min. The time and temperature of processing should be checked with can supplier or with the National Canners Association.

SOURCE: D. K. Tressler and Associates, Westport, Conn.

CANNING PEAS

Peas on the vines are mowed in the field, loaded on trucks by machines resembling hay loaders and hauled to a viner station where they are put through a viner. This is a large inclined rotating, perforated cylinder which is fitted with beater arms which strike the pods with considerable force causing them to burst open. The peas fall through the perforations in the cylinder and are collected for delivery to a cannery. However, at the vining station they are usually cleaned in a fanning mill which separates and eliminates pieces of vines, etc.

At the cannery, the peas are first washed in a special washing machine which not only washes off the vine juice, dirt, etc., but separates pebbles and other heavy material and also lighter materials which float away. Usually, the washed peas are then put through special flotation equipment to eliminate thistle buds and some other foreign matter left in the peas.

The washed peas then pass to grading machines which separate them into five sizes. Next, the peas should be passed over an inspection belt, where workers pick out and eliminate any foreign matter that somehow has passed through the cleaner and washer.

The peas should then be blanched; usually this is done in a reel blancher which consists of a perforated inside cylinder revolving in an outside cylindrical shell containing water heated by steam. The peas should be heated to 170°F or hotter in the blancher. Unless the peas are relatively immature, they should be put through a "quality grader" in order to eliminate starchy peas which sink in the quality grader brine maintained at 38°-40° salinometer.

The blanched and graded peas should be filled immediately into cans; then boiling hot brine is added. This brine should contain both sugar (about 4%) and salt (about 3%).

No. 2½ size cans and smaller need not be exhausted. No. 10 cans should be exhausted for a period long enough to bring the temperature of the peas to 180°F. No. 2 cans (initial temperature 140°) should be processed for 35 min at 240°F or 15 min at 250°F. No. 10 cans (initial temperature 140°F) should be processed for 50 min at 240°F or 15 min at 250°F. Time and temperature of processing should be checked with can supplier or the National Canners Association.

SOURCE: D. K. Tressler and Associates, Westport, Conn.

CANNING PIMIENTOS

Pimientos are large, smooth red, sweet peppers. First they should be graded for size in a rod-type grader. The No. 1 size includes those over 2 in. in diameter. The No. 2 size is approximately 2 in. in diameter. The No. 3's are less than 1¾ in. in diameter. Then the pimientos should be peeled. This is done by heating to loosen the skin. Heating may be accomplished by (1) roasting for about 1 min in a slowly rotating gas-heated cylinder; (2) heating in a vat of cottonseed oil at 400°F for 3-4 min; or (3) by boiling in a 10% lye solution followed by heating under steam pressure. Regardless of the method used to heat the pimientos, they are cooled with powerful sprays of water which wash off most of the skin which has been loosened by the heating; any remaining skin is removed with a knife when the peppers are cored.

The peeled and cored pimientos are flattened and solidly packed into small cans. A citric acid tablet is added to each can to reduce the pH to 4.5 or lower. Because the pimientos are solidly packed usually at a low temperature, the cans must be given a relatively long exhaust: small cans for 12-15 min, No. 2½ cans for 30 min, and No. 10 cans 45 min at 200°F or higher. The length of process will depend on the pH obtained. Consult can supplier or the National Canners Association for time and temperature required to sterilize the pimientos in cans of various sizes.

SOURCE: D. K. Tressler and Associates, Westport, Conn.

CANNED POTATOES

Potatoes are canned in several forms: whole, diced, sliced, strips, and julienne. By far the largest part of the potatoes canned are whole potatoes of less then 1½ in. in diameter. Potatoes in the United States are not grown specifically for canning but the small sizes are not desirable for fresh market.

A good canning potato should not slough or disintegrate during processing. Immature potatoes and those of low specific gravity, less than 1.075, generally are good for canning. Sloughing of the canned product can be prevented by the addition of calcium chloride which tends to firm the tissue.

Procedure

Potatoes are washed and peeled with lye, steam, abrasion, or a combination of these methods. Both batch and continuous high-pressure steam-peeling equipment may be used. Lye peelers may be of the reel or drum type or draper belt in tank. Some small processors use abrasion peelers. Although peeling losses are much greater with this type, the initial cost is lower and operational procedures are simpler. Following lye or steam peeling, reel-type washers are generally used with water sprays under high pressure.

Peeled potatoes are trimmed and then sized if necessary.

Most potatoes are canned whole but some of them, particularly the larger sizes are sliced, diced, julienne stripped, or cut into shoestring size.

Filling and Packing.—Cans with inner hot-dipped or electrolytic plate bodies and inner enameled electrolytic plate ends are filled with whole or cut potatoes by automatic or rotary handpack fillers. Either boiling water or brine of 1.5–3.0% salt is added to the container to the desired level. A salt tablet is added if boiling water is used. Calcium may be added in the form of calcium chloride, calcium sulfate, calcium citrate, monocalcium phosphate, or any mixture of two or more of these salts. Total calcium content must not exceed 0.051% of the net weight of the finished product.

Closing and Processing.—If ordinary closure is made, the closing temperature should be at 160°F or above in order to obtain desirable can vacuum. The processing temperature and time vary with can size and temperature of the can contents at the time the steam is turned on for the process. Temperatures of 240° or 250°F are recommended and time of processing varies from 20 to 55 min. The cans should be cooled to 100°F immediately after processing. Check processing time and temperature with can supplier or the National Canners Association.

SOURCE: *Potatoes: Production, Storing, Processing* by Ora Smith published by Avi Publishing Co., Westport, Conn.

CANNED PUMPKIN AND SQUASH

Pumpkins and squash to be canned should be deep yellow or orange in color. First, they should be thoroughly washed; if they are caked with mud, soaking may be necessary before scrubbing. Stems are cut off, and the pumpkins (or squash) are halved with a large knife or a mechanical cutter. The halves should be put through a rotating tumbler to remove seeds. Then they should be cut into pieces about 6 in. sq. These pieces should be put into retort baskets in which they are steamed at 240°F for about 20 min. Another procedure is to steam the pieces of pumpkin at atmospheric pressure until the flesh is soft. The steamed pumpkin is usually too watery, so it should be pressed, preferably between two continuous meshed wire belts. When sufficient moisture has been removed, the cooked pumpkin is run through a cyclone or tomato pulper to remove the skins, and finally through a finisher or comminutor. Since the pumpkin must be filled into the cans hot, it may be heated in an open kettle or may be pumped through a "preheater" to raise the temperature of the pumpkin to 180°F or higher. When filled at this temperature no exhaust is needed. Enamel-lined cans should be used to prevent discoloration.

No. 2 cans require 75 min processing at 240°F or 60 min at 250°. No. 10 cans require 190 min at 240° or 165 min at 250°F. Processing times and temperatures should be checked with can supplies or the National Canners Association.

SOURCE: D. K. Tressler and Associates, Westport, Conn.

CANNED RHUBARB

This vegetable is canned principally in No. 10 cans for bakers, restaurants, and institutions.

The freshly-cut rhubarb should be trimmed, thoroughly washed, and then cut into pieces ¾ in. in length. Then pieces are filled into No. 10 cans; boiling water is added; and the cans are exhausted for 10 min at 212°F.

An alternate method producing a somewhat better and more solid pack is to put the cans of rhubarb through the exhaust box before adding the boiling water. The rhubarb shrinks and a half more cut rhubarb can be added, thus producing a solid or heavy pack.

Another procedure, sometimes followed, is to hand peel the stalks before they are cut. The cut rhubarb is heated with a little water in a kettle until it softens. Then the hot, softened rhubarb is filled into cans. The juice left in the kettle is used to cover the rhubarb in the cans.

The rhubarb canned raw should be processed for 13 min at 212°F. The precooked rhubarb needs no further processing if the cans are sealed at 180°F or higher.

Processing procedures should be checked with can supplier or the National Canners Association.

SOURCE: D. K. Tressler and Associates, Westport, Conn.

CANNED SAUERKRAUT

Sauerkraut is sufficiently acid and contains enough salt that the product needs little heating in order to obtain a stable canned product. The acidity should be about 1.2%. The kraut to be packed in cans should be heated in a large kettle (preferably of stainless steel) to 165°F and filled at this temperature. Hot kraut brine (juice) is added to assure a proper fill. The cans are passed through an exhaust box and on to the sealer. The cans need no further processing but should be water cooled to 100°F.

SOURCE: D. K. Tressler and Associates, Westport, Conn.

CANNED SPANISH RICE

	Ingredients	Lb	Oz
(A)	Onion, sliced	10	3
	Pepper, diced	7	5
	Fat	2	14
(B)	Cooked Tomatoes	45	10
	Salt		8
	Sugar		11
	Amioca starch (CLEARJEL)	1	
	Bay leaf (to suit)		
(C)	Rice, cooked	32	
	Total weight	100	

Procedure

Sauté (A) over low heat until tender. Mix (B) until uniform and add to (A) with stirring. Simmer for 15 min, stirring until thickened. Remove bay leaf. Add (C). Cook covered, over low heat for 10 min. Fill into cans; close, seal, and process. Check processing time and temperature with the National Canners Association or can supplier.

SOURCE: National Starch and Chemical Corp., Plainfield, N.J.

CANNED SPINACH, SWISS CHARD, MUSTARD, BEET AND DANDELION GREENS

Spinach is machine harvested and must be canned within 8 hr or it may lose its bright green color and toughen. The first operation in the cannery is the cutting of and elimination of the crowns, heavy stalks, yellow leaves, weeds, etc.

The trimmed spinach (or greens) should then be placed on a conveyor which takes it to the washer. Usually, this is a long revolving cylinder rotating at 40-50 rpm. Powerful sprays of water wash the spinach as it turns over and over and the water and dirt fall through the screen walls of the washer.

The washed spinach (or greens) is discharged into a blancher in which it is submerged in steam-heated water at about 212°F for 3-6 min. The blanching water should not be recirculated. The blanched spinach should be discharged on an inspection belt where tough or discolored pieces are picked out and discarded. The inspection belt should pass under light rollers which eliminate excess water taken up during the blanching.

The spinach should then be filled into plain tin cans with enameled ends; 2½% salt brine at 200°F or hotter should be added to fill the cans completely. The cans should be exhausted before closing: No. 2 or No. 2½ for 5-6 min; No. 10 cans require 11-13 min.

Because of the solid nature of canned spinach it requires a long process usually at 250°F. The can supplier or the National Canners Association should be consulted in order to obtain proper processing times and temperatures.

SOURCE: D. K. Tressler and Associates, Westport, Conn.

CANNED SUCCOTASH

Succotash is usually considered to be a mixture of cream-style corn, green lima beans, and tomato purée; ⅓ of each ingredient is often used. Another formula includes 50% corn, 20% lima beans, and 30% tomato purée. The corn and green lima beans are prepared for canning as have been described earlier in this Section.

The ingredients are weighed into a steam-jacketed kettle and heated to boiling. No. 2 cans are usually processed for 60 min at 240°F. Check with can supplier or the National Canners Association for exact time and temperature of processing.

SOURCE: D. K. Tressler and Associates, Westport, Conn.

CANNED SWEET CORN

Whole Grain (Kernel)

Most sweet corn is mechanically harvested. The less mature is usually canned as whole grain corn, the more mature has tougher kernels and so is canned cream-style.

Husking is the first operation. This machine not only husks the corn, but also eliminates most of the silk. The ears of corn are then washed and run over an inspection belt. The more mature ears are picked out, and imperfectly formed and any wormy ears eliminated. The ears of corn then pass to a silking machine in which they are rolled rapidly between a pair of rollers and at the same time brushed with fiber brushes.

The ears then pass to the cutter which cuts deep enough to take most of the kernel but not cut into the cob. The kernels are washed to eliminate bits of cob, silk, and milk. The washed corn then passes over a draining belt before going to a filler which fills the corn into C-enameled No. 2 electrotin plate cans. Boiling hot weak (often 1%) salt brine, sometimes sweetened with sugar is added. The filled cans of corn should be given a short exhaust before closure. No. 2 cans and smaller should be processed at 240°F for 50 min or for 25 min at 250°F. No. 10 cans (initial temperature 160°F) require 80 min at 240°F or 40 min at 250°F. Processing time and temperature should be checked with can supplier or the National Canners Association.

Cream-Style

More mature corn should be packed cream-style. The corn is husked and the husked ears are washed, inspected, and desilked in the manner described above for kernel corn. Special cutters are used for cream-style of cut, they cut the kernels and scrape the cob both in one operation. The cut corn is then passed over a series of vibrating and revolving screens to remove silk, pieces of cob, etc.

The cream-style corn procedure is quite different from this point on inasmuch as the product is prepared batch by batch. The desilked corn should be run into a stainless steel tank equipped with rotating paddles to mix the batch. Measured quantities of corn and water are put in the tank; weighed amounts of salt, sugar, and (usually) cornstarch are added. The cornstarch is added to give a product which, when used by the housewife, will just pour from the can. As an average, 1 gal. of water is added for each 4 gal. of corn. The amount of sugar and salt added varies, but is often 20 lb sugar and 5 lb salt per 100 gal. corn. It is best to make a slurry of the starch with cold water before adding it to a batch, otherwise the corn may be lumpy even though it is agitated continuously. The corn is heated to 160°F in the tank and then in a second blender the temperature is raised to 190°F to gelatenize the starch.

It is important that the temperature of the corn in the cans be at 180°F or higher when closed. If this is the case, No. 2 cans will require processing of 90 min at 240°F or 70 min at 250°F; No. 10 cans will require 180 min processing at 240°F or 155 min at 250°F.

Consult your can supplier or the National Canners Association for data for processing of other sizes of cans at various temperatures.

SOURCE: D. K. Tressler and Associates, Westport, Conn.

CANNING SWEET POTATOES

The essential steps in a good sweet potato canning operation are as follows: (1) receiving at the cannery; (2) dry cleaning; (3) preheating; (4) peeling; (5) inspection, trimming, and sorting; (6) size grading; (7) blanching; (8) filling into cans; (9) syruping; (10) exhausting; (11) closing; (12) heat processing; (13) cooling; and (14) storage.

Cleaning

Loose soil, sand, and some of the extraneous organic materials should be removed by passing the roots through a revolving drum with slots large enough for such material to pass through but not large enough for the sweet potatoes to go through.

Preheating

Preheating in water held at 145°F for 8 min has been found to be useful, and has proved more feasible in commercial production.

Peeling

The peeling operation may be accomplished by one of several alternative methods as follows: (1) mechanical abrasion; (2) sodium hydroxide (lye); (3) longer time in flowing steam; (4) shorter time in high pressure steam; and (5) combinations of two or more of these.

Abrasion

Mechanical abrasion is useful for peeling fresh roots for institutional feeding but is seldom used in commercial processing plants. Use of this technique as the only process in peeling results in excessive yield losses. It is sometimes used in conjunction with one of the other methods of peeling to finish or "polish" the roots.

Use of Lye

Although a 10% lye concentration works very well at temperatures from 200° to 215°F, some commercial processors have found that equally good results can be obtained by use of lye at concentrations of 20-25% with the bath at about 225°F. The optimum combination of lye concentration, bath temperature, and time of exposure will depend upon the variety used, time since the roots were dug, size of roots, and degree of polish needed on the finished product.

In the lye peeling operation the washed roots are conveyed into the hot lye bath in equipment which keeps the roots submerged and permits conveying them through the solution at a controlled rate of speed so as to permit regulation of the time they are exposed to the peeling bath.

As the roots emerge from the lye bath they are discharged into a revolving drum equipped with nozzles which deliver water over the tumbling roots at a pressure of from 90 to 100 psi. The tumbling action and resulting abrasion along with the high pressure, effectively remove skins from the roots. The sweet potatoes may be run over brushes or abrasion peelers to give added polish to the product if the improved quality warrants the added cost.

Inspection, Trimming, and Sorting

The peeled roots are conveyed past workers who perform the inspection, trimming, and sorting. Discolored areas, fibrous ends, and insect- or disease-damaged spots are carefully removed.

Roots that have large discolored or damaged areas should be sorted out and discarded. Excessively trimmed and irregular shaped roots should be separated out and conveyed to the puréed product or for use other than canned whole sweet potatoes.

Size Grading

Size grading has a profound effect on the finished product. A rather large size range is acceptable to the housewife and the trade so long as uniformity of size within the individual container is maintained. Size grading is best accomplished by using a revolving reel with rods at selected spacings. As the roots pass through the reel, the smaller ones drop through first and the larger ones drop out as they pass through the reel.

Blanching

Conveyors should be so arranged to receive the sized roots and convey them through a blancher in which they are held in water at 170°F for 1-3 min.

Filling

The hot, blanched roots should be immediately packed into cans and covered with hot syrup. Plain tin cans of either hot-dipped or electroplated bodies and enameled ends should be used. Syrup of 40-50% sucrose content at 205°F should be used.

Exhausting

After having been filled into suitable cans and having hot syrup added, cans larger than No. 303 should be conveyed through a steam chamber with a retention time sufficient to raise the center temperature to 160°-170°F. The time required to accomplish this will depend upon the can size, in-going temperature, and temperature inside the steam chamber.

No. 303 cans and smaller may be closed without exhausting if hot syrup and a steam-flow closing machine are used.

Closing

As the cans of sweet potatoes come from the exhaust box, lids are seamed onto the cans using a suitable commercial can closing machine. It is generally preferable to use the machine designed by the supplier of cans and lids although this is not necessary if suitable adjustments are made on the can closing machine.

It is good practice to use a steam-flow closing machine. A jet of steam is flowed into the headspace just prior to the lid being seamed on the can. Such a practice has the following beneficial results: (1) air is forced out of the headspace thus reducing the oxygen content of the can; (2) the entrapped steam will condense and aid in development of a good internal can vacuum.

Whether steam-flow closing or mechanical vacuum closing is used on syrup-packed roots the resulting vacuum should range from 10 to 15 in. of mercury with the high side of the range preferred. With vacuum-style sweet potatoes the mechanical vacuum closing machine is preferred and a final vacuum of 26-30 in. of mercury is desirable. Solid and dry packs may be closed under atmospheric pressure without benefit of steam-flow if filled hot and the cans are full. The contraction of the product upon cooling will result in development of adequate vacuum.

Heat Processing

The time at various temperatures required to commercially sterilize canned sweet potatoes should be obtained from the National Canners Association laboratories or other competent laboratories. The heat applied must be sufficient to inactivate spores of *Clostridium botulinum* throughout the container.

Cooling

Immediately after having been retorted, the cans of sweet potatoes must be cooled to about body temperature (95°-105°F). Adequate cooling can be evaluated by vigorously shaking the can and contents and holding the can against the side of the face. If the can feels warm but not hot, cooling is adequate.

SOURCE: *Sweet Potatoes: Production, Processing, Marketing* by Edmond and Ammerman published by Avi Publishing Co., Westport, Conn.

CANNED TOMATOES

A variety of tomato to be satisfactory for canning must be medium-sized, have a smooth contour, have small seed cells and core, be uniformly dark red throughout, and have a good flavor. The first step in preparing tomatoes for canning is to pass them over a sorting belt and remove both decayed and green fruit. Washing is the next operation; the tomatoes must be sprayed with powerful streams of water as they are rolled over and over. This can be carried out on a roller conveyor. After the tomatoes have been thoroughly washed, they are scalded for about 30 sec preferably with steam jets. After scalding, the tomatoes should be sprayed with cold water in order to loosen the skins. Next the tomatoes should be cored and peeled. Coring is effected by pressing the stem end of the tomato down on a revolving knife. Coring may be done before scalding. Tomatoes must be hand peeled and trimmed as no machine has been invented which will peel them satisfactorily. The peeled tomatoes are filled into tin cans with plain bodies and enameled ends. This is done by machine which fills a mixture of tomato meats and juice. If a solid pack is being canned, the cans are filled with meats without any juice and about 0.5% of dry salt is added, often as a tablet.

The standard grade of canned tomatoes consists of ⅔ small tomatoes and ⅓ tomato purée.

If the tomatoes are overripe and somewhat mushy, 0.67% of calcium chloride may be added to keep the tomatoes from going to pieces during processing.

The cans of tomatoes (No. 3 and smaller) should be exhausted for 4 min at 200°F in an exhaust box; No. 10 cans require a 10 min exhaust. No. 2 cans (and smaller) should be processed 35 min at 212°F if air cooled, or for 45 min when water cooled.

No. 10 cans should be processed for 80 min at 212°F if air cooled or 100 min if water cooled.

Check processing times and temperatures with can supplier or with the National Canners Association.

SOURCE: D. K. Tressler and Associates, Westport, Conn.

CANNED TURNIPS

Immature white turnips may be preserved by canning. They should be harvested when they are sweet and not more than 1½ in. in diameter. First, wash them thoroughly, and scrape or trim off the roots. Then steam them just long enough so that the skins can be slipped off. The whole turnips are packed in No. 2 or No. 2½ cans, and the institutional pack in No. 10 cans. Fill the cans with boiling hot 1½% salt brine. Exhaust the No. 2 cans for 5–6 min then close immediately. Process turnips in No. 2½ cans at 240°F for 30 min. Check processing time and temperature with can supplier or the National Canners Association.

SOURCE: D. K. Tressler and Associates, Westport, Conn.

DRIED AND DEHYDRATED VEGETABLE PRODUCTS

DRIED GREEN BEANS

Fresh beans are delivered to the processor in bulk bins. They are dumped, graded for size, sorted for defects, and mechanically snipped to remove pod ends. These operations are the same as those customarily performed in canning and freezing beans. The beans should be washed either before or after these operations. Sizing of beans according to diameter by automatic graders is a routine operation in processing beans. Sizes 1, 2, and 3 have been found to dehydrate poorly while sizes 6 or larger are usually fibrous. Sizes 4 and 5 ($^{21}/_{64}$-in. to $^{23}/_{64}$-in. thickness) yield a good dehydrated product both as to appearance and quality, and are specified in current military specifications for this item.

The snipped pods should be cut transversely into approximately 1-in. segments for cross-cut beans; and transversely into 1½- to 2-in. segments, then sliced length wise for "French style." The cut beans should be blanched for about 4 min in atmospheric steam and promptly cooled with water sprays. A sulfite-bisulfite solution should be sprayed over the blanched material, to produce a sulfur dioxide content of about 500 ppm in the dried product. The blanched, sulfited, cut beans should then be dried immediately, or frozen and held in this state until they are delivered to the dehydrator.

The beans should be spread on a tray or belt for drying whether or not they have been frozen. If dried on trays in a cabinet dehydrator, 6–6½ hr at 145°F, will be required. They should then be transferred to a bin for 48 hr, after which they should be packed in tin cans or moisture proof plastic bags.

SOURCE: *Food Dehydration, 2nd Edition* by Van Arsdel, Copley and Morgan published by Avi Publishing Co., Westport, Conn.

INSTANT LIMA BEAN SOUP

Ingredients	Parts by Weight
Lima bean powder (instantly rehydratable)	81.10
Hydrogenated vegetable fat	9.40
Salt	5.00
Monosodium glutamate	0.80
Onions, powdered, dehydrated	1.00
Smoked-meat flavoring	2.50
Soluble allspice flavoring	0.10
Soluble black pepper flavoring	0.10
	100.00

Procedure

Mix the above ingredients together thoroughly.

To Use

This soup is rehydrated by adding 1½ oz of dry mix to hot water (180°F) and stirring with a spoon (about 1½ min).

SOURCE: Military Specification 35016, 14 November 1962

DEHYDRATED BEETS

Usually, beets are first "dry-washed" by tumbling them in a slightly inclined rotary screen or slotted drum and the loosened dirt falls through the holes. Then the beets proceed to a wet washer, where they are tumbled through a rotating rod-type cylinder while exposed to strong sprays of water.

Beets have been successfully peeled with steam, lye, and abrasion. Abrasive peelers use less water but result in high peeling loss. Lye peeling requires careful controls and thorough washing to remove all traces of lye. Preheating in hot water reduces the load on lye-peeling equipment. Peeling for 2 min in 10% lye at 215°F has been effective in efficient skin removal without excessive loss. Steam peelers are generally operated at 70–100 lb per sq in. for 60–85 sec exposure time. The skins which have been loosened by steam or lye are removed by passing the beets over a series of high-speed rollers covered with rubber or abrasive. High-pressure water sprays wash off the loosened peelings as the beets are tumbled. Peeling and trimming losses may vary from 10 to 30% depending on raw material quality and peeling methods.

The peeled beets are inspected and trimmed; then diced, sliced, or strip-cut to the specified size. The cut material should be conventionally blanched in flowing steam for about 6 min in a continuous blancher. Since betanin, the red pigment of beets, is water-soluble, such operations as blanching, cutting, and washing should be accomplished with a minimum of time and water.

The blanched dice may be dehydrated in tunnel driers on trays, continuous conveyor-belt dehy-

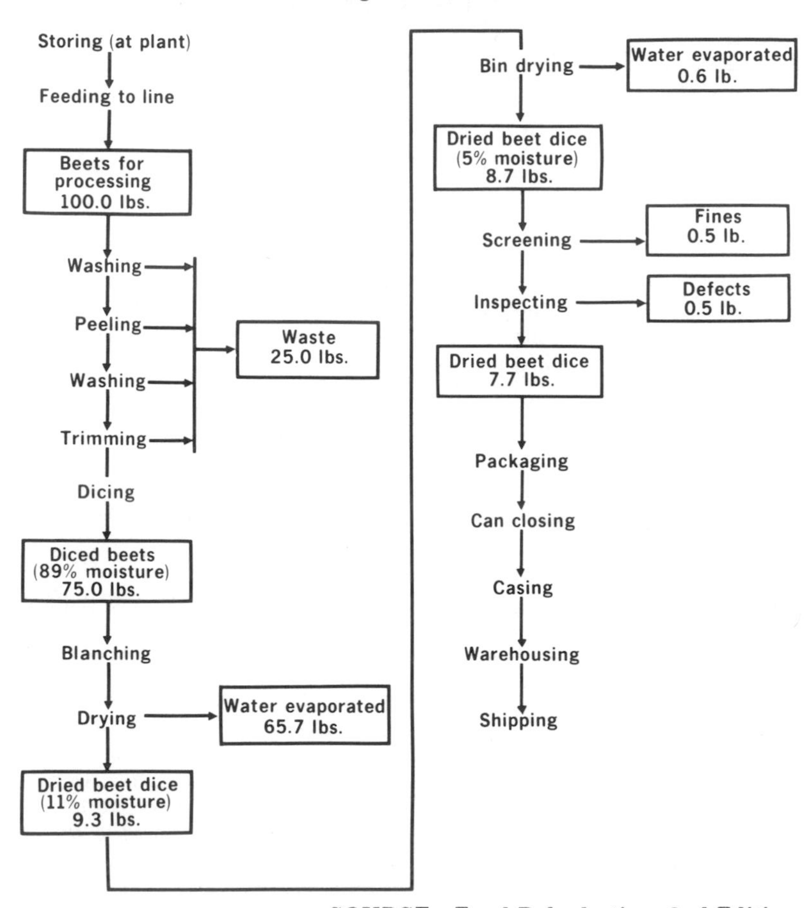

SOURCE: Food Dehydration, 2nd Edition, Vol. 2, Avi Publishing Co., Westport, Conn.

FIG. 11.1. FLOW SHEET FOR BEET DICE DEHYDRATION

drators, or belt-trough driers. Relatively high initial air temperatures of 200°-210°F may be used for dehydrating beets, with maximum second stage temperature of 160°F. The material is taken from the driers at about 11% moisture and may be finished in bin driers at 145°F to a final moisture content of 5%.

The dehydrated beets should be packaged in air-tight packages and stored in a cool place.

SOURCE: *Food Dehydration, 2nd Edition* by Van Arsdel, Copley and Morgan published by Avi Publishing Co., Westport, Conn.

DEHYDRATED CABBAGE

Solid heads of winter cabbage free from insect infestation should be selected. The outer wrapper leaves that are withered, damaged, or discolored are removed by hand on the preparation line. After it is trimmed, the head may be cored with a water-powered rotating knife. More commonly, the cabbage head is sliced in half and each half is pushed against a short length of metal tubing sharpened at one end. The knife edge scoops out the core material, and this falls into a chute and is carried away for disposal. The cored and trimmed halves are washed with strong water sprays to remove dirt and grit. They are then shredded or diced. During World War II, dehydrated cabbage was prepared principally as shreds. The cored, trimmed, washed cabbage halves were shredded by kraut cutters in shreds ¼-⅛ in. in width. A ⅜-in. dice is not the preferred style for both military and commercial uses.

Cabbage has normally been blanched and sulfited before drying, but U.S. Military Specifications for dehydrated cabbage now call for "Style A, unblanched"—to be used for cole slaw, relish, or salad where the crisp texture of fresh cabbage is desired; and "Style B, blanched"—to be used for cooked cabbage.

Since it is difficult to spread warm, limp, blanched cabbage shreds or dice evenly on a tray, the practice in the United States is to spread the cool, crisp unblanched material immediately after shredding or dicing; and blanch, sulfite, and dry it on the same tray. All-wood trays are unsatisfactory for this technique; a drying tray consisting of a wooden frame with ¼-in. galvanized wire cloth bottom has been used successfully. The wire cloth has sometimes been coated with a confectioners' grade mineral oil to prevent sticking of the dried product in the meshes. In order to achieve uniform blanching and drying conditions it is important that the cabbage be loaded evenly on the tray. Blanching and drying are usually done with a tray loading of 1 lb per sq ft. Trays are conveyed through flowing steam, with a residence time of about 80-100 sec. Overblanching will result in mushy cabbage. Sulfiting is done in the blancher. A sulfite solution with a pH not lower than about 7.0-7.5 is advisable, in order to minimize corrosion of the trays and to maintain a bright green color in the final product. A proportion of three parts by weight of sodium sulfite to one part of sodium metabisulfite yields a solution of approximately pH 7.2. A concentration of 0.3-0.7% sulfite/bisulfite mixture, or sufficient to give a concentration of 1000-2000 ppm SO_2 in the finished product, is sprayed over the cabbage at a point ½ to ⅔ of the blancher length from the entrance end of the blancher. Sulfiting too early in the blanching period results in poor retention of sulfite; sulfiting too near the discharge end does not allow sufficient time for drainage.

As the trays move out of the blancher they are automatically stacked onto cars. Since cabbage contains about 93% water, it is possible to remove much of the moisture in the first stage of drying, using relatively high temperatures. Two-stage tunnel driers have been successfully used with an inlet air temperature of 180°F in the first (parrallel air flow) stage, and 145°F in the second (countercurrent air flow) stage. By this system the moisture can be reduced from 93 to about 7% in approximately 6 hr. The dried cabbage is removed from the trays by hand scraping or by a revolving wire-brush. It may then be transferred to finishing bins, where the moisture is lowered from 7 to 4% in about 7 hr using inlet air at 120°F.

The dehydrated cabbage is rather hygroscopic and must be packaged in air-tight moisture-proof containers; usually, tin cans are used.

SOURCE: *Food Dehydration, 2nd Edition* by Van Arsdel, Copley and Morgan published by Avi Publishing Co., Westport, Conn.

COMMERCIAL DEHYDRATION OF CARROTS

Washing

Two methods of washing may be used: (1) "Dry washing" followed by water washing. (2) Water washing only. A thorough water wash to remove remaining dirt is necessary before carrots are processed.

Peeling

Carrots may be readily peeled by either steam or lye. One company, that has used both steam and lye, favors steam because of lower peeling losses and elimination of problems encountered in handling lye. The proposed operation is equipped for steam peeling. Reported conditions for steam peeling range from 40 to 120 sec at 70 lb per sq in. to 25 to 30 sec at 100 lb per sq in. pressure. (Lye peeling requires 3-5 min in a 5% caustic soda solution at 210°F.)

Peeling losses are assumed to be 20% but may vary from below 8 to over 30% depending on the variety, age, size, and condition of the carrots at the time of processing, as well as peeling procedure employed.

Washing (To Remove Peel)

In this operation, loosened skins are washed off the carrots in a rotary rod-type washer. Good washing depends on plenty of water under pressure combined with active tumbling, rolling, and rubbing action of carrots. Excessive water pressure should be avoided as pitting and gouging will result.

Trimming

The "merry-go-round" type of trimming belt is assumed for this operation. The trimming lines normally will require 45 women for a 100-ton per day plant, but the requirements may vary depending on the grade and size of material, peeling efficiency, etc. Feeding to the line should be coordinated with trimming so that the carrots do not travel the "merry-go-round" circuit unduly long.

Dicing

The carrots are cut to ⅜ × ⅜ × $\frac{3}{16}$-in. half-dice. Three dicers are proposed for the operation. Two dicers are adequate to carry the normal load, but one extra dicer is provided to assure uninterrupted production.

Blanching and Sulfiting

After the dicing operation, the product is washed (if desired) by sprays located on the front end of the blancher belt. For the desired capacity, the blancher provided permits a maximum blanching time of 6-7 min when the belt loading is 4 lb per sq ft. Adjustable belt speed is provided so that blanching conditions may be varied.

Sulfiting of carrots, as with most vegetables, is done in a manner which is best determined by trial. Specifications require 500-1000 ppm (as SO_2) in the finished product. The product may be sprayed with a sulfite solution, dipped in a bath of sulfite solution, or subjected to drying air containing sulfur dioxide gas. Sulfite solutions generally used are dilute—approximately 0.2-1.0%.

Drying

Belt-trough driers are generally used for preliminary drying to remove the bulk of the moisture, followed by bins or deep belts.

Screening

Specifications require that not more than 1% by weight of the dehydrated product may pass through a U.S. Standard sieve containing 8-meshes to the inch (0.973-in. openings). Screening is, therefore, necessary to remove material that is too fine in size to comply with these requirements. A magnet is provided at this point to remove pieces of iron and steel.

Filling, Packing, and Sealing

In a filling operation of 330 cans an hour, cans are placed manually into the run which feeds cans to the rotary hand-pack filler. The entire can-carrying circular table revolves, as well as the center bowl carrying the product to be packaged. The cans are automatically placed under the can-filling openings around the edge of the center bowl. The product is manually pushed into the holes by the operators. The center bowl is supplied from an overhead hopper.

Since the presence of oxygen causes undesired changes in the product during storage, specifications require that "Every effort should be made to secure an oxygen content of less than 1% in the container." In order to accomplish this, the air is replaced by inert gas, usually nitrogen.

SOURCE: USDA Western Regional Research Laboratory, Berkeley, Calif.

DEHYDRATED CELERY

Celery is harvested and delivered from the field in tote bins. First washing of the whole celery head is in the flood type washer using six paddle wheels. Approved wetting agent and detergents, automatically metered into the supply water, loosen any adhering field dirt. High pressure spray washers complete the first washing.

Following this thorough prewash, the celery is fed through mechanical cutters. So flexible are these cutters, any desired portion of the stalk can be removed from the celery head and diverted to either the manufacture of celery stalk dice or to celery stalk and leaf flakes. As the length of the celery head, as well as the size of the butt ends, varies considerably in field-run celery, gaging devices control both the butt-end cut and the length of the center stalk sections.

The leafy portion of the celery is cut to specified size, and the leaves are separated from the stalk portion by air. At this point the two streams of material are diverted—the stalks being conveyed to the dicing equipment, the leaves going to the slicers.

Prior to the dicing and slicing, the celery passes over inspection tables and then through both flood-type and rotary-type washers using high pressure sprays.

No wash water is recirculated and all wash water is chlorinated.

Diced celery stalk is blanched in atmospheric steam for about 2 min; leaves for 1 min. Blanching may be omitted if the dried product is to be ground into celery powder, since blanching is reported to cause some loss in flavor. Sulfite/bisulfite solution is sprayed over the blanched material to give a final sulfur dioxide content of 500-1000 ppm.

In a 2-stage tunnel drier system, initial dry-bulb temperatures of 180°F in the hot end of the first stage (parallel flow) and 130°F in the second stage (countercurrent) have been recommended.

SOURCE: *Food Dehydration, 2nd Edition* by Van Arsdel, Copley and Morgan published by Avi Publishing Co., Westport, Conn.

DRY MIX CHILI SAUCE

Ingredients	%
Textaid	20.30
Waxy maize starch (Clearjel)	7.20
Modified cornstarch (Dry Flo)	2.00
Tomato powder	23.20
Chili powder	20.00
Salt	14.60
Sugar	9.10
Onion powder	3.60
	100.00

Procedure

Dry blend ingredients thoroughly.

To Use

To prepare sauce, mix 1 oz of dry mix with 5 oz of water. Heat to boiling with stirring.

SOURCE: National Starch and Chemical Corp., Plainfield, N.J.

DRY MIX COCKTAIL SAUCE

Ingredients	%
Pregelatinized tapioca (Instant Textaid)	12.1
Pregelatinized cornstarch and corn syrup solids (Instant Plus)	10.6
Tomato powder	60.8
Salt	8.7
Spray-dried vegetable shortening (Beatreme)	4.6
Onion powder	1.2
Garlic powder	0.5
Chili powder	1.2
Cayenne powder	0.3
Color (FD&C Red No. 4, to suit)	
	100.0

Procedure

Blend all ingredients well.

To Use

Mix 50 gm of above mixture with 8 oz of boiling water. Chill and serve with seafood.

SOURCE: National Starch and Chemical Co., Plainfield, N.J.

DEHYDRATED SWEET CORN

Corn should be harvested when still young and tender and the kernels full of "milk." The ears are mechanically harvested, promptly hauled to the processing plant, and automatically husked and de-silked. The kernels are cut from the cob and blanched for 2 min in atmospheric steam. Frozen blanched corn can be purchased by the dehydrating plant, if desired, although there is no quality advantage to be gained by inserting a freezing step. The blanched corn is either dipped into, or sprayed with, a sulfite/bisulfite solution adjusted to a pH of about 6.7 and of sufficient concentration to produce a residual sulfur dioxide content of approximately 2000 ppm in the final dried product.

Sweet corn may be dried in tray-tunnel driers or continuous belt driers. In a 2-stage tunnel drying system a dry-bulb temperature of 180°F for air entering the first (parallel flow) stage and 165°F for air entering the second (counterflow) stage has been recommended. The partially dried kernels may be taken from the second stage and dried to a final moisture content of 5% in a bin drier. Pieces of cob, silk, or kernel fragments may be removed by aspiration after drying.

SOURCE: *Food Dehydration, 2nd Edition* by Van Arsdel, Copley and Morgan published by Avi Publishing Co., Westport, Conn.

DRY MIX CREAM SAUCE

Ingredients	%
Instantized amioca starch (Instant Clearjel)	25.0
Beatreme 1126	40.0
Nonfat dry milk powder	33.0
Salt	1.5
Pepper	0.5
Color (FD&C No. 5, to suit)	

Procedure

Blend ingredients together thoroughly.

To Use

Use 1¼ oz of mixture in ½ cup of boiling water and stir until smooth.

SOURCE: National Starch and Chemical Co., Plainfield, N.J.

DEHYDRATED GARLIC

The bulbs are loosened by passing a cutter bar underneath them; they are then pulled by hand and stacked in windrows to cure. After about a week, or when they have dried thoroughly, the bulbs are "topped" by cutting off the leaves and roots with shears. Diseased and damaged bulbs are sorted out in the field. After grading, the garlic is brought to the dehydration plant in 100-lb open mesh bags or in large bulk bins holding about 1000 lb. Garlic stores well under a wide range of temperatures, so that controlled temperature storage usually is not necessary. At temperatures near 40°F garlic tends to sprout, so that long storage in this temperature range should be avoided. At humidities higher than 70% garlic may start to mold.

Drying

The garlic bulb, which may be composed of 6 to 36 cloves, is broken into individual cloves by passing between rubber-covered rollers which exert enough pressure to crack the bulb without crushing the cloves. The loose "paper shell" is removed by screening and aspirating. The cloves are then washed in a flood washer, at which time the root-stubs are floated off. Garlic is sliced, trayed, and dehydrated in a manner similar to that used for onions. After drying, the pink skin which adhered tightly to the fresh clove can be removed by screening and air aspiration. Garlic is commercially dried to about 6.5% moisture.

Dehydrated garlic is sold commercially primarily as powder or "granules." It is also available in sliced, chopped, or minced form. Packaging is similar to that used for onions.

SOURCE: *Food Dehydration, 2nd Edition* by Van Arsdel, Copley and Morgan published by Avi Publishing Co., Westport, Conn.

DEHYDRATED HORSERADISH

If an entire horseradish root is blanched or cooked so that the natural enzymes are destroyed, no flavor-producing substances can be formed in subsequent slicing or grinding. For this reason, when horseradish is to be dehydrated, the enzymes must not be destroyed by blanching nor inhibited by sulfiting. Crushing of the plant tissue must be kept to a minimum during the predrying operations so that the formation of volatile allyl isothiocyanate and other flavorful constituents, and their subsequent loss during drying, is minimized. When the horseradish root is sliced for drying, only a small proportion of cells are broken. The dried slices are ground into a powder or into small granules. Although the grinding ruptures the plant cells, liberating enzyme and substrate, no allyl isothiocyanate is formed, since the enzyme reaction requires water. For this reason, the dried horseradish powder is almost tasteless, yet when mixed with water and allowed to stand a few minutes it becomes extremely pungent.

Horseradish roots must be thoroughly washed by high pressure sprays and scoured with stiff brushes, by hand or mechanical means, since they are not peeled before drying. The roots are sliced about ¼ in. thick and tray-dried. Two-stage tunnels have been recommended, the first stage being parallel flow with the relatively low inlet temperature of about 150°F; an inlet temperature of about 135°F can be used in the secondary counterflow drier. The slices are removed at about 7-8% moisture content and are dried to a final moisture content of 5% in a bin drier. The dried slices are then milled into a powder or granules.

The finished item is used as an ingredient by manufacturers of such products as cocktail and fish sauces, horseradish mustard, or horseradish dressings. A 2½-oz jar of dehydrated horseradish powder is a popular retail item.

SOURCE: *Food Dehydration, 2nd Edition* by Van Arsdel, Copley and Morgan published by Avi Publishing Co., Westport, Conn.

NEWBURGH SAUCE MIX

Ingredients	%
Maggi HPP Type 3H3 Powder	0.90
Monosodium glutamate	0.55
Salt	0.58
Sugar	0.63
Butter or hydrogenated vegetable oil	1.62
Starch	3.50
Nonfat milk solids	3.60
Soluble pepper	0.02
Soluble celery	0.03
Soluble onion	0.09
Oleoresin paprika	0.01
Sherry	3.00
Water	85.47
	100.00

Procedure

Mix in stainless steel bowl with power driven agitator.

SOURCE: Nestlé Company, Food Ingredients Division, 100 Bloomingdale Road, White Plains, N.Y.

DEHYDRATED ONIONS

The process for dehydrating onions consists of the following main steps:

1. Field-run onions are first size-graded to separate the small sizes. Disposition practices for small sizes vary considerably. The small first-quality onions may be selected from the lot and sold in the market. The remainder of the small onions may be later run through the line without being peeled and ground into onion powder after the residual skins are removed in an aspirator.

2. The dry outer layers (paper shell) of onions are removed, usually by flame peeling. Peeling may also be accomplished by cutting off the top and roots to open up the paper-shell layers and then passing the onions through washers that have vigorous brushing action and high pressure water sprays.

3. Flame peeling is followed by washing and coring, and topping either on water-driven rotary knives or by other means to remove tops and root crowns. Inspection, trimming, and washing follow.

4. Slicing is usually done on specially-designed, high-speed cutters. Kraut cutters have been used to some extent.

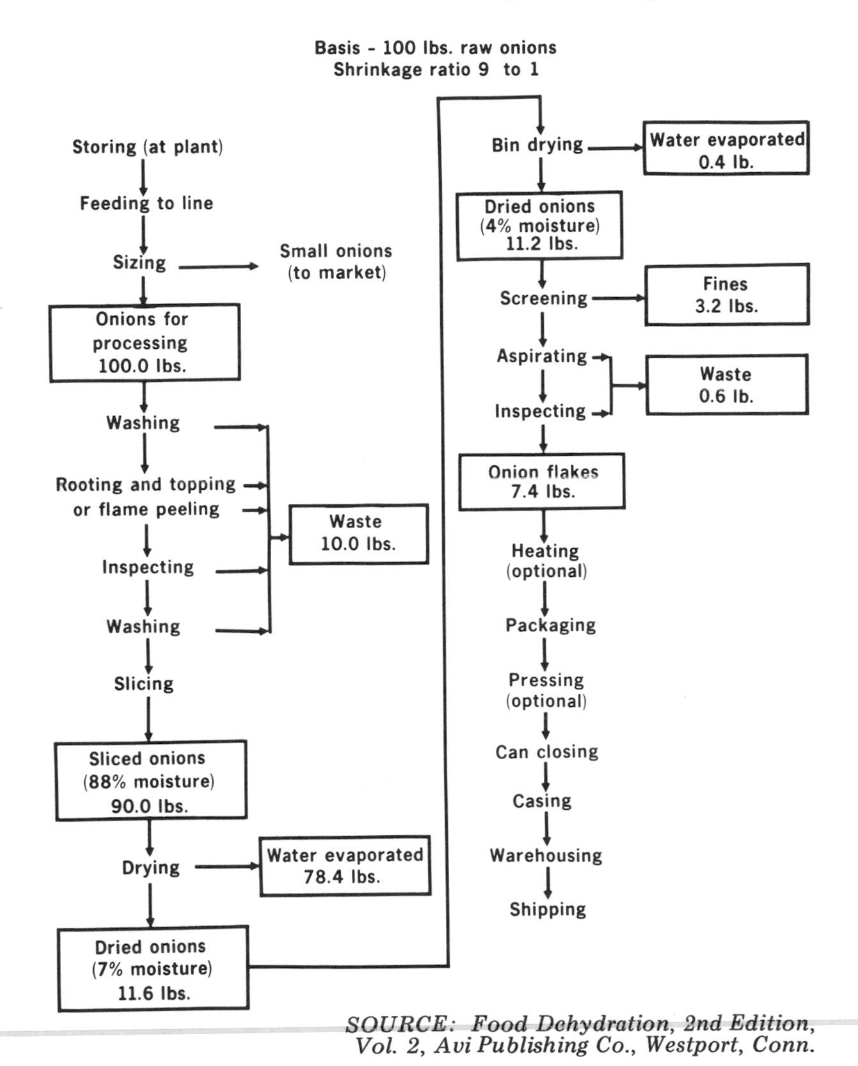

SOURCE: Food Dehydration, 2nd Edition, Vol. 2, Avi Publishing Co., Westport, Conn.

FIG. 11.2. FLOW SHEET FOR ONION DEHYDRATION

5. The sliced onions may then be spread on drying trays which, in turn, are stacked on transfer cars. Tunnel type dehydrators have long been used by the major onion dehydrators. The cars are placed in these tunnels, and hot air is blown across the trays. The onions are dried down to about 10% moisture in this operation, which takes 10–15 hr. Conveyor-belt dehydrators are also satisfactory for drying onions. Air is blown through the bed of onions on the belt, flowing upward in one section of the dryer and downward in another section.

6. Part of the remaining moisture is usually removed in a finishing operation for which the onions are placed in large bins. Warm air is forced upward through the bins. This bin drying and conditioning operation may take around 30 hr, the exact time depending not only on the plant but also on size of the cuts, the desired final moisture content, and the humidity and temperature of the air. In both drying operations (5) and (6), temperatures must be carefully controlled so that browning or scorching will not occur.

7. After the slices are dried, they may be screened for removal of large partially-dried slabs and "fines." The "fines" may amount to ⅓ of the total dehydrated product. Usually, the fines are ground into powder. The slabs may be broken up and redried. The acceptable slices may be cut to desired size, such as flakes. Grinding and packaging of powder should be done in low-humidity surroundings to avoid gumming and caking.

8. Aspirating equipment in which the remaining paper-shell fragments are removed from the dried onions is located at convenient points along the processing line.

9. Following final inspection, the onion flakes or slices are packaged in No. 10 tin cans or larger size cans or drums.

SOURCE: USDA Engineering and Development Laboratory, Western Utilization Research and Development Division, Agricultural Research Service, Berkeley, Calif.

ONION SOUP MIX

Ingredients	%
Salt	41.11
Hydrolyzed plant protein	11.67
Hydrogenated vegetable oil	10.28
Potato flour—redried	9.28
Monosodium glutamate	8.22
Anhydrous dextrose	7.00
Beef extract, dehydrated	6.66
Potato starch, redried	2.83
Cornstarch, redried	2.67
Caramel color	0.28
	100.00

Procedure

Mix thoroughly until a homogenous mixture is obtained.

Package 18 gm of above mix and 21 gm of dehydrated onion slices (which may be a mixture of natural and toasted pieces) in a foil pouch. For reconstitution, stir contents of envelope into 1 qt of boiling water, cover and boil for 10 min.

SOURCE: *Food Dehydration, 2nd Edition* by Van Arsdel, Copley and Morgan published by Avi Publishing Co., Westport, Conn.

DEHYDRATED PARSLEY

The cut parsley falls into field trailers, which haul it quickly to the plant. Here it is unloaded, passed through a reel to remove dirt and field debris, and triple-washed. The parsley is fed at a uniform rate onto a wide conveyor belt, where it is inspected and yellow leaves and other defects are sorted out. Dehydration is accomplished in a 3-stage continuous belt drier in a drying time of only 30 min. Parsley is neither blanched nor sulfited for drying. Final moisture content of the finished product is about 4%. The whole dried parsley emerges into a mechanical and air separating system where the stems are removed from the leaves. The leaves are sold as flakes or granules; leaves and stems are ground for powder. The entire process of parsley dehydration as described above, from field to final package, is accomplished in less than 2 hr.

SOURCE: *Food Dehydration, 2nd Edition* by Van Arsdel, Copley and Morgan published by Avi Publishing Co., Westport, Conn.

DEHYDRATED GREEN PEAS

Green peas are harvested by cutting the vines with a mower, raking into windrows, and vining (separation of peas from other parts of the plant). Mobile viners may go directly into the field or vines may be hauled to stationary vining stations in the field or at the processing plant. Peas deteriorate rapidly after removal from the pod, primarily because of unavoidable mechanical bruising.

After vining, the peas are dry cleaned and size-graded. Sizes 3, 4, and 5 (will pass through a $^{13}/_{32}$-in. mesh screen but not through a $^{10}/_{22}$-in. screen) are recommended for a good quality end product. Smaller sizes usually do not rehydrate well and larger sizes may be too high in starch content. The peas are thoroughly washed in cold water and are sorted to eliminate pods, stems, off-color and other defective units. Blanching may be accomplished in hot water at 210°F or in atmospheric steam for 1-2 min. The drying rate tends to decrease with increasing maturity of the peas, but this effect can be overcome in part by increasing the severity of the blanching treatment. If desired, the blanched peas may be frozen at this stage and held frozen until they can be dehydrated.

The blanched (or frozen and thawed) peas are run through the slitting operation. Commercial machines are available which will handle in excess of 6000 lb per hr, making about a $^{1}/_{8}$-in. slit in each pea. To enable the slitter to do a good job, peas of the same size should be put through any single machine at one time. After the peas have been slit, the sizes can be comingled. The slit peas are dipped into, or sprayed with, a sulfite/bisulfite solution of sufficient concentration to produce a sulfur dioxide content of 300-500 ppm in the dried product.

Drying of the slitted peas may be successfully accomplished with tray-tunnel driers, cabinet driers, continuous belt driers, or belt-trough driers. It is advisable to remove peas from any of these drying systems when they have been reduced to about 8% moisture and continue drying down to 4% moisture in bin driers, using desiccated air at 120°F. In 2-stage tunnel driers, temperatures of 180°F for the initial stage and 160°F for the second stage are recommended. With through-circulation continuous belt driers, temperatures from 190° to 200°F may be used during the early part of the drying cycle.

SOURCE: *Food Dehydration, 2nd Edition* by Van Arsdel, Copley and Morgan published by Avi Publishing Co., Westport, Conn.

DEHYDROFROZEN (DF) PEAS

Varieties of peas suitable for freezing are also preferred for DF peas and preparation is the same for dehydrofreezing as for conventional freezing (see Section 12, Freezing Green Peas). The skins of peas are pierced in order to speed drying and later reconstitution. Piercing can be done in a machine equipped with a rotating drum with a multiplicity of small peripheral cavities. As the drum revolves peas lodging in each cavity are carried under reciprocating pointed 3/64-in. diameter pins, which perforate the seed coat of each pea. Other designs slit the pea skin with knives, draw the peas onto pins by air pressure, or position the peas on flat plates with arrays of holes before pricking.

Peas are dehydrated to 50% weight reduction, usually in less than 45 min at 170°-180°F. Mixing-type driers can be used because the peas can withstand the tumbling, mixing action without significant physical damage. In mixing-type driers, temperatures up to 250°F can be used safely to dry peas in the first stage of multistage drying operations. The products are undamaged if the driers are of the through-flow type and the DF products are stored at 0°F or lower. Quick freezing is done on a belt and the products are held in cold storage in tote-bins until they are repacked into 1-2½ or 50-lb packages.

SOURCE: *The Freezing Preservation of Foods, 4th Edition, Vol. 2* by Tressler, Van Arsdel and Copley published by Avi Publishing Co., Westport, Conn.

DEHYDRATED GREEN PEA SOUP, UNCOOKED

Ingredients	% by weight
Green pea powder	77.0
Salt	6.0
Hydrogenated vegetable fat	4.0
Onion powder	1.5
Smoked meat flavoring	3.0
Sugar	6.0
Monosodium glutamate	1.0
Spices, spice extractives, and seasonings (sufficient to give a properly blended and flavored end product)	

Procedure

Mix thoroughly until a uniform mixture is obtained.

Specifications for Military

The moisture limit is 4.5%, acid insoluble ash 0.05%, crude fiber 2.0%, salt 7.5%, with fat of 5.0 ± 1.0%. Reconstitute in ratio of 1¼ oz powder to 8 oz of water.

SOURCE: Military Specification 30598, 24 October 1962.

INSTANT GREEN PEA SOUP

Ingredients	% by Weight	
Green pea powder, dehydrated	Not less than	77.0
Hydrogenated vegetable fat	Not less than	7.0
Salt (total)	Not more than	7.0
Monosodium glutamate	Not less than	0.75
Onion powder, dehydrated	Not less than	0.60
Smoked meat flavoring	Not less than	1.0
Sugar, spices, and spice flavorings (sufficient to give a properly blended and flavored product)		
Added thiamin hydrochloride (0.5 mg/1¼ oz mix)		

Procedure

Mix thoroughly until a uniform mixture is obtained.

Specifications for Military

Moisture content of this soup mix is limited to 4.5%. Five ounces of mix are reconstituted with 1 qt of water. This is an "instant" soup, requiring only 1½ min of stirring into nearly boiling water (180°F) for its preparation. The headspace of the tins is nitrogen-filled, with a permitted oxygen content after 72 hr of not more than 2%. For smaller packs, laminated envelopes of 0.001-in. polyethylene extruded on 0.00035-in. aluminum foil and 25-30 lb/ream kraft paper, are used.

SOURCE: Military Specification Mil-S-3686 B, 21 September 1962.

DEHYDRATED BELL PEPPERS

Bell peppers are harvested by hand and brought into the plant in 1000-lb bins or bulk trailers. They are washed, inspected, and graded for color and size. The peppers are then fed by hand into an automatic coring machine which removes and ejects the stem, pithy placenta, and seeds. At the same time the pepper is cut into halves. The halves are washed under strong water sprays to remove any remaining seed or pithy material. After inspection and trimming, the halves are fed to a dicer to be cut into ¼, ⅜, ½, or ¾ in. dice. The dice are sprayed with a sulfite/bisulfite solution to give a final sulfur dioxide content of 1000 to 2500 ppm. Most of the dehydrated bell pepper dice currently produced in California are dehydrated in continuous belt-trough driers, although some of the product is still dried in tray-tunnel driers. In the latter type the initial air temperature is about 170°F in the primary stage, and 145°F in the secondary stage. The dice are removed from the belt or trays at about 10% moisture content and are brought down to a final moisture content of 5% in finishing bins.

SOURCE: *Food Dehydration, 2nd Edition* by Van Arsdel, Copley and Morgan published by Avi Publishing Co., Westport, Conn.

DEHYDRATED PIMIENTOS

The pimiento (or pimento) is a thick-walled, heart-shaped, brilliant-red, sweet pepper. Unlike bell peppers, pimientos are never harvested while green and only small quantities are sold on the fresh market. Because of their thick skin, pimientos are usually peeled by flame or lye, cored, and seeded. They are processed either whole or as cut shoestring strips. The bright red color and characteristic flavor of pimientos make them useful for such foods as potato salad, stew, luncheon meats, cheese, etc.

"Perfection" is the pimiento variety usually grown in this country. There is ordinarily a very large placenta or seed core in pimientos, consequently special strains with a smaller placenta have been developed by dehydrators to minimize losses from coring.

Pimientos for dehydrating are harvested when fully mature. They are washed, sorted, and peeled. Flame peeling is the preferred method, although lye peeling can be used. After peeling, the peppers are cored by machine. Dicing and drying operations are similar to those described above for bell peppers, except that pimiento dice are not sulfited.

SOURCE: *Food Dehydration, 2nd Edition* by Van Arsdel, Copley and Morgan published by Avi Publishing Co., Westport, Conn.

DEHYDROFROZEN (DF) PIMIENTOS

In the preparation for drying, pimientos are inspected, flame peeled, washed with high-pressure water sprays, hand trimmed, cored, and again washed to remove any adhering seeds or skin fragments. Drying is done in either of two ways: (1) the pods are sliced or broken into slabs and loaded onto trays for drying in truck-and-tunnel driers; or (2) the pods are diced into ⅜-in. pieces and dried continuously in a belt-trough drier. In belt-trough driers, pimientos dry uniformly and sanitation is simplified because the drying surface can be continuously cleaned during uninterrupted operation. In the belt-trough drier, ⅜-in. diced pimientos can be dried to 66% weight reduction in about 20 min with air at 300°F. The extent of dehydration depends upon the solids content of the pimientos. Finished products with about 22% solids content are desired.

When large slabs of pimiento are dried on trays, the product is chopped into the desired size after drying. A standard freezer-can holding 28 lb of DF pimiento represents 84 lb of single-strength prepared product.

SOURCE: *The Freezing Preservation of Foods, 3rd Edition* by Tressler and Evers published by Avi Publishing Co., Westport, Conn.

SALAD DRESSING DRY MIX

Ingredients	%
Xanthan gum (Keltrol)	9.46
Vegetable oil	0.27
Powdered sugar	43.27
Salt (fine mesh)	47.00
Non nutritive sweetener to taste	
	100.00

Procedure

Spices or flavors are added to base dry mix and then packaged for the consumer. The mix is added to a mixture of 1 cup of water and ⅓ cup of vinegar and shaken for 1 min, vigorously at first and then moderately.

SOURCE: Kelco Co., 20 N. Wacker Drive, Chicago, Illinois.

DEHYDROFROZEN (DF) POTATOES

As the name suggests, dehydrofreezing consists of a combination of dehydration and freezing. Fruits and vegetables which are suited to this process are first dehydrated to approximately half their original weight. No loss in quality results from the partial dehydration. The product is then frozen. Dehydrofreezing effects substantial savings in container, shipping, storage, and handling

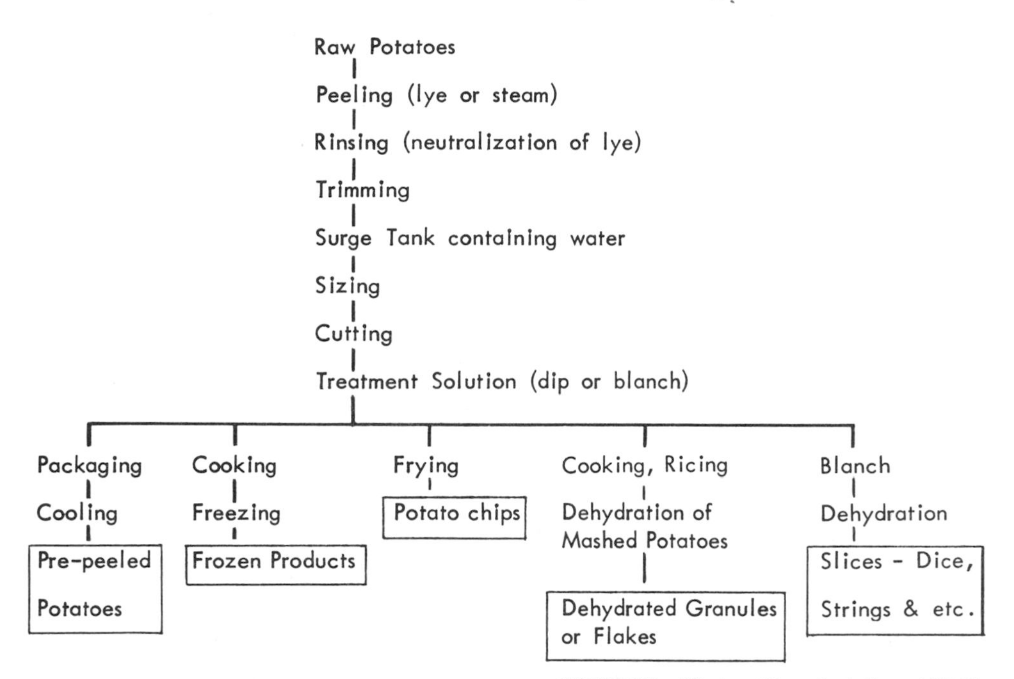

SOURCE: Victor Chemical Co., 155 N. Wacker Drive, Chicago, Illinois

FIG. 11.3. GENERAL PROCESSING STEPS FOR POTATO PRODUCTS

costs since both weight and volume are usually reduced by at least half.

Dehydrofreezing has been applied commercially to several potato products. Dehydrofrozen or "concentrated" mashed potato is prepared by first cooking, mashing, and mixing milk solids and salt with the potato. The mashed product is extruded and dehydrated in a continuous drier to a moisture content of about 12-15%. In this case, the original weight is reduced as much as 75%. The product is frozen, packaged, and distributed to both the institutional and retail trade. It is readily reconstituted by addition of hot water or hot milk and mixing or whipping to the desired consistency. Dehydrofrozen mashed potato flakes with a moisture content of around 12% have recently been introduced. This product contains no added sulfite or antioxidants.

Potatoes are also dehydrofrozen in piece form to around 50% or more weight reduction. The pieces may be dice, e.g., ⅜-in. cubes or so-called stew cuts of approximately 1 × 1 × ½ in. Intermediate sizes, utilizing broken pieces from French-fry cuts or other by-product material, are also dehydrofrozen.

SOURCE: *Processing of Frozen French Fried Potatoes and Other Frozen Potato Products,* USDA Western Utilization Research and Development Division, Berkeley, Calif.

CURING SWEET POTATOES

If sweet potatoes are not properly cured at a high humidity, excessive loss by decay occurs during storage. Further, the quality of the cooked product may be inferior. Curing is best carried out by holding at 85°F and a relative humidity of 85% for a period of 10 days. Curing too long results in excessive sprouting and in a greater loss in weight than necessary. However, if curing is effected at a lower temperature, a longer period should be used. Thus, at 80°F cure for 12-16 days; at 75°F, 20-28 days; and at 70°F, 28-42 days are required.

During curing, sweet potatoes lose water rather rapidly at first, but the rate becomes relatively slow after ten days.

The products are then quick frozen and stored at 0°F.

SOURCE: *The Freezing Preservation of Foods, 4th Edition, Vol. 4* by Tressler, Van Arsdel and Copley published by Avi Publishing Co., Westport, Conn.

INSTANT TOMATO SAUCE

Ingredients	%
Tomato powder	49.5
Hydrogenated vegetable shortening	23.1

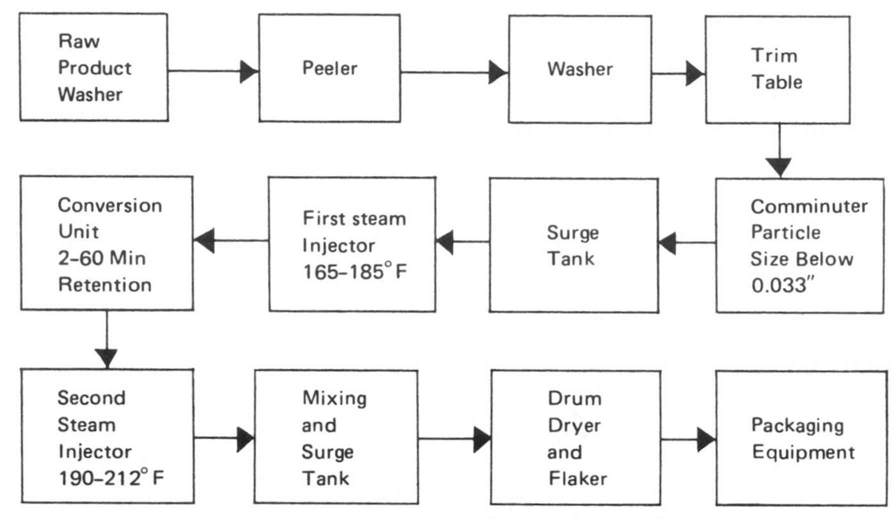

SOURCE: Sweet Potatoes: Production, Processing, Marketing, Avi Publishing Co., Westport, Conn.

FIG. 11.4. AN ENZYME ACTIVATION PROCESS FOR PRODUCING SWEET POTATO FLAKES

	%
Salt	6.6
Oregano	0.5
Onion powder	1.2
Garlic powder	1.2
Basil	0.6
Black pepper	0.8
Instantized starch (instant Textaid)	16.5
Color (to suit)	
	100.0

Procedure

Blend all dry ingredients thoroughly.

To Use

To 1 oz of dry powder, add 5¼ fl oz water with agitation.

SOURCE: National Starch and Chemical Co., Plainfield, N.J.

TOMATO SAUCE MIX
(for Beans with Tomato Sauce)

Ingredients	%
Powdered sugar	62.00
Tomato flakes	22.75
Salt	10.00
Milo starch	3.00
Onion powder	1.60
Garlic powder	0.25
Mustard, dry	0.16
Pepper, white, ground	0.12
Cloves, ground	0.12
	100.00

Procedure

Tomato flakes and onion and garlic powder are very hygroscopic, consequently the mixing and packaging these ingredients must be carried out in an air-conditioned room of low humidity.

SOURCE: *Food Dehydration* by Van Arsdel and Copley published by Avi Publishing Co., Westport, Conn.

DEHYDRATED TOMATO-VEGETABLE SOUP WITH NOODLES

Ingredients	%
Egg noodles	30
Dehydrated tomato flakes	12 (max)
Potato flour	6 (max)
Dehydrated vegetables	6 (max)
Carrot flakes	
White onions, minced	
Cabbage flakes	
Red and green pepper dice	
Celery flakes	
Cut green beans	
Green sweet peas	
Starch, dextrin, flour, sugar	21 (max)

	%
Salt	13 (max)
Hydrogenated vegetable oil	6
Hydrolyzed protein, monosodium glutamate, spices and flavorings	sufficient to make up 100%

Procedure

Moisture limits on the dehydrated vegetables are 4.0% for tomato and onion and 5.0% for the others. Differing sulfite ranges are specified for most of the vegetables ranging from between 100 to 500 ppm for dehydrated celery flakes to between 1000 and 2500 for bell pepper dice. Noodle moisture is limited to 6%. This mix is packaged in a bag with CaO as a desiccant.

Mix thoroughly until a uniform mixture is obtained.

SOURCE: Military Specification 35051, 21 November 1960.

VEGETABLE SOUP MIX

Ingredients	%
Starch	47.58
Salt	14.68
Beef fat	10.61
Beef extract (dehydrated)	9.44
Monosodium glutamate	8.61
Hydrogenated vegetable oil	3.78
Hydrolyzed plant protein	3.70
Spice mix	1.60
	100.00

Spice Mix

Ingredients	%
Celery Cream O'Spice	80.50
Black pepper cream	7.90
White onion powder	5.80
Garlic powder	3.20
Rosemary	2.60
	100.00

Dehydrated Vegetable Blend

Ingredients	%
Onion slices	24.23
Carrot dice	22.61
Celery dice	13.73
Leek flakes	9.53
Green String beans	8.08
Tomato flakes	6.87
Green peas	5.25
Potato dice	4.85
Cabbage flakes	4.04
Parsley flakes	0.81
	100.00

Procedure

The first step is weighing or measuring ingredients for a standard batch which may be done by hand, or it may be completely automated in large-volume plants. In the first case, it is customary to bring the ingredients to a scale and weigh out successively each ingredient required for the batch. By some suitable transport system, the scaled-off components are conveyed to the mixing equipment where they are blended for a sufficient time to bring about uniformity in the mixer. Where all the ingredients are dry powders, it is preferable to have each as uniform in screen size as is convenient in order to prevent segregation of coarse and fine particles during the subsequent handling and filling operations.

Package 26.5 gm of the dry mix with 12.39 gm of the dehydrated vegetable blend in a buried-foil pouch. The contents of 1 envelope are stirred into 3 cups of water which is then brought to a boil, partially covered, and boiled gently for 10–15 min.

SOURCE: *Food Dehydration, 2nd Edition* by Van Arsdel, Copley and Morgan published by Avi Publishing Co., Westport, Conn.

WHITE SAUCE MIX

Ingredients	%
Xanthan gum (Keltrol F)	7.50
Paprika	0.25
White pepper	1.00
Onion powder	1.25
Salt	15.00
Clearjel starch (National Starch and Chemical Co.)	25.00
Whey solids	50.00
	100.00

Procedure

Mix ingredients until a uniform mixture is obtained.

To Use

Disperse 20.0 gm (0.7 oz) in 1 cup of cold milk; slowly heat to boil while stirring.

SOURCE: Kelco Co., 20 N. Wacker Drive, Chicago, Illinois.

FROZEN VEGETABLE PRODUCTS

FROZEN ARTICHOKES

The stems of the artichokes, fresh from the field, are first cut off square at the base, so that the artichokes can stand upright. Next the tops of the artichokes are cut off adjacent to the tips of the outer long scales, so that the scales can be readily spread apart to open up the heads of the artichokes so that they can serve as receptacles or cups for the blanching water with which they are subsequently filled. The spreading apart of the petals is effected under warm water at a temperature of about 145°F. This results in a thorough cleaning or washing of the vegetable. When filled with warm water, the artichokes are removed in an upright position so that very little, if any, water will drain out; they are then placed in upright position on screen trays.

The trays with the artichokes are then blanched under steam in the usual steam box at superatmospheric pressure at a temperature of about 240°F for about 10 min. During blanching, the water in the water-filled artichokes is converted to steam resulting in a thorough blanching of all the interior artichoke scales as well as the hearts or centers of the artichokes, to inactivate the enzymes which would otherwise cause blackening and spoiling of the artichokes upon freezing.

After blanching the artichokes are removed from the steam box and placed on cooling trays and are then banded by placing a rubber band about the periphery of each artichoke to hold the scales in place tight to the center of the artichoke. Next the artichokes are allowed to cool to approximately room temperature; and when cooled they are packaged in suitable cartons and frozen quickly in a freezing chamber at a temperature of about 40°F below zero for about 4 hr. After such freezing, the packaged artichokes are stored under freezing conditions in the usual frozen food storage chamber.

SOURCE: *The Freezing Preservation of Foods, 3rd Edition* by Tressler and Evers published by Avi Publishing Co., Westport, Conn.

FROZEN ASPARAGUS

The first operation in preparing asparagus for freezing usually is to place the "grass" crossways on a belt conveyor with the spears all pointing in one direction, flush with the guard rail at the edge of the belt. The conveying belt passes under a pressure spray washer, then passes girls who rearrange the stalks in perfect order just before the asparagus passes under rotary knives which cut the asparagus about 5 in. from the tip, with 2 more 2-inch cuts made simultaneously. The butt ends are discarded. The short middle cuts are diverted on another belt and are hand sorted for tenderness. The tough cuts are discarded, and the tender cuts either packed for freezing as cuts, or are diverted for canning.

The tips are then conveyed in front of sorters who pick out the very small spears. These small spears are usually diverted for canning. The remaining tips, comprising about 90% of the total tip cuts, are conveyed to a soaking type of washer where any grit is loosened. This soaker-washer is a place where tips may accumulate if temporary delays occur further along the line. As the "grass" is conveyed out of the soaker-washer it is again washed with powerful sprays of water.

The tip cuts are then sorted by hand into three sizes: medium, colossal, and jumbo. Since most of the tips are of medium size, this size is permitted to move past the sorters on the belt and on to the blancher. The other sizes are picked off, allowed to accumulate, and then put in batches on other conveyors leading to the blanchers.

The steam blancher consists of a woven wire belt moving through a steam chamber approximately 30 ft in length. The "grass" emerges on the belt from the blancher; it is then cooled by numerous sprays of cold water. The cooled asparagus is placed in moisture-proof cartons, the weight is checked, the cartons are closed, then overwrapped and placed on trays for freezing in either a multiplate freezer or on racks in a cold air blast at—20°F or below.

After freezing, the cartons are packed into corrugated fiberboard shipping containers usually fitted with corrugated liners.

SOURCE: *The Freezing Preservation of Foods, 3rd Edition* by Tressler and Evers published by Avi Publishing Co., Westport, Conn.

FROZEN BAKED BEANS

California small white beans packed in 100-lb bags are emptied into a hopper which feeds into a shaker-type screen. This removes some of the lighter foreign material. As the beans fall off the screen, they are subjected to a blower fan which further cleans them. The raw product is then flumed into a riffle where heavier foreign matter,

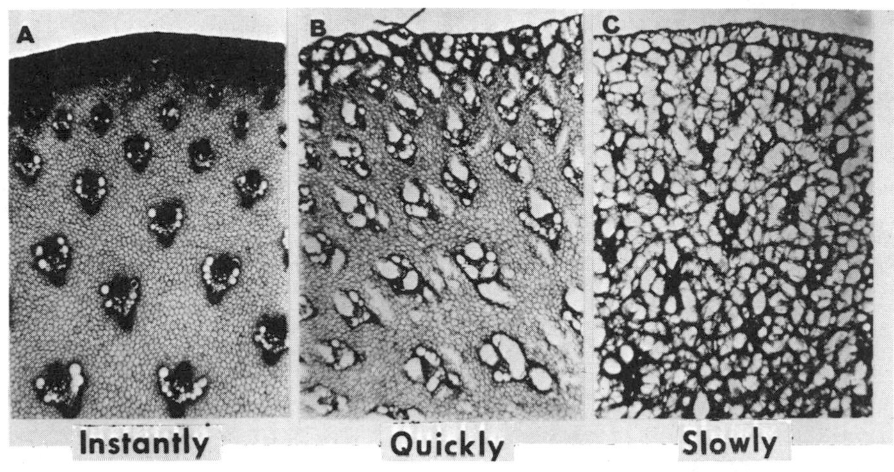

Courtesy of U.S. Department of Agriculture

FIG. 12.1. RATE OF FREEZING ASPARAGUS AFFECTS NUMBER OF CELL WALL RUPTURES

such as stones or sticks, are separated from the beans. A conveyor belt raises the beans and drops them on a wide rubber sorting belt where defective beans are removed. This belt empties the beans into large wooden tubs. Some moisture adheres to the beans from the cleaning process, so they are allowed to stand and drain completely. The beans are not soaked.

A given quality of syrup is combined with several hundred pounds of cleaned beans in an iron pot. The beans are baked for approximately 3 hr in a gas-fired brick oven; then the fire is reduced and the dampers closed to develop the color. After 5 hr from the start of the bake, the beans are stirred, water added to the surface of the beans, and the salt pork placed over the beans on perforated trays. The beans are agitated only 2-3 times during the entire baking process. Usually, water is added only once during the bake. As the beans come from the oven, they are conveyed down a cooling chute where the syrup is diluted. Iron pots of the same type are used to collect the beans and carry them to the packing line. The amount of water added here is in direct proportion to the amount of evaporation during the baking.

The beans are packed in moisture-proof consumer packages and frozen in an air blast at −20°F or lower.

SOURCE: *The Freezing Preservation of Foods, 4th Edition, Vol. 4* by Tressler, Van Arsdel and Copley published by Avi Publishing Co., Westport, Conn.

FREEZING SNAP BEANS, GREEN OR WAX

Most snap beans have a rather bland flavor which is easily lost during preparation, freezing, storage, thawing, and cooking. For this reason, if an attractive product is to be obtained, great pains must be taken in the selection and preparation of the raw material. Therefore, select young tender beans, free from fiber in the side walls. If they must be held for longer than 12 hr they should be kept in cold storage (e.g., 34°F).

First, put the beans through a size grader; select No. 1 (8/64 in. diam); No. 2 (11/64 in. diam); No. 3 (14/64 in. diam) and No. 4 (18/64 in. diam) for freezing; larger beans should be canned.

After size-grading, the beans should be fed into the snippers, which remove the stems and blossom ends from the pods. The snippers are operated either on the automatic batch principle or on a continuous self-adjusted feed basis, the operator only filling the intake hopper of the machine. A short inspection belt, about 10-12 ft long should be attached to the discharge end of all of the snippers. About 4-6 women are needed to inspect the snipped beans, hand-snip all beans which are missed by the machine, and remove all diseased and insect bitten beans, and other foreign material.

Prepare the No. 1 and No. 2 sizes for freezing as whole beans, cross-cut the No. 3 and No. 4 sizes. Cross-cut beans are usually considered as 1-in. cuts by the trade. If a cannery is not operated in conjunction with the freezing plant the No. 5 size may be utilized in the French-style pack by slitting the beans lengthwise. The bean variety must be straight podded if the No. 1 and No. 2 sizes are to be packed whole. Straight pods are also desirable for the French-style pack as crooked beans yield a high percentage of small pieces. Machines are available for cross-cutting and Frenching.

The cut beans should be conveyed on a belt through a steam blancher and blanched for about

3 min; after blanching the beans should be conveyed under sprays of cold water, then given a final inspection.

The French-style product should be packaged by hand and then frozen in a multi-plate freezer. Cross-cut beans may either be automatically packaged by machine and frozen in a multi-plate freezer or they may be individually frozen in a fluidized bed as peas are frozen. Individually frozen cut beans are free-flowing and may be stored in bulk until required for sale, then they are packaged.

SOURCE: *The Freezing Preservation of Foods, 3rd Edition* by Tressler and Evers published by Avi Publishing Co., Westport, Conn.

FROZEN GREEN SHELLED BEANS

Green shelled beans should be handled in a manner similar to Henderson Bush or Fordhook lima beans, i.e., they should be pulled in the field, hauled to the viner and vined, or picked in baskets, hauled to the freezing plant and podded. In preparing the beans for freezing, they should be cleaned first in a fanning mill and then in a washer. Blanching may be carried out either in boiling water for 80 sec, or in steam for 105 sec. After cooling, the beans should be passed over an inspection belt and then either packaged and quick frozen, or frozen in an air blast on trays or on a slowly moving wire belt.

SOURCE: *The Freezing Preservation of Foods, 3rd Edition* by Tressler and Evers published by Avi Publishing Co., Westport, Conn.

FROZEN BROCCOLI

The first factory operation is the sorting and trimming of the heads. A long table is usually constructed with about a 5-in.-wide belt moving lengthwise in the center of the table. Women stand on each side of the table and remove the broccoli from baskets, and sort and trim the product before they place it on the center belt. The women on the sorting belts will average from 40 to 60 lb of trimmed broccoli per hour, depending upon the quality of the raw product and the efficiency of the workers. The stalks are sorted to remove damaged, blossomed, or insect-infested heads. Center heads are split and trimmed so that the head will be about 1½ to 2 in. in diameter. All of the leaves are placed in one direction on the belt, which conveys the broccoli to a cutter that trims the stalks to about 5 in. in length. After the stalks are trimmed and cut to the desired length, they are discharged into a washer.

Some plants use automatic cutters for the elimination of the fibrous butt end. This equipment consists of a special feeding and positioning belt and a revolving knife. The broccoli is placed in small bunches crosswise between the "marcels" of the special belt conveyor in such a position that the fibrous butt ends extend across the narrow open space between one belt assembly and the other. The conveyor carries the spears down the line to the revolving knife which shears off the butt ends. The unwanted butt ends are trapped by a curved metal plate and pass down a chute to a crate below. The edible portions of the broccoli fall from the "marcelled" belt onto a conveyor which carries them down a sorting and trimming table where women workers split the spears into suitable pieces for packing and eliminate all off-grade material. The conveying belt then carries the broccoli to the washer. Usually a spinach washer is used for the washing operation, and the product is discharged from the washer onto a conveyor, which carries the product to the blancher. As a rule, broccoli is steam blanched for 3-5 min. Although some plants blanch for only 2½ min, others may blanch for as long as 7½ min.

The blanched broccoli is cooled in a flume of cold water and then packed into cartons which are frozen either in an air blast at 0°F or lower or in a plate freezer.

SOURCE: *The Freezing Preservation of Foods, 3rd Edition* by Tressler and Evers published by Avi Publishing Co., Westport, Conn.

FROZEN BRUSSELS SPROUTS

Crates of sprouts are tipped on the side before the women who do the trimming on special rapidly rotating trimmers which cut off the base of the sprouts. After trimming, the sprouts are dropped through a chute to a conveyor which moves the trimmed sprouts to a dry rotary rod "deleafer." From this machine the sprouts are elevated to a flume which conveys them to a soaker-washer from which they pass onto the belt of the steam blancher. After passing through the steam blancher, the sprouts drop into a flume in which they are cooled. They are elevated to an inspection belt passing along a packing table on which the women inspect the sprouts and put them into moisture-proof rectangular cartons resting on scales. When the desired weight of sprouts has been placed in a carton, the carton is closed and put on another conveying belt. The cartons are automatically overwrapped with lithographed wrapper, then put on trays with screen bottoms and placed on wheeled racks which are transported into an air blast freezer for freezing at about −30°F.

SOURCE: *The Freezing Preservation of Foods, 3rd Edition* by Tressler and Evers published by Avi Publishing Co., Westport, Conn.

FROZEN CARROTS

Carrots are mechanically topped and dug in the field and loaded into large bulk trailers holding about 50,000 lb. On arrival at the plant the carrots are washed in a presoak tank followed by a tumble washer. The washed carrots are mechanically separated into three basic sizes: *small*, to be used for whole carrots; *medium*, to be used for sliced; and *large*, to be used for diced. The carrots are lined up on belts, pass between rotating knives which cut off the tip and butt ends, and are flumed by water to storage hoppers. After inspection, trimming, and peeling (usually by steam) the larger carrots are mechanically diced or sliced. The slices or dice pass first to an air cleaner, where chips and small pieces are removed by air blast, and then to a blancher. While water blanching is sometimes used, carrots are usually blanched by steam; blanch times vary from 2 to 8 min depending on size, maturity, and texture.

Diced and sliced carrots lend themselves well to fluidized freezing or other IQF techniques. Carrots are unique in that the prepared product is frequently graded for size after freezing. This grading operation takes place in a cold room held at about 30°F. Frozen sliced or crinkle-cut carrots pass over grading screens which divide them into three diameter sizes: small, medium, and large. The frozen diced carrots pass over screens which remove chips and small pieces which are sold separately for use in soups or stews. Carrots are marketed in containers of various sizes, including 10-oz cartons, 2-lb poly bags, 20-lb bags, and 50-lb bags.

Small whole carrots, which have become quite popular in recent years, are processed in much the same way as large carrots. Smaller carrots are not younger than large carrots, since both the large and small ones are harvested at the same time. Where plantings are thicker, more small carrots are obtained. Whole carrots are frequently sold by count: medium are 80 and over per pound, small are 200 per pound, and tiny are 300 per pound. Some packers cut off the tip ends of the smaller size carrots and run these through an abrasive peeler to round off the cut end. The finished product looks like a tiny carrot and is sold as such. Special tiny carrots from Belgium and Holland may have counts ranging from 375 to 450 per pound. These are the "Paris" variety, whose seed does not seem to be obtainable in this country. Because of the growing market for this item, U.S. seed companies are developing varieties of "baby carrots."

SOURCE: *The Freezing Preservation of Foods, 4th Edition, Vol. 2* by Tressler, Van Arsdel and Copley published by Avi Publishing Co., Westport, Conn.

FROZEN CAULIFLOWER

Only compact white heads should be selected for freezing. If cauliflower is allowed to stand in a warm place for more than a few hours the curds may become loose and turn somewhat brown or gray. Therefore, if the product is to be held for long, it must be maintained under refrigeration (32°-34°F) at 85-90% relative humidity.

Ordinarily, the cauliflower is received at the packing plant in crates—12 heads to a crate. These crates are emptied onto a moving belt in front of women who use heavy knives to cut off the base of the stem and the larger outer leaves. The heads then pass along to other workers who trim off more of the leaves and place the heads on another conveyor belt which carries them to other workers who cut out the core with a small ringed knife. The heads then pass on to women who cut and break the heads into individual flowerettes. The flowerettes then pass through a cylindrical rod cleaner which eliminates small pieces of cauliflower, some loose leaves, and foreign material. The cauliflower flowerettes are then elevated to a flume which carries then to a washer containing cold water under violent agitation. This washer eliminates foreign matter and insects. The washed flowerettes are then elevated to a steam blancher operated at 212°F. After being conveyed through a steam blancher, the flowerettes are cooled in a long flume and then elevated to an inspection belt where the larger green leaves are trimmed off. At the end of this inspection belt the flowerettes drop directly into rectangular moisture-proof cartons. The filled cartons pass to an inspection belt where they are check weighed. The packages with the proper weight are placed on an upper belt which transports them to a closing machine. Then the cartons are automatically overwrapped with a lithographed wrapper. The wrapped cartons are put on trays and either placed in a plate freezer or on racks on casters which are moved into an air blast tunnel for freezing.

The blanching time used for cauliflower by different food packers varies from 3 to 10 min; however, most of them use a steam blanch of 4-5 min.

SOURCE: *The Freezing Preservation of Foods, 3rd Edition* by Tressler and Evers published by Avi Publishing Co., Westport, Conn.

FROZEN CORN ON THE COB

Ears of corn selected for the corn-on-the-cob pack should be slightly less mature than those used for whole kernel corn.

After thorough washing, the husked ears are conveyed through a steam blancher and blanched for 6-11 min (long enough to inactivate the enzyme catalase on the tips of the kernels); large ears require longer blanching than small ears. The corn is cooled with water sprays to about 70°F and then sorted to remove irregular and damaged ears. The ears are then trimmed to an even length, generally about 6 in. Then they are wrapped in moisture proof plastic sheeting, packaged, and frozen at -10°F or lower.

SOURCE: *The Freezing Preservation of Foods, 3rd Edition* by Tressler and Evers published by Avi Publishing Co., Westport, Conn.

FROZEN CREAM-STYLE CORN

Frozen cream-style corn is prepared in the same way as for canning (see **Canned Sweet Corn**, Section 10). After husking, silking, and washing the ears are fed into a cream-style corn cutter, which cuts off half of each kernel and scrapes off the remainder with blunt blades. The grains and scrapings are mixed before freezing.

In preparation, the husked ears of corn are delivered by a screw conveyor to a silking machine, which removes pieces of silk, husk, and cob. From the silker the cream-style corn passes into a mixer where it is heated by direct injection of steam to 190°-195°F, diluted with about 20% of brine containing about 1% salt and 2% sugar. The mixture is then cooled by pumping it through a heat exchanger on its way to a carton (usually 12-oz size) filler. Cartons are check-weighed and then conveyed to a freezer. A multi-plate type freezer is commonly used for rectangular cartons; other types are frozen in an air blast at -10°F or lower.

SOURCE: *The Freezing Preservation of Foods, 3rd Edition* by Tressler and Evers published by Avi Publishing Co., Westport, Conn.

FROZEN SWEET CORN
(Whole Grain Kernel)

The first step in preparing corn for freezing is husking. This is done mechanically. The husked corn is washed. Generally, a large reel washer is used, and then corn is conveyed to the cutting machines. Two cutters will handle the entire output of three double huskers.

The blanching operation, which utilizes steam at atmospheric pressure, is carried out on either the husked corn on the cob or after the corn is cut from the cob. The former method must be used for all ear packs and is also used by some processors for the whole kernel corn pack. The chief drawbacks for this method are: A large quantity of steam is required for the blanching operations; the blanchers are enormous in size in order to accommodate the average frozen corn processing line; and blanched corn does not cut as well as raw corn. The advantages of the method are: little or no loss of soluble solids during blanching, and less loss of flavor and sugars during the washing and cleaning operation after cutting.

The advantages of cutting the corn from the cob before blanching are: the use of much less steam during blanching; the blanchers are much smaller in size and have a greater capacity; and the fact that corn cuts easier and cleaner before blanching. Cut corn is blanched from 2 to 4 min. However, if the corn is blanched before cutting from the cob, the ears are steamed for about 6 min.

After corn is blanched it is cooled in cold water. If it has been blanched on the cob, the cool ears are put through a corn cutter. The cut corn is then cleaned in water. The kernels sink, whereas the pieces of silk, husk, and chaff float and are washed out. The cleaned corn is passed over a picking belt where women pick out and discard all foreign material that the cleaner failed to remove.

The "whole kernel" corn is then conveyed to (1) fillers which fill it into retail size cartons, or (2) a continuous belt freezer (e.g., a fluidized bed freezer) on which the kernels are individually frozen in an air blast, or (3) it is frozen on trays in an air blast. On the last method, the corn must be put through a "cluster buster" in order to separate the kernels and obtain a free flowing product.

Free flowing corn kernels may be stored in bins or large containers under refrigeration and packaged later for sale either in retail size containers or in larger institutional packages. Or it may be mixed with other vegetables for mixed vegetables or succotash.

SOURCE: *The Freezing Preservation of Foods, 3rd Edition* by Tressler and Evers published by Avi Publishing Co., Westport, Conn.

FROZEN EGG PLANT

Egg plant, fried in deep fat, is an excellent dish. In preparing this product, the "eggs" are washed, peeled, cut into slices and then into strips, just as potatoes are prepared for French-frying. The strips are blanched for 4 min. After draining, the strips are fried in a continuous deep fat fryer according to the procedure used in cooking French-fried potatoes. The fried product is drained of fat, cooled by fans, then either packaged in rectangular cartons, which are overwrapped, and quick frozen in a plate freezer, or frozen on a belt or on trays in an air blast, then packaged in cartons which are overwrapped.

SOURCE: *The Freezing Preservation of Foods, 4th Edition, Vol. 2* by Tressler, Van Arsdel and Copley published by Avi Publishing Co., Westport, Conn.

FREEZING SOUTHERN GREENS

Collard greens, turnip greens, mustard greens, and kale are leafy green vegetables popular in the Southern states. It is only in recent years that commercial freezing of these vegetables has become common. Popular commercial varieties of turnip greens are Purple Top, Seven-Top, Shogoin, and Just-Rite; Vates is a popular variety of collards; while Siberian and Vates are the usual commercial varieties of kale. All of the vegetables named above are harvested and processed in the same manner as described later in this Section for spinach. Kale is usually packed in whole leaf style, but collard greens and turnip greens are usually packed as chopped.

SOURCE: *The Freezing Preservation of Foods, 3rd Edition* by Tressler and Evers published by Avi Publishing Co., Westport, Conn.

FROZEN INFANT FOOD
(Strained Vegetables with Beef)

Ingredients	Lb	Oz
Ground beef	140	
Carrots	106	
Potatoes	110	
Tomato juice	11	
Celery stalks	35	10
Waxy rice flour	22	
Rice	10	
Dehydrated onion powder	1	
Salt	3	
Monosodium glutamate	1	6
	440	

Yield: 100 gal.

Procedure

The ground beef is cooked in a steam-jacketed kettle in 35 gal. of water for 30 min. The partially cooked meat is then comminuted in a Fitzpatrick mill, or equivalent, and is returned to the kettle. Rice and salt are added and cooking is continued for 15 more minutes. Potatoes are washed, then peeled in an abrasive peeler, or by some other method. Carrots are washed, trimmed, and peeled. Celery is washed and trimmed. After chopping the potatoes, carrots, and celery, they are added to the stew and the cooking continued for about 25 min. The tomato juice, salt, monosodium glutamate, and an aqueous slurry of waxy rice flour and onion powder is stirred in. The batch is then made up to 100 gal. with additional water. The stew is then put through a rotary cylindrical finisher fitted with a screen having 0.033-in. openings. The resultant purée is then pumped through a tubular flash-heater or sterilizer to raise the temperature to about 270°F. It is then immediately cooled to the filling temperature by passing it through a heat exchanger. Finally the product is frozen, usually in an air blast at -20°F.

SOURCE: *The Freezing Preservation of Foods, 4th Edition, Vol. 4* by Tressler, Van Arsdel and Copley published by Avi Publishing Co., Westport, Conn.

FROZEN INFANT FOOD
(Chopped Vegetables with Beef)

The formula used for this product is exactly the same as that for making Strained Vegetables with Beef (the preceding formula).

Procedure

Small pieces (e.g., 1 in. cubes) are cooked in a steam-jacketed kettle in 35 gal. of water for 30 min. The partially cooked meat is chopped in a Buffalo cutter. The remainder of the procedure is exactly that described for making Strained Vegetables with Beef (given above) up to the point where the finished stew is run through the finisher. Instead of putting the product through the finisher, it is either immediately filled into tin cans or cooled and packaged in cartons and frozen.

SOURCE: *The Freezing Preservation of Foods, 4th Edition, Vol. 2* by Tressler, Van Arsdel and Copley published by Avi Publishing Co., Westport, Conn.

FROZEN KALE

The freezing process is the same as that described for Spinach (given later in this Section). Scalding in steam for 5 min is recommended, or 2 min in boiling water is sufficient. However, both steam and water should reach each leaf individually, since the quality is adversely affected by overblanching.

The product should be chilled in cold water, drained, then packed in packages for freezing in an air blast or plate freezer.

SOURCE: *The Freezing Preservation of Foods, 3rd Edition* by Tressler and Evers published by Avi Publishing Co., Westport, Conn.

FROZEN KOHLRABI

To prepare kohlrabi for freezing, it is first washed and peeled. It is then diced into ½-in. cubes. The diced product should be scalded in boiling water for 60 sec. If steam is employed as the blanching medium, a 100-sec scald should be used. The blanched product should be immediately cooled in running cold water, then packaged in moisture-, vaporproof packages, and quick frozen.

SOURCE: *The Freezing Preservation of Foods, 3rd Edition* by Tressler and Evers published by Avi Publishing Co., Westport, Conn.

FROZEN MUSHROOMS

Mushrooms yield a very attractive frozen product. They may be prepared as buttons, large whole mushrooms, and sliced mushrooms. During pulling and trimming, care should be taken to prevent bruising, since the bruises soon discolor. Mushrooms darken and deteriorate rapidly after harvest. Therefore, they should be prepared and frozen the same day they are picked.

If the mushrooms have not been graded according to size prior to their delivery at the freezing plant, they are first sorted in order to eliminate all open and broken mushrooms, and sized. Sizing is usually accomplished by passage through a stainless steel, perforated, rotating cylinder which operates under cold water. The base of the stem is then cut off allowing only about 3/16 in. to remain. After this trimming, the mushrooms are thoroughly washed.

If a fancy light colored mushroom is desired, the tight buttons should then be placed in a vacuum tank, covered with and held under water containing 4 lb of citric acid and 4 lb ascorbic acid per 100 gal. A high vacuum, e.g., about 28 in., is drawn and held for about 3 min. The vacuum is released and then again drawn. This vacuum treatment is not absolutely necessary, but produces frozen mushrooms of better color than would otherwise be obtained.

Steam blanching does not leach out the soluble components of the mushrooms to the same extent as does water blanching; consequently, it yields a more flavorsome product. To prevent excessive shrinking, the minimum period of steaming which will prevent darkening during storage should be employed. For buttons, 105 secs; and for mushrooms 1⅛–1⅜ in. in diameter, a 2½ min steam blanch is sufficient. Larger mushrooms should be steam scalded 3-5 min. Immediately after scalding, they should be cooled, preferably first to 70°F with sprays of cold water, and then in a 1% citric acid solution.

The open, broken, and spotted mushrooms may advantageously be sliced before freezing. In preparing sliced mushrooms, the base of the stem is first trimmed from freshly harvested mushrooms. The trimmed mushrooms are cut into slices about ¼ in. thick and then thoroughly washed. The washed slices are spread on a corrosion-resistant meshed wire belt or trays and steam blanched for 2 min. The blanched slices are immediately cooled, first in 1% citric acid, and then in cold water. After draining thoroughly 15-20 min, the slices are packed in moisture-, vaporproof packages and quick frozen.

SOURCE: *The Freezing Preservation of Foods, 3rd Edition* by Tressler and Evers published by Avi Publishing Co., Westport, Conn.

FROZEN OKRA

The principal variety of okra frozen is Clemson Spineless. The harvested product is sorted at the freezing plant to remove culls and old fibrous or woody fruits. The pods are sized either by hand or mechanically, with both very small and overly large pieces going to a cutting machine to be packed as cut okra. The whole pods are trimmed either by hand or on Hydrouts to remove stems. After a thorough washing, the pods are blanched, either in steam or in hot water, for 2-3 min depending on the size of the pod. Perforation of pods with a needle board prior to blanching will reportedly reduce the incidence of rupture during blanching. The blanched pods should be quickly cooled by spraying or immersion in cold water and then be drained in a dewatering reel or vibrating screen before packaging and freezing. Freeze at 0°F or lower in an air blast or plate freezer.

SOURCE: *The Freezing Preservation of Foods, 4th Edition, Vol. 2* by Tressler, Van Arsdel and Copley published by Avi Publishing Co., Westport, Conn.

FROZEN ONION RINGS

The butts of Bermuda or other large select onions are cut off and air is applied to effect blow-off peeling. They are then put into a water bath to clean them. This done, the onions are run through the slicer to be cut into individual slices, then put into another water bath to separate rings.

Next, the onions go through a vibrator separator onto a stainless steel belt. From there, they go into and through a Stein breading machine, and then, into a continuous cooker at 385°F.

After leaving the cooker, the onions are caught in baskets and precooled, after which they are placed into a blast freezer at -20°F and frozen. Finally, they are packaged and put into a storage freezer at -5°F.

SOURCE: *Quick Frozen Foods*, New York, N.Y.

FREEZING GREEN PEAS

No two companies prepare and freeze peas in exactly the same manner. In all cases the peas are first mowed, and then loaded onto trucks, and hauled to a nearby viner station, or to the freezing plant, where they are threshed out in a viner.

Vines should be delivered to the vining stations immediately after the harvesting or cutting operation. Pea vines should not be cut in large quantities ahead of the delivery trucks which transport the vines to the hullers. Peas show a slower rate of change on the living vine than when cut. Acreage and planting dates should be synchronized to reduce the possibility of large quantities of peas being ready to harvest at the same time. A common rule used by many operators is to plant no more than four acres each day per viner. Vines should not be held at hulling stations in piles for any length of time, since heating and souring of the peas is certain to take place. If peas must be held on vines at viner stations, they should be spread not over 6-8 in. deep on the ground.

After the peas are removed from the viner, they are usually passed through a cleaning (fanning) mill to remove foreign material. After this operation, the cleaned product is generally weighed and a record kept upon which the original basis for payment to the grower is made.

After cleaning, the peas are washed in cold water (usually refrigerated). If the vined peas contain many nightshade berries and thistle buds they may be subjected to a flotation process in which foreign material (floaters) are separated from the sound peas which sink. After a second washing the peas are flumed or pumped by means of a hydroconveyor to the blancher. The peas are heated sufficiently in the blancher with either hot water (the usual type) or steam to inactivate the catalase (an enzyme) and "set" the dark green color. In water at 210°-212°F, blanching for 50-60 sec is sufficient.

After the blanching operation, the peas must be cooled rapidly. This is accomplished by means of water flumes or troughs, the product being carried along in the stream of water; many plants use chlorinated water to keep down bacterial growth. The peas are cooled to prevent bacterial increases, and to cool the product before it passes into the quality separators. The product should be passed through a reel to remove all excess water so that the quality separator brine will be subjected to a minimum amount of dilution. The quality grader does not operate efficiently if it is overloaded or if the peas are warm.

After being discharged from the separator, the peas are washed in fresh water to remove the salt and are transferred in flumes to the picking tables, where all foreign material, yellow peas, splits, and skins are removed. Most packers use from 4 to 6 picking tables (inspection belts) for each line or for one quality separator, blancher, washer, and cleaning mill. In many operations, the peas are caught in buckets as they are discharged from the picking tables, while in others the peas are discharged directly into the filling machine. The product is then packaged or passed through a freezer in the loose state. If the product is packaged before freezing, a telescope pocket type filler is commonly used. The cartons (usually the rectangular folding type) are placed in holders which are attached to an endless chain which passes the packages under the pockets during the filling operation. These fillers can be adapted for either retail or institutional size packages. Capacity on small cartons ranges from 80 to 250 cartons per min, while on the institutional size, the capacity per minute is from 40 to 125. After the weight of the peas has been checked, the cartons are closed by hand, and are generally passed through a wrapping machine, where a waxed overwrap is applied. The packages are then frozen usually in a multi-plate freezer.

Large quantities of peas are also frozen before packaging. This is usually accomplished in a fluidized bed freezer. In this, the peas are spread on a perforated belt. Refrigerated air at 0°F or below is forced up through the perforations in the belt causing "fluidization" of the peas and rapid freezing, because of intimate contact of each pea with rapidly moving cold air. When individually frozen, the peas may be stored in large containers or bins under refrigeration until needed for sale, then the frozen peas are packaged.

Combining Peas with Carrots

The ingredient proportion for this item is 50-75% peas and 25-50% diced or sliced carrots.

SOURCE: *The Freezing Preservation of Foods, 3rd Edition* by Tressler and Evers published by Avi Publishing Co., Westport, Conn.

FROZEN BELL PEPPERS

Bell peppers are harvested by hand and brought into the plant in 1000-lb bins or bulk trailers. They are washed, inspected, and graded for color and size. The peppers are fed by hand into an automatic coring machine which removes and ejects the stem, pithy placenta, and seeds; at the same time the pepper is cut into halves. The halves are washed under strong water sprays to remove any remaining seeds or pithy material. Some operators slice the top off of the stem end and mechanically squeeze out the placenta and seeds. Other operators pass the whole pepper through rollers which crush the pepper, and then remove the placenta and seeds by hand or by screening.

Bell peppers are processed either as whole green,

in which case they are usually not blanched; cored and halved (unblanched or blanched); or diced (unblanched or blanched). Both green and red bell peppers will freeze well unblanched but tend to develop objectionable flavors after about six months' storage. If a freezer is required to supply peppers with low bacterial and mold counts, it is frequently desirable to blanch peppers in water or steam for approximately 2 min. Rapid freezing methods such as belt or fluidized bed freezers, are recommended for diced peppers because slow freezing for this item results in bleeding and adverse texture changes.

Diced bell peppers, either red or green, are usually packed in 3-lb cartons, while whole or halved peppers are usually packed in polyethylene bags, and then frozen at 0°F or lower.

SOURCE: *The Freezing Preservation of Foods, 4th Edition, Vol. 2* by Tressler, Van Arsdel and Copley published by Avi Publishing Co., Westport, Conn.

FROZEN GREEN PEPPERS STUFFED WITH HYDROLYZED PLANT PROTEIN

Ingredients	%
Maggi HPP Type 4BE Powder with partially hydrogenated vegetable oil added	51.30
Celery, microground	1.50
Black pepper, ground	1.10
Laurel, ground	0.10
Onion, ground, toasted	15.00
Monosodium glutamate	6.50
Sugar	5.50
Parsley granules	1.90
Nutmeg, ground	0.40
Coriander, ground	0.70
Egg white solids	16.00
	100.00

Procedure

Blend until uniform 200 gm of ground beef, 75 gm textured soy flour, 30 gm of the seasoning blend, formula above, and 350 cc of milk. Fill adequate amount of this mix into green peppers which have been cut into half (lengthwise) and previously blanched. Package, preferably in aluminum foil containers. Freeze at 0°F.

SOURCE: Nestlé Company, 100 Bloomingdale Road, White Plains, N.Y.

FROZEN SWEET PEPPERS

Sweet peppers may be prepared for freezing by first washing and then cutting into halves or slices. The halves or slices may be scalded for 2 min in either steam or boiling water, and then immediately cooled. Some packers do not blanch them, since the unblanched product does not quickly develop off-flavors during storage. The cooled product should be packaged in moisture-, vapor-proof cartons preferably before freezing.

SOURCE: *The Freezing Preservation of Foods, 3rd Edition, Vol. 1* by Tressler and Evers published by Avi Publishing Co., Westport, Conn.

FROZEN PIMIENTOS

The pimiento (or pimento) is a thick-walled, tough-skinned, heart-shaped, brilliant-red sweet pepper. Unlike bell peppers, pimientos are never harvested while green.

Because of their thick skin, pimientos are usually peeled by flame, hot oil, or lye. They are cored and seeded either before or after the peeling operation. Pimientos are processed either whole, as shoestring strips, or diced. Their bright red color and characteristic flavor make them a useful ingredient for remanufacture in such foods as potato salad, stew, luncheon meats, cheese, etc.

Perfection is the pimiento variety usually grown in the United States.

Because of this large core and the relatively large proportion of peel to flesh, preparation losses from coring and peeling may amount to over 60% of the weight of the harvested peppers. Pimientos are harvested when fully mature in a manner similar to that used for bell peppers. They are washed, sorted, peeled, cored, cut into strips or dice, and frozen.

SOURCE: *The Freezing Preservation of Foods, 4th Edition, Vol. 2* by Tressler, Van Arsdel and Copley published by Avi Publishing Co., Westport, Conn.

AU GRATIN POTATOES

Cooked, diced potatoes are mixed with a sauce consisting of milk, cheddar cheese, salt, monosodium glutamate, and pepper. The mixture is approximately ⅔ potato and ⅓ sauce. Other ingredients such as flour, shortening, and sugar may be added. A topping consisting of cheddar cheese, toasted bread crumbs, and margarine or other formulations are sprinkled on the product before freezing.

SOURCE: *Processing of Frozen French Fried Potatoes and Other Frozen Potato Products*, USDA, Western Utilization Research and Development Division, Berkeley, Calif.

POTATO CAKES

Potato cakes are prepared by incorporating beaten eggs and salt with cold mashed potatoes or grated raw potatoes. The chopped parsley, chopped celery or celery seed, grated onion, small and irregular blanched strips of potatoes rejected from the French-fry line may be used after they have been cooked further on a wire-mesh conveyor in a continuous steam-blancher and then inspected and riced in a pulper. If grated raw potatoes are used, more eggs will be required to hold the cakes together than if either cold mashed potatoes or the steam-blanched, irregular strips from the French-fry line are used. After thorough mixing, the mash is formed into cakes which are dipped in either fine bread or cracker crumbs, or flour, and then fried by the shallow fry method. Midway through the frying, the cakes are flipped over and browned on the other side. After cooling, they are packed in consumer cartons which are closed and overwrapped before freezing, or are placed on a tray as a component of a frozen precooked dinner.

SOURCE: *The Freezing Preservation of Foods, 3rd Edition* by Tressler and Evers published by Avi Publishing Co., Westport, Conn.

HASH BROWN POTATOES

Several methods are used to produce this product. In one process, small whole potatoes are completely cooked, cooled, shredded, and packed loose in cartons before freezing. Sliver and nubbin by-products from the French-fry line are also used. This material is shredded, chopped, or diced and is then blanched or cooked. If the material is blanched or cooked first, provision must be made for adequate cooling in order to avoid sticking or gumming in the cutting equipment.

SOURCE: *Processing of Frozen French Fried Potatoes and Other Frozen Potato Products*, USDA, Western Utilization Research and Development Division, Berkeley, Calif.

MASHED OR WHIPPED POTATOES

Slivers and small pieces of potato are steamed and mashed with mashing rolls or by extruding through a ricer. A finisher can be used to remove lumps and fiber. Salt and milk solids can be added. For whipped potatoes, the mashed material is vigorously beaten. A volumetric piston filler can be used to meter the product into film-lined cartons that are frozen in an air blast. Mashed potatoes for the institutional trade are produced from slices, cuts, or shreds which are blanched or cooked and frozen. Preparation for serving consists of heating in a steam-jacketed kettle or double-boiler. The product is mashed after the addition of milk or water.

SOURCE: *Processing of Frozen French Fried Potatoes and Other Frozen Potato Products*, USDA, Western Utilization Research and Development Division, Berkeley, Calif.

POTATO PATTIES

In the manufacture of potato patties, slivers and short pieces separated from the French-fry line are steam blanched and then cooled and shredded or chopped. Whole small potatoes may be sliced or shredded and processed in the same manner as slivers and nubbins. Another method is partial cooking of small potatoes in steam or hot water before shredding or chopping. Shredding after cooking is thought to give a product with better frying characteristics than does shredding before cooking. The shredded material is mixed with salt or other seasoning and flour. In some cases, onion powder is added for flavor. A patty-forming machine shapes either round or rectangular patties weighing about 3 oz each. The product can be frozen before or after packaging. Waxed paper between patties keeps them separate in cartons.

The potato patty is a versatile product that can be prepared for serving by frying in deep fat or in a skillet, by broiling, by baking, or by boiling and mashing. It can also be prepared as an au gratin dish. Portion control for institutional feeding is also simplified by the use of patties.

SOURCE: *Processing of Frozen French Fried Potatoes and Other Frozen Potato Products*, USDA, Western Utilization Research and Development Division, Berkeley, Calif.

PREPEELED POTATOES

Many hotels and restaurants use fresh prepeeled potatoes that have been cut in strips (Frenched), then treated with a sodium bisulfite or a citric solution to which ascorbic acid has been added, then packaged in vacuumized plastic bags (Cryovac) and refrigerated until used. The procedure in producing a good prepeeled product follows:

Wash potatoes thoroughly, then peel the potatoes either in an abrasive peeler or by soaking the potatoes in a 20% lye solution at 145°F, after which the potatoes are passed under powerful sprays of water to wash off the loose peels and the caustic solution. The peeled potatoes then should be run on a belt and inspected; any poorly peeled potatoes should again be passed through the lye peeling equipment. Eyes which have not been removed should be trimmed out. The peeled, trimmed potatoes should be put through a cutter which slices the potatoes in strips for French-frying. The strips should then be immersed for 30 sec in a solution containing 5000 ppm sodium bisulfite and 5000 ppm of citric acid. The potato strips are drained and then packaged in plastic-lined paper or Cryovac bags. If Cryovac bags are used, they should be vacuumized. After packing in bags, the potato strips should be refrigerated at about 34°F. Under these conditions the potatoes will keep satisfactorily for 2-3 weeks.

SOURCE: D. K. Tressler and Associates, Westport, Conn.

POTATO PUFFS

Slivers, and also small pieces of potatoes are used for the production of frozen potato puffs. The raw material is cooked with steam and mashed and then mixed with flour, eggs, and seasoning in a batter mixer. A basic formula consists of cooked peeled potatoes, 79.5%; butter or margarine, 4.5%; cream (light), 9.0%; egg yolks, 3.5%; and egg whites, 3.5%. Onion flavoring may be added. The mixture is extruded hot in the form of croquettes approximately ¾-in. in diameter by 1½ in. long. These are allowed to cool, then fried in deep fat and frozen.

SOURCE: *Processing of Frozen French Fried Potatoes and Other Potato Products*, USDA, Western Utilization Research and Development Division, Berkeley, Calif.

POTATO WHIRLS

A frozen mashed product known as "potato whirls" is produced in England. Whole potatoes are peeled by abrasion, trimmed to remove eyes and defects, then rapidly sliced mechanically, and cooked in steam-jacked kettles. Eggs, milk, margarine, seasoning, and other ingredients are added during mashing. The final product has a very creamy texture. Individual portions are given a whirl or spiral configuration by means of a chocolate forming machine specially adapted to this purpose; 4 completed whirls are packed in polyethylene in a 7½ oz carton and frozen.

SOURCE: *Processing of Frozen French Fried Potatoes and other Frozen Potato Products*, USDA, Western Utilization Research and Development Division, Berkeley, Calif.

FROZEN RHUBARB

Rhubarb is brought in from the fields either in lug boxes or large tote bins. This vegetable is relatively easy to pack, since it requires no peeling, husking, threshing, or sizing. Most of the waste material, such as the large leaves, are removed in the field and only the stalks are brought in for processing. The stalks are washed by passing under high-pressure sprays and fed to a transverse slicer for cross-cutting into 1-in. slices. Slicing machines handling 4,000-6,000 lb of rhubarb per hour are available.

The cut slices are conveyed into a tank of agitated water for preliminary wash and are spray-rinsed. The washed pieces are run over sorting belts, where defective units such as rot, cuts, and broken pieces are removed.

Unblanched rhubarb is slow to develop off-flavors and this item has sometimes been packed. However, blanched rhubarb not only has a longer storage life but is also easier to pack because of its softer texture. Because of the large surface area in cut rhubarb, steam blanching (1-2 min) is preferable to water blanching.

Before packaging and freezing, the cut rhubarb is mixed with sugar in the proportion of 6 parts of rhubarb to 1 part of sugar. The sugar-rhubarb mixture is filled into cartons and is usually plate frozen.

SOURCE: *The Freezing Preservation of Foods, 4th Edition, Vol. 2* by Tressler, Van Arsdel and Copley published by Avi Publishing Co., Westport, Conn.

FROZEN COOKED RICE
(Using Steamed Polished Rice)

Patna rice is washed in a rod-reel washer. Next, it is conveyed by belt to hoppers and measured into stainless steel-jacketed kettles equipped with removable wire-lined baskets. Water is added in the proportion of 1.28 lb per pound dry rice, and the mass boiled. Following complete absorption of water, the basket of partially cooked rice is lifted out of the kettle by hoist and dumped into a hopper, which feeds the rice into a steamer for completion of cooking. The steamer is similar to a large blancher in general design, and is equipped with stainless steel mesh belts.

Following cooking, the rice is discharged onto a stainless steel mesh belt (to allow draining) conveyed through an air blast cooler and cooled to approximately room temperature. It is then packaged in 12-oz cardboard cartons which are transported to a refrigerated warehouse, where they are frozen and held in storage until marketed.

SOURCE: USDA, Western Regional Research Laboratory, Berkeley, Calif.

FROZEN SPINACH

A mechanical cutter cuts the spinach a few inches from the ground, carries it up on a conveyor belt and loads it into a trailer. Since a large mass of tightly-packed spinach will quickly heat up in the truck, it is common practice to cut spinach at night while the air is cool and haul it to the processing plant for processing next day. At the plant the spinach is raked from the trailer onto a receiving belt. From there it is elevated into a circular mesh reel where the spinach is agitated by means of vanes to remove trash. A powerful fan may be used to blow a strong stream of air through the reel to rid the spinach of insects, bits of dirt, sand, grit, broken leaves, etc. After this "dry cleaning" operation, the spinach is dumped onto an inspection belt, so arranged that the leaves are tumbled onto progressive belts, thus permitting the product to be frequently turned over for inspection and sorting. Sorters remove damaged and yellow leaves as well as extraneous material such as weeds.

The spinach proceeds by belt into a wash tank for a vigorous agitated wash followed by high-pressure water sprays. This wash involves several changes of water and each time is followed by passage over a mesh belt to drain dirty water from the previous wash. Washing of spinach must be particularly thorough so that all traces of sand and silt are removed.

The washed spinach is then wilted and blanched. Spinach may be either wilted and blanched in a single operation, or wilted in a wilting tank, using water maintained at about 130°F, then blanched in boiling water or a steam tunnel for about 2 min. From the blancher the spinach passes into a cold water quench.

Yellow leaves will frequently show up much better after blanching, so there is a final sorting of the blanched spinach in order to remove such discolored material. Some operations may float the leaves in a water trough to enable sorters to select out discolored leaves. The cooled, blanched spinach is elevated by a mesh belt to facilitate draining. Sometimes a roller is used on the conveyor belt to help press out free water; however, such an operation, if not carefully controlled, will press free liquid in the package and buyers therefore sometimes specify a maximum percentage of free liquid.

Spinach is packed in three principal styles: whole leaf; cut leaf (cut on a special Urschel cutter with knives set 2 × 2 in.); and chopped (cut ¼ × ¼ in.). Chopped spinach may be pumped into a filler machine and mechanically filled into paperboard cartons, an operation that is impossible with the whole-leaf style. These are frozen either in a multiplate freezer or in an air blast at -20°F or lower. Sometimes spinach, in various styles, may be bulk frozen in 50- or 100-lb blocks for later use as boil-in-the-bag items.

SOURCE: *The Freezing Preservation of Foods, 4th Edition, Vol. 2* by Tressler, Van Arsdel and Copley published by Avi Publishing Co., Westport, Conn.

FROZEN SUMMER SQUASH

Summer Crookneck squash, when properly prepared and frozen, is an acceptable product. In order to obtain a first class product, it is necessary to harvest the squash before the rind is hard and the seeds large. All that is necessary is to wash the squash, slice it into ½-in. slices, then scald the slices for 3½ min in boiling water. After blanching, the squash is immediately cooled in running water. The cool product is packaged in moisture-vaporproof packages and frozen at 0°F.

SOURCE: *The Freezing Preservation of Foods, 3rd Edition* by Tressler and Evers published by Avi Publishing Co., Westport, Conn.

FROZEN WINTER SQUASH AND PUMPKIN

Fully mature, hard shelled squash are washed, then cut up; and the seeds and stringy material removed. The cut squash is cooked by steaming until it is soft; this requires 30-45 min. A continuous steamer may be used for the purpose. The steamed squash is conveyed to a finisher or pulper which separates most of the rind from the pulp. Use of a screen with about 0.04-in. openings is recommended. The squash is then rapidly cooled to prevent discoloration. This may be done in a shallow metal vat or trough which is partially immersed in running cold water. A screw conveyor may be used to move the squash through the cooling trough. The cool squash is filled into moisture-vaporproof cartons and preferably quick frozen.

SOURCE: *The Freezing Preservation of Foods, 4th Edition, Vol. 2* by Tressler, Van Arsdel and Copley published by Avi Publishing Co., Westport, Conn.

FROZEN SWEET POTATOES

Frozen sweet potatoes are a good product. However, in order to obtain high quality, great care is required in processing. Properly cured sweet potatoes are preferred to those freshly dug.

The first step in preparation for freezing is washing. This may be done in a soaker-washer followed by washing with powerful sprays of water on a conveyor elevator. The washed sweet potatoes should then be peeled. This is best accomplished by treating them in a boiling 10% lye solution for 5-6 min. As the sweet potatoes emerge from the boiling lye solution they should be cooled and washed with sprays of water. The sweet potatoes then should be inspected and trimmed by women who work along a trimming table where the loosened peels are removed. The peeled sweet potatoes should then be cooked preferably in a retort at 10 lb pressure for 5-25 min. A small amount of citric acid (0.3%) may be added to the cooked sweet potatoes and the product allowed to cool and then put through a pulper. Or, if desired, the sweet potatoes may be sliced and then packaged.

SOURCE: *The Freezing Preservation of Foods, 3rd Edition, Vol. 1* by Tressler and Evers published by Avi Publishing Co., Westport, Conn.

FROZEN BAKED SWEET POTATOES

Baking in-the-peel is the best method of cooking sweet potatoes to develop maximum natural sweetness and flavor. Those peeled before baking lack the attractive appearance, sheen, and pronounced aroma and flavor of the ones baked unpeeled. Peeled potatoes baked in aluminum foil or in partially covered pans were superior to similar potatoes baked on a wire rack or baking sheets; but not as good as unpeeled potatoes baked on sheets. It is desirable to grease the surface of unpeeled potatoes with butter or margarine before baking; and after baking they may be peeled and wrapped individually in aluminum foil or other moisture-proof sheets, or they may be packaged in the peel.

Preference was shown by a taste panel for sweet potatoes that were baked for about 10 min at 240°F before freezing, and the baking process completed after the potatoes were thawed. The first heating inactivated enzymes and prevented darkening, while the second heating developed a fresh-from-the-oven flavor.

SOURCE: *The Freezing Preservation of Foods, 4th Edition, Vol. 4* by Tressler, Van Arsdel and Copley published by Avi Publishing Co., Westport, Conn.

GLAZED SWEET POTATOES

The sweet potatoes are washed, inspected, and then cooked until tender either by boiling or steaming. The cooked potatoes are allowed to cool, then the peels are removed with a knife and the peeled potatoes trimmed to remove dark spots. A syrup is prepared by dissolving 32 parts of granulated sugar and 32 parts of brown sugar in 24 parts of water, heating the resultant syrup almost to the boiling point to obtain complete solution of the sugar. Then 9 parts of orange juice and ½ part of butter are added and the whole mixed thoroughly. The peeled sweet potatoes are sliced into ½-in. slices which are then dipped into the hot syrup and packed in liquid-tight, moisture-vapor-proof cartons leaving only ½-in. headspace. Then sufficient syrup is poured over the slices to cover them. Approximately 3 oz of syrup will be used on each 12 oz of sweet potatoes. The packaged product is frozen at −20°F or lower.

If the glazed sweet potatoes are produced on a large scale, the washed potatoes may be lye peeled before cooking.

SOURCE: *The Freezing Preservation of Foods, 4th Edition, Vol. 4* by Tressler, Van Arsdel and Copley published by Avi Publishing Co., Westport, Conn.

FREEZING TOMATOES

Although frozen tomatoes and tomato products are only a little better than canned tomatoes and tomato products, still considerable quantities have been frozen, principally in Europe. The varieties commonly used for canning collapse so completely on freezing and thawing that an inferior product is produced. Consequently, the Italian varieties should be used, since they are more meaty. The addition of calcium salts prior to freezing helps to prevent collapse, probably because of the formation of calcium pectate. Since the slices collapse badly, greater success is obtained by quartering, and treating with calcium salts before freezing. If they are to be used in salads, the quarters should be served before they have completely defrosted. Cryogenic methods of freezing, e.g., in a spray of liquid nitrogen, causes less disruption of the tissues.

Flash pasteurized tomato juice gives a good frozen product although the liquid tends to separate from the pulp when the product is thawed. In preparing juice for freezing only sound, fully ripe, highly colored tomatoes should be used. The tomatoes should be thoroughly washed, then scalded to loosen the skins. The skins and cores should be removed and any green parts removed. The tomatoes should be chopped and then immediately put through a flash heater and raised to 185°-195°F. The juice should then be extracted in a screw-type extractor, and immediately cooled. About 1% of salt should be added, then the product should be packaged and frozen.

SOURCE: *The Freezing Preservation of Foods, 3rd Edition* by Tressler and Evers published by Avi Publishing Co., Westport, Conn.

FROZEN TURNIP GREENS

Turnip greens are frozen principally in Arkansas, Georgia, Maryland, New Jersey, Oklahoma, Tennessee, Texas, and Washington. The tops of young turnips should be used. All of the large coarse leaves and any foreign matter should be eliminated. The greens are washed, blanched, cooled, and drained, following the procedure described for Spinach as given above. See also p. 157.

SOURCE: *The Freezing Preservation of Foods, 3rd Edition* by Tressler and Evers published by Avi Publishing Co., Westport, Conn.

FROZEN TURNIPS

Frozen turnips are prepared for freezing according to the same general procedure indicated for kohlrabi (as described earlier in this Section). Only young tender turnips should be used as old turnips are likely to be stringy or woody. The tops and roots should be cut off. Then the turnips should be peeled and diced in ½-in. cubes. The diced turnips should be steamed for 70–80 sec, then cooled in running water and packaged in cartons. The packaged turnips should be frozen at 0°F or below in air blast or in a plate freezer.

SOURCE: *The Freezing Preservation of Foods, 3rd Edition* by Tressler and Evers published by Avi Publishing Co., Westport, Conn.

FROZEN CHOPPED VEGETABLES

Preparation from Frozen Vegetables

Frozen vegetables packed for remanufacture or in institutional size packages are allowed to thaw overnight in a cool room. The thawed, or nearly thawed, product is chopped in a vegetable chopper, usually adjusted so as to produce an average size of piece not greater than 1/16 in. in diameter. Spinach and other greens, and broccoli, which are commonly frozen in chopped form, are often comminuted to a ¼-in. size, using an Urschel dicer or similar chopper. These frozen chopped vegetables are blanched but not ordinarily cooked by the frozen food packer. They may be used as raw material for the preparation of both precooked chopped junior foods and precooked strained infant foods. The chopped vegetable is transferred to a steam-jacketed kettle; a small amount of water, 0.15% monosodium glutamate, and 0.25% of salt are added, and the vegetable cooked until tender. If the chopped vegetable is packed in tin cans, it is run into a steam-jacketed holding tank, equipped with an agitator, located above an automatic filler which fills the cans with the hot product. If composite or other cartons are used, it should be cooled before filling. If the quantity to be cooled is small, cooling can be done with sufficient rapidity merely by running cold water in the jacket of the kettle while the chopped product is being slowly agitated. If the scale of operations is large, a heat exchanger suitable for handling a semifluid product should be used. Chopped spinach and other relatively fluid products can be pumped through a tubular heat exchanger, provided the pump used will handle fluids containing small pieces of vegetables.

Preparation from Fresh Vegetables

If fresh vegetables are used as the raw material for the making of frozen chopped baby foods, the procedures will be the same as those described above for making the product from frozen raw material, except that it will be necessary to prepare, clean, wash, sort, and do all of the other things required in the usual operations carried out in the preparation of vegetables for freezing.

For strained baby foods, chopped carrots and beets are commonly prepared from the fresh vegetables. Instead of converting these products into a purée, homogenizing, and sterilizing them, it is only necessary to add the desired amount of salt (usually 0.25%) and monosodium glutamate (0.15%), fill hot, if cans are used, or cool and fill into cartons or composite cartons, then quick freeze.

In order to obtain a product from spinach and other greens, and broccoli, suited for feeding both juniors and old persons, it may be advantageous to comminute them to a piece size larger than 1/16 in. in diameter (recommended for feeding very small children). This may be done by an Urschel dicer which chops these vegetables into ¼-in. "dice."

SOURCE: *The Freezing Preservation of Foods, 4th Edition, Vol. 2* by Tressler, Van Arsdel and Copley published by Avi Publishing Co., Westport, Conn.

FROZEN MIXED VEGETABLES

The USDA Standards for Frozen Mixed Vegetables describe this item as a mixture containing three or more of the following basic vegetables:

Beans, green or wax	cut-style ½-in. to 1½-in. cuts
Beans, lima	either large whole green limas or baby limas
Carrots	⅜- to ½-in. cubes
Corn, sweet	whole-kernel yellow corn
Peas	sieve sizes 3 through 5

When 3 vegetables are used, no one vegetable should be more than 40% by weight of the total; when 4 vegetables are used, no single vegetable should be more than 35% or less than 8% by weight of the total; when 5 vegetables are used no single vegetable should be more than 30% or less than 8% by weight. A good quality mix used by one processor is 22% green beans, 22% corn, 22% peas, 22% carrots, and 12% limas. Lima beans almost always are the smallest proportion. Inasmuch as frozen mixed vegetables are combinations of ingredients of different sizes and composition, care must be taken to see that all of the vegetables are so blanched that when the mixture is cooked all pieces will be of uniform "doneness." Lima beans for mixed vegetables should be "double-blanched" and diced carrots should similarly be blanched longer than usual. Frozen mixed vegetables are almost always packed by packers of peas and/or green beans. They may have to order those ingredients which they do not pack themselves from other packers. It is usually not economical, however, for a carrot packer, for example, to buy other components from other freezers.

Virtually all the mixtures described are made from vegetables which have been frozen and packed in bulk during the season. In the off-season the free-flowing vegetables are mixed and packaged while still in the frozen state.

SOURCE: *The Freezing Preservation of Foods, 4th Edition, Vol. 2* by Tressler, Van Arsdel and Copley published by Avi Publishing Co., Westport, Conn.

SUCCOTASH

Succotash is a mixture of whole kernel corn with either lima beans or green beans. When green beans are used the product is designated as "frozen green bean succotash." The USDA Standards for Frozen Succotash recommend that the proportion of ingredients be between 50 and 75% for the corn and between 25 and 50% for the beans.

SOURCE: *The Freezing Preservation of Foods, 4th Edition, Vol. 2* by Tressler, Van Arsdel and Copley published by Avi Publishing Co., Westport, Conn.

FROZEN VEGETABLES FOR STEWS

This mixture of vegetables has become very popular in recent years because it considerably simplifies and eliminates much of the labor necessary for the housewife to make a meat and vegetable stew. Although there are no standards for this item, practically all mixes now on the market consist of large pieces of potatoes, carrots, onions, and celery. These vegetables are all IQF-frozen separately and bulk-stored to be mixed and packaged in the off-season. The potato component is either composed of whole potatoes 1-1½ in. in diameter, or large pieces of irregular size and cut, about 1 oz in weight. The carrots are transverse slices of ⅜-½ in. in length, or they may be irregular cut pieces. Onions are almost always whole onions 1-1½ in. in diameter. The celery component is in the form of transverse ½-in. cuts. One popular mix being packed consists of:

Potatoes	55% large pieces
Carrots	28% large pieces
Onions	12% whole
Celery	5% transverse cuts

A 1½-lb polyethylene bag is a common package for this item.

SOURCE: *The Freezing Preservation of Foods, 4th Edition, Vol. 2* by Tressler, Van Arsdel and Copley published by Avi Publishing Co., Westport, Conn.

VEGETABLE PICKLES AND SPICED PRODUCTS

CANNED BARBECUE PARTY DIP

Ingredients	Lb	Oz
Soaked, cooked pinto beans	315	
Water	70	
Smoked bacon ends	35	
Green peppers, fresh	40	
Onion powder	10	
Canned red peppers, diced	10	
Vinegar, 100-grain	2 (pt)	
Salt	12	8
Chili peppers, ground	4	4
Spanish paprika	1	8
Black pepper, ground		2
Red pepper, ground		0.5
Cumin		14
Oregano		2.5
Garlic powder		2.5

Procedure

Soak beans overnight, drain water, cook until tender. Grind bacon ends through ⅛-in. plate of grinder. Clean green peppers eliminating stems and seeds; dice. Transfer cooked beans to meat chopper; add ground bacon ends and chop to fine consistency. Add water, salt, vinegar, and the remainder of the ingredients except diced green and canned red peppers. Chop bean mixture for 3 min; then add green and red peppers and continue chopping for only an additional 2–3 revolutions.

Fill into 208 × 410 (11 oz) cans. Close under 27 in. vacuum. Process 2 hr at 240°F. Check processing time and temperature with can supplier or the National Canners Association.

SOURCE: Griffith Laboratories, 1415 W. 37th St., Chicago, Illinois.

RANCH STYLE BEANS

Ingredients	Gal.	Lb	Oz
Tomato purée	35		
Cane sugar		12	8
Salt		32	
Cornstarch		45	
Beef fat (rendered)		35	
Chili pepper (34 mesh)		12	
Paprika (domestic)		13	
Onion powder		9	
Garlic powder		2	
Ground cumin seed		8	
Ground oregano		4	
Water to make 200 gal.			

Procedure for Sauce:

Put tomato purée in the steam-jacketed kettle. Add sugar and salt, which should be mixed together with the rest of the ingredients except rendered beef fat. Stir steadily while adding the mixed product to the tomato purée, then add heated beef fat and bring up volume with added hot water to 200 gal. Bring up temperature to 212°F, and cook for 20 min.

Procedure for Beans:

Soak pinto beans overnight at cooler temperature. Next morning cook beans for 12 min in boiling water.

Procedure for Canning

Pack: 8 oz soaked and blanched beans
8 oz hot sauce

Process: 300 × 409 cans (16-oz net) 85 min at 240°F.

Check processing time and temperature with can supplier or the National Canners Association.

SOURCE: D. K. Tressler and Associates, Westport, Conn.

CANTALOUPE PICKLES NO. 1

Ingredients	
Firmed cantaloupe pieces	20 lb
Water	4 gal.
Sugar	25 lb
Vinegar, 40-grain	7 qt
Spices (1:49 parts 70% alcohol):	
Cinnamon oil	40 ml
Clove oil	40 ml
Allspice oil	15 ml
Ginger oil	7 ml

Yield: 65 10-oz jars

Firming Cantaloupe Pieces

Prepare firm-ripe cantaloupes: (a) remove about ⅓ in. of the peel; (b) Remove connecting tissue and soft layer near the seeds; (c) cut meat into desired shapes such as wedges, dice, circles, balls. Place pieces in solution of 0.5% calcium hydroxide for 16 hr at 70°F for firming. Rate of firming will be influenced by the cantaloupe variety, degree of ripeness, size of pieces, temperature, concentration of salt and time of treatment.

Freshen the pieces by soaking in 140°F water for 1 hr with changes at 15-min intervals; or, soak in 70°F water for 3 hr.

Pickling Procedure

Mix water, sugar, and vinegar and bring to boil; add cantaloupe and allow to stand 10 min. Cook slowly for 1 hr or until product becomes translucent around edges and air bubbles form in the center. Then increase heat rapidly until syrup reaches 218°F; add spices, mix thoroughly, and cook to 65° Brix. Pack in sterile containers, seal, and cool quickly.

SOURCE: *Cantaloupe Pickles*, Georgia Experiment Station Circular *NS 15*, Experiment, Georgia.

CANTALOUPE PICKLES NO. 2

Preparation Prior to Pickling

Medium-ripe or half-ripe cantaloupes are best for making pickles.

Separate the peel and green portion from the soft flesh. To accomplish this, the melons are usually cut lengthwise into segments following the ribs of the cantaloupe with a curved knife. The peeled and trimmed product should have a firm texture, no green coloration, and a smooth surface. Then the segments should be cut or diced into desired shapes for preserves or pickles.

Firming the cantaloupe pieces is necessary to produce the desired crispness in the finished product. Firming is best accomplished by soaking the pieces in a solution of calcium hydroxide overnight or for about 15 hr and at a temperature of about 70°F. For each 5 lb of pieces use 2 gal. water and 2 tbsp calcium hydroxide.

After firming, the pieces must be freshened. This consists of thoroughly removing the excess calcium hydroxide from the cantaloupe by washing and soaking. Drain the calcium solution and replace it with fresh warm water (140°F) and let stand for 30 min; then refreshen 2 more times at 15-min intervals after which the pieces are ready for pickling.

Pickling Procedure

Ingredients	
Freshened, firmed cantaloupe	5 lb
Sugar	6½ lb
Water	7 pt
Vinegar, 40-grain	5 cups
Allspice, ground	5 tsp
Cinnamon, ground	5 tsp
Cloves, ground	5 tsp
Ginger, ground	5 tsp

Yield: 12 8-oz jars

Make syrup with sugar, water, and vinegar. Add to cantaloupe pieces. Add to the syrup at this time. (If whole spices are used, tie spices in cloth bag.) Cook slowly (200°F) or simmer for 1 hr. Then boil vigorously for 20 min or until the syrup reaches 217°F. Pack pickle pieces in hot jars, cover with boiling syrup, seal, and cool at once.

SOURCE: Dept. of Food Science, Georgia Experiment Station, Experiment, Georgia.

CAPER FLAVOR

Ingredients	Fl Oz
Oil of garlic	0.25
Oil of dill seed	0.25
Oil of mustard	4.00
Alcohol, 95%	32.00
Propylene glycol	91.00
	127.50

Procedure

Mix thoroughly.

SOURCE: *Food Flavorings, Composition, Manufacture, and Use, 2nd Edition* by Merory published by Avi Publishing Co., Westport, Conn.

CATSUP

Ingredients	Gal.	Lb	Oz
"Cyclone" Tomato juice, 1.020 sp gr	182		
Salt		43	
Sugar		75	
Finely chopped onions		25	
Finely chopped garlic			8 to 16
Ground cinnamon			25
Penang mace, very fine			3.5
Ground cloves			15
Ground allspice			15
Cayenne pepper			3.5
Paprika, powdered (optional)			2
Vinegar, 100-grain, distilled		12	

Yield: 100 gal. catsup

Procedure

The spices are simmered in half of the vinegar in a covered kettle for about ½ hr. The vinegar-spice solution is filtered to remove the extracted spices. The remainder of the vinegar is added to the filtrate and the salt and sugar dissolved in the hot vinegar. The tomato juice is concentrated to about 1.010 sp gr and then the warm vinegar solution of the spices, salt and sugar is slowly added and the boiling in the open steam-jacketed, stainless steel kettle continued until the specific gravity reaches about 1.150 which corresponds to a 33.0% solids content. The powdered paprika is then stirred in. The catsup is filled at 185°F or slightly higher into warm sterile bottles.

NOTE: Spice concentrates may be used in place of ground spices thus eliminating their extraction with hot vinegar. The salt and sugar may be added to the boiling juice instead of to the vinegar.

SOURCE: D. K. Tressler and Associates, Westport, Conn.

CATSUP SUPREME

Ingredients	Gal.	Lb	Oz
1.060 sp gr, heavy tomato purée	100		
Sucrose		200	
High DE corn syrup		70	
Salt		30	
Chopped onions		30	
Cinnamon		1	8
Mace			3
Cloves		1	
Cayenne			4
Chopped garlic			4
Cassia			2
Chili			2
White pepper			2
Cayenne pepper			2
Thyme			2
Paprika			4
Vinegar (100-grain)	15		

Yield: 1320 lb

Procedure

With a portion of vinegar, make up a paste with all the spices except onions and garlic. Add the purée to a steam-jacketed kettle and bring to a boil. Add the sugar, corn syrup, chopped onion, and garlic. Add the salt and then the vinegar and spice mix. Strain and pack at 205°F, or process.

SOURCE: CPC International, Inc., Industrial Division, Englewood Cliffs, N.J.

CHILI COCKTAIL DIP

Ingredients	48 Portions
Softened cream cheese	1 lb
Dairy sour cream	1 qt
Instant minced onion	½ cup
Chili powder	2 tbsp
Lemon juice	1 tbsp
Salt	1 tsp
Instant garlic powder	½ tsp
Milk or cream	3-4 tbsp

Yield: approx 48 portions

Procedure

Combine all ingredients except milk. Blend until smooth. Add milk in small quantities, blending until desired consistency is reached. Let mixture stand at least 2 hr before serving. Serve with potato or corn chips, celery and carrot sticks, or assorted crackers.

SOURCE: American Spice Trade Association, Empire State Building, New York, N.Y.

CHUTNEY

Chutneys are pungent spicy relishes prepared with fruits, spices, and herbs. The name may come from the Hindustani word *chatni* a sweet pickle or relish prepared with sweet fruits, acidified with lemon, lime, and sour herbs, and flavored with hot spices such as chilies and cayenne pepper.

There are a wide variety of chutneys, such as apple chutney, tomato apple chutney, and tomato pear chutney. In the preparation of such products, it is essential to use enough acid, usually vinegar, with the sweetening so that the product will be acid enough to inhibit bacterial spore germination and also keep fairly well after the processed product is opened. One formula calls for 100 lb of sugar made into a heavily spiced syrup and with 5% vinegar. Spices or spice emulsions should depend on preference. The syrup is brought to a boil and poured over prepared fruit slices or chunks in the container. Following sealing a short, 5-min cook in hot water is sufficient.

A typical formula for chutney is given below.

Ingredients	Gal.	Lb	Oz
Water	3.5		
Vinegar (containing 5% gum tragacanth)	2		
Brown sugar		30	
Carrots, chopped		40	
Dates, minced		30	
Raisins		10	
Onions, chopped		10	
Acetic acid, glacial		4	
Salt		5	
Caramel			10
Protein hydrolyzate			10
Ginger, ground			10
Cinnamon, ground			8

	Gal.	Lb	Oz
Paprika, ground			6
Cayenne pepper, ground			4
Pimiento, ground			4
Coriander			2½

Procedure

Boil carrots, dates, and raisins with the water for ½ hr. Add the salt, spices, and seasoning and boil slowly for 15 min more. Add the vinegar and acetic acid. Bring to the boil and then fill into clean jars.

SOURCE: D. K. Tressler and Associates, Westport, Conn.

GREEN TOMATO CHUTNEY

Ingredients	Gal.	Lb	Oz
Green tomatoes (sliced)		40	
Onions (sliced)		20	
Chilies (sliced)		2	
Peppercorns		1	
Mixed spice			3
Ginger			2½
Pepper			2½
Vinegar	5		

Procedure

The tomatoes, onions, and chilies are to be sliced then sprinkled with salt and allowed to stand for 12 hr. Pour in the vinegar and add the pepper, ginger, and sugar. Bring to the boil, then simmer until desired consistency is obtained, usually a soft brown mass. Fill hot and cap immediately.

SOURCE: D. K. Tressler and Associates, Westport, Conn.

TOMATO CHUTNEY

Ingredients	
Tomato purée	12 gal.
Sugar	48 lb
Salt	2 lb
Onions (chopped)	28 lb
Vinegar	5 gal.
Garlic vinegar	2 gal.
Wheat flour	15 lb
Starch	2 lb
Shalots (chopped)	1 lb
Sultanas (chopped)	6 lb
Raisins (chopped)	6 lb
Mace (ground)	4 oz
Ginger (ground)	4 oz
Cloves (ground)	1 oz
Chilies	1 oz
Tomato Color	½-1 to ½ pt

Yield: 35 doz 10-oz bottles

Procedure

The whole batch should be boiled for 1 hr and then passed through sieve.

SOURCE: D. K. Tressler and Associates, Westport, Conn.

TOMATO CHUTNEY NO. 2

Ingredients	Lb	Oz
Tomatoes, peeled and diced	100	
Vinegar	10	
Salt	4	
Sugar	40	
Seedless raisins	8	
Ginger root	2-3	
Dry chili peppers		5

Procedure

Combine all ingredients, bring to a boil and cook until thick. Pack in containers, seal, and cool.

SOURCE: D. K. Tressler and Associates, Westport, Conn.

CORN RELISH

Ingredients	%
Sweet corn kernels	50.00
Chopped green pepper	5.00
Chopped red pepper	5.00
Chopped onion	6.50
Sugar	7.50
Mustard seeds	0.50
Turmeric	0.15
Vinegar	13.00
Water	12.22
Stabilizer (multi-Sta Special)	0.13
	100.00

Procedure

Blend the stabilizer with the water, adding the stabilizer slowly under good agitation in order to avoid lumping of the colloids. When the stabilizer has dispersed, add the vinegar followed by the remainder of the ingredients. Blend gently until a uniform mixture has been achieved.

SOURCE: Germantown Manufacturing Company, 505 Parkway, Broomall, Penn.

BRINING OR CURING CUCUMBERS

Cucumbers are brined in wooden vats. The vats are filled with green cucumbers size graded or of mixed sizes and the vats are fitted with loosely constructed wooden board covers, keyed down firmly with wooden 2 × 4's or 4 × 4's.

The general method of salting is to use a 30°–40°

salometer brine in the bottom of the tank; 1 lb of salt per gallon of water will give approximately a 40° salometer solution.

A layer of 8-10 in. of 40° brine is first placed in the tank to prevent bruising of the cucumbers during filling. The cucumbers are then filled in, additional salt being added during the filling at the rate of 2 lb per bushel of pickles. Additional 40° salometer brine is added in sufficient amounts to keep the cucumbers covered. For proper curing, cucumbers will require 4¼-5 lb of salt per bushel in addition to the salt in the 40° brine. It is, therefore, general custom to place dry salt on the top layer of cucumbers to maintain the initial brine concentration, which otherwise would be diluted by the water in the cucumbers. The brine is recirculated by means of a pump from the bottom of the tank to the top until the salt is dissolved. The initial concentration ranges from 8 to 10% salt. Usually the brine strength is gradually raised by adding enough dry salt to give a holding strength of 16-18% at the end of 4-6 weeks.

The scum which forms on the top of the tanks during fermentation should be removed from time to time, otherwise spoilage of the pickles accompanied by softening may result. The pickles are cured when the original bright green color has changed to dark olive green and the pickles are translucent in appearance and show no white spots or areas when broken.

All tanks or vats used in salting pickles should be provided, as above mentioned, with a loose cover of boards or planks, fitting inside the container a few inches below the top and with cleats, weights, or other suitable means so that the pickles or other vegetables can be kept under the surface of the brine. When the tank is full, cover the pickles with cheesecloth or other suitable material, place the cover in position and fasten it down. Skim off all froth or foam and keep the top covered with 60° brine. When fermentation has ceased, remove scum daily by skimming the tanks. From time to time add sufficient 60° brine to keep the cover submerged. Large tanks used for dry salting must be provided with a pump box or shield on one side so that the brine may be circulated from the bottom of the tank to the top when it is heavier at the bottom than at the top. When completely cured in a 60° salometer brine, pickles will keep satisfactorily for 1 yr or more. If they are kept for 4-5 yr, salt should be added each summer to raise the salt test of the brine 5 to 10° salometer until 90° salometer is reached. Some manufacturers, after curing is completed, cover the liquor at the top of the tanks with a layer of tasteless mineral oil or melted paraffin.

SOURCE: *A Complete Course in Canning, 4th Edition* by Lopez published by Canning Trade, Baltimore, Maryland.

YELLOW CUCUMBER PICKLES

Ingredients	Lb
Cucumbers, large	8
Onions, large	8
Celery, large stalks	8
Sugar	3
Mustard, prepared	1
Mustard, seed	(4 tbsp)
Salt	½
Vinegar	8

Procedure

Peel cucumbers; scrape out seeds. Cut cucumbers, onions, and celery in small cubes. Sprinkle with salt; let stand 2 hr. Rinse well with cold water, drain.

Add sugar, vinegar, mustard seed, and prepared mustard. Bring to a boil and stir to prevent scorching. Pack and seal in sterile jars.

SOURCE: J. G. Woodroof, Griffin, Georgia.

SOUR CUCUMBER PICKLES

Various types of finished pickle products are made from completely cured salt stock by a series of operations—leaching out most of the salt, souring with vinegar, and sweetening with sugar. The leaching or desalting operation is referred to as processing by the industry. The 15-18% of salt in the cured stock is reduced to about 4% by at least 2 changes of water. In the last change the water is heated to about 130°F. After desalting, the stock is covered with distilled vinegar. This is referred to as souring. Sour pickles and processed dills are made directly from the souring operation and are made to contain about 2.0% and 0.8% acetic acid respectively.

SOURCE: *A Complete Course in Canning, 4th Edition* by Lopez published by Canning Trade, Baltimore, Maryland.

SWEET CUCUMBER PICKLES

Sweet pickles are also manufactured from completely cured salt stock, desalted as for sour pickles. The sweetening operation is usually carried out in small tanks, although some packers prefer to sweeten in barrels. To make sweet pickles, the processing stock, after souring in distilled vinegar, is covered with liquor or syrup which contains all of the vinegar and some of the sugar to be used according to the desire of the manufacturer. The remaining sugar is added gradually until the desired sweetness is attained. Enough vinegar and sugar must be added to prohibit fermentation.

The sugar content may vary from 36 to 51% (20° to 28° Baumé) and the acid content from

1.6 to 2.1% acetic acid (16 to 21 grains vinegar). As the sugar content is increased less acid is required for preservation. As an example, a product finished at 51% sugar would require at least 1.6% acetic acid as compared to one finished at 36% sugar, which would require at least 2.1% acetic acid. For sweet pickles containing less than 2% acetic acid and 36% sugar, to prevent fermentation they should be pasteurized for 15 min at a temperature of 165°F followed by prompt cooling. Various formulas are used for the sweet liquor such as the two formulas given below.

Formula No. 1

Ingredients	Gal.	Lb	Oz
Water	50		
Distilled 80-grain vinegar	50		
Granulated sugar		150	
Brown sugar		150	
Whole cloves			12½
Coriander			12½
Mustard seed			12½
Ginger root, broken			12½
Mace			12½

Procedure

The spices should be placed in a bag. A mixture of water, vinegar and the sugars should be heated to 175°-190°F in a covered vessel at which time the bag of spices is added and the sweet liquor with the spices is heated at this temperature for 1 hr in order to impregnate the liquor with the spice flavor.

Formula No. 2

Ingredients	Gal.	Lb	Oz
Distilled 50-grain vinegar	100		
Granulated sugar		400	
Brown sugar		200	
Oil of cloves			1
Oil of cassia			1
Spice mixture of:			
Red pepper			1½
Crushed coriander seed		1	
Crushed allspice		1	
Broken Saigon cinnamon		½	
Whole mustard seed		½	
Crushed mace		½	
Ginger root			6
Crushed anise seed			4
Whole celery seed			8

Procedure

The whole spices are extracted in hot sweetened vinegar solution. The oils are dissolved in ½ pt of alcohol and gradually added to the mixture containing the spice extract.

To Use

The spiced, sweetened vinegar solution should be added to freshened pickles packed in barrels. The barrels should be turned a half turn every day in order to hasten the diffusion of the sweet vinegar into the pickles.

SOURCE: *A Complete Course in Canning, 4th Edition* by Lopez published by Canning Trade, Baltimore, Maryland.

GENUINE DILL PICKLES

Several types of dill, sour, or spiced pickles are fermented in weals in salt brines and may be consumed where cured without further processing. They undergo a typical lactic acid bacterial fermentation during which about 0.7-1.0% acid expressed as lactic acid is produced and distinct changes in texture, flavor, and color occur.

Genuine dill pickles are produced by a natural fermentation of fresh cucumbers in a 30°-40° salinometer brine (7.0-10.6%) to which has been added dill weed and a blend of mixed spices and/or an emulsion of spice oils. Practically all manufacturers have their own spicing formulas. In general, about 10-15 lb of cured dill weed and 1 lb of mixed spices are added per barrel. Combination of spice oils are usually used according to instructions by their manufacturer. "Kosher style" dill pickles are generally more highly seasoned with garlic, onion, and spices. Fermented pickles may be used within a few days but to obtain a complete fermentation and cure with absorption of flavors a period of 3-6 weeks is required at room temperatures. The brine must be covered to exclude air and thus prevent yeast growth on the surface. In the past, this was accomplished by keeping the barrels full to overflowing. Since the salt and acid are so low it is obvious that the pickles are perishable. This is particularly true with some of the extremely low salt fermented pickles in which a 20° salinometer brine is used.

Softening may be delayed by cool storage to delay enzyme activity or by pasteurization at 165°F for 15 min to inactivate enzymes and/or by addition of alum.

SOURCE: *Microbiology of Food Fermentations* by Pederson published by Avi Publishing Co., Westport, Conn.

PASTEURIZED DILL PICKLES

Ingredients	Lb
Water	89
Salt	8
Sugar	2
Acetic acid (or 4lb of 4% vinegar may be used instead of the acetic acid)	1

Procedure

Trim the ends off of cucumbers and cut them in 5-in. lengths. Then cut them lengthwise into quarters and pack the pieces tightly into pint jars. Add pieces of dill, dill seeds, and other spices including a piece of a chili pepper if desired. Fill the jar with hot brine, pasteurize at 165°F for 15 min. The final salt content should be 2.5-3%.

SOURCE: D. K. Tressler and Associates, Westport, Conn.

GHERKINS

Gherkins are small cucumbers. The name probably comes from the Greek *agouris* meaning unripe or youth.

Since small cucumbers, 1-2 in. in length are the most costly cucumbers, they are usually prepared as a very sweet, mildly spiced and acidified pickle. These cucumbers are nearly always placed in salt brines for fermentation (see **Salt Stock** given below in this Section), until a large enough supply has been accumulated to prepare a finished product. They are refreshed immediately before preparing a finished pickle. Each processor should develop his own formula. The spice companies prepare spice emulsions as well as spice mixtures and will advise processors. Spice emulsions have many advantages.

Procedure

The refreshed cucumbers are placed in a 5% vinegar for overnight or a few days. The cucumbers are removed from the vinegar and covered with an 8% vinegar containing 20 lb sugar to 8 gal. of vinegar and the suggested amount of spice emulsion. If a whole spice mixture is used, the spices are placed in a bag and boiled in some of the vinegar to extract flavor. A suggested spice mixture of 1 part allspice, 1 celery seed, 2 cinnamon, 2 cloves, and 4 mustard seed using 4 lb of spice to 100 gal. of pickle will yield a mild flavor. The cucumbers are held in the spice vinegar syrup and the sugar content is progressively increased by addition of more sugar at daily intervale until the desired sweetness is attained. This permits cucumbers to absorb sugar gradually and thus avoid shriveling. Sugar contents of 30% or more are common. Some packers add turmeric to improve color, alum to improve texture, gums to increase colloidal properties and/or polysorbate 80 as an emulsifier.

The gherkins are packed in jars and covered with the heavy syrup. A hot water process of not over 5 min may be used before cooling the product.

SOURCE: D. K. Tressler and Associates, Westport, Conn.

MUSTARD RELISH FOR MEATS

A tangy, easy-to-make relish to serve with roast beef, pot roast, meat loaf, baked ham, ham loaf, roast pork, or pork chops.

Ingredients	
Canned apple sauce	1 No. 10 can
Mustard, prepared	12 oz
Celery seed	2 tbsp

Yield: 50 4-oz portions (scant 3½ qt)

Procedure

Combine all ingredients; blend well. Chill.

SOURCE: Processed Apples Institute, 666 Fifth Ave., New York, N.Y.

PREPARED FRENCH MUSTARD

Ingredients	Gal.	Lb	Oz
Distilled malt vinegar (4% acetic acid)	100		
White mustard flour		100	
Salt		27	8
Ground turmeric		4	3
Ground cayenne pepper		1	10
Ground cloves		1	10
Ground pimiento			13

Procedure

Mill the mustard flour and ground spices together until a smooth powder is obtained. Slowly add the mustard and spice mixture to the vinegar (in which the salt has been dissolved) agitating the mixture steadily. Continue agitation until a smooth mustard, free of lumps, has been obtained. The product should be packed in glass jars.

SOURCE: D. K. Tressler and Associates, Westport, Conn.

CANNED PEPPER-ONION RELISH

Ingredients	Lb
Onions, finely chopped	75
Sweet red pepper, finely chopped	25
Green peppers, finely chopped	25
Sugar	25
Vinegar	50
Salt	1

Yield: 375 pt

Procedure

Combine ingredients in stainless steel steam-jacketed kettle. Boil about 45 min or until slightly thickened. Pack boiling hot relish in clean hot jars to ½ in. of top. Seal. Process in boiling water bath for 5 min. Cool.

Check processing time with container supplier or the National Canners Association.

SOURCE: D. K. Tressler and Associates, Westport, Conn.

GREEN TOMATO RELISH

Ingredients		%
Keltrol	0.7-1.4 oz	0.045-0.09
Green tomatoes, pressed and chopped	44.2 lb	44.19
Salt	1.36 lb	1.36
Sugar	30.93 lb	30.93
Vinegar (100-grain)	264.8 fl oz	17.50
Mustard seed	10.72 oz	0.67
Celery seed	1.0 oz	0.06
Soluble pepper (white)	0.3 oz	0.02
Red peppers, chopped (dehydrated)	4.8 oz	0.30
Onions, fresh, chopped	4.9 oz	4.87
Relish oil (to taste)	0.2 oz	0.01
	100.00 lb	100.00%

Procedure

Dry blend Keltrol with about five times its weight in sugar. Combine all relish ingredients in mixer and start mixer (making sure top of mixer blades is not covered with relish). "Dust" in the Keltrol and blend slowly while mixer is running. Mix normally for 8-12 min; then handle according to the regular procedure for processing relish.

SOURCE: Kelco Co., 20 N. Wacker Drive, Chicago, Illinois.

CHILI PEPPERS

Chili peppers may be dried in the sun in arid climates. The fully ripe chili pepper rods are placed on racks or a roof until they are dry. Often when nearly dry, they are strung together in long strings which may be hung on clothes lines or fences until they are completely dry.

In California, the commercial product is prepared and dehydrated with artificial heat by the process described for bell peppers.

SOURCE: D. K. Tressler and Associates, Westport, Conn.

CANNED PICCALILLI

Ingredients	Lb
Green tomatoes, chopped	200
Sweet red peppers, chopped	25
Green peppers, chopped	25
Onions, chopped	40
Cabbage, chopped	200
Salt	40
Vinegar	150
Brown sugar	200
Whole mixed pickling spices	6

Yield: 400 pt

Procedure

Combine vegetables, mix in salt. Allow to stand overnight. Drain. Discard liquid. Press lightly. Discard press liquor.

Place vinegar in stainless steel steam-jacketed kettle. Add sugar. Put spices in a canvas bag. Add to vinegar. Bring to a boil. Add chopped vegetables and boil slowly at a simmer for 30 min or until there is just enough liquid to moisten vegetables. Remove spice bag and pack the hot piccalilli in glass jars, filling jars to ½ in. of top. Close jars. Process 5 min in boiling water. Cool.

Check processing time with container supplier or the National Canners Association.

SOURCE: D. K. Tressler and Associates, Westport, Conn.

BASIC PICKLE PRODUCT JELLY

Ingredients	100 Lb Batch Gal.	Lb	Qt
Pickle product (drained) or raw materials such as fresh peppers, cucumbers, onions, etc.*		20-30	
Cane sugar (sucrose) or its equivalent in liquid or invert sugar syrup		55	
White vinegar (50-grain) or equivalent amount of a higher grain vinegar			5
Sunkist single-strength lemon juice (or 12 fl oz of Exchange concentrated lemon juice No. 2309)	½		
Pectin solution**	1¼		

The amount of pickle product or raw material may be varied from 20 to 30 lb in the batch. The amounts of vinegar and lemon can also be varied but it is important that the finished product have a pH range of 2.9-3.2 and 60°-63° Brix.

Procedure

1. All of the pickle of raw material ingredients should be finely chopped for portion-pack use, coarse chopped for better visibility in glass packing,

and thin sliced for such items as cucumber-onion jelly. The natural juices released during chopping should be included in the batch.

2. Combine in the kettle all of the ingredients except the pectin solution. Heat to boiling and continue heating until a 72° Brix is reached. The high brix is needed to obtain a satisfactory gel.

3. Determine the pH of the batch and adjust, if necessary, to 2.9 or less. A citric acid solution made up at a rate of 1 lb of anhydrous citric acid to 1 pt of water may be used to adjust the pH. If the pickles or raw materials are unusually high in acid content, it is advisable to hold out a portion of the lemon juice. The pectin solution usually will bring the batch to the desired pH and Brix.

4. Shut off the heat and add the pectin solution with good agitation, mix thoroughly. Fill into containers and seal. The filling temperatures should be from 180°-190° F.

5. Cool the filled and sealed containers in a tunnel or immerse in cool water.

---

*Many combinations of pickle products and raw vegetable materials may be used in producing these jellies; following are a few suggested examples: cucumber-onion, sweet pickle-pineapple, sweet mixed pickle, sweet pepper relish, green tomato, spiced beet, lemonade pickle, pepper relish-orange, sweet pepper sauce, spiced red tomato.

**Pectin Solution: Heat 1¼ gal. of water to near boiling. Add 8-9 oz Jet-Sol Rapid Set Pectin No. 3434 with good agitation. Continue mixing slowly until the pectin is completely dispersed before adding to the batch. It is good practice to run the solution through a screen to ensure a smooth pectin solution. The solution may be made up in larger quantities if it is used the same day.

SOURCE: Sunkist Growers, 720 E. Sunkist St., Ontario, Calif.

MIXED PICKLES OR BREAD AND BUTTER PICKLES

This is a favorite in many homes. They are ordinarily prepared with slices or chunks of cucumbers, sliced onions, green peppers, and/or other vegetables. The cucumbers may be fresh stock held overnight in a 30° salt brine or refreshed salt stock. Proportions are optional. To 80 lb of cucumbers, 10 lb onions, 2 lb green pepper one would use 25 lb or 3 gal. vinegar, 35 lb sugar, and 12 oz of spice in proportion of 1½ turmeric, ½ ground cloves, 2 mustard seed, and 2 celery seed.

The vinegar, sugar, and spices are boiled; the vegetables are added and when warmed are transferred to containers. The syrup is brought to a boil and poured over the vegetables and containers are sealed; after 5 min the product is cooled.

SOURCE: D. K. Tressler and Associates, Westport, Conn.

SWEET PICKLE RELISH

Ingredients		%
Xanthan gum (Keltrol)	0.8-1.6 oz	0.05-0.10
Pickles, chopped, desalted, pressed	49.6 lb	49.63
Sugar	29.8 lb	29.78
Vinegar (100-grain)	297.4 fl oz	19.65
Mustard seed	8.6 oz	0.54
Celery seed	1.1 oz	0.07
Red peppers, chopped (dehydrated)	3.5 oz	0.22
Relish oil (to taste)	0.2 oz	0.01
	100.0 lb	100.00%

Procedure

Dry blend Keltrol with about five times its weight in sugar. Combine all relish ingredients in mixer and start mixer (making sure top of mixer blades are not covered with relish). "Dust" in the Keltrol and blend slowly while mixer is running. Mix normally for 8-12 min.; then handle according to the regular procedure for processing relish.

SOURCE: Kelco Co., 20 N. Wacker Drive, Chicago, Illinois.

SWEET CROSS-CUT SLICED PICKLES

Cross-cut pickles may be prepared from fresh cucumbers or from salt stock cucumbers after refreshing. If fresh cucumbers are used they should be placed in a 30° brine overnight before slicing. The larger cucumbers are used for such pickles. The pickles are sliced into a container and covered with a hot solution of vinegar syrup. A prepared spice emulsion may be preferred and used as recommended by the spice company. After 24 hr the syrup is drained off and an additional 2 lb of sugar is dissolved by heating to boiling. This is repeated after another 24 hr and again if the pickles are not sweet enough. A suggested spice mixture may be 1 part allspice, 1 celery seed, 2 cinnamon, 2 cloves, and 2 mustard seed. On the third or fourth day, drain off the syrup, heat to a rolling boil and pour over the cucumbers which have been packed in sterilized containers. Seal and cool.

SOURCE: D. K. Tressler and Associates, Westport, Conn.

HAMBURGER RELISH

Ingredients		%
Xanthan gum (Keltrol)	1.44 oz	0.09
Pickles, chopped, de-salted, pressed	46.44 lb	46.44
Vinegar (100-grain)	278.3 fl oz	18.39
Onions, fresh, chopped	4.09 lb	4.09
Red peppers, chopped (dehydrated)	3.2 oz	0.20
Sugar	27.86 lb	27.86
Mustard seed	13.12 oz	0.82
Celery seed	0.96 oz	0.06
Relish oil	0.16 oz	0.01
Tomato paste (26%)	2.04 lb	2.04
Soluble paprika (to taste)		—
	100.00 lb	100.00%

Procedure

Mix ingredients to a uniform mixture.

SOURCE: Kelco Co., 20 N. Wacker Drive, Chicago, Illinois.

HORSERADISH RELISH

Since horseradish grows in the ground it must be very thoroughly cleaned. First, it should be soaked in cold water and then brushed and finally washed with powerful sprays of water. The outer brown skin must be peeled off. The peeled horseradish should be sliced and then ground in a vegetable chopper.

Ingredients	Lb
Grated horseradish	10
Vinegar, 100-grain	10
Salt	1

Procedure

Mix all ingredients thoroughly in a stainless steel mixer. Pack into glass jars. Hold product at 40°F or colder.

SOURCE: D. K. Tressler and Associates, Westport, Conn.

HOT DOG RELISH

Ingredients		%
Xanthan gum (Keltrol)	0.7-1.4 oz	0.045-0.09
Pickles, chopped, de-salted, pressed	45.6 lbs	45.63
Vinegar (100-grain)	273.6 fl oz	18.08
Onions, fresh, chopped	4.0 lb	4.02
Red peppers, chopped (dehydrated)	3.2 oz	0.20
Sugar	27.4 lb	27.39
Mustard seed	8.0 oz	0.50
Celery seed	1.0 oz	0.06
Relish oil	0.16 oz	0.01
Prepared mustard	4.02-5.53 lb	4.02-5.53
Soluble turmeric to taste		—
	100.00 lb	100.00%

Procedure

Mix ingredients to a uniform mixture.

SOURCE: Kelco Co., 20 N. Wacker Drive, Chicago, Illinois.

SALT STOCK

The preparation of salt stock is a commercial development designed to handle large quantities of cucumbers rapidly and store them for future use for any one of several types of finished pickles. The combination of acids produced by fermentation and the salt in the brine inhibit enzyme action which may cause softening of the pickle and eventually will stop further bacterial growth.

The cucumbers are immersed in a 30° salt brine and covered with a wooden cover weighted to hold cucumbers under the brine. A lactic acid bacterial fermentation will occur as evidenced by clouding of the brine and evolution of gas. The concentration of salt in the brine will drop due to absorption of salt by the cucumber. Additional salt is added at daily or semiweekly intervals to raise the brine concentration about 5° per week and until a concentration of about 60° is attained. Acidities of 0.7-1.07% should be attained. After the desired salt concentration is attained, the pickles may be covered with a plastic cover.

Salt stock may be stored a year or more. When needed, the salt stock pickles are refreshed in several changes of water, including one hot water to inactivate enzymes. The cucumbers may then be converted to any one of a number of types of pickles. See also Brining or Curing Cucumbers, pp. 170-171.

Other vegetables are salted and fermented in a similar manner for use in blends of pickles.

SOURCE: *Microbiology of Food Fermentations*, by Pederson published by Avi Publishing Co., Westport, Conn.

SAUERKRAUT

Sauerkraut is literally acid cabbage. It is the product of a lactic acid bacterial fermentation of cabbage. It is an easy product to prepare but establishment of proper environmental conditions is essential in ensuring a desirable fermentation.

The solid white heads of properly matured cabbage are cored mechanically and then trimmed to remove green, broken, or dirty leaves. The cabbage is sliced to about 1/32 in. and transported to the vat by belt lines and/or carts. Salt (never more than 2.25%) is distributed uniformly with the shredded cabbage on the belt line or while being packed into the vat. The cut cabbage must be distributed uniformly in the vat. Salt withdraws water and nutrients from the cabbage to furnish substrate for bacterial growth. The salt brine begins to form shortly after shreds are salted, and when the vat is full, there will be sufficient brine to cover the shredded cabbage. When the vat is full, the product is covered with a plastic sheet large enough to extend over the edge of the vat. Sufficient water is placed in this cover to serve as an effective seal and weight. This weight must be sufficient so that the brine effectively covers all of the shredded cabbage. Some adjustment is sometimes required during the fermentation. Fermentation occurs by the activity of 3 and sometimes 4 species of lactic acid bacteria growing in sequence. The rate of fermentation will depend upon the temperature of the cabbage. At about 65°F an acidity of 2.07% will be attained in about 2 months and the kraut is ready for processing. Fermentation is more rapid at higher temperatures and less active at lower temperatures. Sometimes at low temperatures, fermentation is not completed after 6 months or more.

Some sauerkraut is retailed in bulk but most of it is canned or packed in plastic bags. Canning in tin or glass is accomplished by heating the product in excess brine and water to 165°-170°F, filling the container, topping with hot water, sealing at 170°F, followed by cooling. Generally enough water is added to the brine so that a final acidity of 1.1-1.5% calculated as lactic acid and a slightly higher percentage of salt is obtained. Sauerkraut packed in plastic bags is sometimes heated but more often packed with a preservative, such as sulfur dioxide, sodium benzoate and/or potassium sorbate. Sulfur dioxide is not permitted in some states and there are limitations on the amount of sodium benzoate. Ascorbic acid is sometimes added.

In some countries, cabbage is packed as whole heads in salt brine, and in some areas mixtures of vegetables are packed and fermented either in their own brine or in a prepared salt brine. Sauerkraut is prepared in many homes using 5- or 10-gal. crocks or kegs or barrels. More than 2¼% salt should never be used. The cabbage, after trimming, is quartered, the core removed, and shredded by hand shredder. It is packed tightly in the container covered with a plastic cover weighted with water. It may be used a few days after fermentation.

SOURCE: *Microbiology of Food Fermentations* by Pederson published by Avi Publishing Co., Westport, Conn.

TAMALE SPICES

Ingredients	Per 100 Lb Lb	Oz
Chili, powdered	2	8
Paprika, powdered	1	
Cumin, powdered		6
Coriander, powdered		5
Oregano, powdered		3
Celery seed, powdered		2

SOURCE: *Food Flavorings, Composition, Manufacture, and Use, 2nd Edition* by Merory published by Avi Publishing Co., Westport, Conn.

CANNED HOT TAMALES

To Prepare White Mush

Ingredients	Lb	Oz
Cream cornmeal	38	
Prime oleo stock	12	
Granulated sugar	2	8
Salt	2	8
Water	95	

Procedure.—Put 95 lb of water in steam-jacketed kettle equipped with mixer. Bring water to boiling, then slowly add cornmeal. Stir constantly and add oleo stock, sugar, and salt. Chill in trucks; then grind through the ⅛-in. plate of the grinder.

To Prepare Red Mush

Ingredients	Lb	Oz
Pork chuck meat, cooked	18	12
Beef trimmings, Canner Grade cooked	18	12
Beef hearts, trimmed and cooked	12	8
Beef suet	12	8
Water	25	8
Onions, fresh ground	2	8
Cream cornmeal	13	8
Wheat flour	1	8
Tomato purée	6	
Salt	3	4
Hot tamale spice mix (given below)	2	12

Spice Mixture for Red Mush

Ingredients	Lb	Oz
Chili pepper (HVC), ground	120	
Cumin seed, ground	24	
Spanish paprika	15	
Savory, ground	3	12
White pepper, ground	3	12
Thyme, ground	3	12
Cayenne pepper, ground	5	
Mexican sage	2	8

Procedure.—Grind the cooked meats, hearts, onions, and suet through the ¼-in. plate of the grinder. Transfer ground mixture to mixer and add the rest of the ingredients; mix for 3 min. Then put the mixture through the ⅛-in. plate of the grinder.

To Prepare Sauce

Ingredients	Gal.	Lb	Oz
Water	11		
Tomato purée		12	
Onion powder			5
Salt			10
Spanish paprika			10
White pepper or dry soluble pepper			3

Procedure.—Put all ingredients in a steam-jacketed kettle and bring to a boil.

To Make Tamales

A specially-designed machine is used to make and wrap the tamales.

Packaging and Processing

Pack in cans or glass jars and close under vacuum.

Suggested process is 2 hr at 240°F for 300 × 409 cans (16 oz net weight). Check processing time and temperature with can supplier or with the National Canners Association.

SOURCE: D. K. Tressler and Associates, Westport, Conn.

TOMATO ASPIC

There are four known processes or treatments used in the production of low methoxyl pectin, each treatment resulting in a product with different functional characteristice—independent of its methoxyl content. Thus, it is possible to have four low methoxyl pectins of similar demethoxylation, each of which will require variations in formulas and handling when employed in the manufacture of products such as tomato aspic. The formulas and information presented herewith are based upon the use of Exchange low methoxyl pectin and will not necessarily prove satisfactory if used with a low methoxyl pectin produced by a different process from that used in the manufacture of Exchange low methoxyl pectin. A great amount of needless research has been wasted in the recent past by food manufacturers who have attempted to follow published formulas and recipes which were developed in laboratories with laboratory manufactured low methoxyl pectin of a type not available or practical from the industrial producer's standpoint. Therefore, it is of utmost importance that food manufacturers, when using Exchange low methoxyl pectin, follow formulas and procedures developed specifically for its correct use. A standard factory formula for tomato aspic follows

Ingredients	
Tomato or vegetable juice	100 gal.
No. 2309 Exchange concentrated lemon juice	1⅜ gal.
Sugar	40 lb
No. 3467 Exchange low methoxyl pectin	13¾ lb
Calcium chloride $CaCl_2 \times 2H_2O$	1¾ lb
Salt and spice (as desired)	

Procedure

Heat the tomato or vegetable juice to approximately 195°F and withdraw 5 gal. of it into a separate container for dissolving the calcium salt.

Thoroughly mix the 13¾ lb of No. 3467 Exchange pectin with the 40 lb of sugar, and the salt and dry spice if used (spice oils can be added to the hot batch just before packing). Add this pectin, sugar, salt, and dry spice mixture into the remaining 95 gal. of hot tomato juice slowly with thorough mechanical agitation and continue agitation until all of the pectin is in solution (approximately 15 min). Add the 1⅜ gal. of No. 2309 Exchange concentrated lemon juice and any remaining spice oils and heat to 200°F.

Dissolve the 1¾ lb of calcium chloride into the separate 5 gal. of tomato juice and heat to approximately 200°F; then add to the main batch which contains the pectin in solution. Fill immediately.

Yield: approx 105 gal. or 916 lb
pH finished aspic: approx 3.6
Brix finished aspic: approx 13°
Pectin finished aspic: approx 1.5%
Added Ca^{++} ion/pectin ratio: 35 mg/gm

This product, because of its acidity, if filled at 200°F should need no further heat treatment for sterilization. It should then be cooled rapidly for the best gel texture of the product. The overall time held hot should not exceed 30 min.

In the above formula, tomato juice, vegetable juice cocktail, reconstituted tomato juice using tomato paste and water or any combination thereof may be used. However, if the aspic is produced during the tomato season from fresh tomatoes, the juice when prepared must first be heat treated at 205°F for 5 min to inactivate the enzymes native to fresh tomatoes. It is important that all raw tomato or vegetable juice going into the batch be so treated before any pectin is added; otherwise, the loss of gel strength of the pectin will be only a matter of seconds. This includes also that portion of the juice into which the calcium salt is to be dissolved.

SOURCE: Sunkist Growers, 720 E. Sunkist St., Ontario, Calif.

CANNED TOMATO ASPIC

Ingredients	%
Xanthan gum (Keltrol)	0.20
Locust bean gum	0.15
Sugar	4.00
Colflo 67 starch*	1.00
Citric acid	0.70
Sodium citrate	0.50
Salt	0.30
Lemon juice	2.00
Tomato juice	91.15
	100.00

For Can Fill Use:	%
Aspic mix	60.00
Sweet relish	40.00
	100.00

Procedure

Prepare a blend of the dry ingredients and add to the vigorously agitated tomato juice. Add the lemon juice. Heat to 170°F. Add the sweet relish, if desired. Maintain temperature for 15 min to gelatinize the starch. Heat to 210°F, pour into cans, seal, invert cans for 5 min, and cool.

SOURCE: *National Starch & Chemical Co., 750 Third Ave., New York, N.Y. Kelco Co., 20 N. Wacker Drive, Chicago, Illinois.

VINEGAR

Vinegar is a word derived from the French vinaigre meaning sour wine. It may be prepared from almost any substance that contains sugar and other nutrients by an alcoholic fermentation followed by an acetic acid fermentation. The character of each vinegar is dependent upon the character of the substrate. Apple juice and wine are common substrates, but distinctive vinegars are made from other fruit juices. Molasses, honey, syrups are also used and malt vinegars are popular.

Two distinctive microbiological processes are essential. The first is an alcoholic fermentation by yeast resulting in conversion of sugars to alcohol and carbon dioxide as major products. The second is a bacterial fermentation and requires oxygen to convert alcohol to acetic acid.

The Orleans or barrel process is the oldest. It followed the observation that when barrels of wine were partly filled, the wine turned to vinegar. It was a simple step in the art to tilt barrels on their side and fill them only ½–⅔ full. A thin film of bacteria, mother of vinegar, will form on the surface of the alcoholic juice. This will increase in mass and the rate of conversion will increase.

The Schiizenback, Boerhave or continuous generator process has become the established method for production of commercial vinegars. The generator, a large cylindrical tall tank, is designed to provide maximum surface exposure of vinegar stock to the air so that the acetic acid bacteria are present on the surface and it is necessary to pass the stock through the generator several times until a buildup of mother on the surfaces is effected. Rapid conversion will occur after this buildup. Satisfactory equipment must be adapted to control the rate of introduction of air and the rate of flow and distribution of the alcoholic stock. Recently, other aeration principles have been developed based upon processes used in antibiotic production.

SOURCE: *Microbiology of Food Fermentations* by Pederson published by Avi Publishing Co., Westport, Conn.

WATERMELON PICKLE

This type pickle has been a favorite home processed pickle for many years. The green rind and red meat are removed from the rind proper. The rind is cut into any desired shape and then covered with a cold 7½% salt water for 12 hr or overnight. The rinds are then drained, covered with boiling water, and boiled until the rinds are half tender.

A heavy syrup consisting of 30% sugar in 2½% vinegar and a mild spice emulsion is prepared. Spice emulsions are prepared by spice companies, one containing cinnamon and cloves is recommended. The syrup is boiled and then poured over the rinds in containers and the containers are sealed and cooled. If a spice mixture is preferred, one containing 2 parts cloves, 4 cinnamon, 2 celery seed, and 1 allspice is tied in a bag and boiled in the vinegar syrup, using 4 lb spice to 100 gal. of vinegar-sugar solution. A few small pieces of stick cinnamon placed in each container add to appearance.

An imitation watermelon pickle may be prepared from large cucumbers. The cucumbers are lye peeled, the seed sections removed and then handled in a manner similar to watermelon rinds.

SOURCE: D. K. Tressler and Associates, Westport, Conn.

WATERMELON RIND PICKLES

Ingredients	
Watermelon rinds prepared for processing	10 lb
Sugar	12½ lb
White vinegar, 4% acetic acid	7 pt
Water	2 gal.
Allspice	10 tsp each of
Cinnamon	whole spice
Cloves	or 10 drops
Ginger	each of essential oil

Procedure

Trim outer green rind and inner meat containing seeds from firm-ripe watermelon and cut into wedges, squares, or oblong pieces of desired size.

Place rinds in preserving kettle, add water, sugar, and vinegar. Boil until rinds are translucent and the syrup reaches 220°F, or 55% soluble solids. Pack rinds loosely in hot jars, cover with syrup, and seal immediately.

SOURCE: Melon-rind Items by DuPree, Woodroof, and Siewert, *Food Engineering 26*, 45–47, 179–182.

WATERMELON RIND RELISH

Ingredients	Lb	Oz
Watermelon rinds prepared for processing, diced	10	
Onions, chopped	6	
Pimientos, peeled and chopped	4	
White mustard seed		1/5
Red pepper, hot powdered		1/16
Celery seed		1/48
Clove oil		1/190
Salt		1/16
Sugar	8	
Vinegar, white	8	

Yield: approx 36 10-oz jars

Procedure

Mix all ingredients, except clove oil, in a preserving kettle and boil slowly for 1 hr, or until mixture becomes thick and temperature reaches about 215°F. Add clove oil, mix well, pour into hot jars, seal, and cook quickly.

Pimiento and red pepper give watermelon rind relish a pink color, similar to that of the meat of watermelon.

SOURCE: Melon-rind Items by DuPree, Woodroof, and Siewert, *Food Engineering 26*, 45–47, 179–182.

VEGETABLE BASE DRESSINGS AND DIPS

AVOCADO DIP (WITH VARIATIONS)

With Garlic

Ingredients

Avocados, mashed or puréed	8
Sour cream	1 cup
Salad dressing mix	14 oz
Chives, chopped	2 tsp
Vinegar	2 tbsp
Bacon cooked crisp, crumbled	6 slices

Yield: approx 6 cups

Procedure

Combine and chill avocado, sour cream, dressing mix, chives, and vinegar. Sprinkle with crumbled bacon.

Variation.—Add 1 cup crumbled bleu cheese; beat or whirl in electric blender until smooth. Chill.

Without Garlic

Ingredients

Avocados, mashed or puréed	8
Salt	3 tsp
Seasoned salt	1 tsp
Lime juice	1 tbsp
Worcestershire sauce	1 tsp
Tabasco sauce	$\frac{1}{4}$ tsp

Yield: approx 6 cups

Procedure

Combine and chill all ingredients.

With Sour Cream and Anchovy

Ingredients

Avocados, mashed or puréed	8
Sour cream	1 cup
Salt	1 tsp
Anchovy paste	2 tbsp
Lemon juice	4 tbsp

Yield: approx 6 cups

Procedure

Combine all ingredients, cover, and chill.

With Cream Cheese and Chervil

Ingredients

Avocados	8
Cream cheese, softened	6 oz
Lemon juice	$\frac{2}{3}$ cup
Salt	4 tsp
Chervil leaves	1 tsp
Onion powder	$\frac{1}{4}$ tsp
Tabasco sauce	$\frac{1}{2}$ tsp

Yield: approx 7 cups

Procedure

Combine all ingredients and mash or purée until smooth. Cover and chill.

With Cottage Cheese

Ingredients

Avocados, mashed or puréed	8
Cottage cheese	1 lb
Lemon juice	$\frac{1}{2}$ cup
Onion, finely chopped	4 tbsp
Salt	2 tsp
Cayenne pepper	dash

Yield: approx 6 cups

Procedure

Blend avocado with cottage cheese until fairly smooth. Blend in onion and seasonings. Cover and chill.

With Cucumber

Ingredients

Avocados, mashed or puréed	8
Salt	2 tsp
Dill weed, crushed	1 tsp
Garlic powder	dash
Chives, chopped	4 tsp
Vinegar	4 tbsp
Cucumber, pared, chopped	1 cup

Yield: approx 6 cups

Procedure

Combine avocado with seasonings and vinegar. Cover and chill. Stir in cucumber just before serving.

With Pimiento

Ingredients	
Avocados, mashed or puréed	8
Sour cream	1 cup
Lemon juice	4 tbsp
Salt	2 tsp
Tabasco sauce	1 tsp
Garlic powder	dash
Pimiento, canned, diced	1 cup

Yield: approx 6 cups

Procedure

Combine all ingredients. Cover and chill.

SOURCE: California Avocado Advisory Board, Newport Beach, Calif.

BLUE CHEESE DRESSING (WITH TRAGACANTH)

Ingredients	%
Vinegar (10% white)	16.8
Vegetable oil	45.0
Salt (fine flake)	3.4
Egg yolk (dry)	3.5
Sugar (granulated)	3.3
Water	16.6
Onion powder	0.3
Garlic powder	0.1
Celery (soluble)	0.4
Black pepper (ground)	0.2
TIC Gum Tragacanth Pretested 440 USP Powder	0.7
Blue cheese (crumbled)	9.5
Potassium sorbate	0.1
Sodium benzoate	0.1

Procedure

Make emulsion of egg yolk with water, dry ingredients, and vegetable oil. Add vinegar and blue cheese. Pump through colloid mill.

SOURCE: Tragacanth Importing Corp., 141 E. 44th St., New York, N.Y.

SALAD DRESSING WITH BLUE CHEESE

Ingredients	%
Cream cheese	49.50
Salt	2.09
Dehydrated parsley flakes	0.50
Sugar	5.85
Vinegar (distilled)	4.60
Oil	19.50
Blue cheese flavor, (Naarden RR 36359)	0.26
Water	17.70
	100.00

Procedure

Whip cream cheese with an electric mixer. Mix all dry ingredients together. Mix all liquids together. Add alternately to whipped cream cheese, mixing well after each addition. Refrigerate.

This product may need to warm slightly at room temperature in order to be pourable.

SOURCE: Naarden, Inc., 10 Painters Mill Road, Owings Mills, Maryland.

CANNED DRESSING FOR SALADS (pH 3.6)
Hot Fill and Cold Fill Static Cook Formulas

Ingredients	Weight % Amount Form. No. 1	Form. No. 2
Water	36.72	38.57
Corn oil	30.00	30.00
Vinegar (50-grain)	14.00	14.00
Sorbitol solution[1]	10.00	10.00
Microcrystalline cellulose (Avicel RC-501)	5.50	3.00
Salt	1.50	1.50
Starch[2]	1.00	1.00
Xanthan gum[3]		0.40
Monosodium glutamate	0.20	0.20
Polysorbate 60[4]	0.30	
Lemon juice		0.50
Mustard powder	0.30	0.30
Gum tragacanth	0.30	
Celery powder		0.20
Onion powder	0.15	0.15
Garlic powder	0.02	0.02
White pepper	0.01	0.01
Ascorbic acid		0.10
Citric acid		0.05
	100.00	100.00

Procedure for Formulations No. 1 and No. 2

1. Disperse Avicel RC-501 with water in a planetary mixer or other suitable high shear device. Add gum stabilizer, either tragacanth or Keltrol. Mix until smooth.
2. Combine oil and Polysorbate 60 when applicable, add oil in a slow continuous stream, and mix for 15 min.
3. Dry blend all remaining dry ingredients except salt and add to emulsion. Mix for 2 min.

4. Add Sorbitol solution and mix for 2 min.
5. Add combined vinegar, salt, and lemon juice to the emulsion and mix for 5 min.
6. Homogenize at an equivalent 2500 psi on a positive displacement piston homogenizer. If a piston homogenizer is not available, a well-maintained colloid mill at 0.010-in. clearance can be used.

The dressings prepared by the above method can be blended in any desired amount with chunk or finely chopped meats or vegetables. The size of the meat or vegetable pieces and the amount of dressing can be varied to give either a spread or salad consistency. The final preparation can be sealed in metal or glass containers and processed under conditions sufficient to sterilize the salad or spread product in the container.

Steam Injection Preheated Formula

Ingredients	Weight % Amount Form. No. 3
Water	46.72
Corn oil	20.00
Vinegar (50-grain)	14.00
Sorbitol solution[1]	10.00
Microcrystalline cellulose (Avicel RC-501)	5.50
Salt	1.50
Starch[2]	1.00
Monosodium glutamate	0.20
Polysorbate 60[4]	0.30
Mustard powder	0.30
Gum tragacanth	0.30
Onion powder	0.15
Garlic powder	0.02
White pepper	0.01
	100.00

Procedure for Formulation No. 3:

1. Disperse Avicel RC-501 with ½ total water in a planetary mixer or other suitable high shear device. Add tragacanth and mix until smooth.
2. Combine oil and polysorbate 60, add the oil in a slow continuous stream, and mix for 15 min.
3. Dry blend all remaining dry ingredients except salt and add to emulsion. Mix for 2 min.
4. Add Sorbitol solution and mix for 2 min.
5. Add combined vinegar and salt to emulsion and mix for 5 min.
6. Inject live steam into the emulsion slurry and heat to 155°-160°F. (Should pick up ¼ total water content.)
7. Homogenize at an equivalent 2500 psi on a positive displacement piston homogenizer. If a piston homogenizer is not available, a well-maintained colloid mill at 0.010-in. clearance may be used.

---

[1] Sorbo Sorbitol solution; Atlas Chemical Div., ICI America, Inc., Wilmington, Delaware.
[2] Purity 420; National Starch & Chemical Corp., New York, N.Y.
[3] Keltrol; Kelco Company, San Diego, Calif.
[4] Polyoxyethylene (20) sorbitan monostearate; Atlas Chemical Div., ICI America, Inc., Wilmington, Delaware.

SOURCE: Atlas Chemical Division, ICI America, Inc., Wilmington, Delaware.

DRESSING, COLE SLAW

Ingredients	%
Xanthan gum (Keltrol)	0.15
Oil	35.00
Sugar	24.00
Water	22.46
Vinegar (100-grain)	13.63
Egg yolks (dried)	2.00
Salt	1.60
Mustard (very fine powder)	0.90
Onion powder	0.14
Celery salt	0.10
Turmeric powder	0.02
	100.00

Procedure

Dry blend Keltrol with 10% of the total sugar and hydrate with the water and vinegar with rapid agitation. Add spices, salt, egg yolks, and balance of sugar. Add oil slowly and stir until homogeneous. Put through colloid mill at 0.30 in.

SOURCE: Kelco Co., 20 N. Wacker Drive, Chicago, Illinois.

FRENCH TYPE DRESSING

Ingredients	%	Gm
Refined corn oil (Staley)	36.47	1850
Vinegar (50-grain)	17.21	850
Water	2.51	124
Lemon juice	8.10	400
Tomato paste	4.05	200
High fructose corn syrup (Isosweet 100)	25.31	1250
Salt	2.53	125
REDISOL 88 starch	2.00	50
Onion powder (Asmus)	0.61	30
Garlic powder (Asmus)	0.30	15
Paprika (Asmus)	0.41	20

	%	Gm
Mustard powder (Asmus)	0.30	15
White pepper (Asmus)	0.20	10
Totals	100.00	4939

Procedure

1. Slurry all liquids except oil.
2. Dry blend all dry ingredients.
3. Add blended dry ingredients to liquid slurry with agitation.
4. Slowly add oil while mixing at high speed in Hobart type mixer.
5. Emulsify mixture by homogenization through Oakes Colloid Mill, Gifford-Wood jet homogenizer, or similar equipment.

SOURCE: A. E. Staley Mfg. Co., Decatur, Illinois.

FRENCH DRESSING (WITH TRAGACANTH)

Ingredients	%
Water	28.8
Vinegar (10% white)	13.2
Sugar (granulated)	9.5
Salt (fine flake)	3.0
Paprika	1.3
Mustard powder	0.6
Onion powder	0.4
Garlic powder	0.2
Vegetable oil	39.5
White pepper (ground)	0.2
Tomato paste (28-30% solids)	1.3
Tomato catsup (30-33% solids)	1.3
TIC gum tragacanth pretested "C" USP powder	0.7

Procedure

Procedures in mixing and emulsification depend on available equipment, ranging from Hobart Mixer to Colloid Mill. Spicing may be varied. If no paprika specks are desired, oleoresin paprika may be substituted. Soy oil is generally used as the vegetable oil.

SOURCE: Tragacanth Importing Corp., 141 E. 44th St., New York, N.Y.

FRENCH DRESSING (Commercial Formula)

In this formula we suggest the use of dried egg yolk to replace a part of the stabilizer combination used. This provides a final product which is richer in texture and with an enhanced flavor.

Ingredients	%
Water	12.0
Vinegar (cider) 5%	22.0
Sugar (granulated)	8.8
Salt (fine flake)	3.5
Worcestershire sauce	3.5
Paprika	4.5
Mustard, garlic, onion	4.7
Pepper (white)	0.3
Vegetable oil	40.0
Gum tragacanth	0.4
Dried egg yolk solids	0.3

Procedure

The dried egg yolk and stabilizer are mixed together with the rest of the dry ingredients and mixed into the water, vinegar, and Worcestershire sauce with agitation. The oil is then added and the uniform premix is pumped through the colloid mill at a close clearance.

SOURCE: Henningsen Foods, Inc., 60 East Forty-Second Street, New York, N.Y.

INSTANT FRENCH DRESSING

Ingredients	Gm	%
Xanthan gum (Keltrol F)	2.5	0.25
Sugar	115.0	11.50
Salt	40.0	4.00
Spreda tomato powder (Brock Co.)	5.2	0.52
Mustard flour (McCormick DSF 3681)	12.5	1.25
Paprika (McCormick)	13.5	1.35
Water	211.5	21.15
Vinegar (40-grain)	225.0	22.50
Vegetable oil	374.8	37.48
	1,000.0	100.00

Procedure

Add the dry mix to all of the water and vinegar in a small Hobart mixer equipped with a wire whip. Mix at medium speed (Speed No. 2) until all of the dry mix is well dispersed, then switch to high speed (Speed No. 3) and mix for 3-5 min. Then add oil slowly, while mixing at high speed, adding it only as fast as it can be mixed in without forming oil "pools." Mix at high speed for an additional 1-2 min after all oil has been added.

SOURCE: Kelco Co., 20 N. Wacker Drive, Chicago, Illinois.

FRENCH DRESSING

Ingredients	%
Xanthan gum (Keltrol)	0.25
Mustard, powdered	1.25

	%
Paprika, powdered	1.35
Salt	4.00
Vinegar (100-grain)	9.00
Sugar	11.50
Water	34.65
Vegetable oil	38.00
	100.00

Procedure

Hydrate blend of Keltrol with ½ of the amount of sugar in all available water and vinegar under vigorous agitation for 15 min. Add blend of all remaining solids. Add oil slowly at first, then at normal rate. Put through colloid mill at 0.002 in.

SOURCE: Kelco Co., 20 N. Wacker Drive, Chicago, Illinois.

IMITATION FRENCH DRESSING

Ingredients	%
Modified waxy maize starch with corn syrup solids (Purity Gum 539)	2.75
Oil	35.20
Cider vinegar (50-grain)	17.00
Sugar	16.75
Water	9.00
Lemon juice	7.00
Tomato paste	7.00
Salt	2.50
Onion powder	1.00
Garlic powder	0.50
Paprika	0.50
Mustard powder	0.50
Polysorbate 60	0.30
	100.00

Procedure

Slurry vinegar, water, lemon juice, and tomato paste together. Add all dry ingredients to slurry with agitation to develop a uniform blend. Dissolve polysorbate 60 in the oil and add slowly. Mix product at high speed to develop emulsion. Homogenize with colloid mill or piston-type homogenizer to develop final stable emulsion.

Note: FDA Standards of Identity do not allow starch as a stabilizer in French dressings; however, Purity Gum 539 does find application in other types of dressings not covered by the Standards of Identity.

SOURCE: National Starch & Chemical Corp., 1700 Front St., Plainfield, N.J.

LO-CAL FRENCH DRESSING

The following formulation produces dressing with excellent mouthfeel and flavor release. Pourability, in range of 40° to 100°F, is exceptional; superior emulsion stability, without colloid milling, is provided.

Ingredients	%
Algin (Kelcoloid LVF)	0.50
Xanthan gum (Keltrol)	0.50
Garlic powder	0.05
Onion powder	0.10
Mustard	0.50
Paprika	0.60
Egg yolk (fresh)	2.00
Salt	3.50
Lemon juice	5.00
Vegetable oil	6.00
Tomato paste (26%)	7.50
Vinegar (50-grain)	18.00
Water	55.75
Non-nutritive sweetener to taste	
	100.00

Approx 19 cal per fl oz or 3 cal per tsp.

Procedure

Disperse Keltrol and Kelcoloid LVF in the oil and add with good agitation to all water, vinegar, and lemon juice in which the mustard is dispersed. Complete hydration in 10–15 min with stirring. After hydration, add tomato paste and egg yolk. Add blend of all solids and stir with high speed for 10 min. Bottle.

SOURCE: Kelco Co., 20 N. Wacker Drive, Chicago, Illinois.

GREEN GODDESS DRESSING

Ingredients	Gm	%
Xanthan gum (Keltrol)	3.10	0.31
Vinegar (100-grain)	115.40	11.54
Water	378.00	37.80
Vegetable oil	380.00	38.00
Salt	30.00	3.00
Sugar	60.00	6.00
Egg yolk (fresh)	20.00	2.00
Anchovy paste	6.00	0.60
Onion powder (Gentry)	3.00	0.30
Garlic powder (Gentry)	3.00	0.30
Shredded green onions	1.00	0.10
Chopped chives	0.50	0.05
Green color (to suit)		
	1,000.00	100.00

Procedure

Hydrate blend of Keltrol with ½ the amount of sugar in all available water and vinegar containing shredded green onions and chives under vigorous agitation for 15 min. Add egg yolk and then remaining dry ingredients. Add oil slowly at first, then at normal rate. Adjust color if so desired. If desired, colloid mill at 0.002 in.

SOURCE: Kelco Co., 20 N. Wacker Drive, Chicago, Illinois.

HEAT STABLE SALAD DRESSING

This salad dressing maintains its emulsion stability through the use of Purity Gum 539. Dressing processed under retort conditions shows no visible oil separation. Purity 420 provides the smooth, heavy viscosity characteristic of a premium salad dressing.

Ingredients	%
Modified waxy maize starch and corn syrup solids (PURITY GUM 539)	4.00
Modified corn starch (PURITY 420)	2.50
Water	33.13
Corn oil	30.00
White vinegar (50-grain)	14.00
Sorbitol (70% sol.)	10.00
Egg yolk (dried)	2.50
Salt	1.50
Monosodium glutamate	0.60
Onion powder	0.60
Lemon juice	0.50
Mustard powder	0.40
Polysorbate 60	0.20
Garlic powder	0.04
Celery (soluble)	0.02
White pepper	0.01
	100.00

Procedure

Add Purity Gum 539 to water, vinegar, and lemon juice in Hobart mixer. Blend 10 min at speed No. 2. Add Purity 420 and all dry ingredients except dried egg yolks. Blend 2–3 min. Add sorbitol and dried egg yolks. Blend 2–3 min. Add oil with Polysorbate 60. Mix in slowly. Blend 15 min. Mill in colloid mill at 0.010–10.020 in. or homogenize at 1500 psi. Combine salad ingredients at below ratios and process.

Suggested Meat/Dressing Ratio (by Weight)

50 parts tuna, shrimp, crab, or lobster/50 parts dressing

50 parts chicken/50 parts dressing (add 2.00% chicken broth to above formula and subtract from water)

55 parts ham/45 parts dressing (add 2.00% ham broth and 0.20% clove powder. Reduce MSG and lemon juice to 0.30%)

SOURCE: National Starch & Chemical Corp., 1700 Front St., Plainfield, N.J.

HEAT STABLE SALAD DRESSINGS NO. 2

Ingredients	For Chicken Salad %	For Tuna Salad %
Xanthan gum (Keltrol)	0.40	0.40
White pepper	0.01	0.01
Garlic powder	0.02	0.02
Citric acid	0.05	0.05
Ascorbic acid	0.10	0.10
Onion powder	0.15	0.15
Celery salt	0.20	0.20
Monosodium glutamate	0.20	0.20
Mustard powder	0.30	0.30
Lemon juice	0.50	0.50
Purity NCS cornstarch (National Starch & Chemical Corp.)	1.00	0.50
Dehydrated egg yolk		1.00
Salt	1.50	1.50
Avicel RC-501 (American Viscose Div., FMC Corp.)	3.00	2.50
Vinegar (100-grain)	7.00	7.00
Sorbitol solution, 70% (Atlas Chemical Corp.)	10.00	10.00
Vegetable oil	30.00	30.00
Water	45.57	45.57
	100.00	100.00

Procedure

Disperse the Avicel RC-501 in the water with a high sheer mixer or in a planetary mixer, such as a Hobart. Dry blend the Keltrol, starch, egg yolk (when applicable), ascorbic acid, citric acid, monosodium glutamate, mustard powder, celery salt, onion powder, garlic powder, and the white pepper. Add the previous mentioned ingredients and mix for 10 min to dissolve the Keltrol. Add the oil in a slow and continuous stream. Mix for 15 min to allow the formation of the emulsion. Add the sorbitol solution, mix for 2 min. Mix salt and lemon juice with the vinegar; add and mix for 5 min. Take viscosity reading. It should be 2500–3200 cps (measured with the Brookfield Viscometer Model LVF, spindle No. 4 at 60 rpm). Homogenize at 2500 psi, single-stage. Take Viscosity reading. It should be between 3700-5500 cps. Mix with equal parts of diced or shredded meat. Place into can, seal, and process to sterility.

SOURCE: Kelco Co., 20 N. Wacker Drive, Chicago, Illinois.

INSTANT SPOONABLE DRESSING (MAYONNAISE-TYPE)

Ingredients	Gm	%
Xanthan gum (Keltrol F)	5.0	0.5
Instant Clearjel (National Starch)	10.0	1.0
Sugar	20.0	2.0
Salt	15.0	1.5
Dried egg yolk	26.0	2.6
Mustard (McCormick DSF 3681)	10.0	1.0
Ground white pepper (McCormick)	2.0	0.2
Water	237.0	23.7
Vinegar (40-grain)	75.0	7.5
Vegetable oil	600.0	60.0
	1,000.0	100.0

Procedure

Put the dry mix in a small Hobart mixer equipped with a wire whip. Add about 15% of the total oil and mix until all lumps are gone. Then add water and vinegar while mixing at medium speed (speed No. 2). Continue mixing at medium speed for 3 min and switch to high speed (speed No. 3). Add remainder of the oil slowly, while mixing at high speed, and continue mixing at least 2 min after all ingredients have been assembled. (Note: Oil should only be added as fast as it can be incorporated into the mix, and no pools of oil should be allowed to collect on the surface.)

SOURCE: Kelco Co., 20 N. Wacker Drive, Chicago, Illinois.

ITALIAN DRESSING

Ingredients	%
Xanthan gum (Keltrol)	0.2
Oil	55.0
Water	17.6
Cider vinegar (100-grain)	11.8
Sugar	1.5
Salt	4.0
Egg yolks	2.0
Garlic powder	0.4
Onion powder	0.3
Oregano	0.2
Lemon juice (reconstituted)	3.0
Wine vinegar (55-grain)	4.0
	100.0

Procedure

Add blend of Keltrol and sugar to the vinegars with agitation. After Keltrol is hydrated, add egg yolk, lemon juice, and blend of salt and spices and mix thoroughly. Slowly add oil and mix until homogeneous. Put through colloid mill at 0.002 in.

This salad dressing does not separate.

SOURCE: Kelco Co., 20 N. Wacker Drive, Chicago, Illinois.

CREAMY ITALIAN DRESSING

Ingredients	Gm	%
Xanthan gum (Keltrol)	1.5	0.15
Oil (soybean)	550.0	55.00
Water	54.5	5.45
Cider vinegar (50-grain)	236.0	23.60
Wine vinegar (50-grain)	48.2	4.82
Sugar	15.0	1.50
Salt	40.0	4.00
Egg yolks (fresh)	20.0	2.00
Lemon juice	30.0	3.00
Minced onions (Gentry)	1.6	0.16
Minced garlic (Gentry)	2.0	0.20
Italian seasoning (Ehlers)	0.2	0.02
Crushed red peppers(Ehlers)	0.2	0.02
Celery seed (Ehlers)	0.4	0.04
Black pepper (McCormick)	0.4	0.04
Butterscotch shade color (to suit)		
	1,000.0	100.00

Procedure

Intimately dry blend xanthan gum (Keltrol) with sugar and salt. Add this dry blend to all of the water, vinegars, and lemon juice at the point of maximum agitation. Allow to mix at high speed for 5-10 min and add the egg yolks. Then add oil slowly at first, then at a moderate rate, determined by efficiency of incorporation into the mix. Add color, if desired, to darken the mixture. Allow to mix an additional 5 min at high speed after all oil has been added. Add the blend of remaining spices and mix just long enough to disperse them homogeneously throughout the mixture. If so desired, the product may be homogenized or passed through a colloid mill before adding the final spice blend.

SOURCE: Kelco Co., 20 N. Wacker Drive, Chicago, Illinois.

CREAMY ITALIAN DRESSING

Ingredients	%
Keltrol*	0.2
Oil	55.0
Water	17.6
Cider vinegar (100-grain)	11.8
Sugar	1.5
Salt	4.0
Egg yolks	2.0
Garlic powder	0.4
Onion powder	0.3
Oregano	0.2
Lemon juice (reconstituted)	3.0
Wine vinegar (55-grain)	4.0
Total	100.0

Procedure

Add blend of Keltrol and sugar to the vinegars with agitation. After Keltrol is hydrated, add egg yolk, lemon juice, and blend of salt and spices and mix thoroughly. Slowly add oil and mix until homogeneous. Put through colloid mill at 0.002 in.

---

*Keltrol is Kelco's xanthan gum especially developed and authorized for use in foods as a stabilizing, emulsifying, suspending, and bodying agent.

SOURCE: Kelco Company, 20 N. Wacker Drive, Chicago, Illinois.

ITALIAN DRESSING (WITH TRAGACANTH)

Ingredients	%
Vegetable oil	66.0
Vinegar (10% white)	12.0
Water	16.0
Salt (fine flake)	3.5
Sugar (granulated)	1.0
Onion (minced)	0.2
Garlic (chopped)	0.3
Black pepper (coarse)	0.3
Red pepper (crushed)	0.2
TIC gum tragacanth pretested 440 USP powder	0.5

Procedure

TIC pretested gum tragacanth provides product stability during mixing and then settles down. Mix all dry ingredients into water. Add vinegar and oil, with continued agitation. Continue agitation during filling. No milling or homogenizing is necessary.

SOURCE: Tragacanth Importing Corp., 141 E. 44th St., New York, N.Y.

LOW CALORIE ITALIAN-TYPE DRESSING (WITH TRAGACANTH)

Ingredients	%
Vinegar (10% white)	20.00
Vegetable oil	4.00
Water	69.50
Salt	3.40
TIC gum tragacanth pretested 440 USP powder	1.75
Celery (soluble)	0.10
Garlic (chopped)	0.25
Onion (minced)	0.65
Black pepper (coarse)	0.13
Calcium saccharin	0.02
Potassium sorbate	0.10
Sodium benzoate	0.10

Procedure

A good basic formula with low oil component. Viscosity can be varied by modifying amount of TIC pretested gum tragacanth and type of homogenizer. Mix dry ingredients. Add to water with agitation. Next, add vinegar and oil, continuing agitation. Pump through colloid mill or homogenizer.

SOURCE: Tragacanth Importing Corp., 141 E. 44th St., New York, N.Y.

INSTANT ITALIAN DRESSING

Ingredients	Gm	%
Xanthan gum (Keltrol F)	0.6	0.06
Sugar	15.1	1.51
Salt	40.0	4.00
Borden's lemon juice powder	2.4	0.24
Minced garlic (Gentry)	2.0	0.20
Minced onion (Gentry)	1.6	0.16
Ground black pepper (McCormick)	0.4	0.04
Celery seed (Ehler's)	0.4	0.04
Crushed red pepper (Ehler's)	0.2	0.02
Italian seasoning (Ehler's)	0.3	0.03
Water	49.0	4.90
Vinegar (40 grain)	288.0	28.80
Vegetable oil	600.0	60.00
	1,000.0	100.00

Procedure

Put the dry mix in a small Hobart mixer equipped with a wire whip. Add about 15% of the total oil and mix until all lumps are gone. Then add water and vinegar while mixing at medium speed (speed No. 2). Continue mixing at medium speed for 3 min and switch to high speed (speed No. 3). Add balance of the oil slowly, while mixing at high speed, and continue mixing at least 2 min after all ingredients have been assembled. (Note: Oil should only be added as fast as it can be incorporated into the mix, and no pools of oil should be allowed to collect on the surface.)

SOURCE: Kelco Co., 20 N. Wacker Drive, Chicago, Illinois.

MAYONNAISE (50-GAL. BATCH COMMERCIAL FORMULA)

In this formula a 30-lb can of frozen salted (10%) egg yolk is replaced by 11 lb 8 oz of dried egg yolk solids. The water and salt differential is incorporated in the formulation.

Ingredients	Lb	Oz
Dried egg yolk	11	8
Oil	350	
Vinegar (10% white)	17	
Water	50	
Sugar (granulated)	8	
Salt (fine flakes)	4	8
Mustard, onion, celery, etc.	2	4

Procedure

This is mixed in the usual way in a premix tank and followed by pumping the entire batch through a colloid mill. The water for rehydration is added to the premix material left in the bottom of the tank. The dried egg yolk is added to this and mixed for about 2 min until *smooth*. The dried spices, sugar, and salt are added followed by the remainder of the water and vinegar in ratio with the rate of oil addition.

SOURCE: Henningsen, Inc., 60 East Forty-Second Street, New York, N.Y.

RUSSIAN DRESSING (WITH TRAGACANTH)

Ingredients	%
Vegetable oil	50.0
Tomato paste (28–30% solids)	5.0
Sugar (granulated)	3.2
Water	14.8
Vinegar (10% white)	12.5
Carotene solution No. 2 or oleoresin paprika (40,000 CV)	0.2
Salt (fine flake)	1.2
Onion powder	0.4
Mustard powder	0.5
Garlic powder	0.1
Celery (soluble)	0.1
Black pepper (ground)	0.1
Egg yolk (dry)	2.0
Dill pickle relish (drained)	8.5
TIC gum tragacanth pretested "C" USP powder	1.4

Procedure

Mix egg yolk with water. Add dry ingredients and vegetable oil. Add tomato paste and rest of liquid ingredients with agitation. Incorporate drained relish before pumping through colloid mill.

SOURCE: Tragacanth Importing Corp., 141 E. 44th St., New York, N.Y.

CREAMY RUSSIAN DRESSING

Ingredients	%
Xanthan gum (Keltrol)	0.25
Mustard	1.00
Tomato paste (26%)	2.50
Salt	4.00
Pickle relish	7.00
Sugar	12.00
Vinegar (50-grain)	13.50
Water	24.75
Vegetable oil	35.00
	100.00

Procedure

Hydrate blend of Keltrol with ½ amount of sugar in all available water, vinegar, and pickle relish liquor under vigorous agitation for 15 min. Add blend of remaining sugar, salt, and mustard; then add tomato paste. Add oil slowly at first, then at normal rate. Pump through colloid mill at 0.002 in. Add pickle relish solids.

SOURCE: Kelco Co., 20 N. Wacker Drive, Chicago, Illinois.

INSTANT CREAMY RUSSIAN DRESSING

Ingredients	Gm	%
Xanthan gum (Keltrol F)	3.0	0.30
Mustard flour (McCormick DSF 3681)	10.0	1.00
Spreda tomato powder (Brock Co.)	6.5	0.65
Salt	20.0	2.00
Sugar	120.0	12.00
Water	241.5	24.15
Vinegar (40-grain)	179.0	17.90
Vegetable oil	350.0	35.00
Pickle relish (100% drained weight)	70.0	7.00
	1,000.0	100.00

Procedure

Add the dry mix to all of the water and vinegar in a small Hobart mixer equipped with a wire whip. Mix at medium speed (speed No. 2) until all of the dry mix is well dispersed, then switch to high speed (speed No. 3) and mix for 3-5 min. Then add the oil slowly, while mixing at high speed, adding it only as fast as it can be mixed in without forming oil "pools." Mix at high speed for an additional 1-2 min after all oil has been added. Reduce speed to medium (speed No. 2) and add the drained pickle relish.

SOURCE: Kelco Co., 20 N. Wacker Drive, Chicago, Illinois.

LO-CAL CREAMY RUSSIAN DRESSING

Ingredients	100-Lb Batch	%
Xanthan gum (Keltrol)	8.0 oz	0.50
Algin (Kelcoloid R)	8.0 oz	0.50
Minced onion	6.4 oz	0.40
Mustard	8.0 oz	0.50
Egg yolk (fresh)	2.0 lb	2.00
Lemon juice	30.0 fl oz	2.00
Drained pickle relish (sweet)*	4.0 lb	4.00
Salt	4.0 lb	4.00
Tomato paste	4.0 lb	4.00
Vegetable oil	99.0 fl oz	6.00
Vinegar (100-grain)	182.0 fl oz	12.00
Water	970.0 fl oz	64.10
Nonnutritive sweetener (to taste)		
	100.0	100.00

Procedure

Disperse Keltrol and Kelcoloid R in the oil and add with good agitation to all water, vinegar, and lemon juice containing the pickle relish, mustard, tomato paste, and minced onion. Complete hydration in 10-15 min with stirring. After hydration, add egg yolk, salt, and sweetener. Stir at high speed for 10 min.

---

*If the pickle relish is stabilized with Keltrol, eliminate the draining step. In this case it may be necessary to decrease the vinegar in the formula to obtain desired flavor.

SOURCE: Kelco Co., 20 N. Wacker Drive, Chicago, Illinois.

30% OIL SALAD DRESSING (Using Purity 420)

Starch Paste

Ingredients	%
Modified corn starch (Purity 420)	8.0
Water	40.3
Sugar	17.7
Cider vinegar (50-grain)	15.0
White vinegar (50-grain)	15.0
Salt	2.6
Mustard powder	1.1
Onion powder	0.1
Garlic powder	0.1
Paprika powder	0.1
	100.0

Salad Dressing

Ingredients	%
Starch paste	65.0
Oil	30.5
Egg yolk (with 10% sugar)	4.5
	100.0

Procedure

Cook paste to 190°-195°F and hold for 5-10 min. Cool paste to 80°F. Add egg yolk with medium agitation. Add oil slowly with medium agitation; then mix at high speed for 2-3 min to develop primary emulsion. Pass through colloid mill to develop final stable emulsion.

SOURCE: National Starch & Chemical Corp., 1700 Front St., Plainfield, N.J.

SPOONABLE DRESSING (FREEZE-THAW STABLE)

Ingredients	%
Xanthan gum (Keltrol)	0.30
Mustard	0.50
Salt	2.00
HPC starch (National Starch Co.)	2.50
Egg yolk (fresh)	4.00
Sugar	10.00
Vinegar (white) 100-grain	10.00
Water	30.70
Vegetable oil	40.00
	100.00

Procedure

Blend Keltrol, sugar and mustard and add to ½ the total amount of the water and the vinegar with vigorous agitation. Dissolve ⅓ of the total amount of salt in the remaining portion of vinegar and water, disperse the starch and heat the mixture for complete hydration of the starch. Cool the mixture, add egg yolk and mix thoroughly. Add the Keltrol mixture and thoroughly mix. Add oil slowly while stirring. Stir until mixture is uniform, then put through colloid mill. Add and disperse remaining amount of salt necessary to make the desired 2.0% salt concentration.

SOURCE: Kelco Co., 20 N. Wacker Drive, Chicago, Illinois.

SALAD DRESSINGS (Commercial Formula)

The following formulation contains the minimum dried egg yolk content which is equivalent to 4% egg yolk (as liquid yolks) and the minimum 30% of edible vegetable oil.

In these formulations a 30-lb can of frozen salted (10%) egg yolk is replaced by 12 lb 4 oz of dried egg yolk solids, 3 lb of salt and 14 lb 12 oz of water.

Salad Dressing Formula Low Oil Type

Ingredients	%
Dried egg yolk	1.8
Vegetable oil	30.0
Starch paste mixture	68.2

Batch Formula to Replace 30-Lb Can Salt Yolk

Ingredients	Lb	Oz
Dried egg yolk	12	4
Vegetable oil	20	4
Starch paste mixture	46	4

The starch paste mixture is made in the usual way by cooking and cooling a combination of ingredients in the following proportions.

Starch Paste Mixture

Ingredients	%
Vinegar (10%)	17.2
Salt	4.0
Starches	7.7
Sugar	15.0
Spices (mustard, celery, etc.)	1.1
Water	55.0

Procedure

The dried egg yolk solids are added to ⅓ of the cooled starch paste (which may contain the extra water for rehydration of the dried egg yolk). It is also possible to add this replacement water when adding the dried egg yolk to the starch paste. Also, in some formulations, the dry spices are added to the premix instead of cooking in the starch. After mixing, the rest of the starch paste and oil are added with agitation so the premix is completed with 3-4 min.

Just as with frozen egg yolk, a richer or higher quality salad dressing may be produced by increasing the egg yolk and oil levels. If these levels are varied, the manufacturer must be certain to compensate for the salt and water normally present in his formulations when using increased levels of salt yolk.

Salad Dressing Formulas

	Low Oil %	Medium Oil %	High Oil %
Dried egg yolk	1.8	2.3	2.7
Vegetable oil	30.0	37.5	42.5
Starch paste	68.2	60.2	54.8

SOURCE: Henningsen Foods, 60 East Forty-Second Street, Street, New York 17, N.Y.

SEMISOLID SALAD DRESSING

Starch Paste

Ingredients	%
Salad dressing starch (Staley)	7.6
High fructose corn syrup (Isosweet 100)	28.2
Corn syrup (Sweetose 440)	10.0
Vinegar (50-grain)	30.0
Salt	3.0
Water	21.2
	100.0

Salad Dressing

Ingredients	%
Starch paste	60.4
Egg yolk	4.5
Soybean oil (Staley Edsoy)	35.0
Spice blend (Asmus 97T-86)	0.1
	100.0

Procedure

Slurry starch paste ingredients together and process through a continuous high temperature cooker at 195°-200°F; cool to less than 100°F. Mix starch paste, egg yolk, and spice blend with agitation; slowly add oil; mix well. Emulsify through colloid mill. Fill into containers.

Note:

If sugar is used in place of Isosweet 100, use 20.0 lb sugar and 29.4 lb water per 100 lb batch.

SOURCE: A. E. Staley Manufacturing Co., Decatur, Illinois.

STARCH BASE SALAD DRESSING
(For Both High and Low Oil Levels)

Starch Base

Ingredients	Lb
Water	108.8
Vinegar	32.0
Sweetener	37.5
Thick boiling cross-bonded waxy cornstarch	16.0
Salt	6.0
	200.0

Starch level is 8.00%.

Mayonnaise Formula

Ingredients	30.7% Oil Lb	48.0% Oil Lb
Eggs	4.7	7.4
Oil	30.7	48.0
Water	1.8	2.8

Finished Salad Dressing

	100-Lb Batch	
Ingredients	30.7% Oil Lb	48.0% Oil Lb
Cooked starch paste	62.8	41.8
Mayonnaise base	37.2	58.2
	100.0	100.0
Starch level is:	5.02%	3.34%

SOURCE: CPC International, Industrial Division, Englewood Cliffs, N.J.

NONSTARCH SALAD DRESSING
(30% Oil Dressing)

Ingredients	Gal.	Lb
Sodium alginate (Kelcosol)		1.0
Sugar		7.5
Water	4.0	
Egg yolk		3.0
Salt		1.5
Mustard		0.4
Vegetable oil	3.0	
Vinegar (100-grain)	1.0	

Procedure

The Kelcosol is dry mixed with all of the sugar and added to the water with good agitation. Either warm or cold water may be used, but solution will be faster in warm water. When the Kelcosol is thoroughly mixed and dissolved (about 10 min to 30 min depending on the equipment), add separately the egg yolk, salt, and mustard. Then the oil is slowly added until a smooth emulsion is formed. The vinegar is added last in a thin stream and thoroughly mixed in the emulsion. A homogenizer or colloid mill may be used to complete the emulsification.

Advantages of a Nonstarch Salad Dressing

1. No cooking is required and therefore no cooking equipment is necessary. Neither is it necessary to store or hold the stabilized paste overnight.
2. Faster production of a top quality dressing is the result of making the batch in one operation with cold water.
3. High quality dressings with good gloss, smooth texture, and soft body are produced.

SOURCE: Kelco Co., 20 N. Wacker Drive, Chicago, Illinois.

THOUSAND ISLAND DRESSING

Starch Paste

Ingredients	%
Salad dressing starch (Staley)	7.6
High fructose corn syrup (Isosweet 100)	28.2
Corn syrup (Sweetose 4400)	10.0
Vinegar (50-grain)	30.0
Salt	3.0
Water	21.2
	100.0

Salad Dressing

Ingredients	%
Starch paste	35.51
Soybean oil (Staley Edsoy)	35.00
Egg yolks	5.00
Chili sauce	12.00
Spice blend (Asmus 97T-87)	0.41
Sweet relish	12.00
EDTA	0.005
Sodium benzoate	0.075
	100.00

Procedure

1. Slurry starch paste ingredients together and process through a continuous high temperature cooker at 195°-200°F. Cool to less than 100°F.
2. Mix all dry ingredients.
3. Add starch paste, chili sauce, and egg yolks to tank and mix.
4. Slowly add dry-blended ingredients and mix with step No. 3 until uniform.
5. Slowly add chilled oil (45°-50°F) and incorporate by mixing; when all oil has been added, blend for 1 min at high speed.
6. Process mixture through colloid mill, then hold in mixing tank.
7. Add sweet relish.

If sugar is used in place of Isosweet 100, use 20.0 lb sugar and 29.4 lb water per 100 lb batch.

SOURCE: A. E. Staley Mfg. Co., Decatur, Illinois.

WINE DRESSING

Ingredients	Gm	%
Xanthan gum (Keltrol)	3.0	0.30
Salt	40.0	4.00
Sugar	30.0	3.00
Water	250.6	25.06
Wine vinegar (50 grain)	290.0	29.00
Egg yolk (fresh)	20.0	2.00
Natural wine flavors (optional)	4.6	0.46
Lemon juice	10.0	1.00
Minced onion (Gentry)	0.4	0.04
Italian seasoning (Ehler's)	0.2	0.02
Crushed red pepper (Ehler's)	0.4	0.04
Black pepper (McCormick)	0.4	0.04
Oil (soybean)	350.0	35.00
FD&C Red No. 2* (to suit)		
	1,000.0	100.00

Procedure

Dry blend Keltrol with all of the sugar and hydrate in all of the water under vigorous agitation for 10 min. Add the vinegar and remaining dry ingredients, followed by lemon juice and egg yolk.

NOTE: Hold out any particulate spices until last if homogenizing or colloid milling is planned. Add the oil slowly at first then at normal rate. Product may be homogenized or colloid milled at this point if the particulate spices have been held out.

---

*This coloring has been de-listed. It is no longer on the FDA-approved list of food colors and cannot be used. Consult your food color supplier for recommended color substitution.

SOURCE: Kelco Co., 20 Wacker Drive, Chicago, Illinois.

VEGETABLE SOUPS, SAUCES, AND SAUCED PRODUCTS

SOUPS

BEEF CONSOMMÉ

Ingredients	Gal.	Lb	Oz
Beef stock in which vegetables were cooked	100		
Salt		16	
Pulped vegetables (onions, carrots, parsnips)		9	
Beef fat, rendered		2	
Onion powder			4
Garlic powder			½
Celery seeds, ground			1
Turmeric			1
Dry soluble pepper			4
Monosodium glutamate		2½	
Plant protein hydrolyzate		1½	
Beef extract		5	
Caramel color			4
Wheat flour		10	

Procedure

Heat wheat flour and beef fat in steam-jacketed kettle to a deep brown color, then add 8 gal. of beef stock to form a smooth slurry. In another kettle add 92 gal. of beef stock and other ingredients; heat to 200°F; add slurry and cook 10–15 min. Use fresh or process in 211 × 4 size cans 30 min at 250°F.

Check process time and temperature with can supplier or the National Canners Association.

SOURCE: *Food Products Formulary, Vol. 1* by Komarik, Tressler and Long published by Avi Publishing Co., Westport, Conn.

BEEF SOUP STOCK

Ingredients	Gal.	Lb	Oz
Beef with bones, forequarters without fat		1000	
Water	200		
Onions, chopped		20	
Carrots, chopped		50	
Celery, chopped		25	
Parsley, fresh		8	
Cloves, whole		1	
Bay leaves			8
Thyme			8
Garlic, fresh			8
or			
Garlic powder (to taste)			1

Procedure

Remove bones, crush, and place in wire basket. Chop meat and place in wire basket. Simmer water with bones and meat (200°F) 8–10 hr with occasional skimming. Add chopped vegetables, cloves, bay leaves, thyme, and garlic (in cheesecloth bag) and simmer for 1 hr; add water to make 200 gal.

Cut off steam and cool stock by circulating cold water through jacket of kettle allowing sedement to collect in bottom and fat to harden on surface. (A) Remove fat and use in soups where formula calls for it; (B) remove meat, dice or grind and use in soups where formula calls for it; (C) remove vegetables and pulp for thickening soup; and (D) strain broth for use in soups.

SOURCE: *Food Products Formulary, Vol. 1* by Komarik, Tressler and Long published by Avi Publishing Co., Westport, Conn.

BEET SOUP (BORSCHT) BASE

Ingredients	Lb	Oz
Beet powder	49	
Salt	36	
Monosodium glutamate	12	
Plant protein hydrolyzate	6	
Cane sugar	110	
Cornstarch	73	
Vegetable oil	12	
Onion powder	3	12
Citric acid	2	4
Ground celery seed		2
Garlic powder		½
Dry soluble pepper		4

Procedure

Put the salt in a mechanical mixer and while the machine is running, add ground celery seed, dry soluble pepper, garlic powder, and citric acid. Add vegetable oil. After a few minutes add the remainder of the ingredients and mix thoroughly.

Pack in any size drum, tin, or moisture- vapor-proof envelope.

To Use

Use 12 oz per 1 gal. of water.

Make a slurry of 12 oz of beet soup base to 1 qt of water (free of lumps) then add slurry to the remaining 3 qt of hot water. Stir and cook an additional 15 min.

SOURCE: *A Guide to the Selection, Combination, and Cooking of Foods* by Reitz published by Avi Publishing Co., Westport, Conn.

CANNED CONDENSED CREAM OF ASPARAGUS SOUP

Ingredients

Use the same ingredients as given in the following formula Cream of Celery Soup but instead of cooked and pulped celery use cooked and pulped asparagus.

Procedure

Identical with cream of celery soup.

Pack while product is 180°F or hotter.

Suggested Process

211 × 4 size cans (10½ oz net weight) 30 min at 250°F.

Check processing time and temperature with can supplier or with the National Canners Association.

SOURCE: *Food Products Formulary, Vol. 1* by Komarik, Tressler and Long published by Avi Publishing Co., Westport, Conn.

CONDENSED CREAM OF CELERY SOUP

Ingredients	Lb
Beef soup stock	264
Cooked, pulped celery	264
Milk, fresh	264
Wheat flour	8
Cornstarch	2
Salt	16
Butter	8
Monosodium glutamate	2½
Dry soluble pepper	½
Plant protein hydrolyzate	1¼

Procedure

Heat to boiling in steam-jacketed kettle all ingredients except cornstarch and wheat flour, with slow agitation. Make slurry of flour, starch, and 5 gal. of water or soup stock, and add to boiling soup.

Use soup fresh or process in 211 × 4 cans 30 min at 250°F.

Check processing time and temperature with can supplier or the National Canners Association.

SOURCE: *Food Products Formulary, Vol. 1* by Komarik, Tressler and Long published by Avi Publishing Company, Westport, Conn.

CONDENSED CREAM OF CHICKEN SOUP

Ingredients	Lb	Oz
Chicken stock (strained)	800	
Cooked chopped chicken meat	40	
Carrot emulsion	30	
Wheat flour	35	
Cornstarch	6	
Cream (30% butterfat)	20	
Salt	16	
Nonfat dry milk powder	6	
Monosodium glutamate	3	
Plant protein hydrolyzate	1	
Onion powder		8
Garlic powder		⅛
Ground turmeric		1
Dry soluble pepper		4
Ground celery seed		½

Procedure

Heat to boiling in a steam-jacketed kettle, 80 gal. of soup stock, carrot emulsion, seasoning, flavoring, and cream. Make slurry of flour, starch, milk powder, and 20 gal. of chilled soup stock and add to boiling soup. Dice or grind cooked chicken meat through ¼-in. plate of grinder, or dice, and add to the batch.

Use fresh or process in 211 × 4 size cans at 250°F for 30 min.

Check processing time and temperature with can supplier or the National Canners Association.

SOURCE: *Food Products Formulary, Vol. 1* by Komarik, Tressler and Long published by Avi Publishing Co., Westport, Conn.

CANNED CONDENSED CREAM OF MUSHROOM SOUP

Ingredients	Gal.	Lb	Oz
Fresh milk	80		
Chopped mushrooms, ¼-in. size		100	
Butter		12	
Salt		10	
Wheat flour		45	
Cornstarch		11	

	Lb	Oz
Monosodium glutamate	2	8
Plant protein hydrolyzate	1	8
Onion powder		4
Garlic powder		1/8
Ground turmeric		1
Ground celery seed		1/2
Dry soluble pepper		4

Procedure

Put 60 gal. of milk, the butter, chopped mushrooms, and the remainder of the ingredients except flour and starch in a steam-jacketed kettle and bring to boil. Agitate product continuously with a bakery mixer. Make a lump-free slurry of flour and starch with 20 gal. of milk. Add slurry slowly with agitation. Cook an additional 15 min.

Fill into 211 × 4 size cans while product is at 180°F or hotter.

Suggested Process: 211 × 4 size cans (10½ oz net weight) 60 min at 240°F.

Check processing time and temperature with can supplier or with the National Canners Association.

SOURCE: Stephan L. Komarik, 4810 Ronda, Coral Gables, Florida.

CONDENSED CREAM OF MUSHROOM SOUP

Ingredients	Oz
Mushrooms, fresh, 3/8-in. dice	18.00
Water for blanching and broth	16.00
Corn oil	2.00
Cream, 32% butterfat	13.00
Skim milk powder	2.00
Wheat flour	8.00
Derivatized cross-bonded waxy cornstarch	3.50
Salt	2.50
Sugar	0.40
Monosodium glutamate	0.50
Water (total)	64.00
Tomato paste, 26% solids	0.30
Cream of mushroom soup seasoning	0.50

Yield: 1 gal.

Procedure

Wash and dice mushrooms 3/8 in. Blanch in 1½ pt water for approximately 3 min. Volume: 3 pt.

Dry mix milk powder, flour, starch, sugar, salt, monosodium glutamate, and seasoning. Add 1 pt water gradually, blend in tomato paste; add cream and oil, blend well. Volume: approximately 2 pt.

Admit 3½ pt water to kettle, heat to boiling. Add the slurry blend slowly with continuous stirring. Reheat slowly to 190°F, allow starch to develop. Add blanched mushrooms and broth; blend thoroughly. Reheat slowly to 190°F (do not scorch) and fill.* Process at 240°F for 65 min using No 1 can, plain bodies, C-enamel ends and lids.

Check process time and temperature with can supplier or the National Canners Association.

---

*The kettle procedure can be reversed if found desirable, but care should be taken not to break up the mushrooms.

SOURCE: CPC International, Industrial Division, Englewood Cliffs, N.J.

CREAM OF MUSHROOM SOUP BASE

Ingredients	Lb	Oz
Skim milk powder	30	
Butter	20	
Salt	40	
Wheat flour	180	
Cornstarch	44	
Monosodium glutamate	10	
Plant protein hydrolyzate	6	
Dry soluble pepper	2	
Freeze-dried mushroom powder	10	
Onion powder	2	8
Garlic powder		1/2
Oleoresin celery		1/2
Ground turmeric		4

Procedure

Put salt in the mechanical mixer, add oleoresin celery, dry soluble pepper, turmeric, garlic, onion powder, and butter (heated to 160°F), mix until the salt is evenly distributed and is somewhat yellow. While the mixer is running, add the wheat flour, followed by the remainder of the ingredients and make a thorough mixture.

Pack in any size drum, can, jar, or moisture-vaporproof envelope.

To Use

Recommended use is 1 lb per gal. water.

Make a lumpless slurry of the dry mix with 1 qt of water and mix with 3 qt of warm water. Cook 15-20 min.

SOURCE: *A Guide to the Selection, Combination, and Cooking of Foods* by Rietz and Wanderstock published by Avi Publishing Co., Westport, Conn.

CREAM OF MUSHROOM SOUP MIX

Ingredients	%
Potato starch, redried	24.22
Nonfat milk solids	23.52
Salt	10.91
Corn flour, redried	10.25
Potato flour, redried	9.95
Dehydrated mushrooms	9.41
Monosodium glutamate	3.53
Hydrolyzed plant and milk protein	3.53
Dehydrated white onion powder	2.35
Hydrogenated vegetable oil	2.09
Turmeric	0.12
White pepper Cream O' Spice	0.12
	100.00

Procedure

Mix and package in 1½-oz buried-foil pouches.

To Use

Empty contents of package into saucepan; 2 cups of cold water and 1 cup of milk are gradually stirred in. The mixture is then heated with continuous stirring until the soup just comes to a boil. It is then ready to serve.

SOURCE: *Food Dehydration, 2nd Edition* by Van Arsdel, Copley and Morgan published by Avi Publishing Co., Westport, Conn.

ONION SOUP BASE

Ingredients	Lb	Oz
Cheese salt	32	
Butter	20	
Precooked cornstarch	4	
Large size onion flakes (toasted)	8	
Cane sugar	8	
Monosodium glutamate	10	
Plant protein hydrolyzate	6	
Beef extract	10	
Caramel color (dehydrated)	1	
Toasted onion powder	1	
Oleoresin celery		2

Procedure

Heat butter, beef extract, and oleoresin celery to 180°F. Mix thoroughly. Put all the other ingredients in the formula in the mechanical mixer and mix thoroughly. Add the heated butter mixture and mix until a smooth texture is obtained.

Pack in any size drum, can, jar, or moisture-vaporproof envelope.

To Use

Recommended use is 4 oz to 1 gal. of water. Simmer 20 min in water before serving.

SOURCE: *A Guide to the Selection, Combination, and Cooking of Foods* by Rietz and Wanderstock published by Avi Publishing Co., Westport, Conn.

FROZEN FRENCH ONION SOUP

Ingredients	Oz
Fresh onions, sliced	32
Butter	4
Water	132
Espagnole extract	
White pepper	
Dry white wine	
Modified starch	16
Croutons of French bread	1¾
Parmesan or Swiss cheese	

Yield: 120 oz

Procedure

Sauté onions in butter in a deep sauce pan, stirring constantly, until onions are a golden brown.

Add water, Espagnole extract, salt, and pepper. Bring to a boil, reduce heat, and simmer for 5 min.

Slowly add white wine to starch; stir until smooth and add to soup. Heat to 180°F stirring constantly.

Package 12 oz in vacuum pouch. Evacuate bag, then heat-seal.

To Serve

Heat pouch 6 min in boiling water to cover. Pour into hot soup tureen. Float croutons on top of soup and sprinkle 1 tsp of parmesan or Swiss cheese on croutons. Place soup under salamander, flame for 15 sec to melt cheese; do not allow cheese to burn.

SOURCE: *The Freezing Preservation of Foods, 4th Edition, Vol. 4* by Tressler, Van Arsdel and Copley published by Avi Publishing Co., Westport, Conn.

GREEN PEA SOUP MIX (PURÉE STYLE)

Ingredients	%
Green split peas, dehydrated	84.34
Salt	4.85
Smoked dehydrated yeast	2.46
Potato starch	2.23
Hydrogenated vegetable oil	2.10
Sucrose	1.60
Dehydrated onion powder	1.00
Monosodium glutamate	0.95
Carboxymethyl cellulose	0.25
Black pepper Cream O'Spice	0.22
	100.00

Procedure

Package 4 oz of mix in buried-foil pouch.

To Use

In the preparation it is necessary to stir the contents of one envelope into 1½ pt of cold water and mix until smooth. The soup is brought to a boil with frequent stirring, partially covered, and simmered for 3 min.

SOURCE: *Food Dehydration, 2nd Edition* by Van Arsdel, Copley and Morgan published by Avi Publishing Co., Westport, Conn.

PEA SOUP BASE

Ingredients	Lb	Oz
Salt	56	
Pea flour, yellow or green	600	
Wheat flour	80	
Cornstarch	16	
Monosodium glutamate	20	
Plant protein hydrolyzate	12	
Dry soluble pepper	5	
Onion powder	12	
Garlic powder		4
Ground nutmeg		4
Oleoresin celery		4
"Liquid smoke" (to flavor)		

Procedure

Place the salt and oleoresin celery in a mechanical mixer and let mixer run until salt is evenly coated with the resin, then add wheat flour and follow with flavorings, seasonings, and the remainder of the ingredients. If "true smoke flavor" is in liquid form, then add liquid to the salt before mixing.

Pack in any size of drum, can, jar, or moisture-vaporproof envelope.

To Use

Use 1 lb per gal. of water. Make a lumpless slurry of the mix with 1 qt of water and add to 3 qt of simmering water. Cook 15-20 min.

SOURCE: *A Guide to the Selection, Combination, and Cooking of Foods* by Rietz and Wanderstock published by Avi Publishing Co., Westport, Conn.

POTATO SOUP BASE

Ingredients	Lb	Oz
Salt	32	
Monosodium glutamate	12	
Plant protein hydrolyzate	3	
Granular potato flour	70	
Dry whole milk powder	30	
Onion powder	1	
Toasted onion powder	1	
Oleoresin celery } diluted in 2 oz		2
Oleoresin turmeric } propylene glycol		½
Dehydrated parsley flakes		4
Dry soluble pepper	1	
Vegetable shortening	50	

Procedure

Put salt in the mechanical mixer; add diluted oleoresin turmeric and oleoresin celery and mix until the salt turns yellow. Add vegetable shortening and the remainder of the ingredients and mix until even distribution is obtained.

Pack in any size moisture-vaporproof drums, cans, jars or envelopes.

To Use

Use 8 oz to 1 gal. of water. Cook 15 min in simmering water before serving.

SOURCE: Stephen Komarik, 4810 Ronda, Coral Gables, Florida.

CANNED CONDENSED TOMATO SOUP

Ingredients	Gal.	Lb	Oz
Tomato purée (sp gr 1.045) }	50		
and water }	45		
or			
Tomato purée (sp gr 1.022)	95		
Water	5		
Carrot emulsion	1		

	Lb	Oz
Sodium bicarbonate	1	
Wheat flour	18	
Cane sugar	15	
Vegetable oil	10	
Salt	8	
Nonfat dry milk	5	
Butter	5	
Onion powder	1	
Garlic powder		½
Dry soluble pepper		4

And the following essential oils and oleoresins mixed together in 1 lb of sugar:

	Cc
Oil of cloves	3.00
Oil of allspice	2.00
Oil of bay	0.25
Oleoresin capsicum	4.00
Oleoresin celery	6.00

Procedure

Put tomato purée (sp gr 1.022 or 1.045) and water into a steam-jacketed kettle, add carrot emulsion, sugar, salt, butter, and vegetable oil; then add sodium bicarbonate diluted with water to reduce acidity of purée. Bring temperature up to 200°F.

Make a slurry of flour, nonfat dry milk, onion and garlic powders, and flavorings in 5 gal. of water in a bakery mixer. Add slurry to the heated purée with steady stirring and cook an additional 10 min.

Pack product at 180°F or higher.

Suggested Process: 211 × 4 size cans (10½ oz net weight) 30 min at 250°F.

Check processing time and temperature with can supplier or the National Canners Association.

SOURCE: Stephan L. Komarik, 4810 Ronda, Coral Gables, Florida.

CANNED CONDENSED CREAM OF TOMATO SOUP

Follow the method as given in formula given above for Condensed Tomato Soup except that, instead of vegetable oil use creamery butter.

The procedure and process are identical.

Check processing time and temperature with can supplier or with the National Canners Association.

SOURCE: Stephan L. Komarik, 4810 Ronda, Coral Gables, Florida.

CANNED CONDENSED TOMATO RICE SOUP

Ingredients	Gal.	Lb	Oz
Tomato purée (sp gr 1.045)	45		
Water	45		
Chopped whole tomatoes	5		
Carrot emulsion	1		
Sodium bicarbonate		1	
Wheat flour		18	
Cane sugar		15	
Vegetable oil		10	
Salt		8	
Nonfat dry milk		5	
Butter		5	
Chopped parsley		2	
Onion powder		1	
Garlic powder			½
Dry soluble pepper			4

And the following essential oils and resins mixed together in 1 lb of sugar:

	Cc
Oil of cloves	3.00
Oil of allspice	2.00
Oil of bay	0.25
Oleoresin capsicum	4.00
Oleoresin celery	6.00

Reduce acidity of purée with one pound of sodium bicarbonate dissolved in water.

Procedure

Put tomato purée, water, chopped whole tomatoes, carrot emulsion, sugar, salt, butter, vegetable oil, and chopped parsley in a steam-jacketed kettle. Add sodium bicarbonate dissolved in water to reduce acidity of purée; then bring temperature to 200°F. Make a slurry of flour, nonfat dry milk, flavorings, and seasonings in 5 gal. of water in a bakery mixer. Add the slurry to the heated purée with steady stirring and cook an additional 10 min.

Preparation of Rice

Use Patna or Malechized rice only. Cook rice in fine mesh wire basket in boiling water for 30 min.

Filling and Processing

Fill into 211 × 4 size cans in the following proportions: 2 oz blanched rice and 8½ oz hot tomato soup. Filling temperature should be 180°F or higher.

Suggested process: 211 × 4 size cans (10½ oz net weight) 30 min at 250°F.

Check processing time and temperature with can supplier or with the National Canners Association.

SOURCE: Stephan L. Komarik, 4810 Ronda, Coral Gables, Florida.

TOMATO SOUP BASE
Dry Soluble Tomato Soup Seasonings

Ingredients	Cc	Oz
Oil of clove	6	
Oil of allspice	4	
Oil of bay	0.25	
Oleoresin capsicum	8	
Oleoresin celery	12	
Propylene glycol		2

Procedure

Dissolve resins in propylene glycol, add oils, then make a thorough mixture with 2 lb of the corn sugar and 13 oz of the citric acid called for in the ingredients given below.

Ingredients	Lb	Oz
Dehydrated tomato, pulverized	50	
Precooked wheat flour	36	
Corn sugar	30	
Salt	20	
Nonfat dry milk	10	
Onion powder	2	
Dry soluble tomato soup seasonings	2	
Garlic powder		1
Citric acid		13

Procedure

Put salt in the mechanical mixer, add dry soluble seasonings with the citric acid, make a mixture. Add remainder of the ingredients and let machine run until all ingredients are properly distributed and homogeneous.

Pack in any size drum, tin, or moisture-vapor-proof envelope.

To Use

Use 12 oz of soup base per 1 gal. of water.

Make a slurry of soup base and 1 qt of water (free of lumps) then add to the remaining 3 qt of hot water. Stir; then cook 15 min before serving.

SOURCE: *A Guide to the Selection, Combination, and Cooking of Foods* by Rietz and Wanderstock published by Avi Publishing Co., Westport, Conn.

CANNED TOMATO SOUP
(Ready-to-Eat)

Ingredients	%
A	
Tomato pulp (12 gal.)	76.4
Butter	0.2
B	
Fresh onions, chopped	1.1
C	
Salt	0.9
Sugar	1.8
Beef extract	1.1
D	
Stabilized amioca starch (CLEARJEL)	0.2
Flour	0.2
Monosodium glutamate (to suit)	
Ground pepper (to suit)	
Ground cinnamon (to suit)	
Ground mace (to suit)	
Water	18.1
	100.0

Procedure

Place A ingredients in a cooking kettle and bring to a boil. Add B ingredient and simmer for 10 min, adding water to make up for evaporation loss. Add C ingredients half way through the cooking period; and 5 min before the cooking time is up add D ingredients which have been slurried in the water. Boil the batch with constant agitation for 4 min. Pass product through a finishing machine and fill into cans while hot.

SOURCE: National Starch & Chemical Corp., Plainfield, N.J.

CONDENSED OLD-FASHIONED VEGETABLE SOUP

Prepare Vegetable-Macaroni Mixture

Ingredients	%
Carrot strips (½ × ¼ × ¼ in.), blanched	27
Potato strips (½ × ¼ × ¼ in.), blanched	15
Small dried lima beans (soaked overnight)	13
Canned or frozen peas	15
Green beans, sliced ¼ in.	6
Celery, sliced ½ in.	8
Cabbage, chopped	4
Rutabagas, diced ¼-oz pieces	2
Macaroni O's, dry, ⅛-in. diam	10

Prepare Soup Base

Ingredients	Gal.	Lb	Oz
Beef stock (clarified)	100		
Salt		16	
Carrot emulsion		8	
Potato starch		15	
Monosodium glutamate		2	8
Hydrolyzed plant protein		1	4
Cane sugar		1	
Vegetable oil		2	
Rendered beef fat		2	
Cooked beef, finely ground		2	
Toasted onion chips			12
Garlic powder			½
Ground turmeric			1
Dry soluble celery			1
Dry soluble pepper			3
Caramel color			4

Heat stock to 200°F. Make a mixture of salt and flavoring materials and add to stock along with fat, oil, beef and carrot emulsion. Make a slurry of the potato starch and 10 gal. of chilled stock or water and, with steady stirring, add to the hot stock. Cook an additional 10 min.

Fill

Fill cans half full with the vegetable-macaroni mixture. Then fill cans with hot soup base at a temperature not lower than 180°F.

Some manufacturers prefer to add the vegetable-macaroni mixture directly to the soup base before filling cans. In this case, soup has to be thick enough to keep the vegetables in proper suspension and soup should be agitated during the filling procedure.

Suggested Process

211 × 400 cans (10½ oz net) 45 min at 240°F

Check process time and temperature with can supplier or the National Canners Association.

SOURCE: *Food Products Formulary, Vol. 1* by Komarik, Tressler and Long published by Avi Publishing Co., Westport, Conn.

FROZEN VICHYSOISSE

Ingredients	Lb	Oz
Potatoes, sliced	100	0
Onions, sliced	15	0
Leeks, sliced	10	0
Water	104	0
Chicken bouillon cubes, granulated	2	8
White pepper		5
Celery salt		1.75
Cream, light	40	0
	271	14.75

Procedure

Slowly cook in steam-jacketed kettle until vegetables are done, then run batch through pulper or paddle-type finisher. Next, mix 5 gal. of light cream into the pulp. Fill into containers and freeze.

To Use

May be used without dilution. Thaw and serve chilled.

SOURCE: *The Freezing Preservation of Foods, 4th Edition, Vol. 4* by Tressler, Van Arsdel and Copley published by Avi Publishing Co., Westport, Conn.

SAUCES

ALMOND MUSHROOM SAUCE

Ingredients	
Cream of mushroom soup	1 No. 5 tall can
Cream of celery soup	1 No. 1 can
Mushrooms, pieces and stems undrained	1 No. 2½ can
Slivered almonds, blanched	2 cups
Creamery butter	¼ lb
Worcestershire sauce	3 tbsp
Angostura bitters	1 tsp
Kitchen Bouquet (caramel color)	1 tbsp

Procedure

Combine soups and mushrooms in sauce pot. Heat to boiling, stirring frequently. Melt butter in skillet, add almonds and sauté until golden brown. (Avoid overbrowning.) Add immediately to heated soup. Add Worcestershire sauce, bitters, and Kitchen Bouquet. Serve over meat with garnish of toasted slivered or sliced almonds.

SOURCE: California Almond Growers Exchange, Sacramento, Calif.

BARBECUE SAUCE (WITH TRAGACANTH)

Ingredients	%
Tomato paste (28–30% solids)	5.0
Tomato catsup (30–33% solids)	6.0
Prepared mustard	3.0
Vinegar (10% white)	8.0
Water	15.0
Sugar (granulated)	40.0
Corn syrup	10.0
Garlic powder	0.4
Onion powder	1.5
Celery (soluble)	0.5
Black pepper (ground)	0.3
Cayenne pepper (ground)	0.3
BBQ seasoning	3.0
Smoke flavoring	0.2
TIC gum tragacanth pretested "C" USP powder	1.0
Salt (fine flake)	5.8

Procedure

Mix dry ingredients with water. Add tomato products, mustard, and vinegar. Pump through colloid mill.

SOURCE: Tragacanth Importing Corp., 141 E. 44th St., New York, N.Y.

BÉARNAISE SAUCE

Ingredients	%
Water	53.11
Microcrystalline cellulose (Avicel RC-591)	1.50
Vegetable oil	39.61
Mustard powder	1.43
Egg yolk solids	0.18
Vinegar (tarragon)	3.57
Salt	0.45
Xanthan gum (Keltrol)[1]	0.15

Procedure

Disperse Avicel RC-591 in vigorously agitated water and mix for 5 min until smooth and thick. Slowly add the oil in a thin stream to the vortex and continue mixing for an additional 5 min. Combine mustard powder and egg yolk and add to the water-oil mixture. Combine vinegar and salt and add to the emulsion and continue mixing for 10 min. Homogenize at 100–500 psi or equivalent.

[1] Available from Kelco Co., San Diego, Calif.

SOURCE: Avicel Div., American Viscose Co., FMC Corp., Marcus Hook, Penn.

FROZEN BÉARNAISE SAUCE
(Batch Process)

Ingredients	%
Butter	30.0
Egg yolk solids	3.0
Vinegar (50-grain)	3.0
Starch (Freezist M)	5.0
Skim milk	57.4
Dehydrated onion (Asmus)	1.0
Black pepper (Asmus)	0.1
Salt	0.5
Seasoning to suit	

Procedure

Slurry ingredients, except melted fat, in skim milk. Heat to 120°F. Melt butter and add to skim milk ingredients. Heat to 190°F and hold for 5 min. Cool and package in suitable containers for freezing.

SOURCE: A. E. Staley Mfg. Company, Decatur, Illinois.

FROZEN BORDELAISE SAUCE
(Batch Process)

Ingredients	%
Whole milk	85.05
Starch (Freezist M)	5.00
Tomato paste	5.00
Seasoning powder (Vico BF-4)	1.70
Sugar	1.00
Salt	2.00
Black pepper (Asmus)	0.15
Citric acid	0.10
Seasoning to suit	

Procedure

Slurry all ingredients in milk. Heat to 190°F and hold for 5 min. Cool and package in suitable containers for freezing.

SOURCE: A. E. Staley Mfg. Company, Decatur, Ill.

BUTTER SAUCE FOR FROZEN VEGETABLES

This sauce is suitable for use with frozen boil-in-the-bag vegetables in butter sauce. These include peas, lima beans, corn, green beans, broccoli spears, mixed vegetables, spinach, and onions.

Ingredients	Lb
Butter	2.5
Vegetable shortening	0.26
Seasoning	0.30

	Lb
Derivatized cross-bonded waxy corn starch	0.50
Water	14.00

Yield: 2 gal.

Procedure

Heat 1½ gal. water to 200°F. Add shortening and butter; blend well and maintain at 200°F.

Prepare starch slurry with 1 qt water; add to water-butter-shortening blend; mix thoroughly maintaining at 200°F, allowing starch to develop.

Add seasoning and fill.

SOURCE: CPC International, Industrial Division, Englewood Cliffs, N.J.

CATSUP SPICE (OIL)

Mix the following oils:

Ingredients	Gm
Cloves	571.65
Cassia	99.0
Nutmeg	79.20
Pimento berries	99.0
Mace	79.20
Mustard	4.95
Celery seed	67.0
Total	1000.00

SOURCE: *Food Flavorings, Composition, Manufacture, and Use* by Merory published by Avi Publishing Co., Westport, Conn.

CHEESE SAUCE MIX

This formulation produces a dry sauce mix with outstanding heat and freeze-thaw stability. The finished product has excellent flavor release and mouthfeel; and the viscosity remains constant over wide temperature ranges.

Ingredients	%
Xanthan Gum (Keltrol F)	2.58
Onion salt	0.18
Garlic salt	0.18
Salt	1.76
Adipic acid	1.79
Rokatang (Kraftco)	6.41
Beatreme 743 (Beatrice Foods)	15.22
Milk solids (nonfat)	32.20
Cheeztang (Kraftco)	39.68
	100.00

Procedure

Mix ingredients until a uniform mixture is obtained.

To Use

Disperse 2 oz of dry mix in 1 cup of cold milk. Heat to boil, while stirring slowly.

SOURCE: Kelco Co., 20 N. Wacker Drive, Chicago, Illinois.

NEWBURG TYPE CHEESE SAUCE

An imitation cheese sauce utilizing starch phosphate is made up as follows:

Ingredients	%
Starch phosphate	1.00
Paprika	0.73
Salt	0.57
Lecithin	0.40
Fresh whole milk	52.50
Fresh cream (12%)	32.20
Butter	8.30
Egg yolks	4.30

Procedure

Add the first 3 ingredients to the cold milk, with the lecithin melted with the butter. The milk is then stirred into the melted butter; then the mix is removed from the heat and cream and egg yolk stirred in. Heat again just to boiling.

SOURCE: American Maize-Products Company, 250 Park Ave., New York, N.Y.

CHILI SAUCE NO. 1

Chili sauce was originally a spiced sauce made with tomatoes and chili peppers. As prepared commercially now, chili sauce is similar to catsup except that the seeds are not removed from the tomatoes. Tomatoes are washed, blanched, and peeled but they are not pulped or passed through a finisher. As is the case with catsup, the final product should contain enough salt, sugar, and acid so that it is not subject to microbial spoilage for a reasonable length of time after the container is opened. A common formula may start with 5280 lb prepared tomato and 100 lb chopped onion. The blend of tomato, onion, and spice is concentrated by boiling to about ½ the volume. A spice emulsion consisting of a blend of 300 oz cinnamon, 36 oz celery seed, 20 oz cayenne pepper, 14 oz mace, and 8 oz garlic may be used. These spices should be suspended in a bag in the boiling tomato mixture. After concentration, 16 lb of 10% vinegar, 80 lb of salt, and 360 lb sugar are added and concentration is continued until the sauce is thick, that is, reduced to about ½ the volume. While still hot the sauce is filled into containers and sealed. A short, not over

5-min hot water cook should be used before cooling.

SOURCE: D. K. Tressler and Associates, Westport, Conn.

CHILI SAUCE NO. 2

Chili sauce is made following the same general procedure used in making catsup except the tomatoes are peeled, cored, and chopped and not crushed or put through a finisher.

Ingredients	Lb	Oz
Whole peeled tomatoes	420	
Chopped onions	17	8
Whole allspice		4
Whole cloves, headless		5
Cinnamon, stick		1
Mustard		6
Garlic, ground		4
Distilled vinegar (10% acetic acid)	21	
Salt	7	
Sugar	30	

Procedure

The spices (except the mustard) are simmered for 2 hr in a covered vessel with a portion of the vinegar, and then strained out and discarded. The peeled tomatoes should be chopped and then concentrated with about ⅓ of the sugar in a vacuum pan to about ½ their original volume. Add the spiced vinegar, powdered mustard, salt, and the remainder of the sugar to the concentrated chopped tomatoes and continue concentration in the vacuum pan until the volume is only ½ that of the original chopped tomatoes. Fill the hot (185°F) chili sauce into widemouthed bottles, and close with special caps which provide a hermetic seal. If the filling temperature is 185°F or above and the jars are clean and hot, additional pasteurization is not required.

SOURCE: D. K. Tressler and Associates, Westport, Conn.

COCKTAIL SAUCE

A typical cocktail sauce for use on seafoods requires no preparation other than thorough mixing.

Ingredients	%
Catsup	68.0
Vinegar or lemon juice	16.0
Celery, finely chopped	10.0
Horseradish, grated	4.5
Tabasco sauce	0.5
Salt	1.0
	100.0

SOURCE: D. K. Tressler and Associates, Westport, Conn.

FROZEN COCKTAIL SAUCE

This cocktail sauce is suited for use on shrimp, clams, oysters, mixed shellfish cocktails, etc.

Ingredients	%
Catsup	68.0
Vinegar or lemon juice	16.0
Celery, finely chopped	10.0
Horseradish, grated	4.5
Tabasco sauce	0.5
Salt	1.0
	100.0

Procedure

No preparation other than thorough mixing is required. This sauce may be frozen in small consumer-size packages, or it may be placed on cooked shrimp as a component of a cocktail.

SOURCE: *The Freezing Preservation of Foods, 3rd Edition* by Tressler and Evers published by Avi Publishing Co., Westport, Conn.

CANNED CREAM SAUCE

Ingredients	Lb
Whole milk powder, 28% butterfat	24.00
Versa-stabe modified food starch No. 4832	25.50
Vegetable shortening	13.25
Cream sauce seasoning*	19.18
Water	7.25

Procedure

Premix whole milk powder in 6.25 gal. of cold water. Pass through a homogenizer or pulper and finisher, if possible, for a smooth consistency. For ease of handling and better dispersion combine starch and seasoning and disperse in 9.37 gal. of cold water and blend. Keep agitated until ready to use. Admit or meter in 75 gal. of water into a stainless steel steam-jacketed kettle. Add shortening. Heat to approximately 120°F and disperse with agitation. Add milk slurry and bring batch to 180°F and add starch-seasoning slurry with continuous stirring. Allow temperature to reach 190°-195°F (stirring constantly) over a period of 3 or a maximum of 4 min, allowing starch to develop fully. Do not overcook. If air can be removed from batch under vacuum, this procedure is definitely recommended. Fill cans, seam, and sterilize. Retort at 240°F, for 60 min using No. 1 cans with plain bodies and C-enamel ends and lids.

Check processing time and temperature with can supplier or the National Canners Association.

*Cream sauce seasoning contains 0.4% titanium dioxide based on the total weight of the batch.

SOURCE: CPC International, Industrial Division, Englewood Cliffs, N.J.

FROZEN CONDENSED ALL-PURPOSE CREAM SAUCE

Ingredients	Gal.	Lb	Oz
Whole milk	60		
Water	30		
Wheat flour		18	
Cracker flour		18	
Butter		26	
Salt		16	
Monosodium glutamate		4	
Plant protein hydrolyzate		2	
Ground turmeric			1
Onion powder			4
Dry soluble pepper			2
Garlic powder			1/8
Ground celery seeds			1/2
Water to make 70 gal.			

Procedure

Measure out 70 gal. of water in the steam-jacketed kettle and make a mark on a measuring stick at water level. Drain water. Put 50 gal. of milk in the steam-jacketed kettle. Bring up temperature to 200°F add butter and cook milk for 15 min. Add salt which has been previously mixed with seasoning and flavoring. Make slurry in a bakery mixer with 10 gal. of milk, flour, and cracker flour until free of lumps. Add to the heated milk with continuous stirring. Bring up volume with water to 70 gal. and with steady agitation of the sauce cook additional 15 min.

Pack in 5-lb disposable oblong carton molds (5 lb net), or in tin cans and freeze at 0°F or below.

To Use

Since this product is concentrated use 2 pt of water or milk for each 5-lb package. Product should be defrosted before heating. The best method of defrosting is in a refrigerator overnight. Defrosted cream sauce should be vigorously stirred until smooth in texture; then add water or milk and mix evenly in the sauce. Stir occasionally during heating in a double boiler. It is an excellent product for institutional use.

SOURCE: Stephan L. Komarik, 4810 Ronda, Coral Gables, Florida.

FROZEN ALL-PURPOSE INSTITUTIONAL CREAM SAUCE

An institutional all-purpose cream sauce should be packaged in disposable cellophane-lined cartons or in No. 10 cans. It is very important that the frozen sauce should be defrosted before heating. If the sauce is packed in tin containers defrosting may be accelerated in warm water, if sauce is packed in cartons it should be defrosted overnight under refrigeration. After sauce is defrosted, it should be stirred until it is smooth in texture. Heating should be accomplished in a double boiler with occasional stirring.

Utilization of the Heated Sauce

Cheese sauce may be made by addition of processed cheese; horseradish sauce may be made by addition of horseradish; curry sauce may be prepared by addition of curry powder; anchovy butter sauce may be made by addition of chopped anchovy and butter; Béarnaise sauce may be prepared by addition of egg yolks, wine, and fresh taragon.

Cream soups may be made by addition of diced chicken meat, peas, diced pimientos, and milk to proper consistency of cream soup. Maharaja soup may be prepared by addition of precooked celery and some of the broth in which the celery was cooked. Cream of vegetable soup may be prepared by addition of cooked diced vegetables from beef or chicken broth and some soup stock. Cream of mushroom soup may be prepared by the addition of canned sliced or chopped mushrooms and the broth.

Creamed Vegetables.—Creamed peas may be prepared by addition of defrosted and cooked green peas or drained canned peas. Creamed carrots and peas can be prepared by addition of defrosted and cooked green peas or drained canned peas. Creamed spinach may be made by addition of precooked and chopped spinach. Caramel asparagus requires the addition of egg yolk, wine, and fresh tarragon, and precooked, or canned asparagus. Creamed cauliflower may be prepared by the addition of processed cheese and precooked cauliflower.

SOURCE: *A Guide to the Selection, Combination, and Cooking of Foods* by Rietz and Wanderstock published by Avi Publishing Co., Westport, Conn.

CREOLE SAUCE NO. 1

Ingredients	%
Canned or cooked tomatoes	78.0
Butter	5.0
Green peppers, minced	2.5

	%
Mushrooms, finely sliced	6.0
Tomato paste	3.0
Olives, finely sliced	1.0
Garlic, minced	0.5
Salt	0.8
Monosodium glutamate	0.3
Vermouth	2.8
Pepper	0.1
	100.0

Procedure

The garlic and peppers are cooked in the butter until tender. The remaining ingredients, with the exception of the vermouth, are added and the sauce simmered for 10 min. The vermouth is added and the sauce immediately cooled, packaged, and frozen.

SOURCE: *The Freezing Preservation of Foods, 3rd Edition* by Tressler and Evers published by Avi Publishing Co., Westport, Conn.

CREOLE SAUCE NO. 2

Ingredients	%
Vegetable oil	2.94
Chopped onions	11.76
Chopped green peppers	5.88
Tomato purée	37.64
Tomato paste	18.82
Waxy rice flour	1.35
Salt	0.85
Caramel syrup	2.50
Oil of red pepper, 5% solution	0.25
Oil of bay, 2% solution	0.05
Oil of garlic, 2% solution	0.05
Oil of cloves, 5% solution	0.10
Water	17.81
	100.00

Procedure

The oil is heated for two minutes in a steam-jacketed kettle using 20 lb per sq in. pressure in the jacket. The onions are added and cooked 8 min. (This should turn them slightly yellow, but *not* brown.) The chopped green peppers are added and the cooking continued for about 5 min. The tomato purée, tomato paste, and $^3/_4$ of the water are added and the sauce heated with agitation until it simmers; then the caramel syrup, salt, and spice oil solutions are added and the sauce brought to a rolling boil. The waxy rice flour is suspended in cold water and slowly added to the boiling mixture as it is being rapidly agitated. Boiling is continued for 5 min, then the sauce is rapidly cooled by running cold water in the jacket of the kettle. When cool, the sauce is packaged and frozen.

The caramel syrup is prepared by caramelizing sugar to a deep caramel color. This product is dissolved in an equal weight of water, and the resultant solution is concentrated by boiling until half of the water added has been evaporated.

SOURCE: *The Freezing Preservation of Foods, 3rd Edition* by Tressler and Evers published by Avi Publishing Co., Westport, Conn.

HAMBURGER SAUCE

Ingredients	%
Kelset	1.300
Water	36.337
Tomato paste (26% solids)	33.600
Sugar	14.800
Vinegar (100-grain)	9.500
Potassium chloride	1.600
Starch (Textaid*)	1.120
Salt	0.800
Mustard flour	0.600
Spice mix	0.170
Soluble paprika	0.160
Tomato flavor	0.010
FD&C red No. 2**	0.003
	100.000

Procedure

Premix Kelset with 3-5 times its weight of sugar until uniform, and hold. Make slurry using cold (tap) water with the starch and mustard flour; use about 25% of available water in formula. Combine water slurry, sugar, tomato paste, potassium chloride, vinegar, salt, red coloring, soluble paprika, and heat to 190°-200°F while mixing and hold 5-8 min at temperature. While mixing, add Kelset-sugar premix and tomato flavor and continue mixing 1-2 min. Package immediately at 190°F and cool to 75°-95°F.

---

*Textaid is a texturizing starch, made by National Starch Company, New York, N.Y.

**This coloring has been de-listed. It is no longer on the FDA-approved list of foods colors and cannot be used. Consult your food color supplier for recommended color substitutions.

SOURCE: Kelco Co., 20 N. Wacker Drive, Chicago, Illinois.

CREAMY TYPE HAMBURGER SAUCE

Ingredients	%
Xanthan gum (Keltrol)	0.44
Water	49.27

	%
Vegetable oil	21.90
Sugar	7.90
White vinegar (100-grain)	8.10
Sweet pickle relish (drained)*	7.00
Salt	2.30
Mustard powder	1.10
Stange spice mix (No. 2618)	1.87
Sodium benzoate	0.10
Oleoresin paprika (40,000 units)	0.02
	100.00

Procedure

Premix Keltrol with ½ the total weight of sugar until uniform and dissolve in water with strong agitation (7-10 min). Add vegetable oil, slowly, while mixing and mix until smooth. Add remainder of sugar, mustard flour, spice mix, sodium benzoate and soluble paprika while mixing. Add sweet relish, vinegar, salt and mix until uniform.

---

*If the pickle relish is stabilized with Keltrol, eliminate the draining step. In this case, it may be necessary to decrease the vinegar in the formula to obtain desired flavor.

SOURCE: Kelco Co., 20 N. Wacker Drive, Chicago, Illinois.

SAUCY HORSERADISH SAUCE

An excellent sauce to serve with tongue, boiled beef, roast beef, or corned beef.

Ingredients	
Canned applesauce	1 No. 10 can
Horseradish, prepared	6 oz.
Celery, finely diced	1½ lb
Onion, minced	4 oz.

Yield: scant 4 qt; 48 ½-cup portions

Procedure

Combine all ingredients; mix well. Chill.

SOURCE: Processed Apple Institute, 666 Fifth Ave., New York, N.Y.

HOT PEPPER SAUCE

Ingredients	Lb	Cups	Tsp
Sweet red chili peppers, dried	2		
Boiling water	2		
Tomatoes, peeled, chopped	4		
Onions, minced		2	
Oregano			1
Salt			2
Sugar			1

Yield: approx 8 cups

Procedure

Boil peppers in hot water until tender; remove from heat and put through a colander. Chop tomatoes and put in saucepan; add onion, oregano, salt, and sugar and boil until tender; put through a colander. Combine pepper and tomato mixture and again bring to a boil. Serve as an accompaniment to Mexican foods.

SOURCE: J. G. Woodroof, Griffin, Georgia.

HOT SAUCE

Ingredients	Gal.	Lb	Oz
Tomato pulp or purée	350		
Green chili peppers, sliced		50	
Onions, sliced		37	8
Garlic, sliced		1	4
Cayenne pepper, ground		1	4
Salt		35	

Procedure

Concentrate first four ingredients by boiling in an open steam-jacketed kettle to about 215 gal.; then add cayenne pepper and salt. Boil long enough to dissolve the salt and stir to mix the cayenne; then put through a finisher to eliminate all fibrous material. Fill into small cans while boiling hot; if cans are sealed immediately no further processing is necessary.

SOURCE: D. K. Tressler and Associates, Westport, Conn.

MARINARA SPAGHETTI SAUCE BASE

Ingredients	%
Garlic powder	24.55
Salt	16.45
Maggi's hydrolyzed plant protein (type 4BE-2 powder)	12.40
Sugar	11.80
Oregano	0.82
Basil	0.41
Thyme	0.41
Yellow No. 5 (malto dextrin 2%)	9.85
Monosodium glutamate	4.93
Red pepper	0.61
Marjoram	0.21
Torulla yeast	4.10
Rosemary	0.24
Spray-dried cheese	0.82
Dextrose	12.40

Procedure

Mix all ingredients together until homogeneous.

To Use

To an 8 oz-can plum tomatoes and an 8 oz-can tomato sauce add 14 gm of spaghetti sauce base and 2-3 tbsp of olive oil. Bring to a boil while stirring. Reduce heat; cover and cook gently for another 5-10 min.

SOURCE: Food Ingredients Division, Nestlé Company, 100 Bloomingdale Road, White Plains, N.Y.

MUSTARD SAUCE

Ingredients	Lb	Oz
Distilled malt vinegar	65	
Water	28	
Mustard flour	8	
Sugar	4	8
Tapioca starch	4	
Salt	2	
White pepper, ground		8
Turmeric, ground		4

Procedure

Disperse tapioca starch in half of the vinegar using a high speed agitator. Mix the other ingredients including the rest of the vinegar in stainless steel steam-jacketed kettle and then heat to boiling. Allow sauce to simmer for 15 min. Then stir in mixture of starch-vinegar and fill into jars that have been thoroughly cleaned.

SOURCE: D. K. Tressler and Associates, Westport, Conn.

MUSTARD SAUCE

Ingredients	Gal.	Lb	Oz
Water	100		
Mustard flour		120	
Modified thick boiling waxy cornstarch		12	
White pepper			2
Ground mace		1	8
Ground onions		3	
Ground garlic			4
Sugar		100	
Salt		40	
High DE corn syrup		50	
Distilled vinegar (100-grain)	40		
Certified yellow color (to suit)			

Yield: 1450 lb

Procedure

In 10 gal. pails, add 6 gal. of water, 20 lb of mustard flour and in one pail add the white pepper and ground mace. Stir the dry flours into a soft paste using a wooden paddle. Make up a slurry using 5 gal. of water and the 12 lb of waxy cornstarch.

Add the remaining 59 gal. of water to a steam-jacketed kettle and add the sugar and corn syrup. Bring to 190°F and while agitating, add the 5 gal. of starch slurry and keep at 190°F until the starch clears. Add the ground onions, garlic, salt, and six buckets of mustard-mace-pepper paste. Bring to a boil and add the vinegar. Simmer gently for 15 min. Color to suit and strain.

Pack at 185°F for pasteurization.

SOURCE: CPC International, Industrial Division, Englewood, N.J.

PIZZA SAUCE

Ingredients	%
Sodium alginate (Kelset)	0.25
Tomato paste (26% solids)	60.00
Water	36.96
Olive oil	1.20
Salt	1.20
Cheddar cheese (dry)	0.20
Garlic powder	0.08
Ground basil	0.07
Ground black pepper	0.02
Ground oregano	0.02
	100.00

Procedure

Retain approximately 1 gal. vegetable oil or olive oil for every 2¾ lb Kelset used. (This is an approximate ratio of 3 parts oil to 1 part Kelset by weight.) Mix Kelset with oil until uniform and hold for later addition. Combine all ingredients, except Kelset-oil mixture, and bring to 210°-212°F while mixing slowly. Simmer mixture 10-15 min. Add Kelset-oil mixture while agitating and continue mixing for 8-10 min. The sauce is then ready for filling into containers.

SOURCE: Kelco Co., 20 N. Wacker Drive, Chicago, Illinois.

SPAGHETTI SAUCE

Ingredients	%
Special coarse cornstarch (Textaid)	2.370
Water	60.005
Tomato paste	31.600
Olive oil	3.700
Salt	1.060
Cheddar cheese, sharp	0.770
Onion powder	0.190
White pepper	0.126

	%
Sweet basil	0.095
Oregano	0.084

Procedure

Mix all ingredients to uniform consistency or dry blend Textaid with all other dry ingredients and add to batch before heating. Cook to 190°F. For a fresh or frozen sauce, hold at 190°F for 5 min. For a canned product, fill at desired temperature.

SOURCE: National Starch & Chemical Corp., Plainfield, N.J.

SPAGHETTI SAUCE (PLAIN)

Ingredients	%
Sodium alginate (Kelset)	0.26
Tomato paste (26% solids)	72.50
Water	21.82
Vegetable oil	3.25
Salt	0.88
Olive oil	0.55
Sugar	0.48
Romano cheese	0.10
Garlic powder	0.07
Ground basil	0.06
Ground black pepper	0.02
Ground oregano	0.01
	100.00

Procedure

Retain approximately 1 gal. vegetable oil or olive oil for every 2¾ lb Kelset used. (This is an approximate ratio of 3 parts oil to 1 part Kelset by weight.) Mix Kelset with oil until uniform and hold for later addition. Combine all ingredients, except Kelset-oil mixture and bring to 210°-212°F while mixing slowly. Simmer mixture 10-15 min. Add Kelset-oil mixture, while agitating and continue mixing for 8-10 min. The sauce is then ready for filling into containers.

SOURCE: Kelco Co., 20 N. Wacker Drive, Chicago, Illinois.

SPAGHETTI SAUCE (WITH MEAT)

Ingredients	%
Sodium alginate (Kelset)	0.22
Tomato paste (26% solids)	49.50
Water	32.47
Ground beef (fresh)	15.00
Olive oil	0.80
Salt	1.20
Sugar	0.48
Romano cheese	0.15
Garlic powder	0.08
Ground basil	0.07
Ground black pepper	0.02
Ground oregano	0.01
	100.00

Procedure

Follow same basic procedure as outlined above for Spaghetti Sauce (Plain) except, sauté meat and mushrooms in vegetable oil first, then combine with all other ingredients except Kelset-oil mixture, which will be added during last 8-10 min of cooking.

SOURCE: Kelco Co., 20 N. Wacker Drive, Chicago, Illinois.

SPAGHETTI SAUCE (MEATLESS)

Ingredients	Gm
Maggi HPP Type 3H3 powder with partially hydrogenated vegetable oil added	10.00
Maggi HPP Type 3FS powder with partially hydrogenated vegetable oil added	10.00
Roger's Dehydrated Romano cheese No. 8236	50.00
Cornstarch	50.00
Onion, fresh flavor, granulated	10.00
Salt, granulated	60.00
Garlic, granulated	2.00
Celery, microground	1.00
Coriander	1.00
Crushed red pepper	1.00
Sugar, granulated	50.00
Oregano, leaf	2.00
Basil	1.00
	248.00

Procedure

Mix all ingredients together until homogeneous.

To Use

Combine 248 gm of this sauce mix with 3 lb tomato paste (30% solids), 6 oz olive or corn oil, and 1 gal. of water.

SOURCE: Food Ingredients Division, Nestlé Company, 100 Bloomingdale Road, White Plains, N.Y.

SPAGHETTI SAUCE (WITH MUSHROOMS)

Ingredients	%
Sodium alginate (Kelset)	0.22
Tomato paste (26% solids)	59.80

	%
Water	24.38
Mushrooms (freshed, chopped)	11.00
Vegetable oil	2.20
Salt	1.10
Olive oil	1.00
Cheddar cheese (dry)	0.15
Garlic powder	0.07
Ground basil	0.05
Ground black pepper	0.02
Ground oregano	0.01
	100.00

Procedure

Retain approximately 1 gal. of vegetable or olive oil for each 2¾ lb Kelset used. Sauté mushrooms in vegetable oil, then combine mushrooms with all of the other ingredients except Kelset-oil mixture and heat to 210°F (while mixing slowly for about 5 min). Add the Kelset-oil mixture and continue mixing for 8-10 min. While still hot, package without cooling.

SOURCE: Kelco Co., 20 N. Wacker Drive, Chicago, Illinois.

CANNED SPAGHETTI SAUCE WITH MUSHROOMS (Hot Pack)

Ingredients	Lb	Oz	Gal.
Whole tomatoes (canned)			40
Olive oil			2
Tomato paste (28% solids)	10		
Diced mushrooms (canned)	48		
Fresh diced onions (or 5 lb reconstituted dehydrated minced onions)	48		
Salt	6		
Cane sugar	2		
Hydrolyzed plant protein	1	8	
Autolyzed yeast protein	1	8	
Dehydrated diced green peppers		8	
Dehydrated diced celery		8	
Dehydrated parsley		4	
Monosodium glutamate		6	
Dry soluble spaghetti sauce seasoning mix (as given below)		4	

Dry Soluble Seasoning Mix

Ingredients	Lb	Cc
Oleoresin capsicum		4
Oleoresin ginger		1.4
Oleoresin mace		0.16
Oil of dill seed		0.2
Oil of cloves		3.6
Oil of cardamom		0.8
Oil of cassia		2.4
Oil of pimiento		26.4
Oil of bay		0.8
Salt to mix	2	

Use 4 gm per 1 gal. sauce

Procedure

If dehydrated minced onions are used, reconstitute them in the ratio of 1 part onions and 9 parts hot water. Use dehydrated green peppers, celery, and parsley. Put canned whole tomatoes and tomato paste in a steam-jacketed kettle. Add salt, sugar, hydrolyzed and autolyzed proteins, olive oil, fresh or reconstituted onions, and mushrooms. While agitating product with a "Lightning" mixer, add the remainder of the ingredients. Bring temperature to simmering (190°-200°F) and cook an additional 10 min. Can product while hot. Temperature of the product should not drop below 160°F while closing cans.

Suggested Process. 8-oz cans 1 hr at 240°F. Check processing time and temperature with can supplier or the National Canners Association.

SOURCE: Stephan L. Komarik, 4810 Ronda, Coral Gables, Florida.

SPAGHETTI SAUCE SEASONING

Ingredients	Lb	Oz
Oleoresin of celery		33.0
Oleoresin of cloves		14.0
Oil of bay leaves and		4.0
Salt	96	11.0
		100.0

Procedure

Mix thoroughly.

Recommended Use

One pound per 100 lb sauce.

SOURCE: *Food Flavorings, Composition, Manufacture, and Use, 2nd Edition* by Merory published by Avi Publishing Co., Westport, Conn.

SPANISH SAUCE

This sauce is suited for meat and fish entrées.

Ingredients	%
Onions, finely chopped	4.0
Celery, finely chopped	10.0
Green peppers, finely chopped	7.0

	%
Butter or margarine	6.0
Tomatoes, canned	69.0
Waxy rice flour	3.0
Salt	0.90
Pepper	0.08
Cayenne	0.02
	100.00

Procedure

The onions, celery, and green peppers are fried in the butter or margarine. Enough juice is drained from the tomatoes to make a smooth paste of the waxy rice flour. The remainder of the canned tomatoes and the seasonings are cooked with the fried onions, celery, and green peppers in a steam-jacketed kettle until the vegetables are tender. The flour mixture is then added and the sauce is cooked until it is slightly thick.

SOURCE: *The Freezing Preservation of Foods, 3rd Edition* by Tressler and Evers published by Avi publishing Co., Westport, Conn.

SWEET AND SOUR SAUCE (WITH TRAGACANTH)

Step 1

Ingredients	%
Water	24.0
Peaches (dried)	10.0
Corn syrup	20.0
Sugar syrup	20.0
Salt (fine flake)	1.4
White pepper (ground)	0.1

Mix in steam-jacketed kettle with agitation. Heat for 30 min.

Step 2

Mix together the following:

Ingredients	%
TIC gum tragacanth pretested 440 USP powder	0.2
Sugar (granulated)	0.8
Cider vinegar (5%)	12.3
Water (to which onion, celery, and garlic powders have been added)	11.2

Step 3

Incorporate mixture of Step 1 with Step 2 and continue heating until solids reach 52.0–53.0% soluble solids.

SOURCE: Tragacanth Importing Corp., 141 E. 44th St., New York, N.Y.

TOMATO SAUCE MIX FOR BEANS WITH TOMATO SAUCE

Ingredients	%
Powdered sugar	62.00
Tomato flakes	22.75
Salt	10.00
Milo starch	3.00
Onion powder	1.60
Garlic powder	0.25
Mustard, dry	0.16
Pepper, white, ground	0.12
Cloves, ground	0.12
	100.00

Procedure

The mix is prepared by blending the ingredients in a mechanically operated mixer (e.g., Hobart).

Sauce is made simply by stirring it into hot water and continuing agitation until it is smooth.

SOURCE: *Food Dehydration, 2nd Edition* by Van Arsdel, Copley and Morgan published by Avi Publishing Co., Westport, Conn.

FROZEN CONDENSED TOMATO SAUCE

Ingredients	Gal.	Lb	Oz
Tomato paste (28% solids)	15		
Water	35		
Wheat flour		9	
Cracker flour		9	
Cane sugar		15	
Butter		5	
Vegetable oil		10	
Nonfat dry milk		5	
Onion powder		1	
Salt		8	
Garlic powder			½
Dry soluble pepper			4

And the following essential oils and resins mixed together in one pound of sugar.

	Cc
Oil of cloves	3.00
Oil of allspice	2.00
Oil of bay	0.25
Oleoresin capsicum	4.00
Oleoresin celery	6.00

Note

Reduce acidity of tomato paste with 1 lb of sodium bicarbonate diluted with water.

Procedure

Put the tomato paste and 30 gal. of water in a steam-jacketed kettle. Add sodium bicarbonate and bring up temperature to 200°F. Stir while cooking. Add sugar, salt, butter, and vegetable oil. Make a slurry of flours, nonfat dry milk, onion and garlic powders, and flavorings in 5 gal. of water in a bakery mixer. Add this slurry to the batch and cook 10-15 min additional with steady stirring.

For institutional use pack 5 lb net in oblong disposable Cellophane-lined container. Prechill before freezing.

To Use

After the sauce is defrosted and since the product is condensed, add to each 5 lb of tomato sauce 7½ lb of water. Heat sauce, stirring steadily; then serve.

Recommended Uses.—Meat balls with tomato sauce; spaghetti meat sauce (by adding ground braised beef); tomato soup (by adding chopped parsley and chopped canned whole tomatoes); tomato soup with precooked rice.

SOURCE: *A Guide to the Selection, Combination, and Cooking of Foods* by Rietz and Wanderstock published by Avi Publishing Co., Westport, Conn.

FROZEN WHITE SAUCE

Ingredients	%
Skim milk	90.2
Hydrogenated vegetable shortening	4.6
Thickening agent (preferably waxy rice flour or a mixture of waxy rice and waxy maize flours)	4.6
Salt	0.6
	100.0

Procedure

In making white sauce, the shortening is melted in a jacketed kettle equipped with an agitator. The thickening agent is slowly stirred in and then warm (140°F) milk is added and the whole thoroughly mixed. The mixing is continued as the product is heated to the boiling point. Cooking is continued for approximately 1 min after the sauce begins to boil. The salt should be added while the sauce is boiling.

Cheese Sauce Variation

A cheese sauce for use on macaroni, spaghetti, broccoli, and cauliflower can be made by the addition of 2 lb of grated cheese to each 10 lb of the basic white sauce described above.

SOURCE: *The Freezing Preservation of Foods, 3rd Edition* by Tressler and Evers published by Avi Publishing Co., Westport, Conn.

WORCESTERSHIRE SAUCE

Ingredients	Lb	Oz	Gal.
Vinegar, malt			9
Sugar	12	8	
Walnut catsup	4	8	
Soy sauce			0.5
Lemon peel, finely ground			0.5
Salt	3	12	
Cayenne pepper	1	12	
Nutmeg, ground	1	8	
Cloves, ground	1	8	
Garlic, chopped		4	

Procedure

The ingredients are brought to a boil in a stainless steel steam-jacketed kettle, and boiled 10 min. The hot sauce is put through a finisher to remove fibrous matter, and then bottled. The product needs no processing.

SOURCE: D. K. Tressler and Associates, Westport, Conn.

SAUCED PRODUCTS

CANNED BEANS IN BARBECUE SAUCE

Ingredients	Gal.	Lb	Oz
Tomato paste (26-28% solids)	18		
Salt		34	
Molasses		10	
Monosodium glutamate		2	
Corn oil		33	
Vinegar, 100-grain		2	
Soy sauce		5	
Onion powder		12	
Wheat flour		30	
Cornstarch		10	
Cane sugar		15	

	Oz
Spanish paprika	14
Red pepper, ground	7
Cloves, ground	2
Cinnamon, ground	2
Mace, ground	1
Ginger, ground	2

Yield: 200 gal.

Procedure

Mix flour together with all the dry ingredients. Place approximately 50 gal. of cold water in the steam-jacketed kettle. Using a "Lightning" mixer gradually add the mixed dry ingredients. When the slurry is free of lumps bring temperature to 180°F, then add the remaining ingredients. Bring up volume to 200 gal. and raise temperature to 190°F; cook an additional 15 min.

Preparation of Beans.—Soak white navy beans overnight. The best method is to have an overflow on the container in which the beans are soaked to circulate the incoming water; this will prevent the beans from becoming sour during the soaking period. After beans are properly soaked, place them in perforated or wire baskets and blanch them in boiling water for 12-15 min.

Pack.—Fill 8 oz soaked and blanched beans and 8 oz sauce (hot) at 160°F or higher.

Suggested Process.—300 × 409 cans (16 oz net) 120 min at 240°F. Close cans under vacuum. Check processing time and temperature with can supplier or with the National Canners Association.

SOURCE: Stephan L. Komarik, 4810 Ronda, Coral Gables, Florida.

CANNED BAKED BEANS IN PLAIN SAUCE

Preparation of Beans

Soak white navy beans overnight (8 hr). The best method is to have an overflow on the container in which the beans are soaking so that water will circulate and beans will not sour during the soaking period. After beans are soaked, they should be placed in perforated baskets and immersed in boiling water for 12-15 min. The yield of the soaked, blanched beans is approximately 185-190% of the weight of the dried beans.

Beans should then be placed in thin layers ½-in. deep in large pans equipped with ¼-in. mesh screens ¼-in. above bottom of the pan for proper heat circulation. Large revolving bakery ovens can be used to process beans. Bake beans at 300°F for ¾ hr. During baking, beans will shrink 20-30%.

Preparation of Sauce

Ingredients	Gal.	Lb	Oz
Water	200		
Brown sugar (dark)		250	
Salt		35	
Cornstarch		20	
Onion powder		6	
Monosodium glutamate		2	
Mustard, ground		2	
Celery seed, ground			4

Put water in a steam-jacketed kettle. Add all other ingredients and bring to a boil. Maintain sauce at 180°F temperature during filling of cans.

Packing and Processing

Pack 6 oz of baked beans and 10 oz hot sauce in 300 × 409 cans (16 oz net).

Suggested Process.—Process 2 hr at 240°F. Check processing time and temperature with can supplier or with National Canners Association.

SOURCE: Stephan L. Komarik, 4810 Ronda, Coral Gables, Florida.

CANNED RANCH STYLE BEANS (Hot Pack)

Sauce Ingredients	Gal.	Lb
Cane sugar		13
Salt		32
Cornstarch		45
Chili peppers (34 mesh)		12
Paprika, domestic		13
Onion powder		9
Garlic powder		2
Cumin seed, ground		8
Oregano, ground		4
Tomato purée (sp gr 1.045)	35	
Rendered beef fat (oleo stock)		35
Water to make	200	

Procedure

To Prepare Beans.—Soak Mexican pinto beans overnight and precook 12 min in boiling water. Drain.

To Make Sauce.—Mix sugar, salt, starch, and spices together. Put tomato purée in a steam-jacketed kettle equipped with a mixer. Add 50 gal. water and apply steam. While the mixer is in operation, slowly add dry ingredient mixture. Then add preheated rendered beef fat. Bring volume up to 200 gal. and temperature up to 200°F and cook 15 min.

Packing and Processing.—Hold beans and sauce at 160°F or above. Put 8 oz beans and 8 oz sauce in each 16-oz can. Suggested process: 300 × 409 cans (net 16 oz) 120 min at 240°F. Check processing time and temperature with can supplier or with the National Canners Association.

SOURCE: Stephan L. Komarik, 4810 Ronda, Coral Gables, Florida.

BEANS IN TOMATO SAUCE VEGETARIAN STYLE

Prepare Beans

Soak beans no longer than 8 hr and no less than 7 hr. The best method for soaking is to have an overflow on the tank to circulate incoming water so the beans will not sour during the soaking period. After beans are properly soaked, place them in wire baskets and submerge in boiling water for 12–15 min. Drain.

Prepare Sauce

Ingredients	Gal.	Lb	Oz	Cc
Tomato purée (sp. gr. 1.040)	50			
Cane sugar		125		
Corn sugar		37		
Salt		31		
Onion powder			10	
Oil of pimiento				10.80
Oil of cloves				5.00
Oil of nutmeg				4.00
Oil of cassia				0.60
Oleoresin capsicum				5.00
Oleoresin mace				5.00
Water to make	200			

Mix together salt, onion powder, essential oils, and oleoresins for later use.

Put tomato purée in a steam-jacketed kettle, add corn and cane sugars and, with steady stirring, bring to a boil. To the boiling stock add the salt-seasoning mixture and continue stirring to uniformly mix ingredients. Bring volume of sauce up to 200 gal. and raise temperature to 200°F.

Fill Cans

Using 300 × 409 cans (16 oz net), fill each can with 8.8 oz blanched beans, 7.2 oz hot tomato sauce. Hold product at 160°F or higher for filling. Close cans under vacuum.

Suggested Process

Process 300 × 409 cans (16 oz net) 2 hr at 240°F. Check process time and temperature with can supplier or the National Canners Association.

SOURCE: *Food Products Formulary*, *Vol. 1* by Komarik, Tressler and Long published by Avi Publishing Co., Westport, Conn.

CANNED MACARONI WITH CHEESE SAUCE (Hot Pack)

Ingredients	Lb
Yellow American cheddar cheese (aged)	100
Wheat flour	35
Corn oil	30
Cooked carrots	35
Salt	24
Whey powder	15
Sugar	10
Butter	6
Onion powder	1
Monosodium glutamate	1
Dry soluble pepper	1
Water to make 200 gal.	

Procedure

Preparation of the Sauce.—Grind cheddar cheese through the ¼-in. plate of the grinder. Cook carrots under 15 lb pressure in a pressure cooker until they are tender enough to be pulped in the mixer. Put 25 gal. of water in a steam-jacketed kettle equipped with a "Lightning" mixer, and bring up temperature to 140°F. While the agitator is working at low speed, add ground cheese, corn oil, and butter. Cook at a temperature of not over 160°F until the cheese is melted, then add 50 gal. more water; add salt, monosodium glutamate, sugar, and dry soluble pepper. Bring up temperature to 160°F. Make a slurry free of lumps with the flour, whey powder, cooked carrots, and onion powder and 10 gal. of water in a bakery mixer. While the sauce is being agitated, add the slurry to the batch. Bring up temperature to 180°–190°F and cook an additional 15 min.

Preparation of the Macaroni.—Use approximately 1 gal. of water per pound of macaroni. Add 2% salt to the cooking water and bring to a boil. Add macaroni to the boiling water; cook for 12 min. After cooking, wash and rinse in cold water and drain. These operations should not take longer than 30 min. Yield 300%.

Can Fill.—Pack 6 oz cooked macaroni and 10 oz hot sauce in each 16-oz can. Internal temperature should never drop under 160°F before cans are closed. Otherwise close cans under vacuum.

Process.—Suggested process: 300 × 409 cans (net 16 oz) 60 min at 240°F. Check processing time and temperature with can supplier or the National Canners Association.

SOURCE: Stephan L. Komarik, 4810 Ronda, Coral Gables, Florida.

CANNED CORN WITH CREAMED BUTTER SAUCE

Ingredients	Lb
Butter	2.5
Vegetable shortening	0.26
Seasoning	0.30
Versa-stabe modified food starch No. 4832	0.50
Water	14.0

Procedure

Heat 1½ gal. water to 200°F. Add shortening and butter; blend well and maintain at 200°F. Prepare starch slurry with 1 qt water; add to water, butter and shortening blend; mix thoroughly maintaining at 200°F, allowing starch to develop. Add seasoning, blend, and fill.

Fill Ratio.—To a No. 1 tin can with c-enamel add 175 gm corn, top with sauce, and process at 240°F for 70 min.

For Canned Lima Beans

Use same sauce formula as above but water may be increased to 2 gal.

For Canned Peas and Green Beans

Use same sauce formula as above.

Proper processing conditions can best be determined by laboratory evaluations. Also, check processing time and temperature with can supplier or the National Canners Association.

SOURCE: CPC International, Industrial Division, Englewood Cliffs, N.J.

CANNED SPAGHETTI IN TOMATO SAUCE WITH CHEESE (Hot Pack)

Sauce Ingredients	Lb	Oz
Tomato purée (sp gr 1.045)	600	
Aged cheddar cheese	50	
Cane sugar	60	
Salt	42	
Cooked carrots	21	
Corn or cottonseed oil	20	
Dry soluble spaghetti sauce seasoning mix (formula given below)	1	
Wheat flour	50	
Bicarbonate of soda		10
Onion powder	1	
Garlic powder		1
Water to make 200 gal.		

Dry Soluble Seasoning Mix

Ingredients	Lb	Cc
Oleoresin capsicum		4
Oleoresin ginger		1.4
Oleoresin mace		0.16
Oil of dill seed		0.2
Oil of cloves		3.6
Oil of cardamom		0.8
Oil of cassia		2.4
Oil of pimiento		26.4
Oil of bay		0.8
Salt to mix	2	

Use 4 gm per 1 gal. sauce

Procedure

Preparation of Sauce.—Grind cheese through the ¼-in. plate of the grinder. Cook carrots under 15 lb pressure in a pressure kettle until they are tender enough so they can be pulped in a mixer. Put ground cheese, cooked carrots, and 7 gal. warm water (temperature 140°-150°F) in a bakery mixer and make a slurry free from any lumps. Blend sugar, salt, wheat flour, and seasonings together. Put 150 gal. of water in a steam-jacketed kettle, add tomato purée and bicarbonate of soda. Agitate sauce with a "Lightning" mixer and slowly add blended mixture of salt, sugar, etc., then add the slurry of cheese and carrots and the oil. Bring up temperature to 180°F, cook an additional 15 min.

Preparation of Spaghetti.—Use approximately 1 gal. of water containing 2% added salt for each pound of spaghetti. Bring water to boil, add spaghetti which has been previously broken into thirds. Boil spaghetti for 12 min. After cooking, wash and rinse in cold water, then drain and pack. Washing and rinsing should not require more than ½ hr. Yield 300%.

Can Fill.—Fill 5.25 oz cooked spaghetti and 10.75 oz sauce in each 16-oz can.

Process.—Suggested process: 300 × 409 cans (16 oz net) 60 min at 240°F. Check processing time and temperature with can supplier or with the National Canners Association.

SOURCE: Stephan L. Komarik, 4810 Ronda, Coral Gables, Florida.

CANNED TOMATO SAUCE AND SPAGHETTI

Ingredients	%
Water	77.2
Tomato paste	14.9
Starch (Thin-N-Thik 35)	3.0
Dextrose (Staleydex 333)	2.0
Salt	1.8
Paprika (Asmus)	0.6
Onion powder (Asmus)	0.3
Garlic powder (Asmus)	0.2

Procedure

Slurry dry ingredients in water and add tomato paste. Heat to 180°F. Fill cans 35% by weight with cooked and drained spaghetti. Fill cans with sauce. Seal and retort.

Check process time and temperature with can supplier or the National Canners Association.

SOURCE: A. E. Staley Mfg. Co., Decatur, Illinois.

SPECIALTY VEGETABLE ITEMS

BAKED BEANS

Ingredients	Lb	Oz
Beans (preferably California pea)	100	
Soda		1/4
Salt	3	
Water (sufficient to cover beans 1½ in.)		

Procedure

Soak beans overnight, then heat and bring to a boil; lower heat and simmer until skins slip. Then drain liquid into a separate container and add the following ingredients to liquid and mix well:

	Lb	Oz
Mustard		1/4
Cinnamon		1/16
Onion (chopped fine)	5	
Catsup	12	
Pork (salt)	15	
Cane syrup (Tricol medium)	18	

Procedure

Mix this solution well into the beans and place in crock or bean pots. Bake at 325°F for 6-8 hr. Replace water at 1½-hr intervals to assure a nice moist bean. Be sure that moisture is just visible when removing from the oven.

SOURCE: American Molasses Co Div., SuCrest Corp, 120 Wall St., New York, N.Y.

IMITATION CATSUP

Ingredients	%
Kelset	1.300
Water	36.968
Tomato paste (26%)	33.600
Sugar	14.800
Vinegar (100-grain)	9.500
Potassium chloride	1.600
Starch (Textaid*)	1.120
Salt	0.800
Soluble paprika	0.160
Spice mix	0.140
Tomato flavor	0.010
FD&C red No. 2**	0.002
	100.00

Procedure

Premix Kelset with 3-5 times its weight of sugar until uniform, and hold. Make slurry using cold (tap) water with the starch; use about 25% of available water in formula. Combine balance of water, slurry, sugar, tomato paste, potassium chloride, vinegar, salt, red coloring No. 2, and soluble paprika and heat to 190°-200°F. While mixing, hold 5-8 min at temperature. Continue mixing, add Kelset-sugar premix and tomato flavor and mix 1-2 min. Package immediately at 190°F and cool to 75°-95°F.

---

*Textaid is a texturizing starch made by National Starch Company, New York, N.Y.

**This coloring has been de-listed. It is no longer on the FDA-approved list of food colors and cannot be used. Consult your food color supplier for recommended color substitutions.

SOURCE: Kelco Company, 20 N. Wacker Drive, Chicago, Illinois.

IMITATION CATSUP NO. 2

This formulation represents approximately 35% cost reduction in ingredients compared to tomato catsup, yet the texture, consistency, flavor, color, and general characteristics are similar to tomato catsup.

Ingredients	%
Sodium alginate (Kelset)[1]	1.300
Water	36.968
Tomato paste (26%)	33.600
Sugar	14.800
Vinegar (100-grain)	9.500
Potassium chloride	1.600
Starch (textaid)[2]	1.120
Salt	0.800
Soluble paprika[3]	0.160
Spice mix[3]	0.140
Tomato flavor[4]	0.010
FD&C red No. 2*	0.002
	100.00

Procedure

Premix Kelset with 3-5 times its weight of sugar until uniform, and hold. Make slurry using cold (tap) water with the starch; use about 25% of available water in formula. Combine balance of water, slurry, sugar, tomato paste, potassium chloride, vinegar, salt, red coloring 2, soluble paprika, and heat to 190°-200°F. While mixing, hold 5-8 min at temperature. Continue mixing, add Kelset-sugar premix and tomato flavor and mix 1-2 min. Package immediately at 190°F and cool to 75°-95°F.

---

[1] Kelset, Kelco Company, Clark, N.J., Chicago, Los Angeles.
[2] Textaid, National Starch Company, New York City, N.Y.
[3] Catsup Spice Mix SP2618 and soluble paprika, Stange Co., Paterson, N.J.
[4] Tomato flavor (Imitation) F-5310, Givaudan Corp., New York, N.Y., and Tomato flavor 567, Florasynth Co., New York, N.Y.
*This coloring has been de-listed. It is no longer on the FDA-approved list of food colors and cannot be used. Consult your food color supplier for recommended color substitution.

SOURCE: Kelco Co., 20 N. Wacker Drive, Chicago, Illinois.

MEATLESS CHILI WITH BEANS NO. 1

Ingredients	%
Textured vegetable protein (Mira-Tex 210)	5.25
Salt	0.37
Beef red powdered caramel color	0.11
Hard vegetable fat	4.50
Tomato paste	7.48
Onion powder (Vico-Asmus)	0.37
Starch (Tenderfil 8)	0.75
Dextrose (Staleydex 333)	0.15
Sugar	0.37
Chili seasoning (Vico-Asmus) 96R-9	3.51
Kidney beans	27.00
Water	50.14
	100.00

Procedure

Soak kidney beans overnight; then, blanch, cool, and weigh hydrated beans.

Disperse Mira-Tex, flavors, color, spices and Tenderfil 8 in water. Heat mixture to 140°F with agitation and add melted fat. Bring mixture to boil, stir until starch is gelatinized. Add tomato paste and kidney beans, heat to boil, stirring constantly. Adjust volume, fill cans, and sterilize. Check processing time and temperature with can supplier or the National Canners Association.

SOURCE: A. E. Staley Mfg. Company, Decatur, Ill.

MEATLESS CHILI WITH BEANS NO. 2

Ingredients	Lb	Oz
Water to soak and cook beans	245	
Red beans	30	
Ultra-Soy, minced	17	
Beef suet	12	
Hot water	33	
Tomato purée	45	
Salt	3	4
Sugar	3	4
Chili powder	3	
Onion powder	2	8
Monosodium glutamate	1	8
Black pepper		10
Garlic powder		8
Paprika		10
Corn flour	4	
Cornstarch	4	

Procedure

Wash beans and soak overnight. Cook in the same water. Melt beef suet and heat to 200°F. Add hot water slowly with fast agitation to form an emulsion. With slow agitation, add seasonings until well mixed. Add Ultra-Soy and mix 5-6 min. Combine cooked beans, tomato purée, and Ultra-Soy mixture and simmer over low heat 5 min. Process 90 min at 10 lb pressure. Check processing time and temperature with can supplier or the National Canners Association.

SOURCE: Far-Mar Company, Research Division, 960 N. Halstead, Hutchinson, Kansas.

CHOP SUEY

Ingredients	Lb
Beef, cut in bite-size pieces	3 lb
Lean pork, cut in bite-size pieces	2 lb
Celery, cut in pieces	2 stalks
Onions, large	6
Mushrooms, button	½ lb
Soy sauce	8 tbsp
Salt (to taste)	

Procedure

Flour all meat and brown in vegetable oil and drain out of this into heavy pan. Cover meat in boiling water, put onions and celery on top. Let steam for 1½ hr. When about tender, add soy sauce and mushrooms, let cook until meat is tender and gravy is thick. Serve with rice, if desired.

SOURCE: *Favorite Southern Recipes*, Waycross Woman's Club, Waycross, Georgia.

CHOP SUEY WITH SOY PROTEIN

Ingredients	Lb	Oz	Other
Texturized soy protein with beef-like flavor (Bontrae)	10		
Oil			1 cup
Celery, 1-in. cuts	3		
Chives		2	
Onions, diced	3		
Brown sugar			1 cup
Soy sauce			1 pt
Molasses			6 tbsp
Bean sprouts	3		
Pimientos, diced	1		
Cornstarch		10	
White pepper			3 tsp
Ginger			¼ tsp
Beef base		2	
Chicken base		2	
Water	8		

Yield: 50 servings

Procedure

Sauté celery and onions in very hot oil. Add pepper, brown sugar, and ginger. Add chicken base, beef base, and water. Dissolve cornstarch in soy sauce and stir into boiling stock. When sauce is thick, add pimientos, bean sprouts, Bontrae, and chives. Serve over steamed rice.

SOURCE: General Mills, Minneapolis, Minn.

CHOW CHOW

Ingredients	%
Chopped cabbage	30.00
Medium onions	7.50
Chopped green peppers	7.50
Chopped red sweet peppers	7.50
Chopped green tomatoes	15.00
Pickling salt	1.00
Prepared mustard	0.50
Vinegar	21.27
Sugar	9.00
Turmeric	0.10
Ginger	0.10
Mustard seeds	0.20
Celery seeds	0.10
Mixed, whole pickling spices	0.10
Stabilizer (Multi-Sta)	0.13
	100.00

Procedure

Mix until a uniform mixture is obtained.

SOURCE: Germantown Manufacturing Company, 505 Parkway, Broomall, Penn.

CANNED CHOW MEIN

Vegetable Ingredients	%
Blanched bean sprouts	40.0
Blanched celery	42.0
Dehydrated onions	4.0
Dehydrated peppers	1.0
Water chestnuts	8.0
Bamboo shoots	5.0
Sauce Ingredients	
Water	92.7
Starch (Thin-N-Thik 65™)	6.0
Salt	1.3

Procedure

Hydrate onions and peppers prior to mixing with other vegetables. Mix vegetables and fill 211 × 400 cans to 50% by weight. Slurry sauce ingredients in cold water and pour over vegetables.

Seal cans and retort in continuous retort to Fo = 12 (19 min at 260°F). For a static retort, heat slurry to 170°F before filling and process 48 min at 245°F. Check processing time and temperature with can supplier or with National Canners Association.

SOURCE: A. E. Staley Mfg. Co., Decatur, Illinois.

WHIPPED GARLIC SPREAD

Ingredients	Lb	Oz
Margarine	37	8
Shortening	18	12
Carotene coloring		2½
Puréed garlic (Gentry)	6	5
Cayenne pepper (Gentry)		1
Sodium benzoate		1
Potassium sorbate		¼
Monosodium glutamate		1
Citric acid		1¼
Sugar		11
Vinegar (100-grain), fluid ounces		11
Salt		9½
Water, fluid ounces		53

Procedure

The suggested operating procedure given here is based on the use of a Hobart L-800 (80-qt) mixer fitted with a wire-whip blade. The process can easily be adapted to more advanced continuous process techniques. In order to obtain the desired amount of whipping, both the shortening and the margarine should be at room temperature (65°–80°F).

Using No. 1 (slow) speed on the Hobart, blend the margarine, shortening, and carotene coloring until a uniform dispersion has been obtained. Meanwhile, mix the other ingredients together until the salt is dissolved.

Then, change the speed of the Hobart mixer to No. 2 (medium) and commence adding the preceding mixture to the shortening and margarine. The rate of addition should be such that little free water is visible. Approximate time: 3 min.

Continue whipping for about 2 min after all of the water and spices have been added or until the desired consistency has been reached. This can be noted by the color of the product, since it becomes lighter with increasing amount of overrun. The product is now ready to be packaged.

SOURCE: Gentry International, Gilroy, California.

HAM-FLAVORED SALAD SPREAD

Ingredients	%
Cream cheese	94.30
Milk	4.47
Salt	0.50
Smithfield ham flavor (RR 39687)	0.20
Color: Allura Red #40 (3% Sol)	0.03
150X Caramel (50% Sol)	0.50
	100.00

Procedure

Allow cream cheese to soften at room temperature. Add milk and mix until a smooth, creamy texture is obtained. Add flavor, salt, and coloring and mix well. Keep refrigerated.

NOTE: Chopped green peppers, pimientos, and celery may be added to enhance the appearance of the salad spread.

SOURCE: Naarden, Inc., 10 Painters Mill Road, Owings Mills, Maryland.

HOPPING JOHN

Ingredients	
Dried black-eyed peas	10 lb
Boiling water	2 gal.
Salt pork or fat bacon	3 lb
Onion, coarsely chopped	2 lb
Celery leaves	10 sprays
Bay leaves, small	10
Salt	10 tsp
Black pepper	1 tsp
Uncooked rice	2 lb
Minced parsley	1/4 lb

Yield: 60 servings

Procedure

Place peas and boiling water in saucepan and allow to stand for 2 hr. Cut pork or bacon in squares and brown in a hot skillet. After the peas soak, add the pork or bacon, onion, celery leaves, bay leaves, salt, and pepper. Add more boiling water as needed. Simmer in a covered saucepan until the peas are tender. Discard the bay leaves, add the rice and simmer in the covered saucepan until the peas and rice are tender. Add salt and pepper to taste, if desired.

Place the pieces of bacon or salt pork on top of the peas and rice and sprinkle with parsley. The product may be frozen or canned.

SOURCE: *Favorite Southern Recipes*, Waycross Woman's Club, Waycross, Georgia.

EXTRUDED ONION RINGS

Ingredients	%
Instant starch (Dura-Jel)	68
K-Vol Vital wheat	8
Corn meal	24
Chopped green onions	100

Procedure

1. Add mixed, dry ingredients to 60% chopped green onions.
2. Blend together and extrude entire mix through an extruder to develop mix into a dough.
3. Shape product into onion rings.
4. Deep fat fry at 350°F for 1 min.
5. Salt and serve.

SOURCE: A. E. Staley Mfg. Co., Decatur, Illinois.

BREADING ONION RINGS FOR FRENCH FRYING

Requirements for good French fried onion rings are: They should taste good; they should hold their shape; the coating should cover the rings completely without being greasy or too thick; the coating should be flaky and tender, but not pop off during frying; the rings should be vibrant, golden brown, and not lose their crispness as they cool; and the method of preparation should be quick and easy. Rings should brown in less than 2 min at 350°–375°F to avoid overcooking of the onion ring and still get a good color.

Procedure

Carefully inspect the graded and sized onions for defects. Use air to blow off the outer coating; cut onions into ⅜-in. rings and drop into lukewarm water where they more or less separate themselves. Place slices on belt and pass through automatic battering machine, using commercial batter mix of a medium-to-thick viscosity and bread within 4 sec using a commercial breading mix.

Place battered and breaded rings flat in a box using freezer paper to separate layers. Smaller rings are placed inside larger rings to use all possible space. Seal in cartons and freeze. Control portion packing is done by freezing the rings before packing. Rings to be used within 48 hr are refrigerated at 32°-34°F without freezing.

SOURCE: Breading of French Fried Onion Rings, by Stone *Quick Frozen Foods 26*, 5, 77-78.

ONION SALT

Ingredients	%
Granulated onion (Gentry Item 6100-78)	25
Salt	70
Calcium stearate (food grade)	5
	100

Procedure

Blend calcium stearate with granulated onion before adding salt.

SOURCE: Gentry International, Gilroy, California.

GARLIC SALT

Ingredients	%
Granulated garlic (Gentry Item 7100-78)	20
Salt	75
Calcium stearate (food grade)	5
	100

Procedure

Blend calcium stearate with granulated garlic before adding salt.

SOURCE: Gentry International, Gilroy, California.

NATURAL POTATO FLAVOR
(Free of starch)

Potato flavor is made by removing the moisture content of peeled potatoes; the separated juice is mixed with propylene glycol; this mixture is then used to extract the potato peels at a temperature of 120°F for 15 min; the extract is drained off either by gravity or by centrifuge; starch separates in storage within 24 hr.

The natural potato flavor is now successfully used in flour mixes and doughnuts instead of potato flour.

SOURCE: *Food Flavorings, Composition, Manufacture, and Use* by Merory published by Avi Publishing Co., Westport, Conn.

FROZEN POTATO PUFFS

Ingredients	%
Cooked, peeled potatoes	79.5
Butter or margarine	4.5
Cream (light)	9.0
Egg yolk	3.5
Egg white	3.5
	100.0

Whip peeled, boiled potatoes until free of lumps in beater-type mixer. Beat in butter and cream until batch is fluffy. Add well-beaten egg yolks, and then fold in stiffly-beaten egg whites. Form into 1½-2 in. diameter balls, place on greased bake sheets, brush with melted butter, and bake 15-20 min in 375°F oven. Pack cooked, cooled potato balls into consumer size cartons, and freeze.

SOURCE: *The Freezing Preservation of Foods, 4th Edition, Vol. 4* by Tressler, Van Arsdel and Copley published by Avi Publishing Co., Westport, Conn.

CANNED POTATO SALAD

Ingredients	%
Xanthan gum (Keltrol)	0.40
Water	46.19
Vegetable oil	30.00
Sucrose	10.30
Vinegar (100-grain)	8.00
Salt	2.00
Starch (Purity, National Starch & Chemical Corp.)	2.00
Mustard powder	0.50
Celery salt	0.20
Monsodium glutamate	0.20
Onion powder	0.15
Paprika	0.03
Garlic powder	0.02
White pepper	0.01
	100.00

For Can Fill

Ingredients	%	Can Size 303 × 406 Gm	606 × 700 Gm
Diced potatoes	55.00	271.70	1705.00
Chopped raw onions	2.50	12.35	77.50
Rehydrated red and green peppers	2.50	12.35	77.50
Salad dressing	40.00	197.60	1240.00
Total	100.00	494.00	3100.00

Procedure

Blend all dry ingredients. Add dry ingredients to the vigorously agitated water. Mix until Keltrol is in solution. Add the oil in a slow and continuous stream. Mix for 10 min. Add the vinegar. Mix for 5 min. Homogenize the emulsion single-stage, at 2500 psi or colloid mill at 0.025 in. Prepare potatoes. For 303 × 406 cans, cook in 0.1% citric acid solution to the desired final texture. For 603 × 700 cans, blanch in boiling 0.1% citric acid solution for 20 min. Rehydrate the red and green peppers in cold water for at least 30 min. Prepare onions. Heat the salad dressing with moderate agitation to 165°-170°F. Mix the hot dressing with the vegetables, fill without headspace and seal cans. Process in static retort at 240°F until sterile. Check processing time and temperature with can supplier or the National Canners Association.

SOURCE: Kelco Co., 20 N. Wacker Drive, Chicago, Illinois.

SCALLOPED POTATOES WITH BACON-FLAVORED CHIPLETS

Ingredients	%
Margarine or butter	2.7
Flour	1.2
Milk	46.9
Medium potatoes, diced thin	43.3
Salt	0.4
Pepper	0.1
Chopped onion	1.6
Bacon-flavored chiplets	3.8

Procedure

Combine butter, flour, milk, salt, and pepper to make a white sauce. Arrange half the potatoes in greased casserole; add half the white sauce and onion and ¾ of the bacon-flavored chiplets. Add remaining potatoes, onion, and bacon flavored chiplets. Cover with remaining white sauce. Cover. Bake at 350°F for 1 hr. Uncover and continue baking until the top is brown.

SOURCE: Far-Mar Company, Research Division, 960 N. Halstead, Hutchinson, Kansas.

PUMPKIN PIE FILLING

Ingredients	%	Per 100 8-in. Pies Lb	Oz
Pumpkin (strained)	41.40	51	12
Milk (whole fluid)	30.76	38	7
Eggs (whole fluid)	13.94	17	7
Sugar, brown	6.21	7	12
Sugar, granulated	6.21	7	12
Salt	0.82	1	
Cinnamon	0.42		8½
Ginger	0.16		3¼
Nutmeg	0.08		1½
	100.00		

Procedure Using Fresh Eggs

Fresh or canned pumpkin may be used with similar results. However, fresh pumpkin gives a slightly better product. If fresh pumpkin is used, pumpkin is cut and the seeds removed. Pumpkin slices are then steamed under pressure for 15-20 min at 15 lb. If a pressure steamer is not available, it may be steamed in a large kettle on racks at atmospheric pressure for 45 min. The pumpkin is then scraped from the rind, if the hard-rind variety is used. If the soft-rind varieties are used, the pumpkins, without peeling, are run through a purée machine. The strained pumpkin is then ready for use.

Brown or white sugar may be used. However, when white sugar is used the color of the pie is rather yellow, and when brown sugar is used, the pie is dark brown in color. The formula given combines brown and white sugar in equal proportions; the combination of sugars gives a pleasing appearance.

The strained pumpkin is placed in a bakery mixer, eggs are added, then the sugar and salt, which have been previously mixed with the spices; and finally, the milk is slowly added. The product is fluid but sets up when the pie is baked.

SOURCE: *The Freezing Preservation of Foods*, *4th Edition*, *Vol. 4* by Tressler, Van Arsdel and Copley published by Avi Publishing Co., Westport, Conn.

CANNED RICE CREOLE WITH MUSHROOMS

Sauce Ingredients	Lb	Gal.
Tomato purée (sp gr 1.045)		50
Salt	20	

	Lb	Gal.
Cane sugar	20	
Spanish paprika	10	
Dry soluble pepper	1	
Hydrolyzed plant protein	1	
Water to make		100

Premixed Ingredients	Lb
Cooked rice	250
Chopped onions	70
Canned diced green peppers	35
Canned diced pimiento	17
Canned sliced mushrooms	70

Procedure

Preparation of the Premixed Ingredients.—Use 1 gal. of cooking water for 1 lb of rice. Bring water to boil, add rice, and cook for 10 min. Drain water and wash rice. Grind onions through the ¼-in. plate of the grinder. Brines from canned mushrooms and peppers should be added to the sauce (below) before bringing up volume with water. Put all the ingredients in a mechanical mixer and mix thoroughly.

Preparation of the Sauce.—Put 50 gal. of tomato purée in the jacketed kettle, add remainder of the ingredients along with the drained brines from the canned mushrooms and peppers. Bring up volume to 100 gal. and heat to a temperature of 180°-190°F.

To Fill.—Pack 7 oz mixed solids and 9 oz tomato sauce in each 16-oz can and close under 27 in. vacuum.

Suggested Process.—For 300 × 409 cans (16-oz net) 60 min at 240°F. Check processing time and temperature with can supplier or with the National Canners Association.

SOURCE: D. K. Tressler and Associates, Westport, Conn.

RICE PILAF FLAVOR BASE

Ingredients	%
Maggi HPP Type 3H3 powder with partially hydrogenated vegetable oil	5.0
Maggi HPP Type 245 powder with partially hydrogenated vegetable oil	5.0
Salt	20.0
Sugar	4.0
Monosodium glutamate	7.2
Celery, soluble	0.5
Pepper, soluble	0.3
Oleoresin paprika	1.0
Mushroom dice, freeze-dried	5.0
Green peppers, granules	10.0
Onions sliced, dehydrated	12.0
Tomato crystals	24.0
Hydrogenated vegetable oil	6.0

Procedure

Mix flavor base ingredients together until mixture is homogeneous.

To Use

Combine 35 gm of flavor base, 6 gm of freeze-dried shrimp, 140 gm (2 cups) quick-cooking rice, and 1 tbsp butter with 2 cups of cold water. Bring to a boil while stirring. Reduce heat, cover and simmer for 5 min.

SOURCE: Food Ingredients Division, Nestlé Company, 100 Bloomingdale Road, White Plains, N.Y.

SWEET POTATO CHIPS

Sweet potato chips are a promising product, easily made, have an attractive yellow color, excellent flavor, and add variety to parties and snacks.

Select deeply colored varieties, as Goldrush, Allgold, Heartogold, Jersey Orange, or Orlis.

Select smooth, medium-sized potatoes free of disease and growth cracks. Large ones or jumbos may be used after cutting lengthwise into halves and quarters. Trim and preheat 15-20 min in water at 170°-190°F to prevent darkening, and make peeling easier. They may be peeled by (a) immersing in a solution of boiling 10% lye for 5-7 min followed by thorough washing and dipping in a 2% solution of citric acid; (b) subjecting to 10 lb steam pressure and removing the peel by hand. After rinsing, slice to a thickness of 1/32 to ¼ in. with a vegetable slicer.

Place the freshly prepared slices in a deep fat frying basket and immerse for 1½-2 min in a good cooking oil heated to 350°F. The volume of oil and application of heat should be such that the temperature does not drop below 300°F at any time. Decreased rate of bubbling and deepening of color are indications of doneness. Cooking continues after the chips are removed from the oil, and experience will indicate when to remove the chips from the oil for optimum color, flavor, and crispness.

Drain the hot chips on a clean cloth or screen and add salt to taste. If the finished chips are too hard, this indicates the potatoes were not preheated sufficiently, or the slices were too thick; if they are too greasy, this can be corrected by raising the temperature of the oil while cooking;

or if the salt does not stick to the chips, either the salt should be ground more finely, or more hydrogenated fat or coconut oil should be added to the cooking oil.

Use an antioxidant in the oil. Either of the following was found beneficial: 0.03% BHA (butylated hydroxyanisole); 0.03% BHT (butylated hydroxytoluene); 0.15% Tenox II; or 0.015% BHA plus 0.015% BHT.

Package in moistureproof containers; bags of polyethylene, cellophane, or similar materials may be used; tin cans and glass jars are also very satisfactory.

The yield of chips from potatoes varies widely depending upon the condition of the potatoes and method of handling. Generally, there is a loss of about 50% in weight during peeling, trimming, and slicing. There is an additional loss of about 20% in weight of the product during cooking due to evaporation of moisture. This gives a yield of about 25% by weight; however, there is an increase in volume of from 8 to 10 times during cooking; consequently, a bushel of potatoes should yield at least 2 bushels of chips weighing from 10 to 15 lb.

SOURCE: Department of Food Science, Georgia Experiment Station, Experiment, Georgia.

CANNED CONGEALED SWEET POTATO ROLL

Ingredients	Lb
Sweet potato purée	100
Starch (FloJel 60*)	8
Corn syrup, high conversion	8
Water	8
Nonfat dry milk	1.5
Salt	0.1
Ascorbic acid	0.02
EDTA**	0.02
Butter flavor	0.60

Procedure

Heat washed, sound, field-run sweet potatoes to 120°F for 30 min, to facilitate peeling and set the color. Peel by immersing in 10% lye at 212°F for 5-8 min or until peel disintegrates; remove peel in rotary, squirrel-cage washer; and rinse in 2% citric acid solution.

Cook potatoes until soft in steam retort or steam blancher; purée and pump into blending tank. Mix starch and water, cook to 190°F, add corn syrup, milk solids, salt, ascorbic acid, EDTA, and butter flavor and mix thoroughly. Mix this with purée in blending tank and blend thoroughly, in Morehouse Mill or Fitspatrick Community Mill. Fill the purée at 200°F into 210 × 410 cans (juice drink size), seal with steam closure and retort for 60 min at 240°F. Cool quickly and case. Check processing time and temperature with can supplier or the National Canners Association.

---

*Made by National Starch & Chemical Co., 750 3rd Ave., New York, N.Y.

**Made by Geigy Industrial Chemicals, Saw Mill River Road, Ardsley, N.Y.

SOURCE: T. S. Boggess and E. K. Heaton, Georgia Experiment Station, Experiment, Georgia.

SLOPPY JOES (Simulated Meat)

Ingredients	Lb	Oz
Ultra-Soy chiplets 100, caramel colored	32.9	
Beef suet	24.2	
Hot water	42.9	
Salt	1.0	
Wilson Certified BV	1.0	
Catsup	30.0	
Tomato paste	10.0	
Minced onion	2.0	
Vinegar	2.0	
Water (added while cooking)	10.0	
Worchestershire sauce		4
Garlic powder		6
Black pepper		6
Chili powder		6
Ground celery		2
Red and green pepper, dehydrated		6
Liquid smoke		4

Procedure

Melt beef suet and pour over Ultra-Soy and dry seasonings. Mix and let set 5 min. Add hot water, beef flavor, Worchestershire sauce, liquid smoke, and vinegar. Mix well and let set 10 more min. Grind through 3/16-in. plate. Add tomato paste catsup, and additional water and simmer.

SOURCE: Far-Mar Company, Research Division, 960 N Halstead, Hutchinson, Kansas.

MEATLESS SLOPPY JOE

Ingredients	Lb	Oz
Ultra-Soy minced, caramel	19	8
Beef suet	15	
Hot water	56	
Salt	2	6

	Lb	Oz
Maggi RFB powder (Nestlé Co.)	3	
Yeast extract (Ac'Cent-International)	3	
Catsup	30	
Dehydrated toasted minced onion	2	8
Toasted onion powder	1	4
Black pepper		7
Garlic powder		8
Chili powder		8
Ground celery		8
Red and green pepper (dehydrated)		12
Monosodium glutamate	2	8

Sauce Ingredients	Lb	Oz
Catsup	10	
Tomato paste	25	
Water	65	
Vinegar	4	
Worcestershire sauce	4	
Liquid smoke		4
Cold Flo 67 (National Starch & Chemical Co.)	4	

Procedure

Combine sauce ingredients and heat to 200°F stirring constantly.

Heat beef suet to 200°F. Add hot water while stirring to create an emulsion. Add dry seasonings, mixing well. Add Ultra-Soy and continue stirring for 3-5 min. Simmer another 5 min.

Combine sauce and Ultra-Soy, heat together 3-5 min. Fill jars and process at 10 lb pressure for 90 min. Check processing time and temperature with can supplier or the National Canners Association.

SOURCE: Far-Mar Company, Research Division, 960 N. Halstead, Hutchinson, Kansas.

MEATLESS TACO FILLING

Ingredients	Lb	Oz
Vegetable oil or beef suet melted	15	
Hot water	56	
Ultra-Soy minced, caramel	19	8
Tomato powder		5
Tomato purée	8	
Salt	1	
Chili powder		6
Onion powder		8
Corral beef flavor, powder (Pfizer)	3	8
Cumin		8
Ground chili pepper		5
Cayenne		1
Coriander		1
Black pepper		1
Oregano		2
Garlic powder		4
Minced onion		5
Paprika		1

Procedure

Heat beef suet or oil to 200°F in steam-jacketed kettle. With high agitation slowly add hot water and mix for approximately 1 min. With slow agitation add seasonings until well mixed. Add Ultra-Soy and mix slowly for 5-6 min. Simmer 5-10 min longer stirring occasionally.

SOURCE: Far-Mar Company, Research Division, 960 N. Halstead, Hutchinson, Kansas.

CANNED TAMALES

Mexican tamales are made from lye hominy ground into a paste; mixed with ground and cooled cooked beef and seasonings.

Ingredients	Gal.	Lb	Oz
Ground lean beef		40	
Lye hominy meal		20-25	
Ground chili pepper		5	
Tomatoes	4		
Chopped onions		1	
Chopped garlic			2
Salt		2	
Wheat flour		3	

Procedure

Mix ingredients in the order listed to the consistency of a thick paste using broth, juices, or water and cook for 30 min. The wrapper is made from a thick paste of cornmeal, with a little wheat flour for adhesiveness, using water or beef broth. The dough is rolled into thin wafers and the meat mixture is wrapped in it, after being formed in automatic machines.

The tamales are wrapped in corn shucks or specially prepared paper, cut to the proper length, and tightly packed into cans, which are then filled with hot brine containing 15 lb of salt per 100 gal. The cans are exhausted for 5 min, closed, and processed at 240°F for 80 min for No. 2 cans, and longer for larger cans.

Check processing time and temperature with can supplier or the National Canners Association.

SOURCE: D. K. Tressler and Associates, Westport, Conn.

TEMPEH

Tempeh, an important source of protein food in Southeast Asia is made by fermenting dehulled, partially cooked soybean cotyledons with molds, usually a species of the genus *Rhizopus*.

Dry soybeans are washed and soaked overnight at about 77°F. In the morning the seed coats are removed and the beans are boiled for ½ hr. After cooling, they are inoculated with spores of the mold, placed in shallow trays, and held at about 86°F for 20-24 hr. The beans will then be completely covered and bound together by the pure white mycelia of the mold. At this stage the product may be consumed in any one of several forms. The thin mat may be sliced, dipped in salt brine, and fried in vegetable oil to yield a golden brown crisp product resembling bacon. It may be eaten in soups; and sometimes consumed with soy sauce.

Similar products are prepared with copra presscake, peanut presscake, cassava, glutinous rice, locust beans, wheat gluten or blends of these substances.

SOURCE: *Microbiology of Food Fermentations* by Pederson published by Avi Publishing Co., Westport, Conn.

TURKEY "CUTLETS" WITH ALMOND-MUSHROOM SAUCE

Ingredients

Margarine	1 cup
Flour	1 cup
Milk	1½ pt
Rice (3 qt cooked)	1½ lb (raw)
Cooked turkey meat diced in ½-in. cubes	3 lb
Roasted almonds, diced	3⅓ cups
Pimiento, canned, drained and chopped	1 cup
Cream of Mushroom soup	No. 5 tall can
Worcestershire sauce	2 tbsp
Angostura bitters	¼ tsp

Procedure

Make a very thick sauce: melt butter in saucepan, add flour, blend and cook over low heat, stirring constantly, for about 4 min. (Do not let brown.) Add milk, stirring constantly, and cook until thickened. Season with salt and pepper. Add rice, turkey, almonds and pimiento and heat well. Remove from heat and let cool overnight in refrigerator. Shape into 4-oz "cutlets," dip in flour, egg, and bread with crackermeal. Deep fry at 350°F for about 2 min. Drain.

For almond-mushroom sauce: Heat mushroom soup to boiling, add Worcestershire and bitters. Serve cutlet with mushroom sauce; garnish with sliced or slivered almonds.

SOURCE: California Almond Growers Exchange, Sacramento, California.

PRESERVING VEGETABLES WITH SULPHUR DIOXIDE

A few vegetables, such as horseradish, cucumbers, okra, cauliflower, cabbage for sauerkraut, pimientos for use in meats, young onions, and others to be used in soups, pickles, relishes or purées, may be preserved in sulphur dioxide alone or in combination with salt and a calcium salt.

Prepare vegetable as for use and cover with a solution of 2000 ppm sulphur dioxide in a wood or corrosion-resistant vessel with tight cover. Add 1 lb of calcium carbonate and 5 lb of sodium chloride per 100 gal. Agitate or turn daily for 1 week, and weekly for 6 months or longer.

Freshen by boiling in open steam-jacketed kettle for 1 hr, then proceed to process as freshly cooked vegetables.

SOURCE: Georgia Experiment Station Leaflet 7, Experiment, Georgia.

ALMOND PRODUCTS

ALMOND BARK

Ingredients	Lb
Vanilla chocolate coating	15
Milk chocolate coating	5
Select sheller run almonds, roasted	10

Procedure

Melt and temper the chocolate coatings, add almonds, mix well and spread thin on dipping papers; or for a more continuous operation, spread on enrober cooling belt and allow to pass through tunnel where it can be scored or cut or broken into irregular pieces.

SOURCE: California Almond Growers Exchange, Sacramento, California.

BORDEAUX ALMOND CREAMS

Ingredients	Lb	Oz
Sugar	100	
Brown sugar	20	
Cream, 24%	5	
Water	20	
Salt		1½
Vanilla flavor		2
Rum flavor		3
Almond flavor		½
Almonds, select sheller run, roasted and ground	17	

Procedure

Cook sugar, brown sugar, and cream to 242°F. Pour on ball beater, cool to 110°F. Beat, add salt, flavor, and almonds; sweat back and extrude. Coat with dark vanilla chocolate.

SOURCE: California Almond Growers Exchange, Sacramento, California.

ALMOND BRITTLE

Ingredients	Lb	Oz
Sugar	12	
Corn syrup	8	
Dairy butter, salted	2	
Almonds, sheller run, roasted, chopped	6	
Salt		4
Baking soda		12

Procedure

Cook sugar and corn syrup to 285°F. Add butter and stir. Cook to 295°F. Add almonds and stir into batch slowly. Remove batch from heat. Add salt, vanilla flavor, and baking soda. Mix in thoroughly until batch puffs up. Pour on oiled slab. Spread batch quickly. Cut into squares and run through sizer to ¼ in. thick. When cold store in air-tight stock tin.

SOURCE: California Almond Growers Exchange, Sacramento, California.

ALMOND BUTTER FUDGE

Ingredients	Lb	Oz
Sugar, white	12	
Sugar, brown	2	

Courtesy of California Almond Growers Exchange

FIG. 17.1. ALMOND BARK

	Lb	Oz
Corn syrup	3	
Manufacturing cream (20% butterfat)		12
Dairy butter, salted	1	
Salt		1
Vanilla flavor	to taste	
Almonds, roasted, diced	7	

Procedure

Cook sugar, corn syrup and cream to 236°F. Add butter and cook to 238°F. Pour on marble slab and allow to cool. When cool add flavor and spade up. When batch begins to grain add almonds and complete spading. Place in wax-lined trays.

SOURCE: California Almond Growers Exchange, Sacramento, California.

SWISS ALMOND DROPS

Ingredients	
Eggs	12
Sugar	12 cups
Flour	1 lb
Salt	½ tsp
Almonds, toasted, finely chopped	4 lb
Chocolate, semisweet	1½ lb
Vanilla extract	6 tsp

Yield: approx 28 doz

Procedure

Beat eggs until thick; add sugar and continue beating until very thick. Add other ingredients and mix well. Chill until dough has stiffened, about 15 min. Drop by half teaspoonfuls onto greased cookie sheets. Bake at 325°F for 10 min.

SOURCE: *Progressive Farmer* 89, 5, 71.

ALMOND FINGERS

Ingredients	Lb	Oz
Cream together:		
Sugar	2	4
Shortening	1	
Butter		8
Soda		1
Salt		1¼
Add gradually:		
Eggs, whole		8
Mix together and add:		
Molasses	1	
Water		14
Sift together and mix in until smooth:		
Cake flour	3	12
Cinnamon		¼
Cream of tartar		½
Ginger		⅛
Then stir in:		
Almonds, chopped	1	12

Deposit on lightly greased pans, using a canvas bag and a No. 7 or 8 plain round tube, into fingers about 2½-3 in. in length. Allow to dry for a few minutes and flatten out. Wash with an egg wash and bake at about 380°F.

NOTE: If desired, a whole or half blanched almond may be placed on each cookie before baking.

SOURCE: Heggblade-Marguleas-Tenneco, Bakersfield, California.

ALMOND MACAROONS, NO. 1

Ingredients	Lb	Oz
Almond paste	2	8
Sugar, granulated	3	
Egg whites (variable)	1	

Procedure

Break the almond paste into small pieces and add a small quantity of the whites at a time to smooth the paste. Alternate the whites and sugar until both are incorporated. Drop out on paper-lined pans and bake on double pans at 360°F.

NOTE: A soft mix causes hollow bottoms. A stiff mix causes a coarse break on top.

SOURCE: Heggblade-Marguleas-Tenneco, Bakersfield, California.

FANCY MACAROONS

Ingredients	Lb	Oz
Almond paste (broken up)	2	8
Sugar, powdered	1	8
Butter		1

Procedure

Mix together the above items. Then gradually add:

Egg whites (variable)	8

Run out into various shapes, using a No. 5 or 5B star tube, on paper-lined pans. Decorate with nuts, glacé fruit, etc., and allow to dry overnight. Bake at about 330°F, on double pans. As soon as they are baked, remove the papers with the macaroons from the pans. Allow them to cool and then wash the macaroons with a corn syrup glaze. Allow this to set. Then turn the papers over and dampen with water. In a short time the macaroons can readily be removed from the paper.

SOURCE: Heggblade-Marguleas-Tenneco, Bakersfield, California

BLUEBERRY ALMOND TARTS

Ingredients	
Blueberries, fresh, dry-pack frozen, or canned, drained	4 lb
Blueberry pie filling	14½ lb
Almonds, slivered (or almond extract)	2 tbsp
Tart shells, 3-in. baked	100
Grated coconut (as needed)	
Whipped cream or topping (as needed)	

Yield: 100 tarts

Procedure

Fold blueberries into pie filling; mix almonds or almond extract into blueberry mixture. Fill tart shells with mixture. Sprinkle edges with grated coconut and garnish with whipped cream or topping.

SOURCE: North American Blueberry Council, Marmora, N.J.

CALIFORNIA SHRIMP BOAT WITH ALMONDS

Ingredients	
Shrimp (fresh or frozen)	3¾ lb
Tomatoes	5 large
Avocados	5 ripe
Fresh lime juice	¾ cup
Butter	1 cup
Curry powder (optional)	1-2 tbsp
Salt	2½ tsp
Chopped onion	5 cups
Flour	1 cup
Chicken broth	2½ cups
Sour cream	5 cups
Rice, cooked	80 oz
Almonds, sliced or slivered, toasted	10 oz
Lemons	4
Parsley	

Yield: 20 servings

Procedure

Cook and clean shrimp; cut into bite-size pieces. Peel, seed, and chop tomatoes; set aside. Peel and chunk avocados; toss gently with lime juice. Set aside. Melt butter with curry powder (optional) and salt on medium heat. Add onion; sauté until transparent. Stir in flour and cook 1 min. Add broth and cook, stirring, until sauce thickens. Add hot sauce gradually to sour cream, stirring constantly; return to pan. Just before serving, fold in tomato and shrimp. Heat to serving temperature. (Too much heat thins sauce.) Fold in avocado and lime juice. Serve approximately 1⅓ cups shrimp sauce over 4 oz hot rice in 20 individual casserole dishes. Top with toasted sliced or slivered almonds. Garnish with lemon slice and parsley.

SOURCE: California Almond Growers Exchange, Sacramento, California.

ALMOND CARAMEL APPLES

Ingredients	Lb
Sugar	2 lb
Corn syrup	1 lb
Butter or margarine	3 tbsp
Light cream	4 cups
Vanilla	4 tsp
Apples	50
Almonds, chopped	2 lb
Skewers	50

Procedure

Combine sugar, syrup, butter, and cream and stir over low heat until sugar is dissolved. Boil over moderate heat to very firm ball stage (250°F) stirring occasionally to prevent scorching. Remove from heat and stir in vanilla. Insert skewer into each apple and dip apple into syrup. Roll in chopped or diced roasted almonds. Makes 50 apples, depending on size.

SOURCE: California Almond Growers Exchange, Sacramento, California.

CRAB NEWBURG ALMONDINE

Ingredients	Lb	Oz	Measure
Crab meat (Alaska King or Dungeness)	5		
Butter		8	
California dry sherry		6	
Veloute or Basic white sauce	7		
Cream, heavy	1		
Patty shells			20
Almonds, toasted slivered		10	
Lemon garnish			7
Asparagus tips fresh or frozen			100

Yield: 20 portions

Procedure

Saute crab meat in butter until hot. Add sherry and allow crab meat to steam thoroughly. Add crab mixture to Veloute sauce in steam kettle or double boiler. Season to taste. Stir in cream and heat well. Serve 8-oz ladle of crab mixture over patty shell or toast points. Garnish with toasted silvered almonds and fancy cut lemon. Serve five asparagus tips alongside of entrée.

SOURCE: California Almond Growers Exchange, Sacramento, California.

ALMOND DIVINITY KISSES

Ingredients	Lb	Oz
Egg albumin		4
Water		11
Sugar	13	
Corn syrup	5	
Fondant, 80/20		11
Invert sugar	1	6
Salt		1½
Almonds, select, roasted, chopped	4	8
Vanilla		¼

Procedure

Dissolve egg albumin with water. Place invert sugar and egg albumin in Hobart mixer and beat until stiff. Cook sugar and corn syrup to 240°F and add in very fine stream into ingredients in Hobart mixer. Continue beating while adding fondant and salt, and until batch shows signs of grain. Fold in almonds and vanilla. Remove from beater and spoon out into desired sizes and shapes.

SOURCE: California Almond Growers Exchange, Sacramento, California.

FRENCH FRIED OR SALTED ALMONDS

Ingredients	Lb
Almonds, unblanched	100
Cooking oil	100
Salad oil	1
Salt, powder	2

Procedure

Roast almonds in cooking oil at 280°F for 5 min or until slightly brown; drain 2 min and coat with salad oil and salt. Sprinkle salt evenly over the nuts and mix thoroughly by turning several times from the bottom. The cooking oil may be reused several times.

SOURCE: American Spice Trade Association, Empire State Building, New York, N.Y.

ALMOND GEMS

Ingredients	Lb	Oz	Gm
Sugar	20		
Invert sugar	5		
Benzoate of soda			5
Water	6		
Salt		2	
Corn syrup	2½		
Egg albumin in 1 lb water		8	
Glycerine		1	
Invertase		1	
Almonds, roasted medium steel cut or chopped, sheller run	3		

Procedure

Cook sugar, invert sugar, benzoate of soda, salt and water to 247°F. Pour on flat-bed beater which has been covered with 8 oz of glycerine and cool to 100°F. Meanwhile prepare frappé by heating the corn syrup to 200°F. Whip egg albumin solution to peak, add hot corn syrup in fine stream and whip back to peak. Start beater, add flavor and invertase. When first grain appears add frappé and then almonds. Coat with milk or dark chocolate. Sprinkle with, or roll in, roasted small steel cut or chopped almonds.

SOURCE: California Almond Growers Exchange, Sacramento, California.

GLAZED ALMONDS

Ingredients	Lb	Oz
Corn syrup	6	
Sugar	3	
Salt		½
Almonds, 20/22 or 23/25 count, roasted	7½	
Water	2	

Procedure

Cook corn syrup, salt, sugar, and water to 300°F. Thoroughly wash sides of kettle just before batch comes to boil. Add almonds and mix carefully so as to avoid graining. Pour on well-oiled slab and fold several times so that the syrup will be well distributed as it cools. Continue to fold from time to time while removing small portions of the batch with gloved hands. Spread and stretch to form a sheet one almond thick.

SOURCE: California Almond Growers Exchange, Sacramento, California.

ALMOND GOLDEN NUGGETS

Ingredients	Lb	Oz
Brown sugar	5	
Corn syrup	8	
Cream, 20%	13	
Salt		3½

Procedure

Cook sugar, corn syrup, salt, and cream to medium ball. Shut off fire and stir in almonds being careful to avoid graining. Pour on slab and fold a few times while syrup is cooling. Form by hand while still pliable.

SOURCE: California Almond Growers Exchange, Sacramento, California.

ALMOND GOULASH

Ingredients	
Ground beef	4 lb
Onions, diced	1 lb
Green peppers, diced	4
Vegetable oil	4 tbsp
Salt	3 tbsp
Tomato sauce	2 lb
Macaroni	2 lb
Cheese, sharp cheddar	1½ lb
Milk	1½ cup
Almonds, roasted, diced	1½ lb

Yield: 25 servings

Procedure

Brown meat, onions, and green peppers in oil; add salt and tomato sauce. Cover and simmer 20 min. Cook macaroni in salt water 15-20 min. Combine with meat mixture. Stir in cheese, milk, and almonds, and turn into casserole. Bake in moderate oven (350°F) 20-30 min.

SOURCE: California Almond Growers Exchange, Sacramento, California.

STUFFING FOR CORNISH HENS

Ingredients	
Long grain and wild rice	80 oz
Raisins	1¼ cup
Butter, softened	⅔ cup
Almonds, slivered	⅔ cup
Rubbed sage	2½ tsp
Cornish game hens (1-1½ lb each)	20 hens
Salt	4 oz
Butter, melted	1¼ cup
Almonds, slivered	5 oz
Butter	1¼ cup
Cling peach halves	10 halves
Avocados	6
Lemon juice	1 oz
Lettuce leaves	20
Maraschino cherry halves	20

Yield: 20 servings

Procedure

Prepare rice according to package directions. Stir raisins, softened butter, almonds, and sage into rice. Rub cavities of hens with a little salt. Skewer neck skins, to backs. Fill each bird with about ¾ cup rice stuffing; cover opening with foil. Truss bird. Brush with melted butter. Place hens in greased shallow baking pans. Roast in preheated 425°F oven for 15 min. Reduce heat to 350°F and bake 40-50 min longer, or until done. Baste occasionally with melted butter. Saute almonds in butter. Use approximately ¼ oz for garnish. Cut peach halves into 40 slices. Cut avocados into 60 slices. Dip avocado slices in lemon juice. Alternate 3 slices of avocado with 2 slices of peach on lettuce leaf. Garnish with cherry half.

SOURCE: California Almond Growers Exchange, Sacramento, California.

HAPPY DIET ALMOND PLATE

Ingredients	Lb	Oz	Measure
Cooked turkey roll	5	10	
Lettuce			9 leaves
Cottage Cheese	3	6	
Sliced peaches jubilee			36 slices
String beans	2	4	
Sliced almonds		2	
Stuffed green olives			12
Ripe olives (large)			40

Yield: 18 portions

Procedure

Slice boneless turkey roll in 5-oz slices. Dish cottage cheese on lettuce leaf with 3-oz scoop. Place peaches on cottage cheese. Dish up 2-oz serving beans. Make the facial features with the toasted sliced almonds. Use one sliced stuffed olive for nose and eye brows. Use pieces of ripe olives for eyes. Garnish with whole ripe olives.

SOURCE: California Almond Growers Exchange, Sacramento, California.

SUGAR ROASTED ALMONDS

Ingredients	Lb
Sugar, white	40
Sugar, brown	10
Salt	½
Water	16
Almonds, small steel cut	50
Vanilla	1/32

Procedure

Place almonds in ribbed revolving pan equipped with gas burner and preroast slightly. Cook sugar, water, and salt to 221°F. Syrup should be added to nuts in a fine stream a little at a time.

Allow the syrup to crystallize and as soon as the nuts appear dry, repeat the process as many times as necessary to use all of the syrup. Let roll until dry, then place in trays to cool. Keep gas fire as low as practical. This type of roasting imparts a unique flavor to the nut, as well as suggests many new uses for small steel cut for fillings, as well as toppings in candy, ice cream, and bakery goods. The sugar, which is added normally, amounts to about 50% which brings the material cost of the processed nut down to slightly over half the cost of almonds. The labor cost for processing, especially in large quantities, is nominal. Many color variations can be made which can also be flavored. A regular 38-in. (full-size) revolving pan will make the above batch (any size pan may be used).

SOURCE: California Almond Growers Exchange, Sacramento, California.

BUTTER CRUNCH

	Large Batch		Small Batch	
Ingredients	Lb	Oz	Lb	Oz
Granulated sugar	20		8	
Water	2½		1	
Salted dairy butter	10		4	
Lecithin		2		¾
Coconut oil (76° MP)	3-¾		1-½	
Light molasses	1-¼		½	
Oil-roasted diced almonds	2-½		1	
Vanilla, maple or rum flavor, if desired				

Procedure

Place the butter and coconut oil in a pan, add the lecithin, mix occasionally until the butter is melted, then add the granulated sugar, mixing well.

Add the molasses and water and continue to mix and cook the batch to 290°F. Turn off the heat, add nuts, mixing them just long enough to distribute them throughout the batch, then pour the batch onto a lightly oiled, cool metal slab (not too cold) and rapidly spread or level off the batch to the required height avoiding unnecessary agitation of the batch.

When the batch is partly cool, take a long knife and pass it under the batch to release it from the slab, then cut with a roller knife into pieces of desired size and shape.

Coat the batch with milk chocolate or other coating, then garnish or roll the coated centers in finely ground almonds.

SOURCE: American Molasses Co. Div., SuCrest Corp., 120 Wall St., New York, N.Y.

PEACH CHERI ALMONDINE

Ingredients	
Vanilla pie filling or pudding mix	12 oz (2 cups)
Milk	2 qt
Whipping cream	1 cup
Sherry (optional)	¼ cup
Pound cake	1 lb 2 oz (6 × 4½ × 3 in.)
Cling peach halves	24 halves
Strawberry or raspberry preserves or jelly	1–1½ cup
Sweetened whipped cream	1 oz
Almonds, sliced or diced, toasted	4 oz
Maraschino cherries	12

Yield: 24 servings

Procedure

Gradually add milk to pie filling mix; cook over boiling water, stirring occasionally until mixture begins to thicken. Cook 10 min longer, stirring constantly. Cool slightly. Whip cream to soft peaks and fold into cooled pudding. Fold in sherry. Pour ¼ cup of pudding mixture into serving dishes. Cut cake in ½-in. thick slices. Trim slices to fit on the pudding in the dishes (approximately 2-in. rounds). Cut each peach half into 5 slices and place in a ring around inside of dish. Using 2–3 tsp of preserves or jelly, make a ring on the peach slices around edge of dish. Add another ¼ cup of pudding mixture in center. Top with whipped cream, sliced or diced toasted almonds and a maraschino cherry half.

SOURCE: California Almond Growers Exchange, Sacramento, California.

PEANUT PRODUCTS

BOILING AND CANNING FRESH PEANUTS
(Shelled or Unshelled)

Freshly dug, unshelled peanuts have been boiled in weak brine as a Southern delicacy for more than half a century and are highly prized in many parts of the world.

Freshly boiled salted peanuts have characteristic differences from those processed by any other method. The shells are less glossy than those of cured nuts and are smooth and plump in appearance with a light gray color. The kernels have a firm, slightly gelatinous texture, are moist and quite brittle, with a mild nutty flavor. The seed coats are gray in color with prominent veins.

Any variety of peanuts can be used for boiling or canning. Preference is given to the medium-size Runner or the large Virginia type because of the increased eye appeal and ease of shelling.

The procedure for boiling unshelled peanuts for immediate use or local sales is very similar to that for boiling vegetables, and the steps in canning peanuts shelled or unshelled are also similar to those in canning vegetables. The reasons for boiling or canning peanuts in the shell are: (a) "green" peanuts are difficult to shell, (b) a more pleasing and distinctive flavor results, and (c) a desirable, tender texture is obtained.

Harvest peanuts when fully mature, remove from vine and stems, wash in a mild solution of kitchen detergent, and rinse in clear water. Place the peanuts in a boiler and cover with a medium brine (26° salimeter) made by dissolving 10 oz of salt (1 cup) per gallon of water. Cover the vessel and boil for 45 min or until the kernels are tender. Pour off the water and allow peanuts to drain an hour before placing in serving dishes. The peanuts are ready for shelling and eating immediately, or they may be held in refrigerator humidors for as long as five days.

For canning green peanuts in the shell, prepare peanuts and brine the same as for boiling for immediate use (as just described). Pack the cleaned peanuts into No. 3 cans or 1-qt glass jars to within ½ in. of the top, using equal weights of peanuts and hot brine (212°F). Partially submerge containers in upright position in boiling water, or place in steam box, for 10 min. Seal while hot and process 45 min at 10 lb steam pressure (240°F). Cool containers in water, label, and store away from heat.

SOURCE: Department of Food Science, Georgia Experiment Station, Experiment, Georgia.

BOILING UNSHELLED PEANUTS

Wash peanuts thoroughly in water; then soak in clean water for about 30 min before cooking. Cover completely with water.

The cooking period for boiled peanuts varies according to the maturity of the peanuts used and the variety of peanut. The cooking time for a "freshly-pulled" green peanut is shorter than for a peanut which has been stored. The best way to prepare them is to cook them as soon as they are picked.

There is no firm method for cooking boiled peanuts. The shells of some peanuts absorb more salt than others, so it is best to begin with 5 gm of salt per pint of peanuts. Then add more salt to taste later. The texture of the peanut when fully cooked should be similar to that of a cooked dry pea or bean. Boil the peanuts for about 35 min, then taste. If they are not salted enough, add more salt. Taste again in 10 min, both for salt content and to see if the peanuts are fully cooked. If not ready, continue tasting every 5 min until they have a satisfactory texture. Drain peanuts after cooking, or they will continue to absorb salt and become oversalted.

SOURCE: Georgia Agricultural Commodity Commission for Peanuts, Tifton, Georgia.

SALTING PEANUTS IN THE SHELL

Grade peanuts by removing those that are faulty, broken, or cracked. Immerse the peanuts for 5 min, with stirring, in a detergent solution (1.3 oz of Calgon or Quadrafos per gallon) at 100°F, and rinse in clear water.

Immerse peanuts in saturated brine (3 lb salt per gallon of water), at 100°F, subject to 15-20 in. of vacuum for 30 sec, and release vacuum suddenly. Adjust vacuum and number of repetitions of the process to obtain desired saltiness. Rinse in water.

Centrifuge peanuts for 1 min to remove free water; dry in layers 4 in. deep with air at 115°-130°F and 200 fpm velocity. Discontinue drying when moisture content reaches 7%.

Store at 32°-36°F with 50-60% RH for as long as 1 yr.

SOURCE: *Salting Peanuts in the Shell for Roasting*, Georgia Experiment Station Mimeo Series *N.S.68*.

PRODUCTION OF PARTIALLY DEFATTED PEANUTS

Adjust moisture in raw or blanched shelled peanuts to 5-6%. Subject peanuts to 2000 psi hydraulic pressure for 30 min to remove about 77% of oil.

Reconstitute peanuts by immersing in hot water for 12 min, to increase moisture to 40-50%. Salt or other ingredients may be added during this expansion stage. Dry expanded peanuts to 6% moisture with (a) 105°F air blast, (b) radiant heat, or (c) infrared heat in electric rotissierie; or dry-roast or oil-roast (as shown below) immediately.

The partially defatted raw peanuts should contain 68-75% protein, 19-20% oil, and 8% moisture.

SOURCE: Southern Utilization Research and Development Division, Agricultural Research Service, USDA, New Orleans, Louisiana.

ROASTING PEANUTS

To Dry Roast

Dry roast at 350°F in rotary oven for 15-20 min, or until cream colored; remove and allow to "brown" and cool quickly.

To Oil Roast

Oil roast peanuts for "salting" by immersing in peanut (or other vegetable) oil until cream colored; coat while hot with coconut oil; sprinkle with salt; shake off excess salt and cool quickly.

SOURCE: J. G. Woodroof, Griffin, Georgia.

MATERIALS FOR COATING ROASTED, UNBLANCHED PEANUTS

Prime Coating, Atomized	Raw Coating,* 1/32 in. to 1/16 in. Thick, One or More of the Following "Panned"	Stabilizers	Flavorings (Nonsweet)	Flavorings (Sweet)	Colors
Corn syrup, about 50° Brix	Corn flour	Zein	Cheese	Lemon	Appropriate to Seasoning
	Oat flour	BHA	Garlic	Orange	
	Rice flour	BHT	Onion	Banana	
	Whole wheat flour	Baking powder	Hickory smoke	Malt	
	Sweet potato purée		Cayenne	Vanilla	
	White potato purée		Butter		
	Gum arabic		Black walnut		
	Raw peanut butter		Salt		
			Monosodium glutamate		

*Use 1 part raw coating to 3 parts water heated to 240°F.

SOURCE: J. G. Woodroof, Griffin, Georgia.

FLAVORING ROASTED PEANUTS

For 100 lb blanched peanuts, use 100 lb odorless cooking oil, 20 lb of flavored (wood smoke, barbecue, chicken, dairy butter, etc.) cooking oil, and 2 lb of salt powder.

Roast peanuts in odorless cooking oil at 280°F for 8 min, or until slightly brown; remove and roll in flavored cooking oil at room temperature for 8 min; remove and roll in dry salt powder for 2 min; allow to cool and pack under vacuum. The excess oils may be used many times.

SOURCE: J. G. Woodroof, Griffin, Georgia.

PEANUT BUTTER MANUFACTURE

Peanuts are sold by the farmer to a sheller, who shells, cleans and grades the kernels, and delivers them to the manufacturer. Here the peanut goes through six separate steps.

Roasting

Machinery for the roasting of peanuts for peanut butter must be specially designed and the process is a very careful one, since it is here that flavor and color of the peanut butter will be largely determined. Even and complete development of color from the center of each kernel to the surface is sought, and scorching, excessive oiliness and decomposition of the surface fats must be prevented.

Cooling

When the peanuts are discharged from the roasting cylinder they must be cooled quickly to prevent uneven development of color and prevent excessive liberation of oil. This is done by pulling large masses of air through the batch, using powerful suction fans.

Blanching

By means of a rubbing action (as light or vigorous as necessary depending upon type and quality of peanuts), the red skins are removed and blown into a collector, the kernels are split, and the hearts are taken out. The heart is a small irregular piece containing the germ, which may add a bitter taste to the peanut butter. Skins affect both the appearance and palatability of the peanut butter. The materials removed in the blanching process are sold as by-products: the skins for oil extraction and the hearts for feeding poultry or as a bird seed. Peanuts may also be blanched by water-blanching process.

Cleaning and Hand Picking

Although the peanuts already have gone through complicated handpicking and even an electronically-controlled sorting process at the sheller level, all this is done again by the manufacturer to ensure absolute purity. A hand-picking table and a variety of pneumatic separating devices are used to remove not only any foreign material but shriveled or immature peanut kernels.

Grinding

The peanuts are passed through a set of grinding discs under uniform pressure to produce the peanut butter. The disks can be set for any degree of smoothness desired. "Chunky" peanut butter can be produced on some grinding mills with a special set of grinding plates. This permits pieces of approximately the size of ⅛ kernel to be mixed with the finely-ground peanut butter. Other ingredients are added to most brands of peanut butter to prevent oil separation or to impart a distinctive flavor (honey or other sweeteners are common). Salt, too, is an important flavor ingredient. By federal regulation, a product cannot be labeled peanut butter unless its peanut content is at least 90%.

Packing

Peanut butter in bulk for bakers, candy manufacturers, or other large users may be shipped in drums containing 500 lb. A No. 10 can is frequently used for institutions. Glass jars, of course, are most common in the consumer market, and range in size from 6 oz to 5 lb.

SOURCE: Educational Service, The Peanut growers of Alabama and Georgia, 6 East 43rd St., New York, N.Y.

STABILIZED PEANUT BUTTER

The process of manufacturing peanut butter usually consists of the following steps: (1) Roasting. (2) Cooling and splitting. (3) Removal of skins and hearts (the germ of the peanut). (4) Sorting to remove underquality nuts. (5) Combining and feeding of nuts, sugar, salt, and stabilizer to the grinder.

(6) Grinding. (7) Recycle mixing. (8) Deaeration. (9) Cooling usually by means of a scraped surface cooler. (10) Packaging.

Distilled monoglycerides (MYVEROL 18-00, 18-06, or 18-07) and distilled propylene glycol monoesters (e.g., MYVATEX 57 Food Emulsifier) are effective stabilizers for peanut butter, making possible improved flavor, good protection against oil-out, and reduced stickiness. Use of these monoglyceride products is permitted under the United States FDA Definitions and Standards of Identity for Peanut Butter (21 CFR 46.5).

Procedure

Monoglycerides are metered to the grinder along with the roasted peanuts, 1.5% salt, and 2% sugar. The exact quantity of monoglycerides needed depends on the oil content of the peanuts used, processing conditions, and butter consistency desired. For maximum stabilizer efficiency, the use levels and processing temperatures in the data below are suggested.

Monoglycerides produce firmer, stiffer peanut butter at the higher temperatures of the suggested outlet temperature range than at the lower temperatures in the range. A very soft yet stable peanut butter can be made, for example, by reducing the outlet temperature to about 100°F (38°C) and increasing the level of monoglycerides by 0.5-0.75%.

Stabilizer	Normal Use Level, %	Minimum Grinding Temperature	Heat Exchanger Outlet Temperature
MYVEROL 18-00 or 18-07 (distilled monoglycerides)	1.5-2.5	165°F (74°C)	100°-120°F (38°-49°C)
MYVATEX 57 (distilled propylene glycol monoesters)	1.5-2.0	165°F (74°C)	84°-105°F (29°-41°C)

SOURCE: Eastman Chemical Products, D.P.I. Division, P.O. Box 431, Kingsport, Tenn.

PEANUT-HAMBURGERS

Ingredients	
Ground chuck	6 lb
Eggs	6
Onions, chopped	4 oz
Garlic cloves, minced	3
Salt	1 oz
Black pepper	¼ oz
Parsley, chopped	1 oz
Margarine, melted	8 oz
Peanuts, roasted, chopped	12 oz

Yield: 25 patties

Procedure

Combine meat, eggs, onion, garlic, salt, pepper, and parsley. Shape mixture into patties, brush with margarine and roll in peanuts. Brown patties on both sides over medium heat; lower heat and continue cooking meat to desired doneness (rare, medium, well-done). Serve on bun with catsup or relish.

SOURCE: Georgia Agricultural Commodity Commission for Peanuts, Tifton, Georgia.

PEANUT-BEAN SALAD

Ingredients	
Green beans, cut, cooked	2 lb
Wax beans, cut, cooked	2 lb
Red kidney beans, cooked	2 lb
Green bell peppers, medium chopped	2
Onions, medium, finely chopped	2
Sugar	½ lb
Peanut oil	½ lb
Vinegar, white	1 cup
Salt	2 tsp
Peanuts, shelled, boiled	1 cup

Yield: 6½ lb

Procedure

Drain green and wax beans. Wash kidney beans. Drain all beans 3-4 hr. Then bring sugar and vinegar to a boil. Pour over beans while boiling. When cool, add pepper, onion, salad oil, salt, and peanuts. Allow mixture to set overnight if possible.

SOURCE: J. G. Woodroof, Griffin, Georgia.

SQUASH CASSEROLE (WITH PEANUTS)

Ingredients	
Squash, frozen or fresh	32 oz
Pimientos, canned chopped	2 oz
Onions, grated	2 tbsp
Carrots, grated	4 oz
Cream of Chicken soup	11 oz
Sour cream	1 cup
Stuffing, herb seasoned	8 oz
Peanuts, roasted, chopped	8 oz
Margarine	4 oz

Yield: 10 servings

Procedure

Cook squash as for serving and combine with pimiento, onion, and carrots. Blend soup and sour cream and stir into vegetable mixture. Toss together stuffing, chopped peanuts, and margarine. Pour half the stuffing in a shallow 3-qt baking dish. Pour in vegetable-sour cream mixture. Top with remaining stuffing. Bake at 375°F for 30 min.

SOURCE: Georgia Agricultural Commodity Commission for Peanuts, Tifton, Georgia.

PEANUT-APPLE PUDDING WITH NUTMEG SAUCE

Ingredients	Lb	Oz	Other
Rolled wheat		7	
Water	3		
Butter or margarine		12	
Sugar	3		
Eggs			6
Apples, peeled, chopped	4	4	
All-purpose flour	1	8	
Soda		1/4	
Cinnamon		1/4	
Nutmeg		1/4	
Cloves		1/4	
Salt		1 1/2	
Raw peanuts		12	
Raisins		15	

Procedure

Add rolled wheat to boiling water. Let stand until cool. Cream butter and sugar until fluffy. Add eggs and mix well. Stir in finely chopped apples. Add dry ingredients and mix well. Stir in cooled rolled wheat. Add nuts and raisins. Mix. Spread batter in greased 18 × 26 × 1 in. sheet pan and bake at 350°F for 1 hr. Serve warm with Nutmeg Sauce.

Nutmeg Sauce

Ingredients	
Flour	2 oz
Sugar	2 lb
Water, cold	3 lb
Salt	1/2 oz
Butter	5 oz
Nutmeg	1/4 oz

Procedure

Blend flour, sugar, and salt in saucepan. Stir in water. Bring to boil, stirring constantly for 3 min. Remove from heat and stir in butter and nutmeg.

SOURCE: Oklahoma Peanut Commission, P.O. Box D, Madill, Oklahoma.

PEANUT BRITTLE

Ingredients	Lb	Oz
Peanuts, blanched or unblanched	10	
Sugar	10	
Corn syrup	3	
Water	2	
Margarine		2
Baking soda		2

Yield: 20 lb

Procedure

Combine peanuts, sugar, water, and syrup in copper kettle. Cook on medium heat until syrup turns golden color or until peanuts start popping (approximately 20 min). Remove from heat, add margarine and mix well, add soda and stir thoroughly. Pour on greased slab or belt and stretch with hand or machine; invert and continue to stretch until it begins to harden. Cool, score, and break into bars.

SOURCE: Georgia Agricultural Commodity Commission for Peanuts, Tifton, Georgia.

PEANUT PRALINE FROSTING

Ingredients	Lb	Oz
Butter	3	
Warm water		10
Peanuts, roasted	2	4
Brown sugar	3	
Flour		5

Yield: Will frost 4 12 × 20 in. cakes

Procedure

Melt butter and add warm water. Add remaining ingredients. Spread over hot cake. Return to oven at once for approximately 5 min.

SOURCE: Oklahoma Peanut Commission, P.O. Box D, Madill, Oklahoma.

PEANUT BUTTER FOR ICE CREAM

Ingredients	Lb
Peanuts, any variety, freshly roasted to medium brown color, blanched	97.7
Hydrogenated fat, melting point 130°F	1.3
Salt	1.0
Antioxidant, butylated hydroxyanisole	0.02

Procedure

Select peanuts of U.S. Grade No. 1 or higher, in reference to flavor and texture; roast, blanch, and grind to a smooth texture with particles sufficiently fine to pass through a 30-mesh screen; add premelted hydrogenated fat, salt, and antioxidant during grinding, at a temperature of 165°F; cool in a heat exchanger and pack at 85°F in batch-size containers. Peanut butter made according to the above formula, packed in well-filled containers and held at 70°F does not need an antioxidant for the first six months, but for longer periods of holding, an antioxidant should be added.

SOURCE: J. G. Woodroof, Griffin, Georgia.

PEANUT BUTTER ICE CREAM

Ingredients	Lb
Ice cream mix (water 61.26 lb, sugar 14.6 lb, nonfat milk solids 11.7 lb, butterfat 9.8 lb, stabilizer 0.34 lb)	97
Peanut butter	3

Procedure

Add peanut butter to a small portion of the pasteurized/homogenized ice cream ingredients at 35°F, mix thoroughly, then incorporate in entire batch.

Freezing may be by batch or continuous operation. The ice cream may be stored at −20°F for periods of 6 months or longer.

SOURCE: J. G. Woodroof, Griffin, Georgia.

PEANUT BUTTER BANANA PUDDING

Ingredients	Lb	Oz
Peanut butter	7	4
Mashed bananas	6	
Sugar	2	
Nonfat dry milk	2	
Water	10	
Cornstarch	1	
Vanilla		3½
Nutmeg, optional		1

Yield: 100 servings

Procedure

Blend peanut butter, mashed bananas, sugar, nonfat dry milk and half the water at low speed. Blend remaining water and cornstarch until smooth, and blend into peanut butter mixture. Cook over low heat, stirring constantly until mixture bubbles and thickens. Cover and cool, then stir in vanilla.

Portion pudding into serving dishes. Sprinkle with nutmeg, chill before serving.

SOURCE: United Fruit Sales Corporation, Prudential Center, Boston, Mass.

BUTTER PEANUT BRITTLE

Ingredients	Large Batch		Small Batch	
	Lb	Oz	Lb	Oz
Granulated sugar	40		8	
Water	10		2	
Corn syrup, 42 DE	15		3	
Spanish peanuts (raw)	35		7	
Light molasses	10		2	
Dairy salt butter	2			8
Baking soda		4		1
Salt		2		½

Procedure

Place the sugar, corn syrup, water, and molasses into a kettle. Heat, and occasionally stir the batch until it boils. Allow the batch to boil for a minute or two; then add the raw peanuts and continue the boiling and stir the batch occasionally until the peanuts have been roasted to a light-brown color. The temperature at this stage will be approximately 310°-315°F.

Now add the butter, mixing rapidly; then remove the batch from the heat, sift in the baking soda and salt, mixing rapidly. Promptly spread the batch on a lightly oiled slab, spreading it as thinly as possible. Permit the brittle to partially cool; then cut the batch in half, turning each half upside down, stretching the sheet of peanut brittle as thinly as possible. When the batch has cooled to approximately 100°F, place in tins or other airtight containers.

SOURCE: American Molasses Co. Div., SuCrest Corp., 120 Wall St., New York, N.Y.

PEANUT BUTTER CHILI

Ingredients	
Peanut oil	5 tbsp
Ground beef	5 lb
Tomatoes, cooked	5 lb
Kidney beans, cooked	5 lb
Chili, dry mix	5 oz
Water	1 qt
Green pepper, chopped	1 lb
Onions, chopped	1 lb
Peanut butter	2½

Yield: 30 servings

Procedure

Brown beef in oil. Add chili mix and stir. Add water, tomatoes, onion, pepper, and beans. Bring to a boil and reduce heat. Simmer covered for 10 min; add peanut butter.

SOURCE: Georgia Agricultural Commodity Commission for Peanuts, Tifton, Georgia.

PEANUTTY CUSTARD

Ingredients	
Milk	3 gal.
Peanut butter	3 qt
Eggs	3½ qt
Honey	1½ qt
Salt	½ cup + 1 tbsp

Yield: 100 portions

Procedure

Stir milk into peanut butter until smooth. Beat eggs slightly, and mix in honey and salt. Combine the milk and egg mixtures and pour into four baking pans, 12 × 20 × 2 in. Bake at 325°F for 30 min or until custard is set.

SOURCE: Oklahoma Peanut Commission, P.O. Box D, Madill, Oklahoma.

HONEY-PEANUT BUTTER SAUCE

Ingredients	
Honey	2 lb
Water	1¾ qt
Salt	1 tbsp
Peanut butter	3 lb

Procedure

Combine honey, water, and salt. Bring quickly to a boil. Cool slightly. Gradually add this syrup to peanut butter and beat until smooth.

NOTE: Serve on cottage pudding, ice cream, or other desserts.

SOURCE: Oklahoma Peanut Commission, P.O. Box D, Madill, Oklahoma.

PEACH-PEANUT BUTTER CRISP

Ingredients	Lb
Cling peach slices (3 No. 10 cans)	
California prunes, plumped, pitted, coarsely chopped	2
Butter	2
Sugar	4
Flour	2
Peanut butter	4
Rolled wheat	3

Yield: 100 portions (about ⅔ cup provides ¼ cup fruit, ½ oz peanut butter)

Procedure

Drain peaches. (Save syrup for gelatin salads, etc.) Combine peaches and prunes. Measure about 3 qt into each of 2 sheet pans (26 × 18 × 1 in.) Cream fat and sugar; mix in flour until crumbly; mix in peanut butter and rolled wheat until crumbly. Do not overmix. Sprinkle 5 qt (7 lb) peanut butter mixture over each pan of fruit. Bake at 400°F (hot) 20-25 min, until golden brown.

SOURCE: The Peanut Growers of Alabama and Georgia, 10 East 40th St., New York, N.Y.

RAISIN PEANUT BUTTER SQUARES

Ingredients	Lb	Oz
All-purpose flour	3	
Sugar	1½	
Nonfat dry milk		12
Salt		3
Baking powder		4
Rolled wheat	2	6
Shortening		6
Peanut butter	2	5
Eggs	1	5½
Raisins	3	
Water	4	12
Rolled wheat (see note below)		3

Procedure

Blend dry ingredients. Cream fat, peanut butter, and eggs until smooth. Add dry ingredients, raisins, and water to creamed mixture. Stir just until blended. Pour into 4 greased baking pans (about 12 × 20 × 2 in.), about 9 lb or 2 qt ⅔ cup per pan. Sprinkle with rolled wheat (¾ oz or ¼ cup per pan). Bake about 25 min at 425°F (hot oven).

NOTE: 1½ lb (1½ qt) chopped Spanish peanuts (6 oz or 1½ cups per pan) may be used in place of rolled wheat.

SOURCE: The Peanut Growers of Alabama and Georgia, 10 East 40th St., New York, N.Y.

PEANUT BUTTER SALAD DRESSING

Ingredients	
Peanut butter	1 lb 4 oz
Salad oil	
Vinegar	1 lb
Salt	2 oz
Sugar	1 lb 4 oz
Prepared mustard	2 oz
Paprika	½ oz

Procedure

Combine all ingredients and beat to blend until smooth. Store in refrigerator. Shake before using. Portion with No. 40 scoop (1⅗ tbsp). Serve on fruit salad made from fresh apples, bananas, canned pineapple tidbits, miniature marshmallows, and red maraschino cherry pieces. Or, serve on a vegetable salad made from chopped celery, cucumber slices, chopped green sweet peppers, onion rings, canned red kidney beans, canned sweet peas, canned red peppers, and salt to taste.

SOURCE: Georgia Agricultural Commodity Commission for Peanuts, Tifton, Georgia.

MISCELLANEOUS NUT PRODUCTS
Chestnuts, Filberts (Hazelnuts), Pecans, Walnuts

GLACÉED MIXED NUTS

Ingredients

Sugar	3 lb
Corn syrup, light	2 lb
Pecan halves	1 lb
Walnut halves	1 lb
Brazil nuts, whole	1 lb
Hazelnuts or filberts	1 lb
Almonds	1 lb
Candied red cherries	1 lb
Salt	2 tsp
Butter or margarine	8 tbsp
Vanilla extract	4 tsp

Yield: about 10 lb

Procedure

In a 10-qt saucepan, combine sugar, corn syrup, and 1¼ cup water; stir over medium heat until sugar is dissolved.

Continue cooking, without stirring, to 285°F on candy thermometer, or until a little in cold water separates into threads that are hard but not brittle. Meanwhile, preheat oven to 350°F.

Arrange nuts and cherries in a 9 × 9 × 1¾ in. baking pan, sprinkle with salt. Heat in oven 10 min; keep warm.

Generously butter a 17 × 14 in. cookie sheet. Remove syrup from heat as soon as temperature is reached. Quickly add warm nuts, cherries, butter, and vanilla. Stir rapidly just until butter melts. Immediately pour onto buttered cookie sheet and quickly spread to edge with the back of a wooden spoon.

Cool completely on wire rack, about 1½ hr. Loosen from pan with spatula (if candy sticks, warm and remove candy immediately). Then break into irregular pieces. Store in airtight container. If desired, substitute canned salted mixed nuts for all nuts and omit salt.

SOURCE: *Nuts in Family Meals*, USDA Home and Garden Bull. *176*.

CHESTNUT STROGANOFF

Ingredients

Beef, boneless, tender, lean, cut in julienne strips	6 lb
Fat or oil	4 tbsp
Butter or margarine	8 tbsp
Flour	8 tbsp
Onion salt	2 tsp
Paprika	2 tsp
Salt	1 tsp
Beef bouillon or beef broth	6 cups
Sour cream	2 cups
Cooking sherry (optional)	4 tbsp
Chestnuts, cooked, mashed*	4 cups
Baked potatoes, cooked rice, or noodles (as desired)	

Yield: 25 servings

Procedure

Lightly brown the meat in fat or oil in frying pan over moderate heat, and drain off excess fat. Melt butter or margarine in saucepan, and blend in seasonings and flour. Add bouillon or broth slowly, stirring constantly. Stir and cook until smooth and bubbly. Remove from heat. Blend in sour cream, sherry, and chestnuts. Add chestnut sauce to meat. Heat just until mixture bubbles, stirring constantly. Serve over potatoes, rice, or noodles.

---

*To prepare mashed chestnuts: Cook 6 cups shelled, blanched chestnuts in 6 cups boiling water in covered pan for about 30 min or until tender. Drain and mash.

SOURCE: *Nuts in Family Meals*, USDA Home and Garden Bull. *176*.

CHESTNUT STUFFING

Ingredients

Butter or margarine	1 cup
Onions, finely ground	1 cup
Celery, chopped stalk and leaves	1 cup
Mushrooms, chopped	1 cup
Salt	4 tsp
Thyme	2 tsp
Poultry seasoning	2 tsp
Cayenne pepper	dash
Garlic salt	dash
Bread crumbs	8 cups

Chicken or beef bouillon	2 cups
Chestnuts, cooked, finely chopped*	1½ lb

Yield: 25 servings

Procedure

Melt fat in heavy pan. Add onions, celery, mushrooms, and seasoning. Cook a few minutes until celery is tender but still crisp, stirring occasionally. Add bread crumbs, bouillon, and nuts. Mix lightly but well. Put stuffing in baking pans and bake 25-30 min, or until slightly brown. Serve with breast of chicken, veal, or lamb.

---

*Almonds, cashews, filberts, peanuts or pecans may be substituted for chestnuts.

SOURCE: *Nuts in Family Meals*, USDA Home and Garden Bull. *176*.

INSTANT PECAN PIE MIX

Ingredients	100-Lb Batch	
	Lb	Oz
Corn syrup solids (dried DE 24-28)	52	3
Sugar, dark brown	23	12
Whole egg, dried (optional)	7	14
Salt		6
Pecan meats	15	13

Procedure

The dry pie filling mix is made by blending dry corn syrup solids, dark brown sugar, dry whole eggs, salt, and nutmeats in the proportion as shown. The ingredients should be fresh, of the highest quality, and very dry. It is optional whether dry egg powder is added to the mix, or whether one fresh egg is added to each pie along with water, margarine and vanilla in the proportions given below.

The package for dry pecan pie filling should hold 16 oz of the mix or sufficient for one pie, and may be metal, glass or plastic. It must be airtight, moisture-vapor-proof, and preferably vacuum closed. Caking of the ingredients and rancidity of fats are the chief problems.

To Use

For use, the ingredients of each package are mixed with ¾ cup water, 3 tbsp oleomargarine, and 1 tsp vanilla and poured into a pie shell for baking. Bake at 350°F for 50 min or until the crust is golden brown.

When poured into the crust the pecan meats float to the surface.

SOURCE: E. K. Heaton, Georgia Experiment Station, Experiment, Georgia.

PECAN BUTTER

Ingredients	Lb	Oz
Pecan meats, toasted at 375°F for 12 min	100	
Salt	1	
Hydrogenated fat	2	8
Dextrose	2	8
Antioxidant, butylated hydroxyanisole		0.01

Yield: 200 8-oz containers

Procedure

Grind all ingredients together to fineness so that 98% will pass through 200-mesh screen. If the heat generated during grinding is 150°F, or sufficient to melt the hydrogenated fat, no further mixing is necessary, otherwise it is necessary to heat the butter to this temperature, with slow stirring, for 5 min. Package in airtight and greaseproof metal or glass containers of 6-, 8-, or 16-oz size. Vacuum packaging is preferred.

SOURCE: E. K. Heaton, Georgia Experiment Station, Experiment, Georgia.

CANNING PECANS

Pecan meats can be protected from insects, mold, and rapid development of rancidity by hermetic canning as follows:

Dry meats slowly to 3% moisture (until they are crisp and "rattle" when shaken in the hand), using air draft at 250°F or lower.

Pack hot meats in glass or metal containers and seal.

Process under 5 lb steam pressure for 10 min, or in boiling water for 30 min.

Cool and store in dry place, preferably under refrigeration.

SOURCE: *Pecans for Processing*, University of Georgia College of Agriculture Experiment Station Bull. *N.S. 80*.

ORANGE PECAN FROSTING

Ingredients	
Butter or margarine	1¼ lb
Confectioners sugar	5 lb
Egg yolks, beaten	5
Orange juice	1 cup
Orange rind, grated	8 tsp
Pecans, chopped	2½ lb

Procedure

Cream butter. Gradually add 1 cup of the sugar while beating constantly. Add remaining sugar alternately with egg yolk which has been beaten and blended with orange juice and rind. Spread on cooled cake. Sprinkle pecans on top of cake.

SOURCE: Georgia Pecan Growers Association, Albany, Georgia.

PECAN PRALINES, NO. 1

Ingredients	
Sugar	9 lb
Salt	1 tsp
Water	5 lb
Butter/margarine	¼ lb
Maple flavoring	2½ tsp
Pecan halves	5 lb

Yield: 12½ lb

Procedure

Melt ½ of sugar in a frying pan over low heat, stirring constantly, until sugar forms a pale yellow syrup. Remove from heat and let stand 5 min. Add salt, water, and remaining sugar. Stir carefully until caramel is dissolved. Add butter and cook to 263°F (soft ball stage), stirring constantly. Remove from heat. Let cool about 5 min. Add flavoring and pecans and stir until mixture becomes creamy. Drop by teaspoonfuls onto waxed paper.

SOURCE: Georgia Pecan Growers Association, Albany, Georgia.

PECAN PRALINES, NO. 2

Ingredients	Large Batch	Small Batch
	Lb	Lb
Granulated sugar	25	5
Light molasses	5	1
Invert sugar (Nulomoline)	5	1
Evaporated milk	5	1
Coconut oil (76° MP)	1¼	¼
Pecans	10	2½

Procedure

Place the sugar, molasses, Nulomoline, evaporated milk, and coconut oil into a kettle, mix well, stir the batch occasionally until it boils. Then cook the batch to 238°F.

Set the batch aside and allow it to cool to 215°F. Add sufficient pecans. Then rub a little of batch against the side of the kettle to produce a grain, mixing this thoroughly with the batch proper. Then ladle the batch out to form patties.

The use of molasses, which, when combined with granulated sugar will produce a delightfully flavored brown sugar taste.

SOURCE: American Molasses Co. Div., SuCrest Corp., 120 Wall St., New York, N.Y.

SPICED PECANS

Ingredients	
Sugar	1 lb
Evaporated milk	⅔ cup
Cinnamon	2 tsp
Butter or margarine	2 tbsp
Vanilla	2 tsp
Salt	2 tsp
Pecan halves	2 lb

Procedure

In a saucepan or kettle combine sugar, evaporated milk, cinnamon, and butter; bring to rolling boil for 1 min. Stir in vanilla, salt, and pecan halves. Pour onto slightly buttered baking sheet, cool, and separate pecan halves.

SOURCE: J. G. Woodroof, Griffin, Georgia.

CARAMEL PRALINES

Ingredients	Large Batch		Small Batch	
	Lb	Oz	Lb	Oz
Evaporated milk	15		5	
Granulated sugar	15		5	
Light molasses	1½			8
Salted dairy butter		6		2
Coconut oil (86° MP)		6		2
Invert sugar (Nulomoline)	4½		1½	
Corn syrup 42 DE	9		3	
Salt		3		1
Pecans	4½		1½	
Vanilla flavor				

Procedure

Place corn syrup, Nulomoline, coconut oil, butter, molasses, and sugar into a kettle. Add about ⅓ of the evaporated milk, mix well; heat and stir the batch until it boils. Gradually add the remainder of the evaporated milk (a pint at a time), keeping the batch constantly boiling, and stirring constantly. Cook to approximately 244°-246°F; add salt, flavor, and pecans. Mix well, then form the batch into patties of the desired size and, when they are cool, wrap in cellophane.

SOURCE: American Molasses Co., Div., SuCrest Corp., 120 Wall St., New York, N.Y.

PIÑON NUTS

Piñon or pine nuts are salted, used in confections, bakery goods or ice cream. Processing is similar to that of pecans except the response to heat is much more quickly, due to the small size. The composition (about 3.0% moisture, 15% protein, and 60% fat) is similar to that of pecans. Piñon nuts have a very delicate, slightly piny flavor.

SOURCE: *The Composition and Value of Piñon Nuts*, New Mexico Agriculture Experiment Station, State College, New Mexico.

APRICOT WALNUT SQUARES

Ingredients	
Apricots, canned halves	6 lb 12 oz
Cornstarch	2½ oz
Apricot juice	1 lb
Sugar, granulated	2 lb 10 oz
English walnuts, chopped	8 oz
Flour, hard wheat, sifted	2 lb
Baking powder	1½ tbsp
Salt	1½ tsp
Baking soda	1½ tsp
Rolled oats	1 lb 6 oz
Sugar, granulated	2 lb 10 oz
Butter or margarine	2 lb

Yield: 48 squares 3 × 3 × ¼ in. from 1 sheet pan 18 × 26 in.

Procedure

1. Drain apricots; chop coarsely. Reserve 2 cups juice for use in Step 2.
2. Add cornstarch to apricot juice and stir to form a smooth paste.
3. Combine apricots, juice-cornstarch mixture, and the first 2 lb 10 oz of sugar in heavy pot. Stir and cook over low heat until smooth and clear. Remove from heat and cool to lukewarm.
4. Add chopped walnuts to apricot mixture and reserve for use in Step 6.
5. Sift flour, baking powder, salt, and soda together into mixer bowl. Add rolled oats, the second 2 lb 10 oz of sugar and butter or margarine and mix at low speed to form a coarse crumb.
6. Pat ⅔ of flour mixture evenly on bottom of sheet pan. Spread apricot-walnut mixture over flour mixture in sheet pan.
7. Sprinkle remaining flour mixture evenly over apricot-walnut mixture.
8. Bake about 40 min in a preheated moderate (375°F) oven or until lightly browned.
9. Cut each pan 6 × 8.

SOURCE: *Tested Recipes for Nursing Homes*, Theodore R. Sills, Chicago, Illinois.

APPLE 'N FILBERT PUDDING

Ingredients	Lb	Oz
Bread, crusts removed	1	8
Cream, light	1	12
Butter	1	
Sugar		8
Ground filberts		10½
Egg yolks, 9		
Egg whites, 9		
Sugar	½	
Canned apple slices, drained	3¼ (½ No. 10 can)	

Yield: 40 ½-cup servings

Procedure

Soak bread in cream.

Cream butter and sugar; add ground filberts, egg yolks and soaked bread.

Beat mixture well.

Whip egg whites with sugar until stiff; fold into filbert mixture.

Pour half of pudding into buttered 10 × 18-in. pan; cover with layer of apples and pour remaining batter over apples. Bake in 375°F oven for 40-50 min or until set.

Serve with Melba Sauce.

SOURCE: Theodore R. Sills, 39 S. LaSalle St., Chicago, Illinois.

FILBERT BUTTER FOR VEGETABLES

Season 12 lb of freshly-cooked vegetables with 2 cups of sliced or chopped filberts that have been browned in 8 oz of butter or margarine.

Yield: 50 servings

SOURCE: Theodore R. Sills, 39 S. LaSalle St., Chicago, Illinois.

FILBERT-CHEESE SAUCE FOR VEGETABLES

Ingredients	
Medium white sauce	1 gal.
Sharp cheddar cheese, grated or ground	3 lb
Worcestershire sauce	2 tbsp
Cayenne pepper (to taste)	
Filberts, sliced or chopped and toasted	2 cups

Yield: 50 servings

Procedure

Add the cheese, Worcestershire sauce, and cayenne pepper to the white sauce.

Pour over hot cooked vegetable and sprinkle with toasted filberts.

To make au gratin vegetables mix the nuts with buttered crumbs and sprinkle on.

SOURCE: Theodore R. Sills, 39 S. LaSalle St., Chicago, Illinois.

MAPLE FILBERT BUTTER CREAM FROSTING

Ingredients	
Butter or margarine	8 oz
Confectioners' sugar	3 lb 12 oz
Egg whites	8 oz
Salt	1¼ tsp
Vanilla	1¼ tbsp
Maple flavoring	1¼ tbsp
Cream or evaporated milk	¼-¾ cups
Chopped filberts (hazelnuts)	14 oz
Sliced filberts (hazelnuts), for garnish	

Yield: 4 2-layer cakes, 48 or 56 cuts

Procedure

Cream butter in mixer until very soft.

Add sugar and mix on low speed until well blended.

Add egg whites and beat on low speed until light and fluffy.

Add salt, vanilla, and maple flavoring.

Thin with cream until of right consistency to spread easily.

Add chopped filberts. Spread between layers, on sides and top of cake. Garnish with sliced filberts.

SOURCE: Theodore R. Sills, 39 S. LaSalle St., Chicago, Illinois.

FILBERT CRUNCH DESSERT

Ingredients	
Whole eggs	3 cups
Sugar, granulated	2½ lb
Salt	1 tsp
Gingersnaps, finely crushed	1 lb
Filberts, chopped or sliced and toasted	10 oz

Procedure

Beat eggs thoroughly. Gradually beat in sugar and salt and continue beating for several minutes. Fold in toasted nuts and gingersnaps. Spread in greased 9-in. pie pans and bake at 325°F. for 30 minutes. Serve topped with ice cream or whipped cream.

SOURCE: *Institutions Magazine*, Chicago, Illinois.

FILBERT DESSERT ROLL

Ingredients	
Egg yolks	3 doz
Sugar	1 lb 14 oz
Finely ground filberts	2½ lb
Baking powder	2 tbsp
Salt	¾ tsp
Egg whites, stiffly beaten	3 doz
Confectioners' sugar (as needed)	
Vanilla pudding, chocolate pudding, whipped cream or seafoam icing (as needed for filling)	

Yield: 6 cakes

Procedure

Beat egg yolks until thick and lemon colored.

Gradually beat in sugar.

Stir in filberts, baking powder, and salt.

Gently fold in egg whites. Spread batter in 6 greased and paper-lined 10 × 15-in. pans.

Bake at 350° 15 min. Turn out on towels dusted with sifted confectioners' sugar. Trim edges; peel off paper and roll up to cool.

Unroll cakes, spread with desired filling. Roll up and chill. Garnish with additional filling and sliced filberts.

SOURCE: Theodore R. Sills, 39 S. LaSalle St., Chicago, Illinois.

FILBERT NUGGETS

Ingredients	Lb	Oz
Sugar	2	
Shortening	1	10

	Lb	Oz
Salt		½
Eggs		12
Pastry flour	2	8
Filberts, chopped	2	8
Macaroon coconut	2	
Vanilla		½
Filberts for topping (as needed)		

Yield: 11 lb 4 oz batter (360 nuggets)

Procedure

Scale all ingredients except the filberts for topping, and place in mixing bowl.

Mix until well blended.

Roll 12-oz pieces of dough into long round strips; cut into ½-oz pieces.

Place pieces on 18 × 26 in. sheet pans, and pinch dough to create an uneven appearance. For an attractive appearance, pieces of dough may be dipped in additional chopped filberts before placing on pans.

Bake at 375° for 12–15 min.

Note: This is a crunchy type of cookie.

SOURCE: Theodore R. Sills, 39 S. LaSalle St., Chicago, Illinois.

FILBERT MOCK HOLLANDAISE

Ingredients	
Milk, hot	1½ qt
Butter, melted	6 oz
Flour	3 oz
Salt	1 tsp
Pepper	½ tsp
Egg yolks, unbeaten	12
Butter	1 lb
Lemon juice	½ cup
Filberts, sliced and toasted	3⅓ cups

Yield: 50 servings

Procedure

Prepare a white sauce of the first five ingredients.

Add 1 egg yolk at a time, a little butter, and a little lemon juice until all are added. Beat well.

Pour over hot cooked vegetable and sprinkle with toasted filberts.

SOURCE: Theodore R. Sills, 39 S. LaSalle St., Chicago, Illinois.

FILBERT CREAM

Ingredients	
Egg yolks	1⅓ cups
Sugar	1 lb
Milk	1½ lb
Rum	⅓ cup
Vanilla	2 tsp
Milk	8 oz
Gelatine	6 oz
Heavy cream, whipped	2 lb
Chopped toasted filberts	8 oz
Fresh or frozen sugared raspberries or strawberries	6 cups

Yield: 24 servings with 2 oz of sauce

Procedure

Beat egg yolks with sugar until light and creamy. Gradually stir in milk and cook until mixture coats a spoon. Stir in rum and vanilla.

Soften gelatine in remaining milk and stir into hot mixture. Chill until it begins to set. Fold in whipped cream and chopped filberts.

Pour mixture into 2 6-cup oiled molds or 24 ½-cup molds. Chill until firm.

Unmold cream and garnish with whipped cream and raspberries or strawberries, if desired.

SOURCE: Theodore R. Sills, 39 S. LaSalle St., Chicago, Illinois.

CHOCOLATE FILBERT DIAMONDS

Ingredients	Lb	Oz
Toasted filberts		13
Semisweet chocolate squares	2	
Egg whites, unbeaten		8
Confectioners' sugar		14

Yield: 12 doz

Procedure

Put filberts and 12 squares of the chocolate through food grinder using medium blade.

Add egg whites and sugar; blend well.

Shape into rectangle ¼-in. thick on waxed paper or foil; let stand overnight to dry.

Melt remaining chocolate over very low heat; spread over surface of rectangle.

Refrigerate until firm; cut into strips 1 in. wide. Cut diagonally to form diamonds.

SOURCE: Theodore R. Sills, 39 S. LaSalle St., Chicago, Illinois.

FILBERT SOUP

Ingredients	
Butter, melted	1 lb
Celery, diced	2½ lb

Onions, diced	3 lb
Flour, all-purpose	10 oz
Salt	3 tbsp + 1 tsp
Worcestershire sauce	2 tbsp + 1½ tsp
Black pepper	1¼ tsp
Milk	10 lb
Chicken bouillon	9 lb
Filberts, ground	5 cups (1¼ lb)
Filberts, chopped	5 cups (1¼ lb)

Yield: 50–60 servings

Procedure

Heat butter in large kettle and sauté onions and celery.

Stir in flour, salt, Worcestershire sauce, and pepper. Slowly stir in milk, bouillon, and ground filberts.

Blend well and simmer 15 min. Serve hot. Garnish with chopped filberts.

SOURCE: Theodore R. Sills, 39 S. LaSalle St., Chicago, Illinois.

FROSTED FILBERT STRIPS

Ingredients

Egg whites	1 cup
Confectioners' sugar, sifted	2 lb
Toasted filberts, ground	2 lb
Vanilla	1 tbsp
Additional confectioners' sugar	

Yield: 12 doz

Procedure

Beat egg whites until frothy; gradually beat in confectioners' sugar. Continue beating for 15 min.

Divide mixture in half. Add filberts and vanilla to ½ of mixture.

Roll filbert mixture to ¼-in. thickness on a board, using additional sifted confectioners' sugar to prevent mixture from sticking.

Cut into 3 × ¾-in. strips. Place strips on lightly greased baking sheets.

Frost each strip with remaining half of egg white mixture.

Bake in 325° (slow) oven 20 min or until edges are very lightly browned.

SOURCE: Theodore R. Sills, 39 S. LaSalle St., Chicago, Illinois.

GRAHAM-FILBERT TORTE

Ingredients

Egg whites	2 doz
Sugar	14 oz
Egg yolks	2 doz
Sugar	1 lb 5 oz
Vanilla	1½ tbsp
Graham cracker crumbs	1 lb 12 oz
Coarsely ground filberts	1 lb 12 oz
Baking powder	4 tsp
Salt	2 tsp
Vanilla pudding mix	12 oz
Milk	1½ qt
Grated orange rind	¼ cup
Heavy cream, whipped	1 qt
Sliced filberts	1 lb
Mandarin oranges, drained (optional)	1 lb

Yield: 4 9-in. cakes

Procedure

Beat egg whites to soft peaks; gradually beat in the 14 oz of sugar, beating to stiff peaks.

Beat egg yolks till thick and lemon-colored. Gradually beat in the 1 lb 5 oz of sugar and vanilla.

Combine crumbs, filberts, baking powder, and salt; stir into egg yolk mixture.

Fold filbert mixture into egg whites.

Turn into 12 paper-lined 9-in. cake pans. Bake at 350°F 30 min. Cool in pans by inverting on edges of other pans.

Prepare pudding mix with milk and orange rind according to label directions and chill.

Fold only 1 pt of the whipped cream into pudding, reserving remaining whipped cream to garnish top.

Stack layers with pudding in between to form 4 3-layer cakes.

Frost or garnish top with pudding mixture and whipped cream, mandarin oranges (optional) or filberts. Chill until served.

SOURCE: Theodore R. Sills, 39 S. LaSalle St., Chicago, Illinois.

FILDORF SALAD

Ingredients

Mayonnaise or cooked salad dressing	1 pt
Whipped cream	½ cup
Apples, tart, unpeeled, diced	8 lb
Celery, chopped	2 lb
Filberts, sliced or chopped	8 oz
Maraschino cherries, diced	8 oz
Salt	1½ tbsp
Sugar (may omit)	6 oz

Yield: 50 ⅓-cup servings

Courtesy of L. H. MacDaniels

FIG. 19.1. THREE VARIETIES OF FILBERTS, SHELLED AND UNSHELLED

(A) Barcelona—thick shell; (B) hybrid with *C. americana*—thin shell; and (C) hybrid with thick shell.

Procedure

Mix together mayonnaise and whipped cream.

Add each apple to dressing as soon as diced.

Add celery, filberts, maraschino cherries, salt, and sugar. Blend together and serve with No. 12 dipper on crisp lettuce.

SOURCE: Theodore R. Sills, 39 S. LaSalle St., Chicago, Illinois.

LINZER TARTLETS

Ingredients	Lb	Oz
Butter	1	
All-purpose flour		6
Sugar		8
Filberts, ground		12
Cake crumbs, sifted		7
Chocolate, grated		3
Jam		14
Filberts, chopped		2

Yield: 25 servings

Procedure

Combine butter, flour, sugar, filberts, crumbs, and chocolate to form a dough; chill for ½ hr.

Roll dough to ⅛ in. thickness, cut with circle cutter; bake on ungreased baking sheet for 10 min at 300°F.; remove and cool.

Spread jam on baked circle, place another circle of baked dough on top and frost with Chocolate Icing and sprinkle with chopped filberts.

Chocolate Icing

Ingredients	Oz
Sugar	8
Water	3½
Chocolate, melted	4½
Butter	½

Procedure

Cook together sugar and water until it spins a heavy thread; add to melted chocolate, stirring constantly until smooth and mixture coats a spoon.

SOURCE: Theodore R. Sills, 39 S. LaSalle St., Chicago, Illinois.

MARMORA MERINGUE CRINKLES

Ingredients	
Egg whites	1½ cups
Salt	¼ tsp
Brown sugar, firmly packed, sifted	2 lb 12 oz
Toasted filberts, ground	2 lb
Vanilla	2 tsp
Granulated sugar	

Yield: 10 doz

Procedure

Beat egg whites and salt together until soft peaks form.

Gradually add brown sugar, ¼ cup at a time, beating well after each addition.

Fold in filberts and vanilla. Chill.

Drop by teaspoonfuls into bowl of granulated sugar. Lightly shape into 1-in. balls.

Place on greased baking sheets and bake in 325°F (slow) oven 20–30 min or until lightly browned.

SOURCE: Theodore R. Sills, 39 S. LaSalle St., Chicago, Illinois.

TURKISH TARTELLES

Ingredients	
Butter or margarine	¾ lb
Granulated sugar	3 cups
Lemon peel, grated	2 tsp
Egg yolks	½ cup
All-purpose flour, sifted	3 cups
Egg whites	¼ cup
Water	2 tbsp
Toasted filberts (hazelnuts), finely chopped	2 cups (8 oz)
Nutmeg	½ tsp
Cinnamon	1 tbsp

Yield: 12 doz

Procedure

Cream butter with 2 cups sugar and lemon peel.

Beat in egg yolks gradually.

Add flour and stir until blended. *Chill* dough until firm.

Shape into ½-in. balls. Flatten balls on greased baking sheets.

Beat egg whites with water until foamy.

Combine filberts with remaining cup of sugar and the spices.

Brush dough with egg whites and sprinkle with filbert mixture.

Bake in 375°F oven 8–10 min or until lightly browned.

SOURCE: Theodore R. Sills, 39 S. LaSalle St., Chicago, Illinois.

APPENDIX

COOKING TEMPERATURES OF WATER
(From Sea Level to 7500 ft Altitude with Barometric Pressure Constant in Relation to That At Sea Level of 760 MM)

Altitude Ft	Boiling Point of Water °F	Altitude Ft	Boiling Point of Water °F
Sea level	212	4000	204
500	211	4500	203
1000	210	5000	202
1500	209	5500	201
2000	208	6000	200
2500	207	6500	199
3000	206	7000	198
3500	205	7500	197

BOILING POINT OF SUGAR SOLUTIONS

Strength %	Boiling Point °F	Strength %	Boiling Point °F
40.0	214.3	95.0	284.0
50.0	215.0	97.0	303.0
60.0	217.5	98.2	320.0
65.0	219.0	99.5	330.0
80.0	230.0	99.6	340.0
90.0	253.0		

DATA FOR PREPARING JELLIES CONFORMING TO FEDERAL REGULATIONS USING FRUIT JUICES OF DIFFERENT SOLUBLE SOLIDS CONCENTRATIONS

TABLE A.1

CRAB APPLE

Average Soluble Solids Content—15.4%				
% Soluble Solids in Juice	Pounds Sugar Per 5 Gallons Juice	Gallons Juice Per 100 Pounds Sugar	Pounds Juice Per 100 Pounds Sugar	Pounds Juice Per Gallon
11.0	38	13¼	115	8.69
11.2	38½	13	112½	8.70
11.4	39½	12¾	110½	8.70
11.6	40	12½	108½	8.71
11.8	40½	12¼	107	8.72
12.0	41½	12	105	8.72
12.2	42½	12	103½	8.73
12.4	43	11½	101½	8.74
12.6	43½	11½	100	8.75
12.8	44½	11¼	98½	8.75
13.0	45	11	97	8.76
13.2	46	10¾	95½	8.77
13.4	46½	10¾	94	8.77
13.6	47½	10½	93	8.78
13.8	48	10½	91½	8.79
14.0	49	10¼	90	8.80
14.2	49½	10	89	8.80
14.4	50½	10	87½	8.81
14.6	51	9¾	86½	8.82
14.8	52	9¾	85	8.82
15.0	52½	9½	84	8.83
15.5	54½	9¼	81½	8.85
16.0	56	9	79	8.87
16.5	58	8½	76½	8.88
17.0	60	8½	74	8.90
17.5	62	8¼	72	8.92
18.0	64	8	70	8.94
18.5	65½	7¾	68	8.96
19.0	67½	7½	66½	8.98
19.5	69½	7¼	65	8.99
20.0	71½	7	63	9.01

SOURCE: *The Almanac of the Canning, Freezing, Preserving Industries* published by The Canning Trade, Baltimore, Maryland.

DATA FOR PREPARING JELLIES CONFORMING TO FEDERAL REGULATIONS USING FRUIT JUICES OF DIFFERENT SOLUBLE SOLIDS CONCENTRATIONS

TABLE A.2

APRICOT, CHERRY, ALL PLUM, GRAPE, PINEAPPLE

Average Soluble Solids Content—14.3%

% Soluble Solids in Juice	Pounds Sugar Per 5 Gallons Juice	Gallons Juice Per 100 Pounds Sugar	Pounds Juice Per 100 Pounds Sugar	Pounds Juice Per Gallon
9.0	33	15	130	8.62
9.2	34	14¾	127	8.63
9.4	34½	14½	124½	8.63
9.6	35½	14¼	122	8.64
9.8	36	14	119	8.65
10.0	37	13½	117	8.66
10.2	37½	13¼	115	8.66
10.4	38½	13	112½	8.67
10.6	39½	12¾	110½	8.68
10.8	40	12½	108	8.68
11.0	41	12¼	106½	8.69
11.2	41½	12	104½	8.70
11.4	42½	11¾	102½	8.70
11.6	43½	11¾	101	8.71
11.8	44	11½	99	8.72
12.0	44½	11¼	97½	8.72
12.2	45½	11	96	8.73
12.4	46½	10¾	94½	8.74
12.6	47	10¾	93	8.75
12.8	48	10½	91½	8.75
13.0	48½	10¼	90	8.76
13.5	50½	10	86½	8.78
14.0	52½	9½	83½	8.80
14.5	54½	9¼	81	8.81
15.0	56½	9	78	8.83
15.5	58½	8½	75½	8.85
16.0	60½	8¼	73	8.87
16.5	62½	8	71	8.88
17.0	64½	7¾	69	8.90
17.5	66½	7½	67	8.92
18.0	68½	7¼	65	8.94
18.5	71	7	63	8.96
19.0	73	7	61½	8.98
19.5	75	6¾	60	8.99
20.0	77	6½	58½	9.01
20.5	79	6½	57	9.03
21.0	81	6¼	56	9.05
21.5	83½	6	54½	9.07
22.0	85½	6	53	9.09
22.5	87½	5¾	52	9.11
23.0	90	5½	51	9.13
23.5	91½	5½	50	9.14
24.0	94	5½	49	9.16
24.5	96	5¼	48	9.18
25.0	98	5	47	9.20

SOURCE: *The Almanac of the Canning, Freezing, Preserving Industries* published by The Canning Trade, Baltimore, Maryland.

DATA FOR PREPARING JELLIES CONFORMING TO FEDERAL REGULATIONS USING FRUIT JUICES OF DIFFERENT SOLUBLE SOLIDS CONCENTRATIONS

TABLE A.3

APPLE, QUINCE

Average Soluble Solids Content—13.3%				
% Soluble Solids in Juice	Pounds Sugar Per 5 Gallons Juice	Gallons Juice Per 100 Pounds Sugar	Pounds Juice Per 100 Pounds Sugar	Pounds Juice Per Gallon
8.0	31½	16	136½	8.59
8.2	32½	15½	133	8.59
8.4	33	15	130	8.60
8.6	34	14¾	127	8.61
8.8	35	14½	124	8.61
9.0	35½	14	121½	8.62
9.2	36½	13¾	118½	8.63
9.4	37	13½	116	8.63
9.6	38	13¼	114	8.64
10.0	39½	12¾	109½	8.66
10.2	40½	12½	107	8.67
10.4	41	12¼	105	8.67
10.6	42	12	103	8.68
10.8	43	11¾	101	8.68
11.0	43½	11½	99½	8.69
11.2	44½	11¼	97½	8.70
11.4	45½	11	96	8.70
11.6	46	10¾	94	8.71
11.8	47	10¾	93	8.72
12.0	48	10½	91	8.72
12.2	48½	10¼	89½	8.73
12.4	49½	10	88	8.74
12.6	50½	10	87	8.75
12.8	51	9¾	85½	8.75
13.0	52	9¾	84	8.76
13.2	53	9½	83	8.77
13.4	53½	9¼	81½	8.77
13.6	54½	9¼	80½	8.78
13.8	55½	9	79	8.79
14.0	56	9	78	8.80
14.2	57	8¾	77	8.80
14.4	58	8¾	76	8.81
14.6	59	8½	75	8.82
14.8	60	8½	74	8.82
15.0	60½	8¼	73	8.83
15.5	62½	8	70½	8.85
16.0	65	7¾	68½	8.87
16.5	67	7½	66	8.88
17.0	69	7¼	64½	8.90
17.5	71½	7	62½	8.92
18.0	73½	6¾	60½	8.94
18.5	76	6¾	59	8.96
19.0	78	6½	57½	8.98

SOURCE: *The Almanac of the Canning, Freezing, Preserving Industries* published by The Canning Trade, Baltimore, Maryland.

DATA FOR PREPARING JELLIES CONFORMING TO FEDERAL REGULATIONS USING FRUIT JUICES OF DIFFERENT SOLUBLE SOLIDS CONCENTRATIONS

TABLE A.4

ORANGE

Average Soluble Solids Content—12.5%

% Soluble Solids in Juice	Pounds Sugar Per 5 Gallons Juice	Gallons Juice Per 100 Pounds Sugar	Pounds Juice Per 100 Pounds Sugar	Pounds Juice Per Gallon
9.0	38	13¼	114	8.62
9.2	38½	13	111½	8.63
9.4	39½	12¾	109	8.63
9.6	40½	12¼	107	8.64
9.8	41½	12	104½	8.65
10.0	42	11¾	102½	8.66
10.2	43	11½	100½	8.66
10.4	44	11¼	98½	8.67
10.6	45	11¼	96½	8.68
10.8	45½	11	95	8.68
11.0	46½	10¾	93	8.69
11.2	47½	10½	91½	8.70
11.4	48½	10¼	90	8.70
11.6	49½	10¼	88½	8.71
11.8	50	10	87	8.72
12.0	51	9¾	85½	8.72
12.2	52	9½	84	8.73
12.4	53	9½	82½	8.74
12.6	53½	9¼	81½	8.74
12.8	54½	9¼	80	8.75
13.0	55½	9	79	8.76
13.2	56½	8¾	77½	8.77
13.4	57½	8¾	76½	8.77
13.6	58½	8½	75½	8.78
13.8	59	8½	74½	8.79
14.0	60	8⅓	73	8.80
14.2	61	8¼	72	8.80
14.4	62	8	71	8.81
14.6	63	8	70	8.82
14.8	63½	7¾	69½	8.82
15.0	64½	7¾	68½	8.83
15.5	67	7½	66	8.85
16.0	69½	7¼	64	8.87
16.5	71½	7	62	8.88
17.0	74	6¾	60½	8.90

SOURCE: *The Almanac of the Canning, Freezing, Preserving Industries* published by The Canning Trade, Baltimore, Maryland.

DATA FOR PREPARING JELLIES CONFORMING TO FEDERAL REGULATIONS USING FRUIT JUICES OF DIFFERENT SOLUBLE SOLIDS CONCENTRATIONS

TABLE A.5

CRANBERRY, LOGANBERRY, RED RASPBERRY, RED CURRANT

Average Soluble Solids Content—10.5%

% Soluble Solids in Juice	Pounds Sugar Per 5 Gallons Juice	Gallons Juice Per 100 Pounds Sugar	Pounds Juice Per 100 Pounds Sugar	Pounds Juice Per Gallon
7.0	34½	14½	123	8.55
7.2	35½	14	120	8.56
7.4	36½	13¾	116½	8.57
7.6	37½	13¼	113½	8.57
7.8	39	13	110½	8.58
8.0	40	12½	108	8.59
8.2	41	12¼	105	8.59
8.4	42	12	102½	8.60
8.6	43	11¾	100	8.61
8.8	44	11½	98	8.61
9.0	45	11¼	96	8.62
9.2	46	11	94	8.63
9.4	47	10¾	92	8.63
9.6	48	10½	90	8.64
9.8	49	10¼	88	8.65
10.0	50	10	86	8.66
10.2	51	9¾	84½	8.67
10.4	52	9½	83	8.67
10.6	53½	9½	81½	8.68
10.8	54½	9¼	80	8.68
11.0	55½	9	78½	8.69
11.2	56½	9	77	8.70
11.4	57½	8¾	76	8.70
11.6	58½	8½	74½	8.71
11.8	59½	8½	73	8.72
12.0	60½	8¼	72	8.72
12.2	61½	8¼	71	8.73
12.4	63	8	69½	8.74
12.6	64	8	68½	8.75
12.8	65	7¾	67½	8.75
13.0	66	7¾	66½	8.76
13.2	67	7½	65½	8.77
13.4	68	7½	64½	8.77
13.6	69	7¼	63½	8.78
13.8	70	7¼	62½	8.79
14.0	71½	7	61½	8.80
14.5	74	6¾	59½	8.81
15.0	76½	6½	57½	8.83
15.5	79½	6¼	55½	8.85
16.0	82	6	54	8.87
16.5	85	6	52½	8.88
17.0	87½	5¾	51	8.90
17.5	90½	5½	49½	8.92
18.0	93	5½	48	8.94

SOURCE: *The Almanac of the Canning, Freezing, Preserving Industries* published by The Canning Trade, Baltimore, Maryland.

DATA FOR PREPARING JELLIES CONFORMING TO FEDERAL REGULATIONS USING FRUIT JUICES OF DIFFERENT SOLUBLE SOLIDS CONCENTRATIONS

TABLE A.6

BLACKBERRY, YOUNGBERRY, BOYSENBERRY, DEWBERRY OTHER THAN LOGANBERRY

Average Soluble Solids Content—10.0%				
% Soluble Solids in Juice	Pounds Sugar Per 5 Gallons Juice	Gallons Juice Per 100 Pounds Sugar	Pounds Juice Per 100 Pounds Sugar	Pounds Juice Per Gallon
7.0	36½	13¾	117	8.55
7.2	37½	13¼	114	8.56
7.4	38½	13	110½	8.57
7.6	40	12½	108	8.57
7.8	41	12¼	105	8.58
8.0	42	12	102½	8.59
8.2	43	11¾	100	8.59
8.4	44½	11¼	97	8.60
8.6	45½	11	95	8.61
8.8	46½	10¾	93	8.61
9.0	47½	10½	91	8.62
9.2	48½	10¼	89	8.63
9.4	49½	10¼	87	8.63
9.6	51	10	85½	8.64
9.8	52	9¾	83½	8.65
10.0	53	9½	82	8.66
10.2	54	9¼	80	8.67
10.4	55	9	79	8.67
10.6	56	9	77	8.68
10.8	57	8¾	76	8.68
11.0	58	8½	74½	8.69
11.2	59½	8½	73	8.70
11.4	60½	8¼	72	8.70
11.6	61½	8¼	71	8.71
11.8	62½	8	69½	8.72
12.0	64	8	68½	8.72
12.2	65	7¾	67	8.73
12.4	66	7½	66	8.74
12.6	67	7½	65	8.75
12.8	68	7¼	64	8.75
13.0	69½	7¼	63	8.76
13.5	72	7	61	8.78
14.0	75	6¾	58½	8.80
14.5	78½	6½	56½	8.81
15.0	81	6¼	54½	8.83
15.5	84	6	53	8.85
16.0	86½	5¾	51	8.87
16.5	89½	5¾	49½	8.88
17.0	92½	5½	48	8.90
17.5	95	5¼	47	8.92
18.0	98	5	45½	8.94

SOURCE: *The Almanac of the Canning, Freezing, Preserving Industries* published by The Canning Trade, Baltimore, Maryland.

DATA FOR PREPARING JELLIES CONFORMING TO FEDERAL REGULATIONS USING FRUIT JUICES OF DIFFERENT SOLUBLE SOLIDS CONCENTRATIONS

TABLE A.7

GRAPEFRUIT, PRICKLY PEAR

Average Soluble Solids Content—9.1%

% Soluble Solids in Juice	Pounds Sugar Per 5 Gallons Juice	Gallons Juice Per 100 Pounds Sugar	Pounds Juice Per 100 Pounds Sugar	Pounds Juice Per Gallon
7.0	40	12½	106½	8.55
7.2	41½	12	103½	8.56
7.4	42½	11¾	100½	8.57
7.6	44	11½	98	8.57
7.8	45	11	95½	8.58
8.0	46	10¾	93	8.59
8.2	47½	10½	91	8.59
8.4	48½	10¼	88½	8.60
8.6	49½	10	86½	8.61
8.8	51	9¾	84½	8.61
9.0	52	9½	83	8.62
9.2	53½	9½	81	8.63
9.4	54½	9¼	79½	8.63
9.6	55½	9	77½	8.64
9.8	57	8¾	76	8.65
10.0	58	8½	74½	8.66
10.2	59½	8½	73	8.66
10.4	60½	8¼	71½	8.67
10.6	62	8	70½	8.68
10.8	63	8	69	8.68
11.0	64	7¾	68	8.69
11.2	65½	7¾	66½	8.70
11.4	66½	7½	65½	8.70
11.6	68	7½	64½	8.71
11.8	69	7¼	63	8.72
12.0	70	7	62	8.72
12.2	71½	7	61	8.73
12.4	73	6¾	60	8.74
12.6	74	6¾	59	8.75
12.8	75	6¾	58	8.75
13.0	76½	6½	57½	8.76
13.2	77½	6½	56½	8.77
13.4	79	6¼	55½	8.77
13.6	80	6¼	55	8.78
13.8	81½	6¼	54	8.79
14.0	82½	6	53	8.80

SOURCE: *The Almanac of the Canning, Freezing, Preserving Industries* published by The Canning Trade, Baltimore, Maryland.

DATA FOR PREPARING JELLIES CONFORMING TO FEDERAL REGULATIONS USING FRUIT JUICES OF DIFFERENT SOLUBLE SOLIDS CONCENTRATIONS

TABLE A.8

BLACK RASPBERRY

Average Soluble Solids Content—11.1%				
% Soluble Solids in Juice	Pounds Sugar Per 5 Gallons Juice	Gallons Juice Per 100 Pounds Sugar	Pounds Juice Per 100 Pounds Sugar	Pounds Juice Per Gallon
8.0	37½	13¼	114	8.59
8.2	38½	13	111	8.59
8.4	39½	12¾	108	8.60
8.6	40½	12½	106	8.61
8.8	41½	12	103½	8.61
9.0	42½	11¾	101	8.62
9.2	43½	11½	99	8.63
9.4	44½	11¼	97	8.63
9.6	45½	11	95	8.64
9.8	46½	10¾	93	8.65
10.0	47½	10½	91	8.66
10.2	48½	10½	89	8.67
10.4	49½	10	87½	8.67
10.6	50½	10	86	8.68
10.8	51½	9¾	84	8.68
11.0	52½	9½	83	8.69
11.2	53½	9½	81	8.70
11.4	54½	9¼	80	8.70
11.6	55½	9	78½	8.71
11.8	56½	9	77	8.72
12.0	57½	8¾	76	8.72
12.2	58½	8½	74½	8.73
12.4	59½	8½	73½	8.74
12.6	60½	8¼	72	8.75
12.8	61½	8¼	71	8.75
13.0	62½	8	70	8.76
13.5	65	7¾	67½	8.78
14.0	67½	7½	65	8.80
14.5	70	7¼	63	8.81
15.0	73	7	61	8.83
15.5	75½	6¾	59	8.85
16.0	78	6½	57	8.87
16.5	80½	6¼	55	8.88
17.0	83	6	53½	8.90
17.5	85½	6	52	8.92
18.0	88½	5¾	50½	8.94

SOURCE: *The Almanac of the Canning, Freezing, Preserving Industries* **published by The Canning Trade, Baltimore, Maryland.**

DATA FOR PREPARING JELLIES CONFORMING TO FEDERAL REGULATIONS USING FRUIT JUICES OF DIFFERENT SOLUBLE SOLIDS CONCENTRATIONS

TABLE A.9

STRAWBERRY

Average Soluble Solids Content—8.0%				
% Soluble Solids in Juice	Pounds Sugar Per 5 Gallons Juice	Gallons Juice Per Pounds 100 Sugar	Pounds Juice Per 100 Pounds Sugar	Pounds Juice Per Gallon
5.0	32	15	131	8.49
5.2	33½	14¾	126	8.49
5.4	35	14¼	121	8.50
5.6	36½	13¾	117	8.51
5.8	37½	13¼	113	8.51
6.0	39	13	109	8.52
6.2	40½	12½	106	8.53
6.4	42	12	102½	8.53
6.6	43	11¾	99	8.54
6.8	44½	11¼	96½	8.55
7.0	45½	11	93½	8.55
7.2	47	10½	91	8.56
7.4	48½	10¼	88½	8.57
7.6	50	10	86	8.57
7.8	51	9¾	84	8.58
8.0	52½	9½	82	8.59
8.2	54	9¼	80	8.59
8.4	55	9	78	8.60
8.6	56½	9	76	8.61
8.8	58	8¾	74½	8.61
9.0	59	8½	73	8.62
9.2	60½	8¼	71½	8.63
9.4	62	8¼	70	8.63
9.6	63½	8	68½	8.64
9.8	65	7¾	67	8.65
10.0	66	7½	65½	8.66

SOURCE: *The Almanac of the Canning, Freezing, Preserving Industries* published by The Canning Trade, Baltimore, Maryland.

DATA FOR PREPARING JELLIES CONFORMING TO FEDERAL REGULATIONS USING FRUIT JUICES OF DIFFERENT SOLUBLE SOLIDS CONCENTRATIONS

TABLE A.10

GUAVA

Average Soluble Solids Content—7.7%

% Soluble Solids in Juice	Pounds Sugar Per 5 Gallons Juice	Gallons Juice Per 100 Pounds Sugar	Pounds Juice Per 100 Pounds Sugar	Pounds Juice Per Gallon
5.0	33½	14¾	126	8.49
5.2	35	14¼	121½	8.49
5.4	36½	13¾	117	8.50
5.6	38	13¼	112½	8.51
5.8	39	12¾	108½	8.51
6.0	40½	12¼	105	8.52
6.2	42	12	101½	8.53
6.4	43½	11½	98½	8.53
6.6	44½	11¼	95½	8.54
6.8	46	10¾	92½	8.55
7.0	47½	10½	90	8.55
7.2	49	10¼	87½	8.56
7.4	50½	10	85	8.57
7.6	51½	9¾	83	8.57
7.8	53	9½	81	8.58
8.0	54½	9¼	79	8.59
8.2	56	9	77	8.60
8.4	57	8¾	75	8.60
8.6	58½	8½	73½	8.61
8.8	60½	8¼	71½	8.61
9.0	62½	8¼	70	8.62
9.2	63	8	68½	8.63
9.4	64½	7¾	67	8.63
9.6	66	7½	65½	8.64
9.8	67	7½	64½	8.65
10.0	68½	7¼	63	8.66

SOURCE: *The Almanac of the Canning, Freezing, Preserving Industries* published by The Canning Trade, Baltimore, Maryland.

SPICE AND HERB CHART

Spice	Appetizers	Soups	Salads and Dressings	Vegetables	Meats and Sauces	Desserts and Baked Goods
Allspice	Pickles, relishes, cocktail meatballs, pickled beets, fruit compote.	Green pea, vegetable beef, minestrone, asparagus, tomato.	Cottage cheese, fruit salad, cheese dressing.	Eggplant, spinach, beets, squash, turnips, red cabbage, carrots.	Beef stew, meat loaf, hamburgers, baked ham, roast lamb, pot roast, cranberry sauce, meat gravies, tomato sauce.	Mincemeat, tapioca and chocolate puddings, spice cake, fruit cake, baked bananas, cookies, pie.
Bay leaves	Hot tomato juice, pickles, pickled beets.	Bouillon, bouillabaisse, fish chowders, lobster bisque, vegetable, minestrone, oxtail, potato, tomato, turtle.	Seafood salad, tomato aspic, chicken aspic, beet salad, French dressing.	Potatoes, artichokes, carrots, beets, eggplant, lentils, onions, rice, squash, zucchini.	Beef stew, meat pie, corned beef, pot roast, roast beef, veal, meat sauces, lamb, spare ribs, gravies.	
Caraway	Soft cheese spreads, pickles.	Cream soups, clam chowder, borscht, vegetable.	Potato salad, sour cream dressing, spiced vinegar, cole slaw.	Cabbage, cauliflower, potatoes, carrots, onions, turnips, broccoli, brussels sprouts, sauerkraut.	Sauerbraten, roast pork, beef a la mode, liver, kidney stew.	Rye bread, muffins, rolls, coffee cakes, cookies, loaf cake.
Cayenne	Deviled eggs, seafood sauces, cottage and cream cheese spreads, pickles.	Clam and oyster stews, fish chowder, cream soups, shrimp gumbo, vegetable.	Tuna, shrimp, chicken, macaroni, seafood, mayonnaise, thousand island dressing, sour cream.	Green beans, lima beans, cauliflower, cut corn, kale, broccoli.	Pork chops, veal stew, ham croquettes, barbecued beef, sandwich filling, meat sauces.	
Celery seed (salt, flakes, seed)	Deviled eggs, ham spread, tomato juice, kraut juice, cream cheese spreads, pickles.	Cream of celery or tomato, fish chowders and bisques, vegetable, bean, potato, bouillon.	Cole slaw, potato, egg, tuna, vegetable, kidney beans, salad dressings, sour cream.	Cabbage, stewed tomatoes, potatoes, cauliflower, turnips, braised lettuce.	Meat loaf, pot roast, meat stews, short ribs of beef, braised lamb.	Rolls, biscuits, salty breads.
Chili powder	Avocado and cheese dips, seafood cocktail sauce.	Corn soup, pepperpot, fish and clam chowders, tomato, bean, shrimp gumbo, vegetable, chili soup.	French dressing, kidney bean salad, thousand island dressing, chili sauce.	Vegetable relishes, green peas, eggplant, rice, tomatoes, corn Mexicali, green beans, lima beans.	Chili con carne, arroz con pollo, tamales, meat loaf, hamburgers, stews, sauces.	

Spice	Appetizers	Soups	Salads and Dressings	Vegetables	Meats and Sauces	Desserts and Baked Goods
Cinnamon (ground and stick)	Cinnamon toast, sweet gherkins, hot spiced beverages, pickled fruits.		Fruit salad, dressings for fruit salads.	Sweet potatoes, squash, pumpkins, spinach, turnips, green beans, beets, parsnips.	Pork chops, ham, sauce for pork and lamb.	Chocolate and rice pudding, stewed fruits, apple desserts, buns, coffee cake, muffins, spice cake, molasses cookies.
Cloves (whole and ground)	Sweet gherkins, pickled fruits, hot spiced wines, fruit punch.	Beef, bean, cream of tomato, cream of pea, mulligatawney.	Topping for fruit salad.	Beets, baked beans, candied sweet potatoes, squash.	Ham (whole) and pork roast, stews, gravies, sausage, boiled tongue.	Preserved and stewed fruits, apple, mince and pumpkin pies, chocolate, rice and tapioca pudding, stewed pears.
Curry powder	Tomato juice, sauce for dips, sweet pickles, deviled eggs, salted nuts.	Clam and fish chowders, tomato soup, cream of mushroom, oyster stew.	Fruit and meat salads, mayonnaise, French dressing.	Rice, creamed onions, creamed potatoes, scalloped tomatoes, carrots, corn, celery, lima beans.	Curried lamb, veal croquettes, stews.	
Dill	Cottage cheese, anchovy spread, cheddar cheese spread, pickles, sour cream dips, stuffed eggs.	Split pea soup, cream of tomato, navy bean, borscht, chicken, lobster bisque, turkey, fish chowder.	Cole slaw, cucumber, green bean, lettuce, mixed green, potato, seafood, mayonnaise, sour cream, French dressing.	Carrots, beets, cabbage, lima beans, green beans, turnips, eggplant, cauliflower, zucchini, squash.	Beef: pot roast, corned, stew, barbecued, hamburger; lamb chops or stew; roast pork.	
Ginger (ground)	Pickles, broiled grapefruit, chutney.	Bean soup, onion, potato.	Ginger pears, French dressing.	Beets, carrots, squash, baked beans.	Broiled beef, lamb, veal, pot roast, stews, chopped beef.	Ginger bread; cakes; cookies; pumpkin pie; custards; baked, stewed, preserved fruits; Indian pudding.
Marjoram	Fruit punch, cream and cottage cheese dips, cheddar cheese spreads, pickles.	Onion soup, clam, oyster, Boston clam chowder, minestrone, oxtail, spinach.	Mixed green salad, asparagus, chicken, fruit, seafood.	Carrots, eggplant, peas, spinach, string beans, onions, summer squash, tomatoes, celery, broccoli, brussels sprouts.	Roast beef, pork, veal, stews, meat pies, loaf, pot roast, short ribs, spare ribs.	

Mustard (ground)	Pickles, pickled onions, ham spreads, Chinese hot sauce, hot English mustard, deviled eggs.	Lobster bisque, bean, onion.	Egg salad, shrimp, lobster, potato, fruit, salad dressings.	Asparagus, beets, broccoli, brussels sprouts, cabbage, onions, green beans, potatoes, baked beans.	Baked ham, kidneys, pickled meat, sauces.	Molasses cookies, gingerbread.
Oregano	Cheese spreads, pizza, vegetable juice, avocado dip, creamed and cottage cheese spreads.	Bean, beef, vegetable, tomato, lentil, minestrone, navy bean, onion, spinach.	Salad dressings, seafood, avocado, green bean, mixed green, potato, tomato, tomato aspic.	Peas, onions, potatoes, spinach, green beans, stewed tomatoes, mushrooms.	Swiss steak, beef stew, broiled and roast lamb, meat loaf, sauces, gravies, spare ribs, veal scallopini.	
Paprika	Canapes, deviled eggs, cream cheese spreads, stuffed celery, seafood creamed, seafood cocktails.	Cream soups, chicken soup, chowders.	Cole slaw, potato salad, mayonnaise, French dressing.	Cauliflower, potatoes, celery, creamed vegetables.	Hungarian goulash, ham, gravies.	
Poppy seed	Cheese spreads, cottage cheese, cheese dips.	Onion soup.	Green salads, salad dressings.	Peas, potatoes, rutabaga, sweet potatoes, carrots, zucchini.	Noodle dishes.	Coffee cake, cookies, pie crusts, bread, rolls, pastries.
Rosemary	Deviled eggs, pickles, sour cream dips.	Mock turtle, chicken, lentil, minestrone, split pea, spinach, chowders.	Meat, salad, fruit salad.	Peas, potatoes, mushrooms, onions, celery, lima beans, green beans, broccoli, cucumbers.	Roast and broiled lamb, beef, pork, veal, beef stew, pie, pot roast, Swiss steak, spare ribs.	
Saffron		Chicken, bouillabaisse, lobster bisque, turkey.	Seafood salads.	Rice.	Gravy for roast chicken, roast turkey, roast veal, Spanish sauce, rabbit.	Rolls, breads, buns, cake, frostings, and icings.
Sage	Cheese spreads.	Consomme, fish and corn chowders, cream soups, asparagus, chicken, cream of tomato, minestrone, turkey.	Salad greens, salad dressing.	Brussels sprouts, lima beans, peas, tomatoes, carrots, eggplant, winter squash, turnips.	Beef: barbecue, stew, pie, roast, pot roast; barbecued lamb; roast lamb; pork; veal stew.	
Sesame seed	Soft cheeses.	Most soups.	Cole slaw, salad dressings.	Asparagus, green beans, tomatoes, spinach, noodle and vegetable casseroles, potatoes, rice.	Meat pies, Hawaiian ham steak.	Top dressings on pies, cookies, coffee cake, rolls, breads, buns, crumpets.

Spice	Appetizers	Soups	Salads and Dressings	Vegetables	Meats and Sauces	Desserts and Baked Goods
Tarragon	Vegetable juice cocktail, liver paté, herb butters, cheese spreads, seafood cocktails, stuffed eggs, pickles.	Bean, chicken, consomme, seafood chowders and bisques, mushroom, pea, tomato, turtle.	Asparagus, celery, chicken, cole slaw, cucumber, egg, green bean, kidney bean, mixed green, tomato.	Asparagus, beans, broccoli, cabbage, cauliflower, celery root, mushrooms, potatoes, spinach, tomatoes.	Meat marinades, broiled steak, pot roast, braised lamb, lamb stew, veal stew, Béarnaise sauce, brown gravies.	

SOURCE: John Wagner & Sons, Ivyland, Penn.

HERBS, PEPPERS, SPICES, SEEDS, and SEASONING / Notes on How to Use Them

A

Allspice, Ground—Flavor resembles combination of cinnamon, nutmeg, and cloves. Delicious in cookies, cakes and relishes.

Allspice, Whole—Use sparingly in soups, stews, and sauces.

Anise Seed, Ground—Originally from Southern Europe. These seeds lend a delightful flavor to salads, shrimp, and crab dishes.

Anise Seed, Whole—Delicious to sprinkle on cookies, sweet rolls, and coffee cake before baking.

Apple Pie Seasoning—A delightful blend of seasonings to give apple pie the "spicy" touch.

Arrowroot—Used as a thickening agent in sauces such as vegetable and meat sauces. Neutral in flavor.

B

Barbecue Sauce Seasoning—A delicious blend of spices and herbs to use in making a barbecue sauce for meat, poultry, and seafood.

Barbecue Seasoning—Skillfully blended all-purpose barbecue seasoning. Can be used in dry form or as a base for barbecue or cocktail sauce.

Basil, Leaf—Widely used in French and Italian dishes. Delicious flavoring in soups, stews, and meat loaf.

Basil, Powdered—Excellent in stuffings for fowl and sauces for spaghetti and other Italian dishes.

Bay Leaves—Lends a delicious flavor to stews, soups, tomato dishes, and stuffings for fish and fowl.

Beef Soup Base—With a combination of the finest seasonings, to make beef soups and gravies.

Borie's Scotch Bonnet—A highly flavored sherry-and-pepper sauce for use in soups, dressings, and stews.

Bouquet Garni—A blend of several fine herbs for use in making flavorful soups, stews, and gravies.

C

Caraway Seed—Originally from Holland and North Africa, these seeds add greatly to the flavor of rye bread, sauerkraut, soup stock, and stewed meats.

Cardamom Seed, Whole and Ground—Originally from India, cardamom lends a sweet flavor to breads, pastries, and cookies.

Celery Seasoning Salt—Adds celery's delicate flavor to meats, stews, soups, and salads.

Celery Seed, Ground—From Southern France. Adds a delightful flavor to fish, salads, tomatoes, and salad dressing.

Celery Seed, Whole—Adds delicious flavor to potato salad, soup, and stews.

Charcoal Salt—A very special blended seasoning to use on steaks, chops, and hamburgers for a delicious barbecue taste and appearance.

Chervil—Adds a moderately pungent flavor to salads, soups, fish sauces, and egg dishes.

Chicken Soup Base—A delightful combination of herbs and spices for making chicken soup. Also, use in casseroles and cream sauces.

Chili Powder—To use in adding that true Mexican flavor to chili con carne.

Cinnamon, Ground—Indispensable seasoning for apple pie, apple sauce, sweet rolls, coffee cakes, and rum grogs and demitasse.

Cinnamon Sugar—Delicious on pancakes, toast, French toast, waffles, fruit sauces, cake and cookie batters.

Cloves, Ground—The flower buds of an Indonesian tree, cloves lend their delicious flavor to soups, stews, and fruit desserts.

Cookery Seasoning—Mixture of black pepper, salt, herbs, and spices. Use in cooking or on the table. Adds zest to meats, soups, sauces, eggs, and salad dressing.

Coriander, Whole and Ground—Native of the Mediterranean countries; for use in gingerbread, spice cookies, Danish pastries, roast pork, beef broth, and meat sauces.

Cream of Tartar—Most frequently used in candy making and cake icings.

Corn-on-Cob Seasoning—Adds zest to meats, soups, sauces, salad dressings, and corn on the cob.

Creole Seasoning—A blend of pungent spices indispensable in Creole recipes, thin soups, gumbos, and ragouts.

Curry Powder—A subtle mixture of many Eastern herbs and spices imported from Madras, India. Used for lamb, rice, fish, soups, venison, kidney stews, sauces, and mushrooms.

Cumin Seed—Native to the Mediterranean area, this spice gives a warm, aromatic taste to stews, roast meats, and root vegetables.

D

Dill Seasoning Salt—An unusual, delightful seasoning. Use as you would salt to add flavor to eggs, cheese, meats, salads, and potatoes.

Dill Seed—Famous for its use in pickling, meats, soups, salads, eggs, and fried potatoes.

Dill Weed—This exceptional herb is delicious when used in creamed dishes, potatoes, salads.

F

Fennel Seed—A classic herb from the parsley family for use in Scandinavian hot breads, cakes, and cookies. Delicious, too, in many Spanish and Italian dishes.

Fenugreek—A product of Morocco. Most frequently used in dishes of Greek origin. Also may be used as a substitute for curry.

Fried Chicken Seasoning—A delicious blend of spices and herbs to season chicken, roast turkey, Cornish hens, pheasant, and egg plant.

G

Garlic Flakes—For every dish that requires garlic. These dehydrated flakes have eight times the strength of fresh garlic so should be used sparingly.

Garlic, Instant Granulated—Delicious in sauces, all potato recipes, meats, and stews. Can be used freely in any recipe which calls for garlic flavoring.

Garlic, Minced—One of the oldest and widely used of spices. Delicious in stews, meat loaf, salad dressings, meat balls, and potato salad.

Garlic Salt Chips—Sprinkle generously over roast beef and lamb before roasting. Use for that hidden garlic touch in soups, stews, gravies, and sauces.

Garlic Seasoning Salt—Use to flavor meats, stews, fish, and eggs.

Ginger, Crystallized—Frequently used in Chinese and Japanese cookery. Also in making chutney and as a confection.

Ginger Garlic Seasoning Salt—A delicious blend of ginger and garlic to be used on lamb, in stews and roast meats. Use with cream cheese as a chip dip.

Ginger, Whole and Ground—The finest ginger comes from Jamaica and the British West Indies. Whole, it is used to give distinctive flavoring to chutney, pickles, conserves, and apple sauce. Ground, it is used widely for all types of spice cakes, cookies, and sweet buns. Especially delicious in Oriental dishes.

Golden Rice Seasoning—A delicious blend of herbs and spices for flavoring rice dishes.

Good Taste—An all-purpose seasoning salt prepared from the finest spices and herbs to add zest and savor to a wide variety of foods.

Gumbo Filé—To use in any gumbo soup.

H

Hamburger Seasoning—Excellent for indoor and outdoor cooking. Can be used on all ground meats before or after cooking.

Herb Blend for Eggs and Cheese—To make your egg and cheese dishes delightfully different and casually easier.

Herb Blend for Fish—A choice blend of fine herbs to add zest and savor to your fish dishes.

Herb Blend for Meat—The prize blend of a famous chef to add distinctive flavor to meats.

Herb Blend for Poultry and Game—Add small amount to dressing or sprinkle lightly on poultry or game before roasting.

Herb Blend for Salads—A blend of the finest obtainable herbs. Adds piquant distinction to dressings and salads.

Herb Blend for Soups—A correctly proportioned blend of herbs to make your cooking casually easy. Adds a delicious flavor to soups.

Herb Blend for Vegetables—A very special blend of seasonings to add a zestful touch to vegetables and spaghetti sauces.

Hickory Smoked Salt—A gourmet's seasoning to sprinkle on steaks, chops, and hamburgers before cooking to impart a fine wood-smoke flavor.

Horseradish—A zesty horseradish powder to use in making prepared horseradish.

J

Juniper Berries—An aromatic berry in chopped form to use dry with poultry and meat.

L

Lemon Flavored Sugar—The ideal sweetening for tea—both hot and iced.

Lemon Peel—Use in sauces and marinade for poultry, lamb, and veal. Add to cake batters, dessert sauces and toppings, meringues and custards.

M

Marjoram, Leaf and Powdered—The perennial herb of the mint family of France. Used in stuffings, chopped meats, stews, soups, and salad dressings.

Meat Ball Seasoning—A famous chef's special seasoning for meat balls, spaghetti sauce, meat loaf, stuffed peppers, and shrimp dishes.

Mint Leaves—Mint leaves impart an aromatic flavor popular for beverages, meats, confections, and desserts.

Monosodium Glutamate—MSG has no flavor of its own but increases the natural flavor of many dishes.

Mushroom Flakes—Cultivated in the heart of the mushroom country. Excellent added to sauces, gravies, meats, and vegetables.

Mushroom Powder—A quick way of adding mushroom flavor to all foods.

Mushroom Salt—Easy to use as a seasoning on

roasts, sauces, gravies, eggs, barbecues, and omelets.

Mustard Seed, Ground and Whole—A native to Europe and Southwest Asia this spice is widely used with meats, sauces, fish, and mayonnaise.

N

Newburg Seasoning—Used by one of the leading chef's of Maryland's Eastern Shore to add a delicious flavor to lobster, shrimp, or crabmeat.

Nutmeg, Ground and Whole—Originates in the East Indies. This spice gives an aromatic odor and slightly bitter taste to custards, puddings, pumpkin, and fruit pies. Delicious sprinkled on egg-nog. Use a nutmeg grinder for the whole nutmeg.

O

Onion Chips—Small chips of onion to be used whenever onions are needed in soups, stews, roast meats, and hamburger.

Onion Flakes, Fried Flavor—A delicious addition to any dish requiring an onion flavor.

Onion, Instant Granulated—Use freely in any recipe which calls for onion flavoring. Delicious in sauces, potato recipes, meats, and stews.

Onion, Minced Green—Colorful and delicious garnish for all salads, potato, and tomato dishes, vichysoisse and tomato juice.

Onion, Minced White—Adds delicate flavor to all dishes where onion is used—salad dressing, roast beef, steaks, chops, hashed brown potatoes.

Onion Powder—For that "touch of onion" to be used in stews, roast meats, fish and fowl, potato salad, and Italian sauces.

Onion Powder, Roasted—Gives the delectable taste of roasted onions to meat gravies, sauces, fowl, and hamburger.

Onion Seasoning Salt—Adds a delicious onion flavor to meats, stews, fish, salads, and eggs.

Onion Soup, French—With a delightful combination of seasonings; for making onion soup and onion dips.

Orange Peel—Delicious in baked goods, duck and barbecue sauces. Add to butter, honey or syrup for toppings.

Oregano—This herb is widely used in the seasoning of Mexican and Italian dishes, pork and tomato sauces and bean dishes.

Oriental Mustard Seed—Used extensively in Oriental dishes. These seeds are very hot and should be used sparingly.

P

Paprika—Widely used as a garnish and in goulash, meat stews, hashes, fish, and game.

Parsley—Used as a colorful garnish. This herb is used in soups, sauces, baked fish, potatoes, and salads.

Pea Soup Mix—A savory mixture for making a delicious pea soup.

Pepper, Cayenne—A very hot red pepper. Delicious to use with shrimp and crab dishes and chili sauce. Also add to hot Mexican and Spanish dishes.

Pepper, Creole—A Louisiana pepper similar to Cayenne. Very popular in Southern and Creole dishes.

Pepper, Lampong, Black Cracked—For those who prefer a more pungent pepper flavor. Especially good in soups and salads.

Pepper, Lampong, Black Ground Fine—This rare extremely fine black pepper is a delight to all gourmets.

Pepper Lampong, Black Ground—By far the most generally used of all spices. This pepper is ground immediately prior to packing to retain full flavor.

Pepper, Lampong, Black Medium—A pungent pepper particularly good in stews, soups, and salads.

Pepper, Malabar, Black Ground—The finest of all black pepper. The most generally used of all spices at table and in cooking.

Pepper, White, Ground—A mild variety of pepper. Ground white pepper is used chiefly in sauces where it is preferable not to have black pepper.

Peppers, Green Bell, Diced—Dehydrated bell peppers. Use with spaghetti sauce, meat loaf, and stews.

Peppers, Green Bell, Ground—Dehydrated bell peppers to use in sauces for spaghetti, string beans, egg plant, and liver.

Peppers, Red Bell, Diced—Dehydrated bell peppers. Try in egg dishes, meat loaf, and stews.

Peppers, Red, Crushed—Use sparingly for a hot touch to Italian dishes, casseroles, stews, hamburgers, and potted meats.

Peppercorns, Garlic—A delightful touch of garlic added to the finest available peppercorns.

Peppercorns, Lampong, Black—Grown in the Netherlands East Indies. For use in peppermills to achieve pungent, freshly ground pepper.

Peppercorns, Malabar, Black—These rare, extremely fine black peppercorns are used in soups, pickling, and meat stews and whenever fine pepper is required. Used principally in peppermills.

Peppercorns, White—These are the finest of natural black peppercorns with the dark outer shell removed. Preferred by those who want a more delicate, less pungent flavor.

Pickling Spice, Whole—A skillful blend of pungent spices and fine herbs to use in making a wide variety of pickles and relishes.

Pizza Seasoning—To use in making pizza sauce

or to sprinkle over pizza at time of eating. Add to salads, veal cutlets, and roast lamb.

Poivre Aromatique—Blended after the formula of an old French Huguenot family. Adds a delightful pungent taste to soups, stews, stuffings, meat loaf, and tomato juice.

Poppy Seed—This Asian herb has a nut-like flavor and odor. Delicious for toppings on rolls, bread, or cookies.

Poultry Seasoning—The ideal blend of herbs and spices to add to bread stuffing for fowl, fish, and pork roasts.

Pumpkin Pie Spice—Developed by a famous pastry chef. Delicious in gingerbread, cookies, pies, and buns.

R

Red Bell Pepper and Onion Blend—A delicious combination to mix with cottage cheese.

Roast Meat Seasoning—For indoor and outdoor cookery. Excellent for stews, meat loaf, hash, croquettes, gravies, mock turtle soup, stewed rabbit, and game.

Rosemary, Leaf and Powdered—Gives a pleasant delicate flavor to meats, soups, fish, and salads.

S

Saffron—A native of Spain and the Mediterranean region. A true gourmet's flavoring for fish, soups, boiled rice, curry, and fish sauces.

Sage Leaf—Grown in Dalmatia, this herb has a spicy aroma and should be used sparingly in soups, meats, and all bread stuffings for fowl, fish, and pork. Sage leaf powdered is delicious in vegetables, boiled fish, and stews.

Salt Crystals—Salt in crystalline form. May be used as is in cooking or may be freshly ground in a salt mill for table use.

Savory, Leaf and Powdered—This fragrant Spanish herb lends a delightful flavor to soups, stuffings, cabbage, stewed meats, and boiled mutton. In powdered form savory is delicious in egg dishes, cold sauces, and salad dressings.

Seafood Seasoning—An expert blend of spices and herbs to sprinkle generously over fish or seafood.

Seasoning Salt—A mixture of peppers, salts, herbs, and spices to be used in cooking or on the table.

Sesame Seed—A small seed from the Orient with a nut-like flavor to use on rolls, breads, cookies, and cakes.

Shrimp Seasoning—Add 1½ tbsp shrimp seasoning to 3½ cups water. Bring to boil. Add 1 lb raw shrimp, boil 8 min. Remove from water.

Steak Seasoning, Garlic—For those who prefer a touch of garlic on their steak. Also excellent on lamb, pot roast, gravies, pork, and rib roast.

T

Tarragon—Famous for flavoring turtle soup, eggs, meat sauces, salad greens, and many vegetables, and a "must" for sauce Béarnaise.

Thyme—Delicious in bread stuffings, fish sauces, soups, gumbos, shellfish dishes, meats, and vegetables.

Tomato Purée Flakes—Dehydrated tomatoes to use in tomato sauces and purées.

Turmeric—Used in soups, pickles, and other dishes where a rich yellow color is desired. Use to color rice where saffron is not used.

V

Vanilla Bean—A dried, cured fruit of the orchid family. The vanilla bean is used for baking, desserts, candy, and syrups.

Vanilla Flavored Sugar—A combination of vanilla beans and sugars to use in baking and desserts.

Vegetable and Salad Blend—An ideal mixture of dried vegetables to use in soups, cottage cheese salads, and cheese dips.

SOURCE: John Wagner & Sons, Ivyland, Penn.

CONVERSION OF CENTIGRADE DEGREES INTO FAHRENHEIT DEGREES

C°	F°	C°	F°	C°	F°
52	125.6	94	201.2	136	276.8
54	129.2	96	204.8	138	280.4
56	132.8	98	208.4	140	284.0
58	136.4	100	212.0	142	287.6
60	140.0	102	215.6	144	291.2
62	143.6	104	219.2	146	294.8
64	147.2	106	222.8	148	298.4
66	150.8	108	226.4	150	302.0
68	154.4	110	230.0	152	305.6
70	158.0	112	233.6	154	309.2
72	161.6	114	237.2	156	312.8
74	165.2	116	240.8	158	316.4
76	168.8	118	244.4	160	320.0
78	172.4	120	248.0	162	323.6
80	176.0	122	251.6	164	327.4
82	179.6	124	255.2	166	330.8
84	183.2	126	258.8	168	334.4
86	186.8	128	262.4	170	338.0
88	190.4	130	266.0	172	341.6
90	194.0	132	269.6	174	345.2
92	197.6	134	273.2	176	348.8

METRIC MEASUREMENT CONVERSIONS

Volume

1 hectoliter = 100 liters
1 dekaliter = 10 liters
1 deciliter = 0.1 liter
1 centiliter = 0.01 liter
1 milliliter = 0.001 liter

1 teaspoon = 5 milliliters
1 tablespoon = 15 milliliters
1 cup = 250 milliliters
1 pint = 550.3 milliliters
1 quart = 1101.2 milliliters
1 gallon = 4404.8 milliliters

Weight

1 kilogram = 1000 grams
1 hectogram = 100 grams
1 dekagram = 10 grams
1 decigram = 0.1 gram
1 centigram = 0.01 gram
1 milligram = 0.001 gram

1 ounce = 438 grams
1 pound = 7008 grams
1 ton = 907.18 kilograms

Temperature

Degrees Centigrade		Degrees Fahrenheit	
0	=	32	Freezing point of water
10	=	50	A warm winter day
20	=	60	A mild spring day
30	=	86	Quite warm, almost hot
37	=	98.6	Normal body temperature
40	=	104	Heat wave conditions
100	=	212	Boiling point of water

Length

1 kilometer = 1000 meters
1 hectometer = 100 meters
1 dekameter = 10 meters
1 decimeter = 0.1 meter
1 centimeter = 0.01 meter
1 millimeter = 0.001 meter

1 inch = 2.5400 centimeters
1 foot = 30.4801 centimeters
1 yard = 91.4402 centimeters
1 mile = 1.60512 kilometers

INDEX